Essential Readings in Juvenile Justice

Edited by

David L. Parry

Endicott College

PEARSON

Prentice
Hall

Upper Saddle River, New Jersey 07458

Library of Congress Cataloging-in-Publication Data

Essential readings in juvenile justice / edited by David L. Parry.-- 1st ed.
    p. cm.
  ISBN 0-13-098186-9
  1. Juvenile justice, Administration of--United States. 2. Juvenile courts--United States. 3. Juvenile delinquency--United States. I. Parry, David L.

KF9778.E84 2004
345.73'08--dc22

                          2004000988

Publisher: Stephen Helba
Executive Editor: Frank Mortimer, Jr.
Assistant Editor: Korrine Dorsey
Production Editor: Linda Duarte, Pine Tree Composition
Production Liaison: Barbara Marttine Cappuccio
Director of Manufacturing and Production: Bruce Johnson
Managing Editor: Mary Carnis
Manufacturing Buyer: Cathleen Petersen
Creative Director: Cheryl Asherman
Cover Design Coordinator: Miguel Ortiz
Cover Image: André Burian/CORBIS
Editorial Assistant: Barbara Rosenberg
Marketing Manager: Tim Peyton
Formatting and Interior Design: Pine Tree Composition
Printing and Binding: Phoenix Book Tech Park

Pearson Education LTD.
Pearson Education Singapore, Pte. Ltd
Pearson Education, Canada, Ltd
Pearson Education–Japan
Pearson Education Australia PTY, Limited
Pearson Education North Asia Ltd
Pearson Educaçion de Mexico, S.A. de C.V.
Pearson Education Malaysia, Pte. Ltd

10 9 8 7 6 5 4 3 2 1
ISBN 0-13-098186-9

Brief Contents

Contents

Contents

Preface

As an instructor committed to making primary source material the centerpiece of even most undergraduate classes (either instead of or in conjunction with a traditional textbook, depending on the level of the course), I have repeatedly found myself frustrated with the absence of an appropriate book of readings for my 300-level juvenile justice course—one pitched at an accessible level for my students, yet providing uncompromising and informative readings on the full range of juvenile justice subject matter that I normally cover in a semester. The field is so rich in writings that may fairly be described as "essential" for anyone seeking more than a cursory understanding of how our juvenile justice system works and why it works the way it does that I have often wondered why someone didn't try to pull all of this material together under a single cover. This book is intended to approximate that ideal. It is sufficiently meaty to sustain graduate students, yet the readings have been carefully chosen and edited to maximize their accessibility for undergraduates as well.

My intent has been to provide a penetrating, yet eminently accessible overview of the entire field of juvenile justice, and to do so in a manner that systematically integrates published scholarship, case law, and other pertinent materials in a mosaic affording readers an opportunity to directly view the multiple layers of law, policy, and analysis that guide contemporary juvenile justice system practices. I have drawn together a wide array of documents including classic statements of traditional juvenile court philosophy, landmark Supreme Court cases, groundbreaking examinations of juvenile court history and contemporary juvenile justice system practices, influential juvenile justice legislation, and model standards for juvenile justice agency policy and procedure. All of this I have done with an eye toward touching upon the entire range of juvenile justice topics one normally finds referenced only in single-author textbooks and in widely scattered books, articles, monographs, court decisions, and other isolated sources—many of which are hard to find (even if available on the Internet) and, once found, daunting to wade through in their original, unabridged form.

In order to augment the accessibility of the material and, just as important, to manage the integration of all the selections into a single volume of reasonable size, I have limited most selections to no more than seven or eight pages in length, editing them in such a way as to preserve the essential points and the flow of the authors' arguments, but omitting nonessential passages and those that seem comparatively unlikely to provoke discussion or excite more than a passing interest. Many selections have been cut down even further, following the model of law school casebooks in which even landmark Supreme Court cases are often reduced to just three or four pages of key passages. In several instances, extremely brief readings—some under a page in length—are introduced as succinct counterpoints to positions taken in other selections or to provide points of departure for classroom discussion of issues that do not receive focused attention elsewhere. Also, reference lists following some selections have been adapted to omit sources that are not cited in included passages, and I have omitted nearly all footnotes—and in-text case citations as well—in excerpts from Supreme Court cases and law review articles, where content-laden notes and citations to statutes and precedent-setting cases often rival the main text in overall length.

I have also inserted a variety of learning aids designed to help students get the most out of their reading. Each chapter begins with a brief introduction designed to place the selections in a broader context by describing relevant historical developments, outlining general practices and issues pertaining to the chapter topic, highlighting points that receive insufficient coverage in the included selections or for which the selections assume greater familiarity with the subject matter than many readers are likely to have, and, finally, summarizing the selections and showing how they relate to each other and to other aspects of juvenile justice. Individual selections are in each instance followed by a set of review questions designed to focus attention on key concepts, highlight any ideas that are notably similar to or in conflict with ones raised in earlier selections, elucidate ways in which points raised in the selection relate to overarching themes or broader trends in juvenile justice policy, and guide readers toward a fuller understanding of the implications of particular practices and issues. Rounding out each chapter is a list of further readings for those who wish to explore particular aspects of juvenile justice in greater depth. This feature will be especially helpful as a resource for students who are asked to write library-based research papers addressing juvenile justice system practices.

The book is organized into 10 chapters, each addressing a major aspect of juvenile justice. Chapter 1 frames many of the themes to be developed in subsequent parts of the book. The selections include a synopsis of juvenile justice system structure and process, statistical breakdowns of juvenile arrest patterns and juvenile court case flow, a summary of the findings of developmental psychologists with respect to reasoning ability and judgment in adolescents and the implications for juvenile justice, and assessments of special problems confronted by minority youth and females in the juvenile justice system. Together, these selections offer a panoramic overview of the juvenile justice system and process, and they raise many of the central issues that are investigated more thoroughly in later chapters.

Chapter 2 traces the evolution of delinquency control measures leading up to the emergence of juvenile courts at the beginning of the 20th century. Included are Anthony Platt's article-length summary of his classic work on the child-saving movement that culminated in creation of the first juvenile court in Chicago, Judge Julian Mack's first-person account of that court and its underlying philosophy, an excerpt from the 1899 Illinois Juvenile Court Act establishing the court, and the pivotal *Ex Parte Crouse* and *Commonwealth v. Fisher* cases that bracketed the child-saving era. These selections combine to give the reader a thorough understanding of the philosophical underpinnings of the juvenile justice system, at least as it existed prior to the comparatively recent drift toward increased formality and punitiveness.

The sweeping changes in juvenile justice first called for in the seminal discussion of juvenile delinquency and youth crime in the 1967 report of the President's Commission on Law Enforcement and Administration of Justice, and then mandated by the Supreme Court in a series of decisions handed down between 1966 and 1975, are documented in Chapter 3. In this chapter the reader gains a sense of the widespread disenchantment with a system that, despite continued lip service to the lofty ideals espoused by Judge Mack and other 19th century reformers, had by the 1960s degenerated into one in which young offenders seemed to receive "the worst of both worlds . . . neither the protections accorded to adults nor the solicitous care and regenerative treatment postulated for children" (*Kent v. U.S.,* 383 U.S. 541, 556 [1966]). Rounding out the chapter—and exemplifying the reformist spirit of the times—are authoritative summaries of two extraordinarily influential sets of model standards for juvenile justice system operation.

The law enforcement response to juvenile delinquency is the focus of Chapter 4. After extensive examination in the 1960s and 1970s, police–juvenile interactions have received surprisingly little attention in the recent scholarly literature. I looked hard for a set of readings that would effectively convey a sense of the special problems associated with policing juveniles and ways in which contemporary police–juvenile interactions differ from those involving adults. The result is a blend of standards, cases, and both classic and contemporary articles highlighting arrest decisions, interrogation, search and seizure (school searches), gang suppression tactics, and the implications of the recent ascendance of community policing for interactions between law enforcement officials and juveniles.

Chapters 5–7 examine the intermediate stages of the juvenile justice process, addressing the many decisions normally falling to an "intake" officer (often a probation officer assigned specifically to work with newly referred youth), prosecutor, or other juvenile court gatekeeper after a youth is referred by the police or another source for further processing. Chapter 5 introduces the intake screening process via two sets of model standards offering alternative views of the responsibilities of intake officers and prosecutors in reviewing cases and deciding in each case whether to file a "petition" initiating formal court action or instead to "divert" the child away from juvenile court and handle the case informally. Additional readings probe issues related to the proliferation of diversion programs for minor offenders, relate one State's statutory provisions for case screening and diversion agreements, and assess the teen court phenomenon that has taken root as an alternative to formal juvenile court processing in many jurisdictions across the country.

Detention of accused juvenile offenders pending the outcome of court action, the focus of Chapter 6, is addressed through excerpts from a landmark Supreme Court case granting judges wide latitude in deciding whether to detain juveniles awaiting adjudication hearings; a set of model standards enumerating far more restrictive criteria for detention decisions; passages in the Juvenile Justice and Delinquency Prevention Act of 1974 (as amended most recently in 2002) detailing its familiar deinstitutionalization, separation, jail removal, and disproportionate minority confinement mandates; and an article addressing trends and reforms in juvenile detention.

Chapter 7, wrapping up consideration of intermediate-stage decisions and processes, includes selections outlining the various mechanisms for transferring juveniles to adult criminal court and their attendant problems, criminal court outcomes for transferred juveniles, and the impact of transfer on the likelihood of recidivism. A passage from law professor Victor L. Streib's meticulously maintained website cataloguing all death sentences imposed on juvenile offenders since 1973 and brief excerpts from two Supreme Court cases addressing the Constitutionality of the death penalty for juveniles round out the material on transfer.

In Chapter 8, attention shifts to practices and issues related to adjudication and disposition of delinquency cases in juvenile court. The chapter begins with passages from Edward Humes' compelling account of his observations over a 1-year period in a Los Angeles juvenile court. It then continues through a series of selections examining cross-jurisdictional variations in juvenile court formality, the role of the prosecutor in delinquency cases, the extent and influence of legal representation in juvenile court, and issues related to the process of pleading guilty in delinquency cases. The chapter ends with consideration of the variety of statutory provisions for sentencing young offenders, factors that influence juvenile court dispositions and, in the final selection, the advent of blended sentencing statutes that in a growing number of states permit judges to combine juvenile and adult sanctions— or choose between the two—for certain categories of juvenile offender.

The entire range of juvenile correctional intervention strategies is touched upon in Chapter 9. The results of a national assessment of conditions of confinement in juvenile detention and correctional facilities open the chapter. This is followed by a review of the rise and fall of the notion of a Constitutional right to treatment in juvenile correctional law and an assessment of alternative legal foundations for ensuring rehabilitative care in institutions for juvenile offenders. From here, and for the balance of the chapter, attention shifts to successful intervention strategies via an extended selection describing in rich detail a wide variety of exemplary community-based and institutional programs for juvenile offenders.

Finally, Chapter 10 draws together several disparate images of the future direction of the juvenile justice system. The first of these comes from an influential manifesto for attacking serious, violent, and chronic delinquency through vigorous prevention efforts and implementation of a system of "graduated sanctions." This is followed by Professor Barry Feld's astonishingly compelling case for abolishing the juvenile court's delinquency jurisdiction altogether and, closing the book, the case for restorative justice and the "balanced approach" as presented by Gordon Bazemore and Susan E. Day.

Acknowledgments

I would like to extend my heartfelt thanks to the many people without whose assistance this book would not have been possible. I have been blessed with the opportunity to work with an extraordinary group of people at Prentice Hall. The indefatigable efforts of Frank Mortimer, Kim Davies, Cheryl Adam, Susan Beauchamp, Sarah Holle, Tim Peyton, Corrina Schultz, Jennifer Walters, and other members of the Prentice Hall team in variously encouraging, advising, and prodding me have finally paid off. I am also deeply indebted to the many authors whose work is represented here, to the publishers who permitted me to reprint copyrighted material and in many instances to adapt it as necessary to effectively blend with and complement other selections, and to Linda Duarte and her colleagues at Pine Tree Composition, Inc., who painstakingly transformed the manuscript into final copy. For their gracious efforts in helping me locate copies of the primary sources from which these readings are drawn, special thanks are due to Dick Irving of the University at Albany Libraries; Tom Cesarz, Betty Roland, and Abby Nelson of the Diane M. Halle Library at Endicott College; and Richard Adamo and Robin Bates of the Essex Law Library in Salem, Massachusetts. Catherine Doyle, Heidi Hsia, and Dennis Mondoro of the Office of Juvenile Justice and Delinquency Prevention (OJJDP) were especially helpful in steering me in fruitful directions, as were Howard Snyder, Melissa Sickmund, and Hunter Hurst III of the National Center for Juvenile Justice. Thanks are also due to reviewers William Kelly, Peter Kratcoski, Roger Levesque, Susan McGuire, Ronald D. Server, Kim Tobin, and Michael Vasu, and to Donna Bishop, Barry Feld, Chuck Frazier, Ed Humes, Barry Krisberg, Irving Piliavin, Joe Sanborn, and Victor Streib for their sage advice at crucial junctures. Others who helped in various ways along the way include Colleen Cantner of the Academy of Criminal Justice Sciences; Robert Pearson of the American Academy of Political and Social Science; Nicole Maggio, Amanda Petteruti, and Richard Vittenson of the American Bar Association; Susan Clayton of the American Correctional Association; Susan Walker of Harvard Law Review; Alison Kinney of the Institute of Judicial Administration; Charles Parker of MCB University Press; Jean Holt of the National District Attorneys Association; Barbara Hunt of Northwestern University School of Law; Kelly Rogers of Rowman and Littlefield Publishing Group; Peter Marino of Sage Publications; Lydia Zelaya of Simon and Schuster; Rhonda Grubbs of Temple Law Review; Marlena Davidian of Transaction Publishers; Perry Cartwright and Michele Johnson of the University of Chicago Press; and Jennifer Thomas and Will Vincent of the University Press of New England. I also want to thank the generations of students who suffered through my attempts to approximate the juvenile justice anthology I really wanted them to read by piecing together from multiple sources many of the selections that ultimately found their way into this book. Finally, I want to thank Carrie, Matt, and Keith, who put up with too much time away from them and kept me sane through all of this.

Delinquency and Public Policy: Concepts, Processes, and Issues

Accounting for nearly 2.4 million arrests each year, young people under 18 years of age represent about one out of every six arrests in the United States (Snyder, 2002). About two-thirds of the juveniles[1] who are arrested each year will find their way to juvenile court, but only about 58% of these will be formally "petitioned" (charged). Roughly 66% of those against whom delinquency petitions are filed will ultimately be "adjudicated" delinquent—a formal ruling by a juvenile court judge, followed in most instances by a judicially-imposed "disposition" involving some form of supervised probation or correctional placement. (Office of Juvenile Justice and Delinquency Prevention, 2003). For all of these youth, though, the juvenile justice system they will encounter is very different from the one their parents may have experienced in their own youth. The spread of gang violence, a flurry of highly publicized school shootings, and widespread disillusionment with the rehabilitative ideology that was once the hallmark of juvenile justice have in recent years fostered get-tough policies and a move away from the diversion-oriented practices of just a few years ago. Attention has shifted from concern about the potentially harmful effects of juvenile court intervention to calls for harsher punishment, aggressive responses to gang activity and school violence, and transfer of serious and violent young offenders to adult criminal courts where they may face lengthy prison terms or even the death penalty.

This book introduces the juvenile justice system that has evolved in the United States from the day in 1825 that the first House of Refuge for young offenders opened its doors, to the creation of the first juvenile court in 1899, to the U.S. Supreme Court's declaration in the

---

[1]Under the laws of most states, persons under the age of 18 are designated "juveniles" who are subject to the exclusive jurisdiction of the juvenile court. Several states, though, set the age at which jurisdiction shifts to adult criminal court at 17, and three set it even lower—at 16. In many states, however, the maximum age for juvenile court jurisdiction is lowered for certain very serious offenses, and "transfer" provisions allow younger juveniles to be tried in adult court for other offenses under certain circumstances.

1960s that "neither the Fourteenth Amendment nor the Bill of Rights is for adults alone" (see p. 90), to the present, when more than 70 young Americans sit on death rows around the nation for crimes they committed when they were 16 or 17 years old and an increasing number of voices are calling for radically restructuring or even "abolishing" the juvenile court.

We begin our exploration of the juvenile justice system with a group of readings that frame many of the themes to be developed in this book. These selections offer a panoramic overview of the juvenile justice system and process, and they raise many of the central issues that are investigated more thoroughly in later chapters.

The first selection is drawn from a voluminous compendium of information compiled by researchers at the National Center for Juvenile Justice (NCJJ) for inclusion in *Juvenile Offenders and Victims: 1999 National Report*—one of many NCJJ reports published by the Office of Juvenile Justice and Delinquency Prevention (OJJDP), the branch of the U.S. Department of Justice charged with responsibility for coordinating federal juvenile justice initiatives and with supporting research and policy development at the state level. The excerpt included here traces major developments in juvenile justice from the founding of the nation's first juvenile court through recent efforts to crack down on juvenile crime. It then introduces us to the major steps or stages in the juvenile justice process and the alternative means of handling cases available to decision makers at each step. The reading introduces many terms we will encounter in later chapters and highlights concepts we will address in much greater detail as we proceed. It is followed by a chart—taken from OJJDP's online *Statistical Briefing Book*—offering statistical information compiled by researchers at NCJJ on the handling of cases at major decision points in the juvenile justice process.

In yet another OJJDP-sponsored report, NCJJ researcher Howard Snyder helps us gain an understanding of the social context in which the juvenile justice system operates by introducing us to the nature and scope of juvenile delinquency (i.e., offenses that would be considered crimes if committed by an adult) as indicated by arrest statistics. This brief selection includes several tables and charts offering highlights from NCJJ's reassessment of data on juvenile offenses included in the Federal Bureau of Investigation's Uniform Crime Reports for 2000 and other sources of statistical information. It gives a sense of the magnitude of the delinquency problem, the kinds of offenses most frequently committed by juveniles, the salience of juveniles among all persons arrested for different types of criminal acts, and changes over time in the frequency of violent and property offenses committed by juveniles.

The next selection provides us with a very different perspective on juvenile justice. In it, authors Elizabeth S. Scott and Thomas Grisso review the contributions of developmental psychology to our understanding of the ways in which the cognitive capacities (i.e., reasoning skills) and judgment of young people differ from those of adults as well as the ways in which developmental factors affect adolescents' decision making about criminal behavior and their ability to understand concepts they will encounter in interactions with police, probation officers, and judges.

The last two selections in this introductory chapter focus on special problems confronting officials at every step of the juvenile justice process. First, authors Carl E. Pope, Rick Lovell, and Heidi Hsia summarize the results of their exhaustive review of contemporary studies examining racial disparities in case outcomes at different stages of the juvenile justice process. Disproportionate confinement of minority youth in juvenile detention and correctional facilities prompted Congress in 1988 to amend the Juvenile Justice and Delinquency Prevention Act of 1974 (Pub. L. No. 93-415, 42 U.S.C. § 5601 *et seq.*) to require states receiving "formula" grants from the federal government to make efforts to reduce the number of minority youth held in secure facilities.[2] Pope's earlier OJJDP-sponsored review of literature on minorities in the juvenile justice system—conducted in collaboration with co-author William Feyerherm (Pope & Feyerherm, 1990a, 1990b, 1995)—represented an important early step in assessing the scope of the problem and mapping a plan for reducing minority overrepresentation. The report included here updates and extends the original review, offering an overview of studies conducted between 1989 and 2001.

Finally, Meda Chesney-Lind discusses the special problems related to female youth in the juvenile justice system. After briefly summarizing the distinctive backgrounds of female delinquents and the special needs they bring with them into the juvenile justice system, she focuses on the limited availability of appropriate correctional programming for girls and the pressing need for dispositional alternatives that provide developmentally sound services suited to their needs.

REFERENCES

Office of Juvenile Justice and Delinquency Prevention. (2003). National estimates of juvenile court processing for delinquency cases, 2000. (2003). *OJJDP Statistical Briefing Book.* Online. Available: http://ojjdp.ncjrs.org/ojstatbb/asp/JCSCF_Display.asp?ID=qa06601&year=2000&group=1&type=2. August 11, 2003. Data Source: National Juvenile Court Data Archive. National Center for Juvenile Justice. Pittsburgh, PA.

Pope, Carl E., and Feyerherm, William (1990a). Minority status and juvenile justice processing—Part I. *Criminal Justice Abstracts, 22*(2), 327–336.

Pope, Carl E., and Feyerherm, William (1990b). Minority status and juvenile justice processing—Part II. *Criminal Justice Abstracts, 22*(3), 527–542.

Pope, Carl E., and Feyerherm, William (1995). *Minorities and the Juvenile Justice System: Research Summary.* Washington, DC: Office of Juvenile Justice and Delinquency Prevention.

Snyder, Howard N. (2002). *Juvenile Arrests 2000.* Washington, DC: Office of Juvenile Justice and Delinquency Prevention.

[2]The disproportionate minority confinement (DMC) provision, which became a "core requirement" of the formula grant program in 1992, was modified in 2002 to expressly require states to address disproportionate minority contact with all components of the juvenile justice system. We will return to the Juvenile Justice and Delinquency Prevention Act—and to the DMC mandate—in later chapters.

Juvenile Justice System Structure and Process

Howard N. Snyder and Melissa Sickmund

The first juvenile court in the United States was established in Chicago in 1899, 100 years ago. In the long history of law and justice, juvenile justice is a relatively new development. The juvenile justice system has weathered significant modifications in the past 30 years, resulting from Supreme Court decisions, Federal legislation, and changes in State legislation.

Perceptions of a juvenile crime epidemic in the early 1990's fueled public scrutiny of the system's ability to effectively control violent juvenile offenders. As a result, States have adopted numerous legislative changes in an effort to crack down on juvenile crime. While some differences between the criminal and juvenile justice system have diminished in recent years, the juvenile justice system remains unique, guided by its own philosophy and legislation and implemented by its own sets of agencies. . . .

THE JUVENILE JUSTICE SYSTEM WAS FOUNDED ON THE CONCEPT OF REHABILITATION THROUGH INDIVIDUALIZED JUSTICE

Early in U.S. history, children who broke the law were treated the same as adult criminals

Throughout the late 18th century, "infants" below the age of reason (traditionally age 7) were presumed to be incapable of criminal intent and were, therefore, exempt from prosecution and punishment. Children as young as 7, however, could stand trial in criminal court for offenses committed and, if found guilty, could be sentenced to prison or even to death.

The 19th-century movement that led to the establishment of the juvenile court in the U S. had its roots in 16th-century European educational reform movements. These earlier reform movements changed the perception of children from one of miniature adults to one of persons with less than fully developed moral and cognitive capacities.

As early as 1825, the Society for the Prevention of Juvenile Delinquency was advocating the separation of juvenile and adult offenders. Soon, facilities exclusively for juveniles were established in most major cities. By mid-century, these privately operated youth

Source: Howard N. Snyder and Melissa Sickmund. (1999). *Juvenile Offenders and Victims: 1999 National Report.* Washington, DC: Office of Juvenile Justice and Delinquency Prevention. Copyright 1999 by the National Center for Juvenile Justice. Adapted by permission.

"prisons" were under criticism for various abuses. Many States then took on the responsibility of operating juvenile facilities.

The first juvenile court in this country was established in Cook County, Illinois, in 1899

Illinois passed the Juvenile Court Act of 1899, which established the Nation's first juvenile court. The British doctrine of *parens patriae* (the State as parent) was the rationale for the right of the State to intervene in the lives of children in a manner different from the way it intervenes in the lives of adults. The doctrine was interpreted to mean that, because children were not of full legal capacity, the State had the inherent power and responsibility to provide protection for children whose natural parents were not providing appropriate care or supervision. A key element was the focus on the welfare of the child. Thus, the delinquent child was also seen as in need of the court's benevolent intervention.

Juvenile courts flourished for the first half of the 20th century

By 1910, 32 States had established juvenile courts and/or probation services. By 1925, all but two States had followed suit. Rather than merely punishing delinquents for their crimes, juvenile courts sought to turn delinquents into productive citizens—through treatment.

The mission to help children in trouble was stated clearly in the laws that established juvenile courts. This benevolent mission led to procedural and substantive differences between the juvenile and criminal justice systems.

During the next 50 years, most juvenile courts had exclusive original jurisdiction over all youth under age 18 who were charged with violating criminal laws. Only if the juvenile court waived its jurisdiction in a case could a child be transferred to criminal court and tried as an adult. Transfer decisions were made on a case-by-case basis using a "best interests of the child and public" standard, and were thus within the realm of individualized justice.

The focus on offenders and not offenses, on rehabilitation and not punishment, had substantial procedural impact

Unlike the criminal justice system, where district attorneys select cases for trial, the juvenile court controlled its own intake. And unlike criminal prosecutors, juvenile court intake considered extra-legal as well as legal factors in deciding how to handle cases. Juvenile court intake also had discretion to handle cases informally, bypassing judicial action.

In the courtroom, juvenile court hearings were much less formal than criminal court proceedings. In this benevolent court—with the express purpose of protecting children—due process protections afforded criminal defendants were deemed unnecessary. In the early juvenile courts, and even in some to this day, attorneys for the State and the youth are not considered essential to the operation of the system, especially in less serious cases.

A range of dispositional options was available to a judge wanting to help rehabilitate a child. Regardless of offense, outcomes ranging from warnings to probation supervision to training school confinement could be part of the treatment plan. Dispositions were tailored to "the best interests of the child." Treatment lasted until the child was "cured" or became an adult (age 21), whichever came first.

As public confidence in the treatment model waned, due process protections were introduced

In the 1950's and 1960's, many came to question the ability of the juvenile court to succeed in rehabilitating delinquent youth. The treatment techniques available to juvenile justice professionals never reached the desired levels of effectiveness. Although the goal of rehabilitation through individualized justice—the basic philosophy of the juvenile justice system—was not in question, professionals were concerned about the growing number of juveniles institutionalized indefinitely in the name of treatment.

In a series of decisions beginning in the 1960's, the U.S. Supreme Court required that juvenile courts become more formal—more like criminal courts. Formal hearings were now required in waiver situations, and delinquents facing possible confinement were given protection against self-incrimination and rights to receive notice of the charges against them, to present witnesses, to question witnesses, and to have an attorney. Proof "beyond a reasonable doubt" rather than merely "a preponderance of evidence" was now required for an adjudication. The Supreme Court, however, still held that there were enough "differences of substance between the criminal and juvenile courts . . . to hold that a jury is not required in the latter.". . .

Meanwhile, Congress, in the Juvenile Delinquency Prevention and Control Act of 1968, recommended that children charged with noncriminal (status) offenses be handled outside the court system. A few years later, Congress passed the Juvenile Justice and Delinquency Prevention Act of 1974, which as a condition for State participation in the Formula Grants Program required deinstitutionalization of status offenders and nonoffenders as well as the separation of juvenile delinquents from adult offenders. (In the 1980 amendments to the 1974 Act, Congress added a requirement that juveniles be removed from adult jail and lockup facilities.) Community based programs, diversion, and deinstitutionalization became the banners of juvenile justice policy in the 1970's.

In the 1980's, the pendulum began to swing toward law and order

During the 1980's, the public perceived that serious juvenile crime was increasing and that the system was too lenient with offenders. Although there was substantial misperception regarding increases in juvenile crime, many States responded by passing more punitive laws. Some laws removed certain classes of offenders from the juvenile justice system and handled them as adult criminals in criminal court. Others required the juvenile justice system to be more like the criminal justice system and to treat certain classes of juvenile offenders as criminals but in juvenile court.

As a result, offenders charged with certain offenses are *excluded* from juvenile court jurisdiction or face *mandatory* or *automatic waiver* to criminal court. In some States, concurrent jurisdiction provisions give prosecutors the discretion to file certain juvenile cases directly in criminal court rather than juvenile court. In some States, some adjudicated juvenile offenders face *mandatory sentences*.

The 1990's have been a time of unprecedented change as state legislatures crack down on juvenile crime

Five areas of change have emerged as States passed laws designed to crack down on juvenile crime. These laws generally involve expanded eligibility for criminal court processing and adult correctional sanctioning and reduced confidentiality protections for a subset of juvenile offenders. Between 1992 and 1997, all but three States changed laws in one or more of the following areas:

- Transfer provisions—Laws made it easier to transfer juvenile offenders from the juvenile justice system to the criminal justice system (45 States).

- Sentencing authority—Laws gave criminal and juvenile courts expanded sentencing options (31 States).

- Confidentiality—Laws modified or removed traditional juvenile court confidentiality provisions by making records and proceedings more open (47 States).

In addition to these areas, there was change relating to:

- Victims rights—Laws increased the role of victims of juvenile crime in the juvenile justice process (22 States).

- Correctional programming—As a result of new transfer and sentencing laws, adult and juvenile correctional administrators developed new programs.

The 1980's and 1990's have seen significant change in terms of treating more juvenile offenders as criminals. Recently, States have been attempting to strike a balance in their juvenile justice systems among system and offender accountability, offender competency development, and community protection. Juvenile code purpose clauses also incorporate restorative justice language (offenders repair the harm done to victims and communities and accept responsibility for their criminal actions). Many States have added to the purpose clauses of their juvenile codes phrases such as:

- Hold juveniles accountable for criminal behavior.

- Provide effective deterrents.

- Protect the public from criminal activity.

- Balance attention to offenders, victims, and the community.

- Impose punishment consistent with the seriousness of the crime. . . .

YOUNG LAW VIOLATORS GENERALLY ENTER THE JUVENILE JUSTICE SYSTEM THROUGH LAW ENFORCEMENT

Each State's processing of law violators is unique

Juvenile case processing of law violators varies from State to State. Even within States, case processing often varies from community to community, reflecting local practice and tradition. Consequently, any description of juvenile justice processing in the U.S. must be general, outlining a common series of decision points.

Law enforcement diverts many juvenile offenders out of the justice system

At arrest, a decision is made either to send the matter further into the justice system or to divert the case out of the system, often into alternative programs. Usually, law enforcement makes this decision, after talking to the victim, the juvenile, and the parents and after reviewing the juvenile's prior contacts with the juvenile justice system. . . .

     Federal regulations discourage holding juveniles in adult jails and lockups. Law enforcement must detain a juvenile in secure custody for a brief period in order to contact a parent or guardian or to arrange transportation to a juvenile detention facility, Federal regulations require that the juvenile be securely detained for no longer than 6 hours and in an area that is not within sight or sound of adult inmates.

Most juvenile court cases are referred by law enforcement

Law enforcement accounted for 85% of all delinquency cases referred to juvenile court in 1996. [This percentage changed very little from year to year throughout the 1990s—*Ed.*] The remaining referrals were made by others such as parents, victims, schools, and probation officers.

The intake department screens cases referred to juvenile court for formal processing

The court intake function is generally the responsibility of the juvenile probation department and/or the prosecutor's office. Intake decides whether to dismiss the case, to handle the matter informally, or to request formal intervention by the juvenile court.

     To make this decision, an intake officer or prosecutor first reviews the facts of the case to determine whether there is sufficient evidence to prove the allegation. If not, the case is dismissed. If there is sufficient evidence, intake then determines whether formal intervention is necessary.

About half of all cases referred to juvenile court intake are handled informally. Most informally processed cases are dismissed. In the other informally processed cases, the juvenile voluntarily agrees to specific conditions for a specific time period. These conditions often are outlined in a written agreement, generally called a "consent decree." Conditions may include such things as victim restitution, school attendance, drug counseling, or a curfew.

In most jurisdictions, a juvenile may be offered an informal disposition only if he or she admits to committing the act. The juvenile's compliance with the informal agreement often is monitored by a probation officer. Consequently, this process is sometimes labeled "informal probation."

If the juvenile successfully complies with the informal disposition, the case is dismissed. If, however, the juvenile fails to meet the conditions, the intake decision may be revised to prosecute the case formally, and the case then proceeds just as it would have if the initial decision had been to refer the case for an adjudicatory hearing.

If the case is to be handled formally in juvenile court, intake files one of two types of petitions: a delinquency petition requesting an adjudicatory hearing or a waiver petition requesting a waiver hearing to transfer the case to criminal court.

A delinquency petition States the allegations and requests the juvenile court to *adjudicate* (or judge) the youth a delinquent, making the juvenile a ward of the court. This language differs from that used in the criminal court system, where an offender is *convicted* and sentenced.

In response to the delinquency petition, an adjudicatory hearing is scheduled. At the adjudicatory hearing (trial), witnesses are called and the facts of the case are presented. In nearly all adjudicatory hearings, the determination that the juvenile was responsible for the offense(s) is made by a judge; although, in some States, the juvenile has the right to a jury trial. . . .

During the processing of a case, a juvenile may be held in a secure detention facility

Juvenile courts may hold delinquents in a secure juvenile detention facility if this is determined to be in the best interest of the community and/or the child.

After arrest, law enforcement may bring the youth to the local juvenile detention facility. Juvenile probation officers or detention workers then review the case to decide whether the juvenile should be detained pending a hearing by a judge. In all States, a detention hearing must be held within a time period defined by statute, generally within 24 hours.

At the detention hearing, a judge reviews the case and determines whether continued detention is warranted. . . .

Detention may extend beyond the adjudicatory and dispositional hearings. If residential placement is ordered, but no placement beds are available, detention may continue until a bed becomes available.

The juvenile court may transfer the case to criminal court

A waiver petition is filed when the prosecutor or intake officer believes that a case under jurisdiction of the juvenile court would be handled more appropriately in criminal court. The court decision in these matters follows a review of the facts of the case and a determination that there is probable cause to believe that the juvenile committed the act. With this established, the court then considers whether jurisdiction over the matter should be waived and the case transferred to criminal court.

The judge's decision in such cases generally centers on the issue of whether the juvenile is amenable to treatment in the juvenile justice system. The prosecution may argue that the juvenile has been adjudicated several times previously and that interventions ordered by the juvenile court have not kept the juvenile from committing subsequent criminal acts. The prosecutor may also argue that the crime is so serious that the juvenile court is unlikely to be able to intervene for the time period necessary to rehabilitate the youth.

If the judge decides that the case should be transferred to criminal court, juvenile court jurisdiction is waived and the case is filed in criminal court. If the judge does not approve the waiver request, an adjudicatory hearing is scheduled in juvenile court. . . .

Prosecutors file certain cases directly in criminal court

In more than half of the States, the legislature has decided that in certain cases (generally those involving serious offenses) juveniles should be tried as criminal offenders. The law excludes such cases from juvenile court; prosecutors must file them in criminal court. In a smaller number of States, the legislature has given both the juvenile and adult courts original jurisdiction in certain cases. Thus, prosecutors have discretion to file such cases in either criminal court or juvenile court.

Between the adjudication decision and the disposition hearing, probation staff prepares an investigation report

Once the juvenile is adjudicated delinquent in juvenile court, probation staff develop a disposition plan. To prepare this plan, probation staff assess the youth, available support systems, and programs. To assist in this process, the court may order psychological evaluations, diagnostic tests, or a period of confinement in a diagnostic facility.

At the disposition hearing, probation staff present dispositional recommendations to the judge. The prosecutor and the youth may also present dispositional recommendations. After considering the recommendations, the judge orders a disposition in the case.

Most cases placed on probation also receive other dispositions

Most juvenile dispositions are multifaceted. A probation order often includes additional requirements such as drug counseling, weekend confinement in the local detention center, and community or victim restitution. The term of probation may be for a specified period of time or it may be open ended. Review hearings are held to monitor the juvenile's progress and to hear reports from probation staff. After conditions of probation have been successfully met, the judge terminates the case. . . .

The judge may order residential placement

. . .Residential commitment may be for a specific or indeterminate time period. The facility may be publicly or privately operated and may have a secure, prison-like environment or a more open (even home-like) setting. In many States, when the judge commits a juvenile to the State department of juvenile corrections, the department determines where the juvenile will be placed and when the juvenile will be released. In other States, the judge controls the type and length of stay; in these situations, review hearings are held to assess the progress of the juvenile.

Juvenile aftercare is similar to adult parole

Upon release from an institution, the juvenile is often ordered to a period of aftercare or parole. During this period, the juvenile is under supervision of the court or the juvenile corrections department. If the juvenile does not follow the conditions of aftercare, he or she may be recommitted to the same facility or may be committed to another facility.

Status offense and delinquency case processing differ

A delinquent offense is an act committed by a juvenile for which an adult could be prosecuted in criminal court. There are, however, behaviors (such as alcohol possession or use) that are law violations only for juveniles and/or young adults because of their status. These "status offenses" may include such behaviors as running away from home, truancy, ungovernability, curfew violations, and underage drinking.

In many ways, the processing of status offense cases parallels that of delinquency cases. Not all States, however, consider all of these behaviors to be law violations. Many States view such behaviors as indicators that the child is in need of supervision. These States handle status offense matters more like dependency cases than delinquency cases, responding to the behaviors through the provision of social services.

While many status offenders enter the juvenile justice system through law enforcement, in many States the initial, official contact is a child welfare agency. . . .

The Juvenile Justice and Delinquency Prevention Act discourages the holding of status offenders in secure juvenile facilities for detention or placement. This policy has been labeled *deinstitutionalization of status offenders.* There is an exception to the general policy: a status offender may be confined in a secure juvenile facility if he or she has violated a valid court order, such as a probation order requiring the youth to attend school and observe a curfew.

Review Questions

1. What were the distinguishing characteristics of juvenile courts during the early part of the 20th century?

2. What important changes have been introduced in juvenile courts and juvenile justice during the past 40–50 years? Do you think these changes have fundamentally altered the way juvenile courts function? In your view, have the changes improved the juvenile justice system or have they had a negative impact?

3. What are the principal steps or stages in the juvenile justice process and what are the basic options available to decision makers at each stage? Are there any steps you think should be eliminated? Added?

Are there any options that you think should *not* be available? Are there options that *should* be available but are not?

4. Which steps in the juvenile justice process—and which options at each step—are similar to procedures used in criminal cases involving adults? Which ones are unique? Do you think the juvenile justice process should be more (or less) like the process for adults accused of criminal offenses?

5. What is a *status offense?* How is juvenile justice system processing of status offenders similar to processing of delinquency cases? How is it different?

National Estimates of Juvenile Court Processing for Delinquency Cases, 2000

National Center for Juvenile Justice, as compiled in the OJJDP Statistical Briefing Book

- Cases referred to juvenile court are first screened by an intake department (either within or outside the court). The intake department may decide to dismiss the case for lack of legal sufficiency or to resolve the matter formally (petitioned) or informally (nonpetitioned).

Source: National estimates of juvenile court processing for delinquency cases, 2000. (2003). *OJJDP Statistical Briefing Book.* Online. Available: http://ojjdp.ncjrs.org/ojstatbb/asp/JCSCF_Display.asp?ID=qa06601&year= 2000&group=1&type=2. August 11, 2003. Data Source: National Juvenile Court Data Archive. National Center for Juvenile Justice. Pittsburgh, PA. Reprinted courtesy of the National Center for Juvenile Justice and the United States Department of Justice, Office of Juvenile Justice and Delinquency Prevention.

Figure 1–1 National estimates of juvenile court processing for delinquency cases, 2000

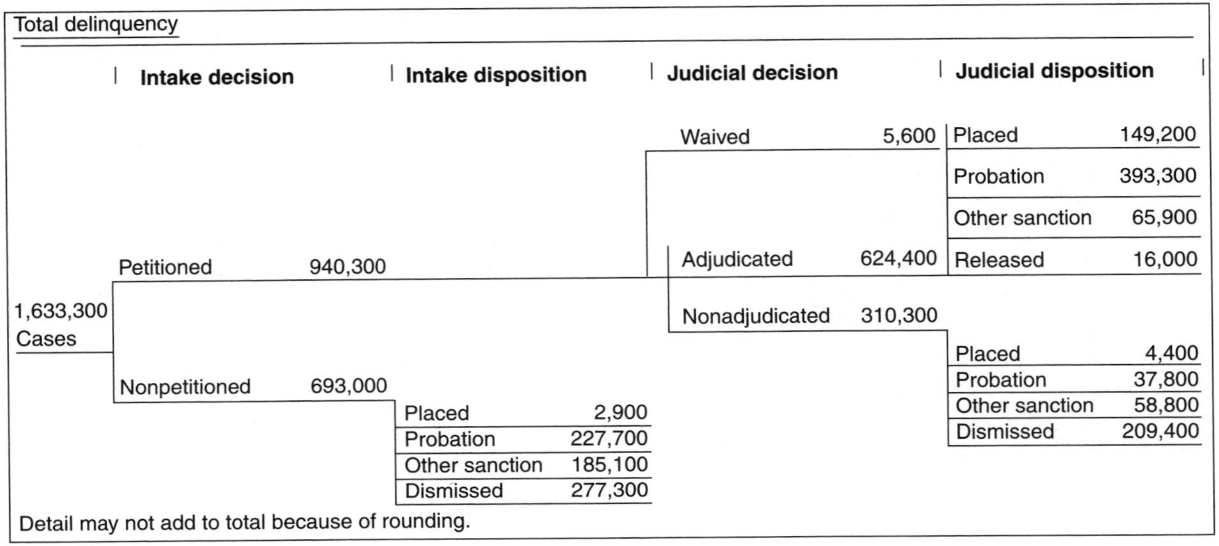

Total delinquency

Intake decision	Intake disposition	Judicial decision	Judicial disposition
		Waived 5,600	Placed 149,200
Petitioned 940,300			Probation 393,300
			Other sanction 65,900
		Adjudicated 624,400	Released 16,000
		Nonadjudicated 310,300	
Nonpetitioned 693,000	Placed 2,900		Placed 4,400
	Probation 227,700		Probation 37,800
	Other sanction 185,100		Other sanction 58,800
	Dismissed 277,300		Dismissed 209,400

1,633,300 Cases

Detail may not add to total because of rounding.

13

- In 2000, 58% (940,300 of 1,633,300) of all delinquency cases disposed by juvenile courts were handled formally while 42% (693,000 of 1,633,300) were handled informally.

- Among nonpetitioned cases, 40% (277,300 of 693,000) were dismissed at intake, often for lack of legal sufficiency. In the remaining cases (60%, or 415,700 of 693,000), youth voluntarily agreed to informal sanctions, including referral to a social service agency, informal probation, or the payment of fines or some form of voluntary restitution.

- If the intake department decides that a case should be handled formally within the juvenile court, a petition is filed and the case is placed on the court calendar (or docket) for an adjudicatory hearing. On the other hand, the intake department may decide that a case should be removed from juvenile court and handled instead in criminal (adult) court. In these cases, a petition is usually filed in juvenile court requesting a waiver/transfer hearing, during which the juvenile court judge is asked to waive jurisdiction over the case.

- In 2000, 66% (624,400 of 940,300 cases) of all formally processed delinquency cases resulted in the youth being adjudicated delinquent. In 33% (310,300 of 940,300) of these cases, the youth was not adjudicated and 1% (5,000 of 940,300) were judicially waived to criminal court.

- At the disposition hearing, the juvenile court judge determines the most appropriate sanction, generally after reviewing a predisposition report prepared by the probation department. The range of options available to a court typically includes commitment to an institution; placement in a group or foster home or other residential facility; probation (either regular or intensive supervision); referral to an outside agency, day treatment, or mental health program; or imposition of a fine, community service, or restitution.

- Youth in 24% (149,200 of 624,400) of adjudicated delinquency cases were placed in a residential facility. In another 63% (393,300 of 624,400) of these adjudicated cases, youth were placed on formal probation.

REVIEW QUESTIONS

1. Which ways of handling cases at each stage of the juvenile justice process are most common? Which are least common? Are the percentages reported for outcomes at each stage what you expected? Why or why not?

2. Why do you think certain dispositions are so much more frequently employed than others? What sorts of offenders do you think tend to receive dispositions that are only rarely imposed on others? Why are such alternatives available to decision makers?

3. Are there options you think should be used more often? Less often? Why?

Juvenile Arrests 2000

Howard N. Snyder

In 2000, law enforcement agencies in the United States made an estimated 2.4 million arrests of persons under age 18.[1] According to the Federal Bureau of Investigation (FBI), juveniles accounted for 17% of all arrests and 16% of all violent crime arrests in 2000. The substantial growth in the number of juvenile violent crime arrests that began in the late 1980s peaked in 1994. In 2000, for the sixth consecutive year, the rate of juvenile arrests for Violent Crime Index offenses—murder, forcible rape, robbery, and aggravated assault—declined. Specifically, between 1994 and 2000, the juvenile arrest rate for Violent Crime Index offenses fell 41%. As a result, the juvenile violent crime arrest rate in 2000 was the lowest since 1985. The juvenile murder arrest rate fell 74% from its peak in 1993 to 2000, when it reached its lowest level since at least the 1960s.

These findings are derived from data reported annually by local law enforcement agencies across the country to the FBI's Uniform Crime Reporting (UCR) Program. Based on these data, the FBI prepares its annual *Crime in the United States* report, which summarizes crimes known to the police and arrests made during the reporting calendar year. This information is used to characterize the extent and nature of juvenile crime that comes to the attention of the justice system. Other recent findings from the UCR Program include the following:

- Of the nearly 1,600 juveniles murdered in 2000, 38% were under 5 years of age, 68% were male, 52% were white, and 52% were killed with a firearm.

- Juveniles were involved in 9% of murder arrests, 14% of aggravated assault arrests, 33% of burglary arrests, 25% of robbery arrests, and 24% of weapons arrests in 2000.

- Juvenile murder arrests increased substantially between 1987 and 1993. In the peak year of 1993, there were about 3,800 juvenile arrests for murder. Between 1993 and 2000, juvenile arrests for murder declined, with the number of arrests in 2000 (1,200) less than one-third that in 1993.

[1]Throughout this Bulletin, persons under age 18 are referred to as juveniles. . . .

Source: Howard N. Snyder. (2002). *Juvenile Arrests 2000.* Washington, DC: Office of Juvenile Justice and Delinquency Prevention. Adapted courtesy of the National Center for Juvenile Justice and the United States Department of Justice, Office of Juvenile Justice and Delinquency Prevention.

Figure 1–2

The number of juvenile arrests in 2000—2.4 million—was 5% below the 1999 level and 15% below the 1996 level

Most Serious Offense	2000 Estimated Number of Juvenile Arrests	Percent of Total Juvenile Arrests		Percent Change		
		Female	Under Age 15	1991–2000	1996–2000	1999–2000
Total	**2,369,400**	**28%**	**32%**	**3%**	**−15%**	**−5%**
Crime Index Total	617,600	28	38	−28	−27	−5
Violent Crime Index	98,900	18	33	−17	−23	−4
Murder and nonnegligent manslaughter	1,200	11	13	−65	−55	−13
Forcible rape	4,500	1	39	−26	−17	−5
Robbery	26,800	9	27	−29	−38	−5
Aggravated assault	66,300	23	36	−7	−14	−4
Property Crime Index	518,800	30	39	−30	−28	−5
Burglary	95,800	12	39	−38	−30	−5
Larceny-theft	363,500	37	40	−24	−27	−6
Motor vehicle theft	50,800	17	26	−51	−34	−3
Arson	8,700	12	65	−7	−17	−7
Nonindex						
Other assaults	236,800	31	43	37	−1	0
Forgery and counterfeiting	6,400	34	12	−20	−24	−7
Fraud	10,700	32	18	−3	−15	−5
Embezzlement	2,000	47	6	132	48	11
Stolen property (buying, receiving, possessing)	27,700	16	29	−40	−33	−1
Vandalism	114,100	12	44	−21	−19	−4
Weapons (carrying, possessing, etc.)	37,600	10	33	−26	−28	−10
Prostitution and commercialized vice	1,300	55	13	−13	−4	−3
Sex offense (except forcible rape and prostitution)	17,400	7	52	−4	8	5
Drug abuse violations	203,900	15	17	145	−4	0
Gambling	1,500	4	18	−27	−30	−22
Offenses against the family and children	9,400	37	38	92	−8	2
Driving under the influence	21,000	17	3	14	13	−3
Liquor law violations	159,400	31	10	20	4	−6
Drunkenness	21,700	20	13	−3	−19	−3
Disorderly conduct	165,700	28	38	33	−9	−8
Vagrancy	3,000	23	28	−33	−7	27
All other offenses (except traffic)	414,200	26	28	35	−5	−5
Suspicion	1,200	22	23	−76	−53	−29
Curfew and loitering	154,700	31	28	81	−16	−11
Runaways	142,000	59	39	−18	−29	−6

◆ In 2000, there were an estimated 1,200 juvenile arrests for murder. Between 1996 and 2000, juvenile arrests for murder fell 55%.

◆ Females accounted for 23% of juvenile arrests for aggravated assault and 31% of juvenile arrests for other assaults (i.e., simple assaults and intimidations) in 2000. Females were involved in 59% of all arrests for running away from home and 31% of arrests for curfew and loitering law violations.

◆ Between 1991 and 2000, there were substantial declines in juvenile arrests for murder (65%), motor vehicle theft (51%), and burglary (38%) and major increases in juvenile arrests for drug abuse violations (145%) and curfew and loitering law violations (81%).

Note: Detail may not add to totals because of rounding.

Data source: *Crime in the United States 2000* (Washington, DC: U.S. Government Printing Office, 2001), tables 29, 32, 34, 36, 38, and 40. Arrest estimates were developed by the National Center for Juvenile Justice.

Figure 1–3

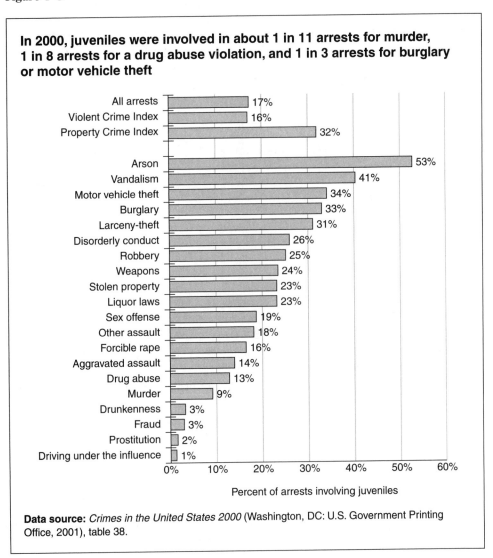

In 2000, juveniles were involved in about 1 in 11 arrests for murder, 1 in 8 arrests for a drug abuse violation, and 1 in 3 arrests for burglary or motor vehicle theft

Category	Percent
All arrests	17%
Violent Crime Index	16%
Property Crime Index	32%
Arson	53%
Vandalism	41%
Motor vehicle theft	34%
Burglary	33%
Larceny-theft	31%
Disorderly conduct	26%
Robbery	25%
Weapons	24%
Stolen property	23%
Liquor laws	23%
Sex offense	19%
Other assault	18%
Forcible rape	16%
Aggravated assault	14%
Drug abuse	13%
Murder	9%
Drunkenness	3%
Fraud	3%
Prostitution	2%
Driving under the influence	1%

Percent of arrests involving juveniles

Data source: *Crimes in the United States 2000* (Washington, DC: U.S. Government Printing Office, 2001), table 38.

- Juvenile arrest rates for burglary declined 63% between 1980 and 2000.
- Between 1990 and 2000, the juvenile proportion of all arrests for drug abuse violations increased from 8% to 13%.

Figure 1–4

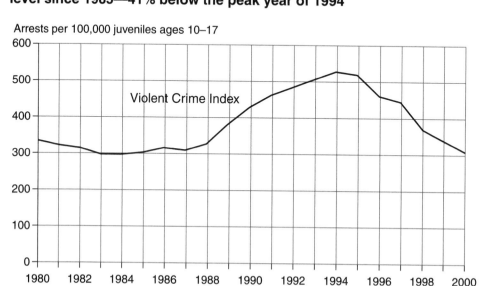

The juvenile Violent Crime Index arrest rate in 2000 was at its lowest level since 1985—41% below the peak year of 1994

Arrests per 100,000 juveniles ages 10–17

◆ All the growth in the juvenile violent crime arrest rate that began in the latter part of the 1980s was erased by 2000.

Data source: Analysis of arrest data from the FBI and population data from the U.S. Bureau of the Census.

- Juvenile arrests for curfew and loitering violations increased 81% between 1991 and 2000. In 2000, 28% of curfew arrests involved juveniles under age 15 and 31% involved females.

- In 2000, 59% of arrests for running away from home involved females and 39% involved juveniles under age 15.

- Arrests of juveniles accounted for 12% of all violent crimes cleared by arrest in 2000—specifically, 5% of murders, 12% of forcible rapes, 16% of robberies, and 12% of aggravated assaults.

Figure 1–5

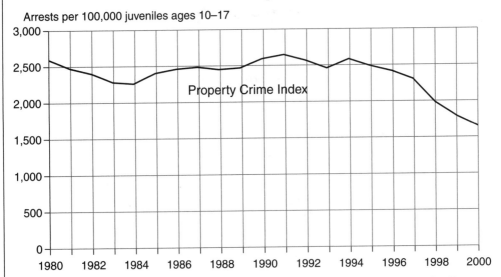

After years of relative stability, the juvenile arrest rate for Property Crime Index offenses fell 37% between 1994 and 2000

Arrests per 100,000 juveniles ages 10–17

Property Crime Index

◆ The relatively stable juvenile arrest rate trend between 1980 and 1997 for Property Crime Index offenses stands in stark contrast to the Violent Crime Index arrest rate trend.

Data source: Analysis of arrest data from the FBI and population data from the U.S. Bureau of the Census.

REVIEW QUESTIONS

1. How many juveniles were arrested in 2000? Which offenses were most common among juveniles? Which were least common?

2. For which offenses did females and youth under age 15 represent the largest percentages of juvenile arrests? For which offenses were the percentages of these two groups lowest? Why do you think the percentages of females and younger juveniles vary so much for different offenses?

3. For which offenses did juveniles represent the largest proportions of all arrests? The smallest proportions? What do you think accounts for these patterns?

4. What trends in juvenile arrests for violent offenses and for property offenses do you see in the charts on pp. 18 and 19? What do you think accounts for these trends?

Youthful Offending in a Developmental Framework

Elizabeth S. Scott and Thomas Grisso

Developmental psychology offers a useful perspective from which to examine and evaluate the changing conceptions of adolescence that have been reflected in the legal responses to juvenile crime during this century. It also clarifies the role that delinquent behavior may play in adolescence. In this [selection], we clarify that many youths engage in criminal activity during adolescence but do not persist into adulthood—a phenomenon that can be explained most satisfactorily in developmental and social terms.[1] We then narrow the focus to examine developmental influences on decision-making that may distinguish the choices of adolescents from those of adults. Our interest here is in factors that may affect the un-

[1]We explore this phenomenon and sketch a theoretical account developed by Terrie Moffitt linking adolescent antisocial behavior to societal constraints on the assumption of adult roles. . . . [As they indicate in this footnote, authors Scott and Grisso ground the first part of their discussion in criminologist Terrie Moffitt's well-known taxonomy of "adolescence-limited" and "life-course-persistent" offenders (see Terrie Moffitt [1993]. Adolescent-limited and life-course-persistent antisocial behavior: A developmental taxonomy. *Psychological Review,* 100, 674–701.) Although Scott and Grisso concentrate most of their attention in Section A on Moffitt's view of factors influencing the "onset" of delinquency followed by later "desistance" among adolescence-limited offenders, you may find that their brief explanation of his distinction between these youth and the much smaller group of "life-course-persistent" offenders helps make the rest of the discussion a little easier to follow. More germane to a full understanding of the arguments advanced in the remainder of the selection, pay close attention to Moffitt's view of developmental influences on adolescence-limited offenders and the way the authors use his ideas as a springboard for the discussion to follow—*Ed.*]

Source: Elizabeth S. Scott and Thomas Grisso. (1997). The evolution of adolescence: A developmental perspective on juvenile justice reform. *Journal of Criminal Law and Criminology, 88*(1), 137–189. Copyright 1997 by Northwestern University School of Law. Reprinted by special permission of Northwestern University School of Law, *Journal of Criminal Law and Criminology.*

derstanding, reasoning and—perhaps most importantly—the judgment of youths who engage in criminal conduct. Finally, we explore how these developmental influences may affect choices made in the criminal justice context—both choices associated with criminal conduct and choices made by youthful defendants in the criminal process.

A. ANTISOCIAL BEHAVIOR AS A PART OF ADOLESCENCE

Substantial evidence indicates that many adolescents become involved in criminal activity in their teens and desist by the time they reach young adulthood. Beginning in early adolescence, criminal behavior increases through age 16 and declines sharply from age 17 onward. Self-report studies indicate that most teenage males engage in some criminal conduct, leading criminologists to conclude that participation in delinquency is "a normal part of teen life." For most adolescent delinquents, desistance from antisocial behavior also seems to be a predictable component of the maturation process. Only a small group of young offenders will persist in a life of crime.

A representative sample of adolescents involved in criminal activity will include a large group whose antisocial conduct is "adolescence-limited" and a much smaller group whose conduct is "life-course-persistent." Although some youths in the latter group initiate antisocial behavior in adolescence, many display a variety of problem behaviors, beginning early in life and persisting through adolescence into adulthood. Of those whose adolescent delinquent conduct is a continuation of earlier antisocial behavior, many, although certainly not all, will become career criminals. However, as Moffitt points out, most youths who engage in delinquent conduct have little notable history of antisocial conduct in childhood; nor will the conduct continue into adulthood. Involvement in criminal activity and other antisocial behavior begins in adolescence and tends to follow a "natural onset and recovery process."

The developmental forces that contribute to the onset and desistance of delinquent adolescent behavior are not well understood. Moffitt offers a plausible etiological theory under which the tendency of adolescents to engage in antisocial behavior can be understood as linked to the gap experienced by contemporary youth between early biological maturity and late social maturity and independence. Moffitt argues that adolescents are striving for elusive autonomy from parental and adult authority in a context in which most privileges of adult status are withheld. Many adolescents may be inclined to mimic their antisocial peers, who appear to have attained adult status in many ways. Through antisocial conduct, the adolescent attenuates the ties of childhood and demonstrates that he can act independently. Under Moffitt's theory, youthful antisocial risk-taking acts are personal statements of independence by individuals who are precluded from yet assuming legitimate adult roles. Desistance in young adulthood is explained under the theory as the adaptive response to changed contingencies, as more legitimate adult roles become available. Delinquent behavior becomes costly rather than rewarding, as many young adults perceive that it threatens now-available conventional opportunities and may foreclose future goals. In short, they come to realize that they have something to lose.[2]

B. REASONING AND JUDGMENT IN ADOLESCENT DECISION MAKING

In this [selection], we shift the focus from a general explanatory account of youthful involvement in crime to an examination of particular developmental influences on individual decision making that may shape the choices of youthful actors in ways that distinguish them from adults. Most familiar, and of particular importance in assessing the competence of younger adolescents to participate in criminal proceedings, are elements of cognitive development—reasoning and understanding. More salient to decisions about participation in criminal conduct are psychosocial factors such as peer influence, temporal perspective (a tendency to focus on short-term versus long-term consequences), and risk perception and preference. These psychosocial factors may affect decision-making in powerful ways that may distinguish juveniles from adults. We designate these psychosocial influences as "judgment" factors, and argue that immature judgment in adolescence may contribute to choices about involvement in crime.[3] This framework is largely consistent with Moffitt's theory, but focuses on internal dynamic influences on adolescent decision-making that are associated with this developmental stage, whereas Moffitt's emphasis is on changing external contingencies.

1. Cognitive Capacity: The Process of Decision-making

It is generally recognized that decision-making capacities increase through childhood into adolescence and that, although there is great variability among individuals, preadolescents

---

[2] . . . Moffitt distinguishes adolescent-limited delinquents entering adulthood from life-course-persistent youths on a number of grounds that account for the failure of youths in the latter group to desist in their antisocial behavior when they become adults. Adolescents for whom delinquency is limited to this developmental stage will not bear the cumulative effects of lifelong antisocial conduct. Typically, they will have engaged in delinquent activity for a shorter time and of a less serious nature than will their life-persistent counterparts, and thus may be less likely to have experienced damaging consequences. They are also more likely to have acquired social and academic skills that prepare them for adult roles. Finally, their delinquency does not reflect deeply entrenched personality disorder as may often be true of life-course-persistent offenders. . . .

[3] The judgment framework that we describe [in Subsection 2—*Ed.*] was developed and applied to adolescent decision making by Elizabeth Scott, N.D. Reppucci and Jennifer Woolard in earlier work. *See* Elizabeth S. Scott et al., *Evaluating Adolescent Decision-making in Legal Contexts,* 19 LAW & HUM. BEHAV. 221 (1995); Elizabeth S. Scott, *Judgment and Reasoning in Adolescent Decision-making,* 37 VILL. L. REV. 1607 (1992). The impact of psychosocial factors on adolescent decision-making was further developed by Lawrence Steinberg and Elizabeth Cauffman. *See* Lawrence Steinberg & Elizabeth Cauffman, *Maturity of Judgment in Adolescence: Psychosocial Factors in Adolescent Decision-making,* 20 LAW & HUM. BEHAV. 249 (1996). . . .

and younger teens differ substantially from adults in their abilities. Development occurs along several lines. The capacities to process information and to think hypothetically develop into adolescence, and cognitive performance improves generally due to knowledge gained in specific domains. Moreover, cognitive skills acquired earlier mature and develop into adolescence.

The question of how adolescents' capacities for understanding and reasoning in making decisions compare with that of adults has received much attention among policy analysts and children's rights advocates in recent years—although largely not in the context of juvenile justice policy. Proponents of broader self-determination rights for minors, drawing on child development theory and empirical research, have argued that, by about age fourteen, adolescents' cognitive decision-making abilities are similar to those of adults. This argument holds that adolescents are capable of making informed and competent decisions about medical treatment and other matters, and should have the legal authority to do so. The evidence for these claims is drawn in part from Piaget's stage theory of cognitive development and from several empirical studies of minors' ability to understand and reason about medical and abortion decisions, to understand treatment issues in psychotherapy, and to understand their Fifth Amendment rights and the meaning of Miranda waivers.

Together, this scientific research and theory support the claim that adolescents are more competent decision-makers than has been presumed under paternalistic policies, but the scientific evidence for the claim that their cognitive decision-making capacity is comparable to that of adults is unclear. We and others have made this argument elsewhere, and thus we will sketch only the most salient points. First, Piaget's strict stage theory of cognitive development is no longer accepted among cognitive psychologists. Further, the studies that support the claim of competence are small and mostly involve middle class subjects of average intelligence. Only a handful compare the decision-making of minors with that of adults. Finally, the studies of adolescent decision-making have been conducted in laboratory settings in which the decision is hypothetical and "pre-framed" in the sense that all relevant information is provided to the subjects. This format yields little useful data about how decisions are made in informal unstructured settings (such as the street), in which decision-makers must rely on their own experience and knowledge in making choices. Moreover, research offers little evidence of how minors may function relative to adults in stressful situations in which decisions have salience to their lives.

In sum, scientific authority indicates that, in general, the cognitive capacity for reasoning and understanding of preadolescents and many younger teens differs substantially in some regards from that of older teens and adults. Tentative authority also supports the conclusion that, by mid-adolescence, youthful capacities for reasoning and understanding approximate those of adults. Whether and how these capacities are employed, however, may be quite variable, and adolescent performance is not necessarily like that of adults in various contexts. Because the research was largely undertaken in structured settings, the findings may be more useful in shedding light on questions about competence to stand trial than on cognitive capacity as it affects choices relevant to criminal conduct.

2. Judgment Factors in Decision-making

Psychosocial developmental factors may also influence decision-making by adolescents in ways that are relevant to competence to stand trial and criminal responsibility. Particularly salient in this context might be factors such as (1) conformity and compliance in relation to peers, (2) attitude toward and perception of risk, and (3) temporal perspective. If these factors influence decision-making, the impact is not on cognitive competence, narrowly defined, but rather on "judgment" (as the term is used in common parlance). The traditional presumption (in juvenile justice and in many other policy areas) that minors are not fully accountable and need legal protection rests in part on a view that their judgment is immature. In essence, the intuition is that developmentally-linked predispositions and responses systematically affect decision making of adolescents in ways that may incline them to make choices that threaten harm to themselves and to others. Whereas cognitive competence affects the process of decision-making, immature judgment is reflected in outcomes, in that developmental factors influence values and preferences, which in turn shape the cost–benefit calculus. The influence of these factors (peer influence, attitude toward risk, and temporal perspective) will change as the individual matures and values and preferences change—resulting in different choices.

a. Peer Influence

It is widely assumed that peer influence plays an important role in adolescent crime, and evidence supports the claim that teens are more subject to this influence than are adults. Peer influence seems to operate through two means: social comparison and conformity. Through social comparison, adolescents measure their own behavior by comparing it to others. Social conformity to peers, which peaks at about age fourteen, influences adolescents to adapt their behavior and attitudes to that of their peers. Peer influence could affect adolescent decision-making in several ways. In some contexts, adolescents might make choices in response to direct peer pressure. More indirectly, adolescent desire for peer approval could affect the choices made, without any direct coercion. Finally, as Moffitt suggests, peers may provide models for behavior that adolescents believe will assist them to accomplish their own ends.

b. Attitude Toward Risk

Research evidence also indicates that adolescents differ from adults in their attitude toward and perception of risk. It is well established that adolescents and young adults generally take more risks with health and safety than do older adults by engaging more frequently in behavior such as unprotected sex, drunk driving and criminal conduct. This inclination may result because adolescents are less aware of risks than are adults, because they calculate the probability of risks differently, or because they value them differently. In some contexts, adolescent risk preferences may be linked to other developmental factors. For example, adolescents may be more averse than adults to risking social ostracism.

c. Temporal Perspective

Differences between adults and adolescents in attitude toward risk are related to differences in temporal perspective. Adolescents seem to discount the future more than adults do, and to weigh more heavily short-term consequences of decisions—both risks and benefits—a response that in some circumstances can lead to risky behavior. This tendency may be linked to the greater uncertainty that young people have about their future, an uncertainty that makes short-term consequences seem more salient. It may also reflect the difference in experience between teens and adults. It may simply be harder for an adolescent than for an adult to contemplate the meaning of a consequence that will have an impact ten or fifteen years into the future.

In general, the fact that adolescents have less experience than adults seems likely to affect decision-making in tangible and intangible ways. Although the relative inexperience of adolescents has not been contested as a general proposition, the relevance of inexperience to decision-making and judgment is uncertain.

C. THE IMPACT OF DEVELOPMENTAL FACTORS ON DECISION-MAKING ABOUT OFFENDING

The research evidence on the impact of immaturity of reasoning and judgment on adolescent decision-making is sketchy, and, thus, assertions about the effects must be very tentative. With this caveat, it seems probable that developmental factors associated with adolescence could affect decision-making in several ways. First, adolescents may use information differently from adults. They may consider different or fewer options in thinking about their available choices or in identifying consequences when comparing alternatives. The extent and sources of the differences in use of information are unclear. It is plausible that dissimilar and more limited experience and knowledge, as well as attitudes toward risk, temporal perspective, and peer influence, are all implicated. These differences may be most evident in unstructured informal settings, where information is not provided, and individuals must make choices based on their own knowledge and experience. Thus, adolescents on the street, who are making choices that lead to criminal conduct, may be less able than adults to consider alternative options that could extricate them from a precarious situation. Secondly, substantial theoretical arguments hold that while older adolescents may have adult-like capacities for reasoning, they may not deploy those capacities as uniformly across different problem-solving situations as do adults, and they may do so less dependably in ambiguous or stressful situations. Finally, adolescents, for developmental reasons, could differ from adults in the subjective value that is assigned to perceived consequences in the process of making choices. Influenced by the developmental factors that we have described, adolescents may weigh costs and benefits differently (or view as a benefit what adults would count as a cost).

These developmentally driven differences could be important to choices about participation in crime. Consider the following example. A youth hangs out with his buddies on the street. Someone suggests holding up a nearby convenience store. The boy's decision to go along with the plan may proceed in the following way. He has mixed feelings about the proposal, but doesn't think of ways to extricate himself—although perhaps a more mature person might develop a strategy. The possibility that one of his friends has a gun and the consequences of that may not occur to him. He goes along, mostly because he fears rejection by his friends, a consequence that he attaches to a decision not to participate—and that carries substantial negative weight. Also the excitement of the hold-up and the possibility of getting some money are attractive. These weigh more heavily in his decision than the cost of possible apprehension by the police, or the long-term costs to his future life of conviction of a serious crime.

The example presents, in our view, a quite plausible account of the influence of the developmental factors that we have described on the decisions of adolescents to engage in criminal conduct. The choice, although it may reflect a lack of knowledge and experience, may not be irrational, because the youth is choosing the option that promotes subjective utility, given his values. The decision does, however, implicate immaturity of judgment—at least from a societal perspective—because it causes harm to a victim, and threatens harm to the youth himself.

If these influences on decision-making are developmental and not simply reflective of individual idiosyncratic preferences for risk-taking, they should abate with maturity. This prediction is consistent with the pattern of desistance from delinquent conduct in late adolescence or early adulthood that we have described. In general, it is reasonable to argue that the developmental factors of peer influence, temporal perspective, and risk perception and preference contribute to delinquent behavior and that their declining influence contributes to desistance. Although the factors contributing to desistance have not been adequately studied, researchers have linked desistance in late adolescence to a longer-term perspective and to changing patterns of peer relationships. As Moffitt postulates, young adults may cease to commit crimes because they come to understand that the decision to offend carries the risk of lost future opportunities. In other words, a cost–benefit calculus leads to a conclusion that choosing crime no longer maximizes subjective utility.

What is not clear is whether the source of the change is exogenous or endogenous. Moffitt seems to suggest that the calculus shifts because external contingencies change. A focus on psychosocial influences that contribute to immaturity of judgment suggests that desistance can be linked to developmental maturation. Based on the developmental research and theory that we have described, we are inclined to believe that much adolescent participation in crime is the result of interaction between developmental influences on decision-making and external contingencies that affect individuals during this stage. Very recent studies have begun to demonstrate the relationship between psychosocial developmental factors and the quality of youths' choices compared to those of adults. Further research is required, however, to determine the degree to which these developmental factors directly affect the decisions of youths participating in delinquent activity.

D. THE IMPACT OF DEVELOPMENTAL FACTORS ON DECISION-MAKING IN THE CRIMINAL PROCESS

Increasingly, under the legislative reforms of recent years, youths who are charged with crimes are tried as adults, or face severe punishment for their offenses even if they are tried in juvenile court. In this context, it becomes relevant to ask whether developmental factors are likely to influence the capacities of youthful defendants to participate in their defense. The importance of this inquiry is clear in light of the constitutional requirement that criminal defendants be competent to participate in the proceedings against them. Historically, questions of competence to stand trial have arisen in cases involving mentally ill and mentally retarded defendants. As younger defendants face adult criminal proceedings and punishment, cases involving trial incompetence due to immaturity are likely to increase.

Richard Bonnie has described two broad types of abilities associated with the defendants' legal competence to participate in criminal proceedings. The first is the capacity to assist counsel. This involves the defendant's ability to understand and appreciate the meaning of the legal procedure and her rights within that process, and the ability to assist counsel in developing a defense. The second concept is decisional competence, referring to defendants' capacities for reasoning and judgment needed to make decisions in the process, including decisions to waive important rights. In these areas of ability, developmental immaturity may impede the capacity of juvenile defendants to participate in criminal proceedings. As compared to the scant empirical data about youthful decisions to offend, substantial research has examined different dimensions of juveniles' capacities as they could affect their participation in trials. A recent comprehensive review of research suggests that delinquent adolescents are at risk of being less competent participants in their defense then are adults, and that this risk is especially great for youths under the age of 14.

Studies on youths' understanding of matters related to trials, such as the roles of participants and the trial process, have found that youths under the age of 14 typically are deficient in their knowledge of the legal process and its basic purposes. In contrast, few differences in basic understanding of trial-related matters have been observed between adolescents 14 to 17 years of age and adults, when the populations studied were "average" adolescents. Similarly, a conventional grasp of the nature of legal rights typically has developed by mid-adolescence. Moreover, fundamental abilities of sensation, perception, and memory ordinarily have matured by early adolescence, suggesting that adolescents on average should be as capable as adults of providing accurate information to their attorneys from their experience.

Delinquent youths, however, are more likely than average to have disabilities—for example, emotional disturbances, learning and attention deficit disorders, or poorer intellectual capacities—that may contribute to delays in the development of capacities for understanding, communication, and the ability to attend to the trial process as it unfolds. Studies of delinquent youths' understanding of the trial process and capacity to assist counsel have found important deficiencies, often distinguishing these juveniles from adults and from "average" adolescents. Compared to adults, both delinquent and non-delinquent adolescents who have lower intelligence test scores, problematic educational histories, learning disabilities, and mental disorders have shown poorer comprehension of basic information about the legal process. Other evidence has suggested that delinquent youths' experience with courts, attorneys, and law enforcement officers does not reliably compensate for these tendencies toward poorer understanding of information related to the trial process and rights.

Defendants must also be able to make decisions in the trial process, and thus, reasoning and judgment capacities are implicated, as well as understanding. The direct evidence is sketchy about how adolescents compare with adults in their capacities to reason about important legal decisions and in their valuation of the consequences of those decisions. As we have described, capacities associated with reasoning and problem solving are in a formative stage in the primary school years. One study, for example, found that youths between ten and thirteen-years-of-age were significantly less likely than older adolescents to think "strategically" about pleading decisions, when hypothetical conditions varied as to evidence of guilt and seriousness of accusations. Research finding younger adolescents to be less capable of imagining risky consequences during hypothetical problem solving, and to consider a more constricted number and range of consequences, also suggests that they may have difficulty considering the merits of plea agreements and making other decisions about their defense. As we have indicated, most studies have found few differences between older adolescents (ages fifteen to seventeen) and adults in formal decision-making functions. Again, however, most of these studies have involved non-delinquent youths, without documented disabilities, processing hypothetical rather than real decision problems (in non-stressful settings), focused on medical treatment rather than criminal or delinquency adjudication.

Beyond the formal ability to understand and process information, youthful judgment may differ from that of adults in ways that could affect the ability to assist counsel and to make decisions. How defendants respond to attorneys' advice and weigh the consequences of their choices in the trial process may be affected by psychosocial factors such as peer and adult influence, temporal perspective, and risk preference and perception. Such differences might influence youths' judgments about the value of accepting plea bargains and of waiving important rights in the legal process. In one study, for example, delinquent youths, in considering the waiver of Miranda rights, focused more than adults on immediate consequences of waiver (release from custody) rather than the impact of the decision on later events in court. A more subtle issue is the effect of psychosocial factors on the attorney–client relationship, particularly on the inclination to trust the attorney and to value her advice, as compared, for example, to advice from peers.

In the trend toward treating more and younger juveniles charged with crimes as adults, little attention has been paid to whether youthful defendants can competently participate in the process. Yet it is uncontroversial that competence is a critical requirement for fair criminal proceedings. The research evidence suggests that many youths may be less competent than adults to assist counsel and make important decisions in their defense.

REVIEW QUESTIONS

1. What is developmental psychology? How is it relevant to juvenile justice?

2. What do authors Scott and Grisso mean when they claim that antisocial behavior is "a part of adolescence" (p. 21)? How is this claim supported by criminologist Terrie Moffitt's view of developmental influences on "adolescence-limited" offenders?

3. In what ways and to what extent does the cognitive capacity (i.e., reasoning ability) of adolescents differ from that of adults?

4. What factors influence the judgment of adolescents? In what ways and to what extent does their judgment differ from that of adults?

5. How do developmental factors affect adolescents' decisions about committing delinquent acts? In what ways do you think the role of developmental factors in adolescent misconduct should influence juvenile justice system intervention with delinquent youth? Do you think such considerations should also be taken into account in determining whether to transfer a juvenile accused of a serious offense to criminal court for trial as an adult? Why or why not?

6. In what ways are developmental factors relevant to the ability of adolescents to understand their legal rights and to comprehend police and court procedures? How, if at all, do you think this should influence decisions about transferring serious juvenile offenders to adult court? What safeguards do you think should be used by police, intake officers, probation officers, and judges to ensure that juveniles adequately understand proceedings in their cases?

Disproportionate Minority Confinement: A Review of the Research Literature from 1989 Through 2001

Carl E. Pope, Rick Lovell, and Heidi M. Hsia

Concerns about the overrepresentation of minority youth in secure confinement have long been noted, and much research has been devoted to this issue. It is only within the past decade or so, however, that national attention has been directed to the impact of race on juvenile justice decisionmaking. In the 1988 amendments to the Juvenile Justice and Delinquency Prevention (JJDP) Act of 1974 (Pub. L. No. 93–415, 42 U.S.C. 5601 *et seq.*), Con-

Source: Carl E. Pope, Rick Lovell, and Heidi M. Hsia. (2002). *Disproportionate Minority Confinement: A Review of the Research Literature From 1989 Through 2001.* Washington, DC: Office of Juvenile Justice and Delinquency Prevention. Adapted courtesy of the United States Department of Justice, Office of Juvenile Justice and Delinquency Prevention.

gress required that States participating in the Formula Grants Program determine if disproportionate minority confinement (DMC) exists and, if so, demonstrate efforts to reduce it. In the words of the Act, States must "address efforts to reduce the proportion of juveniles detained or confined in secure detention facilities, secure correctional facilities, jails, and lockups who are members of minority groups if such proportion exceeds the proportion such groups represent in the general population." For the purposes of the JJDP Act, the Office of Juvenile Justice and Delinquency Prevention (OJJDP) defined minority populations as African Americans, American Indians, Asians, Pacific Islanders, and Hispanics (OJJDP Regulations, 28 CFR Part 31). In the 1992 amendments to the JJDP Act, DMC was elevated to a core requirement, with future funding eligibility tied to State compliance.[1]

As outlined by OJJDP, addressing DMC involves five phases of ongoing activities:

- Identifying the extent to which DMC exists.

- Assessing the reasons for DMC if it exists.

- Developing an intervention plan to address these identified reasons.

- Evaluating the effectiveness of strategies to address DMC.

- Monitoring DMC trends over time.

To implement DMC efforts, States have sponsored numerous studies at the State and local levels and published many reports of their findings. There are now three national reports that summarize States' DMC efforts at each phase since the enactment of the amendment (Feyerherm, 1993; Hamparian and Leiber, 1997; and Hsia and Hamparian, 1998). Additionally, major reports have been published that describe lessons learned from five OJJDP-sponsored DMC pilot States (Devine, Coolbaugh, and Jenkins, 1998), present updated DMC national data (Snyder and Sickmund, 1999; Poe-Yamagata and Jones, 2000), and examine the transfer of juvenile offenders to adult court (Males and Macallair, 2000; Juszkiewicz, 2000).

In addition to the State and national DMC reports, a variety of social science journals have published a body of research that examines race and juvenile justice processing. As part of the first OJJDP-funded DMC research effort, Pope and Feyerherm (1990) undertook an analysis of DMC-related literature published between January 1969 and February 1989. The results of this analysis of 46 research articles clearly showed that there were substan-

---

[1][Amendments to the JJDP Act enacted in 2002 broadened the scope of the DMC requirement to expressly target disproportionate minority contact with all components of the juvenile justice system. The Act now specifies that participating States must "address juvenile delinquency prevention efforts and system improvement efforts designed to reduce, without establishing or requiring numerical standards or quotas, the disproportionate number of juvenile members of minority groups, who come into contact with the juvenile justice system." (see p. 244). Note that this selection, although originally published before the 2002 amendments were enacted, addresses decision making at all stages of the juvenile justice process—*Ed.*]

tial differences in the processing of minority youth within many juvenile justice systems. These differences could not be attributed solely to the presence of legal characteristics or other factors. Instead, approximately two-thirds of the reviewed research indicated that a youth's racial status made a difference at selected stages of juvenile processing. Moreover, these findings were independent of the type of research design employed. In other words, studies employing various types of methodologies were equally likely to find differences: research finding evidence of racial bias was no more or less sophisticated than research finding no such evidence. Differential outcomes could occur at any stage of juvenile processing and, in some instances, were cumulative (i.e., racial differences became more pronounced the further the youth penetrated into the system). Clearly, this was cause for concern.

The purpose of this Bulletin is to extend the earlier analysis by examining research found in professional academic journals and edited books during the subsequent 12-year period. Conference papers or presentations are excluded from the current review, as are unpublished State studies or plans, except when portions of these may have formed the basis for a journal publication. A methodological format similar to that employed in the earlier study is used. The question is simple: What does the existing periodical research now tell us about the processing of minority youth through the juvenile justice system? This Bulletin details the results of this analysis. . . .

METHODOLOGY

The present review includes DMC studies published in professional academic journals and scholarly books from March 1989 through December 2001. Like the earlier research summary (Pope and Feyerherm, 1990), it focuses on empirical research studies of the official processing of minority youth. It does not directly encompass research on the full range of conditions that might place minority youth at risk of coming into contact with law enforcement and/or the courts. The focus of this review is on decisions made within the juvenile justice system and on studies that bear on the question of whether race appears to be related to the outcomes of those decisions.

The first stage of the review involved a search for the target literature. Five data-based library searches covering the targeted time period were conducted. . . . This process produced a total of 126 potentially relevant documents that warranted additional review to determine whether the studies sufficiently addressed DMC.

The next stage in the review involved the selection of the substantive materials for inclusion in the examination. . . . The process resulted in the selection of 34 publications relevant to the review. . . .

The third stage of the examination required an intensive, critical review of the 34 documents selected. The investigators thoroughly reviewed the selected publications, each initially taking a subset of one-half of the targeted works. A matrix was developed to standardize the categorization and extraction of key features from each of the studies. . . .

To enhance reliability, the investigators each reviewed the subset of articles initially examined by the other, as well as verifying the information extracted and categorized by the other. The initial 25 of the 34 obtained were sent to two consultant reviewers who also examined these works and verified the information extracted and categorized by the investigators. The final stage was analyzing and synthesizing the matrix information.

ANALYSIS

Characteristics of the Studies Reviewed

Across the studies, the minority groups of interest included African American (27 studies), Hispanic or Latino (11 studies), American Indian (4 studies), and Asian American (2 studies), with the majority of the studies focusing on more than one minority group. It is important to note that four studies used the category "other" to aggregate data on minority groups other than African American, and five studies employed a general categorization of "nonwhite" for analysis. The studies reviewed targeted a variety of sites covering diverse jurisdictions from many areas of the United States, with the largest number of the studies from the Midwest (14). Other studies focused on the East (7 studies, many in Pennsylvania), Florida (3 studies), Washington and California (4 studies), and Arizona (1 study). Five of the studies involved national databases or multiregional sites. Data collection involved a variety of sources and approaches. Most (19) of the studies were primarily quantitative in nature, several (12) combined quantitative and qualitative approaches, and a few (3) studies were primarily qualitative in nature.

The studies examined an array of processing points and outcomes, including arrest, detention, petition, adjudication, and disposition. Disposition (20 studies) and petition (13 studies) were the most frequently examined processing points, and more than half (18) of the studies examined multiple decision points in juvenile justice processing. Several independent variables were in evidence across the studies, most centering on the legal and social characteristics of the youth being processed (e.g., offense characteristics, prior record). More than 80% of the studies employed multivariate analytic approaches, most often logistic regression—an approach that facilitates an assessment of the relative importance of individual factors or groups of factors that may explain the outcome and the degrees to which these factors relate to the outcome of interest.

Of the 46 studies included in the earlier DMC literature review (Pope and Feyerherm, 1990), 19 were published during the 1970s and 27 during the 1980s. The present review yielded 34 published studies from 1989 through 2001. Four of the studies included in this review were published in an edited book. Thirty empirical studies directly relevant to DMC were published in academic journals over the 12-year period, with none published during the year 2000. Taken in perspective, the number of empirical studies published during this time period is surprisingly small.

Salient Findings From the Review

The majority of the studies reviewed (25 out of 34) report race effects in the processing of youth [i.e., differences in the way youth of different races are treated—Ed.]. Eight studies reported direct or indirect effects, and 17 studies revealed mixed results (i.e., race effects were present at some decision points yet not present at others, or race effects were apparent for certain types of offenders or certain offenses but not for others). Of the remaining nine studies in the present review, one found no race effects and eight reported that the effects related to DMC outcomes could not be determined. Effects in these latter studies were categorized as "unknown" because data were not analyzed for DMC outcomes. However, these studies were included in this review because they were empirical and because they can assist in identifying factors of potential importance in DMC research.

The current review mirrors Pope and Feyerherm's previous DMC literature review, in which the majority of studies were also found to show race effects. The results of the current review differ from the previous DMC review in that a greater proportion of the studies showed "mixed" effects (17 out of 34 in the current review compared with 8 out of 46 in the earlier review). Nevertheless, the preponderance of the research over three decades documents evidence of racial disparities, at least at some stages within the juvenile justice system.

Taken together, the research findings support the existence of disparities and potential biases in juvenile justice processing. However, the causes and mechanisms of these disparities are complex. Important contributing factors may include inherent system bias, effects of local policies and practices, and social conditions (such as inequality, family situation, or underemployment) that may place youth at risk. Further, overrepresentation may result from the interaction of factors. Also, the most significant factors may vary by jurisdiction.

The previous DMC review noted increasing sophistication in the methodologies employed by researchers examining this issue. This pattern continued with the studies examined in the present review. More than 80 percent of the studies employed complex designs and used multivariate analytic techniques. These techniques increase the potential for identifying indirect effects, particularly for showing interaction effects that could help identify variables that relate to race—often called surrogate variables (e.g., family situation). This may also lead to more qualification of results. Increasing precision and using combinations of approaches represent the main methods for identifying the causes and mechanisms leading to existing disparities.

Although the current review found increasing precision in study methodologies and more "mixed results" in study findings, this does not mean that disproportionality has decreased. Rather, it reveals that locating the source(s) of disproportionality is complex. For example, a linear "cumulative disadvantage" is not in evidence (i.e., disproportionality does not increase from petition to disposition). Significant differences between minorities and whites may not occur at all decision points, and where a decision point shows a significant difference, the legally relevant variables (e.g., prior record, current offense) that are analyzed may not be the source. Therefore, the increasing precision in study methodology leads to a focus on other variables of potential importance and/or other sources, as well as refinement of the reasons why disproportionality occurs.

The results of the studies in this review add to the understanding that disparate outcomes may occur at any stage of juvenile processing. Although seven studies found that differences between minority and majority youth increased as youth were processed through decision stages, as was reported in the previous DMC review, this review does not provide strong support about accumulation of disadvantage because 17 studies produced mixed results regarding race effects. This points to the need to focus on similarly situated offenders and questions concerning when, how, and to what degree they become dissimilar or disadvantaged. As with the previous review, this review found few studies that examined police decisionmaking. Further, there was little attention to the interaction of the effects of decisions by corrections officials.

The current review shows that researchers are paying increasing attention to minority groups other than African Americans. The current review yielded 11 studies that examined issues related to Hispanics, 4 that included American Indians, and 2 that included Asians, while the earlier review examined 6 studies on Hispanics, 1 on American Indians, and 1 on Asians. However, research concerning American Indians and Asian Americans remained very sparse during the last 12 years. Between March 1989 and December 2001, there were five studies that used the category "nonwhite" and two studies that grouped all non-African American minorities as "other."

This review shows that the body of knowledge concerning DMC is growing, albeit very slowly, and the research is increasing in complexity. It highlights the diversity present across the studies in terms of perspectives, approaches, designs, definitions, and measures. As discussed earlier, the delivery of juvenile justice services varies from jurisdiction to jurisdiction—what happens in one locale is not necessarily what happens in another. The same is true for research: Variations across methods, time frames, and measures, among other considerations, make comparisons across the studies very difficult. This may be inevitable in the development of a body of research-based knowledge. Nevertheless, greater emphasis is needed on the state of knowledge, gaps in the knowledge base, issues regarding methodology, and explication of meaningful policy implications. Many variables remain unmeasured. For example, there is little information on the attitudes of youth and the relationship of those attitudes to the decisions of officials. Similarly, information on the history of drug/alcohol abuse among family members or guardians is not consistently recorded and is largely unavailable.

Overall, as found in the previous DMC review, the majority of studies continue to provide evidence of race effects, direct or indirect, at certain stages of juvenile justice processing and in certain jurisdictions. Accounting for these effects remains difficult. Data on disproportionality often are adequate for identifying rather broad patterns, but inadequate for a precise understanding of which factors are most important and how these factors operate to produce the observed results. . . .

CONCLUSION

Considering the evidence from this and the previous DMC literature review, it is clear that the issue of race is central to the administration of juvenile justice in this country. The majority of the empirical studies over the past three decades report race effects—direct, indirect, or, more often, mixed. The number of studies reporting mixed results highlights the complexity of the problem.

It is clear that the state of knowledge is far from complete. More precise research-based information is needed, as are additional efforts to identify gaps in the knowledge base, encourage targeted research to fill these gaps, conduct well-focused efforts to address DMC-related issues, and build sustained partnerships between DMC researchers and practitioners at both the national and the local level. . . .

REFERENCES

Devine, P., Coolbaugh, K., and Jenkins, S. (1998). *Disproportionate Minority Confinement: Lessons Learned From Five States* [Bulletin]. Washington, DC: U.S. Department of Justice, Office of Justice Programs, Office of Juvenile Justice and Delinquency Prevention.

Feyerherm, W. (1993). *The Status of the States: A Review of State Materials Regarding Overrepresentation of Minority Youth in the Juvenile Justice System* [Report]. Washington, DC: U.S. Department of Justice, Office of Justice Programs, Office of Juvenile Justice and Delinquency Prevention.

Hamparian, D., and Leiber, M.J. (1997). *Disproportionate Confinement of Minority Youth in Secure Facilities: 1996 National Report*. Report. Washington, DC: U.S. Department of Justice, Office of Justice Programs, Office of Juvenile Justice and Delinquency Prevention.

Hsia, H.M., and Hamparian, D. (1998). *Disproportionate Minority Confinement: 1997 Update*. Bulletin. Washington, DC: U.S. Department of Justice, Office of Justice Programs, Office of Juvenile Justice and Delinquency Prevention.

Juszkiewicz, J. 2000. *Youth Crime/Adult Time: Is Justice Served*. Washington, DC: Youth Law Center.

Males, M., and Macallair, D. (2000). *The Color of Justice: An Analysis of Juvenile Adult Court Transfer in California*. Washington, DC: Youth Law Center.

Poe-Yamagata, E., and Jones, M. (2000). *And Justice for Some: Differential Treatment of Minority Youth in the Justice System*. Washington, DC: Youth Law Center.

Pope, C.E., and Feyerherm, W. (1990). Minority status and juvenile justice processing. *Criminal Justice Abstracts* 22(2):327–336 (part I); 22(3):527–542 (part II).

Snyder, H.N., and Sickmund, M. (1999). *Minorities in the Juvenile Justice System*. Bulletin. Washington, DC: U.S. Department of Justice, Office of Justice Programs, Office of Juvenile Justice and Delinquency Prevention.

REVIEW QUESTIONS

1. This report was based on a review of 34 studies examining handling of minorities in the juvenile justice system that were conducted between 1989 and 2001. What were the major findings? You may find it helpful to try to "unpack" each paragraph of the "salient findings" section on pp. 32-34 by translating them into more easily understandable terminology and exploring the implications of each point the authors raise.

2. What do the authors conclude about the processing of minority youth? To what extent does this conclusion seem warranted

by the results of their review of the literature? Based on their discussion, do you believe that racial discrimination is sufficiently extensive to be considered a major problem in the juvenile justice system?

3. The Juvenile Justice and Delinquency Prevention Act's disproportionate minority confinement (DMC) requirement, discussed at the beginning of this selection, will again draw our attention in Chapter 6. Differential treatment of minority youth is a focus of selections in other chapters as well. It should be evident that the question of racial disparity arises at every stage of the juvenile justice process. What do you think State governments should do to try to ensure fair treatment of minority youth in the juvenile justice system? Should the federal government play a role? Is there anything individual agencies or organizations involved in processing of juvenile offenders can do to combat racial discrimination?

What About the Girls? Delinquency Programming as if Gender Mattered

Meda Chesney-Lind

The FBI noted in 1999 that every year, girls account for one out of four arrests of young people in America. Despite this, young women almost always are invisible when the delinquency "problem" is discussed and largely forgotten when programs for "delinquents" are crafted.

CHARACTERISTICS OF GIRLS AT RISK

According to Girls Inc., a national organization serving girls (i.e., Girl Scouts), girls at risk for becoming involved in the juvenile justice system face problems regarding school and community situations, family circumstances, and individual/peer characteristics. These problems are, in many ways, similar to those faced by boys, however, they take on special dimensions as a result of the way gender works in the lives of young women.

Clearly, young women residing in poverty-ridden and often violent communities face the greatest challenges of growing up optimally. Triply marginalized by age, race and gender, structural inequity and institutional racism haunt the lives of girls in these neighbor-

Source: Meda Chesney-Lind. (2001, February). What about the girls? Delinquency programming as if gender mattered. *Corrections Today, 63*(1), 38–45. Copyright by American Correctional Association. Reprinted with permission of the American Correctional Association, Lanham, Md.

hoods. Lack of educational and employment opportunities increases despair and the probability of engaging in self-destructive, delinquent activities (including horizontal violence against other girls); this is especially true for girls who reside in communities in which crime and gang violence are prevalent.

Recently, the coping strategies of young minority women, particularly those who drift into gangs, have been demonized by the media. A closer look at the data on girls and violence, including gang violence, reveals a much more complex picture. Certainly, we need to get beyond either denial or demonization of girls' violence to a perspective that puts the behavior in its psychological and social contexts.

Educational neglect is another salient risk factor related to youth involvement in delinquency. A 1990 report by the American Correctional Association (ACA) found that 78% of female juvenile offenders had neither completed high school nor obtained a general equivalency diploma. Likewise, substance abuse is another prominent characteristic of particularly at-risk girls. Nearly two-thirds of the girls in U.S. training schools need substance abuse treatment at intake and more than half are multiply addicted.

Related to the drug problem, reported ACA, are rates of sexual abuse, which are disconcertingly high among at-risk girls. Girls in the juvenile justice system have experienced particularly high levels of abuse; more than 60% have been victims of some form of physical abuse and 54% reported being victims of sexual abuse. As of 1990, nearly 90% of these girls reported that the first incident of sexual and/or physical abuse occurred before age 15. Not surprisingly, a link between victimization and subsequent delinquent and/or self-destructive behavior is evident.

Girls often respond to abuse by fighting back, "acting out" and/or running away from home. Recent studies show that more than 70% of girls on the streets have run away to flee violence in their homes. As a result, runaway girls are at further risk of victimization and often resort to prostitution, petty theft and drug dealing to survive. ACA also reported that more than 80% of girls in the system have run away from home and a staggering 50% have run away from home six or more times. . . .

SHORTCHANGING GIRLS: PROBLEMS WITH TRADITIONAL DELINQUENCY PROGRAMS

Researcher Christine Alder points out that serving girls effectively will require different and innovative strategies since "young men tend to be more noticeable and noticed than young women." Girls involved in the juvenile justice system are particularly invisible in terms of programming. For example, one national study of 443 delinquency program evaluations conducted since 1950 revealed that 34.8 percent of these programs only served males and 42.4 percent served primarily boys. Conversely, in 1992, only a meager 2.3% of delinquency programs served only girls, and 5.9 percent served primarily girls, according to researcher M.W. Lipsey. Other surveys of youth programming show similar levels of programmatic neglect of girls' issues.

The Minnesota Women's Fund noted that the most frequent risk factors for girls and boys differ, and that for girls, the list includes emotional stress, physical and sexual abuse, negative body image, eating disorders, suicide and pregnancy. For boys, the list includes alcohol, multiple drug use, accidental injury and delinquency. While clearly not all girls at risk will end up in the juvenile justice system, this gendered examination of youth problems sets a standard for examination of delinquency prevention and intervention programs.

Most programs and services are narrowly focused on a specific, often stereotypical issue to the exclusion of interrelating factors that place young women at risk. Programs tend to emphasize a single issue, often teen pregnancy and mothering. They may focus on substance abuse, sexual abuse or, more recently, gang violence; these patterns are largely a result of issue-specific funding initiatives that have been concerned with one "problem" at a time. Similarly, programs tend to be more intervention-oriented than preventive, concentrating more on girls who are already in trouble than on girls who are at risk of getting into trouble, according to the Ms. Foundation for Women.

PROGRAMMING AS IF GIRLS MATTERED

Effective girls' programs should address the following: physical and sexual violence (from parents, boyfriends, pimps, and others), risk of HIV/AIDS, pregnancy and motherhood, drug and alcohol dependency, family problems, unemployment and employment training, finding safe housing, managing stress, and developing a sense of efficacy and empowerment. Many of these needs are universal and should be part of programs for all youths, according to juvenile justice experts Ira Schwartz and Frank Orlando. However, most of these are particularly important for young women.

Programs also must be scrutinized to assure that they are culturally specific as well as gender-specific. As increasing numbers of minority girls are drawn into the juvenile justice system (and bootstrapped into correctional settings), while their white counterparts are deinstitutionalized, there is a need for programs to be rooted in specific cultures. According to researchers Hortensia Amaro, Maria Agular and Peggy Orenstein, since it is clear that minority girls have different experiences of their gender, as well as different experiences with the dominant institutions in the society, programs to divert and deinstitutionalize must be shaped by the unique developmental issues confronting minority girls, as well as building in the specific cultural resources available in ethnic communities.

Given what is known about at-risk girls' characteristics, problems and needs, what can girls' programs do to help? Programs, particularly those that are issue-specific, need to provide transition and aftercare services that support young women in maintaining the progress they have made. Girls' programs also need to create separate time and space for girls, separate from boys, so that issues related to sexism will not be overshadowed by boys' more disruptive behavior.

Programs, particularly prevention programs for girls, need to begin at earlier ages. Many at-risk girls may engage in delinquent behavior simply because there is little else to occupy their free time. Structured recreation that gets past the "girls watching boys play sports" approach should be vigorously explored. Girls already embedded within the juvenile justice system frequently state that had they had opportunities to engage in meaningful, interesting activities, they probably would not have fallen into the system. In the words of one girl at the Hawaii Youth Correctional Facility, having "something to do, like a job or something" could have helped her to be delinquency-free. Likewise, another girl in the facility stated that "if you're smart and strong enough and keep busy, you can stay out of trouble."

Finally, programs should invariably work to empower girls and advocate for change that will benefit them. This entails not only building on girls' innate strengths, skills and creativity to develop their voices and their abilities to assert themselves, but also identifying and challenging barriers that girls, particularly marginalized girls, face in our society.

REFERENCES

Alder, Christine. 1995. *Delinquency prevention with young women.* Paper presented at the Delinquency Prevention Conference, Terrigal, New South Wales, Australia.

Amaro, Hortensia. 1995. Love, sex and power. Considering women's realities in HIV prevention. *American Psychologist,* 50(6) 437–447.

Amaro, Hortensia and Agular, Maria. 1994. *Programa Mama: Mom's project: A Hispanic/Latino family approach to substance abuse prevention.* Center for Substance Abuse Prevention, Mental Health Services Administration.

American Correctional Association. 1990. *The female offender: What does the future hold?* Lanham, MD: American Correctional Association.

Federal Bureau of Investigation. 1999. *Crime in the United States, 1998.* Washington, DC: Government Printing Office, p. 219.

Girls Inc. 1996. *Prevention and parity: Girls in juvenile justice.* Indianapolis, Girls Inc. National Resource Center.

Lipsey, M.W. 1992. Juvenile delinquency treatment: A meta-analytic inquiry into the variability of effects. In *Meta-analysis for explanation: A casebook,* eds. T.A. Cook, H. Cooper, D.S. Cordray, H. Hartmann, L.V. Hedges, R.J. Light, T.A. Louis, & E. Mosleller, (83-126). New York: Russell Sage.

Orenstein, Peggy. 1994. *School girls.* New York: Doubleday.

Schwartz, I.M., and F. Orlando. 1991. *Programming for young women in the juvenile justice system.* Ann Arbor, University of Michigan Center for the Study of Youth Policy.

REVIEW QUESTIONS

1. What are the major characteristics of girls at risk for juvenile justice system involvement, according to the reports cited by Chesney-Lind at pp. 36-37? How do these characteristics seem to differ from those of their male counterparts and in what ways do they seem similar? How do the "risk factors" for girls that are identified on p. 38 differ from those for boys? Are there any ways in which they are similar?

2. What are the implications of gender-based differences in the characteristics and risk

factors Chesney-Lind identifies for the kinds of services needed by female offenders in the juvenile justice system?

3. How are available juvenile justice system services different for boys and girls? Why and in what ways does the author believe that girls are "shortchanged" by traditional delinquency programs? What additional services does she argue should be made available for girls?

4. Consider the points raised in this selection about the characteristics of "at-risk" fe-

males in the context of Scott and Grisso's discussion of adolescent development earlier in this chapter. In what ways and to what extent do you think girls' reasoning and judgment differs from that of boys? Do you think gender differences in psychological development have an impact on decisions about committing delinquent acts? Do developmental differences influence the respective abilities of male and female youth to understand their legal rights and comprehend police and court procedures?

FURTHER READING

American Bar Association and National Bar Association. (2001). *Justice by Gender: The Lack of Appropriate Prevention, Diversion and Treatment Alternatives for Girls in the Justice System.* Washington, DC: American Bar Association and National Bar Association. Available online: http://www.abanet.org/crimjust/juvjus/justicebygenderweb.pdf

Bernard, Thomas J. (1992). *The Cycle of Juvenile Justice.* New York: Oxford University Press.

Chesney-Lind, Meda, and Shelden, Randall G. (2004). *Girls, Delinquency and Juvenile Justice* (3rd ed.). Belmont, CA: Wadsworth.

Feld, Barry C. (1999). *Bad Kids: Race and the Transformation of the Juvenile Court.* New York: Oxford University Press.

Grisso, Thomas, and Schwartz, Robert G. (Eds.). (2000). *Youth on Trial: A Developmental Perspective on Juvenile Justice.* Chicago: University of Chicago Press.

Leonard, Kimberly Kempf, Pope, Carl E., and Feyerherm, William H. (Eds.). (1995).

Minorities in Juvenile Justice. Thousand Oaks, CA: Sage.

McCord, Joan, Widom, Cathy Spatz, and Crowell, Nancy A. (Eds.). (2001) *Juvenile Crime, Juvenile Justice.* Washington, DC: National Academy Press.

Moffitt, Terrie (1993). Adolescent-limited and life-course-persistent antisocial behavior: A developmental taxonomy. *Psychological Review, 100,* 674–701.

Rosenheim, Margaret K. (Ed.). (2001). *A Century of Juvenile Justice.* Chicago: University of Chicago Press.

Snyder, Howard N., and Sickmund, Melissa (1999). *Juvenile Offenders and Victims: 1999 National Report.* Washington, DC: Office of Juvenile Justice and Delinquency Prevention. Available online: http://www.ncjrs.org/html/ojjdp/nationalreport99/toc.html

2

Juvenile Courts and the Invention of Delinquency

It may come as a surprise to students of our modern juvenile justice system that young offenders were not always treated differently from adult criminals. Separate correctional institutions for juvenile offenders did not emerge in the United States until well into the 19th century, however, and distinctive juvenile courts did not begin to appear until almost the 20th.

Although some historians point to the English Bridewells (after London's Bridewell Palace, used as a workhouse for paupers and vagrants beginning in the mid-16th century) as early antecedents of contemporary juvenile correctional institutions (see Krisberg & Austin, 1993), the first known institution established specifically to house wayward youth was the New York House of Refuge. Opened in 1825 by the Society for the Reformation of Juvenile Delinquents (formerly the Society for the Prevention of Pauperism), the New York House of Refuge was designed to provide an alternative to the jails, workhouses, and other facilities in which delinquent, dependent, and neglected youth had formerly been housed side-by-side with adult criminals.

Houses of Refuge modeled after New York's soon sprang up in Boston (1826) and Philadelphia (1828). These institutions became the vanguard of a burgeoning movement among wealthy philanthropists to extend their largesse in yet another direction via charitable efforts to rescue and reform youth growing up in the squalid slums of the young nation's largest cities and thereby to relieve a major source of disorder and social upheaval among immigrants and the poor (Mennel, 1973; see also Schlossman, 1977; Krisberg & Austin, 1993).

Early court decisions lauded the intervention of these new institutions in the lives of troubled adolescents. The most significant of these, *Ex Parte Crouse,* an 1839 case involving a girl committed to the Philadelphia House of Refuge, is reproduced as the first selection in this chapter. In *Crouse,* the Pennsylvania Supreme Court resurrected the common law concept of *parens patriae* to justify the state's intervention to supercede the role of a child's parents in guiding the child away from a life of crime. Recall from Chapter 1 that *parens patriae*—a term most commonly translated as "father of the country" or "parent of the country" and generally referring to the obligation of the state to protect and care for people who cannot care for themselves—became the dominant rationale for state intervention in the lives of troubled youth. The *Crouse* case was instrumental in introducing the doctrine to the American lexicon and cementing it in an essentially new role as the principal legal foundation for separate treatment of young offenders without the encumbrance of Constitutional safeguards guaranteed to adult defendants in criminal court.

Despite the pronouncements of their proponents and the blessing of the courts, though, youth confined in Houses of Refuge were exposed to a harsh institutional regimen that entailed rigid discipline, long hours of strenuous work, corporal punishment and, not infrequently, extended periods of solitary confinement. The accounts of early observers offer a telling glimpse into the daily life of a refuge inmate:

> At sunrise, the children are warned, by the ringing of a bell, to rise from their beds. Each child makes his own bed, and steps forth, on a signal, into the Hall. They then proceed, in perfect order, to the Wash Room. Thence they are marched to parade in the yard, and undergo an examination as to their dress and cleanliness; after which, they attend morning prayer. The morning school then commences, where they are occupied in summer, until 7 o'clock. A short intermission is allowed, when the bell rings for breakfast; after which, they proceed to their respective workshops, where they labor until 12 o'clock, when they are called from work, and one hour allowed them for washing and eating their dinner. At one, they again commence work, and continue at it until five in the afternoon, when the labor of the day terminates. Half an hour is allowed for washing and eating their supper, and at half-past five, they are conducted to the school room where they continue at their studies until 8 o'clock. Evening Prayer is performed by the Superintendent; after which, the children are conducted to their dormitories, which they enter, and are locked up for the night, when perfect silence reigns throughout the establishment. The foregoing is the history of a single day, and will answer for every day in the year, except Sundays, with slight variations during stormy weather, and the short days in winter. (Society for the Reformation of Juvenile Delinquents, *Annual Report,* 1835; quoted in Mennel, 1973, pp. 18–19 [footnote omitted]. Reprinted by permission of The University Press of New England.)

> Nothing short of excessive ignorance can entertain for a moment the idea that the inmates of the Refuge are contented. In summer, they are about fourteen hours under orders daily. On parade, at table, at their work, and in school, they are not allowed to converse. They rise at five o'clock in summer—are hurried into the yard—hurried into the dining-room—hurried at their work and at their studies. For every trifling commission or omission which it is deemed wrong to do or to omit to do, they are "cut" with rattan. Every day they experience a series of painful excitements. The endurance of the whip, or the loss of a meal—deprivation of play or the solitary cell. On every hand their walk is bounded; while Restriction and Constraint are their most intimate companions. Are they contented? (Elijah Devoe, *The Refuge System,* 1848; quoted in Mennel, 1973, p. 27 [footnote omitted]. Reprinted by permission of The University Press of New England.)

Dissatisfaction with the methods employed in Houses of Refuge proliferated as the century progressed, giving rise to a new generation of reformers who came to be known as "child savers." Anthony Platt, in a widely publicized book, described the role of the child savers both in redirecting juvenile correctional interventions in the last half of the 19th century and in instituting a series of reforms that culminated in the initiation of the first juvenile court and replacement of Houses of Refuge with a new type of institution that collectively came to be known as reformatories, reform schools, or, somewhat later, training schools. Platt's article-length summary of the major themes developed in *The Child Savers* appears as the second selection in this chapter.

As Platt recounts, the efforts of the child savers culminated as the 19th century drew to a close and a wave of reformist spirit swept through the country during a period that came to be known (though Platt doesn't mention it by name) as the Progressive Era. The Progressive Era spawned massive changes in American society including women's suffrage, workplace safety laws, child labor laws, welfare, and indeterminate sentences for adult criminals. Not least among the reforms initiated during this period was the introduction of the country's first juvenile court, established in Chicago in 1899. To be sure, juvenile delinquency cases had already begun to receive special handling in Boston, Colorado, and elsewhere, most commonly as a result of the efforts of charismatic, child-focused judges such as Denver's Ben Lindsey. A number of these developments were concisely summarized by the President's Commission on Law Enforcement and Administration of Justice in the groundbreaking 1967 report of its Task Force on Juvenile Delinquency and Youth Crime:

> In 1861 the mayor of Chicago was authorized to appoint a commissioner to hear and decide minor charges against boys between 6 and 17 years and to place them on probation or in a reformatory, power which the judges received in 1867. In 1869 a Massachusetts statute provided for the presence in court of an agent of the State in cases where the child might be committed to the State reformatory; the agent was also charged with finding foster homes in suitable cases and paying subsequent visits to them. A law of 1870 required separate hearing of children's cases in Suffolk County (Boston) and authorized a representative of the Commonwealth to investigate cases, attend trials, and protect children's interests. The separate trial statute was extended throughout the Commonwealth in 1872, followed in 1877 by provision for separate sessions, dockets, and court records in juvenile cases. New York established separate trials, dockets, and records in 1892. Rhode Island in 1898 instituted segregation of children under 16 years awaiting trial, separate arraignments and trials, special dockets and records, and presence at juvenile proceedings of public and private agents to protect the interests of the child. (p. 3)

Still, it took the Illinois Juvenile Court Act of 1899 to codify for the first time the operation of a truly separate court for young people. The Act—reproduced as the third selection in this chapter—authorized circuit and county courts to designate a separate courtroom as the "juvenile court" and provided for a process by which a "petition" to the court could be filed on behalf of any child believed to be "neglected," "dependent," or "delinquent," as these terms were defined in the statute. The Act also authorized the juvenile court to assign a probation officer to conduct any needed investigations, represent the child's interests in court, and supervise the child following adjudication. The act further authorized the court to assign a guardian and/or commit the youth to a suitable "family home," training school, or other appropriate institution if deemed necessary.

The philosophy and operation of the Chicago juvenile court are described in our next selection—a classic *Harvard Law Review* article penned by Julian Mack, one of the first judges of the court and one of its most eloquent supporters. Judge Mack described the philosophical underpinnings of the court, the qualities he considered most desirable in its judges, the role of probation officers, and the basic operations of the court. His discussion is now regarded as the seminal statement of the ideals and practices underlying the traditional juvenile court.

Commonwealth v. Fisher, the 1905 case appearing as the final selection in this chapter, reinforced the doctrine of *parens patriae* and ratified the authority of juvenile court judges to remove youth from homes they deemed unsatisfactory—even in the absence of a jury trial or other trappings of the criminal process. Curiously, this case involved the same court (the Pennsylvania Supreme Court) and the same institution (the Philadelphia House of Refuge—although, in light of Platt's discussion, nearly everything but the name on the gate had undoubtedly changed in the interim) as the *Crouse* case decided nearly 70 years earlier. Although its decision applied only to juvenile courts in Pennsylvania, *Fisher* continues to be cited as the landmark case legitimating the *parens patriae* authority of juvenile court judges to adjudicate cases in an informal, nonadversarial atmosphere and to hand down decisions consistent with their perception of the best interests of the child—completely disregarding, if they wish, any or all of the Constitutional rights guaranteed to an adult facing trial in criminal court.

REFERENCES

Krisberg, Barry, and Austin, James F. (1993). *Reinventing Juvenile Justice.* Newbury Park, CA: Sage.

Mennel, Robert M. (1973). *Thorns and Thistles: Juvenile Delinquents in the United States, 1825-1940.* Hanover, NH: University Press of New England.

Schlossman, Steven L. (1977). *Love and the American Delinquent: The Theory and Practice* of *"Progressive" Juvenile Justice, 1825–1920.* Chicago: University of Chicago Press.

Task Force on Juvenile Delinquency. (1967). *Task Force Report: Juvenile Delinquency and Youth Crime—Report on Juvenile Justice and Consultants' Papers.* The President's Commission on Law Enforcement and Administration of Justice. Washington, DC: U.S. Government Printing Office.

Ex Parte Crouse

The Supreme Court of Pennsylvania
4 Whart. 9 (1839)

This was a habeas corpus directed to the keeper and managers of the "House of Refuge," in the county of Philadelphia, requiring them to produce before the court one Mary Ann Crouse, an infant, detained in that institution. The petition for the habeas corpus was in the name of her father.

By the return to the writ it appeared, that the girl had been committed to the custody of the managers by virtue of a warrant under the hand and seal of Morton McMichael, Esq., a justice of the peace of the county of Philadelphia, which recited that complaint and due proof had been made before him by Mary Crouse, the mother of the said Mary Ann Crouse, "that the said infant by reason of vicious conduct, has rendered her control beyond the power of the said complainant, and made it manifestly requisite that from regard to the moral and future welfare of the said infant she should be placed under the guardianship of the managers of the House of Refuge;" and the said alderman certified that in his opinion the said infant was "a proper subject for the said House of Refuge." Appended to the warrant of commitment were the names and places of residence of the witnesses examined, and the substance of the testimony given by them respectively, upon which the adjudication of the magistrate was founded.

The House of Refuge was established in pursuance of an Act of Assembly passed on the 23d day of March 1826. The sixth section of that act declared that the managers should, "at their discretion, receive into the said House of Refuge, such children who shall be taken up or committed as vagrants, or upon any criminal charge, or duly convicted of criminal offences, as may be in the judgment of the Court of Oyer and Terminer, or of the Court of Quarter Sessions of the peace of the county, or of the Mayor's Court of the city of Philadelphia, or of any alderman or justice of the peace, or of the managers of the almshouse and house of employment, be deemed proper objects." By a supplement to the act passed on the 10th day of April 1835, it was declared, that in lieu of the provisions of the act of 1826, it should be lawful for the managers of the House of Refuge "at their discretion, to receive into their care and guardianship, infants, males under the age of twenty-one years, and females under the age of eighteen years committed to their custody in either of the following modes, viz First: Infants committed by an alderman or justice of the peace on the complaint and due proof made to him by the parent, guardian or next friend of such infant, that by reason of incorrigible or vicious conduct such infant has rendered his or her control beyond the power of such parent, guardian or next friend, and made it manifestly requisite that from regard for the morals and future welfare of such infant, he or she should be placed under the guardianship of the managers of the House of Refuge. Second: Infants committed by the authority aforesaid, where complaint and due proof have been made that such infant is a proper subject for the guardianship of the managers of the House of Refuge, in consequence of vagrancy, or of incorrigible or vicious conduct, and that from the moral depravity or otherwise of the parent or next friend in whose custody such infant may be, such parent or next friend is incapable or unwilling to exercise the proper care and discipline over such incorrigible or vicious infant. Third: Infants committed by the courts of this Commonwealth in the mode provided by the act to which this is a supplement." . . .

PER CURIAM.—The House of Refuge is not a prison, but a school. Where reformation, and not punishment, is the end, it may indeed be used as a prison for juvenile convicts who would else be committed to a common gaol; and in respect to these, the constitutionality of the act which incorporated it, stands clear of controversy. It is only in respect of the application of its discipline to subjects admitted on the order of the court, a magistrate or the managers of the Almshouse, that a doubt is entertained. The object of the charity is reformation, by training its inmates to industry; by imbuing their minds with principles of morality and religion; by furnishing them with means to earn a living; and, above all, by separating them from the corrupting influence of improper associates. To this end may not the natural parents, when unequal to the task of education, or unworthy of it, be superseded by the *parens patriae,* or common guardian of the community? It is to be remembered that the public has a paramount interest in the virtue and knowledge of its members, and that of strict right, the business of education belongs to it. That parents are ordinarily intrusted with it is because it can seldom be put into better hands; but where they are incompetent or corrupt, what is there to prevent the public from withdrawing their faculties, held, as they obviously are, at its sufferance? The right of parental control is a natural, but not an unalienable one. It is not excepted by the declaration of rights out of the subjects of ordinary legislation; and it consequently remains subject to the ordinary legislative power which, if wantonly or inconveniently used, would soon be constitutionally restricted, but the competency of which, as the government is constituted, cannot be doubted. As to abridgment of indefeasible rights by confinement of the person, it is no more than what is borne, to a greater or less extent, in every school; and we know of no natural right to exemption from restraints which conduce to an infant's welfare. Nor is there a doubt of the propriety of their application in the particular instance. The infant has been snatched from a course which must have ended in confirmed depravity; and, not only is the restraint of her person lawful, but it would be an act of extreme cruelty to release her from it.

Remanded.

REVIEW QUESTIONS

1. What kinds of children could be placed in the Philadelphia House of Refuge? What sorts of proceedings were necessary before a child could be placed there?

2. How did Mary Ann Crouse get placed in the House of Refuge? Who wanted to have her placed there? Who brought the *habeas corpus* action seeking her release? Can you

discern the legal grounds for the *habeas corpus* petition?

3. Did the Pennsylvania Supreme Court order Mary Ann Crouse released? What was the rationale for their decision?

4. What is meant by *parens patriae*? What circumstances justify the government in using its *parens patriae* authority to remove a child from his or her parents' custody?

5. What impression of the Philadelphia House of Refuge do you get from reading this case? Was it designed to help children? Was it a pleasant place to live? Do you think the court would have decided the case differently if it was aware of conditions such as those described in the introduction to this chapter?

The Rise of the Child-Saving Movement: A Study in Social Policy and Correctional Reform

Anthony Platt

This paper analyzes the nature and origins of the reform movement in juvenile justice and juvenile corrections at the end of the nineteenth century. Delinquency raises fundamental questions about the objects of social control, and it was through the child-saving movement that the modern system of delinquency-control emerged in the United States. The child-savers were responsible for creating a new legal institution for penalizing children (juvenile court) and a new correctional institution to accommodate the needs of youth (reformatory). The origins of "delinquency" are to be found in the programs and ideas of these reformers, who recognized the existence and carriers of delinquent norms.

IMAGES OF DELINQUENCY

The child-saving movement, like most moral crusades, was characterized by a "rhetoric of legitimization," built on traditional values and imagery. From the medical profession, the child-savers borrowed the imagery of pathology, infection, and treatment; from the tenets

Source: Anthony Platt. (1969). The rise of the child-saving movement: A study in social policy and correctional reform. *The Annals of the American Academy of Political and Social Science, 381,* 21–38. Copyright 1969 by the American Academy of Political and Social Science. Adapted by permission.

of Social Darwinism, they derived their pessimistic views about the intractability of human nature and the innate moral defects of the working class; finally, their ideas about the biological and environmental origins of crime may be attributed to the positivist tradition in European criminology and to antiurban sentiments associated with the rural, Protestant ethic.

American criminology in the last century was essentially a practical affair. Theoretical concepts of crime were imported from Europe, and an indiscriminating eclecticism dominated the literature. Lombrosian positivism and Social Darwinism were the major sources of intellectual justification for crime workers. The pessimism of Darwinism, however, was counterbalanced by notions of charity, religious optimism, and the dignity of suffering which were implicit components of the Protestant ethic. . . .

Nature versus Nurture

. . . The organization of correctional workers through national representatives and their identification with the professions of law and medicine operated to discredit the tenets of Darwinism and Lombrosian theory. Correctional workers did not think of themselves merely as the custodians of a pariah class. The self-image of penal reformers as doctors rather than guards and the domination of criminological research in the United States by physicians helped to encourage the acceptance of "therapeutic" strategies in prisons and reformatories. . . . Perhaps what is more significant is that physicians furnished the official rhetoric of penal reform. Admittedly, the criminal was "pathological" and "diseased," but medical science offered the possibility of miraculous cures. Although there was a popular belief in the existence of a "criminal class" separated from the rest of mankind by a "vague boundary line," there was no good reason why this class could not be identified, diagnosed, segregated, changed, and controlled.

By the late 1890's, most correctional administrators agreed that hereditary theories of crime were overfatalistic. The superintendent of the Kentucky Industrial School of Reform told delegates to a national conference on corrections that heredity is "unjustifiably made a bugaboo to discourage efforts at rescue. We know that physical heredity tendencies can be neutralized and often nullified by proper counteracting precautions." E.R.L. Gould, a sociologist at the University of Chicago, similarly criticized biological theories of crime for being unconvincing and sentimental. "Is it not better," he said, "to postulate freedom of choice than to preach the doctrine of the unfettered will, and so elevate criminality into a propitiary sacrifice?"

Charles Cooley was one of the first sociologists to observe that criminal behavior depended as much upon social and economic circumstances as it did upon the inheritance of biological traits. "The criminal class," he said, "is largely the result of society's bad workmanship upon fairly good material." In support of this argument, he noted that there was a "large and fairly trustworthy body of evidence" to suggest that many "degenerates" could be converted into "useful citizens by rational treatment."

Urban Disenchantment

Another important influence on nineteenth-century criminology was a disenchantment with urban life—an attitude which is still prevalent in much "social problems" research. Immigrants were regarded as "unsocialized," and the city's impersonality compounded their isolation and degradation. "By some cruel alchemy," wrote Julia Lathrop, "we take the sturdiest of European peasantry and at once destroy in a large measure its power to rear to decent livelihood the first generation of offspring upon our soil." The city symbolically embodied all the worst features of industrial life. . . .

Programs which promoted rural and primary group concepts were encouraged because slum life was regarded as unregulated, vicious, and lacking social rules. Its inhabitants were depicted as abnormal and maladjusted, living their lives in chaos and conflict. It was consequently the task of social reformers to make city life more wholesome, honest, and free from depravity. Beverley Warner told the National Prison Association in 1898 that philanthropic organizations all over the country were making efforts to get the children out of the slums, even if only once a week, into the radiance of better lives. . . . It is only by leading the child out of sin and debauchery, in which it has lived, into the circle of life that is a repudiation of things that it sees in its daily life, that it can be influenced.

Although there was a wide difference of opinion among experts as to the precipitating causes of crime, it was generally agreed that criminals were abnormally conditioned by a multitude of biological and environmental forces, some of which were permanent and irreversible. Biological theories of crime were modified to incorporate a developmental view of human behavior. If, as it was believed, criminals are conditioned by biological heritage and brutish living conditions, then prophylactic measures must be taken early in life. Criminals of the future generations must be reached. "They are born to cringe," wrote the penologist Enoch Wines in 1880, "brought up for it. They must be saved."

MATERNAL JUSTICE

The 1880's and 1890's represented for many middle-class intellectuals and professionals a period of discovery of the "dim attics and damp cellars in poverty-stricken sections of populous towns" and of "innumerable haunts of misery throughout the land." The city was suddenly discovered to be a place of scarcity, disease, neglect, ignorance, and "dangerous influences." Its slums were the "last resorts of the penniless and the criminal"; here humanity reached its lowest level of degradation and despair.

The discovery of problems posed by "delinquent" youth was greatly influenced by the role of feminist reformers in the child-saving movement. It was widely agreed that it was a woman's business to be involved in regulating the welfare of children, for women were considered the "natural caretakers" of wayward children. Women's claim to the public care of children had some historical justification during the nineteenth century, and their role in child-rearing was considered paramount. Women were regarded as better teachers than men and were also more influential in child-training at home. The fact that public education also came more under the direction of women teachers in the schools increased the predominance of women in the raising of children.

Child-saving was a predominantly feminist movement, and it was regarded even by antifeminists as female domain. The social circumstances behind this appreciation of maternalism were women's emancipation and the accompanying changes in the character of traditional family life. Educated middle-class women now had more leisure time but a limited choice of careers. Child-saving was a reputable task for women who were allowed to extend their housekeeping functions into the community without denying antifeminist stereotypes of woman's nature and place. . . .

Child-saving may be understood as a crusade which served symbolic and status functions for native, middle-class Americans, particularly feminist groups. Middle-class women at the turn of the century experienced a complex and far-reaching status revolution. Their traditional functions were dramatically threatened by the weakening of domestic roles and the specialized rearrangement of family life. One of the main forces behind the child-saving movement was a concern for the structure of family life and the proper socialization of young persons, since it was these concerns that had traditionally given purpose to a woman's life. Professional organizations—such as settlement houses, women's clubs, bar associations, and penal organizations—regarded child-saving as a problem of women's rights, whereas their opponents seized upon it as an opportunity to keep women in their proper place. Child-saving organizations had little or nothing to do with militant supporters of the suffragette movement. In fact, the new role of social worker was created by deference to antifeminist stereotypes of a "woman's place."

A Woman's Place

Feminist involvement in child-saving was endorsed by a variety of penal and professional organizations. Their participation was usually justified as an extension of their housekeeping functions so that they did not view themselves, nor were they regarded by others, as competitors for jobs usually performed by men. Proponents of the "new penology" insisted that reformatories should resemble home life, for institutions without women were likely to do more harm than good to inmates. According to G. E. Howe, the reformatory system provided "the most ample opportunities for woman's transcendant influence."

Female delegates to philanthropic and correctional conferences also realized that correctional work suggested the possibility of useful careers. Mrs. W. P. Lynde told the National Conference of Charities and Correction in 1879 that children's institutions offered the "truest and noblest scope for the public activities of women in the time which they can spare from their primary domestic duties." Women were exhorted by other delegates to make their lives meaningful by participating in welfare programs, volunteering their time and services, and getting acquainted with less privileged groups. They were told to seek jobs in institutions where "the woman-element shall pervade . . . and soften its social atmosphere with motherly tenderness."

Although the child-savers were responsible for some minor reforms in jails and re-formatories, they were more particularly concerned with extending governmental control over a whole range of youthful activities that had previously been handled on an informal basis. The main aim of the child-savers was to impose sanctions on conduct unbecoming youth and to disqualify youth from enjoying adult privileges. As Bennett Berger has com-mented, "adolescents are not made by nature but by being excluded from responsible par-ticipation in adult affairs, by being rewarded for dependency, and penalized for precocity."

The child-saving movement was not so much a break with the past as an affirmation of faith in traditional institutions. Parental authority, education at home, and the virtues of rural life were emphasized because they were in decline at this time. The child-saving move-ment was, in part, a crusade which, through emphasizing the dependence of the social or-der on the proper socialization of children, implicitly elevated the nuclear family and, more especially, the role of women as stalwarts of the family. The child-savers were prohibition-ists, in a general sense, who believed that social progress depended on efficient law en-forcement, strict supervision of children's leisure and recreation, and the regulation of illicit pleasures. What seemingly began as a movement to humanize the lives of adolescents soon developed into a program of moral absolutism through which youth was to be saved from movies, pornography, cigarettes, alcohol, and anything else which might possibly rob them of their innocence.

Although child-saving had important symbolic functions for preserving the social prestige of a declining elite, it also had considerable practical significance for legitimizing new career-openings for women. The new role of social worker combined elements of an old and partly fictitious role—defenders of family life—and elements of a new role—social servant. Social work was thus both an affirmation of cherished American values and an in-strumentality for women's emancipation.

JUVENILE COURT

The essential preoccupation of the child-saving movement was the recognition and control of youthful deviance. It brought attention to, and thus "invented," new categories of youth-ful misbehavior which had been hitherto unappreciated. The efforts of the childsavers were institutionally expressed in the juvenile court, which, despite recent legislative and consti-tutional reforms, is generally acknowledged as their most significant contribution to pro-gressive penology.

The juvenile-court system was part of a general movement directed towards remov-ing adolescents from the criminal-law process and creating special programs for delinquent, dependent, and neglected children. Regarded widely as "one of the greatest advances in child welfare that has ever occurred," the juvenile court was considered "an integral part of total welfare planning.". . .

The juvenile court was a special tribunal created by statute to determine the legal sta-tus of children and adolescents. Underlying the juvenile-court movement was the concept of *parens patriae* by which the courts were authorized to handle with wide discretion the problems of "its least fortunate junior citizens." The administration of juvenile justice differed in many important respects from the criminal-court processes. A child was not accused of a crime but offered assistance and guidance; intervention in his life was not supposed to carry the stigma of criminal guilt. Judicial records were not generally available to the press or public, and juvenile-court hearings were conducted in relative privacy. Juvenile-court procedures were typically informal and inquisitorial. Specific criminal safeguards of due process were not applicable because juvenile proceedings were defined by statute as civil in character.

The original statutes enabled the courts to investigate a wide variety of youthful needs and misbehavior. As Joel Handler has observed, "the critical philosophical position of the reform movement was that no formal, legal distinctions should be made between the delinquent and the dependent or neglected." Statutory definitions of "delinquency" encompassed (1) acts that would be criminal if committed by adults; (2) acts that violated county, town, or municipal ordinances; and (3) violations of vaguely defined catch-alls—such as "vicious or immoral behavior," "incorrigibility," and "truancy—which "seem to express the notion that the adolescent, if allowed to continue, will engage in more serious conduct."

The juvenile-court movement went far beyond a concern for special treatment of adolescent offenders. It brought within the ambit of governmental control a set of youthful activities that had been previously ignored or dealt with on an informal basis. It was not by accident that the behavior selected for penalizing by the child-savers—sexual license, drinking, roaming the streets, begging, frequenting dance halls and movies, fighting, and being seen in public late at night—was most directly relevant to the children of lower-class migrant and immigrant families.

The juvenile court was not perceived by its supporters as a revolutionary experiment, but rather as a culmination of traditionally valued practices. The child-saving movement was "antilegal," in the sense that it derogated civil rights and procedural formalities, while relying heavily on extra-legal techniques. The judges of the new court were empowered to investigate the character and social life of predelinquent as well as delinquent children; they examined motivation rather than intent, seeking to identify the moral reputation of problematic children. The requirements of preventive penology and child-saving further justified the court's intervention in cases where no offense had actually been committed, but where, for example, a child was posing problems for some person in authority such as a parent or teacher or social worker.

The Personal Touch

. . . Juvenile court judges had to be carefully selected for their skills as expert diagnosticians and for their appreciation of the "helping" professions. Miriam Van Waters, for example, regarded the juvenile court as a "laboratory of human behavior" and its judges as "experts with scientific training and specialists in the art of human relations." It was the judge's task to "get the whole truth about a child" in the same way that a "physician searches for every detail that bears on the condition of a patient."

The child-savers' interest in preventive strategies and treatment programs was based on the premise that delinquents possess innate or acquired characteristics which predispose them to crime and distinguish them from law-abiding youths. Delinquents were regarded as constrained by a variety of biological and environmental forces, so that their proper treatment involved discovery of the "cause of the aberration" and application of "the appropriate corrective or antidote." "What the trouble is with the offender," noted William Healy, "making him what he is, socially undesirable, can only be known by getting at his mental life, as it is an affair of reactive mechanisms."

The use of terms like "unsocialized," "maladjusted," and "pathological" to describe the behavior of delinquents implied that "socialized" and "adjusted" children conform to middle-class morality and participate in respectable institutions. The failure empirically to demonstrate psychological differences between delinquents and nondelinquents did not discourage the child-savers from believing that rural and middle-class values constitute "normality." The unique character of the child-saving movement was its concern for predelinquent offenders—"children who occupy the debatable ground between criminality and innocence"—and its claim that it could transform potential criminals into respectable citizens by training them in "habits of industry, self-control and obedience to law." This policy justified the diminishing of traditional procedures in juvenile court. If children were to be rescued, it was important that the rescuers be free to provide their services without legal hindrance. Delinquents had to be saved, transformed, and reconstituted. "There is no essential difference," said Frederick Wines, "between a criminal and any other sinner. The means and methods of restoration are the same for both."

THE REFORMATORY SYSTEM

It was through the reformatory system that the child-savers hoped to demonstrate that delinquents were capable of being converted into law-abiding citizens. The reformatory was initially developed in the United States during the middle of the nineteenth century as a special form of prison discipline for adolescents and young adults. Its underlying principles were formulated in Britain by Matthew Davenport Hill, Alexander Maconochie, Walter Crofton, and Mary Carpenter. If the United States did not have any great penal theorists, it at least had energetic penal administrators who were prepared to experiment with new programs. The most notable advocates of the reformatory plan in the United States were Enoch Wines, Secretary of the New York Prison Association; Theodore Dwight, the first Dean of Columbia Law School; Zebulon Brockway, Superintendent of Elmira Reformatory in New York; and Frank Sanborn, Secretary of the Massachusetts State Board of Charities.

The reformatory was distinguished from the traditional penitentiary by its policy of indeterminate sentencing, the "mark" system, and "organized persuasion" rather than "coercive restraint." Its administrators assumed that abnormal and troublesome individuals could become useful and productive citizens. . . . But, as Brockway observed at the first meeting of the National Prison Congress in 1870, the "new penology" was toughminded and devoid of "sickly sentimentalism. . . . Criminals shall either be cured, or kept under such continued restraint as gives guarantee of safety from further depredations."

Reformatories, unlike penitentiaries and jails, theoretically repudiated punishments based on intimidation and repression. They took into account the fact that delinquents were "either physically or mentally below the average." The reformatory system was based on the assumption that proper training can counteract the impositions of poor family life, a corrupt environment, and poverty, while at the same time toughening and preparing delinquents for the struggle ahead. "The principle at the root of the educational method of dealing with juvenile crime," wrote William Douglas Morrison, "is an absolutely sound one. It is a principle which recognizes the fact that the juvenile delinquent is in the main, a product of adverse individual and social conditions."

The reformatory movement spread rapidly through the United States, and European visitors crossed the Atlantic to inspect and admire the achievements of their pragmatic colleagues. Mary Carpenter, who visited the United States in 1873, was generally satisfied with the "generous and lavish expenditures freely incurred to promote the welfare of the inmates, and with the love of religion." Most correctional problems with regard to juvenile delinquents, she advised, could be remedied if reformatories were built like farm schools or "true homes." At the Massachusetts Reform School, in Westborough, she found an "entire want of family spirit," and, in New York, she complained that there was no "natural life" in the reformatory. "All the arrangements are artificial," she said; "instead of the cultivation of the land, which would prepare the youth to seek a sphere far from the dangers of large cities, the boys and young men were being taught trades which will confine them to the great centers of an overcrowded population." She found similar conditions in Philadelphia where "hundreds of youth were there congregated under lock and key," but praised the Connecticut Reform School for its "admirable system of agricultural training." If she had visited the Illinois State Reformatory at Pontiac, she would have found a seriously overcrowded "minor penitentiary" where the inmates were forced to work ten hours a day manufacturing shoes, brushes, and chairs.

To Cottage and Country

Granted the assumption that "nurture" could usually overcome most of nature's defects, reformatory-administrators set about the task of establishing programs consistent with the aim of retraining delinquents for law-abiding careers. . . . The heritage of biological imagery and Social Darwinism had a lasting influence on American criminology, and penal reformers continued to regard delinquency as a problem of individual adjustment to the demands of industrial and urban life. Delinquents had to be removed from contaminating situations, segregated from their "miserable surroundings," instructed, and "put as far as possible on a footing of equality with the rest of the population."

The trend from congregate housing in the city to group living in the country represented a significant change in the organization of penal institutions for young offenders. The family or cottage plan differed in several important respects from the congregate style of traditional prisons and jails. According to William Letchworth, in an address delivered before the National Conference of Charities and Correction in 1886:

> A fault in some of our reform schools is their great size. In the congregating of large numbers, individuality is lost. . . . These excessive aggregations are overcome to a great extent in the cottage plan. . . . The internal system of the reformatory school should be as nearly

as practicable as that of the family, with its refining and elevating influences; while the awakening of the conscience and the inculcation of religious principles should be primary aims.

The new penology emphasized the corruptness and artificiality of the city; from progressive education, it inherited a concern for naturalism, purity, and innocence. It is not surprising, therefore, that the cottage plan also entailed a movement to a rural location. The aim of penal reformers was not merely to use the countryside for teaching agricultural skills. The confrontation between corrupt delinquents and unspoiled nature was intended to have a spiritual and regenerative effect. The romantic attachment to rural values was quite divorced from social and agricultural realities. It was based on a sentimental and nostalgic repudiation of city life. Advocates of the reformatory system generally ignored the economic attractiveness of city work and the redundancy of farming skills. . . .

The "new" reformatory suffered, like all its predecessors, from overcrowding, mismanagement, "boodleism," understaffing, and inadequate facilities. Its distinctive features were the indeterminate sentence, the movement to cottage and country, and agricultural training. Although there was a decline in the use of brutal punishments, inmates were subjected to severe personal and physical controls: military exercises, "training of the will," and long hours of tedious labor constituted the main program of reform.

SUMMARY AND CONCLUSIONS

The child-saving movement was responsible for reforms in the ideological and institutional control of "delinquent" youth. The concept of the born delinquent was modified with the rise of a professional class of penal administrators and social servants who promoted a developmental view of human behavior and regarded most delinquent youth as salvageable. The child-savers helped to create special judicial and correctional institutions for the processing and management of "troublesome" youth.

There has been a shift during the last fifty years or so in official policies concerning delinquency. The emphasis has shifted from one emphasizing the criminal nature of delinquency to the "new humanism" which speaks of disease, illness, contagion, and the like. It is essentially a shift from a legal to a medical emphasis. The emergence of a medical emphasis is of considerable significance, since it is a powerful rationale for organizing social action in the most diverse behavioral aspects of our society. For example, the child-savers were not concerned merely with "humanizing" conditions under which children were treated by the criminal law. It was rather their aim to extend the scope of governmental control over a wide variety of personal misdeeds and to regulate potentially disruptive persons. The child-savers' reforms were politically aimed at lower-class behavior and were instrumental in intimidating and controlling the poor.

The child-savers made a fact out of the norm of adolescent dependence. "Every child is dependent," wrote the Illinois Board of Charities in 1899, "even the children of the wealthy. To receive his support at the hands of another does not strike him as unnatural, but quite the reverse." The juvenile court reached into the private lives of youth and disguised basically punitive policies in the rhetoric of "rehabilitation." The child-savers were prohibitionists, in a general sense, who believed that adolescents needed protection from even their own inclinations.

The basic conservatism of the child-saving movement is apparent in the reformatory system which proved to be as tough-minded as traditional forms of punishment. Reformatory programs were unilateral, coercive, and an invasion of human dignity. What most appealed to correctional workers were the paternalistic assumptions of the "new penology," its belief in social progress through individual reform, and its nostalgic preoccupation with the "naturalness" and intimacy of a preindustrial way of life.

The child-saving movement was heavily influenced by middle-class women who extended their housewifely roles into public service. Their contribution may also be seen as a "symbolic crusade" in defense of the nuclear family and their positions within it. They regarded themselves as moral custodians and supported programs and institutions dedicated to eliminating youthful immorality. Social service was an instrumentality for female emancipation, and it is not too unreasonable to suggest that women advanced their own fortune at the expense of the dependency of youth.

REVIEW QUESTIONS

1. Who were the child savers? What sort of people were they? What social conditions gave rise to the child saving movement?

2. What were the main values and beliefs underlying the child saving movement? How were these values and beliefs translated into policy in the juvenile court? In the reformatory?

3. Recall the discussion of Houses of Refuge in the introduction to this chapter and in the *Ex Parte Crouse* case. How were reformatories different from Houses of Refuge? Were they more consistent with the *parens patriae* philosophy as described in *Crouse*?

An Act to Regulate the Treatment and Control of Dependent, Neglected and Delinquent Children

Illinois Juvenile Court Act approved April 21, 1899

SECTION 1. *Be it enacted by the People of the State of Illinois, represented in the General Assembly:* DEFINITIONS.] This as shall apply only to children under the age of 16 years not now or hereafter inmates of a State institution, or any training school for boys or industrial school for girls or some institution incorporated under the laws of this State, except as provided in sections twelve (12) and eighteen (18). For the purposes of this act the words dependent child and neglected child shall mean any child who for any reason is destitute or homeless or abandoned; or dependent upon the public for support; or has not proper parental care or guardianship; or who habitually begs or receives alms; or who is found living in any house of ill fame or with any vicious or disreputable person; or whose home, by reason of neglect, cruelty or depravity on the part of its parents, guardian or other person in whose care it may be, is an unfit place for such a child; and any child under the age of 8 years who is found peddling or selling any articles or singing or playing any musical instrument upon the streets or giving any public entertainment. The words delinquent child shall include any child under the age of 16 years who violates any law of this State or any city or village ordinance. The word child or children may mean one or more children, and the word parent or parents may be held to mean one or both parents, when consistent with the intent of this act. The word association shall include any corporation which includes in its purposes the care of disposition of children coming within the meaning of this act.

§ 2. JURISDICTION.] The circuit and county courts of the several counties in this State shall have original jurisdiction in all cases coming within the terms of this act. In all trials under this act any person interested therein may demand a jury of six, or the judge of his own motion may order a jury of the same number, to try the case.

§ 3. JUVENILE COURT.] In counties having over 500,000 population the judges of the circuit court shall, at such times as they shall determine, designate one or more of their number whose duty it shall be to hear all cases coming under this act. A special court room, to be designated as the juvenile court room, shall be provided for the hearing of such cases, and the findings of the court shall be entered in a book or books to be kept for that purpose and known as the "Juvenile Record," and the court may, for convenience, be called the "Juvenile Court."

§ 4. PETITION TO THE COURT.] Any reputable person, being resident in the county, having knowledge of a child in his county who appears to be either neglected, dependent or delinquent, may file with the clerk of a court having jurisdiction in the matter a petition in writing, setting forth the facts, verified by affidavit. It shall be sufficient that the affidavit is upon information and belief.

§ 5. SUMMONS.] Upon the filing of the petition a summons shall issue requiring the person having custody or control of the child, or with whom the child may be, to appear with the child at a place and time stated in the summons, which time shall be not less than 24 hours after service. The parents of the child, if living, and their residence is [if] known, or its legal guardian, if one there be, or if there is neither parent nor guardian, or if his or her residence is not known, then some relative, if there be one and his residence is known, shall be notified of the proceedings, and in any case the judge may appoint some suitable person to act in behalf of the child. If the person summoned as herein provided shall fail, without reasonable cause, to appear and abide the order of the court, or to bring the child, he may be proceeded against as in case of contempt of court. In case the summons can not be served or the party served fails to obey the same, and in any case when it shall be made to appear to the court that such summons will be ineffectual, a warrant may issue on the order of the court, either against the parent or guardian or the person having custody of the child or with whom the child may be, or against the child itself. On there turn of the summons or other process, or as soon thereafter as may be, the court shall proceed to hear and dispose of the case in a summary manner. Pending the final disposition of any case the child may be retained in the possession of the person having the charge of same, or may be kept in some suitable place provided by the city or county authorities.

§ 6. PROBATION OFFICERS.] The court shall have authority to appoint or designate one or more discreet persons of good character to serve as probation officers during the pleasure of the court; said probation officers to receive no compensation from the public treasury. In case a probation officer shall be appointed by any court, it shall be the duty of the clerk of the court, if practicable, to notify the said probation officer in advance when any child is to be brought before the said court; it shall be the duty of the said probation officer to make such investigation as may be required by the court; to be present in court in order to represent the interests of the child when the case is heard; to furnish to the court such information and assistance as the judge may require; and to take such charge of any child before and after trial as may be directed by the court.

§ 7. DEPENDENT AND NEGLECTED CHILDREN.] When any child under the age of sixteen (16) years shall be found to be dependent or neglected within the meaning of this act, the court may make an order committing the child to the care of some suitable State institution, or to the care of some reputable citizen of good moral character, or to the care of some training school or an industrial school, as provided by law, or to the care of some association willing to receive it embracing in its objects the purpose of caring or obtaining homes for dependent or neglected children, which association shall have been accredited as hereinafter provided.

§ 8. GUARDIANSHIP.] In any case where the court shall award a child to the care of any association or individual in accordance with the provisions of this act the child shall, unless otherwise ordered, become a ward and be subject to the guardianship of the association or individual to whose care it is committed. Such association or individual shall have authority to place such child in a family home, with or without indenture, and may be made party to any proceeding for the legal adoption of the child, and may be its or his attorney or agent appear in any court where such proceedings are pending and assent to such adoption. And such assent shall be sufficient to authorize the court to enter the proper order or decree of adoption. Such guardianship shall not include the guardianship of any estate of the child.

§ 9. DISPOSITION OF DELINQUENT CHILDREN.] In the case of a delinquent child the court may continue the hearing from time to time, and may commit the child to the care and guardianship of a probation officer duly appointed by the court, and may allow said child to remain in its own home, subject to the visitation of the probation officer; such child to report to the probation officer as often as may be required and subject to be returned to the court for further proceedings, whenever such action may appear to be necessary; or the court may commit the child to the care and guardianship of the probation officer, to be placed in a suitable family home, subject to the friendly supervision of such probation officer; or it may authorize the said probation officer to board out the said child in some suitable family home, in case provision is made by voluntary contribution or otherwise for the payment of the board of such child, until a suitable provision may be made of the child in a home without such payment; or the court may commit the child, if a boy, to a training school of boys, or if a girl, to an industrial school for girls. Or, if the child is found guilty of any criminal offense, and the judge is of the opinion that the best interest requires it, the court may commit the child to any institution within said county incorporated under the laws of this State for the care of delinquent children, or provided by a city for the care of such offenders, or may commit the child, if a boy over the age of ten years, to the State reformatory, or if a girl over the age of ten years, to the State Home for Juvenile Female Offenders. In no case shall a child be committed beyond his or her minority. A child committed to such institution shall be subject to the control of the board of manager thereof, and the said board shall have power to parole such child on such conditions as it may prescribe, and the court shall, on the recommendation of the board, have power to discharge such child from custody whenever in the judgment of the court his or her reformation shall be complete; or the court may commit the child to the care and custody of some association that will receive it embracing in its objects the care of neglected and dependent children and that has been duly accredited as hereinafter provided.

§ 10. TRANSFER FROM JUSTICES AND POLICE MAGISTRATES.] When, in any county where a court is held as provided in section three of this act, a child under the age of 16 years is arrested with or without warrant, such child may, instead of being taken before a justice of the peace or police magistrate, be taken directly before such court; or if the child is taken before a justice of the peace or police magistrate, it shall be the duty of such justice of the peace or police magistrate to transfer the care [case] to such court, and the officer having the child in charge to take such child before that court upon petition as herein provided. In any case the court shall require notice to be given and investigation to be made as in other cases under this act, and may adjourn the hearing from time to time for the purpose.

§ 11. CHILDREN UNDER TWELVE YEARS NOT TO BE COMMITTED TO JAIL.] No court or magistrate shall commit a child under twelve (12) years of age to a jail or police station, but if such child is unable to give bail it may be committed to the care of the sheriff, police officer or probation officer, who shall keep such child in some suitable place provided by the city or county outside of the inclosure of any jail or police station. When any child shall be sentenced to confinement in any institution to which adult convicts are sentenced it shall be unlawful to confine such child in the same building with such adult convicts, or to confine such child in the same yard or inclosure with such adult convicts, or to bring such child into any yard or building in which such adult convicts may be present.

§ 12. AGENTS OF JUVENILE REFORMATORIES.] It shall be the duty of the superintendent of the State Reformatory at Pontiac and the board of managers of the State Home for Juvenile Female Offenders at Geneva, and the board of managers of any other institution to which juvenile delinquents may be committed by the courts, to maintain an agent of such institution for the purpose of ascertaining and reporting to said court whether they are suitable homes; to assist children paroled or discharged from such institution in finding suitable employment, and to maintain a friendly supervision over paroled inmates during the continuance of their parole; such agents shall hold office subject to the pleasure of the board making the appointment, and shall receive such compensation as such board may determine out of any funds appropriated for such institution applicable thereto. . . .

§ 21. CONSTRUCTION OF THE ACT.] This act shall be liberally construed, to the end that its purpose may be carried out, to-wit: That the care, custody and discipline of a child shall approximate as nearly as may be that which should be given by its parents, and in all cases where it can properly be done the child be placed in an improved family home and become a member of the family by legal adoption or otherwise.

APPROVED April 21, 1899.

REVIEW QUESTIONS

1. What types of behavior might bring a minor to the attention of the juvenile courts established by the Illinois Juvenile Court Act of 1899 (i.e., how broad was the jurisdiction of juvenile courts established under the Act)? What *categories* of youth are defined in the act as subject to juvenile court jurisdiction? What sorts of behavior or other problems are included within each category?

2. What was the age range of youth subject to juvenile court jurisdiction under each of the three categories of youth defined in the Act?

3. What procedures were established by the Act for handling cases within each category (e.g., filing petitions, ensuring the presence of the child and other appropriate parties in court, committing a child to a state institution or other out-of-home placement, placing a child on probation)? In what ways did procedures differ for neglected, dependent, and delinquent children and in what ways were children in different categories to be treated alike?

4. For how long could a delinquent child be committed to a state institution under the Act and how was an appropriate release date to be determined?

5. How did the procedures mandated by the Act differ from those of adult criminal courts?

The Juvenile Court

Julian W. Mack

The past decade marks a revolution in the attitude of the state toward its offending children, not only in nearly every American commonwealth, but also throughout Europe, Australia, and some of the other lands. The problem of the delinquent child, though juristically comparatively simple, is, in its social significance, of the greatest importance, for upon its wise solution depends the future of many of the rising generation. The legal questions, while not complicated, have, nevertheless, given rise to some discussion and to some slight dissent from the standpoint of constitutional law.

The first thought which suggests itself in connection with the juvenile court is, What is there distinctively new about it? We are familiar with the conception that the state is the higher or the ultimate parent of all of the dependents within its borders. We know that, whatever may have been the historical origin of the practice, for over two centuries, as evidenced by judgments both of the House of Lords and of the Chancellors, the courts of chancery in England have exercised jurisdiction for the protection of the unfortunate child. . . .

. . .The judges of the juvenile court, in exercising jurisdiction, have, in accordance with the most advanced philanthropic thought, recognized that the lack of proper home care can best be supplied by the true foster parent. Though the orphan asylums of the civilized world have ever been valuable and their recent improvement is marked, nevertheless, following the splendid lead of Massachusetts, greater effort is being put forth everywhere to solve the problem of the permanently dependent or neglected child by finding for it a foster home where it shall receive that individualized love and care that a true father gives to and would always desire for his own little ones.

While in most jurisdictions the juvenile-court laws make provision for the dependent as well as the neglected, the truant and the delinquent child, some of the best workers in this field have objected to a court's having anything to do with the strictly dependent child, the child whose parents must ask assistance, merely because of poverty or misfortune. If friends or the church fail to supply the necessary help, and the aid of the state is to be sought, it should be granted through poor law or relief commissioners. The court should be called upon to act only in the case of a persistent truant, or a victim of neglect or wrongdoing, either on the part of others or of itself. It is particularly in dealing with those

Source: Julian W. Mack. (1909). The juvenile court. *Harvard Law Review, 23,* 104–122. Copyright © 1909 by the Harvard Law Review Association. Adapted by permission.

children who have broken the law or who are leading the kind of life which will inevitably result in such breach, that the new and distinctive features of the juvenile-court legislation appear.

Our common criminal law did not differentiate between the adult and the minor who had reached the age of criminal responsibility, seven at common law and in some of our states, ten in others, with a chance of escape up to twelve, if lacking in mental and moral maturity. The majesty and dignity of the state demanded vindication for infractions from both alike. The fundamental thought in our criminal jurisprudence was not, and in most jurisdictions is not, reformation of the criminal, but punishment; punishment as expiation for the wrong, punishment as a warning to other possible wrongdoers. The child was arrested, put into prison, indicted by the grand jury, tried by a petit jury, under all the forms and technicalities of our criminal law, with the aim of ascertaining whether it had done the specific act—nothing else—and if it had, then of visiting the punishment of the state upon it.

It is true that during the last century ameliorating influences mitigated the severity of the old regime; in the last fifty years our reformatories have played a great and very beneficent part in dealing with juvenile offenders. They supplanted the penitentiary. In them the endeavor was made, while punishing, to reform, to build up, to educate the prisoner so that when his time should have expired he could go out into the world capable at least of making an honest living. And in course of time, in some jurisdictions, the youths were separated from the older offenders even in stations, jails, and workhouses; but, nevertheless, generally in this country, the two classes were huddled together. The result of it all was that instead of the state's training its bad boys so as to make of them decent citizens, it permitted them to become the outlaws and outcasts of society; it criminalized them by the very methods that it used in dealing with them. It did not aim to find out what the accused's history was, what his heredity, his environments, his associations; it did not ask how he had come to do the particular act which had brought him before the court. It put but one question, "Has he committed this crime?" It did not inquire, "What is the best thing to do for this lad?" It did not even punish him in a manner that would tend to improve him; the punishment was visited in proportion to the degree of wrongdoing evidenced by the single act; not by the needs of the boy, not by the needs of the state.

To-day, however, the thinking public is putting another sort of question. Why is it not just and proper to treat these juvenile offenders, as we deal with the neglected children, as a wise and merciful father handles his own child whose errors are not discovered by the authorities? Why is it not the duty of the state, instead of asking merely whether a boy or a girl has committed a specific offense, to find out what he is, physically, mentally, morally, and then if it learns that he is treading the path that leads to criminality, to take him in charge, not so much to punish as to reform, not to degrade but to uplift, not to crush but to develop, not to make him a criminal but a worthy citizen.

And it is this thought—the thought that the child who has begun to go wrong, who is incorrigible, who has broken a law or an ordinance, is to be taken in hand by the state, not as an enemy but as a protector, as the ultimate guardian, because either the unwillingness or inability of the natural parents to guide it toward good citizenship has compelled the intervention of the public authorities; it is this principle, which, to some extent theretofore applied in Australia and a few American states, was first fully and clearly declared, in the Act under which the Juvenile Court of Cook County, Illinois, was opened in Chicago, on July 1, 1899, the Hon. R. S. Tuthill presiding. Colorado followed soon after, and since that time similar legislation has been adopted in over thirty American jurisdictions, as well as in Great Britain and Ireland, Canada, and the Australian colonies. In continental Europe and also in Asia the American juvenile courts have been the object of most careful study, and either by parliamentary or administrative measures similar courts have been established, or at least some of their guiding principles have been enforced. . . .

Juvenile-court legislation has assumed two aspects. In Great Britain, in New York, and in a few other jurisdictions the protection is accomplished by suspending sentence and releasing the child under probation, or, in case of removal from the home, sending it to a school instead of to a jail or penitentiary. The criminal proceeding remains, however. The child is charged with the commission of a definite offense, of which it must be found either guilty or not guilty. If not guilty of the one certain act, it is discharged, however much it may need care or supervision. If guilty, it is then dealt with, but as a criminal. . . .

. . . But in Illinois, and following the lead of Illinois, in most jurisdictions, the form of procedure is totally different and wisely so. It would seem to be obvious that, if the common law could fix the age of criminal responsibility at seven, and if the legislature could advance that age to ten or twelve, it can also raise it to sixteen or seventeen or eighteen, and that is what, in some measure, has been done. Under most of the juvenile court laws a child under the designated age is to be proceeded against as a criminal only when in the judgment of the judge of the juvenile court, either as to any child, or in some states as to one over fourteen or over sixteen years of age, the interests of the state and of the child require that this be done. It is to be observed that the language of the law should be explicit in order to negative the jurisdiction of the criminal courts in the first instance. In the absence of such express provision the Supreme Court of New Hampshire in State v. Burt recently upheld a criminal conviction. On the other hand, the Supreme Court of Louisiana has decided in the case of State v. Reed that a criminal proceeding against one within the age limit must be quashed and the case transferred to the juvenile court.

To get away from the notion that the child is to be dealt with as a criminal; to save it from the brand of criminality; the brand that sticks to it for life; to take it in hand and instead of first stigmatizing and then reforming it, to protect it from the stigma,—this is the work which is now being accomplished by dealing even with most of the delinquent children through the court that represents the parens patriae power of the state, the court of chancery. Proceedings are brought to have a guardian or representative of the state appointed to look after the child, to have the state intervene between the natural parent and the child because the child needs it, as evidenced by some of its acts, and because the parent is either unwilling or unable to train the child properly. . . .

. . . If a child must be taken away from its home, if for the natural parental care that of the state is to be substituted, a real school, not a prison in disguise, must be provided. Whether the institutional life be only temporary until a foster home can be found, or for a longer period until the child can be restored to its own home or be given its complete freedom, the state must . . . furnish the proper care. This cannot be done in one great building, with a single dormitory for all of the two or three or four hundred or more children, in which there will be no possibility of classification along the lines of age or degrees of delinquency, in which there will be no individualized attention. What is needed is a large area, preferably in the country,—because these children require the fresh air and contact with the soil even more than does the normal child,—laid out on the cottage plan, giving opportunity for family life, and in each cottage some good man and woman who will live with and for the children. Locks and bars and other indicia of prisons must be avoided; human love, supplemented by human interest and vigilance, must replace them. In such schools there must be opportunity for agricultural and industrial training, so that when the boys and girls come out, they will be fitted to do a man's or woman's work in the world, and not be merely a helpless lot, drifting aimlessly about. . . .

Private philanthropy has supplemented, and doubtless in the future will supplement the work of the state in providing for the delinquents. To a large extent it is denominational, though many organizations are non-sectarian. None have accomplished more good or give promise of greater continued usefulness than the George junior Republics and similar organizations that stand for self-government, self-reliance, and redemption through honest labor. . . .

. . . [T]aking a child away from its parents and sending it even to an industrial school is, as far as possible, to be avoided; and . . . when it is allowed to return home, it must be under probation, subject to the guidance and friendly interest of the probation officer, the representative of the court. To raise the age of criminal responsibility from seven or ten to sixteen or eighteen, without providing for an efficient system of probation, would indeed be disastrous. Probation is, in fact, the keynote of juvenile-court legislation.

But even in this there is nothing radically new. Massachusetts has had probation, not only in the case of minors, but even in the case of adults, for nearly 40 years, and several other states now have provisions for the suspension of a criminal sentence in the case of adults, permitting the defendant to go free, but subject to the control of a probation officer. Wherever juvenile courts have been established, a system of probation has been provided for, and even where as yet the juvenile court system has not been fully developed, some steps have been taken to substitute probation for imprisonment of juvenile offenders.

Most of the children who come before the court are, naturally, the children of the poor. In many cases the parents are foreigners, frequently unable to speak English, and without an understanding of American methods and views. What they need, more than anything else, is kindly assistance; and the aim of the court, in appointing a probation officer for the child, is to have the child and the parents feel, not so much the power, as the friendly interest of the state; to show them that the object of the court is to help them to train the child right; and therefore the probation officers must be men and women fitted for these tasks.

Their duties are oftentimes of the most delicate nature. Tact, forbearance, and sympathy with the child, as well as a full appreciation of the difficulties that the poorer classes, and especially the immigrants, are confronted with in our large cities, are indispensable. . . .

The procedure and practice of the juvenile court is simple. In the first place the number of arrests is greatly decreased. The child and the parents are notified to appear in court, and unless the danger of escape is great, or the offense very serious, or the home totally unfit for the child, detention before hearing is unnecessary. Children are permitted to go on their own recognizance or that of their parents, or on giving bail. Probation officers should be and often are authorized to act in this respect. If, however, it becomes necessary to detain the children either before a hearing or pending a continuance, or even after the adjudication, before they can be admitted into the home or institution to which they are to be sent, they are no longer kept in prisons or jails, but in detention homes. In some states, the laws are mandatory that the local authorities provide such homes managed in accordance with the spirit of this legislation. These are feasible even in the smallest communities, inasmuch as the simplest kind of a building best meets the need.

The jurisdiction to hear the cases is generally granted to an existing court having full equity powers. In some cities, however, special courts have been provided, with judges devoting their entire time to this work. If these special courts can constitutionally be vested with full and complete chancery and criminal jurisdiction, much is to be said in favor of their establishment. In the large cities particularly, the entire time of one judge may well be needed. It has been suggested from time to time that all of the judges of the municipal or special sessions courts be empowered to act in these cases, but while it would be valuable in metropolitan communities to have more than one detention home and court house, nevertheless it would seem to be even more important to have a single juvenile court judge. The British government has adopted this policy for London.

By the Colorado Act of 1909 provision is made for hearings before masters in chancery, designated as masters of discipline, to be appointed by the juvenile court judge and to act under his directions. This may prove to be the best solution of a difficult problem, combining as it does the possibility of a quick disposition of the simpler cases in many sections of a large city or county, with a unity of administration through the supervisory power of a single judge.

The personality of the judge is an all-important matter. . . . The public at large, sympathetic to the work, and even the probation officers who are not lawyers, regard him as one having almost autocratic power. Because of the extent of his jurisdiction and the tremendous responsibility that it entails, it is, in the judgment of the writer, absolutely essential that he be a trained lawyer thoroughly imbued with the doctrine that ours is a "government of laws and not of men."

He must, however, be more than this. He must be a student of and deeply interested in the problems of philanthropy and child life, as well as a lover of children. He must be able to understand the boys' point of view and ideas of justice; he must be willing and patient enough to search out the underlying causes of the trouble and to formulate the plan by which, through the cooperation, ofttimes, of many agencies, the cure may be effected.

In some very important jurisdictions the vicious practice is indulged in of assigning a different judge to the juvenile court work every month or every three months. It is impossible for these judges to gain the necessary experience or to devote the necessary time to the study of new problems. The service should under no circumstances be for less than one year, and preferably for a longer period. In some of our cities, notably in Denver, the judge has discharged not only the judicial functions, but also those of the most efficient probation officer. Judge Lindsey's love for the work and his personality has enabled him to exert a powerful influence on the boys and girls that are brought before him. While doubtless the best results can be obtained in such a court, lack of time would prevent a judge in the largest cities from adding this work to his strictly judicial duties, even were it not extremely difficult to find the necessary combination of elements in one man.

The problem for determination by the judge is not, Has this boy or girl committed a specific wrong, but What is he, how has he become what he is, and what had best be done in his interest and in the interest of the state to save him from a downward career. It is apparent at once that the ordinary legal evidence in a criminal court is not the sort of evidence to be heard in such a proceeding. A thorough investigation, usually made by the probation officer, will give the court much information bearing on the heredity and environment of the child. This, of course, will be supplemented in every possible way; but this alone is not enough. The physical and mental condition of the child must be known, for the relation between physical defects and criminality is very close. It is, therefore, of the utmost importance that there be attached to the court, as has been done in a few cities, a child study department, where every child, before hearing, shall be subjected to a thorough psychophysical examination. In hundreds of cases the discovery and remedy of defective eyesight or hearing or some slight surgical operation will effectuate a complete change in the character of the lad.

The child who must be brought into court should, of course, be made to know that he is face to face with the power of the state, but he should at the same time, and more emphatically, be made to feel that he is the object of its care and solicitude. The ordinary trappings of the courtroom are out of place in such hearings. The judge on a bench, looking down upon the boy standing at the bar, can never evoke a proper sympathetic spirit. Seated at a desk, with the child at his side, where he can on occasion put his arm around his shoulder and draw the lad to him, the judge, while losing none of his judicial dignity, will gain immensely in the effectiveness of his work.

The object of the juvenile court and of the intervention of the state is, of course, in no case to lessen or to weaken the sense of responsibility either of the child or of the parent. On the contrary, the aim is to develop and to enforce it. Therefore it is wisely provided in most of the recent acts that the child may be compelled when on probation, if of working age, to make restitution for any damage done by it. Moreover, the parents may not only be compelled to contribute to the support even of the children who are taken away from them and sent to institutions, but following Colorado, in many states, they, as well as any other adults, may be made criminally liable for their acts or neglect contributing to a child's dependency or delinquency. . . .

Valuable, however, as is the introduction of the juvenile court into our system of jurisprudence, valuable both in its effect upon the child, the parents, and the community at large, and in the great material saving to the state which the substitution of probation for imprisonment has brought about, nevertheless it is in no sense a cure-all. Failures will result from probation, just as they have resulted from imprisonment. As Judge Lindsey has said:

"It does not pretend to do all the work necessary to correct children or to prevent crime. It is offered as a method far superior to that of the old criminal court system of dealing with the thing rather than the child. That method was more or less brutal. The juvenile court system has a danger in becoming one of leniency, but as between this method and that of the criminal court, it is much to be preferred. But the dangers of leniency as well as those of brutality can be avoided in most cases. Juvenile-court workers must not be sentimentalists any more than brutalists. In short, the idea is a system of probation work, which contemplates cooperation with the child, the home, the school, the neighborhood, the church, and the businessman in its interests and that of the state. Its purpose is to help all it can, and to hurt as little as it can; it seeks to build character—to make good citizens rather than useless criminals. The state is thus helping itself as well as the child, for the good of the child is the good of the state."

But more than this, the work of the juvenile court is, at the best, palliative, curative. The more important, indeed the vital thing, is to prevent the children from reaching that condition in which they have to be dealt with in any court, and we are not doing our duty to the children of to-day, the men and women of to-morrow, when we neglect to destroy the evils that are leading them into careers of delinquency, when we fail not merely to uproot the wrong, but to implant in place of it the positive good. It is to a study of the underlying causes of juvenile delinquency and to a realization of these preventive and positive measures that the trained professional men of the United States, following the splendid lead of many of their European brethren, should give some thought and some care. The work demands the united and aroused efforts of the whole community, bent on keeping children from becoming criminals, determined that those who are treading the downward path shall be halted and led back.

REVIEW QUESTIONS

1. What are the most significant reasons given by Judge Mack for establishment of the Cook County juvenile court?
2. What was the underlying philosophy of the Cook County juvenile court? What procedures were to be used? What kinds of evidence were relevant? How did its procedures differ from those of adult criminal courts and from earlier approaches to handling juvenile offenders?
3. What characteristics does Judge Mack believe are important in a juvenile court judge? How does the way he believes they should handle cases differ from the approach of judges in adult criminal courts? Do you agree that these are the ideal characteristics in a juvenile court judge? If not, what characteristics would you emphasize?
4. What was the role of probation and probation officers in the juvenile court described by Judge Mack?
5. What did he think "training schools" (as institutions for delinquents were then beginning to be called) should look like and how did he think they should be run?

Commonwealth v. Fisher

The Supreme Court of Pennsylvania
213 Pa. 48, 62 A. 198 (Pa. 1905)

BROWN, J. In a proceeding conducted in the court of quarter sessions of the county of Philadelphia under the provisions of the act of April 23, 1903 (P. L. 274), Frank Fisher, the appellant, was committed by that court to the House of Refuge. From the order so committing him an appeal was taken to the superior court, which affirmed it. The constitutionality of the act of 1903 was the sole question before the court in that case, and is renewed here. The objections of the appellant to the constitutionality of the act, as presented by counsel, are: (a) Under its provisions the defendant was not taken into court by due process of law. (b) He was denied his right of trial before a jury on the charge of the felony for which he had been arrested. (c) The tribunal before which he appeared, and which heard the case and committed him to the House of Refuge, was an unconstitutional body, and without jurisdiction. (d) The act provides different punishments for the same offense by a classification of individuals according to age. (e) The act contains more subjects than one, some of which are not expressed in the title. In considering these objections, the order in which they are made will not be followed.

The act is entitled "An act defining the powers of the several courts of quarter sessions of the peace, within this commonwealth, with reference to the care, treatment and control of dependent, neglected, incorrigible and delinquent children, under the age of 16 years, and providing for the means in which such power may be exercised." By this title notice of the purpose of the act is distinctly given. It is a single one. It is to define what powers the state, as the general guardian of all of its children, commits to the several courts of quarter sessions in exercising special guardianship over children under the age of 16 years needing the substitution of its guardianship for that of parents or others. . . .

The objection that "the act offends against a constitutional provision in creating, by its terms, different punishments for the same offense by a classification of individuals," overlooks the fact, hereafter to be noticed, that it is not for the punishment of offenders but for the salvation of children, and points out the way by which the state undertakes to save, not particular children of a special class, but all children under a certain age, whose salvation may become the duty of the state, in the absence of proper parental care or disregard of it by wayward children. No child under the age of 16 years is excluded from its beneficent provisions. Its protecting arm is for all who have not attained that age and who may need its protection. It is for all children of the same class. That minors may be classified for their best interests and the public welfare has never been questioned in the legislation relating to them. . . .

✗ No new court is created by the act under consideration. In its title it is called an act to define the powers of an already existing and ancient court. In caring for the neglected or unfortunate children of the Commonwealth, and in defining the powers to be exercised by that court in connection with these children, recognized by the state as its wards requiring its care and protection, jurisdiction is conferred upon that court as the appropriate one, and not upon a new one created by the act. . . . It is a mere convenient designation of the court of quarter sessions to call it, when caring for children, a 'juvenile court'; but no such court, as an independent tribunal, is created. It is still the court of quarter sessions before which the proceedings are conducted, and though that court, in so conducting them, is to be known as the 'juvenile court,' the records are still those of the court of quarter sessions.

In pressing the objection that the appellant was not taken into custody by due process of law, the assumption, running through the entire argument of the appellant, is continued that the proceedings of the act of 1903 are of a criminal nature for the punishment of offenders for crimes committed, and that the appellant was so punished. But he was not, and he could not have been without due process of law; for the constitutional guaranty is that no one charged with a criminal offense shall be deprived of life, liberty, or property without due process of law. To save a child from becoming a criminal, or from continuing in a career of crime, to end in maturer years in public punishment and disgrace, the Legislature surely may provide for the salvation of such a child, if its parents or guardian be unable or unwilling to do so, by bringing it into one of the courts of the state without any process at all, for the purpose of subjecting it to the state's guardianship and protection. The natural parent needs no process to temporarily deprive his child of its liberty by confining it in his own home, to save it and to shield it from the consequences of persistence in a career of waywardness; nor is the state, when compelled, as parens patriae, to take the place of the father for the same purpose, required to adopt any process as a means of placing its hands upon the child to lead it into one of its courts. When the child gets there, and the court, with power to save it, determines on its salvation, and not its punishment, it is immaterial how it got there. The act simply provides how children who ought to be saved may reach the court to be saved. If experience should show that there ought to be other ways for it to get there, the Legislature can, and undoubtedly will, adopt them, and they will never be regarded as undue processes for depriving a child of its liberty or property as a penalty for crime committed.

The last reason to be noticed why the act should be declared unconstitutional is that it denies the appellant a trial by jury. Here again is the fallacy that he was tried by the court for any offense. "The right of trial by jury shall remain inviolate," are the words of the Bill of Rights, and no act of the Legislature can deny this right to any citizen, young or old, minor or adult, if he is to be tried for a crime against the commonwealth. But there was no trial for any crime here, and the act is operative only when there is to be no trial. The very purpose of the act is to prevent a trial, though, if the welfare of the public require that the minor should be tried, power to try it is not taken away from the court of quarter sessions; for the eleventh section expressly provides that nothing in the preceding sections "shall be in derogation of the powers of the courts of quarter sessions and oyer and terminer to try, upon an indictment, any delinquent child, who, in due course, may be brought to trial." This section was entirely unnecessary, for without it a delinquent child can be tried only by a jury for a crime charged; but, as already stated, the act is not for the trial of a child charged with a crime, but is mercifully to save it from such an ordeal, with the prison or penitentiary in its wake, if the child's own good and the best interests of the state justify such salvation. Whether the child deserved to be saved by the state is no more a question for a jury than whether the father, if able to save it, ought to save it. If the latter ought to save, but is powerless to do so, the former, by the act of 1903, undertakes the duty; and the Legislature, in directing how that duty is to be performed in a proper case, denies the child no right of a trial by a jury, for the simple reason that by the act it is not to be tried for anything. The court passes upon nothing but the propriety of an effort to save it, and, if a worthy subject for an effort of salvation, that effort is made in the way directed by the act. The act is but an exercise by the state of its supreme power over the welfare of its children, a power under which it can take a child from its father and let it go where it will, without committing it to any guardianship or any institution, if the welfare of the child, taking its age into consideration, can be thus best promoted. . . .

      . . . [T]he proceeding is not one according to the course of the common law, in which the right of trial by jury is guarantied, but a mere statutory proceeding for the accomplishment of the protection of the helpless, which object was accomplished before the Constitution without the enjoyment of a jury trial. There is no restraint upon the natural liberty of children contemplated by such a law, none whatever, but rather the placing of them under the natural restraint, so far as practicable, that should be, but is not, exercised by parental authority. It is the mere conferring upon them that protection to which, under the circumstances, they are entitled as a matter of right. It is for their welfare and that of the community at large. The design is not punishment, nor the restraint imprisonment, any more than is the wholesome restraint which a parent exercises over his child. The severity in either case must necessarily be tempered to meet the necessities of the particular situation. There is no probability, in the proper administration of the law, of the child's liberty being unduly invaded. Every statute which is designed to give protection, care, and training to children, as a needed substitute for parental authority and performance of parental duty, is but a recognition of the duty of the state, as the legitimate guardian and protector of children where other guardianship fails. No constitutional right is violated, but one of the most important duties which organized society owes to its helpless members is performed, just in the measure that the law is framed with wisdom and is carefully administered. The conclusions above expressed are in accordance with adjudications elsewhere, with but very few exceptions.

      None of the objections urged against the constitutionality of the act can prevail. The assignments of error are therefore all overruled, and the order of the superior court, affirming the commitment below, is affirmed.

REVIEW QUESTIONS

1. What were Frank Fisher's objections to his placement in the House of Refuge? Which of his rights under the United States Constitution did he believe had been violated?
2. How did the Pennsylvania Supreme Court rule on each issue? What was its reasoning with respect to each issue? In what ways was the court's reasoning similar to the reasoning used almost 70 years earlier in *Ex parte Crouse?* In what ways was it different?
3. Do you think the Supreme Court of Pennsylvania made the right decision in this case? Why or why not?
4. Note that this case was decided by the same court (the Pennsylvania Supreme Court) and involved the same institution (the Philadelphia House of Refuge) as the *Ex parte Crouse* case. Recall Platt's discussion earlier in this chapter of the child savers and the development of reformatories in the late 19th century. Based on Platt's discussion, how much do you think the Philadelphia House of Refuge had changed in the years since the court issued its decision in *Ex parte Crouse?* Would these changes have made institutional conditions more (or less) consistent with the *parens patriae* philosophy?

FURTHER READING

Fox, Sanford J. (1970). Juvenile justice reform: An historical perspective. *Stanford Law Review, 22,* 1187–1239.

Hawes, Joseph M. (1971). *Children in Urban Society: Juvenile Delinquency in Nineteenth Century America.* New York: Oxford University Press.

Lerman, Paul. (1977). Delinquency and social policy: A historical perspective. *Crime and Delinquency, 23*(4), 383–393.

Mennel, Robert M. (1973). *Thorns and Thistles: Juvenile Delinquents in the United States, 1825-1940.* Hanover, NH: University Press of New England.

_____. (1982). Attitudes and policies toward juvenile delinquency in the United States. *Crime and Justice: An Annual Review of Research, 4,* 191–224.

Platt, Anthony M. (1969). *The Child Savers: The Invention of Delinquency.* Chicago: University of Chicago Press.

Rendleman, Douglas R. (1971). Parens patriae: From chancery to the juvenile court. *South Carolina Law Review, 23,* 205–229.

Rothman, David J. (1980). *Conscience and Convenience: The Asylum and its Alternatives in Progressive America.* Boston: Little, Brown.

Schlossman, Steven L. (1977). *Love and the American Delinquent: The Theory and Practice of "Progressive" Juvenile Justice, 1825–1920.* Chicago: University of Chicago Press.

CHAPTER

3

The Constitutionalization of Juvenile Justice and the Movement for Reform

The idea of a separate, rehabilitative court for juveniles spread rapidly at the dawn of the 20th century. Within a decade following initiation of the Illinois juvenile court in 1899, juvenile courts had been established in 22 states. By 1925 they were present in all but two. As the juvenile justice system developed, though, reality increasingly diverged from the idealistic conceptions of Judge Mack and other Progressive reformers. In urban juvenile courts especially, spiraling caseloads prompted increasingly streamlined procedures, and the therapeutic correctional resources envisioned by early reformers largely failed to materialize. By the 1960s, critics were accusing juvenile courts of sending young offenders to institutions that were virtually indistinguishable from adult prisons, following perfunctory proceedings that dispensed with any semblance of the Constitutional rights guaranteed to adults charged with criminal offenses. As early as 1948 the U.S. Supreme Court had suggested that due process of law might apply to juveniles just as it applies to adults (*Haley v. Ohio*, 332 U.S. 596 [1948]; see also *Gallegos v. Colorado*, 370 U.S. 49 [1962]). But it was not until well into the due process revolution of the 1960s that the Court began in earnest to examine the operation of the juvenile court.

This chapter traces the "Constitutionalization" and reform of juvenile justice during the 1960s and 1970s. We begin with an excerpt from the influential 1967 report of the President's Commission on Law Enforcement and the Administration of Justice. Entitled *The Challenge of Crime in a Free Society,* this report summarized the findings of nine separate task forces that had examined nearly every aspect of the administration of justice in the United States. The selection included here is from a chapter summarizing—largely verbatim—the report of the Task Force on Juvenile Delinquency. The *Task Force Report: Juvenile Delinquency and Youth Crime* is among the most influential documents in the history of juvenile justice. The passage reprinted here from the Commission's final report appears in nearly identical language—but with additional commentary and in a different order of presentation—in the *Task Force Report.*

Even before the President's Commission issued its report, the U.S. Supreme Court had handed down its first major decision affecting juvenile justice. In *Kent v. United States* the Court reviewed the decision of a juvenile court judge in Washington, D.C. (the *only* juvenile court judge serving our nation's capital at the time) to "waive" juvenile court jurisdiction and transfer the case of a mentally ill 16-year-old boy charged with housebreaking, robbery, and rape to the District Court for prosecution as an adult. Speaking for the Court, Justice Abe Fortas heralded a veritable revolution in juvenile justice with his charge that "there is no place in our system of law for reaching a result of such tremendous consequences without ceremony—without hearing, without effective assistance of counsel, without a statement of reasons" and his warning that, absent court-imposed standards of due process, "there may be grounds for concern that the child receives the worst of both worlds: that he gets neither the protections accorded to adults nor the solicitous care and regenerative treatment postulated for children" (see p. 83).

The following year, at about the same time that the President's Commission released its report, Justice Fortas turned the juvenile justice system on its ear, delivering a decision in *In re Gault* that mandated many of the same procedural safeguards applicable in adult criminal cases: the right to notice of charges; the privilege against self-incrimination; the right to confront and cross-examine witnesses; and, most notably, the right to counsel—a right that had only recently been guaranteed for adult felons who could not afford to pay for their own lawyers (*Gideon v. Wainwright*, 372 U.S. 335 [1963]) and that would only later be extended to adults charged with misdemeanors for which they might face short periods of incarceration in a local jail (*Argersinger v. Hamlin*, 407 U.S. 25 [1972]).

Gault was followed in 1970 by *In re Winship*, which extended yet another procedural safeguard to juveniles—the right to proof beyond reasonable doubt. To reach this decision, however, the Court had to overcome a peculiar hurdle: It had never explicitly guaranteed that *adults* charged with crimes enjoyed such a right! But the court made short work of the matter, holding first that proof beyond reasonable doubt is indeed Constitutionally required in adult criminal courts, and then going on to hold that the differences between the adult and juvenile systems are insufficient to justify a lesser standard for young people charged with delinquent acts.

The *Gault* and *Winship* decisions were feared by many—including some members of the Supreme Court—to signal the death knell for the juvenile court experiment. So when an opportunity arose in a 1971 case—*McKeiver v. Pennsylvania*—to consider whether to extend the Sixth Amendment right to a jury trial to juvenile delinquency cases, the Court balked. Writing for only four members of the Court (a fifth Justice concurred in the judgments but not in the plurality's rationale, and a sixth concurred in the judgment in one of the two consolidated cases but dissented in the other), Justice Harry Blackmun lamented the many shortcomings of the juvenile court but shied away from the risk of stifling further experimentation by introducing "the traditional delay, the formality, and the clamor of the adversary system" that he believed would accompany jury trials (see p. 108).

The next selection—*Breed v. Jones*, decided in 1975—concludes the line of cases by which the Supreme Court established the basic Constitutional parameters of modern juvenile court proceedings. *Breed v. Jones* involved what may seem a less substantial issue than those addressed in the earlier cases. But in holding that the Fifth Amendment's double jeopardy clause bars transfer to adult court for retrial *after* the juvenile has been adjudicated delinquent, the Court firmly reiterated the position underlying its *Gault* and *Winship* decisions that, "in terms of potential consequences, there is little to distinguish an adjudicatory hearing such as was held in this case from a traditional criminal prosecution." "[I]t is simply too late in the day to conclude," observed Chief Justice Warren Burger in his majority opinion, "that a juvenile is not put in jeopardy at a proceeding whose object is to determine whether he has committed acts that violate a criminal law and whose potential consequences include both the stigma inherent in such a determination and the deprivation of liberty for many years" (see p. 112).

By the time *Breed v. Jones* was decided the combined effects of the *Task Force Report* and *In re Gault* had engendered a groundswell of support for completing the transformation of the juvenile court—moving it further away from the informal, nonadversarial, and predominantly rehabilitative orientation advocated by the child-savers, and toward implementation of due process safeguards and sanctions more in keeping with the severity of the offense rather than the perceived treatment needs of the offender. Even before the Supreme Court issued its decision in *Breed v. Jones,* Congress had moved to define an assertive role for the federal government in juvenile justice through passage of the Juvenile Justice and Delinquency Prevention Act of 1974. Signed into law by President Gerald Ford in September 1974, the JJDP Act has been subsequently amended and updated in half a dozen major reauthorizations (in 1977, 1980, 1984, 1988, 1992, and 2002). The Act became a formidable force for change in juvenile justice systems nationwide, and the Office of Juvenile Justice and Delinquency Prevention (OJJDP) established pursuant to its provisions became an enormously powerful vehicle for developing delinquency prevention initiatives, fostering policy innovations at the state level, funding juvenile justice research, and sponsoring nationwide reforms spanning the full spectrum of juvenile justice system interventions. We encountered some of OJJDP's many publications addressing juvenile justice policies and practices in Chapter 1, and we will read several more in subsequent chapters of this book. As we proceed, we will also learn more about some of the specific provisions of the JJDP Act—such as the disproportionate minority confinement (DMC) mandate discussed by Pope, Lovell, and Hsia in Chapter 1, which we will revisit in Chapter 6 along with the "deinstitutionalization," "separation," and "jail removal" requirements with which states participating in the Act's formula grant program must also comply.

Among its many provisions, the JJDP Act as it was originally enacted included one establishing a National Advisory Committee for Juvenile Justice and Delinquency Prevention, and directing the Committee to develop national standards for juvenile justice administration. By 1980, following an exhausting process of preparation, submission, review, and modification, the Committee had adopted a single-volume set of standards and commentary running more than 500 pages in length. The standards—another significant link in the chain of juvenile justice reform efforts initiated in the wake of the *Task Force Report* and *In re Gault*—are summarized here in a selection drawn from the OJJDP Administrator's Letter of Transmittal (addressed "To the President and Congress of the United States") and the Foreword to the volume produced by the Committee.

Another, even more ambitious, effort to develop standards for juvenile justice had been undertaken as a joint effort of the Institute of Judicial Administration and the American Bar Association even before the National Advisory Committee began its work. Toiling throughout the 1970s to complete its monumental task, the IJA-ABA Juvenile Justice Standards Project produced an encyclopedic 23-volume set of standards at almost the same time as the National Advisory Committee completed its work. The IJA-ABA standards were considered by many to be the definitive statement of necessary juvenile justice system reform, culminating a full decade of work involving some 300 juvenile justice experts from across the country. Recently republished by the ABA—in a single-volume format omitting the extensive commentary accompanying the standards in each of the original volumes—the IJA-ABA standards continue to exert a dominant influence on juvenile justice policy. We close this chapter with a recap of the project and its underlying principals as recalled in an introduction prepared for the new edition by Barbara Flicker, who served for a time as director of the Juvenile Justice Standards Project and remained a key figure throughout its duration, authoring the original summary volume and serving as Executive Editor for the entire set of standards published in 1980 and 1981. (Note: In addition to the introductory discussions of juvenile justice standards in this chapter, we will encounter an extended excerpt from the IJA-ABA standards in Chapter 5, while brief passages from the National Advisory Committee standards will be found in Chapter 4 and again in Chapter 6.)

Juvenile Delinquency and Youth Crime

*The President's Commission on Law Enforcement
and Administration of Justice*

THE JUVENILE COURT AND RELATED AGENCIES

. . . Studies conducted by the Commission, legislative inquiries in various States, and reports by informed observers compel the conclusion that the great hopes originally held for the juvenile court have not been fulfilled. It has not succeeded significantly in rehabilitating delinquent youth, in reducing or even stemming the tide of delinquency, or in bringing justice and compassion to the child offender. To say that juvenile courts have failed to

Source: The President's Commission on Law Enforcement and Administration of Justice. (1967). *The Challenge of Crime in a Free Society.* Washington, DC: U.S. Government Printing Office.

achieve their goals is to say no more than what is true of criminal courts in the United States. But failure is most striking when hopes are highest.

One reason for the failure of the juvenile courts has been the community's continuing unwillingness to provide the resources—the people and facilities and concern—necessary to permit them to realize their potential and prevent them from acquiring some of the undesirable features typical of lower criminal courts in this country. In some jurisdictions, for example, the juvenile court judgeship does not have high status in the eyes of the bar, and while there are many juvenile court judges of outstanding ability and devotion, many are not. One crucial presupposition of the juvenile court philosophy—mature and sophisticated judge, wise and well versed in law and the science of human behavior—has proved in fact too often unattainable. A recent study of juvenile court judges in the United States revealed that half had no undergraduate degree; a fifth had received no college education at all; a fifth were not members of the bar. Almost three-quarters devote less than a quarter of their time to juvenile and family matters, and judicial hearings often turn out to be little more than attenuated interviews of 10 to 15 minutes' duration.

Similarly, more than four-fifths of the juvenile judges polled in a recent survey reported no psychologist or psychiatrist available to them on a regular basis—over half a century after the juvenile court movement set out to achieve the coordinated application of the behavioral and social sciences to the misbehaving child. Clinical services to diagnose and to assist in devising treatment plans are the exception, and even where they exist, the waiting lists are so long that their usefulness is more theoretical than real.

The dispositional alternatives available even to the better endowed juvenile courts fall far short of the richness and the relevance to individual needs envisioned by the court's founders. In most places, indeed, the only alternatives are release outright, probation, and institutionalization. Probation means minimal supervision at best. A large percentage of juvenile courts have no probation services at all, and in those that do, caseloads typically are so high that counseling and supervision take the form of occasional phone calls and perfunctory visits instead of the careful, individualized service that was intended. Institutionalization too often means storage—isolation from the outside world—in an overcrowded, understaffed security institution with little education, little vocational training, little counseling or job placement or other guidance upon release. Intermediate and auxiliary measures such as halfway houses, community residential treatment centers, diversified institutions and programs, intensive community supervision have proved difficult to establish.

But it is by no means true that a simple infusion of resources into juvenile courts and attendant institutions would fulfill the expectations that accompanied the court's birth and development. There are problems that go much deeper. The failure of the juvenile court to fulfill its rehabilitative and preventive promise stems in important measure from a grossly overoptimistic view of what is known about the phenomenon of juvenile criminality and of what even a fully equipped juvenile court could do about it. Experts in the field agree that it is extremely difficult to develop successful methods for preventing serious delinquent acts through rehabilitative programs for the child. What research is making increasingly clear is that delinquency is not so much an act of individual deviancy as a pattern of behavior produced by a multitude of pervasive societal influences well beyond the reach of the actions of any judge, probation officer, correctional counselor, or psychiatrist.

The same uncritical and unrealistic estimates of what is known and can be done that make expectation so much greater than achievement also serve to justify extensive official action and to mask the fact that much of it may produce more harm than good. Official action may actually help to fix and perpetuate delinquency in the child through a process in which the individual begins to think of himself as delinquent and organizes his behavior accordingly. That process itself is further reinforced by the effect of the labeling upon the child's family, neighbors, teachers, and peers, whose reactions communicate to the child in subtle ways a kind of expectation of delinquent conduct. The undesirable consequences of official treatment are maximized in programs that rely on institutionalizing the child. The most informed and benign official treatment of the child therefore contains within it the seeds of its own frustration and itself may often feed the very disorder it is designed to cure.

The limitations, both in theory and in execution, of strictly rehabilitative treatment methods, combined with public anxiety over the seemingly irresistible rise in juvenile criminality, have produced a rupture between the theory and the practice of juvenile court dispositions. While statutes, judges, and commentators still talk the language of compassion and treatment, it has become clear that in fact the same purposes that characterize the use of the criminal law for adult offenders—retribution, condemnation, deterrence, incapacitation—are involved in the disposition of juvenile offenders too. These are society's ultimate techniques for protection against threatening conduct; it is inevitable that they should be used against threats from the young as well as the old when other resources appear unavailing. . . .

The difficulty is not that this compromise with the rehabilitative idea has occurred, but that it has not been acknowledged. Juvenile court laws and procedures that can be rationalized solely on the basis of the original optimistic theories endure as if the vitality of those theories were undiluted. Thus, for example, juvenile courts retain expansive grounds of jurisdiction authorizing judicial intervention in relatively minor matters of morals and misbehavior, on the ground that subsequent delinquent conduct may be indicated, as if there were reliable ways of predicting delinquency in a given child and reliable ways of redirecting children's lives. Delinquency is adjudicated in informal proceedings that often lack safeguards fundamental for protecting the individual and for assuring reliable determinations, as if the court were a hospital clinic and its only objective were to discover the child's malady and to cure him.

The Commission does not conclude from its study of the juvenile court that the time has come to jettison the experiment and remand the disposition of children charged with crime to the criminal courts of the country. As trying as are the problems of the juvenile courts, the problems of the criminal courts, particularly those of the lower courts that would fall heir to much of the juvenile court jurisdiction, are even graver; and the ideal of separate treatment of children is still worth pursuing. What is required is rather a revised philosophy of the juvenile court, based on recognition that in the past our reach exceeded our grasp. The spirit that animated the juvenile court movement was fed in part by a humanitarian compassion for offenders who were children. That willingness to understand and treat people who threaten public safety and security should be nurtured, not turned aside as hopeless sentimentality, both because it is civilized and because social protection itself demands constant search for alternatives to the crude and limited expedient of condemnation and punishment. But neither should it be allowed to outrun reality. The juvenile court is a court of law, charged like other agencies of criminal justice with protecting the community against threatening conduct. Rehabilitation of offenders through individualized handling is one way of providing protection, and appropriately the primary way in dealing with children. But the guiding consideration for a court of law that deals with threatening conduct is nevertheless protection of the community. The juvenile court, like other courts, is therefore obliged to employ all the means at hand, not excluding incapacitation, for achieving that protection. What should distinguish the juvenile from the criminal courts is their greater emphasis on rehabilitation, not their exclusive preoccupation with it.

This chapter outlines a series of interlocking proposals aimed at what the Commission believes are basic deficiencies in the system of juvenile justice. . . . The essence of those relating to the juvenile court and institutions closely connected with it is as follows:

- The formal sanctioning system and pronouncement of delinquency should be used only as a last resort. In place of the formal system, dispositional alternatives to adjudication must be developed for dealing with juveniles, including agencies to provide and coordinate services and procedures to achieve necessary control without unnecessary stigma. Alternatives already available, such as those related to court intake, should be more fully exploited.

- The range of conduct for which court intervention is authorized should be narrowed.

- The cases that fall within the narrowed jurisdiction of the court and filter through the screen of pre-judicial, informal disposition modes would largely involve offenders for whom more vigorous measures seem necessary. Court adjudication and disposition of those offenders should no longer be viewed solely as a diagnosis and prescription for cure, but should be frankly recognized as an authoritative court judgment expressing society's claim to protection. While rehabilitative efforts should be vigorously pursued in deference to the youthfulness of the offenders and in keeping with the general commitment to individualized treatment of all offenders, the incapacitative, deterrent, and condemnatory purposes of the judgment should not be disguised. Accordingly, the adjudicatory hearing should be consistent with basic principles of due process. Counsel and evidentiary restrictions are among the essential elements of fundamental fairness in juvenile as well as adult criminal courts.

REVIEW QUESTIONS

1. What problems in the juvenile justice system does the President's Commission cite in support of its argument that "the great hopes originally held for the juvenile court have not been fulfilled" (p. 75)? Are any or all of these problems traceable to the

underlying philosophy of juvenile courts as expressed by Judge Mack and by the Pennsylvania Supreme Court in the *Fisher* case? Or are they a result of failure to follow through with the plans of the founders of the juvenile court?

2. Why doesn't the Commission recommend abolishing the juvenile court?

3. What kinds of reforms does the Commission think are needed in the juvenile justice system? Do you think adopting such reforms would alleviate the problems identified by the Commission? Would they improve the juvenile justice system? Or would they make juvenile courts too much like adult criminal courts? Would the kinds of reforms the Commission advocates create other problems?

Kent v. United States

The Supreme Court of the United States
383 U.S. 541 (1966)

MR. JUSTICE FORTAS delivered the opinion of the Court. . . .

Morris A. Kent, Jr., first came under the authority of the Juvenile Court of the District of Columbia in 1959. He was then aged 14. He was apprehended as a result of several housebreakings and an attempted purse snatching. He was placed on probation, in the custody of his mother who had been separated from her husband since Kent was two years old. Juvenile Court officials interviewed Kent from time to time during the probation period and accumulated a "Social Service" file.

On September 2, 1961, an intruder entered the apartment of a woman in the District of Columbia. He took her wallet. He raped her. The police found in the apartment latent fingerprints. They were developed and processed. They matched the fingerprints of Morris Kent, taken when he was 14 years old and under the jurisdiction of the Juvenile Court. At about 3 p.m. on September 5, 1961, Kent was taken into custody by the police. Kent was then 16 and therefore subject to the "exclusive jurisdiction" of the Juvenile Court. He was still on probation to that court as a result of the 1959 proceedings.

Upon being apprehended, Kent was taken to police headquarters where he was interrogated by police officers. It appears that he admitted his involvement in the offense which led to his apprehension and volunteered information as to similar offenses involving housebreaking, robbery, and rape. His interrogation proceeded from about 3 p.m. to 10 p.m. the same evening.

Some time after 10 p.m. petitioner was taken to the Receiving Home for Children. The next morning he was released to the police for further interrogation at police headquarters, which lasted until 5 p.m.

The record does not show when his mother became aware that the boy was in custody, but shortly after 2 p.m. on September 6, 1961, the day following petitioner's apprehension, she retained counsel.

Counsel, together with petitioner's mother, promptly conferred with the Social Service Director of the Juvenile Court. In a brief interview, they discussed the possibility that the Juvenile Court might waive jurisdiction . . . and remit Kent to trial by the District Court. Counsel made known his intention to oppose waiver.

Petitioner was detained at the Receiving Home for almost a week. There was no arraignment during this time, no determination by a judicial officer of probable cause for petitioner's apprehension.

During this period of detention and interrogation, petitioner's counsel arranged for examination of petitioner by two psychiatrists and a psychologist. He thereafter filed with the Juvenile Court a motion for a hearing on the question of waiver of Juvenile Court jurisdiction, together with an affidavit of a psychiatrist certifying that petitioner "is a victim of severe psychopathology" and recommending hospitalization for psychiatric observation. Petitioner's counsel, in support of his motion to the effect that the Juvenile Court should retain jurisdiction of petitioner, offered to prove that if petitioner were given adequate treatment in a hospital under the aegis of the Juvenile Court, he would be a suitable subject for rehabilitation.

At the same time, petitioner's counsel moved that the Juvenile Court should give him access to the Social Service file relating to petitioner which had been accumulated by the staff of the Juvenile Court during petitioner's probation period, and which would be available to the Juvenile Court judge in considering the question whether it should retain or waive jurisdiction. Petitioner's counsel represented that access to this file was essential to his providing petitioner with effective assistance of counsel.

The Juvenile Court judge did not rule on these motions. He held no hearing. He did not confer with petitioner or petitioner's parents or petitioner's counsel. He entered an order reciting that after "full investigation, I do hereby waive" jurisdiction of petitioner and directing that he be "held for trial for [the alleged] offenses under the regular procedure of the U.S. District Court for the District of Columbia." He made no findings. He did not recite any reason for the waiver. He made no reference to the motions filed by petitioner's counsel. We must assume that he denied, sub silentio, the motions for a hearing, the recommendation for hospitalization for psychiatric observation, the request for access to the Social Service file, and the offer to prove that petitioner was a fit subject for rehabilitation under the Juvenile Court's jurisdiction.[1]

Presumably, prior to entry of his order, the Juvenile Court judge received and considered recommendations of the Juvenile Court staff, the Social Service file relating to petitioner, and a report dated September 8, 1961 (three days following petitioner's apprehension), submitted to him by the Juvenile Probation Section. The Social Service file and the September 8

---

[1] It should be noted that at this time the statute provided for only one Juvenile Court judge. Congressional hearings and reports attest the impossibility of the burden which he was supposed to carry. The statute was amended in 1962 to provide for three judges for the court.

report were later sent to the District Court and it appears that both of them referred to petitioner's mental condition. The September 8 report spoke of "a rapid deterioration of [petitioner's] personality structure and the possibility of mental illness." As stated, neither this report nor the Social Service file was made available to petitioner's counsel.

The provision of the Juvenile Court Act governing waiver expressly provides only for "full investigation." It states the circumstances in which jurisdiction may be waived and the child held for trial under adult procedures, but it does not state standards to govern the Juvenile Court's decision as to waiver. The provision reads as follows:

> "If a child sixteen years of age or older is charged with an offense which would amount to a felony in the case of an adult, or any child charged with an offense which if committed by an adult is punishable by death or life imprisonment, the judge may, after full investigation, waive jurisdiction and order such child held for trial under the regular procedure of the court which would have jurisdiction of such offense if committed by an adult; or such other court may exercise the powers conferred upon the juvenile court in this subchapter in conducting and disposing of such cases."

Petitioner appealed from the Juvenile Court's waiver order to the Municipal Court of Appeals, which affirmed, and also applied to the United States District Court for a writ of habeas corpus, which was denied. On appeal from these judgments, the United States Court of Appeals held on January 22, 1963, that neither appeal to the Municipal Court of Appeals nor habeas corpus was available. In the Court of Appeals' view, the exclusive method of reviewing the Juvenile Court's waiver order was a motion to dismiss the indictment in the District Court.

Meanwhile, on September 25, 1961, shortly after the Juvenile Court order waiving its jurisdiction, petitioner was indicted by a grand jury of the United States District Court for the District of Columbia. The indictment contained eight counts alleging two instances of housebreaking, robbery, and rape, and one of housebreaking and robbery. On November 16, 1961, petitioner moved the District Court to dismiss the indictment on the grounds that the waiver was invalid. He also moved the District Court to constitute itself a Juvenile Court. . . . After substantial delay occasioned by petitioner's appeal and habeas corpus proceedings, the District Court addressed itself to the motion to dismiss on February 8, 1963. The District Court denied the motion to dismiss the indictment. The District Court ruled that it would not "go behind" the Juvenile Court judge's recital that his order was entered "after full investigation." It held that "The only matter before me is as to whether or not the statutory provisions were complied with and the Courts have held . . . with reference to full investigation, that that does not mean a quasi judicial or judicial hearing. No hearing is required."

On March 7, 1963, the District Court held a hearing on petitioner's motion to determine his competency to stand trial. The court determined that petitioner was competent.[2]

---

[2]The District Court had before it extensive information as to petitioner's mental condition, bearing upon both competence to stand trial and the defense of insanity. The court had obtained the "Social Service" file from the Juvenile Court and had made it available to petitioner's counsel. On Oc-

At trial, petitioner's defense was wholly directed toward proving that he was not criminally responsible because "his unlawful act was the product of mental disease or mental defect." Extensive evidence, including expert testimony, was presented to support this defense. The jury found as to the counts alleging rape that petitioner was "not guilty by reason of insanity." Under District of Columbia law, this made it mandatory that petitioner be transferred to St. Elizabeths Hospital, a mental institution, until his sanity is restored. On the six counts of housebreaking and robbery, the jury found that petitioner was guilty.[3]

Kent was sentenced to serve five to 15 years on each count as to which he was found guilty, or a total of 30 to 90 years in prison. The District Court ordered that the time to be spent at St. Elizabeths on the mandatory commitment after the insanity acquittal be counted as part of the 30- to 90-year sentence. Petitioner appealed to the United States Court of Appeals for the District of Columbia Circuit. That court affirmed. . . .

Petitioner attacks the waiver of jurisdiction on a number of statutory and constitutional grounds. He contends that the waiver is defective because no hearing was held; because no findings were made by the Juvenile Court; because the Juvenile Court stated no reasons for waiver; and because counsel was denied access to the Social Service file which presumably was considered by the Juvenile Court in determining to waive jurisdiction. . . .

We agree with the Court of Appeals that the statute contemplates that the Juvenile Court should have considerable latitude within which to determine whether it should retain jurisdiction over a child or—subject to the statutory delimitation—should waive jurisdiction. But this latitude is not complete. At the outset, it assumes procedural regularity sufficient in the particular circumstances to satisfy the basic requirements of due process

---

tober 13, 1961, the District Court had granted petitioner's motion of October 6 for commitment to the Psychiatric Division of the General Hospital for 60 days. On December 20, 1961, the hospital reported that "It is the concensus [sic] of the staff that Morris is emotionally ill and severely so . . . we feel that he is incompetent to stand trial and to participate in a mature way in his own defense. His illness has interfered with his judgment and reasoning ability. . . ." The prosecutor opposed a finding of incompetence to stand trial, and at the prosecutor's request, the District Court referred petitioner to St. Elizabeths Hospital for psychiatric observation. According to a letter from the Superintendent of St. Elizabeths of April 5, 1962, the hospital's staff found that petitioner was "suffering from mental disease at the present time, Schizophrenic Reaction, Chronic Undifferentiated Type," that he had been suffering from this disease at the time of the charged offenses, and that "if committed by him [those criminal acts] were the product of this disease." They stated, however, that petitioner was "mentally competent to understand the nature of the proceedings against him and to consult properly with counsel in his own defense."

[3] The basis for this distinction—that petitioner was "sane" for purposes of the housebreaking and robbery but "insane" for the purposes of the rape—apparently was the hypothesis, for which there is some support in the record, that the jury might find that the robberies had anteceded the rapes, and in that event, it might conclude that the housebreakings and robberies were not the products of his mental disease or defect, while the rapes were produced thereby.

and fairness, as well as compliance with the statutory requirement of a "full investigation." The statute gives the Juvenile Court a substantial degree of discretion as to the factual considerations to be evaluated, the weight to be given them and the conclusion to be reached. It does not confer upon the Juvenile Court a license for arbitrary procedure. The statute does not permit the Juvenile Court to determine in isolation and without the participation or any representation of the child the "critically important" question whether a child will be deprived of the special protections and provisions of the Juvenile Court Act. It does not authorize the Juvenile Court, in total disregard of a motion for hearing filed by counsel, and without any hearing or statement or reasons, to decide—as in this case—that the child will be taken from the Receiving Home for Children and transferred to jail along with adults, and that he will be exposed to the possibility of a death sentence instead of treatment for a maximum, in Kent's case, of five years, until he is 21.

We do not consider whether, on the merits, Kent should have been transferred; but there is no place in our system of law for reaching a result of such tremendous consequences without ceremony—without hearing, without effective assistance of counsel, without a statement of reasons. It is inconceivable that a court of justice dealing with adults, with respect to a similar issue, would proceed in this manner. It would be extraordinary if society's special concern for children, as reflected in the District of Columbia's Juvenile Court Act, permitted this procedure. We hold that it does not.

1. The theory of the District's Juvenile Court Act, like that of other jurisdictions, is rooted in social welfare philosophy rather than in the corpus juris. Its proceedings are designated as civil rather than criminal. The Juvenile Court is theoretically engaged in determining the needs of the child and of society rather than adjudicating criminal conduct. The objectives are to provide measures of guidance and rehabilitation for the child and protection for society, not to fix criminal responsibility, guilt and punishment. The State is *parens patriae* rather than prosecuting attorney and judge. But the admonition to function in a "parental" relationship is not an invitation to procedural arbitrariness.

2. Because the State is supposed to proceed in respect of the child as *parens patriae* and not as adversary, courts have relied on the premise that the proceedings are "civil" in nature and not criminal, and have asserted that the child cannot complain of the deprivation of important rights available in criminal cases. It has been asserted that he can claim only the fundamental due process right to fair treatment. . . .

While there can be no doubt of the original laudable purpose of juvenile courts, studies and critiques in recent years raise serious questions as to whether actual performance measures well enough against theoretical purpose to make tolerable the immunity of the process from the reach of constitutional guaranties applicable to adults. There is much evidence that some juvenile courts, including that of the District of Columbia, lack the personnel, facilities and techniques to perform adequately as representatives of the State in a *parens patriae* capacity, at least with respect to children charged with law violation. There is evidence, in fact, that there may be grounds for concern that the child receives the worst of both worlds: that he gets neither the protections accorded to adults nor the solicitous care and regenerative treatment postulated for children.

This concern, however, does not induce us in this case to accept the invitation to rule that constitutional guaranties which would be applicable to adults charged with the serious offenses for which Kent was tried must be applied in juvenile court proceedings concerned with allegations of law violation. The Juvenile Court Act and the decisions of the United States Court of Appeals for the District of Columbia Circuit provide an adequate basis for decision of this case, and we go no further.

3. It is clear beyond dispute that the waiver of jurisdiction is a "critically important" action determining vitally important statutory rights of the juvenile. . . . The Juvenile Court is vested with "original and exclusive jurisdiction" of the child. This jurisdiction confers special rights and immunities. He is, as specified by the statute, shielded from publicity. He may be confined, but with rare exceptions he may not be jailed along with adults. He may be detained, but only until he is 21 years of age. The court is admonished by the statute to give preference to retaining the child in the custody of his parents "unless his welfare and the safety and protection of the public can not be adequately safeguarded without . . . removal." The child is protected against consequences of adult conviction such as the loss of civil rights, the use of adjudication against him in subsequent proceedings, and disqualification for public employment.

The net, therefore, is that petitioner—then a boy of 16—was by statute entitled to certain procedures and benefits as a consequence of his statutory right to the "exclusive" jurisdiction of the Juvenile Court. In these circumstances, considering particularly that decision as to waiver of jurisdiction and transfer of the matter to the District Court was potentially as important to petitioner as the difference between five years' confinement and a death sentence, we conclude that, as a condition to a valid waiver order, petitioner was entitled to a hearing, including access by his counsel to the social records and probation or similar reports which presumably are considered by the court, and to a statement of reasons for the Juvenile Court's decision. We believe that this result is required by the statute read in the context of constitutional principles relating to due process and the assistance of counsel. . . .

We are of the opinion that the Court of Appeals misconceived the basic issue and the underlying values in this case. It did note . . . that the determination of whether to transfer a child from the statutory structure of the Juvenile Court to the criminal processes of the District Court is "critically important." We hold that it is, indeed, a "critically important" proceeding. The Juvenile Court Act confers upon the child a right to avail himself of that court's "exclusive" jurisdiction. As the Court of Appeals has said, "[I]t is implicit in [the Juvenile Court] scheme that non-criminal treatment is to be the rule—and the adult criminal treatment, the exception which must be governed by the particular factors of individual cases."

Meaningful review requires that the reviewing court should review. It should not be remitted to assumptions. It must have before it a statement of the reasons motivating the waiver including, of course, a statement of the relevant facts. It may not "assume" that there are adequate reasons, nor may it merely assume that "full investigation" has been made. Accordingly, we hold that it is incumbent upon the Juvenile Court to accompany its waiver order with a statement of the reasons or considerations therefor. We do not read the statute as requiring that this statement must be formal or that it should necessarily include conventional findings of fact. But the statement should be sufficient to demonstrate that the statutory requirement of "full investigation" has been met; and that the question has received the careful consideration of the Juvenile Court; and it must set forth the basis for the order with sufficient specificity to permit meaningful review.

Correspondingly, we conclude that an opportunity for a hearing which may be informal must be given the child prior to entry of a waiver order. . . .

The right to representation by counsel is not a formality. It is not a grudging gesture to a ritualistic requirement. It is of the essence of justice. Appointment of counsel without affording an opportunity for hearing on a "critically important" decision is tantamount to denial of counsel. There is no justification for the failure of the Juvenile Court to rule on the motion for hearing filed by petitioner's counsel, and it was error to fail to grant a hearing.

We do not mean by this to indicate that the hearing to be held must conform with all of the requirements of a criminal trial or even of the usual administrative hearing; but we do hold that the hearing must measure up to the essentials of due process and fair treatment.

With respect to access by the child's counsel to the social records of the child, we deem it obvious that since these are to be considered by the Juvenile Court in making its decision to waive, they must be made available to the child's counsel. . . .

We do not agree with the Court of Appeals' statement, attempting to justify denial of access to these records, that counsel's role is limited to presenting "to the court anything on behalf of the child which might help the court in arriving at a decision; it is not to denigrate the staff's submissions and recommendations." On the contrary, if the staff's submissions include materials which are susceptible to challenge or impeachment, it is precisely the role of counsel to "denigrate" such matter. There is no irrebuttable presumption of accuracy attached to staff reports. If a decision on waiver is "critically important" it is equally of "critical importance" that the material submitted to the judge—which is protected by the statute only against "indiscriminate" inspection—be subjected, within reasonable limits having regard to the theory of the Juvenile Court Act, to examination, criticism and refutation. While the Juvenile Court judge may, of course, receive *ex parte* analyses and recommendations from his staff, he may not, for purposes of a decision on waiver, receive and rely upon secret information, whether emanating from his staff or otherwise. The Juvenile Court is governed in this respect by the established principles which control courts and quasi-judicial agencies of the Government.

For the reasons stated, we conclude that the Court of Appeals and the District Court erred in sustaining the validity of the waiver by the Juvenile Court. . . .

Ordinarily we would reverse the Court of Appeals and direct the District Court to remand the case to the Juvenile Court for a new determination of waiver. If on remand the decision were against waiver, the indictment in the District Court would be dismissed. However, petitioner has now passed the age of 21 and the Juvenile Court can no longer exercise jurisdiction over him. In view of the unavailability of a redetermination of the waiver question by the Juvenile Court, it is urged by petitioner that the conviction should be vacated and the indictment dismissed. In the circumstances of this case . . . we do not consider it appropriate to grant this drastic relief. Accordingly, we vacate the order of the Court of Appeals and the judgment of the District Court and remand the case to the District Court for a hearing *de novo* on waiver, consistent with this opinion. If that court finds that waiver was inappropriate, petitioner's conviction must be vacated. If, however, it finds that the waiver order was proper when originally made, the District Court may proceed, after consideration of such motions as counsel may make and such further proceedings, if any, as may be warranted, to enter an appropriate judgment.

Reversed and remanded.

APPENDIX TO OPINION OF THE COURT [omitted—*Ed.*]

Mr. Justice Stewart, with whom Mr. Justice Black, Mr. Justice Harlan and Mr. Justice White join, dissenting.

This case involves the construction of a statute applicable only to the District of Columbia. Our general practice is to leave undisturbed decisions of the Court of Appeals for the District of Columbia Circuit concerning the import of legislation governing the affairs of the District. It appears, however, that two cases decided by the Court of Appeals subsequent to its decision in the present case may have considerably modified the court's construction of the statute. Therefore, I would vacate this judgment and remand the case to the Court of Appeals for reconsideration in the light of its subsequent decisions.

Review Questions

1. What *issue* was before the Court in *Kent v. U.S.?* How did the court resolve the issue (i.e., what was its *holding*)? What *reasons* did Justice Fortas give for the Court's decision? What *facts* of the case were pertinent to the Court's decision? (Note: Law school students are typically asked to write a *brief* of each court case they read. Their briefs typically summarize the facts, issue(s), and holding in the case, as well as the reasoning given by the author of the *majority opinion*. Other justices will often write separate *opinions* in which they state their reasons for *concurring* with or *dissenting* from the decision of the majority and law students will typically summarize the reasoning in these opinions also. You may find it helpful to brief the U.S. Supreme Court cases in this book as a way to help you spot essential information and familiarize yourself with the most important aspects of each case. Even if you choose not to brief cases, you will find it helpful to identify the facts, issue(s), holding and reasoning as you are reading.)

2. What did the Supreme Court find wrong with the way in which the juvenile court judge "waived" juvenile court jurisdiction and transferred the case to the District Court for prosecution of Morris Kent as an adult? What Constitutional rights did the Supreme Court say a juvenile in Kent's situation must be granted before the case can be transferred? Why did the Court believe each of these rights was essential to the fairness of the proceeding?

3. What is the Court's impression of the traditional juvenile court?

4. Speaking for the court in *Kent,* Justice Fortas observes that "there may be grounds for concern that the child receives the worst of both worlds . . ." (p. 83). What does he mean by this and how does he support his argument?

5. What do you make of Justice Fortas' observation in footnote 1 (p. 80) that the delinquency statute in force in Washington, D.C. at the time of Kent's transfer to adult court provided for but one juvenile court judge? Would the judicial style described by Judge Mack as essential in juvenile court be possible given the caseload this judge must have confronted in a city known for its astronomical rates of crime and delinquency?

6. What did the Court say must happen to Morris Kent as a result of its decision?

In re Gault

The Supreme Court of the United States
387 U.S. 1 (1967)

MR. JUSTICE FORTAS delivered the opinion of the Court. . . .

I.

On Monday, June 8, 1964, at about 10 a.m., Gerald Francis Gault and a friend, Ronald Lewis, were taken into custody by the Sheriff of Gila County. Gerald was then still subject to a six months' probation order which had been entered on February 25, 1964, as a result of his having been in the company of another boy who had stolen a wallet from a lady's purse. The police action on June 8 was taken as the result of a verbal complaint by a neighbor of the boys, Mrs. Cook, about a telephone call made to her in which the caller or callers made lewd or indecent remarks. It will suffice for purposes of this opinion to say that the remarks or questions put to her were of the irritatingly offensive, adolescent, sex variety.

At the time Gerald was picked up, his mother and father were both at work. No notice that Gerald was being taken into custody was left at the home. No other steps were taken to advise them that their son had, in effect, been arrested. Gerald was taken to the Children's Detention Home. When his mother arrived home at about 6 o'clock, Gerald was not there. Gerald's older brother was sent to look for him at the trailer home of the Lewis family. He apparently learned then that Gerald was in custody. He so informed his mother. The two of them went to the Detention Home. The deputy probation officer, Flagg, who was also superintendent of the Detention Home, told Mrs. Gault "why Jerry was there" and said that a hearing would be held in Juvenile Court at 3 o'clock the following day, June 9.

Officer Flagg filed a petition with the court on the hearing day, June 9, 1964. It was not served on the Gaults. Indeed, none of them saw this petition until the habeas corpus hearing on August 17, 1964. The petition was entirely formal. It made no reference to any factual basis for the judicial action which it initiated. It recited only that "said minor is under the age of eighteen years, and is in need of the protection of this Honorable Court; [and that] said minor is a delinquent minor." It prayed for a hearing and an order regarding "the care and custody of said minor." Officer Flagg executed a formal affidavit in support of the petition.

On June 9, Gerald, his mother, his older brother, and Probation Officers Flagg and Henderson appeared before the Juvenile Judge in chambers. Gerald's father was not there. He was at work out of the city. Mrs. Cook, the complainant, was not there. No one was sworn at this hearing. No transcript or recording was made. No memorandum or record of the substance of the proceedings was prepared. Our information about the proceeding and the subsequent hearing on June 15 derives entirely from the testimony of the Juvenile Court Judge, Mr. and Mrs. Gault and Officer Flagg at the habeas corpus proceeding conducted two months later. From this, it appears that at the June 9 hearing Gerald was questioned by the judge about the telephone call. There was conflict as to what he said. His mother recalled that Gerald said he only dialed Mrs. Cook's number and handed the telephone to his friend, Ronald. Officer Flagg recalled that Gerald had admitted making the lewd remarks. Judge McGhee testified that Gerald "admitted making one of these [lewd] statements." At the conclusion of the hearing, the judge said he would "think about it." Gerald was taken back to the Detention Home. He was not sent to his own home with his parents. On June 11 or 12, after having been detained since June 8, Gerald was released and driven home. There is no explanation in the record as to why he was kept in the Detention Home or why he was released. At 5 p.m. on the day of Gerald's release, Mrs. Gault received a note signed by Officer Flagg. It was on plain paper, not letter-head. Its entire text was as follows:

> "Mrs. Gault:
>
> "Judge McGHEE has set Monday June 15, 1964 at 11:00 A. M. as the date and time for further Hearings on Gerald's delinquency
>
> "/s/ Flagg"

At the appointed time on Monday, June 15, Gerald, his father and mother, Ronald Lewis and his father, and Officers Flagg and Henderson were present before Judge McGhee.

Witnesses at the habeas corpus proceeding differed in their recollections of Gerald's testimony at the June 15 hearing. Mr. and Mrs. Gault recalled that Gerald again testified that he had only dialed the number and that the other boy had made the remarks. Officer Flagg agreed that at this hearing Gerald did not admit making the lewd remarks. But Judge McGhee recalled that "there was some admission again of some of the lewd statements. He—he didn't admit any of the more serious lewd statements." Again, the complainant, Mrs. Cook, was not present. Mrs. Gault asked that Mrs. Cook be present "so she could see which boy that done the talking, the dirty talking over the phone." The Juvenile Judge said "she didn't have to be present at that hearing." The judge did not speak to Mrs. Cook or communicate with her at any time. Probation Officer Flagg had talked to her once—over the telephone on June 9.

At this June 15 hearing a "referral report" made by the probation officers was filed with the court, although not disclosed to Gerald or his parents. This listed the charge as "Lewd Phone Calls." At the conclusion of the hearing, the judge committed Gerald as a juvenile delinquent to the State Industrial School "for the period of his minority [that is, until 21], unless sooner discharged by due process of law." An order to that effect was entered. It recites that "after a full hearing and due deliberation the Court finds that said minor is a delinquent child, and that said minor is of the age of 15 years."

No appeal is permitted by Arizona law in juvenile cases. On August 3, 1964, a petition for a writ of habeas corpus was filed with the Supreme Court of Arizona and referred by it to the Superior Court for hearing.

At the habeas corpus hearing on August 17, Judge McGhee was vigorously cross-examined as to the basis for his actions. He testified that he had taken into account the fact that Gerald was on probation. He was asked "under what section of . . . the code you found the boy delinquent?"

. . . In substance, he concluded that Gerald came within ARS § 8-201-6 (a), which specifies that a "delinquent child" includes one "who has violated a law of the state or an ordinance or regulation of a political subdivision thereof." The law which Gerald was found to have violated is ARS § 13-377. This section of the Arizona Criminal Code provides that a person who "in the presence or hearing of any woman or child . . . uses vulgar, abusive or obscene language, is guilty of a misdemeanor. . . ." The penalty specified in the Criminal Code, which would apply to an adult, is $5 to $50, or imprisonment for not more than two months. The judge also testified that he acted under ARS § 8-201-6 (d) which includes in the definition of a "delinquent child" one who, as the judge phrased it, is "habitually involved in immoral matters."

Asked about the basis for his conclusion that Gerald was "habitually involved in immoral matters," the judge testified, somewhat vaguely, that two years earlier, on July 2, 1962, a "referral" was made concerning Gerald, "where the boy had stolen a baseball glove from another boy and lied to the Police Department about it." The judge said there was "no hearing," and "no accusation" relating to this incident, "because of lack of material foundation." But it seems to have remained in his mind as a relevant factor. The judge also testified that Gerald had admitted making other nuisance phone calls in the past which, as the judge recalled the boy's testimony, were "silly calls, or funny calls, or something like that."

The Superior Court dismissed the writ, and appellants sought review in the Arizona Supreme Court. That court stated that it considered appellants' assignments of error as urging (1) that the Juvenile Code . . . is unconstitutional because it does not require that parents and children be apprised of the specific charges, does not require proper notice of a hearing, and does not provide for an appeal; and (2) that the proceedings and order relating to Gerald constituted a denial of due process of law because of the absence of adequate notice of the charge and the hearing; failure to notify appellants of certain constitutional rights including the rights to counsel and to confrontation, and the privilege against self-incrimination; the use of unsworn hearsay testimony; and the failure to make a record of the proceedings. Appellants further asserted that it was error for the Juvenile Court to remove Gerald from the custody of his parents without a showing and finding of their unsuitability, and alleged a miscellany of other errors under state law.

The Supreme Court handed down an elaborate and wide-ranging opinion affirming dismissal of the writ and stating the court's conclusions as to the issues raised by appellants and other aspects of the juvenile process. In their jurisdictional statement and brief in this Court, appellants do not urge upon us all of the points passed upon by the Supreme Court of Arizona. They urge that we hold the Juvenile Code of Arizona invalid on its face or as applied in this case because, contrary to the Due Process Clause of the Fourteenth Amendment, the juvenile is taken from the custody of his parents and committed to a state institution pursuant to proceedings in which the Juvenile Court has virtually unlimited discretion, and in which the following basic rights are denied:

1. Notice of the charges;
2. Right to counsel;
3. Right to confrontation and cross-examination;
4. Privilege against self-incrimination;
5. Right to a transcript of the proceedings; and
6. Right to appellate review.

We shall not consider other issues which were passed upon by the Supreme Court of Arizona. We emphasize that we indicate no opinion as to whether the decision of that court with respect to such other issues does or does not conflict with requirements of the Federal Constitution.

II.

 . . . [W]hatever may be their precise impact, neither the Fourteenth Amendment nor the Bill of Rights is for adults alone.

We do not in this opinion consider the impact of these constitutional provisions upon the totality of the relationship of the juvenile and the state. We do not even consider the entire process relating to juvenile "delinquents." For example, we are not here concerned with the procedures or constitutional rights applicable to the pre-judicial stages of the juvenile process, nor do we direct our attention to the post-adjudicative or dispositional process. We consider only the problems presented to us by this case. These relate to the proceedings by which a determination is made as to whether a juvenile is a "delinquent" as a result of alleged misconduct on his part, with the consequence that he may be committed to a state institution. As to these proceedings, there appears to be little current dissent from the proposition that the Due Process Clause has a role to play. The problem is to ascertain the precise impact of the due process requirement upon such proceedings.

From the inception of the juvenile court system, wide differences have been tolerated—indeed insisted upon—between the procedural rights accorded to adults and those of juveniles. In practically all jurisdictions, there are rights granted to adults which are withheld from juveniles. In addition to the specific problems involved in the present case, for example, it has been held that the juvenile is not entitled to bail, to indictment by grand jury, to a public trial or to trial by jury. It is frequent practice that rules governing the arrest and interrogation of adults by the police are not observed in the case of juveniles.

The history and theory underlying this development are well-known, but a recapitulation is necessary for purposes of this opinion. The Juvenile Court movement began in this country at the end of the last century. From the juvenile court statute adopted in Illinois in 1899, the system has spread to every State in the Union, the District of Columbia, and Puerto Rico. The constitutionality of Juvenile Court laws has been sustained in over 40 jurisdictions against a variety of attacks.

The early reformers were appalled by adult procedures and penalties, and by the fact that children could be given long prison sentences and mixed in jails with hardened criminals. They were profoundly convinced that society's duty to the child could not be confined by the concept of justice alone. They believed that society's role was not to ascertain whether the child was "guilty" or "innocent," but "What is he, how has he become what he is, and what had best be done in his interest and in the interest of the state to save him from a downward career." The child—essentially good, as they saw it—was to be made "to feel that he is the object of [the state's] care and solicitude," not that he was under arrest or on trial. The rules of criminal procedure were therefore altogether inapplicable. The apparent rigidities, technicalities, and harshness which they observed in both substantive and procedural criminal law were therefore to be discarded. The idea of crime and punishment was to be abandoned. The child was to be "treated" and "rehabilitated" and the procedures, from apprehension through institutionalization, were to be "clinical" rather than punitive.

These results were to be achieved, without coming to conceptual and constitutional grief, by insisting that the proceedings were not adversary, but that the state was proceeding as *parens patriae*. The Latin phrase proved to be a great help to those who sought to rationalize the exclusion of juveniles from the constitutional scheme; but its meaning is murky and its historic credentials are of dubious relevance. The phrase was taken from chancery practice, where, however, it was used to describe the power of the state to act *in loco parentis* for the purpose of protecting the property interests and the person of the child. But there is no trace of the doctrine in the history of criminal jurisprudence. At common law, children under seven were considered incapable of possessing criminal intent. Beyond that age, they were subjected to arrest, trial, and in theory to punishment like adult offenders. In these old days, the state was not deemed to have authority to accord them fewer procedural rights than adults.

The right of the state, as *parens patriae,* to deny to the child procedural rights available to his elders was elaborated by the assertion that a child, unlike an adult, has a right "not to liberty but to custody." He can be made to attorn to his parents, to go to school, etc. If his parents default in effectively performing their custodial functions—that is, if the child is "delinquent"—the state may intervene. In doing so, it does not deprive the child of any rights, because he has none. It merely provides the "custody" to which the child is entitled. On this basis, proceedings involving juveniles were described as "civil" not "criminal" and therefore not subject to the requirements which restrict the state when it seeks to deprive a person of his liberty.

Accordingly, the highest motives and most enlightened impulses led to a peculiar system for juveniles, unknown to our law in any comparable context. The constitutional and theoretical basis for this peculiar system is—to say the least—debatable. And in practice, as we remarked in the *Kent* case, the results have not been entirely satisfactory. Juvenile Court history has again demonstrated that unbridled discretion, however benevolently motivated, is frequently a poor substitute for principle and procedure. In 1937, Dean Pound wrote: "The powers of the Star Chamber were a trifle in comparison with those of our juvenile courts. . . ." The absence of substantive standards has not necessarily meant that children receive careful, compassionate, individualized treatment. The absence of procedural rules based upon constitutional principle has not always produced fair, efficient, and effective procedures. Departures from established principles of due process have frequently resulted not in enlightened procedure, but in arbitrariness. . . .

It is claimed that juveniles obtain benefits from the special procedures applicable to them which more than offset the disadvantages of denial of the substance of normal due process. As we shall discuss, the observance of due process standards, intelligently and not ruthlessly administered, will not compel the States to abandon or displace any of the substantive benefits of the juvenile process. . . .

. . . [T]he features of the juvenile system which its proponents have asserted are of unique benefit will not be impaired by constitutional domestication. For example, the commendable principles relating to the processing and treatment of juveniles separately from adults are in no way involved or affected by the procedural issues under discussion. Further, we are told that one of the important benefits of the special juvenile court procedures is that they avoid classifying the juvenile as a "criminal." The juvenile offender is now classed as a "delinquent." There is, of course, no reason why this should not continue. It is disconcerting, however, that this term has come to involve only slightly less stigma than the term "criminal" applied to adults. It is also emphasized that in practically all jurisdictions, statutes provide that an adjudication of the child as a delinquent shall not operate as a civil disability or disqualify him for civil service appointment. There is no reason why the application of due process requirements should interfere with such provisions.

Beyond this, it is frequently said that juveniles are protected by the process from disclosure of their deviational behavior. As the Supreme Court of Arizona phrased it in the present case, the summary procedures of Juvenile Courts are sometimes defended by a statement that it is the law's policy "to hide youthful errors from the full gaze of the public and bury them in the graveyard of the forgotten past." This claim of secrecy, however, is more rhetoric than reality. Disclosure of court records is discretionary with the judge in most jurisdictions. Statutory restrictions almost invariably apply only to the court records, and even as to those the evidence is that many courts routinely furnish information to the FBI and the military, and on request to government agencies and even to private employers. Of more importance are police records. In most States the police keep a complete file of juvenile "police contacts" and have complete discretion as to disclosure of juvenile records. Police departments receive requests for information from the FBI and other law-enforcement agencies, the Armed Forces, and social service agencies, and most of them generally comply. Private employers word their application forms to produce information concerning juvenile arrests and court proceedings, and in some jurisdictions information concerning juvenile police contacts is furnished private employers as well as government agencies.

In any event, there is no reason why, consistently with due process, a State cannot continue, if it deems it appropriate, to provide and to improve provision for the confidentiality of records of police contacts and court action relating to juveniles. . . .

Further, it is urged that the juvenile benefits from informal proceedings in the court. The early conception of the Juvenile Court proceeding was one in which a fatherly judge touched the heart and conscience of the erring youth by talking over his problems, by paternal advice and admonition, and in which, in extreme situations, benevolent and wise institutions of the State provided guidance and help "to save him from a downward career." Then, as now, goodwill and compassion were admirably prevalent. But recent studies have, with surprising unanimity, entered sharp dissent as to the validity of this gentle conception. They suggest that the appearance as well as the actuality of fairness, impartiality and orderliness—in short, the essentials of due process—may be a more impressive and more therapeutic attitude so far as the juvenile is concerned. . . . Of course, it is not suggested that juvenile court judges should fail appropriately to take account, in their demeanor and conduct, of the emotional and psychological attitude of the juveniles with whom they are confronted. While due process requirements will, in some instances, introduce a degree of order and regularity to Juvenile Court proceedings to determine delinquency, and in contested cases will introduce some elements of the adversary system, nothing will require that the conception of the kindly juvenile judge be replaced by its opposite, nor do we here rule upon the question whether ordinary due process requirements must be observed with respect to hearings to determine the disposition of the delinquent child.

Ultimately, however, we confront the reality of that portion of the Juvenile Court process with which we deal in this case. A boy is charged with misconduct. The boy is committed to an institution where he may be restrained of liberty for years. It is of no constitutional consequence—and of limited practical meaning—that the institution to which he is committed is called an Industrial School. The fact of the matter is that, however euphemistic the title, a "receiving home" or an "industrial school" for juveniles is an institution of confinement in which the child is incarcerated for a greater or lesser time. His world becomes "a building with whitewashed walls, regimented routine and institutional hours. . . ." Instead of mother and father and sisters and brothers and friends and classmates, his world is peopled by guards, custodians, state employees, and "delinquents" confined with him for anything from waywardness to rape and homicide.

In view of this, it would be extraordinary if our Constitution did not require the procedural regularity and the exercise of care implied in the phrase "due process." Under our Constitution, the condition of being a boy does not justify a kangaroo court. The traditional ideas of Juvenile Court procedure, indeed, contemplated that time would be available and care would be used to establish precisely what the juvenile did and why he did it—was it a prank of adolescence or a brutal act threatening serious consequences to himself or society unless corrected? Under traditional notions, one would assume that in a case like that of Gerald Gault, where the juvenile appears to have a home, a working mother and father, and an older brother, the Juvenile Judge would have made a careful inquiry and judgment as to the possibility that the boy could be disciplined and dealt with at home, despite his previous transgressions. Indeed, so far as appears in the record before us, except for some conversation with Gerald about his school work and his "wanting to go to . . . Grand Canyon with his father," the points to which the judge directed his attention were little different from those that would be involved in determining any charge of violation of a penal statute. The essential difference between Gerald's case and a normal criminal case is that safeguards available to adults were discarded in Gerald's case. The summary procedure as well as the long commitment was possible because Gerald was 15 years of age instead of over 18.

If Gerald had been over 18, he would not have been subject to Juvenile Court proceedings. For the particular offense immediately involved, the maximum punishment would have been a fine of $5 to $50, or imprisonment in jail for not more than two months. Instead, he was committed to custody for a maximum of six years. If he had been over 18 and had committed an offense to which such a sentence might apply, he would have been entitled to substantial rights under the Constitution of the United States as well as under Arizona's laws and constitution. The United States Constitution would guarantee him rights and protections with respect to arrest, search and seizure, and pretrial interrogation. It would assure him of specific notice of the charges and adequate time to decide his course of action and to prepare his defense. He would be entitled to clear advice that he could be represented by counsel, and, at least if a felony were involved, the State would be required to provide counsel if his parents were unable to afford it. If the court acted on the basis of his confession, careful procedures would be required to assure its voluntariness. If the case went to trial, confrontation and opportunity for cross-examination would be guaranteed. So wide a gulf between the State's treatment of the adult and of the child requires a bridge sturdier than mere verbiage, and reasons more persuasive than cliche can provide. . . .

We now turn to the specific issues which are presented to us in the present case.

III.
NOTICE OF CHARGES.

Appellants allege that the Arizona Juvenile Code is unconstitutional or alternatively that the proceedings before the Juvenile Court were constitutionally defective because of failure to provide adequate notice of the hearings. . . .

. . . Notice, to comply with due process requirements, must be given sufficiently in advance of scheduled court proceedings so that reasonable opportunity to prepare will be afforded, and it must "set forth the alleged misconduct with particularity." It is obvious, as we have discussed above, that no purpose of shielding the child from the public stigma of knowledge of his having been taken into custody and scheduled for hearing is served by the procedure approved by the court below. The "initial hearing" in the present case was a hearing on the merits. Notice at that time is not timely; and even if there were a conceivable purpose served by the deferral proposed by the court below, it would have to yield to the requirements that the child and his parents or guardian be notified, in writing, of the specific charge or factual allegations to be considered at the hearing, and that such written notice be given at the earliest practicable time, and in any event sufficiently in advance of the hearing to permit preparation. Due process of law requires notice of the sort we have described—that is, notice which would be deemed constitutionally adequate in a civil or criminal proceeding. It does not allow a hearing to be held in which a youth's freedom and his parents' right to his custody are at stake without giving them timely notice, in advance of the hearing, of the specific issues that they must meet. Nor, in the circumstances of this case, can it reasonably be said that the requirement of notice was waived.

IV.
RIGHT TO COUNSEL.

Appellants charge that the Juvenile Court proceedings were fatally defective because the court did not advise Gerald or his parents of their right to counsel, and proceeded with the hearing, the adjudication of delinquency and the order of commitment in the absence of counsel for the child and his parents or an express waiver of the right thereto. The Supreme Court of Arizona pointed out that "[t]here is disagreement [among the various jurisdictions] as to whether the court must advise the infant that he has a right to counsel." . . . It referred to a provision of the Juvenile Code which it characterized as requiring "that the probation officer shall look after the interests of neglected, delinquent and dependent children, including representing their interests in court. The court argued that "The parent and the probation officer may be relied upon to protect the infant's interests." Accordingly it rejected the proposition that "due process requires that an infant have a right to counsel." It said that juvenile courts have the discretion, but not the duty, to allow such representation; it referred specifically to the situation in which the Juvenile Court discerns conflict between the child and his parents as an instance in which this discretion might be exercised. We do not agree. Probation officers, in the Arizona scheme, are also arresting officers. They initiate proceedings and file petitions which they verify, as here, alleging the delinquency of the child; and they testify, as here, against the child. And here the probation officer was also superintendent of the Detention Home. The probation officer cannot act as counsel for the child. His role in the adjudicatory hearing, by statute and in fact, is as arresting officer and witness against the child. Nor can the judge represent the child. There is no material difference in this respect between adult and juvenile proceedings of the sort here involved. In adult proceedings, this contention has been foreclosed by decisions of this Court. A proceeding where the issue is whether the child will be found to be "delinquent" and subjected to the loss of his liberty for years is comparable in seriousness to a felony prosecution. The juvenile needs the assistance of counsel to cope with problems of law, to make skilled inquiry into the facts, to insist upon regularity of the proceedings, and to ascertain whether he has a defense and to prepare and submit it. The child "requires the guiding hand of counsel at every step in the proceedings against him." Just as in *Kent v. United States* we indicated our agreement with the United States Court of Appeals for the District of Columbia Circuit that the assistance of counsel is essential for purposes of waiver proceedings, so we hold now that it is equally essential for the determination of delinquency, carrying with it the awesome prospect of incarceration in a state institution until the juvenile reaches the age of 21. . . .

We conclude that the Due Process Clause of the Fourteenth Amendment requires that in respect of proceedings to determine delinquency which may result in commitment to an institution in which the juvenile's freedom is curtailed, the child and his parents must be notified of the child's right to be represented by counsel retained by them, or if they are unable to afford counsel, that counsel will be appointed to represent the child.

At the habeas corpus proceeding, Mrs. Gault testified that she knew that she could have appeared with counsel at the juvenile hearing. This knowledge is not a waiver of the right to counsel which she and her juvenile son had, as we have defined it. They had a right expressly to be advised that they might retain counsel and to be confronted with the need for specific consideration of whether they did or did not choose to waive the right. If they were unable to afford to employ counsel, they were entitled in view of the seriousness of the charge and the potential commitment, to appointed counsel, unless they chose waiver. Mrs. Gault's knowledge that she could employ counsel was not an "intentional relinquishment or abandonment" of a fully known right.

V.
CONFRONTATION, SELF-INCRIMINATION, CROSS-EXAMINATION.

Appellants urge that the writ of habeas corpus should have been granted because of the denial of the rights of confrontation and cross-examination in the Juvenile Court hearings, and because the privilege against self-incrimination was not observed. The Juvenile Court Judge testified at the habeas corpus hearing that he had proceeded on the basis of Gerald's admissions at the two hearings. Appellants attack this on the ground that the admissions were obtained in disregard of the privilege against self-incrimination. If the confession is disregarded, appellants argue that the delinquency conclusion, since it was fundamentally based on a finding that Gerald had made lewd remarks during the phone call to Mrs. Cook, is fatally defective for failure to accord the rights of confrontation and cross-examination which the Due Process Clause of the Fourteenth Amendment of the Federal Constitution guarantees in state proceedings generally.

Our first question, then, is whether Gerald's admission was improperly obtained and relied on as the basis of decision, in conflict with the Federal Constitution. . . .

. . . Specifically, the question is whether, in such a proceeding, an admission by the juvenile may be used against him in the absence of clear and unequivocal evidence that the admission was made with knowledge that he was not obliged to speak and would not be penalized for remaining silent. In light of *Miranda v. Arizona,* we must also consider whether, if the privilege against self-incrimination is available, it can effectively be waived unless counsel is present or the right to counsel has been waived. . . .

It would indeed be surprising if the privilege against self-incrimination were available to hardened criminals but not to children. The language of the Fifth Amendment, applicable to the States by operation of the Fourteenth Amendment, is unequivocal and without exception. And the scope of the privilege is comprehensive. . . .

Against the application to juveniles of the right to silence, it is argued that juvenile proceedings are "civil" and not "criminal," and therefore the privilege should not apply. It is true that the statement of the privilege in the Fifth Amendment, which is applicable to the States by reason of the Fourteenth Amendment, is that no person "shall be compelled in any criminal case to be a witness against himself." However, it is also clear that the availability of the privilege does not turn upon the type of proceeding in which its protection is invoked, but upon the nature of the statement or admission and the exposure which it invites. The privilege may, for example, be claimed in a civil or administrative proceeding, if the statement is or may be inculpatory.

It would be entirely unrealistic to carve out of the Fifth Amendment all statements by juveniles on the ground that these cannot lead to "criminal" involvement. In the first place, juvenile proceedings to determine "delinquency," which may lead to commitment to a state institution, must be regarded as "criminal" for purposes of the privilege against self-incrimination. To hold otherwise would be to disregard substance because of the feeble enticement of the "civil" label-of-convenience which has been attached to juvenile proceedings. . . .

It is also urged, as the Supreme Court of Arizona here asserted, that the juvenile and presumably his parents should not be advised of the juvenile's right to silence because confession is good for the child as the commencement of the assumed therapy of the juvenile court process, and he should be encouraged to assume an attitude of trust and confidence toward the officials of the juvenile process. This proposition has been subjected to widespread challenge on the basis of current reappraisals of the rhetoric and realities of the handling of juvenile offenders.

In fact, evidence is accumulating that confessions by juveniles do not aid in "individualized treatment," as the court below put it, and that compelling the child to answer questions, without warning or advice as to his right to remain silent, does not serve this or any other good purpose. . . .

Further, authoritative opinion has cast formidable doubt upon the reliability and trustworthiness of "confessions" by children. . . .

We conclude that the constitutional privilege against self-incrimination is applicable in the case of juveniles as it is with respect to adults. We appreciate that special problems may arise with respect to waiver of the privilege by or on behalf of children, and that there may well be some differences in technique—but not in principle—depending upon the age of the child and the presence and competence of parents. The participation of counsel will, of course, assist the police, Juvenile Courts and appellate tribunals in administering the privilege. If counsel was not present for some permissible reason when an admission was obtained, the greatest care must be taken to assure that the admission was voluntary, in the sense not only that it was not coerced or suggested, but also that it was not the product of ignorance of rights or of adolescent fantasy, fright or despair.

The "confession" of Gerald Gault was first obtained by Officer Flagg, out of the presence of Gerald's parents, without counsel and without advising him of his right to silence, as far as appears. The judgment of the Juvenile Court was stated by the judge to be based on Gerald's admissions in court. Neither "admission" was reduced to writing and, to say the least, the process by which the "admissions" were obtained and received must be characterized as lacking the certainty and order which are required of proceedings of such formidable consequences. Apart from the "admissions," there was nothing upon which a judgment or finding might be based. There was no sworn testimony. Mrs. Cook, the complainant, was not present. The Arizona Supreme Court held that "sworn testimony must be required of all witnesses including police officers, probation officers and others who are part of or officially related to the juvenile court structure." We hold that this is not enough. No reason is suggested or appears for a different rule in respect of sworn testimony in juvenile courts than in adult tribunals. Absent a valid confession adequate to support the determination of the Juvenile Court, confrontation and sworn testimony by witnesses available for cross-examination were essential for a finding of "delinquency" and an order committing Gerald to a state institution for a maximum of six years. . . .

. . .We now hold that, absent a valid confession, a determination of delinquency and an order of commitment to a state institution cannot be sustained in the absence of sworn testimony subjected to the opportunity for cross-examination in accordance with our law and constitutional requirements.

VI.
APPELLATE REVIEW AND TRANSCRIPT OF PROCEEDINGS.

Appellants urge that the Arizona statute is unconstitutional under the Due Process Clause because, as construed by its Supreme Court, "there is no right of appeal from a juvenile court order. . . ." The court held that there is no right to a transcript because there is no right to appeal and because the proceedings are confidential and any record must be destroyed after a prescribed period of time. Whether a transcript or other recording is made, it held, is a matter for the discretion of the juvenile court.

This Court has not held that a State is required by the Federal Constitution "to provide appellate courts or a right to appellate review at all." In view of the fact that we must reverse the Supreme Court of Arizona's affirmance of the dismissal of the writ of habeas corpus for other reasons, we need not rule on this question in the present case or upon the failure to provide a transcript or recording of the hearings—or, indeed, the failure of the Juvenile Judge to state the grounds for his conclusion. . . .

For the reasons stated, the judgment of the Supreme Court of Arizona is reversed and the cause remanded for further proceedings not inconsistent with this opinion.

It is so ordered.

Mr. Justice Black, concurring.

. . .This holding strikes a well-nigh fatal blow to much that is unique about the juvenile courts in the Nation. For this reason, there is much to be said for the position of my Brother Stewart that we should not pass on all these issues until they are more squarely presented. But since the majority of the Court chooses to decide all of these questions, I must either do the same or leave my views unexpressed on the important issues determined. In these circumstances, I feel impelled to express my views. . . .

Where a person, infant or adult, can be seized by the State, charged, and convicted for violating a state criminal law, and then ordered by the State to be confined for six years, I think the Constitution requires that he be tried in accordance with the guarantees of all the provisions of the Bill of Rights made applicable to the States by the Fourteenth Amendment. Undoubtedly this would be true of an adult defendant, and it would be a plain denial of equal protection of the laws—an invidious discrimination—to hold that others subject to heavier punishments could because they are children, be denied these same constitutional safeguards. I consequently agree with the Court that the Arizona law as applied here denied to the parents and their son the right of notice, right to counsel, right against self-incrimination, and right to confront the witnesses against young Gault. Appellants are entitled to these rights, not because "fairness, impartiality and orderliness—in short, the essentials of due process"—require them and not because they are "the procedural rules which have been fashioned from the generality of due process," but because they are specifically and unequivocally granted by provisions of the Fifth and Sixth Amendments which the Fourteenth Amendment makes applicable to the States. . . .

Mr. Justice White, concurring.

I join the Court's opinion except for Part V. I also agree that the privilege against compelled self-incrimination applies at the adjudicatory stage of juvenile court proceedings. I do not, however, find an adequate basis in the record for determining whether that privilege was violated in this case. . . .

For somewhat similar reasons, I would not reach the questions of confrontation and cross-examination which are also dealt with in Part V of the opinion.

Mr. Justice Harlan, concurring in part and dissenting in part.

Each of the 50 States has created a system of juvenile or family courts, in which distinctive rules are employed and special consequences imposed. The jurisdiction of these courts commonly extends both to cases which the States have withdrawn from the ordinary processes of criminal justice, and to cases which involve acts that, if performed by an adult, would not be penalized as criminal. Such courts are denominated civil, not criminal, and are characteristically said not to administer criminal penalties. One consequence of these systems, at least as Arizona construes its own, is that certain of the rights guaranteed to criminal defendants by the Constitution are withheld from juveniles. This case brings before this Court for the first time the question of what limitations the Constitution places upon the operation of such tribunals. For reasons which follow, I have concluded that the Court has gone too far in some respects, and fallen short in others, in assessing the procedural requirements demanded by the Fourteenth Amendment. . . .

. . .[C]onsiderations . . . which I believe to be fair distillations of relevant judicial history . . . suggest three criteria by which the procedural requirements of due process should be measured here: first, no more restrictions should be imposed than are imperative to assure the proceedings' fundamental fairness; second, the restrictions which are imposed should be those which preserve, so far as possible, the essential elements of the State's purpose; and finally, restrictions should be chosen which will later permit the orderly selection of any additional protections which may ultimately prove necessary. In this way, the Court may guarantee the fundamental fairness of the proceeding, and yet permit the State to continue development of an effective response to the problems of juvenile crime.

Measured by these criteria, only three procedural requirements should, in my opinion, now be deemed required of state juvenile courts by the Due Process Clause of the Fourteenth Amendment: first, timely notice must be provided to parents and children of the nature and terms of any juvenile court proceeding in which a determination affecting their rights or interests may be made; second, unequivocal and timely notice must be given that counsel may appear in any such proceeding in behalf of the child and its parents, and that in cases in which the child may be confined in an institution, counsel may, in circumstances of indigency, be appointed for them; and third, the court must maintain a written record, or its equivalent, adequate to permit effective review on appeal or in collateral proceedings. These requirements would guarantee to juveniles the tools with which their rights could be fully vindicated, and yet permit the States to pursue without unnecessary hindrance the purposes which they believe imperative in this field. Further, their imposition now would later permit more intelligent assessment of the necessity under the Fourteenth Amendment of additional requirements, by creating suitable records from which the character and deficiencies of juvenile proceedings could be accurately judged. . . .

Finally, I turn to assess the validity of this juvenile court proceeding under the criteria discussed in this opinion. Measured by them, the judgment below must, in my opinion, fall. Gerald Gault and his parents were not provided adequate notice of the terms and purposes of the proceedings in which he was adjudged delinquent; they were not advised of their rights to be represented by counsel; and no record in any form was maintained of the proceedings. It follows, for the reasons given in this opinion, that Gerald Gault was deprived of his liberty without due process of law, and I therefore concur in the judgment of the Court.

Mr. Justice Stewart, dissenting.

The Court today uses an obscure Arizona case as a vehicle to impose upon thousands of juvenile courts throughout the Nation restrictions that the Constitution made applicable to adversary criminal trials. I believe the Court's decision is wholly unsound as a matter of constitutional law, and sadly unwise as a matter of judicial policy.

Juvenile proceedings are not criminal trials. They are not civil trials. They are simply not adversary proceedings. Whether treating with a delinquent child, a neglected child, a defective child, or a dependent child, a juvenile proceeding's whole purpose and mission is the very opposite of the mission and purpose of a prosecution in a criminal court. The object of the one is correction of a condition. The object of the other is conviction and punishment for a criminal act. . . .

A State in all its dealings must, of course, accord every person due process of law. And due process may require that some of the same restrictions which the Constitution has placed upon criminal trials must be imposed upon juvenile proceedings. For example, I suppose that all would agree that a brutally coerced confession could not constitutionally be considered in a juvenile court hearing. But it surely does not follow that the testimonial privilege against self-incrimination is applicable in all juvenile proceedings. Similarly, due process clearly requires timely notice of the purpose and scope of any proceedings affecting the relationship of parent and child. But it certainly does not follow that notice of a juvenile hearing must be framed with all the technical niceties of a criminal indictment.

In any event, there is no reason to deal with issues such as these in the present case. The Supreme Court of Arizona found that the parents of Gerald Gault "knew of their right to counsel, to subpoena and cross examine witnesses, of the right to confront the witnesses against Gerald and the possible consequences of a finding of delinquency." It further found that "Mrs. Gault knew the exact nature of the charge against Gerald from the day he was taken to the detention home." And, as MR. JUSTICE WHITE correctly points out, no issue of compulsory self-incrimination is presented by this case.

I would dismiss the appeal.

REVIEW QUESTIONS

1. What *facts* were important to the Court's decision in *Gault*? What *issues* was it asked to resolve? What was its *holding* with respect to each of these issues? What was the *reasoning* underlying its resolution of each issue?

2. What specific rights were extended to accused juvenile delinquents in the Gault case? Why did the court consider each of these rights essential to the fairness of juvenile court proceedings?

3. What rights did the Court expressly *decline* to make available in juvenile court adjudication hearings? What was its reasoning?

4. Justice Fortas' majority opinion seems to take a dim view of the traditional juvenile court and its *parens patriae* philosophy. Why?

5. In his concurring opinion, Justice Black argues that "[t]his holding strikes a well-nigh

fatal blow to much that is unique about the juvenile courts in this nation" (p. 99). Why do you think he said this? Do you agree with him? Why did he decide to concur in the Court's decision anyway?

6. Justice Harlan concurred in part and dissented in part. With which parts of the majority's decision did he agree and with which parts did he disagree? What was his reasoning? Do you agree with his argument?

7. What is the basis for Justice Stewart's dissent? Do you agree with him?

8. In your opinion, are the rights extended to juveniles in the *Gault* case essential to the fairness of the proceedings in juvenile court, or do they make the proceedings unnecessarily adversarial and too much like those in adult criminal courts?

In re Winship

The Supreme Court of the United States
397 U.S. 358 (1970)

MR. JUSTICE BRENNAN delivered the opinion of the Court.

. . .This case presents the single, narrow question whether proof beyond a reasonable doubt is among the "essentials of due process and fair treatment" required during the adjudicatory stage when a juvenile is charged with an act which would constitute a crime if committed by an adult.

Section 712 of the New York Family Court Act defines a juvenile delinquent as "a person over seven and less than sixteen years of age who does any act which, if done by an adult, would constitute a crime." During a 1967 adjudicatory hearing, conducted pursuant to § 742 of the Act, a judge in New York Family Court found that appellant, then a 12-year-old boy, had entered a locker and stolen $112 from a woman's pocketbook. The petition which charged appellant with delinquency alleged that his act, "if done by an adult, would constitute the crime or crimes of Larceny." The judge acknowledged that the proof might not establish guilt beyond a reasonable doubt, but rejected appellant's contention that such proof was required by the Fourteenth Amendment. The judge relied instead on § 744 (b) of the New York Family Court Act which provides that "[a]ny determination at the conclusion of [an adjudicatory] hearing that a [juvenile] did an act or acts must be based on a preponderance of the evidence." During a subsequent dispositional hearing, appellant was ordered placed in a training school for an initial period of 18 months, subject to annual extensions of his commitment until his 18th birthday—six years in appellant's case. The Appellate Division of the New York Supreme Court, First Judicial Department, affirmed without opinion. The New York Court of Appeals then affirmed by a four-to-three vote, expressly sustaining the constitutionality of § 744 (b). We noted probable jurisdiction. We reverse.

I.

. . .Lest there remain any doubt about the constitutional stature of the reasonable-doubt standard, we explicitly hold that the Due Process Clause protects the accused [in an adult criminal court—*Ed.*] against conviction except upon proof beyond a reasonable doubt of every fact necessary to constitute the crime with which he is charged.

II.

We turn to the question whether juveniles, like adults, are constitutionally entitled to proof beyond a reasonable doubt when they are charged with violation of a criminal law. The same considerations that demand extreme caution in factfinding to protect the innocent adult apply as well to the innocent child. We do not find convincing the contrary arguments of the New York Court of Appeals. *Gault* rendered untenable much of the reasoning relied upon by that court to sustain the constitutionality of § 744 (b). The Court of Appeals indicated that a delinquency adjudication "is not a 'conviction'; that it affects no right or privilege, including the right to hold public office or to obtain a license; and a cloak of protective confidentiality is thrown around all the proceedings." The court said further: "The delinquency status is not made a crime; and the proceedings are not criminal. There is, hence, no deprivation of due process in the statutory provision [challenged by appellant]. . . ." In effect the Court of Appeals distinguished the proceedings in question here from a criminal prosecution by use of what *Gault* called the " 'civil' label-of-convenience which has been attached to juvenile proceedings." But *Gault* expressly rejected that distinction as a reason for holding the Due Process Clause inapplicable to a juvenile proceeding. The Court of Appeals also attempted to justify the preponderance standard on the related ground that juvenile proceedings are designed "not to punish, but to save the child." Again, however, *Gault* expressly rejected this justification. We made clear in that decision that civil labels and good intentions do not themselves obviate the need for criminal due process safeguards in juvenile courts, for "[a] proceeding where the issue is whether the child will be found to be 'delinquent' and subjected to the loss of his liberty for years is comparable in seriousness to a felony prosecution."

Nor do we perceive any merit in the argument that to afford juveniles the protection of proof beyond a reasonable doubt would risk destruction of beneficial aspects of the juvenile process. Use of the reasonable-doubt standard during the adjudicatory hearing will not disturb New York's policies that a finding that a child has violated a criminal law does not constitute a criminal conviction, that such a finding does not deprive the child of his civil rights, and that juvenile proceedings are confidential. Nor will there be any effect on the informality, flexibility, or speed of the hearing at which the factfinding takes place. And the opportunity during the post-adjudicatory or dispositional hearing for a wide-ranging review of the child's social history and for his individualized treatment will remain unimpaired. Similarly, there will be no effect on the procedures distinctive to juvenile proceedings that are employed prior to the adjudicatory hearing.

The Court of Appeals observed that "a child's best interest is not necessarily, or even probably, promoted if he wins in the particular inquiry which may bring him to the juvenile court." It is true, of course, that the juvenile may be engaging in a general course of conduct inimical to his welfare that calls for judicial intervention. But that intervention cannot take the form of subjecting the child to the stigma of a finding that he violated a criminal law and to the possibility of institutional confinement on proof insufficient to convict him were he an adult.

We conclude, as we concluded regarding the essential due process safeguards applied in *Gault,* that the observance of the standard of proof beyond a reasonable doubt "will not compel the States to abandon or displace any of the substantive benefits of the juvenile process."

Finally, we reject the Court of Appeals' suggestion that there is, in any event, only a "tenuous difference" between the reasonable-doubt and preponderance standards. The suggestion is singularly unpersuasive. In this very case, the trial judge's ability to distinguish between the two standards enabled him to make a finding of guilt that he conceded he might not have made under the standard of proof beyond a reasonable doubt. Indeed, the trial judge's action evidences the accuracy of the observation of commentators that "the preponderance test is susceptible to the misinterpretation that it calls on the trier of fact merely to perform an abstract weighing of the evidence in order to determine which side has produced the greater quantum, without regard to its effect in convincing his mind of the truth of the proposition asserted."

III.

In sum, the constitutional safeguard of proof beyond a reasonable doubt is as much required during the adjudicatory stage of a delinquency proceeding as are those constitutional safeguards applied in *Gault*—notice of charges, right to counsel, the rights of confrontation and examination, and the privilege against self-incrimination. We therefore hold, in agreement with Chief Judge Fuld in dissent in the Court of Appeals, "that, where a 12-year-old child is charged with an act of stealing which renders him liable to confinement for as long as six years, then, as a matter of due process . . . the case against him must be proved beyond a reasonable doubt."

Reversed.

MR. JUSTICE HARLAN, concurring. [omitted–*Ed.*]

MR. CHIEF JUSTICE BURGER, with whom MR. JUSTICE STEWART joins, dissenting.

The Court's opinion today rests entirely on the assumption that all juvenile proceedings are "criminal prosecutions," hence subject to constitutional limitations. This derives from earlier holdings, which, like today's holding, were steps eroding the differences between juvenile courts and traditional criminal courts. The original concept of the juvenile court system was to provide a benevolent and less formal means than criminal courts could provide for dealing with the special and often sensitive problems of youthful offenders. Since I see no constitutional requirement of due process sufficient to overcome the legislative judgment of the States in this area, I dissent from further straitjacketing of an already overly restricted system. What the juvenile court system needs is not more but less of the trappings of legal procedure and judicial formalism; the juvenile court system requires breathing room and flexibility in order to survive, if it can survive the repeated assaults from this Court. . . .

My hope is that today's decision will not spell the end of a generously conceived program of compassionate treatment intended to mitigate the rigors and trauma of exposing youthful offenders to a traditional criminal court; each step we take turns the clock back to the pre-juvenile-court era. I cannot regard it as a manifestation of progress to transform juvenile courts into criminal courts, which is what we are well on the way to accomplishing.

We can only hope the legislative response will not reflect our own by having these courts abolished.

MR. JUSTICE BLACK, dissenting. [omitted—Ed.]

REVIEW QUESTIONS

1. What right was granted to juveniles in this case? Why did the majority consider it important?
2. Do you agree with the court that proof beyond reasonable doubt is essential to the fairness of adjudication hearings in juvenile court? Will this make juvenile court proceedings too adversarial? Are there other rights that should also be granted in juvenile court?
3. Do you share Chief Justice Burger's concern about the impact of this case on the juvenile justice system?

McKeiver v. Pennsylvania

The Supreme Court of the United States
403 U.S. 528 (1971)

The requests of appellants in No. 322 [*McKeiver v. Pennsylvania*—*Ed.*] for a jury trial were denied, and they were adjudged juvenile delinquents under Pennsylvania law. The State Supreme Court, while recognizing the applicability to juveniles of certain due process procedural safeguards, held that there is no constitutional right to a jury trial in juvenile court. Appellants argue for a right to a jury trial because they were tried in proceedings "substantially similar to a criminal trial," and note that the press is generally present at the trial and that members of the public also enter the courtroom. Petitioners in No. 128 [*In re Burrus et al.*, which was consolidated with *McKeiver* for joint consideration when it reached the U.S. Supreme Court—*Ed.*] were adjudged juvenile delinquents in North Carolina, where their jury trial requests were denied and in proceedings where the general public was excluded. [From the syllabus of the decision prepared by the Reporter of Decisions—*Ed.*]

MR. JUSTICE BLACKMUN announced the judgments of the Court and an opinion in which THE CHIEF JUSTICE, MR. JUSTICE STEWART, and MR. JUSTICE WHITE join.

These cases present the narrow but precise issue whether the Due Process Clause of the Fourteenth Amendment assures the right to trial by jury in the adjudicative phase of a state juvenile court delinquency proceeding. . . .

V.

The Pennsylvania juveniles' basic argument is that they were tried in proceedings "substantially similar to a criminal trial." They say that a delinquency proceeding in their State is initiated by a petition charging a penal code violation in the conclusory language of an indictment; that a juvenile detained prior to trial is held in a building substantially similar to an adult prison; that in Philadelphia juveniles over 16 are, in fact, held in the cells of a prison; that counsel and the prosecution engage in plea bargaining; that motions to suppress are routinely heard and decided; that the usual rules of evidence are applied; that the customary common-law defenses are available; that the press is generally admitted in the Philadelphia juvenile courtrooms; that members of the public enter the room; that arrest and prior record may be reported by the press (from police sources, however, rather than from the juvenile court records); that, once adjudged delinquent, a juvenile may be confined until his majority in what amounts to a prison; and that the stigma attached upon delinquency adjudication approximates that resulting from conviction in an adult criminal proceeding.

The North Carolina juveniles particularly urge that the requirement of a jury trial would not operate to deny the supposed benefits of the juvenile court system; that the system's primary benefits are its discretionary intake procedure permitting disposition short of adjudication, and its flexible sentencing permitting emphasis on rehabilitation; that realization of these benefits does not depend upon dispensing with the jury; that adjudication of factual issues on the one hand and disposition of the case on the other are very different matters with very different purposes; that the purpose of the former is indistinguishable from that of the criminal trial; that the jury trial provides an independent protective factor; that experience has shown that jury trials in juvenile courts are manageable; that no reason exists why protection traditionally accorded in criminal proceedings should be denied young people subject to involuntary incarceration for lengthy periods; and that the juvenile courts deserve healthy public scrutiny.

VI.

All the litigants here agree that the applicable due process standard in juvenile proceedings, as developed by *Gault* and *Winship,* is fundamental fairness. As that standard was applied in those two cases, we have an emphasis on factfinding procedures. The requirements of notice, counsel, confrontation, cross-examination, and standard of proof naturally flowed from this emphasis. But one cannot say that in our legal system the jury is a necessary component of accurate fact-finding. There is much to be said for it, to be sure, but we have been content to pursue other ways for determining facts. Juries are not required, and have not been, for example, in equity cases, in workmen's compensation, in probate, or in deportation cases. Neither have they been generally used in military trials. . . .

We must recognize, as the Court has recognized before, that the fond and idealistic hopes of the juvenile court proponents and early reformers of three generations ago have not been realized. The devastating commentary upon the system's failures as a whole, contained in the President's Commission on Law Enforcement and Administration of Justice, Task Force Report: Juvenile Delinquency and Youth Crime, reveals the depth of disappointment in what has been accomplished. Too often the juvenile court judge falls far short of that stalwart, protective, and communicating figure the system envisaged. The community's unwillingness to provide people and facilities and to be concerned, the insufficiency of time devoted, the scarcity of professional help, the inadequacy of dispositional alternatives, and our general lack of knowledge all contribute to dissatisfaction with the experiment.

The Task Force Report, however, also said, "To say that juvenile courts have failed to achieve their goals is to say no more than what is true of criminal courts in the United States. But failure is most striking when hopes are highest."

Despite all these disappointments, all these failures, and all these shortcomings, we conclude that trial by jury in the juvenile court's adjudicative stage is not a constitutional requirement. We so conclude for a number of reasons:

1. The Court has refrained, in the cases heretofore decided, from taking the easy way with a flat holding that all rights constitutionally assured for the adult accused are to be imposed upon the state juvenile proceeding. . . .

2. There is a possibility, at least, that the jury trial, if required as a matter of constitutional precept, will remake the juvenile proceeding into a fully adversary process and will put an effective end to what has been the idealistic prospect of an intimate, informal protective proceeding.

3. The Task Force Report, although concededly pre-*Gault*, is notable for its not making any recommendation that the jury trial be imposed upon the juvenile court system. This is so despite its vivid description of the system's deficiencies and disappointments. Had the Commission deemed this vital to the integrity of the juvenile process, or to the handling of juveniles, surely a recommendation or suggestion to this effect would have appeared. The intimations, instead, are quite the other way. Further, it expressly recommends against abandonment of the system and against the return of the juvenile to the criminal courts.

4. The Court specifically has recognized by dictum that a jury is not a necessary part even of every criminal process that is fair and equitable.

5. The imposition of the jury trial on the juvenile court system would not strengthen greatly, if at all, the factfinding function, and would, contrarily, provide an attrition of the juvenile court's assumed ability to function in a unique manner. It would not remedy the defects of the system. Meager as has been the hoped-for advance in the juvenile field, the alternative would be regressive, would lose what has been gained, and would tend once again to place the juvenile squarely in the routine of the criminal process.

6. The juvenile concept held high promise. We are reluctant to say that, despite disappointments of grave dimensions, it still does not hold promise, and we are par-

ticularly reluctant to say, as do the Pennsylvania appellants here, that the system cannot accomplish its rehabilitative goals. So much depends on the availability of resources, on the interest and commitment of the public, on willingness to learn, and on understanding as to cause and effect and cure. In this field, as in so many others, one perhaps learns best by doing. We are reluctant to disallow the States to experiment further and to seek in new and different ways the elusive answers to the problems of the young, and we feel that we would be impeding that experimentation by imposing the jury trial. The States, indeed, must go forward. If, in its wisdom, any State feels the jury trial is desirable in all cases, or in certain kinds, there appears to be no impediment to its installing a system embracing that feature. That, however, is the State's privilege and not its obligation.

7. Of course there have been abuses. The Task Force Report has noted them. We refrain from saying at this point that those abuses are of constitutional dimension. They relate to the lack of resources and of dedication rather than to inherent unfairness.

8. There is, of course, nothing to prevent a juvenile court judge, in a particular case where he feels the need, or when the need is demonstrated, from using an advisory jury.

9. "The fact that a practice is followed by a large number of states is not conclusive in a decision as to whether that practice accords with due process, but it is plainly worth considering in determining whether the practice 'offends some principle of justice so rooted in the traditions and conscience of our people as to be ranked as fundamental.'" It therefore is of more than passing interest that at least 29 States and the District of Columbia by statute deny the juvenile a right to a jury trial in cases such as these. The same result is achieved in other States by judicial decision. In 10 States statutes provide for a jury trial under certain circumstances.

10. Since *Gault* and since *Duncan* [v. *Louisiana,* the 1968 Supreme Court case extending the Constitutional right to a jury trial, previously guaranteed only in federal courts, to adults charged with criminal offenses in state courts—*Ed.*] the great majority of States, in addition to Pennsylvania and North Carolina, that have faced the issue have concluded that the considerations that led to the result in those two cases do not compel trial by jury in the juvenile court. . . .

12. If the jury trial were to be injected into the juvenile court system as a matter of right, it would bring with it into that system the traditional delay, the formality, and the clamor of the adversary system and, possibly, the public trial. . . .

13. Finally, the arguments advanced by the juveniles here are, of course, the identical arguments that underlie the demand for the jury trial for criminal proceedings. The arguments necessarily equate the juvenile proceeding—or at least the adjudicative phase of it—with the criminal trial. Whether they should be so equated is our issue. Concern about the inapplicability of exclusionary and other rules of evidence, about the juvenile court judge's possible awareness of the juvenile's prior record and of the contents of the

social file; about repeated appearances of the same familiar witnesses in the persons of juvenile and probation officers and social workers—all to the effect that this will create the likelihood of pre-judgment—chooses to ignore, it seems to us, every aspect of fairness, of concern, of sympathy, and of paternal attention that the juvenile court system contemplates.

If the formalities of the criminal adjudicative process are to be superimposed upon the juvenile court system, there is little need for its separate existence. Perhaps that ultimate disillusionment will come one day, but for the moment we are disinclined to give impetus to it.

Affirmed.

MR. JUSTICE WHITE, concurring. . . .

For me there remain differences of substance between criminal and juvenile courts. They are quite enough for me to hold that a jury is not required in the latter. Of course, there are strong arguments that juries are desirable when dealing with the young, and States are free to use juries if they choose. They are also free, if they extend criminal court safeguards to juvenile court adjudications, frankly to embrace condemnation, punishment, and deterrence as permissible and desirable attributes of the juvenile justice system. But the Due Process Clause neither compels nor invites them to do so.

MR. JUSTICE BRENNAN, concurring in the judgment in No. 322 and dissenting in No. 128.

I agree with the plurality opinion's conclusion that the proceedings below in these cases were not "criminal prosecutions" within the meaning of the Sixth Amendment. For me, therefore, the question in these cases is whether jury trial is among the "essentials of due process and fair treatment" required during the adjudication of a charge of delinquency based upon acts that would constitute a crime if engaged in by an adult. This does not, however, mean that the interests protected by the Sixth Amendment's guarantee of jury trial in all "criminal prosecutions" are of no importance in the context of these cases. The Sixth Amendment, where applicable, commands that these interests be protected by a particular procedure, that is, trial by jury. The Due Process Clause commands, not a particular procedure, but only a result: in my Brother BLACKMUN's words, "fundamental fairness . . . [in] fact-finding." In the context of these and similar juvenile delinquency proceedings, what this means is that the States are not bound to provide jury trials on demand so long as some other aspect of the process adequately protects the interests that Sixth Amendment jury trials are intended to serve.

In my view, therefore, the due process question cannot be decided upon the basis of general characteristics of juvenile proceedings, but only in terms of the adequacy of a particular state procedure to "protect the [juvenile] from oppression by the Government," and to protect him against "the compliant, biased, or eccentric judge."

Examined in this light, I find no defect in the Pennsylvania cases before us. The availability of trial by jury allows an accused to protect himself against possible oppression by what is in essence an appeal to the community conscience, as embodied in the jury that hears his case. To some extent, however, a similar protection may be obtained when an accused may in essence appeal to the community at large, by focusing public attention upon the facts of his trial, exposing improper judicial behavior to public view, and obtaining, if necessary, executive redress through the medium of public indignation. Of course, the Constitution, in the context of adult criminal trials, has rejected the notion that public trial is an adequate substitute for trial by jury in serious cases. But in the context of juvenile delinquency proceedings, I cannot say that it is beyond the competence of a State to conclude that juveniles who fear that delinquency proceedings will mask judicial oppression may obtain adequate protection by focusing community attention upon the trial of their cases. For, however much the juvenile system may have failed in practice, its very existence as an ostensibly beneficent and noncriminal process for the care and guidance of young persons demonstrates the existence of the community's sympathy and concern for the young. Juveniles able to bring the community's attention to bear upon their trials may therefore draw upon a reservoir of public concern unavailable to the adult criminal defendant. In the Pennsylvania cases before us, there appears to be no statutory ban upon admission of the public to juvenile trials. Appellants themselves, without contradiction, assert that "the press is generally admitted" to juvenile delinquency proceedings in Philadelphia. Most important, the record in these cases is bare of any indication that any person whom appellants sought to have admitted to the courtroom was excluded. In these circumstances, I agree that the judgment in No. 322 must be affirmed.

The North Carolina cases, however, present a different situation. North Carolina law either permits or requires exclusion of the general public from juvenile trials. In the cases before us, the trial judge "ordered the general public excluded from the hearing room and stated that only officers of the court, the juveniles, their parents or guardians, their attorney and witnesses would be present for the hearing," notwithstanding petitioners' repeated demand for a public hearing. The cases themselves, which arise out of a series of demonstrations by black adults and juveniles who believed that the Hyde County, North Carolina, school system unlawfully discriminated against black school children, present a paradigm of the circumstances in which there may be a substantial "temptation to use the courts for political ends." And finally, neither the opinions supporting the judgment nor the respondent in No. 128 has pointed to any feature of North Carolina's juvenile proceedings that could substitute for public or jury trial in protecting the petitioners against misuse of the judicial process. Accordingly, I would reverse the judgment in No. 128.

MR. JUSTICE HARLAN, concurring in the judgments. . . .

I concur in the judgments in these cases . . . on the ground that criminal jury trials are not constitutionally required of the States, either as a matter of Sixth Amendment law or due process. . . .

MR. JUSTICE DOUGLAS, with whom MR. JUSTICE BLACK and MR. JUSTICE MARSHALL concur, dissenting.

These cases from Pennsylvania and North Carolina present the issue of the right to a jury trial for offenders charged in juvenile court and facing a possible incarceration until they reach their majority. I believe the guarantees of the Bill of Rights, made applicable to the States by the Fourteenth Amendment, require a jury trial. . . .

Conviction of each of these crimes would subject a person, whether juvenile or adult, to imprisonment in a state institution. In the case of these students the possible term was six to 10 years; it would be computed for the period until an individual reached the age of 21. Each asked for a jury trial which was denied. The trial judge stated that the hearings were juvenile hearings, not criminal trials. But the issue in each case was whether they had violated a state criminal law. The trial judge found in each case that the juvenile had committed "an act for which an adult may be punished by law" and held in each case that the acts of the juvenile violated one of the criminal statutes cited above. The trial judge thereupon ordered each juvenile to be committed to the state institution for the care of delinquents and then placed each on probation for terms from 12 to 24 months.

. . .[W]here a State uses its juvenile court proceedings to prosecute a juvenile for a criminal act and to order "confinement" until the child reaches 21 years of age or where the child at the threshold of the proceedings faces that prospect, then he is entitled to the same procedural protection as an adult. . . .

In the present cases imprisonment or confinement up to 10 years was possible for one child and each faced at least a possible five-year incarceration. No adult could be denied a jury trial in those circumstances. The Fourteenth Amendment, which makes trial by jury provided in the Sixth Amendment applicable to the States, speaks of denial of rights to "any person", not denial of rights to "any adult person"; and we have held indeed that where a juvenile is charged with an act that would constitute a crime if committed by an adult, he is entitled to be tried under a standard of proof beyond a reasonable doubt. . . .

These cases should be remanded for trial by jury on the criminal charges filed against these youngsters.

APPENDIX TO OPINION OF DOUGLAS, J., DISSENTING [omitted—*Ed.*]

REVIEW QUESTIONS

1. Why does Justice Blackmun say juveniles do not have the right to a jury trial in delinquency adjudication hearings? Is his reasoning consistent with the reasoning in *Gault* and *Winship*, or does he take a different view of juvenile court proceedings?

2. Which justices agree with Justice Blackmun's reasoning and which ones disagree? Note that although he announced the *judgment* of the court, only three other justices agreed with his *reasoning* and joined his opinion. But at least *five* justices (a majority of the nine-member court) must agree what the holding should be in order for a decision to be reached. Which other justices agreed with the judgment of the Court? How was their reasoning different from Justice Blackmun's? What do you make of Justice Brennan's opinion? Why did he think denial of the right to a jury trial was Constitutionally acceptable in one case but not in the other? Do you agree with him?

3. What is the basis for Justice Douglas' dissent? Do you find his argument more compelling than Justice Blackmun's?

4. The Court's decisions in *Winship* and *McKeiver* have been argued to reflect conflicting views of juvenile court philosophy and practice and, in consequence, of the

extent to which the procedural rights available to juveniles charged with delinquent acts should mirror those available to adults facing criminal charges. Which of these decisions seems more consistent with your own view of the juvenile court and the procedural safeguards that should be present?

Or do *both* decisions square with your own perspective (i.e., do you believe that a right to trial by jury would make juvenile court too much like criminal court but the requirement of proof beyond reasonable doubt does not)?

Breed v. Jones

The Supreme Court of the United States
421 U.S. 519 (1975)

Mr. Chief Justice Burger delivered the opinion of the Court. [This was a unanimous decision—*Ed.*]

We granted certiorari to decide whether the prosecution of respondent as an adult, after Juvenile Court proceedings which resulted in a finding that respondent had violated a criminal statute and a subsequent finding that he was unfit for treatment as a juvenile, violated the Fifth and Fourteenth Amendments to the United States Constitution. . . .

The parties agree that, following his transfer from Juvenile Court, and as a defendant to a felony information, respondent was entitled to the full protection of the Double Jeopardy Clause of the Fifth Amendment, as applied to the States through the Fourteenth Amendment. In addition, they agree that respondent was put in jeopardy by the proceedings on that information, which resulted in an adjudication that he was guilty of robbery in the first degree and in a sentence of commitment. Finally, there is no dispute that the petition filed in Juvenile Court and the information filed in Superior Court related to the "same offense" within the meaning of the constitutional prohibition. The point of disagreement between the parties, and the question for our decision, is whether, by reason of the proceedings in Juvenile Court, respondent was "twice put in jeopardy." . . .

We believe it is simply too late in the day to conclude, as did the District Court in this case, that a juvenile is not put in jeopardy at a proceeding whose object is to determine whether he has committed acts that violate a criminal law and whose potential consequences include both the stigma inherent in such a determination and the deprivation of liberty for many years. For it is clear under our cases that determining the relevance of constitutional policies, like determining the applicability of constitutional rights, in juvenile proceedings, requires that courts eschew "the 'civil' label-of-convenience which has been attached to juvenile proceedings," and that "the juvenile process . . . be candidly appraised."

As we have observed, the risk to which the term jeopardy refers is that traditionally associated with "actions intended to authorize criminal punishment to vindicate public justice." Because of its purpose and potential consequences, and the nature and resources of the State, such a proceeding imposes heavy pressures and burdens—psychological, physical, and financial—on a person charged. The purpose of the Double Jeopardy Clause is to require that he be subject to the experience only once "for the same offense."

In *In re Gault* this Court concluded that, for purposes of the right to counsel, a "proceeding where the issue is whether the child will be found to be 'delinquent' and subjected to the loss of his liberty for years is comparable in seriousness to a felony prosecution." The Court stated that the term "delinquent" had "come to involve only slightly less stigma than the term 'criminal' applied to adults" and that, for purposes of the privilege against self-incrimination, "commitment is a deprivation of liberty. It is incarceration against one's will, whether it is called 'criminal' or 'civil.'"

Thus, in terms of potential consequences, there is little to distinguish an adjudicatory hearing such as was held in this case from a traditional criminal prosecution. . . .

. . . We therefore conclude that respondent was put in jeopardy at the adjudicatory hearing. Jeopardy attached when respondent was "put to trial before the trier of the facts," that is, when the Juvenile Court, as the trier of the facts, began to hear evidence.

Petitioner argues that, even assuming jeopardy attached at respondent's adjudicatory hearing, the procedure by which he was transferred from Juvenile Court and tried on a felony information in Superior Court did not violate the Double Jeopardy Clause. The argument is supported by two distinct, but in this case overlapping, lines of analysis. First, petitioner reasons that the procedure violated none of the policies of the Double Jeopardy Clause or that, alternatively, it should be upheld by analogy to those cases which permit retrial of an accused who has obtained reversal of a conviction on appeal. Second, pointing to this Court's concern for "the juvenile court's assumed ability to function in a unique manner," petitioner urges that, should we conclude traditional principles "would otherwise bar a transfer to adult court after a delinquency adjudication," we should avoid that result here because it "would diminish the flexibility and informality of juvenile court proceedings without conferring any additional due process benefits upon juveniles charged with delinquent acts."

We cannot agree with petitioner that the trial of respondent in Superior Court on an information charging the same offense as that for which he had been tried in Juvenile Court violated none of the policies of the Double Jeopardy Clause. For, even accepting petitioner's premise that respondent "never faced the risk of more than one punishment," we have pointed out that "the Double Jeopardy Clause . . . is written in terms of potential or risk of trial and conviction, not punishment.". . .

Respondent was subjected to the burden of two trials for the same offense; he was twice put to the task of marshaling his resources against those of the State, twice subjected to the "heavy personal strain" which such an experience represents. We turn, therefore, to inquire whether either traditional principles or "the juvenile court's assumed ability to

function in a unique manner" supports an exception to the "constitutional policy of final-
ity" to which respondent would otherwise be entitled.

In denying respondent's petitions for writs of habeas corpus, the California Court of
Appeal first, and the United States District Court later, concluded that no new jeopardy
arose as a result of his transfer from Juvenile Court and trial in Superior Court. In the view
of those courts, the jeopardy that attaches at an adjudicatory hearing continues until there
is a final disposition of the case under the adult charge. . . .

. . .[T]he fact that the proceedings against respondent had not "run their full course"
within the contemplation of the California Welfare and Institutions Code, at the time of
transfer, does not satisfactorily explain why respondent should be deprived of the constitutional protection against a second trial. If there is to be an exception to that protection in
the context of the juvenile-court system, it must be justified by interests of society, reflected
in that unique institution, or of juveniles themselves, of sufficient substance to render tolerable the costs and burdens, noted earlier, which the exception will entail in individual
cases. . . .

We do not agree with petitioner that giving respondent the constitutional protection
against multiple trials in this context will diminish flexibility and informality to the extent
that those qualities relate uniquely to the goals of the juvenile-court system. . . .

A requirement that transfer hearings be held prior to adjudicatory hearings affects not
at all the nature of the latter proceedings. More significantly, such a requirement need not
affect the quality of decisionmaking at transfer hearings themselves. In *Kent v. United States*
the Court held that hearings under the statute there involved "must measure up to the essentials of due process and fair treatment." However, the Court has never attempted to prescribe criteria for, or the nature and quantum of evidence that must support, a decision to
transfer a juvenile for trial in adult court. We require only that, whatever the relevant criteria, and whatever the evidence demanded, a State determine whether it wants to treat a juvenile within the juvenile-court system before entering upon a proceeding that may result
in an adjudication that he has violated a criminal law and in a substantial deprivation of liberty, rather than subject him to the expense, delay, strain, and embarrassment of two such
proceedings.

Moreover, we are not persuaded that the burdens petitioner envisions would pose a
significant problem for the administration of the juvenile-court system. . . .

Quite apart from our conclusions with respect to the burdens on the juvenile-court
system envisioned by petitioner, we are persuaded that transfer hearings prior to adjudication will aid the objectives of that system. What concerns us here is the dilemma that the
possibility of transfer after an adjudicatory hearing presents for a juvenile, a dilemma to
which the Court of Appeals alluded. Because of that possibility, a juvenile, thought to be
the beneficiary of special consideration, may in fact suffer substantial disadvantages. If he
appears uncooperative, he runs the risk of an adverse adjudication, as well as of an unfavorable dispositional recommendation. If, on the other hand, he is cooperative, he runs the
risk of prejudicing his chances in adult court if transfer is ordered. We regard a procedure
that results in such a dilemma as at odds with the goal that, to the extent fundamental fairness permits, adjudicatory hearings be informal and nonadversary. Knowledge of the risk

of transfer after an adjudicatory hearing can only undermine the potential for informality and cooperation which was intended to be the hallmark of the juvenile-court system. Rather than concerning themselves with the matter at hand, establishing innocence or seeking a disposition best suited to individual correctional needs, the juvenile and his attorney are pressed into a posture of adversary wariness that is conducive to neither.

We hold that the prosecution of respondent in Superior Court, after an adjudicatory proceeding in Juvenile Court, violated the Double Jeopardy Clause of the Fifth Amendment, as applied to the States through the Fourteenth Amendment. The mandate of the Court of Appeals, which was stayed by that court pending our decision, directs the District Court "to issue a writ of habeas corpus directing the state court, within 60 days, to vacate the adult conviction of Jones and either set him free or remand him to the juvenile court for disposition." Since respondent is no longer subject to the jurisdiction of the California Juvenile Court, we vacate the judgment and remand the case to the Court of Appeals for such further proceedings consistent with this opinion as may be appropriate in the circumstances.

So ordered.

REVIEW QUESTIONS

1. What right did this case add to the ones *Kent* decided must be made available to juveniles facing waiver of juvenile court jurisdiction and transfer to adult criminal court? Why did the court believe this right was Constitutionally required?

2. Compare Justice Burger's reasoning in the majority opinion in this case with his dissent in *Winship*. Has his view of the juvenile justice system changed in the intervening five years? Or has the juvenile court changed sufficiently to require a different perspective? Or is there another explanation for differences between the two opinions?

3. Do you believe that the Court's decisions in *Kent, Gault, Winship, McKeiver,* and *Breed* carved out the proper balance between the informality of the traditional juvenile court and the procedural safeguards applicable in criminal courts? Why or why not?

Standards for the Administration
of Juvenile Justice

National Advisory Committee for Juvenile Justice
and Delinquency Prevention

LETTER OF TRANSMITTAL

To the President and Congress of the United States:

I have the honor of transmitting herewith the Report of the National Advisory Committee for Juvenile Justice and Delinquency Prevention: *Standards for the Administration of Juvenile Justice,* prepared in accordance with the provisions of Section 247 of the Juvenile Justice and Delinquency Prevention Act (Public Law No. 93-415, as amended by Public Law No. 95-417).

The JJDP Act created a major Federal initiative to respond to the "enormous annual cost and unmeasurable loss of human life, personal security, and wasted human resources," caused by juvenile delinquency and delegated the responsibility for administering and coordinating the programs established under that initiative to the Office of Juvenile Justice and Delinquency Prevention, Law Enforcement Assistance Administration. As part of this effort, the Act called for development of national standards for the administration of juvenile justice. This report represents the culmination of the first phase of an ongoing process to generate improvements in the juvenile justice system. These standards provide direction for change and can be used as a benchmark for measuring progress toward improving the quality of justice for young people in the United States.

The Report, which reflects the basic principles and policies of the JJDP Act, offers specific strategies, criteria and approaches that can be used in accomplishing some of the important objectives of the Act. Over the past decade a number of state and national groups, including many supported by LEAA, have carefully re-examined existing laws and practices and formulated criminal and juvenile justice standards and model legislation. This effort, which has benefited from these activities, represents a significant contribution to the field in its own right. It will serve as an important resource for use by policy makers, planners,

Source: National Advisory Committee for Juvenile Justice and Delinquency Prevention. (1980). *Standards for the Administration of Juvenile Justice.* Washington, DC: U.S. Government Printing Office. Adapted courtesy of the United States Department of Justice, Office of Juvenile Justice and Delinquency Prevention.

youth advocates, legislators, judges, juvenile services agency administrators and other juvenile justice professionals and practitioners in all parts of the country.

Respectfully submitted,

Ira M. Schwartz

FOREWORD

. . . In its initial report submitted in September 1975, the Subcommittee on Standards outlined the tasks before it:

- To propose a set of recommendations addressing the full range of law enforcement, judicial, prevention, correctional, service and planning activities affecting youth;

- To organize these recommendations so that groups and agencies performing similar functions would be governed by the same set of principles; and

- To distill the best thinking from the standards, models, and public policies proposed and adopted by national and state standards, commissions, professional organizations, advocacy groups, and agencies.

It also pledged to submit the first group of standards by September 1976, and the remainder six months thereafter.

Following submission of this plan, work began in earnest. Meeting on the average of every six weeks, the subcommittee reviewed materials presented by the National Institute for Juvenile Justice and Delinquency Prevention on the patterns of existing state laws, the proposed recommendations of the National Task Force on Standards and Goals for Juvenile Justice and Delinquency Prevention, the Institute of Judicial Administration/American Bar Association Joint Commission on Juvenile Justice Standards, and the positions adopted by other state and national organizations and agencies, and considered draft standards. By September 1976, the standards on adjudication had been completed. The work continued and in March 1977, the standards on administration, intervention, and supervision, together with a set of prevention strategies, were submitted in "advanced draft" form—i.e., without the explanatory commentary.

The pace then slowed as the personnel from the Office of Juvenile Justice and Delinquency Prevention who had served as staff to the subcommittee, became increasingly engaged in other duties, and as uncertainty grew over whether the authority to recommend standards under the Juvenile Justice and Delinquency Prevention Acts was vested in the subcommittee or full National Advisory Committee. With the passage of the 1977 Amendments to the Act clarifying that the duty to recommend standards lay with the National Advisory Committee as a whole, and with the advent of an independent staff of consultants for the committee, work on the commentary was renewed. By August 1979, the entire set of standards, strategies, and commentary was ready for final review, and after extensive discussion, this volume of recommendations was overwhelmingly adopted by the National Advisory Committee on September 21, 1979.

The volume is divided into six chapters. The first five contain the proposed standards and strategies and are divided along the functional lines noted above. The sixth chapter presents a general implementation plan outlining criteria considered in assessing the various implementation mechanisms available, and two implementation strategies which appear to meet those criteria. . . .

The chapter on the Prevention Function includes a recommended definition of delinquency prevention together with thirty-seven possible prevention strategies. These strategies are presented not as prescriptive standards, but as illustrations of the types of services and actions which states and communities should consider in developing a comprehensive prevention program that addresses local needs and takes advantage of already available resources. . . .

The chapter entitled the Administration Function contains standards on the role and responsibilities of the local, state and federal levels of government for the planning, management, and evaluation of the juvenile service system. The standards emphasize the need for a coordinated, multi-level planning process. . . .

The Intervention Function chapter concentrates on the point at which a public official makes contact with a juvenile and/or family because of alleged delinquency or non-criminal misbehavior, or to protect a juvenile in danger of serious harm who has no adult with whom he/she has substantial ties, or who is willing and able to provide protection against that harm. . . . The standards recommended in this chapter define the situations in which intervention is appropriate; set forth criteria to guide decisions to refer individuals to the intake unit and decisions to take a juvenile into custody; and delineate the procedures and rights which should apply following intervention. They reflect the principle of using the least restrictive or intrusive alternative to achieve the objectives of the intervention. . . .

The standards on the Adjudication Function recommend establishment of a family court with jurisdiction over nearly all legal matters affecting children. In addition, they provide for the qualifications for and method of selection of family court judges and staff, the rights of the parties in judicial and administrative adjudicatory proceedings, some of the procedures which should apply to such proceedings, and the alternatives, criteria, and procedures for intake, detention, and dispositional decisions.

The final chapter of standards concerns the Supervision Function. It is directed to those agencies and programs supervising juveniles and families subject to the jurisdiction of the family court over delinquency, noncriminal misbehavior, neglect and abuse. . . . Although the National Advisory Committee strongly urges the reliance on community supervision, in-home services, and small community-based residential programs to the maximum extent possible, it recognizes that training schools and other large congregate facilities for juveniles will not disappear from the American landscape overnight. Accordingly, the standards in this chapter recommend that such facilities be structured and provided with the necessary services, staff, and resources to accomplish the treatment objectives they were established to perform. . . .

Binding all these recommendations together are five basic themes:

I. The family remains the basic unit of our social order—governmental policies, programs, and practices should be designed to support and assist families, not usurp their functions;

II. Together with any grant of authority by or to a governmental entity must be the establishment of limits on the exercise and duration of that authority and mechanisms to assure accountability—guildelines and review procedures should be established for all intervention, intake, custody, and dispositional decisions;

III. Age is not a valid basis for denying procedural protections when fundamental rights are threatened. . . .

IV. Whenever there is a choice among various alternatives, the option which least intrudes upon liberty and privacy should be preferred . . .; and

V. When rehabilitation forms a basis for the imposition of restraints on liberty, an obligation arises to offer a range of services reasonably designed to achieve the rehabilitative goals within the shortest period of time—governmental intervention justified upon the doctrine of *parens patriae* trigger at least a moral duty to provide the resources necessary to fulfill the promise of care and assistance.

The standards are, of course, fully consistent with the Act's prohibitions against confinement of nonoffenders in detention and correctional facilities and the commingling of juveniles in any facility with adults accused or found guilty of having committed a criminal offense. . . .

Margaret C. Driscoll,
Chairperson of the Subcommittee on Standards, 1980

Lawrence Semski,
Chairperson of the Subcommittee on Standards, 1977–1979

Wilfred W. Nuernberger,
Chairperson of the Subcommittee on Standards, 1975–1977

REVIEW QUESTIONS

1. The *Standards for the Administration of Juvenile Justice* developed by the National Advisory Committee for Juvenile Justice and Delinquency Prevention were a major out-growth of the concerns about juvenile justice system practices initially raised in the report of the President's Commission and repeatedly addressed in the U.S. Supreme

Court cases we have encountered in this chapter. What were the major purposes underlying development of the *Standards*? What prompted their creation? What process was involved in developing them and who was involved?

2. The National Advisory Committee standards were designed as guidelines for policymakers seeking to improve state and local juvenile justice services. Although their creation was mandated by the Juvenile Justice and Delinquency Prevention Act of 1974, the standards themselves were not laws and did not carry the force of law. However, they had a major impact on juvenile justice as a result of their influence on policymakers nationwide. What can you deduce from the brief summaries of the respective chapters of the *Standards* about the kinds of guidance offered in each one? What specific guidelines can you find in these summaries?

3. Carefully review the five "basic themes" listed near the end of the selection and try to discern how each of them might be implemented at different stages of the juvenile justice process. Which of these themes seem most closely related to the reforms advocated by the President's Commission? Which ones seem most important to you? Which ones seem least important? Explain your reasoning.

Introduction to the IJA-ABA Juvenile Justice Standards

Barbara Flicker

DEVELOPMENT OF THE STANDARDS

The Juvenile Justice Standards Project was initiated in 1971 at the Institute of Judicial Administration, a nonprofit research and educational national court organization located at the New York University School of Law. It began as an afterthought to the ABA Project for *Standards for Criminal Justice,* for which IJA served as secretariat. Staff members first had considered annotating the twelve volumes of criminal justice standards to show how the juvenile law diverged, but they found the fundamental disparities more extensive than they had anticipated. The criminal justice standards did not address the issues presented by the separate courts and agencies established to handle problems affecting juveniles and their

Source: Barbara Flicker. (1996). Introduction. In Institute of Judicial Administration—American Bar Association. *Juvenile Justice Standards Annotated: A Balanced Approach* (pp. xv–xxi). Robert E. Shepherd, Jr., editor. Chicago: American Bar Association. Copyright © 1996 American Bar Association. Reprinted by permission.

families. IJA began to plan a modest project to produce a single volume devoted to juvenile justice. Ten years and twenty-three volumes later, the *IJA-ABA Juvenile Justice Standards* were completed.

The project was an arduous task executed by about three hundred dedicated professionals throughout the nation, including prominent representatives of every discipline connected to the juvenile justice system: the law, the judiciary, medicine, social work, psychiatry, psychology, sociology, corrections, political science, law enforcement, education, and architecture. Scholars and practitioners joined task forces and working groups to perform research, analysis, drafting, reviewing, revising, and editing functions, supported by IJA professional and clerical staff.

The structure of the project was as intricate as the volumes of standards it produced. A planning committee chaired by the late Chief Judge Irving R. Kaufman of the United States Court of Appeals for the Second Circuit met in October 1971, followed by meetings of six planning subcommittees to identify the issues in the juvenile justice field and the areas to be covered. In February 1973, the ABA became cosponsor of the project and the IJA-ABA Joint Commission on *Juvenile Justice Standards* was established as its governing body, chaired by Chief Judge Kaufman. The Joint Commission consisted of twenty-nine members, of which half were lawyers and judges. A Minority Group Advisory Committee was created in 1973.

Four drafting committees supervised the work of the thirty scholars who were assigned as reporters to draft the individual volumes. The chairs of the drafting committees were members of the joint Commission. Each volume and its reporter or reporters came within the jurisdiction of one of the drafting committees: Drafting Committee I: Intervention in the Lives of Children, Co-chairs William S. White and Margaret K. Rosenheim; II: Court Roles and Procedures, Chair Charles Z. Smith; III: Treatment and Corrections, Chair Allen F. Breed; and IV: Administration, Chair Daniel L. Skoler.

As the reporters met with their drafting committees or work groups within the committees, issues arose and were submitted to the Joint Commission for resolution at its periodic meetings. After the reporters' manuscripts were approved by the drafting committees, they were reviewed by the project staff and transmitted to the joint Commission with pertinent comments on matters of cross-volume consistency. The members of the joint Commission independently reviewed the contents of each volume on the agenda, followed by discussions of broad principles, as well as minute details of text and format. The volumes then were returned to the reporters with instructions for revisions.

In 1975 and 1976 all twenty-three volumes were published as tentative drafts and distributed widely to individuals and organizations concerned with juvenile justice for their comments and suggestions. The ABA assigned the volumes to the appropriate sections, committees, and other entities specializing in the areas covered by each volume, with the task of coordinating the resulting recommendations handled by the Committee on Juvenile Justice of the Section of Criminal Justice and its chair, Livingston Hall and the Juvenile Justice Standards Review Committee of the Section of Family Law, chaired by Marjorie Childs.

The reports, comments, and suggestions of the various individuals and groups, including the ABA entities, were submitted to the Executive Committee of the Joint

Commission, which had been authorized to respond on behalf of the commission. It met in 1977 and 1978 to consider the proposed changes in the tentative drafts. Relatively minor changes were approved and the published tentative drafts were sent to the ABA House of Delegates, accompanied by minutes describing the Executive Committee's decisions with respect to the revisions to be made in the volumes. The ABA House of Delegates approved seventeen volumes in 1979 and three more in August 1980. Of the remaining three volumes, *The Standards Relating to Schools and Education* was withdrawn from consideration by the House of Delegates as too specialized, *The Standards Relating to Noncriminal Misbehavior* was tabled by the delegates as too controversial, and *The Standards Relating to Abuse and Neglect* was returned for revision. A revised volume on abuse and neglect was approved by the Joint Commission and published with the final revised drafts of all twenty-three IJA-ABA juvenile justice standards volumes in 1980, but the project ended in 1981 and no further submissions were made to the House of Delegates.

BASIC PRINCIPLES

Despite the complex and time-consuming path followed by the standards volumes from inception to final publication, it was straightforward for the underlying principles. As issue papers were analyzed and the subjects to be covered were identified, a pattern of interweaving concepts emerged and a value system that permeated all of the *Standards* became apparent.

The strongest influence was the 1967 Supreme Court decision in *In re Gault.* The Joint Commission adopted a due process model governed by equity and fairness, rejecting the more popular medical model premised on a need for treatment as the basis for the court's jurisdiction. From that choice, several principles flowed with logical precision, as follows:

1. Sanctions should be proportionate to the seriousness of the offense.
2. Sentences or dispositions should be fixed or determinate as declared by the court after a hearing, not indeterminate as determined by correctional authorities based on subsequent behavior or administrative convenience.
3. The least restrictive alternative to accomplish the purpose of the intervention should be the choice of decision makers at every stage, with written reasons for finding less drastic remedies inadequate required of every official decision maker.

Another feature of the juvenile justice system envisioned by the Joint Commission would require access to adequate and appropriate community-based services on a voluntary basis to the families and children who need them. This vision is set forth in full in the volume, *Standards Relating to Youth Service Agencies.* A network of social, educational, vocational, health, and other services would be made available to every juvenile and family, not imposed as official sanctions or dependent on welfare eligibility. Unfortunately, access to community-based services geared to the legitimate needs of the local residents is one of the unfulfilled goals of the standards. The principles that result from the assumption that communities would provide voluntary youth services and from the *Standards'* rejection of involuntary intervention without a finding of delinquency, child abuse, or neglect are:

4. Noncriminal misbehavior (status offenses or conduct that would not be a crime if committed by an adult) should be removed from juvenile court jurisdiction.
5. Limitations should be imposed on detention, treatment, or other intervention prior to adjudication and disposition.

A third element in the value system that distinguishes the *IJA-ABA Standards* is accountability in an open society in which the rights and responsibilities of individuals and agencies would be clearly delineated, protected, and enforced. The applicable principles are:

6. Visibility and accountability of decision making should replace closed proceedings and unrestrained official discretion.
7. Juveniles should have the right to decide on actions affecting their lives and freedom, unless they are found incapable of making reasoned decisions.
8. Parental roles in juvenile proceedings should be redefined with particular attention to possible conflicts between the interests of parent and child.
9. There should be a right to counsel for all affected interests at all crucial stages of proceedings and an unwaivable right to counsel for juveniles.

Finally, the project relied on its idealized design of the family court as the centerpiece of its idealized juvenile justice system. Organized as a separate division of the court of original trial jurisdiction, with judges rotated at fixed intervals from the other trial courts and all of the personnel (judges, lawyers, police officers, corrections officials, social workers, and related service providers) trained to handle the special problems of families and children brought into contact with the judicial system, the family court would be uniquely equipped to implement the standards. It would be expected to deal effectively with all but the most egregious cases and even then to retain jurisdiction until every reasonable effort had failed and the criminal justice system could be shown to be more effective. The much-breached assumption that juvenile offenses would not be tried in criminal court except as a last resort is embodied in the tenth principle as follows:

10. Strict criteria should be established for waiver of juvenile court jurisdiction to regulate the transfer of juveniles to adult criminal court.

REVIEW QUESTIONS

1. Although created during the same decade as the National Advisory Committee standards we encountered in the previous selection—and arising from the same reformist spirit—the IJA-ABA standards followed a very different path of development and their scope ended up being far broader. How did the project begin? Who was involved? What process was followed in preparing the 23 volumes of standards?

2. Review the nine "basic principles" underlying the work of the IJA-ABA Juvenile Justice Standards Project. What does each one suggest about the way the juvenile justice system should function? What are the implications of each principle for handling of offenders at different stages of the juvenile justice process?

3. How do the principles underlying the IJA-ABA standards differ from the "basic themes" running through the National Advisory Committee standards? How are they similar? Which of the IJA-ABA principles seem most responsive to the concerns and recommendations of the President's Commission?

4. Like the National Advisory Committee standards, those promulgated by the IJA-ABA did not carry the force of law. Rather, the standards—and the principles underlying them—were devised as guidelines that the authors hoped juvenile justice system officials would follow in developing policies for their own jurisdictions. Which of the principles enumerated in this selection do you think should be adhered to in developing juvenile justice system policies today and in the future? Which ones should be ignored? Why?

FURTHER READING

del Carmen, Rolando V., Parker, Mary, and Reddington, Frances P. (1998). *Briefs of Leading Cases in Juvenile Justice*. Cincinnati, OH: Anderson.

Institute of Judicial Administration—American Bar Association. (1996). *Juvenile Justice Standards Annotated: A Balanced Approach*. Robert E. Shepherd, Jr., editor. Chicago: American Bar Association.

Manfredi, Christopher P. (1998). *The Supreme Court and Juvenile Justice*. Lawrence, KS: University Press of Kansas.

National Advisory Committee for Juvenile Justice and Delinquency Prevention. (1980). *Standards for the Administration of Juvenile Justice*. Washington, DC: U.S. Government Printing Office.

Task Force on Juvenile Delinquency. (1967). *Task Force Report: Juvenile Delinquency and Youth Crime—Report on Juvenile Justice and Consultants' Papers*. The President's Commission on Law Enforcement and Administration of Justice. Washington, DC: U.S. Government Printing Office.

CHAPTER

4

Policing Juveniles

Accounting for roughly 85% of delinquency cases referred to the nation's juvenile courts each year, police officers represent the primary gatekeepers of the juvenile justice system. As we learned in Chapter 1, nearly one out of every six arrests nationwide involves a person under 18 years of age. Untold numbers of additional youth are stopped and questioned, then dealt with by some method short of arrest. It should be abundantly clear, then, that understanding the nature of the police role in handling juvenile offenders as well as the problems and issues that arise in connection with their interactions with youth provides a crucial link in our efforts to comprehend the ways in which our society and its juvenile justice institutions respond to delinquent behavior.

Although the methods the police employ in their interactions with juveniles in many ways resemble those used with adults, they are necessarily different in a number of important respects. The selections in this chapter provide an overview of the police response to the unique characteristics and needs of juvenile offenders, and to the institutional problems presented by the salience of adolescents among the individuals—suspected offenders as well as victims, witnesses, and others—with whom law enforcement officials interact on a regular basis.

The first selection, although written some four decades ago, provides one of the most vivid portraits of street encounters between police officers and juveniles ever written. Some of the terminology used by Piliavin and Briar in *Police Encounters with Juveniles* is unquestionably dated, but their description of the decision-making process and the alternatives available to officers in deciding how to respond to juvenile misbehavior remains fresh, their assessment of factors influencing police dispositions of juvenile cases continues to stir heated debate, and the article has justifiably become a classic in the field of juvenile policing.

To highlight the gulf between factors that have been found to influence police decisions in the field and those that *should* be taken into account, we next examine two brief excerpts from the National Advisory Committee standards that we learned about in the last chapter. The Committee's *Criteria for Taking a Juvenile Into Custody—Delinquency* and *Criteria for Referral to Intake—Delinquency* offer an illuminating normative counterpoint to Piliavin and Briar's empirical observations about police decision making. Where Piliavin and Briar found personal characteristics such as race, grooming, and, most importantly, demeanor to weigh heavily in police dispositions of juvenile cases, these two sets of standards enumerate much more limited sets of criteria that the Committee deemed reasonable for police to consider.

The next selection—a passage from another classic study, this one originally published in 1967—delves into the nature of police interrogation of juvenile suspects. Written by Aaron Cicourel as part of an exhaustive qualitative examination of ways in which juvenile justice system officials produce the information that becomes part of a juvenile's official file, the reading outlines the mechanisms used by police in street encounters and in stationhouse interrogations to make sense of an event, to obtain information consistent with their initial impressions, and to translate their perception of "what happened" into a written report.

The fact that the police interrogation tactics outlined by Cicourel often involve an array of subterfuges designed to draw a reluctant suspect into a confession or admission that might later be used against him or her in court highlights the question of what special protections are necessary or appropriate to safeguard the juvenile's Constitutional rights (i.e., the right to counsel and the privilege against self-incrimination) during interrogation. *Fare v. Michael C.*, the leading U.S. Supreme Court case addressing the matter, examines the meaning of the right to counsel during police interrogation when the suspect is a juvenile. In this case, the issue was whether a juvenile's request to speak with his probation officer is legally equivalent to a request for an attorney, in which case further questioning would be prohibited.

The Court held in the *Michael C.* case that the nature of the probation officer's role is so different from that of an attorney that a request to speak with the former prior to interrogation cannot be regarded as a *per se* invocation of the Sixth Amendment right to counsel. Instead, it held that such a request is but one of many factors that should be taken into account in determining whether the "totality of circumstances" indicates that the juvenile wishes to assert his or her Fifth Amendment right to remain silent.

Resolution of the Constitutional issue leaves open the *policy* issue of whether the presence of *some* supportive adult (attorney, parent, guardian, or friend) is necessary to offset problems associated with juveniles' immature cognitive capacity and judgment, as addressed in the selection by Scott and Grisso in Chapter 1. The National Advisory Committee standard for *Procedures Applicable to the Interrogation of Juveniles*, which follows the *Michael C.* case in this chapter, specifies a right to the presence of both an attorney and a parent or other adult "with whom the juvenile has substantial ties" during interrogation, and it prohibits use in court of any statement made by a juvenile in police custody in the absence of a supportive adult. The standard goes on to emphasize the importance, in view of concerns similar to those raised by Scott and Grisso, of ensuring not only that the child fully understands all of his or her Constitutional rights, but that any statement given by the child "is not the product of adolescent fantasy, fright, or despair." Other ways to ensure fair interrogation of juveniles are raised in the review questions that follow the standard.

The scope of a juvenile's Fourth Amendment right against unreasonable search and seizure is addressed in the next three selections, all landmark Supreme Court cases focusing on the right of public school officials to conduct searches that would almost certainly be found unconstitutional if conducted by police officers operating outside the school environment. First, in *New Jersey v. T.L.O.*, the Court confronted the authority of school officials to search a child's person and belongings in the absence of probable cause and/or a warrant, as is normally required before police can conduct such a search. In justifying a lesser "reasonable suspicion" standard, the Court pointed to the special nature of the school environment and the unique problems encountered by teachers and administrators in their efforts to keep students safe and maintain sufficient order to accommodate the learning process. In the second case, *Vernonia School District 47J v. Acton*, the court addressed the Constitutionality of mandatory drug testing of student athletes, concluding, once again, that the uniqueness of the public school setting justifies departure from the restrictions the Fourth Amendment places on searches in other contexts. Finally, in *Board of Education of Independent School District No. 92 of Pottawatomie County v. Earls,* the Court extended the logic of *Vernonia* to embrace drug testing of students involved in *any* school-sponsored extracurricular activities.

Our examination of police interactions with juveniles concludes with excerpts from two journal articles examining contemporary policing styles as they relate to juvenile offenders. In the first, Eric Fritsch, Tory Caeti and Robert Taylor focus on gang suppression efforts, reviewing previous literature on the police role in dealing with gangs and the effect of police actions on gang activity before discussing the implications of their own investigation of an anti-gang initiative in Dallas, Texas. In the second, Gordon Bazemore and Scott Senjo "revisit" some of the same issues examined by Piliavin and Briar in the selection that opened this chapter, this time focusing on ways in which community-oriented policing (COP) affects police encounters with juveniles.

Police Encounters with Juveniles

Irving Piliavin and Scott Briar

As the first of a series of decisions made in the channeling of youthful offenders through the agencies concerned with juvenile justice and corrections, the disposition decisions made by police officers have potentially profound consequences for apprehended juveniles. Thus

Source: Irving Piliavin and Scott Briar. (1964). Police Encounters with Juveniles. *American Journal of Sociology,* 70, 206–214. © 1964 by The University of Chicago. Adapted by permission.

arrest, the most severe of the dispositions available to police, may not only lead to confinement of the suspected offender but also bring him loss of social status, restriction of educational and employment opportunities, and future harassment by law-enforcement personnel. According to some criminologists, the stigmatization resulting from police apprehension, arrest, and detention actually reinforces deviant behavior. Other authorities have suggested, in fact, that this stigmatization serves as the catalytic agent initiating delinquent careers. Despite their presumed significance, however, little empirical analysis has been reported regarding the factors influencing, or consequences resulting from, police actions with juvenile offenders. Furthermore, while some studies of police encounters with adult offenders have been reported, the extent to which the findings of these investigations pertain to law-enforcement practices with youthful offenders is not known.

The above considerations have led the writers to undertake a longitudinal study of the conditions influencing, and consequences flowing from, police actions with juveniles. In the present paper findings will be presented indicating the influence of certain factors on police actions. Research data consist primarily of notes and records based on nine months' observation of all juvenile officers in one police department. The officers were observed in the course of their regular tours of duty. While these data do not lend themselves to quantitative assessments of reliability and validity, the candor shown by the officers in their interviews with the investigators and their use of officially frowned-upon practices while under observation provide some assurance that the materials presented below accurately reflect the typical operations and attitudes of the law-enforcement personnel studied.

The setting for the research, a metropolitan police department serving an industrial city with approximately 450,000 inhabitants, was noted within the community it served and among law-enforcement officials elsewhere for the honesty and superior quality of its personnel. Incidents involving criminal activity or brutality by members of the department had been extremely rare during the 10 years preceding this study; personnel standards were comparatively high; and an extensive training program was provided to both new and experienced personnel. Juvenile Bureau members, the primary subjects of this investigation, differed somewhat from other members of the department in that they were responsible for delinquency prevention as well as law enforcement, that is, juvenile officers were expected to be knowledgeable about conditions leading to crime and delinquency and to be able to work with community agencies serving known or potential juvenile offenders. Accordingly, in the assignment of personnel to the Juvenile Bureau, consideration was given not only to an officer's devotion to and reliability in law enforcement but also to his commitment to delinquency prevention. Assignment to the Bureau was of advantage to policemen seeking promotions. Consequently, many officers requested transfer to this unit, and its personnel comprised a highly select group of officers.

In the field, juvenile officers operated essentially as patrol officers. They cruised assigned beats and, although concerned primarily with juvenile offenders, frequently had occasion to apprehend and arrest adults. Confrontations between the officers and juveniles occurred in one of the following three ways, in order of increasing frequency: (1) encounters resulting from officers' spotting officially "wanted" youths; (2) encounters taking place at or near the scene of offenses reported to police headquarters; and (3) encounters occurring as the result of officers' directly observing youths either committing offenses or in "suspicious circumstances." However, the probability that a confrontation would take place between officer and juvenile, or that a particular disposition of an identified offender would be made, was only in part determined by the knowledge that an offense had occurred or that a particular juvenile had committed an offense. The bases for and utilization of non-offenses related criteria by police in accosting and disposing of juveniles are the foci of the following discussion.

SANCTIONS FOR DISCRETION

In each encounter with juveniles, with the minor exception of officially "wanted" youths, a central task confronting the officer was to decide what official action to take against the boys involved. In making these disposition decisions, officers could select any one of five discrete alternatives:

1. outright release
2. release and submission of a "field interrogation report" briefly describing the circumstances initiating the police–juvenile confrontation
3. "official reprimand" and release to parents or guardian
4. citation to juvenile court
5. arrest and confinement in juvenile hall.

Dispositions 3, 4, and 5 differed from the others in two basic respects. First, with rare exceptions, when an officer chose to reprimand, cite, or arrest a boy, he took the youth to the police station. Second, the reprimanded, cited, or arrested boy acquired an official police "record," that is, his name was officially recorded in Bureau files as a juvenile violator.

Analysis of the distribution of police disposition decisions about juveniles revealed that in virtually every category of offense the full range of official disposition alternatives available to officers was employed. This wide range of discretion resulted primarily from two conditions. First, it reflected the reluctance of officers to expose certain youths to the stigmatization presumed to be associated with official police action. Few juvenile officers believed that correctional agencies serving the community could effectively help delinquents. For some officers this attitude reflected a lack of confidence in rehabilitation techniques; for others, a belief that high case loads and lack of professional training among correctional workers vitiated their efforts at treatment. All officers were agreed, however, that juvenile justice and correctional processes were essentially concerned with apprehension and punishment rather than treatment. Furthermore, all officers believed that some aspects of these processes (e.g., judicial definition of youths as delinquents and removal of delinquents from the community), as well as some of the possible consequences of these processes (e.g., intimate institutional contact with "hard-core" delinquents, as well as parental, school, and conventional peer disapproval or rejection), could reinforce what previously might have been only a tentative proclivity toward delinquent values and behavior. Consequently, when officers found reason to doubt that a youth being confronted was highly committed toward deviance, they were inclined to treat him with leniency.

Second, and more important, the practice of discretion was sanctioned by police-department policy. Training manuals and departmental bulletins stressed that the disposition of each juvenile offender was not to be based solely on the type of infraction he committed. Thus, while it was departmental policy to "arrest and confine all juveniles who have committed a felony or misdemeanor involving theft, sex offense, battery, possession of dangerous weapons, prowling, peeping, intoxication, incorrigibility, and disturbance of the peace," it was acknowledged that "such considerations as age, attitude and prior criminal record might indicate that a different disposition would be more appropriate." The official justification for discretion in processing juvenile offenders, based on the preventive aims of the Juvenile Bureau, was that each juvenile violator should be dealt with solely on the basis of what was best for him. Unofficially, administrative legitimation of discretion was further justified on the grounds that strict enforcement practices would overcrowd court calendars and detention facilities, as well as dramatically increase juvenile crime rates—consequences to be avoided because they would expose the police department to community criticism.

In practice, the official policy justifying use of discretion served as a demand that discretion be exercised. As such, it posed three problems for juvenile officers. First, it represented a departure from the traditional police practice with which the juvenile officers themselves were identified, in the sense that they were expected to justify their juvenile disposition decisions not simply by evidence proving a youth had committed a crime—grounds on which police were officially expected to base their dispositions of non-juvenile offenders—but in the *character* of the youth. Second, in disposing of juvenile offenders, officers were expected, in effect, to make judicial rather than ministerial decisions. Third, the shift from the offense to the offender as the basis for determining the appropriate disposition substantially increased the uncertainty and ambiguity for officers in the situation of apprehension because no explicit rules existed for determining which disposition different types of youths should receive. Despite these problems, officers were constrained to base disposition decisions on the character of the apprehended youth, not only because they wanted to be fair, but because persistent failure to do so could result in judicial criticism, departmental censure, and, they believed, loss of authority with juveniles.

DISPOSITION CRITERIA

Assessing the character of apprehended offenders posed relatively few difficulties for officers in the case of youths who had committed serious crimes such as robbery, homicide, aggravated assault, grand theft, auto theft, rape, and arson. Officials generally regarded these juveniles as confirmed delinquents simply by virtue of their involvement in offenses of this magnitude. However, the infraction committed did not always suffice to determine the appropriate disposition for some serious offenders; and, in the case of minor offenders, who comprised over 90 per cent of the youths against whom police took action, the violation per se generally played an insignificant role in the choice of disposition. While a number of minor offenders were seen as serious delinquents deserving arrest, many others were perceived either as "good" boys whose offenses were atypical of their customary behavior, as pawns of undesirable associates or, in any case, as boys for whom arrest was regarded as an unwarranted and possibly harmful punishment. Thus, for nearly all minor violators and for some serious delinquents, the assessment of character—the distinction between serious delinquents, "good" boys, misguided youths, and so on—and the dispositions which followed from these assessments were based on youths' personal characteristics and not their offenses.

Despite this dependence of disposition decisions on the personal characteristics of these youths, police officers actually had access only to very limited information about boys at the time they had to decide what to do with them. In the field, officers typically had no data concerning the past offense records, school performance, family situation, or personal adjustment of apprehended youths. Furthermore, files at police headquarters provided data only about each boy's prior offense record. Thus both the decision made in the field— whether or not to bring the boy in—and the decision made at the station—which disposition to invoke—were based largely on cues which emerged from the interaction between the officer and the youth, cues from which the officer inferred the youth's character. These cues included the youth's group affiliations, age, race, grooming, dress, and demeanor. Older juveniles, members of known delinquent gangs, Negroes, youths with well-oiled hair, black jackets, and soiled denims or jeans (the presumed uniform of "tough" boys), and boys who in their interactions with officers did not manifest what were considered to be appropriate signs of respect tended to receive the more severe dispositions.

Other than prior record, the most important of the above clues was a youth's *demeanor.* In the opinion of juvenile patrolmen themselves the demeanor of apprehended juveniles was a major determinant of their decisions for 50–60 percent of the juvenile cases they processed. A less subjective indication of the association between a youth's demeanor and police disposition is provided by Table 4.1, which presents the police dispositions for sixty-six youths whose encounters with police were observed in the course of this study. For purposes of this analysis, each youth's demeanor in the encounter was classified as

Table 4.1   SEVERITY OF POLICE DISPOSITION BY YOUTH'S DEMEANOR

Severity of Police Disposition	*Youth's Demeanor*		*Total*
	Co-operative	*Unco-operative*	
Arrest (most severe)	2	14	16
Citation or official reprimand	4	5	9
Informal reprimand	15	1	16
Admonish and release (least severe)	24	1	25
Total	45	21	66

either cooperative or unco-operative. The results clearly reveal a marked association between youth demeanor and the severity of police dispositions.

The cues used by police to assess demeanor were fairly simple. Juveniles who were contrite about their infractions, respectful to officers, and fearful of the sanctions that might be employed against them tended to be viewed by patrolmen as basically law-abiding or at least "salvageable." For these youths it was usually assumed that informal or formal reprimand would suffice to guarantee their future conformity. In contrast, youthful offenders who were fractious, obdurate, or who appeared nonchalant in their encounters with patrolmen were likely to be viewed as "would-be tough guys" or "punks" who fully deserved the most severe sanction: arrest. . . .

Although anger and disgust frequently characterized officers' attitudes toward recalcitrant and impassive juvenile offenders, their manner while processing these youths was typically routine, restrained, and without rancor. While the officers' restraint may have been due in part to their desire to avoid accusation and censure, it also seemed to reflect their inurement to a frequent experience. By and large, only their occasional "needling" or insulting of a boy gave any hint of the underlying resentment and dislike they felt toward many of these youths.

PREJUDICE IN APPREHENSION AND DISPOSITION DECISIONS

Compared to other youths, Negroes and boys whose appearance matched the delinquent stereotype were more frequently stopped and interrogated by patrolmen—often even in the absence of evidence that an offense had been committed—and usually were given more severe dispositions for the same violations. Our data suggest, however, that these selective apprehension and disposition practices resulted not only from the intrusion of long-held prejudices of individual police officers but also from certain job-related experiences of law-enforcement personnel. First, the tendency for police to give more severe dispositions to Negroes and to youths whose appearance corresponded to that which police associated with delinquents partly reflected the fact, observed in this study, that these youths also were much more likely than were other types of boys to exhibit the sort of recalcitrant demeanor which police construed as a sign of the confirmed delinquent. Further, officers assumed, partly on the basis of departmental statistics, that Negroes and juveniles who "look tough" (e.g., who wear chinos, leather jackets, boots, etc.) commit crimes more frequently than do other types of youths. In this sense, the police justified their selective treatment of these youths along epidemiological lines: that is, they were concentrating their attention on those youths whom they believed were most likely to commit delinquent acts. . . .

As regards prejudice per se, eighteen of twenty-seven officers interviewed openly admitted a dislike for Negroes. However, they attributed their dislike to experiences they had, as policemen, with youths from this minority group. The officers reported that Negro boys were much more likely than non-Negroes to "give us a hard time," be unco-operative, and show no remorse for their transgressions. Recurrent exposure to such attitudes among Negro youth, the officers claimed, generated their antipathy toward Negroes. . . .

IMPLICATIONS

It is apparent from the findings presented above that the police officers studied in this research were permitted and even encouraged to exercise immense latitude in disposing of the juveniles they encountered. That is, it was within the officers' discretionary authority, except in extreme limiting cases, to decide which juveniles were to come to the attention of the courts and correctional agencies and thereby be identified officially as delinquents. In exercising this discretion policemen were strongly guided by the demeanor of those who were apprehended, a practice that ultimately led, as seen above, to certain youths (particularly Negroes and boys dressed in the style of "toughs") being treated more severely than other juveniles for comparable offenses.

But the relevance of demeanor was not limited only to police disposition practices. Thus, for example, in conjunction with police crime statistics the criterion of demeanor led police to concentrate their surveillance activities in areas frequented or inhabited by Negroes. Furthermore, these youths were accosted more often than others by officers on patrol simply because their skin color identified them as potential troublemakers. These discriminatory practices—and it is important to note that they are discriminatory, even if based on accurate statistical information—may well have self-fulfilling consequences. Thus it is not unlikely that frequent encounters with police, particularly those involving youths innocent of wrongdoing, will increase the hostility of these juveniles toward law-enforcement personnel. It is also not unlikely that the frequency of such encounters will in time reduce their significance in the eyes of apprehended juveniles, thereby leading these youths to regard them as "routine." Such responses to police encounters, however, are those which law-enforcement personnel perceive as indicators of the serious delinquent. They thus serve to vindicate and reinforce officers' prejudices, leading to closer surveillance of Negro districts, more frequent encounters with Negro youths, and so on in a vicious circle. Moreover, the consequences of this chain of events are reflected in police statistics showing a disproportionately high percentage of Negroes among juvenile offenders, thereby providing "objective" justification for concentrating police attention on Negro youths.

To a substantial extent, as we have implied earlier, the discretion practiced by juvenile officers is simply an extension of the juvenile-court philosophy, which holds that in making legal decisions regarding juveniles, more weight should be given to the juvenile's character and life-situation than to his actual offending behavior. The juvenile officer's disposition decisions—and the information he uses as a basis for them—are more akin to the discriminations made by probation officers and other correctional workers than they are to decisions of police officers dealing with non-juvenile offenders. The problem is that such clinical-type decisions are not restrained by mechanisms comparable to the principles of due process and the rules of procedure governing police decisions regarding adult offenders.

Consequently, prejudicial practices by police officers can escape notice more easily in their dealings with juveniles than with adults.

The observations made in this study serve to underscore the fact that the official delinquent, as distinguished from the juvenile who simply commits a delinquent act, is the product of a social judgment, in this case a judgment made by the police. He is a delinquent because someone in authority has defined him as one, often on the basis of the public face he has presented to officials rather than of the kind of offense he has committed.

REVIEW QUESTIONS

1. What alternatives were available to police officers in the department studied by Piliavin and Briar in deciding what action to take in their encounters with juveniles?
2. How much *discretion* did officers have in determining which disposition to use?
3. What criteria did the authors find to be important in police decisions about how to handle cases involving juveniles?

Which of these criteria do you consider to be appropriate? Which ones are inappropriate? Why?
4. Based on your reading of this selection, what factors seem most influential in police decisions about what action to take in encounters with juveniles? In what ways, if any, do these differ from the criteria that you believe *should* be taken into account?

Criteria for Taking a Juvenile into Custody and Referral to Intake—Delinquency

National Advisory Committee for Juvenile Justice and Delinquency Prevention

CRITERIA FOR TAKING A JUVENILE INTO CUSTODY—DELINQUENCY

Whenever practicable, an order issued by a family court judge should be obtained prior to taking into custody a juvenile alleged to have committed a delinquent act.

An order should not be issued nor a juvenile taken into custody without an order unless there is probable cause to believe that the juvenile falls within the jurisdiction of

Source: National Advisory Committee for Juvenile Justice and Delinquency Prevention. (1980). *Standards for the Administration of Juvenile Justice.* Washington, DC: U.S. Government Printing Office. Adapted courtesy of the United States Department of Justice, Office of Juvenile Justice and Delinquency Prevention.

the family court over delinquency described in Standard 3.111, and it is determined that issuance of a summons or citation would not adequately protect the jurisdiction or process of the family court; would not adequately protect the juvenile from an imminent threat of serious bodily harm; or would not adequately reduce the risk of the juvenile inflicting serious bodily harm on others or committing serious property offenses prior to adjudication.

In making this determination, the family court judge or law enforcement officer should consider:

a. The nature and seriousness of the alleged offense;

b. The juvenile's record of delinquency offenses, including whether the juvenile is currently subject to dispositional authority of the family court or released pending adjudication, disposition, or appeal;

c. The juvenile's record of willful failures to appear following the issuance of a summons or citation; and

d. The availability of noncustodial alternatives, including the presence of a parent, guardian, or other suitable persons able and willing to provide supervision and care for the juvenile and to assure his/her compliance with a summons or citation.

Written rules and regulations should be developed to guide custody decisions in delinquency matters. . . .

CRITERIA FOR REFERRAL TO INTAKE—DELINQUENCY

Law enforcement agencies should promulgate written regulations for guiding decisions to refer to the intake unit a juvenile alleged to have committed an act which would be a crime or major traffic offense if committed by an adult. In determining whether referral would best serve the interests of the community and the juvenile, law enforcement officers should consider whether there is probable cause to believe the juvenile is subject to the jurisdiction of the family court over delinquency, and:

a. Whether a complaint has already been filed;

b. The seriousness of the alleged offense;

c. The role of the juvenile in that offense;

d. The nature and number of contacts with the law enforcement agency and the family court that the juvenile has had, and the results of those contacts;

e. The juvenile's age and maturity; and

f. The availability of appropriate persons or services outside the juvenile justice system willing and able to provide care, supervision, and assistance to the juvenile.

A juvenile should not be referred to the intake unit solely because he/she denies the allegations or because the complainant or victim insists.

REVIEW QUESTIONS

1. In what ways do these standards restrict the discretion of police officers in deciding whether to take a juvenile into custody and/or refer him or her to intake? What criteria apply? What considerations should be taken into account?

2. In what ways are the criteria for referral to intake different from those for taking a juvenile into custody? In what ways are they the same? Do you agree that different criteria should apply for these two decisions? Why or why not?

3. Which of the factors Piliavin and Briar found to influence police decision making would be permitted under these standards? Which ones would be prohibited? What factors not mentioned by Piliavin and Briar would be taken into account?

4. Do you think police departments should establish criteria such as the ones outlined in these standards to govern police decision making in encounters with juveniles, or should officers be allowed to use their own discretion?

Process and Structure in Juvenile Justice

Aaron V. Cicourel

The police must locate events and objects they investigate in some legal context, or characterize the situation in such a way that their presence or interference can be warranted now and later on if further justification is required. The police must map the event and social objects into socially and legally relevant categories as a condition for inference and action. The officer's tacit knowledge combines with information he has received, and his own observations of the action scene, to provide him with a preliminary mapping, but he invariably asks fairly standardized questions about "what happened" and who were the principal actors involved. The initial search procedures combine with prior assumptions and information to give the scene structure, but body motion, facial expressions, voice intonation, and the like, can make problematic the

Source: Aaron V. Cicourel. (1995). *The Social Organization of Juvenile Justice.* New Brunswick, NJ: Transaction Publishers. Originally published in 1968 by Heinemann Educational Books Ltd. Copyright © 1995 by Transaction Publishers. Reprinted by permission of Transaction Publishers.

routine use of social and legal categories, and alter or "push" the interpretation of events and objects into categories calling for more or less "serious" action. "Normal" appearances are crucial here for routine action. Two general classes of encounters are common in juvenile cases: (1) patrol being called to the scene or they may be passing a situation that is viewed as suspicious, and (2) juvenile officers making telephone or personal inquiries in the field or at the station. In the first class of encounters, appearances are critical for invoking a presumption of guilt and deciding "what happened." Practical solutions are immediate, for readily available categories usually exist for subsuming the events described by the participants. For example, a street fight, a variety store clerk with a male or female juvenile accused of stealing candy or cosmetics, juveniles with "questionable" grounds for not being in school, and a juvenile unable to identify his ownership of a car or establish an appropriate link with the owner, are all viewed as routine objects and events easily categorized. The "game" is understandable because it is possible to map some general features of the objects and events involved, with categories and general practices "known" to fall within the policeman's proper domain of activities. When the patrol officer finds that the situation does not readily fit available categories for deciding "what happened," he may take down more than the routine kind of face sheet data and description and bring everyone involved down to the station for further interrogation or for detention, until a juvenile officer or detective (depending on the policy of the organization) can pursue the matter further. The imputed suspicions of the patrolman may be communicated in the official report as something like "they couldn't give a straight story as to what they were up to around the garage so I brought them in." Or the report may say "The same suspects have been known to break into houses in the X area so the undersigned decided it was best to have the juvenile bureau talk to them." The initial remarks, however, may be loaded or indirect, depending upon how much information the officer had prior to arrival or what was immediately observable as he pulled up, and, of course, the particular style the officer employs for such occasions: "What's up?" "What's going on around here?" "O.K., what are you guys up to?" "O.K., who did it?" "Which one of you started it?" "O.K., now, who are you? What are you doing here?" "In trouble again, huh?" "O.K., let's have it." "O.K., what else did you take?" If the patrolman is involved with a more complicated problem involving witnesses and several possible offenders, the initial question may be followed by more systematic attempts to establish the sequence and timing of "what happened." The critical feature of the initial remarks, coupled with any prior information related or observed, is that some attempt at mapping the objects and events into a readily understandable police situation is signaled by the language used and the categories therein. Thus the body motion, facial expressions, voice intonation, a known past record by the juveniles involved provide the officer with an initial basis for inferences, judgments, routinized evaluations as revealed in the language categories he employs. My field experiences, however, differ little from those reported elsewhere and I would not be adding much to repeat similar descriptions.

The case of interrogations by juvenile officers in the field or at the station is another matter for several reasons.

1. The juvenile officer is skilled in his ability to interview suspects and has had considerable experience with virtually every "type" known to the police. There is little that is likely to surprise him and he will seldom lack appropriate categories with which to classify, evaluate, or summarize any concrete case.

2. The juvenile officer can pursue the case and contact different witnesses or others relevant to the case such as school officials, parents, neighbors, and victims. He can draw upon whatever information the police have on the suspect and supplement it by other contacts. Thus the "picture" can be fairly complete prior to the interrogation. The language of the interview is often more managed than those encounters experienced by patrolmen in the field.

3. The juvenile officer has had experience with a variety of offenders and possible dispositions, troublesome parents, probation, and a particular style of interviewing he follows, depending upon the initial assumptions he makes about the case at hand. The interrogation, therefore, is often based upon some fairly definite interpretations of "what happened" and a kind of plan of action for reaching a particular disposition. The alternatives that might emerge here are contingent upon the suspect's demeanor, the details he reveals about participation in activities under investigation, his past record, the kind of imputations the officer makes about his home situation, and the control the officer assumes can be exercised by the parents and police over his future conduct.

4. Because the juvenile officer has more information available and accessible, and because of his knowledge of probation-court procedures, he is able to manipulate the interview more than the patrolman. The juvenile officer, therefore, becomes a critical gatekeeper in the administration of juvenile justice because the same information can lead him to make quite different recommendations. Thus he is in a position to bargain with the juvenile and negotiate terms under which some disposition will be accomplished. The bargaining and negotiations reveal how members "close" activities, resolve contingencies, and arrive at seemingly "clear" accounts as to "what happened."

The juvenile officer interview is oriented by a variety of hunches, theories, rules of thumb, general procedures, and on the spot strategies for dealing with different juvenile suspects. The officer's past experience and the information available prior to the interview, lead him to make quick evaluations of his client as soon as there is a confrontation. The interrogation, therefore, is highly structured in the sense that the information revealed by the juvenile is evaluated quickly in terms of a set of categories which the officer invokes by means of questions posed for the suspect. The interrogation is designed to confirm the officer's suspicions or firm beliefs about "what happened" and how the particular suspect is implicated. The language used links the juvenile to particular activities, relations with peers, family, school officials, and the like, locates the suspect in a network of social relationships, and imputes routine motives and grounds to his action. For example:

> **POLICE OFFICER:**   Hi, you Jack Jones?
>
> **JUVENILE:**   Yaa, that's me.
>
> **OFF:**   Fine, sit down, Jack, I wanta ask ya a few questions about that dance out at the————Club last Saturday night. You were there, weren't you?
>
> **JUV:**   Yaa, I guess I was there. Why?
>
> **OFF:**   I wanta ask ya a few questions, that's all.

The officer may not reveal that the juvenile is the prime suspect in an incident involving an assault with a deadly weapon, that is, not until he can establish certain factors as to the youth's presence, for instance, his knowledge of what happened, his friends, his whereabouts at the time of the incident, his general manner of talking, the confidence he reveals about his affairs and their description. But the officer does seek to establish some immediate conditions for preparing the youth for a particular line of questioning. The initial gambit seeks to establish a nonthreatening setting if the officer assumes the juvenile's presence cannot be clearly established by witnesses. If this information is available to him (i.e., there are witnesses of the youth at the dance), then the opening line may include a "pleasant" or "neutral" tone of voice and seemingly a routine line of questioning without any apparent implications about the guilt or innocence of the youth. The meaning of the message and the particular line of questioning are constrained by the social context. Now it is possible that the officer has no prior information, the suspect is a kind of shot in the dark, and he intends to bluff his way while "playing it by ear." The officer may plunge into the following: "Why do you cheat, lie, and act this way?" The decision to "bluff" a "hard line" may be motivated by the fact that a serious offense was committed and there are few leads to follow. The many possibilities, however, are endless, but they are not all "independent" cases; some can be analyzed for routinized patterns. The officer engages in a preliminary mapping of events and objects into social categories to establish the relevance of prior knowledge, present assumptions, and what is "happening." The language employed, therefore, may or may not reflect the initial strategy of the policeman's intentions, but locates officer and juvenile in a preliminary network of relationships. The officer seeks to keep the suspect in a state of "informational imbalance." The sense of bargaining or fatality that is communicated can vary with the particular officer's style of interviewing, his estimation of who is guilty or implicated, the juvenile's demeanor, the juvenile's past record, and how much information the officer possesses that can be used to convey particular power conditions he has available. Now each of these conditions is not available to the officer as an explicit and obvious possibility he will or can utilize to "nail down" the case, but the conditions are revealed to the researcher in two ways. First, the interview itself, as it unfolds, reveals something of the officer's strategy. Second, in discussing cases with officers, general conditions of interrogation are described over and over again in distinct cases and cut across officers.

Some idea of police interrogation strategies can be obtained from reading the official policy of large metropolitan juvenile bureaus such as the following from a large city in southern California:

> *Interrogation.* Juveniles are to be interrogated, keeping in mind the same procedures and techniques used with adults, with one exception: the interrogation of a female under the age of eighteen years regarding sex matters shall be conducted by a policewoman, except if none is available and the situation demands immediate investigation.
>
> Many times a juvenile is anxious to tell the entire story about his suspected crimes immediately upon arrest. After a period of waiting in a police station without being interrogated, he may gain composure or he may think about the reaction of his parents when they learn of his arrest. This waiting period may afford him a good opportunity to think of an excuse or a story to cover his arrest. Many admissions have no doubt been lost by the fact that officers failed to interrogate juvenile suspects properly upon initial contact.
>
> Juveniles are more inclined to "cop out" than an adult, and a good interrogation will result often in the admission of other crimes and the identification of accomplices.

Notice how the above general statement of policy and strategy stresses the importance of interrogation under conditions where the juvenile may not be "composed." The "suspect" appears to be viewed as "guilty," even though the language does not make the apparent presumption clear. The statement makes explicit reference to the possibility of obtaining information about "other crimes and the identification of accomplices." What remains unclear, of course, is how one "interrogate(s) juvenile(s) properly."

REVIEW QUESTIONS

1. What is Cicourel's main argument about police interrogation of juveniles?
2. How is interrogation by juvenile officers different from questioning by patrol officers? *Why* is it different?
3. In what ways, if at all, does Cicourel's discussion suggest that police interrogation of juveniles differs from interrogation of adults? In particular, does interrogation of juveniles appear to involve tactics that are designed to exploit developmental factors such as those discussed by Scott and Grisso in Chapter 1?

4. To what extent, if at all, do you believe procedures involved in police interrogation of juveniles should be different from procedures applicable in cases involving adults? Should the same Constitutional rights accorded adult suspects apply (i.e., right to counsel, privilege against self-incrimination)? Should additional rights be granted (e.g., right to presence of a parent or guardian, *unwaivable* right to presence of an attorney)? Should the way in which officers question suspects be modified for juveniles? Is your answer to any of

these questions affected by consideration of the ways in which the developmental factors discussed by Scott and Grisso influence juveniles' understanding of and willingness to waive their Constitutional rights or to appreciate the implications of statements they might make?

Fare v. Michael C.

The Supreme Court of the United States
442 U.S. 707 (1979)

Mr. Justice Blackmun delivered the opinion of the Court.

In *Miranda v. Arizona* this Court established certain procedural safeguards designed to protect the rights of an accused, under the Fifth and Fourteenth Amendments, to be free from compelled self-incrimination during custodial interrogation. The Court specified, among other things, that if the accused indicates in any manner that he wishes to remain silent or to consult an attorney, interrogation must cease, and any statement obtained from him during interrogation thereafter may not be admitted against him at his trial.

In this case, the State of California, in the person of its acting chief probation officer, attacks the conclusion of the Supreme Court of California that a juvenile's request, made while undergoing custodial interrogation, to see his *probation officer* is *per se* an invocation of the juvenile's Fifth Amendment rights as pronounced in *Miranda*.

I.

Respondent Michael C. was implicated in the murder of Robert Yeager. The murder occurred during a robbery of the victim's home on January 19, 1976. A small truck registered in the name of respondent's mother was identified as having been near the Yeager home at the time of the killing, and a young man answering respondent's description was seen by witnesses near the truck and near the home shortly before Yeager was murdered.

On the basis of this information, Van Nuys, Cal., police took respondent into custody at approximately 6:30 p.m. on February 4. Respondent then was 16 1/2 years old and on probation to the Juvenile Court. He had been on probation since the age of 12. Approximately one year earlier he had served a term in a youth corrections camp under the supervision of the Juvenile Court. He had a record of several previous offenses, including burglary of guns and purse snatching, stretching back over several years.

Upon respondent's arrival at the Van Nuys station house two police officers began to interrogate him. The officers and respondent were the only persons in the room during the interrogation. The conversation was tape-recorded. One of the officers initiated the interview by informing respondent that he had been brought in for questioning in relation to a murder. The officer fully advised respondent of his *Miranda* rights. The following exchange then occurred, as set out in the opinion of the California Supreme Court:

> **Q:** . . . Do you understand all of these rights as I have explained them to you?
>
> **A:** Yeah.
>
> **Q:** Okay, do you wish to give up your right to remain silent and talk to us about this murder?
>
> **A:** What murder? I don't know about no murder.
>
> **Q:** I'll explain to you which one it is if you want to talk to us about it.
>
> **A:** Yeah, I might talk to you.
>
> **Q:** Do you want to give up your right to have an attorney present here while we talk about it?
>
> **A:** Can I have my probation officer here?
>
> **Q:** Well I can't get a hold of your probation officer right now. You have the right to an attorney.
>
> **A:** How I know you guys won't pull no police officer in and tell me he's an attorney?
>
> **Q:** Huh?
>
> **A:** [How I know you guys won't pull no police officer in and tell me he's an attorney?]
>
> **Q:** Your probation officer is Mr. Christiansen.
>
> **A:** Yeah.
>
> **Q:** Well I'm not going to call Mr. Christiansen tonight. There's a good chance we can talk to him later, but I'm not going to call him right now. If you want to talk to us without an attorney present, you can. If you don't want to, you don't have to. But if you want to say something, you can, and if you don't want to say something you don't have to. That's your right. You understand that right?
>
> **A:** Yeah.
>
> **Q:** Okay, will you talk to us without an attorney present?
>
> **A:** Yeah I want to talk to you."

Respondent thereupon proceeded to answer questions put to him by the officers. He made statements and drew sketches that incriminated him in the Yeager murder.

Largely on the basis of respondent's incriminating statements, probation authorities filed a petition in Juvenile Court alleging that respondent had murdered Robert Yeager . . . and that respondent therefore should be adjudged a ward of the Juvenile Court. . . . Respondent thereupon moved to suppress the statements and sketches he gave the police during the interrogation. He alleged that the statements had been obtained in violation of *Miranda* in that his request to see his probation officer at the outset of the questioning constituted an invocation of his Fifth Amendment right to remain silent, just as if he had requested the assistance of an attorney. Accordingly, respondent argued that since the interrogation did not cease until he had a chance to confer with his probation officer, the statements and sketches could not be admitted against him in the Juvenile Court proceedings. . . .

In support of his suppression motion, respondent called his probation officer, Charles P. Christiansen, as a witness. Christiansen testified that he had instructed respondent that if at any time he had "a concern with his family," or ever had "a police contact," he should get in touch with his probation officer immediately. The witness stated that, on a previous occasion, when respondent had had a police contact and had failed to communicate with Christiansen, the probation officer had reprimanded him. This testimony, respondent argued, indicated that when he asked for his probation officer, he was in fact asserting his right to remain silent in the face of further questioning.

In a ruling from the bench, the court denied the motion to suppress. It held that the question whether respondent had waived his right to remain silent was one of fact to be determined on a case-by-case basis, and that the facts of this case showed a "clear waiver" by respondent of that right. . . .

On appeal, the Supreme Court of California took the case by transfer from the California Court of Appeal and, by a divided vote, reversed. The court held that respondent's "request to see his probation officer at the commencement of interrogation negated any possible willingness on his part to discuss his case with the police [and] thereby invoked his Fifth Amendment privilege." . . .

The court accordingly held that the probation officer would act to protect the minor's Fifth Amendment rights in precisely the way an attorney would act if called for by the accused. In so holding, the court found the request for a probation officer to be a *per se* invocation of Fifth Amendment rights in the same way the request for an attorney was found in *Miranda* to be, regardless of what the interrogation otherwise might reveal. . . .

The State of California petitioned this Court for a writ of certiorari. MR. JUSTICE REHNQUIST, as Circuit Justice, stayed the execution of the mandate of the Supreme Court of California. Because the California judgment extending the *per se* aspects of *Miranda* presents an important question about the reach of that case, we thereafter issued the writ.

II.

We note at the outset that it is clear that the judgment of the California Supreme Court rests firmly on that court's interpretation of federal law. This Court, however, has not heretofore extended the *per se* aspects of the *Miranda* safeguards beyond the scope of the holding in the *Miranda* case itself.[1] We therefore must examine the California court's decision to determine

[1]Indeed, this Court has not yet held that *Miranda* applies with full force to exclude evidence obtained in violation of its proscriptions from consideration in juvenile proceedings, which for certain purposes have been distinguished from formal criminal prosecutions. We do not decide that is-

whether that court's conclusion so to extend *Miranda* is in harmony with *Miranda's* underlying principles. For it is clear that "a State may not impose . . . greater restrictions as a matter of federal constitutional law when this Court specifically refrains from imposing them."

The rule the Court established in *Miranda* is clear. In order to be able to use statements obtained during custodial interrogation of the accused, the State must warn the accused prior to such questioning of his right to remain silent and of his right to have counsel, retained or appointed, present during interrogation. "Once [such] warnings have been given, the subsequent procedure is clear."

> "If the individual indicates in any manner, at any time prior to or during questioning, that he wishes to remain silent, the interrogation must cease. At this point he has shown that he intends to exercise his Fifth Amendment privilege; any statement taken after the person invokes his privilege cannot be other than the product of compulsion, subtle or otherwise. . . . If the individual states that he wants an attorney, the interrogation must cease until an attorney is present. At that time, the individual must have an opportunity to confer with the attorney and to have him present during any subsequent questioning. If the individual cannot obtain an attorney and he indicates that he wants one before speaking to police, they must respect his decision to remain silent."

Any statements obtained during custodial interrogation conducted in violation of these rules may not be admitted against the accused, at least during the State's case in chief. . . .

The rule in *Miranda*, however, was based on this Court's perception that the lawyer occupies a critical position in our legal system because of his unique ability to protect the Fifth Amendment rights of a client undergoing custodial interrogation. Because of this special ability of the lawyer to help the client preserve his Fifth Amendment rights once the client becomes enmeshed in the adversary process, the Court found that "the right to have counsel present at the interrogation is indispensable to the protection of the Fifth Amendment privilege under the system" established by the Court. Moreover, the lawyer's presence helps guard against overreaching by the police and ensures that any statements actually obtained are accurately transcribed for presentation into evidence. . . .

A probation officer is not in the same posture with regard to either the accused or the system of justice as a whole. Often he is not trained in the law, and so is not in a position to advise the accused as to his legal rights. Neither is he a trained advocate, skilled in the representation of the interests of his client before both police and courts. He does not assume the power to act on behalf of his client by virtue of his status as adviser, nor are the communications of the accused to the probation officer shielded by the lawyer–client privilege.

Moreover, the probation officer is the employee of the State which seeks to prosecute the alleged offender. He is a peace officer, and as such is allied, to a greater or lesser extent, with his fellow peace officers. He owes an obligation to the State, notwithstanding the obligation he may also owe the juvenile under his supervision. In most cases, the probation offi-

---

sue today. In view of our disposition of this case, we assume without deciding that the *Miranda* principles were fully applicable to the present proceedings.

cer is duty bound to report wrongdoing by the juvenile when it comes to his attention, even if by communication from the juvenile himself. Indeed, when this case arose, the probation officer had the responsibility for filing the petition alleging wrongdoing by the juvenile and seeking to have him taken into the custody of the Juvenile Court. It was respondent's probation officer who filed the petition against him, and it is the acting chief of probation for the State of California, a probation officer, who is petitioner in this Court today.

In these circumstances, it cannot be said that the probation officer is able to offer the type of independent advice that an accused would expect from a lawyer retained or assigned to assist him during questioning. Indeed, the probation officer's duty to his employer in many, if not most, cases would conflict sharply with the interests of the juvenile. For where an attorney might well advise his client to remain silent in the face of interrogation by the police, and in doing so would be "exercising [his] good professional judgment . . . to protect to the extent of his ability the rights of his client," a probation officer would be bound to advise his charge to cooperate with the police. . . .

By the same token, a lawyer is able to protect his client's rights by learning the extent, if any, of the client's involvement in the crime under investigation, and advising his client accordingly. To facilitate this, the law rightly protects the communications between client and attorney from discovery. We doubt, however, that similar protection will be afforded the communications between the probation officer and the minor. Indeed, we doubt that a probation officer, consistent with his responsibilities to the public and his profession, could withhold from the police or the courts facts made known to him by the juvenile implicating the juvenile in the crime under investigation.

We thus believe it clear that the probation officer is not in a position to offer the type of legal assistance necessary to protect the Fifth Amendment rights of an accused undergoing custodial interrogation that a lawyer can offer. . . . A probation officer simply is not necessary, in the way an attorney is, for the protection of the legal rights of the accused, juvenile or adult. He is significantly handicapped by the position he occupies in the juvenile system from serving as an effective protector of the rights of a juvenile suspected of a crime. . . .

Nor do we believe that a request by a juvenile to speak with his probation officer constitutes a *per se* request to remain silent. As indicated, since a probation officer does not fulfill the important role in protecting the rights of the accused juvenile that an attorney plays, we decline to find that the request for the probation officer is tantamount to the request for an attorney. And there is nothing inherent in the request for a probation officer that requires us to find that a juvenile's request to see one necessarily constitutes an expression of the juvenile's right to remain silent. As discussed below, courts may take into account such a request in evaluating whether a juvenile in fact had waived his Fifth Amendment rights before confessing. But in other circumstances such a request might well be consistent with a desire to speak with the police. In the absence of further evidence that the minor intended in the circumstances to invoke his Fifth Amendment rights by such a request, we decline to attach such overwhelming significance to this request.

We hold, therefore, that it was error to find that the request by respondent to speak with his probation officer *per se* constituted an invocation of respondent's Fifth Amendment right to be free from compelled self-incrimination. It therefore was also error to hold that because the police did not then cease interrogating respondent the statements he made during interrogation should have been suppressed.

III.

Miranda further recognized that after the required warnings are given the accused, "[i]f the interrogation continues without the presence of an attorney and a statement is taken, a heavy burden rests on the government to demonstrate that the defendant knowingly and intelligently waived his privilege against self-incrimination and his right to retained or appointed counsel." We noted in *North Carolina v. Butler* that the question whether the accused waived his rights "is not one of form, but rather whether the defendant in fact knowingly and voluntarily waived the rights delineated in the *Miranda* case." Thus, the determination whether statements obtained during custodial interrogation are admissible against the accused is to be made upon an inquiry into the totality of the circumstances surrounding the interrogation, to ascertain whether the accused in fact knowingly and voluntarily decided to forgo his rights to remain silent and to have the assistance of counsel. . . .

. . .Where the age and experience of a juvenile indicate that his request for his probation officer or his parents is, in fact, an invocation of his right to remain silent, the totality approach will allow the court the necessary flexibility to take this into account in making a waiver determination. At the same time, that approach refrains from imposing rigid restraints on police and courts in dealing with an experienced older juvenile with an extensive prior record who knowingly and intelligently waives his Fifth Amendment rights and voluntarily consents to interrogation.

In this case, we conclude that the California Supreme Court should have determined the issue of waiver on the basis of all the circumstances surrounding the interrogation of respondent. . . .

. . .The transcript of the interrogation reveals that the police officers conducting the interrogation took care to ensure that respondent understood his rights. They fully explained to respondent that he was being questioned in connection with a murder. They then informed him of all the rights delineated in *Miranda*, and ascertained that respondent understood those rights. There is no indication in the record that respondent failed to understand what the officers told him. Moreover, after his request to see his probation officer had been denied, and after the police officer once more had explained his rights to him, respondent clearly expressed his willingness to waive his rights and continue the interrogation.

Further, no special factors indicate that respondent was unable to understand the nature of his actions. He was a 16½-year-old juvenile with considerable experience with the police. He had a record of several arrests. He had served time in a youth camp, and he had been on probation for several years. He was under the full-time supervision of probation authorities. There is no indication that he was of insufficient intelligence to understand the rights he was waiving, or what the consequences of that waiver would be. He was not worn down by improper interrogation tactics or lengthy questioning or by trickery or deceit.

On these facts, we think it clear that respondent voluntarily and knowingly waived his Fifth Amendment rights. Respondent argues, however, that any statements he made during interrogation were coerced. . . .

Review of the entire transcript reveals that respondent's claims of coercion are without merit. As noted, the police took care to inform respondent of his rights and to ensure that he understood them. The officers did not intimidate or threaten respondent in any way. Their questioning was restrained and free from the abuses that so concerned the Court in *Miranda*. The police did indeed indicate that a cooperative attitude would be to respondent's benefit, but their remarks in this regard were far from threatening or coercive. And respondent's allegation that he repeatedly asked that the interrogation cease goes too far: at some points he did state that he did not know the answer to a question put to him or that he could not, or would not, answer the question, but these statements were not assertions of his right to remain silent.

IV.

We hold, in short, that the California Supreme Court erred in finding that a juvenile's request for his probation officer was a *per se* invocation of that juvenile's Fifth Amendment rights under *Miranda*. We conclude, rather, that whether the statements obtained during subsequent interrogation of a juvenile who has asked to see his probation officer, but who has not asked to consult an attorney or expressly asserted his right to remain silent, are admissible on the basis of waiver remain a question to be resolved on the totality of the circumstances surrounding the interrogation. On the basis of the record in this case, we hold that the Juvenile Court's findings that respondent voluntarily and knowingly waived his rights and consented to continued interrogation, and that the statements obtained from him were voluntary, were proper, and that the admission of those statements in the proceeding against respondent in Juvenile Court was correct.

The judgment of the Supreme Court of California is reversed, and the case is remanded for further proceedings not inconsistent with this opinion.

It is so ordered.

Mr. Justice Marshall, with whom Mr. Justice Brennan and Mr. Justice Stevens join, dissenting. . . .

. . . I believe *Miranda* requires that interrogation cease whenever a juvenile requests an adult who is obligated to represent his interests. Such a request, in my judgment, constitutes both an attempt to obtain advice and a general invocation of the right to silence. . . . A juvenile in these circumstances will likely turn to his parents, or another adult responsible for his welfare, as the only means of securing legal counsel. Moreover, a request for such adult assistance is surely inconsistent with a present desire to speak freely. . . .

On my reading of *Miranda*, a California juvenile's request for his probation officer should be treated as a *per se* assertion of Fifth Amendment rights. . . .

Mr. Justice Powell, dissenting.

Although I agree with the Court that the Supreme Court of California misconstrued *Miranda v. Arizona*, I would not reverse the California court's judgment. This Court repeatedly has recognized that "the greatest care" must be taken to assure that an alleged confession of a juvenile was voluntary. Respondent was a young person, 16 years old at the time of his arrest and the subsequent prolonged interrogation at the station house. Although respondent had had prior brushes with the law, and was under supervision by a probation officer, the taped transcript of his interrogation—as well as his testimony at the suppression hearing—demonstrates that he was immature, emotional, and uneducated, and therefore was likely to be vulnerable to the skillful, two-on-one, repetitive style of interrogation to which he was subjected.

When given *Miranda* warnings and asked whether he desired an attorney, respondent requested permission to "have my probation officer here," a request that was refused. That officer testified later that he had communicated frequently with respondent, that respondent had serious and "extensive" family problems, and that the officer had instructed respondent to call him immediately "at any time he has a police contact, even if they stop him and talk to him on the street." The reasons given by the probation officer for having so instructed his charge were substantially the same reasons that prompt this Court to examine with special care the circumstances under which a minor's alleged confession was obtained. After stating that respondent had been "going through problems," the officer observed that "many times the kids don't understand what is going on, and what they are supposed to do relative to police. . . ." This view of the limited understanding of the average 16-year-old was borne out by respondent's question when, during interrogation, he was advised of his right to an attorney: "How I know you guys won't pull no police officer in and tell me he's an attorney?" It was during this part of the interrogation that the police had denied respondent's request to "have my probation officer here."

The police then proceeded, despite respondent's repeated denial of any connection to the murder under investigation, persistently to press interrogation until they extracted a confession. In *In re Gault*, in addressing police interrogation of detained juveniles, the Court stated:

> "If counsel was not present for some permissible reason when an admission was obtained [from a child], the greatest care must be taken to assure that the admission was voluntary, in the sense not only that it was not coerced or suggested, but also that it was not the product of ignorance of rights or of adolescent fantasy, fright or despair."

It is clear that the interrogating police did not exercise "the greatest care" to assure that respondent's "admission was voluntary." In the absence of counsel, and having refused to call the probation officer, they nevertheless engaged in protracted interrogation.

Although I view the case as close, I am not satisfied that this particular 16-year-old boy, in this particular situation, was subjected to a fair interrogation free from inherently coercive circumstances. For these reasons, I would affirm the judgment of the Supreme Court of California.

REVIEW QUESTIONS

1. Why does the Court say that a probation officer cannot protect a juvenile's rights during interrogation the way an attorney would?

2. How does the Court say the determination should be made as to whether a juvenile has asserted his or her right to remain silent?

3. Do you think Michael C. should have been allowed to have his probation officer present during the interrogation? If not, do you think an attorney—or Michael C.'s parents—should have been called? Or should the police have stopped questioning him? Do you think he "invoked" his right to counsel when he asked for his probation officer? His right against self-incrimination?

4. Compare Justice Blackmun's comments about the probation officer's inability to fulfill the role of an attorney during interrogation with Justice Fortas' discussion in *Gault* of the probation officer's inability to protect the youth's interests in court (see pp. 95-96). Is Justice Blackmun's argument consistent with the decision in *Gault*? Would a different outcome (i.e., holding that Michael C. *did* have a right to have his probation officer present) have been consistent with *Gault*? Do you think the decisions in the *Gault* and *Michael C.* cases provided equally satisfactory mechanisms for safeguarding the rights of accused delinquents at the respective stages of the juvenile justice process? Why or why not?

Procedures Applicable to the Interrogation of Juveniles

National Advisory Committee for Juvenile Justice and Delinquency Prevention

Juveniles accused of committing a delinquent offense or engaging in noncriminal misbehavior should not be questioned regarding such offenses or such conduct, and formal oral or written statements by those juveniles should not be accepted, unless it has been explained in language understandable by the juvenile:

a. That the juvenile has a right to remain silent;

b. That any statement which the juvenile makes may be used against him/her in a subsequent court proceeding;

Source: National Advisory Committee for Juvenile Justice and Delinquency Prevention. (1980). *Standards for the Administration of Juvenile Justice.* Washington, DC: U.S. Government Printing Office. Adapted courtesy of the United States Department of Justice, Office of Juvenile Justice and Delinquency Prevention.

   c. That the juvenile has a right to have an attorney present;

   d. That the juvenile has a right to have an attorney appointed when any of the circumstances listed in Standard 3.132 apply [i.e., whenever counsel is not retained, an "adverse interest" exists between child and parent, or the interests of justice require appointment of independent counsel—Ed.];

   e. That the juvenile has a right to have present his/her parent, guardian, or primary caretaker, or another adult who is within a reasonable distance and with whom the juvenile has substantial ties; and

   f. That the juvenile has a right to stop answering questions at any time.

No statement made by any juvenile while in the custody of a law enforcement officer shall be admissible against the juvenile as part of the government's case-in-chief, unless such statement was made either in the presence of a parent or other adult described in paragraph (e) above or in the presence of the juvenile's attorney.

     Before accepting a formal written or oral statement from a juvenile, law enforcement officers or other public officials working in their behalf should assure that the juvenile fully understands the matters explained and that the statement is voluntary, not only in the sense that it is not coerced or suggested, but also that it is not the product of adolescent fantasy, fright, or despair.

REVIEW QUESTIONS

1. Do the guidelines in this standard provide fundamentally different criteria for assessing the reasonableness of police interrogation of juveniles than the Supreme Court's decision in *Fare v. Michael C.*?

2. The standard specifies a right to the presence of both an attorney and a parent, guardian, or other adult "with whom the juvenile has substantial ties" during interrogation. Do you think a juvenile should always be allowed to have a parent present during interrogation? Why or why not?

3. The standard also permits use in court of statements made in the presence of a parent or other supportive adult even if an attorney is not present. Do you think having a parent present during interrogation would protect the rights of a juvenile suspect better than a probation officer would? As well as an attorney would? Would it be better to *require* the presence of an attorney during interrogation?

4. In what ways does this standard address the concerns raised by Scott and Grisso in Chapter 1 about the impact of developmental factors on the ability of adolescents to understand their rights and make rational decisions about waiving them? To what extent do you think it alleviates those concerns?

5. All things considered, do you think this standard provides a sounder foundation for safeguarding juveniles' rights during interrogation than the "totality of circumstances" approach taken by the Supreme Court in *Fare v. Michael C?* Why or why not?

New Jersey v. T.L.O.

The Supreme Court of the United States
469 U.S. 325 (1985)

Justice White delivered the opinion of the Court. . . .

I.

On March 7, 1980, a teacher at Piscataway High School in Middlesex County, N.J., discovered two girls smoking in a lavatory. One of the two girls was the respondent T.L.O., who at that time was a 14-year-old high school freshman. Because smoking in the lavatory was a violation of a school rule, the teacher took the two girls to the Principal's office, where they met with Assistant Vice Principal Theodore Choplick. In response to questioning by Mr. Choplick, T.L.O.'s companion admitted that she had violated the rule. T.L.O., however, denied that she had been smoking in the lavatory and claimed that she did not smoke at all.

Mr. Choplick asked T.L.O. to come into his private office and demanded to see her purse. Opening the purse, he found a pack of cigarettes, which he removed from the purse and held before T.L.O. as he accused her of having lied to him. As he reached into the purse for the cigarettes, Mr. Choplick also noticed a package of cigarette rolling papers. In his experience, possession of rolling papers by high school students was closely associated with the use of marihuana. Suspecting that a closer examination of the purse might yield further evidence of drug use, Mr. Choplick proceeded to search the purse thoroughly. The search revealed a small amount of marihuana, a pipe, a number of empty plastic bags, a substantial quantity of money in one-dollar bills, an index card that appeared to be a list of students who owed T.L.O. money, and two letters that implicated T.L.O. in marihuana dealing.

Mr. Choplick notified T.L.O.'s mother and the police, and turned the evidence of drug dealing over to the police. At the request of the police, T.L.O.'s mother took her daughter to police headquarters, where T.L.O. confessed that she had been selling marihuana at the high school. On the basis of the confession and the evidence seized by Mr. Choplick, the State brought delinquency charges against T.L.O. in the Juvenile and Domestic Relations Court of Middlesex County. Contending that Mr. Choplick's search of her purse violated the Fourth Amendment, T.L.O. moved to suppress the evidence found in her purse as well as her confession, which, she argued, was tainted by the allegedly unlawful search. The Juvenile Court denied the motion to suppress. Although the court concluded that the Fourth Amendment did apply to searches carried out by school officials, it held that "a school official may properly conduct a search of a student's person if the official has a reasonable suspicion that a crime has been or is in the process of being committed, or reasonable cause to believe that the search is necessary to maintain school discipline or enforce school policies."

Applying this standard, the court concluded that the search conducted by Mr. Choplick was a reasonable one. . . .

On appeal from the final judgment of the Juvenile Court, a divided Appellate Division affirmed the trial court's finding that there had been no Fourth Amendment violation, but vacated the adjudication of delinquency and remanded for a determination whether T.L.O. had knowingly and voluntarily waived her Fifth Amendment rights before confessing. T.L.O. appealed the Fourth Amendment ruling, and the Supreme Court of New Jersey reversed the judgment of the Appellate Division and ordered the suppression of the evidence found in T.L.O.'s purse. . . .

 Although we originally granted certiorari to decide the issue of the appropriate remedy in juvenile court proceedings for unlawful school searches, our doubts regarding the wisdom of deciding that question in isolation from the broader question of what limits, if any, the Fourth Amendment places on the activities of school authorities prompted us to order reargument on that question. Having heard argument on the legality of the search of T.L.O.'s purse, we are satisfied that the search did not violate the Fourth Amendment.

II.

 In determining whether the search at issue in this case violated the Fourth Amendment, we are faced initially with the question whether that Amendment's prohibition on unreasonable searches and seizures applies to searches conducted by public school officials. We hold that it does.

It is now beyond dispute that "the Federal Constitution, by virtue of the Fourteenth Amendment, prohibits unreasonable searches and seizures by state officers." Equally indisputable is the proposition that the Fourteenth Amendment protects the rights of students against encroachment by public school officials. . . .

. . .Today's public school officials do not merely exercise authority voluntarily conferred on them by individual parents; rather, they act in furtherance of publicly mandated educational and disciplinary policies. In carrying out searches and other disciplinary functions pursuant to such policies, school officials act as representatives of the State, not merely as surrogates for the parents, and they cannot claim the parents' immunity from the strictures of the Fourth Amendment.

III.

To hold that the Fourth Amendment applies to searches conducted by school authorities is only to begin the inquiry into the standards governing such searches. Although the underlying command of the Fourth Amendment is always that searches and seizures be reasonable, what is reasonable depends on the context within which a search takes place. The determination of the standard of reasonableness governing any specific class of searches requires "balancing the need to search against the invasion which the search entails." On one side of the balance are arrayed the individual's legitimate expectations of privacy and personal security; on the other, the government's need for effective methods to deal with breaches of public order. . . .

How, then, should we strike the balance between the schoolchild's legitimate expectations of privacy and the school's equally legitimate need to maintain an environment in which learning can take place? It is evident that the school setting requires some easing of the restrictions to which searches by public authorities are ordinarily subject. The warrant requirement, in particular, is unsuited to the school environment: requiring a teacher to obtain a warrant before searching a child suspected of an infraction of school rules (or of the criminal law) would unduly interfere with the maintenance of the swift and informal disciplinary procedures needed in the schools. Just as we have in other cases dispensed with the warrant requirement when "the burden of obtaining a warrant is likely to frustrate the governmental purpose behind the search," we hold today that school officials need not obtain a warrant before searching a student who is under their authority.

The school setting also requires some modification of the level of suspicion of illicit activity needed to justify a search. Ordinarily, a search—even one that may permissibly be carried out without a warrant—must be based upon "probable cause" to believe that a violation of the law has occurred. However, "probable cause" is not an irreducible requirement of a valid search. The fundamental command of the Fourth Amendment is that searches and seizures be reasonable, and although "both the concept of probable cause and the requirement of a warrant bear on the reasonableness of a search, . . . in certain limited circumstances neither is required.". . . Where a careful balancing of governmental and private interests suggests that the public interest is best served by a Fourth Amendment standard of reasonableness that stops short of probable cause, we have not hesitated to adopt such a standard.

We join the majority of courts that have examined this issue in concluding that the accommodation of the privacy interests of schoolchildren with the substantial need of teachers and administrators for freedom to maintain order in the schools does not require strict adherence to the requirement that searches be based on probable cause to believe that the subject of the search has violated or is violating the law. Rather, the legality of a search of a student should depend simply on the reasonableness, under all the circumstances, of the search. Determining the reasonableness of any search involves a twofold inquiry: first, one must consider "whether the . . . action was justified at its inception"; second, one must determine whether the search as actually conducted "was reasonably related in scope to the circumstances which justified the interference in the first place." Under ordinary circumstances, a search of a student by a teacher or other school official[1] will be "justified at its

---

[1]We here consider only searches carried out by school authorities acting alone and on their own authority. This case does not present the question of the appropriate standard for assessing the legality of searches conducted by school officials in conjunction with or at the behest of law enforcement agencies, and we express no opinion on that question.

inception" when there are reasonable grounds for suspecting that the search will turn up evidence that the student has violated or is violating either the law or the rules of the school.[2] Such a search will be permissible in its scope when the measures adopted are reasonably related to the objectives of the search and not excessively intrusive in light of the age and sex of the student and the nature of the infraction. . . .

IV.

There remains the question of the legality of the search in this case. . . . Our review of the facts surrounding the search leads us to conclude that the search was in no sense unreasonable for Fourth Amendment purposes.

The incident that gave rise to this case actually involved two separate searches, with the first—the search for cigarettes—providing the suspicion that gave rise to the second—the search for marihuana. Although it is the fruits of the second search that are at issue here, the validity of the search for marihuana must depend on the reasonableness of the initial search for cigarettes, as there would have been no reason to suspect that T.L.O. possessed marihuana had the first search not taken place. Accordingly, it is to the search for cigarettes that we first turn our attention.

The New Jersey Supreme Court pointed to two grounds for its holding that the search for cigarettes was unreasonable. First, the court observed that possession of cigarettes was not in itself illegal or a violation of school rules. Because the contents of T.L.O.'s purse would therefore have "no direct bearing on the infraction" of which she was accused (smoking in a lavatory where smoking was prohibited), there was no reason to search her purse. Second, even assuming that a search of T.L.O.'s purse might under some circumstances be reasonable in light of the accusation made against T.L.O., the New Jersey court concluded that Mr. Choplick in this particular case had no reasonable grounds to suspect that T.L.O. had cigarettes in her purse. At best, according to the court, Mr. Choplick had "a good hunch."

Both these conclusions are implausible. T.L.O. had been accused of smoking, and had denied the accusation in the strongest possible terms when she stated that she did not smoke at all. Surely it cannot be said that under these circumstances, T.L.O.'s possession of cigarettes would be irrelevant to the charges against her or to her response to those charges. T.L.O.'s possession of cigarettes, once it was discovered, would both corroborate the report that she had been smoking and undermine the credibility of her defense to the charge of smoking. To be sure, the discovery of the cigarettes would not prove that T.L.O. had been smoking in the lavatory; nor would it, strictly speaking, necessarily be inconsistent with her claim that she did not smoke at all. But it is universally recognized that evidence, to be rel-

---

[2]We do not decide whether individualized suspicion is an essential element of the reasonableness standard we adopt for searches by school authorities. . . . Because the search of T.L.O.'s purse was based upon an individualized suspicion that she had violated school rules, we need not consider the circumstances that might justify school authorities in conducting searches unsupported by individualized suspicion.

evant to an inquiry, need not conclusively prove the ultimate fact in issue, but only have "any tendency to make the existence of any fact that is of consequence to the determination of the action more probable or less probable than it would be without the evidence." The relevance of T.L.O.'s possession of cigarettes to the question whether she had been smoking and to the credibility of her denial that she smoked supplied the necessary "nexus" between the item searched for and the infraction under investigation. Thus, if Mr. Choplick in fact had a reasonable suspicion that T.L.O. had cigarettes in her purse, the search was justified despite the fact that the cigarettes, if found, would constitute "mere evidence" of a violation.

Of course, the New Jersey Supreme Court also held that Mr. Choplick had no reasonable suspicion that the purse would contain cigarettes. This conclusion is puzzling. A teacher had reported that T.L.O. was smoking in the lavatory. Certainly this report gave Mr. Choplick reason to suspect that T.L.O. was carrying cigarettes with her; and if she did have cigarettes, her purse was the obvious place in which to find them. Mr. Choplick's suspicion that there were cigarettes in the purse was not an "inchoate and unparticularized suspicion or 'hunch'"; rather, it was the sort of "common-sense conclusio[n] about human behavior" upon which "practical people"—including government officials—are entitled to rely. . . . Accordingly, it cannot be said that Mr. Choplick acted unreasonably when he examined T.L.O.'s purse to see if it contained cigarettes.

Our conclusion that Mr. Choplick's decision to open T.L.O.'s purse was reasonable brings us to the question of the further search for marihuana once the pack of cigarettes was located. The suspicion upon which the search for marihuana was founded was provided when Mr. Choplick observed a package of rolling papers in the purse as he removed the pack of cigarettes. Although T.L.O. does not dispute the reasonableness of Mr. Choplick's belief that the rolling papers indicated the presence of marihuana, she does contend that the scope of the search Mr. Choplick conducted exceeded permissible bounds when he seized and read certain letters that implicated T.L.O. in drug dealing. This argument, too, is unpersuasive. The discovery of the rolling papers concededly gave rise to a reasonable suspicion that T.L.O. was carrying marihuana as well as cigarettes in her purse. This suspicion justified further exploration of T.L.O.'s purse, which turned up more evidence of drug-related activities: a pipe, a number of plastic bags of the type commonly used to store marihuana, a small quantity of marihuana, and a fairly substantial amount of money. Under these circumstances, it was not unreasonable to extend the search to a separate zippered compartment of the purse; and when a search of that compartment revealed an index card containing a list of "people who owe me money" as well as two letters, the inference that T.L.O. was involved in marihuana trafficking was substantial enough to justify Mr. Choplick in examining the letters to determine whether they contained any further evidence. In short, we cannot conclude that the search for marihuana was unreasonable in any respect.

Because the search resulting in the discovery of the evidence of marihuana dealing by T.L.O. was reasonable, the New Jersey Supreme Court's decision to exclude that evidence from T.L.O.'s juvenile delinquency proceedings on Fourth Amendment grounds was erroneous. Accordingly, the judgment of the Supreme Court of New Jersey is

Reversed.

JUSTICE POWELL, with whom JUSTICE O'CONNOR joins, concurring. [omitted—*Ed.*]

JUSTICE BLACKMUN, concurring in the judgment. [omitted—*Ed.*]

JUSTICE BRENNAN, with whom JUSTICE MARSHALL joins, concurring in part and dissenting in part.

I fully agree with Part II of the Court's opinion. Teachers, like all other government officials, must conform their conduct to the Fourth Amendment's protections of personal privacy and personal security. . . .

I do not, however, otherwise join the Court's opinion. Today's decision sanctions school officials to conduct full-scale searches on a "reasonableness" standard whose only definite content is that it is not the same test as the "probable cause" standard found in the text of the Fourth Amendment. In adopting this unclear, unprecedented, and unnecessary departure from generally applicable Fourth Amendment standards, the Court carves out a broad exception to standards that this Court has developed over years of considering Fourth Amendment problems. Its decision is supported neither by precedent nor even by a fair application of the "balancing test" it proclaims in this very opinion. . . .

I emphatically disagree with the Court's decision to cast aside the constitutional probable-cause standard when assessing the constitutional validity of a schoolhouse search. The Court's decision jettisons the probable-cause standard—the only standard that finds support in the text of the Fourth Amendment—on the basis of its Rorschach-like "balancing test." Use of such a "balancing test" to determine the standard for evaluating the validity of a full-scale search represents a sizable innovation in Fourth Amendment analysis. This innovation finds support neither in precedent nor policy and portends a dangerous weakening of the purpose of the Fourth Amendment to protect the privacy and security of our citizens. Moreover, even if this Court's historic understanding of the Fourth Amendment were mistaken and a balancing test of some kind were appropriate, any such test that gave adequate weight to the privacy and security interests protected by the Fourth Amendment would not reach the preordained result the Court's conclusory analysis reaches today. Therefore, because I believe that the balancing test used by the Court today is flawed both in its inception and in its execution, I respectfully dissent. . . .

JUSTICE STEVENS, with whom JUSTICE MARSHALL joins, and with whom JUSTICE BRENNAN joins as to Part I, concurring in part and dissenting in part. . . .

. . . Although I join Part II of the Court's opinion, I continue to believe that the Court has unnecessarily and inappropriately reached out to decide a constitutional question. More importantly, I fear that the concerns that motivated the Court's activism have produced a holding that will permit school administrators to search students suspected of violating only the most trivial school regulations and guidelines for behavior. . . .

The majority . . . does not contend that school administrators have a compelling need to search students in order to achieve optimum enforcement of minor school regulations. To the contrary, when minor violations are involved, there is every indication that the informal school disciplinary process, with only minimum requirements of due process, can function effectively without the power to search for enough evidence to prove a criminal case. In arguing that teachers and school administrators need the power to search students based on a lessened standard, the United States as *amicus curiae* relies heavily on empirical evidence of a contemporary crisis of violence and unlawful behavior that is seriously undermining the process of education in American schools. A standard better attuned to this concern would permit teachers and school administrators to search a student when they have reason to believe that the search will uncover evidence that the student is violating the law or engaging in conduct that is seriously disruptive of school order, or the educational process. . . .

Like the New Jersey Supreme Court, I would view this case differently if the Assistant Vice Principal had reason to believe T.L.O.'s purse contained evidence of criminal activity, or of an activity that would seriously disrupt school discipline. There was, however, absolutely no basis for any such assumption—not even a "hunch."

In this case, Mr. Choplick overreacted to what appeared to be nothing more than a minor infraction—a rule prohibiting smoking in the bathroom of the freshmen's and sophomores' building. It is, of course, true that he actually found evidence of serious wrongdoing by T.L.O., but no one claims that the prior search may be justified by his unexpected discovery. As far as the smoking infraction is concerned, the search for cigarettes merely tended to corroborate a teacher's eyewitness account of T.L.O.'s violation of a minor regulation designed to channel student smoking behavior into designated locations. Because this conduct was neither unlawful nor significantly disruptive of school order or the educational process, the invasion of privacy associated with the forcible opening of T.L.O.'s purse was entirely unjustified at its inception.

A review of the sampling of school search cases relied on by the Court demonstrates how different this case is from those in which there was indeed a valid justification for intruding on a student's privacy. In most of them the student was suspected of a criminal violation; in the remainder either violence or substantial disruption of school order or the integrity of the academic process was at stake. Few involved matters as trivial as the no-smoking rule violated by T.L.O. The rule the Court adopts today is so openended that it may make the Fourth Amendment virtually meaningless in the school context. Although I agree that school administrators must have broad latitude to maintain order and discipline in our classrooms, that authority is not unlimited. . . .

I respectfully dissent.

REVIEW QUESTIONS

1. What considerations did the Court take into account in trying to decide whether the search of T.L.O.'s purse violated her Fourth Amendment right against unreasonable search and seizure? How important was the setting (i.e., a public school)? How important was the scope of the search? Did the nature of the offense T.L.O. was suspected of committing make a difference?

2. Did the court decide that the search for cigarettes was Constitutional? What about the search for marijuana? What was the Court's rationale for its decision with respect to each of these phases of the search of T.L.O.'s purse?

3. Do you agree with the Court's decision in this case? Why or why not?

4. How compelling do you find Justice Stevens' argument that a search such as the one performed in this case should be permissible only if a more serious offense or rule violation were suspected?

5. Do you think the Court's view of the case would have been different if the search had been conducted by a police officer rather than the school's assistant vice principal? Why or why not?

Vernonia School District 47J v. Acton

The Supreme Court of the United States
515 U.S. 646 (1995)

JUSTICE SCALIA delivered the opinion of the Court.

The Student Athlete Drug Policy adopted by School District 47J in the town of Vernonia, Oregon, authorizes random urinalysis drug testing of students who participate in the District's school athletics programs. We granted certiorari to decide whether this violates the Fourth and Fourteenth Amendments to the United States Constitution. . . .

Fourth Amendment rights, no less than First and Fourteenth Amendment rights, are different in public schools than elsewhere; the "reasonableness" inquiry cannot disregard the schools' custodial and tutelary responsibility for children. For their own good and that of their classmates, public school children are routinely required to submit to various physical examinations, and to be vaccinated against various diseases. . . . Particularly with regard to medical examinations and procedures, therefore, "students within the school environment have a lesser expectation of privacy than members of the population generally."

Legitimate privacy expectations are even less with regard to student athletes. School sports are not for the bashful. They require "suiting up" before each practice or event, and showering and changing afterwards. Public school locker rooms, the usual sites for these activities, are not notable for the privacy they afford. The locker rooms in Vernonia are typical: no individual dressing rooms are provided; shower heads are lined up along a wall, unseparated by any sort of partition or curtain; not even all the toilet stalls have doors. As the United States Court of Appeals for the Seventh Circuit has noted, there is "an element of 'communal undress' inherent in athletic participation."

There is an additional respect in which school athletes have a reduced expectation of privacy. By choosing to "go out for the team," they voluntarily subject themselves to a degree of regulation even higher than that imposed on students generally. In Vernonia's public schools, they must submit to a preseason physical exam (James testified that his included the giving of a urine sample), they must acquire adequate insurance coverage or sign an insurance waiver, maintain a minimum grade point average, and comply with any "rules of conduct, dress, training hours and related matters as may be established for each sport by the head coach and athletic director with the principal's approval." Somewhat like adults who choose to participate in a "closely regulated industry," students who voluntarily participate in school athletics have reason to expect intrusions upon normal rights and privileges, including privacy.

Having considered the scope of the legitimate expectation of privacy at issue here, we turn next to the character of the intrusion that is complained of. We recognized in *Skinner* [*v. Railway Labor Executives' Assn.—Ed.*] that collecting the samples for urinalysis intrudes upon "an excretory function traditionally shielded by great privacy." We noted, however, that the degree of intrusion depends upon the manner in which production of the urine sample is monitored. Under the District's Policy, male students produce samples at a urinal along a wall. They remain fully clothed and are only observed from behind, if at all. Female students produce samples in an enclosed stall, with a female monitor standing outside listening only for sounds of tampering. These conditions are nearly identical to those typically encountered in public restrooms, which men, women, and especially school children use daily. Under such conditions, the privacy interests compromised by the process of obtaining the urine sample are in our view negligible.

The other privacy-invasive aspect of urinalysis is, of course, the information it discloses concerning the state of the subject's body, and the materials he has ingested. In this regard it is significant that the tests at issue here look only for drugs, and not for whether the student is, for example, epileptic, pregnant, or diabetic. Moreover, the drugs for which the samples are screened are standard, and do not vary according to the identity of the student. And finally, the results of the tests are disclosed only to a limited class of school personnel who have a need to know; and they are not turned over to law enforcement authorities or used for any internal disciplinary function. . . .

Finally, we turn to consider the nature and immediacy of the governmental concern at issue here, and the efficacy of this means for meeting it. . . .

That the nature of the concern is important—indeed, perhaps compelling—can hardly be doubted. . . . School years are the time when the physical, psychological, and addictive effects of drugs are most severe. "Maturing nervous systems are more critically impaired by intoxicants than mature ones are; childhood losses in learning are lifelong and profound"; "children grow chemically dependent more quickly than adults, and their record of recovery is depressingly poor." And of course the effects of a drug-infested school are visited not just upon the users, but upon the entire student body and faculty, as the educational process is disrupted. In the present case, moreover, the necessity for the State to act is magnified by the fact that this evil is being visited not just upon individuals at large, but upon children for whom it has undertaken a special responsibility of care and direction. Finally, it must not be lost sight of that this program is directed more narrowly to drug use by school athletes, where the risk of immediate physical harm to the drug user or those with whom he is playing his sport is particularly high. . . .

As for the immediacy of the District's concerns: We are not inclined to question—indeed, we could not possibly find clearly erroneous—the District Court's conclusion that "a large segment of the student body, particularly those involved in interscholastic athletics, was in a state of rebellion," that "[d]isciplinary actions had reached 'epidemic proportions,'" and that "the rebellion was being fueled by alcohol and drug abuse as well as by the student's misperceptions about the drug culture."

As to the efficacy of this means for addressing the problem: It seems to us self-evident that a drug problem largely fueled by the "role model" effect of athletes' drug use, and of particular danger to athletes, is effectively addressed by making sure that athletes do not use drugs. Respondents argue that a "less intrusive means to the same end" was available, namely, "drug testing on suspicion of drug use." We have repeatedly refused to declare that only the "least intrusive" search practicable can be reasonable under the Fourth Amendment. Respondents' alternative entails substantial difficulties—if it is indeed practicable at all. It may be impracticable, for one thing, simply because the parents who are willing to accept random drug testing for athletes are not willing to accept accusatory drug testing for all students, which transforms the process into a badge of shame. Respondents' proposal brings the risk that teachers will impose testing arbitrarily upon troublesome but not drug-likely students. It generates the expense of defending lawsuits that charge such arbitrary imposition, or that simply demand greater process before accusatory drug testing is imposed. And not least of all, it adds to the ever-expanding diversionary duties of schoolteachers the new function of spotting and bringing to account drug abuse, a task for which they are ill prepared, and which is not readily compatible with their vocation. In many respects, we think, testing based on "suspicion" of drug use would not be better, but worse.

Taking into account all the factors we have considered above—the decreased expectation of privacy, the relative unobtrusiveness of the search, and the severity of the need met by the search—we conclude Vernonia's Policy is reasonable and hence constitutional. . . .

Justice Ginsburg, concurring. [omitted—*Ed.*]

Justice O'Connor, with whom Justice Stevens and Justice Souter join, dissenting.

The population of our Nation's public schools, grades 7 through 12, numbers around 18 million. By the reasoning of today's decision, the millions of these students who participate in interscholastic sports, an overwhelming majority of whom have given school officials no reason whatsoever to suspect they use drugs at school, are open to an intrusive bodily search.

In justifying this result, the Court dispenses with a requirement of individualized suspicion on considered policy grounds. First, it explains that precisely because every student athlete is being tested, there is no concern that school officials might act arbitrarily in choosing who to test. Second, a broad-based search regime, the Court reasons, dilutes the accusatory nature of the search. In making these policy arguments, of course, the Court sidesteps powerful, countervailing privacy concerns. Blanket searches, because they can involve "thousands or millions" of searches, "pos[e] a greater threat to liberty" than do suspicion-based ones, which "affec[t] one person at a time." Searches based on individualized suspicion also afford potential targets considerable control over whether they will, in fact, be searched because a person can avoid such a search by not acting in an objectively suspicious way. And given that the surest way to avoid acting suspiciously is to avoid the underlying wrongdoing, the costs of such a regime, one would think, are minimal.

But whether a blanket search is "better" than a regime based on individualized suspicion is not a debate in which we should engage. In my view, it is not open to judges or government officials to decide on policy grounds which is better and which is worse. For most of our constitutional history, mass, suspicionless searches have been generally considered *per se* unreasonable within the meaning of the Fourth Amendment. And we have allowed exceptions in recent years only where it has been clear that a suspicion-based regime would be ineffectual. Because that is not the case here, I dissent.

REVIEW QUESTIONS

1. What is the issue in *Vernonia*? What is the Court's holding?
2. Why does the Court say that student athletes have a lesser expectation of privacy than other students?
3. How does the nature of the "intrusion" (i.e., the drug testing) influence the Court's decision?
4. Why is the evidence of student athletes' involvement in the drug problem in Vernonia important to the Court's decision?
5. Do you agree with Justice O'Connor's dissenting view that drug testing of students should only be permitted when there is "individualized suspicion"?
6. Imagine that you were one of the justices of the U.S. Supreme Court when it decided *Vernonia School District 47J v. Acton.* Write an "opinion" in which you either dissent or concur with the majority opinion. Be sure to fully justify your position, raising and refuting opposing arguments and citing Justice Scalia's majority opinion, Justice O'Connor's dissent, and/or other relevant readings for support.

Board of Education of Independent School District No. 92 of Pottawatomie County v. Earls

The Supreme Court of the United States
536 U.S. 822 (2002)

JUSTICE THOMAS delivered the opinion of the Court.

The Student Activities Drug Testing Policy implemented by the Board of Education of Independent School District No. 92 of Pottawatomie County (School District) [which administers Tecumseh High School and all other public schools in Tecumseh, Oklahoma—Ed.] requires all students who participate in competitive extracurricular activities to submit to drug testing. Because this Policy reasonably serves the School District's important interest in detecting and preventing drug use among its students, we hold that it is constitutional. . . .

In *Vernonia*, this Court held that the suspicionless drug testing of athletes was constitutional. The Court, however, did not simply authorize all school drug testing, but rather conducted a fact-specific balancing of the intrusion on the children's Fourth Amendment rights against the promotion of legitimate governmental interests. Applying the principles of *Vernonia* to the somewhat different facts of this case, we conclude that Tecumseh's Policy is also constitutional.

We first consider the nature of the privacy interest allegedly compromised by the drug testing. . . .

Respondents argue that because children participating in nonathletic extracurricular activities are not subject to regular physicals and communal undress, they have a stronger expectation of privacy than the athletes tested in *Vernonia*. This distinction, however, was not essential to our decision in *Vernonia*, which depended primarily upon the school's custodial responsibility and authority.

In any event, students who participate in competitive extracurricular activities voluntarily subject themselves to many of the same intrusions on their privacy as do athletes. Some of these clubs and activities require occasional off-campus travel and communal undress. All of them have their own rules and requirements for participating students that do not apply to the student body as a whole. For example, each of the competitive extracurricular activities governed by the Policy must abide by the rules of the Oklahoma Secondary Schools Activities Association, and a faculty sponsor monitors the students for compliance with the various rules dictated by the clubs and activities. This regulation of extracurricular activities further diminishes the expectation of privacy among schoolchildren. We therefore conclude that the students affected by this Policy have a limited expectation of privacy.

Next, we consider the character of the intrusion imposed by the Policy. . . .

Under the Policy, a faculty monitor waits outside the closed restroom stall for the student to produce a sample and must "listen for the normal sounds of urination in order to guard against tampered specimens and to insure an accurate chain of custody." The monitor then pours the sample into two bottles that are sealed and placed into a mailing pouch along with a consent form signed by the student. This procedure is virtually identical to that reviewed in *Vernonia*, except that it additionally protects privacy by allowing male students to produce their samples behind a closed stall. Given that we considered the method of collection in *Vernonia* a "negligible" intrusion, the method here is even less problematic.

In addition, the Policy clearly requires that the test results be kept in confidential files separate from a student's other educational records and released to school personnel only on a "need to know" basis. . . .

Moreover, the test results are not turned over to any law enforcement authority. Nor do the test results here lead to the imposition of discipline or have any academic consequences. Rather, the only consequence of a failed drug test is to limit the student's privilege of participating in extracurricular activities. . . .

Given the minimally intrusive nature of the sample collection and the limited uses to which the test results are put, we conclude that the invasion of students' privacy is not significant.

Finally, this Court must consider the nature and immediacy of the government's concerns and the efficacy of the Policy in meeting them. This Court has already articulated in detail the importance of the governmental concern in preventing drug use by schoolchildren. The drug abuse problem among our Nation's youth has hardly abated since *Vernonia* was decided in 1995. In fact, evidence suggests that it has only grown worse. . . .

Additionally, the School District in this case has presented specific evidence of drug use at Tecumseh schools. Teachers testified that they had seen students who appeared to be under the influence of drugs and that they had heard students speaking openly about using drugs. A drug dog found marijuana cigarettes near the school parking lot. Police officers once found drugs or drug paraphernalia in a car driven by a Future Farmers of America member. And the school board president reported that people in the community were calling the board to discuss the "drug situation." We decline to second-guess the finding of the District Court that "[v]iewing the evidence as a whole, it cannot be reasonably disputed that the [School District] was faced with a 'drug problem' when it adopted the Policy.". . .

Furthermore, this Court has not required a particularized or pervasive drug problem before allowing the government to conduct suspicionless drug testing. . . .

Given the nationwide epidemic of drug use, and the evidence of increased drug use in Tecumseh schools, it was entirely reasonable for the School District to enact this particular drug testing policy. We reject the Court of Appeals' novel test that "any district seeking to impose a random suspicionless drug testing policy as a condition to participation in a school activity must demonstrate that there is some identifiable drug abuse problem among a sufficient number of those subject to the testing, such that testing that group of students will actually redress its drug problem." Among other problems, it would be difficult to administer such a test. As we cannot articulate a threshold level of drug use that would suffice to justify a drug testing program for schoolchildren, we refuse to fashion what would in effect be a constitutional quantum of drug use necessary to show a "drug problem."

Respondents also argue that the testing of nonathletes does not implicate any safety concerns, and that safety is a "crucial factor" in applying the special needs framework. They contend that there must be "surpassing safety interests" or "extraordinary safety and national security hazards" in order to override the usual protections of the Fourth Amendment. Respondents are correct that safety factors into the special needs analysis, but the safety interest furthered by drug testing is undoubtedly substantial for all children, athletes and nonathletes alike. We know all too well that drug use carries a variety of health risks for children, including death from overdose.

We also reject respondents' argument that drug testing must presumptively be based upon an individualized reasonable suspicion of wrongdoing because such a testing regime would be less intrusive. In this context, the Fourth Amendment does not require a finding of individualized suspicion, and we decline to impose such a requirement on schools attempting to prevent and detect drug use by students. . . .

Finally, we find that testing students who participate in extracurricular activities is a reasonably effective means of addressing the School District's legitimate concerns in preventing, deterring, and detecting drug use. While in *Vernonia* there might have been a closer fit between the testing of athletes and the trial court's finding that the drug problem was "fueled by the 'role model' effect of athletes' drug use," such a finding was not essential to the holding. *Vernonia* did not require the school to test the group of students most likely to use drugs, but rather considered the constitutionality of the program in the context of the public school's custodial responsibilities. Evaluating the Policy in this context, we conclude that the drug testing of Tecumseh students who participate in extracurricular activities effectively serves the School District's interest in protecting the safety and health of its students.

Within the limits of the Fourth Amendment, local school boards must assess the desirability of drug testing schoolchildren. In upholding the constitutionality of the Policy, we express no opinion as to its wisdom. Rather, we hold only that Tecumseh's Policy is a reasonable means of furthering the School District's important interest in preventing and deterring drug use among its schoolchildren. Accordingly, we reverse the judgment of the Court of Appeals.

It is so ordered.

JUSTICE BREYER, concurring. [omitted—*Ed.*]

JUSTICE O'CONNOR, with whom JUSTICE SOUTER joins, dissenting. [omitted—*Ed.*]

JUSTICE GINSBURG, with whom JUSTICE STEVENS, JUSTICE O'CONNOR, and JUSTICE SOUTER join, dissenting.

Seven years ago, in *Vernonia School Dist. 47J* v. *Acton,* this Court determined that a school district's policy of randomly testing the urine of its student athletes for illicit drugs did not violate the Fourth Amendment. In so ruling, the Court emphasized that drug use "increase[d] the risk of sports-related injury" and that Vernonia's athletes were the "leaders" of an aggressive local "drug culture" that had reached "epidemic proportions." Today, the Court relies upon *Vernonia* to permit a school district with a drug problem its superintendent repeatedly described as "not . . . major" to test the urine of an academic team member solely by reason of her participation in a nonathletic, competitive extracurricular activity—participation associated with neither special dangers from, nor particular predilections for, drug use.

"[T]he legality of a search of a student," this Court has instructed, "should depend simply on the reasonableness, under all the circumstances, of the search." Although "'special needs' inhere in the public school context," those needs are not so expansive or malleable as to render reasonable any program of student drug testing a school district elects to install. The particular testing program upheld today is not reasonable, it is capricious, even perverse: Petitioners' policy targets for testing a student population least likely to be at risk from illicit drugs and their damaging effects. I therefore dissent. . . .

. . .[T]his case resembles *Vernonia* only in that the School Districts in both cases conditioned engagement in activities outside the obligatory curriculum on random subjection to urinalysis. The defining characteristics of the two programs, however, are entirely dissimilar. The Vernonia district sought to test a subpopulation of students distinguished by their reduced expectation of privacy, their special susceptibility to drug-related injury, and their heavy involvement with drug use. The Tecumseh district seeks to test a much larger population associated with none of these factors. It does so, moreover, without carefully safeguarding student confidentiality and without regard to the program's untoward effects. A program so sweeping is not sheltered by *Vernonia;* its unreasonable reach renders it impermissible under the Fourth Amendment.

REVIEW QUESTIONS

1. Speaking for the Court in *Pottawatomie*, Justice Thomas notes that the decision seven years earlier in *Vernonia* had entailed "a fact-specific balancing of the intrusion on the children's Fourth Amendment rights against the promotion of legitimate governmental interests" (p. 162). He then sequentially addresses three distinct components of the analysis the Court employed in *Vernonia* and applies them to the facts presented in *Pottawatomie*. What are these three considerations and how does Justice Thomas respond to each of them?

2. Justice Ginsburg concurred in *Vernonia*, but then dissented in *Pottawatomie*. What rationale does she offer for permitting random searches of student athletes but not of those involved in other extracurricular activities? Do you agree with her argument that the decision in *Pottawatomie* is inconsistent with the Court's reasoning in *Vernonia*?

3. Suppose that, instead of only testing students involved in extracurricular activities, school officials tested *all* students for drug use. Do you think the outcome would be different if such a case reached the Supreme Court? What if the testing were conducted by police officers? What if, instead of random drug tests, school officials—or the police—brought drug-sniffing dogs into classrooms? In any of these scenarios, would the outcome be different if the case arose in an elementary school rather than a middle school or high school? What if it arose in the college you attend?

4. The Supreme Court has not specifically addressed the scope of police authority to conduct searches on school grounds. Except where a person *consents* to a search, the Court's interpretations of the Fourth Amendment in non-school contexts generally preclude police officers from conducting searches without a warrant unless they

have *probable cause* and some *exigent circumstance* (i.e., emergency situation) justifies failure to obtain a warrant before searching. A major exception to this rule is that police may *frisk* the outer clothing of a person for weapons (but not other evidence) if they have a *reasonable suspicion* (a lower standard than probable cause) that the person is armed and engaged in illegal activity. The logic of the stop-and-frisk cases was employed by the Court in the *T.L.O.–Vernonia–Pottawatomie* line of cases to justify searches without probable cause based on the "reasonableness, under all the circumstances, of the search" and, more specifically, on "whether the . . . action was justified at its inception" and "was reasonably related in scope to the circumstances which justified the interference in the first place" (*T.L.O.*, p. 153). These cases, however, focus entirely on the authority of public school officials to conduct searches in situations where searches by police officers acting outside the school setting would almost certainly be found to violate the Fourth Amendment. How do you think the Court would respond to cases similar to those presented here if the searches at issue were conducted on school grounds by police officers rather than school officials? Would it find them Constitutional? Why or why not?

Gang Suppression Through Saturation Patrol, Aggressive Curfew, and Truancy Enforcement: A Quasi-Experimental Test of the Dallas Anti-Gang Initiative

Eric J. Fritsch, Tory J. Caeti, and Robert W. Taylor

For years, police agencies have pursued tactics designed to deal with the proliferation of gangs and gang violence. According to the National Youth Gang Survey, the primary strategy in many jurisdictions is suppression (Spergel and Curry 1990). Suppression tactics include tactical patrols by law enforcement, vertical prosecution by district attorneys, and intensive supervision by probation departments. Generally, suppression involves the arrest,

Source: Eric J. Fritsch, Tory J. Caeti, and Robert W. Taylor. (1999). Gang suppression through saturation patrol, aggressive curfew, and truancy enforcement: A quasi-experimental test of the Dallas Anti-Gang Initiative. *Crime and Delinquency,* 45(1), 122–139. Copyright © 1999 by Sage Publications, Inc. Reprinted by permission of Sage Publications, Inc.

prosecution, and incarceration of gang members. Although suppression is the primary strategy in many jurisdictions, it is also frequently viewed as the least effective (Spergel and Curry 1990).

In 1996, the Dallas Police Department received an anti-gang initiative grant from the Office of Community Oriented Policing Services to combat violent gang activity. The grant period lasted from June 1, 1996, through May 31, 1997. In 1996, the city of Dallas had 79 gangs with 6,145 documented gang members. In addition, there were 1,332 gang-related incidents recorded in 1996. The Dallas Police Department targeted five areas, made up of a varying number of patrol beats, which were home to seven of the most violent gangs in Dallas. In the year preceding the grant, the targeted gangs accounted for 18 percent of the known gang members in Dallas and were responsible for approximately 35 percent of the gang-related violent crimes.

The primary objective of the grant was to fund overtime enforcement in the five targeted areas in hopes of significantly decreasing violent gang activity through suppression. Gang Unit officers teamed with Interactive Community Policing (ICP) officers to develop innovative enforcement strategies for each of the targeted areas. Subsequently, teams of six to eight officers were assembled and received overtime pay to implement the developed strategy. These officers were freed from calls for service and instead spent their time implementing and carrying out the particular enforcement strategy. Although tactics such as "buy-bust" operations and warrant service were employed during the grant period, the vast majority of overtime funds were spent on three suppression tactics: aggressive curfew enforcement—juvenile curfew ordinances were strictly enforced whenever suspected gang members were encountered; aggressive truancy enforcement—officers worked closely with local school districts in enforcing truancy laws; and saturation patrol—officers conducted high-visibility patrols in target areas, stopping and frisking suspected gang members or other suspicious persons that they observed and making arrests when appropriate. The research reported in this article assessed the effectiveness of these strategies in reducing gang-related violence and gang-related offenses reported to the police.

LITERATURE REVIEW

The Police Role in Dealing with Gangs

Several authors, while noting that gangs per se probably cannot be eradicated, believe that the police can manage and, in effect, suppress the more negative aspects of gang activity (Huff and McBride 1993; Owens and Wells 1993; Rush 1996). The various strategies adopted by law enforcement to deal with gangs have been well documented (Dart 1992; Huff and McBride 1993; Jackson and McBride 1996; Johnson, Webster, Connors, and Saenz 1995; Klein 1993, 1995; Knox 1994; Spergel 1995; Weston 1993). Some have advocated the use of specialized patrols, especially foot patrol (Wilson and Kelling 1989); others have embraced a philosophy best represented by the GREAT program, which integrates schools and law enforcement and teaches resistance (Howell 1996); and still others have advocated traditional and nontraditional law enforcement suppression techniques (Houston 1996; Johnson et al. 1995; Needle and Stapleton 1983; Rush 1996). However, empirical evaluations of the prescribed strategies have been few in number.

Gang suppression by law enforcement has also often included a broad range of tactics that frequently have taken the form of crackdowns. Crackdowns typically have involved "a sharp increase in law enforcement resources applied to the previously under-enforced laws, with a clear goal of enhancing general deterrence of the misconduct" (Sherman 1990b, p. 2). Most often, crackdowns have been effective initially, have had a short residual deterrent effect, and have been followed by an eventual return to preintervention levels of crime (Sherman 1990b). Generally, greater successes have been found in strategies focusing on specific offenses, offenders, and places than by simply increasing presence (Sherman 1990b). Although Sherman (1990b) has provided an extensive review of police crackdowns, including those emphasizing suppression of drug sales, drunk driving, prostitution, subway crime, and various other serious and nonserious crimes, no gang-specific crackdowns were examined or discussed in his review.

Gang crackdowns have not been evaluated systematically (Klein 1995). Some authors have dismissed the use of the crackdown entirely. "In the case of youth gang interdiction, this tactic is analogous to an attempt to put out a forest fire with a water bucket" (Shelden, Tracy, and Brown 1997, p. 212). However, a crackdown can be, and often is, a coordinated effort by a law enforcement agency to stop a certain type of crime or an offender using more than simple police presence. Indeed, the role of crime analysis in directing and supporting police crackdowns is growing; however, to date, very little empirical research examining well-coordinated crackdowns directed by crime analysis has been conducted. The studies that have been done have shown dramatic results, as was the case in the Minneapolis "hotspots" research (Sherman 1990b) and the Kansas City Gun Experiment (Sherman, Shaw, and Rogan 1995).

Gang problems and behaviors vary widely from city to city as well as within cities (Weisel and Painter 1997). In accordance, it is doubtful that one strategy will be effective across and within all jurisdictions. Some law enforcement agencies have adopted a philosophy of total suppression, in which any gang member or wanna-be has been targeted, such as in the Los Angeles Police Department's (LAPD) Community Resources Against Street Hoodlums (CRASH) (Freed 1986; Klein 1993). Others, such as the Los Angeles Sheriff's Operation Safe Streets (OSS), have adopted a philosophy of target suppression, in which the police have only targeted hard-core gang members (Freed 1986; Klein 1993). Still others, such as the Oxnard, California, Police Department's Gang-Oriented Comprehensive Action Program (GOCAP) and the Westminster, California, Tri-Agency Resource Gang Enforcement Team (TARGET), have focused on information sharing and intelligence gathering to identify, arrest, and successfully prosecute gang members (Kent and Smith 1994; Owens and Wells 1993).

Most of the current prescriptive literature has focused on community-oriented tactics. Some have recommended that the police stop trying to eradicate gangs and that they communicate with gang youths in such a way as to demonstrate respect, acceptance, and concern for gang youths (Spergel 1995). The literature has also concluded that law enforcement alone cannot solve the gang problem—in fact, the typical police organization is ill-equipped and poorly structured to deal with gangs (Rush 1996). Dealing with gangs requires a comprehensive approach that involves all members of the criminal justice community, schools, community leaders, and the like (Owens and Wells 1993; Rush 1996). A fundamental problem with all of the aforementioned strategies, but especially the latter, has been the lack of reliable, well-documented, well-designed, empirical evaluations of the strategies and tactics employed (Klein 1993, 1995; Knox 1994; Spergel 1995). In fact, some of the evaluations of the tactics have been gleaned from newspapers (Freed 1986).

A recent review of several gang efforts has questioned the efficacy of police responses in dealing with the problem (Weisel and Painter 1997). In describing the gang enforcement tactics in five major cities in the United States, Weisel and Painter (1997) noted that "none of the agencies engaged in any identifiable long-term planning process or conducted research to monitor the changing nature of the problem. None . . . engaged in meaningful evaluations of effectiveness of specialized or other departmental efforts related exclusively to gang enforcement" (p. 83). In fact, some evaluative statements have been based on hunches because of the lack of empirical data. For example, Klein (1993) has said, "my informed hunch is that suppression programs, left to their own devices, may deter a few members but also increase the internal cohesiveness of the group" (p. 312). Indeed, much of the current literature has concluded that traditional law enforcement tactics alone will have little effect on reducing, managing, or suppressing gangs (Huff and McBride 1993; Rush 1996; Shelden et al. 1997; Spergel 1995).

Empirical Evaluations of the Effect of Police on Gang Activity

Spergel (1995) has concluded that the strategy of targeting gangs and gang members only for suppression purposes is flawed. However, in evaluating the effectiveness of suppression, Spergel also noted that "We have no systematic or reliable assessments of the effectiveness of a gang suppression strategy by criminal justice agencies, particularly law enforcement" (p. 198). Indeed, his analysis of the literature assessing the effectiveness of gang suppression by law enforcement consisted of a series of anecdotal comments from newspaper articles—hardly a scientific source. Klein (1995) reviewed several sweep programs that were undertaken in California. Operation Hammer, which was conducted by the LAPD, was a preannounced, media-covered gang sweep of Los Angeles that resulted in 1,453 juveniles being arrested; however, 1,350 were released without formal charges being filed. In the end, the operation was characterized by Klein and some LAPD officials as "all show" that was only for public relations. However, Klein also reported that when he rode along with Los Angeles County Sheriff's officials on a gang sweep that was not announced, not covered, and that was coordinated among several different targeted areas, the results were much different. Whereas Operation Hammer provided serious gang members with good laughing material, the Sheriff's sweep produced no humor among the arrestees that night.

Evaluations of community-based gang prevention programs are increasing. However, many of these have been qualitative and did not measure the impact of the program on crime in general or even on gang-related crime. For example, Thurman, Giacomazzi, Reisig, and Mueller (1996) evaluated a community-based gang prevention program implemented in Mountlake Terrace, Washington. Their evaluation included direct observation, focus group interviews, and official crime statistics. The program purported to provide an alternative outlet in which youths at risk or already involved in a gang could spend their time (Thurman et al. 1996). The official crime statistics used in the study were general calls for service to the police, with no breakdown given between gang-related calls for service and regular calls for service. Although Thurman et al. concluded that the intervention "appears to be a cost-effective gang prevention and intervention program" (p. 292), no data on crime; effect on the number of gang members, gang-related crimes, or gang-related calls for service; or other statistical evidence were offered to support this conclusion. Furthermore, the extent and scope of the gang problem in the area, the demographic characteristics of the community, and the crime statistics for the community were not discussed. The authors concluded that the program "offers an effective alternative to traditional law enforcement approaches which typically rely on police crackdowns and curfews to regulate gang activity" (Thurman et al. 1996, p. 279), yet no evidence was offered to show that these latter techniques were ineffective or have not been effective in the past—either nationally or in Mountlake Terrace.

Palumbo, Eskay, and Hallett (1992) evaluated three gang prevention programs, including Arizona New Turf, GREAT, and Community Reliance Resource Effort (CARE). They found that although all of the programs were well implemented, there was no effect on the gang problem, even though police officers, students, and members of the community felt positively about the programs. Indeed, the majority of the community-based programs may fall victim to a common criticism—they sound good, feel good, look good, but do not work good. Many of the evaluations of these community programs have relied on qualitative data that typically show that everyone surveyed or interviewed thought the program was effective and useful, but no quantitative empirical support has been offered to indicate the impact on the gang problem, gang-related crime, or the gang members served by the program.

Much of the current literature has been dismissive, perhaps prematurely, of the ability of the police to suppress gang activity in that there are virtually no empirical studies that support such a claim. As Klein (1993) noted,

> The message is not so much that suppression does or does not "work": evidence one way or the other is sorely lacking. *There are logical, as well as experiential, reasons to believe that suppression programs can have deterrent effects and thus, by our reasoning, can contribute substantially to gang and drug activity prevention.* (p. 308; emphasis in original)

Curfew and Truancy Enforcement

The literature assessing curfew and truancy enforcement is still in its infancy; most existing studies have focused on tactics, descriptions of programs, and legal issues (Friend 1994; Garrett and Brewster 1994; "Juvenile Curfews" 1994; Ruefle and Reynolds 1995; Watzman 1994). Curfews have received attention recently because of their perceived effectiveness in reducing juvenile crime and juvenile victimization. Much anecdotal reference about their effectiveness has appeared in the popular media (LeBoeuf 1996; Ruefle and Reynolds

1995), but the existing academic literature on curfew and truancy enforcement has been limited to a few articles on the number of arrests and the various types of ordinances that have been enacted.

Hunt and Weiner (1977) studied a Detroit curfew that was specifically designed to reduce criminal gang activity by youths. They used before and after comparisons of crime rates and criminal temporal activity and concluded that the curfew enforcement seemed to effectively reduce or suppress the relative level of crime during curfew hours, although they also found evidence of temporal displacement (i.e., gang-related crime increased during noncurfew hours). Ruefle and Reynolds (1995) surveyed metropolitan police departments serving populations of more than 200,000 and found that curfews in one form or another existed in 59 (77percent) of the 77 largest American cities. The Dallas Police Department's internal analysis revealed that following adoption of its aggressive curfew enforcement program, juvenile victimization during curfew hours dropped 17.7 percent and juvenile arrests dropped 14.6 percent from the previous year (Click 1994). Statistics from Phoenix, Arizona, revealed that 21 percent of all curfew violators were gang members. Furthermore, a 10 percent decrease in juvenile arrests for violent crimes occurred following implementation of an aggressive curfew program (LeBoeuf 1996). Decreases in various other juvenile crimes occurred in several other metropolitan areas (Chicago, Denver, Jacksonville, New Orleans, North Little Rock) that employed curfew programs (LeBoeuf 1996).

Truancy has been linked to a variety of negative consequences for youths (e.g., drug use, delinquency, unemployment) and for society (i.e., daytime crime, auto theft, vandalism) (Garry 1996; J. R. Martin, Schulze, and Valdez 1988; Rohrman 1993). However, the impact of aggressive truancy enforcement on crime rates remains essentially unevaluated. One evaluated program used a small squad of officers to enforce truancy laws; although numerous arrests were made, the impact on felonies and misdemeanors in the area was nominal (J. R. Martin et al. 1988). However, the study did not control for whether the crimes under study were committed by adults or by juveniles.

METHODOLOGY

A quasi-experimental design was used for the evaluation reported in this article. The main objective of the initiative was to decrease gang-related violence in the five targeted areas. The five areas were composed of patrol beats and were selected on the basis of two criteria. First, the areas had experienced a large amount of gang violence in the preceding year. Second, they overlapped some of the defined Enterprise Zones and Renaissance Areas in Dallas. Enterprise Zones are designated by the city to encourage economic development in an area, and businesses receive tax breaks for locating in the Zones. A Renaissance Zone is an area in which neighborhood organizations use federal funds to design and implement programs to reduce crime and disorder.

To estimate the impact of the enforcement strategies on crime, it was important to select control areas for comparison purposes. Four control areas were selected based on a two-stage selection process. First, the number of violent gang-related offenses from June 1,

1995, through May 31, 1996, for each patrol beat in the same patrol division as the corresponding target area was determined from data provided by the Dallas Police Department Gang Unit. Second, the beats with the largest number of violent gang-related offenses during the time period were matched with a corresponding target area and served as control areas. The target and control areas were sufficiently similar to allow comparison and estimation of the efficacy of the gang suppression effort.

Two data sets were used to measure the anti-gang initiative's impact on crime. First, offenses reported to the police from June 1, 1995, through May 31, 1997, were obtained from the Crime Analysis Unit of the police department. Murder, rape, robbery, aggravated assault, burglary, auto theft, theft, arson, other assault, criminal mischief, drug offenses, and weapon offenses were analyzed. The last two offenses were measured by number of arrests rather than reported offenses. Second, data from the Gang Unit on all of the gang-related offenses reported to the police from June 1, 1995, through May 31, 1997, were collected. Several offenses were aggregated into the category of violent gang-related offenses.

Because of the small sample size, gang-related property crimes were not analyzed. Final determination of whether an offense was gang related was made by Gang Unit detectives after a follow-up investigation based on police department criteria for gang-related crime. Report formats clearly indicated that the offense was gang related by both a checked box and a narrative. Annual precomparisons and postcomparisons of crime in general and gang-related violence in particular were analyzed for each target and control area to determine the anti-gang initiative's impact on crime. For each comparison, a paired samples t test was computed to determine statistically significant differences between the mean values over two time periods. In instances in which statistically significant differences existed, efforts were made to determine the particular strategy employed during the time period (curfew enforcement, truancy enforcement, or saturation patrol). . . .

DISCUSSION AND CONCLUSION

This study found that, consistent with previous research, undirected saturation patrol has little effect on reducing crime (Sherman 1990b). In short, simply adding more police officers without direction was not effective. Unfortunately, this conclusion has been overgeneralized to mean that policing and patrol does not work. Fortunately, other research has shown that directed patrol (whether directed toward offenders, places, victims, or offenses) was effective in varying degrees (Abrahamse, Ebener, Greenwood, Fitzgerald, and Kosin 1991; S. E. Martin 1986; S. E. Martin and Sherman 1986; Sherman, 1990a, 1990b, 1992; Sherman et al. 1995). The research reported in this article provides support for the latter statement because the aggressive enforcement of truancy and curfew laws was effective in reducing gang-related violence in target areas. This finding needs replication, particularly in a true experimental design.

Enforcement of curfew and truancy is frequently a low-priority task of officers, but it can have an impact on gang violence and may potentially have an even greater impact on juvenile victimization. For example, the number of homicides in Dallas (citywide) that involved a juvenile victim (excluding child abuse deaths) dropped from 18 during the year prior to the anti-gang initiative to 7 during the initiative. Furthermore, the number of gang-related juvenile homicide victims dropped from 6 during the first time period to 2 during the second (Caeti 1997).

We also found little effect on the number of offenses reported to the police. Increased officer presence did not lead to a decrease in offenses reported to the police. Sherman (1990b, 1992) reported that both increases and decreases in calls for service have been noted as the result of a crackdown. Thus, the validity of using calls for service as a measure of effectiveness must be questioned. In addition, freeing officers from responding to calls for service did not lead to greater officer-initiated activity, such as drug and weapons arrests. The question "What do officers do with their time?" needs greater empirical attention. Furthermore, suppressible crime was not affected greatly by the initiative overall. Perhaps this was because the enforcement activities that relied on curfew and truancy enforcement only had appreciable effects on the crimes that juvenile offenders commit. Indeed, criminal mischief and weapons offenses decreased dramatically in the targeted areas. Individuals who commit robberies and other serious felonies may be unaffected by curfew or truancy enforcement because they may be adults and/or not in the school system.

Many police scholars have concluded that traditional police activities and goals (preventive patrol, rapid response, investigations, etc.) have failed to achieve crime reduction and have increased problems of police–citizen alienation (Kelling 1978). However, more recently, Kelling (1996), in discussing how to define the bottom line in policing, noted the following:

> A basic purpose of police is crime prevention. The idea that police cannot do anything about crime and that they stand helpless in the face of demographics, drugs, gangs, or whatever is unacceptable—often . . . a "cop-out" that covers lack of strategic commitment and absence of planning and implementation. (p. 31)

Police gang suppression activity may not affect gang membership or the conditions that create gangs. However, it is possible that those activities affect the nefarious effects of gangs—crime and violence.

Would we really care if kids joined gangs if gangs did not engage in criminal activity? Probably not; in fact, some positive gang values (group cohesiveness, loyalty, respect, discipline, etc.) are encouraged to a large extent in legitimate activities, such as youth sports, clubs, and various other groups. In any case, the gang suppression activities of law enforcement probably cannot and perhaps should not be concerned with the "whys" of gangs. As Spergel (1995) noted,

> The police cannot be held responsible for basic failures of youth socialization; lack of social and economic achievement by families, deficiencies of schools, decreased employment opportunities for African-American youth, the extensive street presence and accessibility of sophisticated weaponry, and the extensive racism and social isolation that appear to be highly correlated with the gang problem in some low-income minority communities. (p. 191)

The police should, however, concern themselves with a more narrow mission of developing effective strategies to address the crime problems that gangs create. The idea that the police can change the underlying socioeconomic conditions that give rise to gangs or to the infinite reasons why kids join gangs is naive and unrealistic. This is not to say that other community agencies should not focus on such endeavors. The simple fact of the matter is that the police are designed, organized, staffed, and trained to deal with crime, not social services.

Although strategies that use offender-, place-, and crime-specific techniques are in their infancy and require greater empirical attention, much of the recent literature that has evaluated such strategies is promising (Sherman 1990b, 1992). For example, when over-time-funded officers were freed from calls for service in Houston, substantial reductions in suppressible crimes soon followed (Hoover and Caeti 1994). The philosophy is that

> police agencies can impact the level of crime and disorder in a community. The police do make a difference. Saying that crime and disorder are a product of social and economic forces the police cannot and should not affect is rejected. (Hoover and Caeti 1994, p. 1)

The police should coordinate with other public agencies in their efforts to deal with gangs, and these efforts should be focused on the criminal problems that gangs create. Interagency cooperation and information-sharing models provide promise as well, especially the ability to successfully prosecute serious and habitual offenders (Owens and Wells 1993). Recent technological advances in the areas of computer mapping, object-oriented databases, management information systems, and offender identification and tracking all bode well for the ability of the police to increase their effectiveness in managing crime, particularly gang crime. More empirical evaluation research is needed concerning which law enforcement strategies can lead to reductions in gang violence and victimization through gang violence.

REFERENCES

Abrahamse, Allan F., Patricia A. Ebener, Peter W. Greenwood, Nora Fitzgerald, and Thomas E. Kosin. 1991. "An Experimental Evaluation of the Phoenix Repeat Offender Program." *Justice Quarterly* 8:141–72.

Caeti, Tory J. 1997. "Who's Killing Our Kids? An Analysis of Juvenile Homicide Victims in Dallas 1993–1997." Research Initiation Grant Project, University of North Texas, Denton.

Click, Benjamin R. 1994. "Statistics in Dallas Encouraging." *Police Chief* 61 (12):33–6.

Dart, Robert W. 1992. "Chicago's 'Flying Squad' Tackles Street Gangs" *Police Chief* 59:96–8.

Freed, David. 1986. "Policing Gangs: Case of Contrasting Styles." Pp. 288–91 in *The Modern Gang Reader*, edited by M. W. Klein, C. L. Maxson, and J. Miller. Los Angeles: Roxbury.

Friend, Charles E. 1994. "Juvenile Curfew." *Policy Review* 6:1–4.

Garrett, Dennis A. and David Brewster. 1994. "Curfew: A New Look at an Old Tool." *Police Chief* (December):29–61.

Garry, Eileen M. 1996. "Truancy: First Step to a Lifetime of Problems." *Juvenile Justice Bulletin* (October).

Hoover, Larry T. and Tory J. Caeti. 1994. "Crime-Specific Policing in Houston." *Texas Law Enforcement Management and Administrative Statistics Program Bulletin* 1 (9).

Houston, James. 1996. "What Works: The Search for Excellence in Gang Intervention Programs." *Journal of Gang Research* 3:1–16.

Howell, James C. 1996. *Youth Gang Violence Prevention and Intervention: What Works.* Washington, DC: National Institute of Justice.

Huff, C. Ronald and Wesley D. McBride. 1993. "Gangs and the Police." Pp. 401–16 in *The Gang Intervention Handbook*, edited by A. P. Goldstein and C. R. Huff. Champaign, IL: Research Press.

Hunt, A. Lee and Ken Weiner. 1977. "The Impact of a Juvenile Curfew: Suppression and Displacement in Patterns of Juvenile Offenses." *Journal of Police Science and Administration* 5:407–12.

Jackson, Robert K. and Wesley D. McBride. 1996. *Understanding Street Gangs.* Incline Village, NV: Copperhouse.

Johnson, Claire M., Barbara A. Webster, Edward F. Connors, and Diana J. Saenz. 1995. "Gang Enforcement Problems and Strategies: National Survey Findings." *Journal of Gang Research* 3:1–18.

"Juvenile Curfews and Gang Violence: Exiled on Main Street." 1994. *Harvard Law Review* 107 (7):1693–710.

Kelling, George L. 1978. "Police Field Services and Crime: The Presumed Effects of a Capacity," *Crime & Delinquency* 24:173–84.

———. 1996. "Defining the Bottom Line in Policing: Organizational Philosophy and Accountability." Pp. 23–36 in *Quantifying Quality in Policing*, edited by L. T. Hoover. Washington, DC: Police Executive Research Forum.

Kent, Douglas R. and Peggy Smith. 1994. "The Tri-Agency Resource Gang Enforcement Team: A Selective Approach to Reduce Gang Crime." Pp. 292–96 in *The Modern Gang Reader*, edited by M. W. Klein, C. L. Maxson, and J. Miller. Los Angeles: Roxbury.

Klein, Malcolm W. 1993. "Attempting Gang Control by Suppression: The Misuse of Deterrence Principles," Pp. 304–13 in *The Modern Gang Reader*, edited by M. W. Klein, C. L. Maxson, and J. Miller. Los Angeles: Roxbury.

———. 1995. *The American Street Gang: Its Nature, Prevalence, and Control.* New York: Oxford University Press.

Knox, George W. 1994. *An Introduction to Gangs.* Bristol, IN: Wyndham Hall.

LeBoeuf, Donni. 1996. *Curfew: An Answer to Juvenile Delinquency and Victimization?* Washington, DC: Office of Juvenile Justice and Delinquency Prevention.

Martin, Joe R., Arnie D. Schulze, and Mike Valdez. 1988. "Taking Aim at Truancy." *FBI Law Enforcement Bulletin* 57:8–12.

Martin, Susan E. 1986. "Policing Career Criminals: An Examination of an Innovative Crime Control Program." *Journal of Criminal Law and Criminology* 77:1159–82.

Martin, Susan E. and Lawrence W. Sherman. 1986. "Catching Career Criminals: Proactive Policing and Selective Apprehension." *Justice Quarterly*, 3:171–92.

Needle, Jerome A. and W. V. Stapleton. 1983. *Police Handling of Youth Gangs.* Washington, DC: American Justice Institute, National Juvenile Justice System Assessment Center.

Owens, Robert P. and Donna K. Wells. 1993. "One City's Response to Gangs." *Police Chief* 58:25–7.

Palumbo, Dennis J., R. Eskay, and Michael A. Hallett. 1992. *Do Gang Prevention Strategies Actually Reduce Crime?* Washington, DC: National Institute of Justice.

Rohrman, Doug. 1993. *Combating Truancy in Our Schools: A Community Effort.* Washington, DC: National Institute of Justice.

Ruefle, William and Kenneth Mike Reynolds. 1995. "Curfews and Delinquency in Major American Cities." *Crime & Delinquency* 41:347–63.

Rush, Jeffrey P. 1996. "The Police Role in Dealing With Gangs." Pp. 85–92 in *Gangs: A Criminal Justice Approach*, edited by J. M. Miller and J. P. Rush. Cincinnati, OH: Anderson.

Shelden, Randall G., Sharon K. Tracy, and William B. Brown. 1997. *Youth Gangs in American Society*. Belmont, CA: Wadsworth.

Sherman, Lawrence W. 1990a. "Police Crackdowns." *National Institute of Justice Reports* (March/April).

_____. 1990b. "Police Crackdowns: Initial and Residual Deterrence." *Crime and Justice: A Review of Research* 12:1–48.

_____. 1992. "Attacking Crime: Police and Crime Control." Pp. 159–230 in *Crime and Justice: A Review of Research*, vol. 14, edited by M. Tonry and N. Morris. Chicago: University of Chicago Press.

Sherman, Lawrence W., James W. Shaw, and Dennis P. Rogan. 1995. "The Kansas City Gun Experiment." *National Institute of Justice: Research in Brief*.

Spergel, Irving A. 1995. *The Youth Gang Problem*. New York: Oxford University Press.

Spergel, Irving A. and G. David Curry. 1990. "Strategies and Perceived Agency Effectiveness in Dealing With the Youth Gang Problem." Pp. 288–309 in *Gangs in America*, edited by C. R. Huff. Newbury Park, CA: Sage.

Thurman, Quint C., Andrew L. Giacomazzi, Michael D. Reisig, and David G. Mueller. 1996. "Community-Based Gang Prevention and Intervention: An Evaluation of the Neutral Zone." *Crime & Delinquency* 42:279–95.

Watzman, Nancy. 1994. "Curfew Revival Gains Momentum." *Governing* 7:20–1.

Weisel, Deborah L. and Ellen Painter. 1997. *The Police Response to Gangs: Case Studies of Five Cities*. Washington, DC: Police Executive Research Forum.

Weston, Jim. 1993. "Community Policing: An Approach to Youth Gangs in a Medium-Sized City." *Police Chief* 60 (August):80–4.

Wilson, James Q. and George L. Kelling. 1989. "Making Neighborhoods Safe." *Atlantic Monthly* (February):46–52.

REVIEW QUESTIONS

1. What does the previous research reviewed by the authors of this selection have to say about the police role in dealing with gangs? About the effect of police intervention on gang activity? About curfew and truancy enforcement?

2. What gang suppression tactics were employed in the areas targeted by the Dallas anti-gang initiative? How was the initiative implemented and how did the authors go about testing its effectiveness?

3. What did the authors find out about the effectiveness of each of the tactics employed in the initiative? How do these findings compare to the findings from previous research on gang suppression efforts?

4. What conclusions do the authors draw about strategies police should use in order to more effectively combat the crime and violence associated with gangs?

Police Encounters with Juveniles Revisited: An Exploratory Study of Themes and Styles in Community Policing

Gordon Bazemore and Scott Senjo

INTRODUCTION

A primary focus of classic studies of policing in the 1960s and 1970s was on police inter-action with juveniles (Black and Reiss, 1970; Lundman et al., 1978; Piliavin and Briar, 1964). During this time both students of delinquent behavior and police researchers em-phasized the role of the police as gatekeeper to the juvenile justice system. In addition, re-searchers underscored the importance of the relationship between police and juveniles in determining patterns of arrest as well as minimizing additional conflict (Siegal and Senna, 1994; Werthman and Piliavin, 1967).

Beginning in the late 1970s and continuing through the 1980s, research interest in the police/juvenile relationship appeared to wane. But as researchers turned attention to other issues, both policing and the police/juvenile relationship were undergoing change. It is there-fore unclear the extent to which studies conducted between 20 and 30 years ago accurately portray the complexity of the police/juvenile relationship today. Specifically, these findings cannot take account of changes that may be emerging from one of the most significant re-forms in the past half century of law enforcement, community-oriented policing (COP).

As it has appeared on the scene in the past decade, proponents have argued that com-munity-oriented policing represents a "third era" of policing based on a new paradigm that differs significantly from both the traditional or watchman policing and the professional, or legalistic policing models (Kelling and Moore, 1988; Moore and Stephens, 1991; Wilson and Kelling, 1982). Although debate continues about the meaning and definition of COP, there is general agreement that the new model rejects a singular focus on law enforcement as the primary function of the police (Mastrofski et al., 1995). In addition, there appears to be a growing consensus that community policing implies a different style of policing,

Source: Gordon Bazemore and Scott Senjo. (1997). Police encounters with juveniles revisited: An exploratory study of themes and styles in community policing. *Policing: An International Journal of Police Strategy and Man-agement, 20*(1), 60–82. Copyright 1997 by MCB University Press. Adapted by permission.

organizational structure, and culture to support this change in style (Moore and Stephens, 1991; Sparrow et al., 1990). To the extent that interaction between COP officers and citizens is based on a different set of agency principles and values (Moore and Stephens, 1991), rather than simply a change in tactics (Goldstein, 1987, 1990), one may anticipate that distinctive patterns of police–citizen interaction will emerge in departments and communities in which community policing is being implemented.

Critical to the effectiveness of community policing, therefore, is a significant behavioral change in the way police interact with the public and an attitudinal change in the view police hold of citizens as clients or "customers" (Bazemore and Cole, 1993; Moore and Stephens, 1991). Accompanying this transformation in behavior and attitude may also be a change in officers' perception of their own role in the response to crime (Mastrofski et al., 1995). As police interact with neighborhood residents and others in a nonadversarial context, the views these citizens hold of police are in turn expected to change, further impacting on citizens' willingness to work with the police, as well as citizens' perception of safety and quality of life in their neighborhoods.

Together these changes are believed to alter the relationship between police and citizens, and to provide the critical theoretical link between community policing and a reduction in crime and fear. But despite a growing body of research and a general consensus that citizen involvement and participation is central to the effectiveness of community policing, little is known about this "community" dimension. Moreover, there is relatively little research on what COP officers actually do and think that is different from traditional officers. Empirical accounts of these hypothesized differences have been especially lacking with respect to police/juvenile interaction.

Although some have implied that COP may change the traditionally antagonistic dynamic of police/juvenile interaction and lead to more creative, informal patterns of processing and intervention (Guarino Ghezzi, 1994; Siegal and Senna, 1994), there have been few attempts to replicate the classic observational studies of police encounters with juveniles in this new context. Will COP officers adopt a different style of interaction with juveniles on the street and, if so, what is the nature of this difference? Will they develop distinctive professional orientations and ideologies toward juvenile crime and the police role in its prevention and control? The exploratory study discussed in this paper provides an opportunity to examine these issues in two target neighborhoods as part of a larger evaluation of the impact of COP on citizens' views of the police, citizen participation and changes in police tactics.

Based on approximately ten months of field observation during the first year of implementation of community policing in a dense, highly urbanized city in South Florida, this study's primary objective was to explore differences between COP officers and officers assigned to traditional units in other areas of the city in the nature and style of police/juvenile encounters.

This paper examines behavioral and ideological orientations in the COP officer response to juveniles and examines officer views of the police role in such encounters. In doing so, we raise questions about potential changes in police interaction, ideological orientation and strategies of engagement with juveniles that may be expected to emerge under COP. These questions address underlying issues that may become critical policy concerns in community policing as well as juvenile justice and should begin to form the basis of a new research agenda for students of policing.

LITERATURE REVIEW

As the initial gatekeeper to the juvenile justice system, police are granted perhaps the most critical discretion of any decision maker in the response to juvenile crime (Siegal and Senna, 1994; Vollmer, 1936): whether or not to arrest and pursue formal processing. The role of police in determining the type and level of diversion has also long been recognized. Recently some have also noted that the police often play a vital role in building deviant identities for young people even when interaction remains at a strictly informal level (Mehan, 1993).

Given this discretion and the potential for impact on the future of young people, the nature of interaction between police and juveniles is especially important. Both the view that juveniles hold toward the police, which may be based on misunderstandings of police intent (Guarino Ghezzi, 1994), and the ideology of police toward their role in interactions with juveniles can be critical factors in determining whether youths are ignored by officers, referred to services or otherwise assisted, warned, counselled, arrested or harassed.

Several themes from the classic observational studies of juvenile justice and social control in the 1960s and 1970s have come to be part of the common wisdom about the police–juvenile relationship (Werthman and Piliavin, 1967; Whitehead and Lab, 1990). First, these studies portray police–adolescent interaction as problematic and imply that the police–juvenile relationship is almost necessarily and universally characterized by tension and antagonism (Piliavin and Briar, 1964; Werthman and Piliavin, 1967; Whitehead and Lab, 1990). Second, since the majority of encounters between police and juveniles involve relatively minor and nuisance offenses, the bulk of police work with juveniles centers around order maintenance and social services (Whitehead and Lab, 1990; Werthman and Piliavin, 1967). Third, these studies confirm that youths have a low arrest rate and that between one third and 40 percent of all juvenile cases are handled informally within police departments or referred to local community services (Lundman, 1974; OJJDP, 1992; Uniform Crime Reports, 1991). As the data on low arrest imply, with the exception of serious offenses, police exercise a great deal of discretion in the "low visibility decision making" that characterizes the response to juvenile crime (Black and Reiss, 1970; Goldman, 1963; Piliavin and Briar, 1964). Fourth, when this discretion is played out in the decision to arrest, it is based both on the response to the characteristics of the individual offender such as race, gender (Black, 1980; Smith and Visher, 1981; Visher, 1983) and demeanor (Black and Reiss, 1970; Lundman et al., 1978) and on characteristics of the offense including seriousness, whether there was a complaint from a victim and other legal variables (Black and Reiss, 1970; Lundman et al., 1978; Werthman and Piliavin, 1967).

One notable early exception to the emphasis on offense and offender in these studies was Wilson's (1967) classic observational study of police department policy and officer style. In comparing higher arrest rates in Western city with those of Eastern city, Wilson attributed this difference to the legalistic style of the Western city officers and the more informal watchman style of Eastern city officers. Both styles were a function of department policy, rather than simply individual variation in officer preference (Wilson, 1967). By focussing on the characteristics of police departments rather than offense characteristics, youth characteristics, or individual officer preference as explanatory factors in police exercise of discretion, Wilson's study raised initial questions about whether patterns of arrest and informal handling were a constant in policing juveniles or varied as a function of policy and organizational culture.

Although Wilson's categorization of departments and policing styles appears out of date today, more recently a number of other researchers have emphasized the interplay between policy, "operational style" and the exercise of discretion in policing. These writers have emphasized the role of organizational structure and departmental philosophy and culture in shaping policing style (Brown, 1989; Ericson, 1982; Smith, 1984). Smith and Klein (1984) note, for example, that the degree of bureaucracy and professionalism of departments is directly related to the number of arrests. Stability of assignment, scale of patrol (Mastrofski, 1981), number of supervisors (Langworthy, 1983) and supervisor span of control have also been linked to operational style, patterns in use of discretion and arrest outcomes. A focus on the implications of policy, cultural factors and organizational characteristics is most salient in examining the impact of community-oriented policing.

COP, Communities and Juveniles

Organizationally, community policing appears to demand changes in some of the very policy and organizational characteristics researchers have argued may most affect policing style and outcomes (Mastrofski and Ritti, 1995). For example, proponents of COP have argued that the increase in officer discretion, reduction in supervisor span of control, decrease in size of beats, increased stability of assignments and greater encouragement of officer initiative associated with this approach will increase creativity and initiative in crime prevention and order maintenance (e.g., Moore and Stephens, 1991; Sparrow et al., 1990).

Ultimately, as a new policing paradigm focussed on developing a cooperative relationship between police officers and communities, COP can be distinguished both theoretically and tactically from the professional model of policing. Tactically, community policing gives priority to a range of programs and practices such as foot patrol, bicycle patrol, crime watch and citizen patrols, and a general expansion in the social services which get officers out into the community (Moore and Trojanowitz, 1988). The theory underlying the expected impact of community policing on crime has two primary components. First, as Wilson and Kelling (1982, p. 15) observe, "a lot of serious crime is adventitious, not the result of inexorable social forces or personal failings." By reducing the opportunities for criminal activity through addressing the physical and psychological barriers to social order, social control can be maintained. Second, fear of crime leads to citizen reluctance to participate in public life in the neighborhood, which translates into a yielding of control from citizens to criminals. COP attempts to empower citizens by restoring ownership and pride in neighborhood institutions, thus creating a greater feeling of efficacy, a greater interest in community affairs and events, and an increased willingness to participate in efforts to reduce crime. COP also attempts to empower police officers by expanding their discretion and encouraging creativity in solving problems in ways which do not necessarily involve arrest and encouraging "community building" aimed at enhancing the preventive capacity of neighborhood institutions (Rosenbaum, 1988; Skogan, 1990).

In recent years, juvenile crime has assumed a prominent position in the headlines of newspapers around the country. While there is some debate about whether and to what extent juvenile crime is actually increasing (Elliott, 1993; Jones and Krisberg, 1994), police in many cities do appear to be arresting and processing more young people. Some express concern that juveniles now present new and greater challenges to policing (OJJDP, 1992; Siegal and Senna, 1994). But as arrests now increase and processing escalates, juvenile justice systems appear to be increasingly unable to accommodate new referrals and are under attack from a wide variety of sources (Lemov, 1994; Bazemore and Washington, 1995). Community policing would appear to have direct implications for the response to youth crime and the role of officers in prevention, diversion and law enforcement.

Key Questions and Expectations

What would COP mean for policing juveniles? With regard to the theory and tactics of COP, there appear to be three implications which may alter the police–juvenile relationship and ultimately influence outcomes such as arrest and diversion. First, frequency of contact and level of intimacy should increase as a result of efforts to prevent and reduce opportunities for crime by greater presence in the neighborhood. Second, the already wide discretion exercised by police is expected to increase under COP as police are encouraged to place increased emphasis on solving underlying problems believed to cause crime (Siegal and Senna, 1994), to increase the proportion of officer activity directed at order maintenance (Reiss, 1992; Wilson and Kelling, 1982), and to work with neighborhoods in "community building" efforts (Mastrofski et al., 1995). Third, both problem solving and order maintenance activities are expected to result in more proactive efforts to engage citizens and more opportunities for police to participate in community life than has been the case under the professional model of policing.

Each of these differences may be expected to result in patterns of interaction with juveniles that are different from those which characterize traditional policing. While each of the anticipated changes in approach and context in community policing suggest potential for constructive change in the police/juvenile relationship (Guarino Ghezzi, 1994), these changes in youth engagement and style are neither inherently good or bad. For example, when officers are given added discretion, this discretion may be used to craft a creative alternative to making an arrest (Mastrofski et al., 1995). In other cases, the exercise of discretion has itself been part of the problem. Even when use of discretion is well intended (e.g., to give a youth a second chance), some juveniles may interpret its exercise as discriminatory (Guarino Ghezzi, 1994). The current study allows for an exploratory examination of COP officer orientation and behavior toward juveniles. Although it is limited in focus in that we lack data on arrest outcomes, our emphasis is on several key themes of variation in the juvenile/police relationship and on the impact of changes that result from community policing on police/juvenile interaction. . . .

DISCUSSION AND CONCLUSION

In many respects the implementation of community policing holds promise for altering the historically antagonistic relationship between juveniles and the police. Community policing is, for example, expected to increase opportunities for prevention and deterrence and to expand the discretion needed for creative problem solving and diversion. It is, however, unclear to what extent the role of officers may change in the response to youth and to juvenile crime.

This paper has examined the behavior and attitudes of community police officers in the context of carrying out law enforcement, surveillance, order maintenance and crime prevention functions. While tentative and exploratory, findings from the current study do document a distinctive style of interaction with young people among community police, a different attitude toward juveniles and a unique view of the appropriate role of officers in the response to youth crime and in support of youth development. Officers assigned to the COP target neighborhoods engaged in a variety of neighborhood based, preventive, coalition building activities that may be expected to improve the situation of young people generally and provide a model which other officers may emulate. Specifically, COP officer efforts to enhance prevention, creative diversion, advocacy and parental support at least in part support the optimism of community policing advocates. These findings also provide support for a new research agenda in policing that begins to reexamine the police/juvenile relationship in the context of the community policing agenda, as well as the reality of new patterns of youth crime.

On the other hand, the limitations of this study leave open the question of whether or not community policing may actually increase arrests and whether COP may in some cases result in expanded efforts to remove troublesome young people from the neighborhood as an order maintenance tactic. While we did not witness such activity, we also cannot rule out the possibility that the generally helpful monitoring and surveillance activities of the COP officers we observed might for other officers degenerate into harassment. Perhaps the most discouraging outcome of the Beach City case study was the ambivalence of some senior police managers in providing support for innovative prevention and problem solving activities by maintaining the commitment of resources to the COP initiative and ensuring that police were given appropriate incentives for creative local diversion. In this regard, this research provides additional support for critics of community policing who question the commitment of administrators to reallocating resources needed to sustain a genuine community presence (Mastrofski and Ritti, 1995).

Finally, more general questions about the meaning of community policing for young people and the response to juvenile crime should be addressed in future research and debated by both police and youth service policy makers and researchers. To what extent do the presumed positive changes in the partnership relationship with adults in community policing apply to juveniles? Will community police be more likely to view juveniles as adolescents with needs rather than as suspects? Will they be less fearful of juveniles than adult offenders, or will they be even more likely to view youth as "symbolic assailants" who can be even more dangerous than adults because of their unpredictability (Skolnick, 1966)? Will young people be treated by officers as citizens with an interest in crime prevention and a role to play in neighborhood safety or will they be viewed and treated primarily as part of the problem to be addressed? More generally, will juveniles be viewed as part of the "community" being served by community policing (Chan, 1994)?

Generally, our findings are consistent with the more positive and hopeful answers to these questions. The potential for positive interaction and the expansion of police in the helping role, described by Guarino Ghezzi (1994) as "reintegrative policing," seems greater with community policing if for no other reason than the prospects for greater understanding among COP officers of young people and their neighborhoods. Changes in juvenile justice and the emerging communitarian response to youth crime (Braithwaite and Mugford, 1994; Moore and O'Connell, 1994) also assume that police officers will be able to adopt new roles both in traditional surveillance and enforcement activities, and in the sanctioning and reintegrative process. Family group conferencing models now being implemented in various cities in the USA, after almost a decade of experience with these approaches in New Zealand and Australia (Alder and Wundersitz, 1994), assign police officers a role as facilitator, and often mediator, in a community conference including the young offender, the victim and his/her supporters, the youth's family and others. Informed by the theory known as reintegrative shaming (Braithwaite, 1989), as these and other restorative justice approaches to juvenile crime (Bazemore and Umbreit, 1995) gain increased acceptance, police will inevitably be asked to continue this "role stretch" to accommodate. It will be left to researchers to examine critically the extent to which police officers are willing to make this shift in a manner consistent with these new communitarian philosophies.

REFERENCES

Alder, C. and Wundersitz, J. (1994). *Family Conferencing and Juvenile Justice: The Way Forward or Misplaced Optimism?*, Australian Institute of Criminology, Canberra, Australia.

Bazemore, G. and Cole, A. (1993). "Implementing and evaluating community policing: a case study in an urban community," paper presented at the SECOPA National Conference, Orlando, FL, October.

Bazemore, G. and Umbreit, M. (1995). "Rethinking the sanctioning function in juvenile court: retributive or restorative responses to youth crime," *Crime and Delinquency*, Vol. 41 No. 3, pp. 296–316.

Bazemore, G. and Washington, C. (1995). "Charting the future of the juvenile justice system: reinventing mission and management," *Spectrum: The Journal of State Government*, Vol. 68 No. 2, pp. 51–66.

Black, D. (1980). *The Manners and Customs of the Police*, Academic Press, New York, NY.

Black, D. and Reiss, A. (1970). "Police control of juveniles," *American Sociological Review*, Vol. 35, pp. 63–77.

Braithwaite, J. (1989). *Crime, Shame and Reintegration*. Cambridge University Press, New York, NY.

Braithwaite, J. and Mugford, S. (1994). "Conditions of successful reintegration ceremonies: dealing with juvenile offenders," *The British Journal of Criminology*, Vol. 34 No. 2, pp. 139–71.

Brown, L.P. (1989). "Community policing: a practical guide for police officials," *The Police Chief*, August, pp. 72–82.

Chan, J. (1994). "Policing youth in 'ethnic' communities: is community policing the answer?," in White, R. and Alder, C. (Eds). *The Police and Young People in Australia*, Cambridge University Press, Melbourne, Australia.

Elliott, D.F. (1993). "Serious violent offenders: onset, developmental course, and termination," The American Society of Criminology, 1993 Presidential address, *Criminology*, Vol. 32, pp. 1–2.

Ericson, R. (1982). *Reproducing Order: A Study of Police Patrol Work*, University of Toronto Press, Toronto.

Goldman, N. (1963). *The Differential Selection of Juvenile Offenders for Court Appearance*. National Council on Crime and Delinquency, Washington, DC.

Goldstein, H. (1987). "Toward community oriented policing: potential, basic requirements and threshold questions," *Crime and Delinquency*, Vol. 33, pp. 6–30.

Goldstein, H. (1990). *Problem Oriented Policing*, McGraw Hill, New York, NY.

Guarino Ghezzi, S. (1994). "Reintegrative police surveillance of juvenile offenders: forging an urban model," *Crime and Delinquency*, Vol. 40 No. 2, pp. 131–53.

Jones, M. and Krisberg, B. (1994). "Images and reality: juvenile crime, youth violence and public policy," National Council on Crime and Delinquency, San Francisco, CA.

Kelling, G. and Moore, M. (1988). "The evolving strategy of policing," *Perspectives on Policing*, No. 4, National Institute of Justice and Harvard University, Washington, DC.

Langworthy, R. (1983). "Effects of police agency size on the use of police employees: a reexamination of Ostrom, Parks and Whitaker," *Police Studies*, Vol. 5 No. 4, pp. 11–19.

Lemov, P. (1994). "The assault on juvenile justice," *Governing*, December, pp. 26–31.

Lundman, R. (1974). "Domestic police citizen encounters," *Journal of Police Science and Administration*, Vol. 2 No. 1, pp. 22–7.

Lundman, R., Sykes, R. and Clark, J. (1978). "Police control of juveniles: a replication," *Journal of Research in Crime and Delinquency*, Vol. 15 No. 1, pp. 74–91.

Mastrofski, S. (1981). "Surveying clients to assess police performance: focussing on the police citizen encounter," *Evaluation Review*, Vol. 5 No. 3, pp. 397–408.

Mastrofski, S. and Ritti, R. (1995). "Making sense of community policing: a theory based analysis," paper presented at the American Society of Criminology National Conference, Boston, MA, November.

Mastrofski, S. Worden, R. and Snypes, J. (1995). "Law enforcement in a time of community policing," *Criminology*, Vol. 33 No. 4, pp. 539–63.

Mehan, A. (1993). "Internal police records and the control of juveniles: politics and policing in a suburban town," *The British Journal of Criminology*, Vol. 33 No. 4, pp. 504–24.

Moore, D. and O'Connell, T. (1994). "Family conferencing in Wagga Wagga: a communitarian model of justice," in Adler, C. and Wrendersitz, J. (Eds). *Family Conferencing and Juvenile Justice: The Way Forward or Misplaced Optimism?*, Australian Studies in Law, Crime and Justice: Australian Institue of Criminology, Canberra, ACT.

Moore, M. and Stephens, D. (1991). *Beyond Command and Control: The Strategic Management of Police Departments*, Police Executive Research Forum, Washington, DC.

Moore, M. and Trojanowicz, R. (1988). "Policing and the fear of crime," *Perspectives on Policing*, National Institute of Justice, US Department of Justice and Harvard University, Washington, DC.

OJJDP. (1992). *Juvenile Justice Bulletin*. OJJDP Update on Statistics, Office of Juvenile Justice and Delinquency Prevention, Washington, DC.

Piliavin, I. and Briar, S. (1964). "Delinquency, situational inducements and commitment to conformity," *Social Problems*, Vol. 13 No. 1, pp. 35–45.

Reiss, A. (1992). "Police organizations in the twentieth century," in Tonry, M. and Morris, N. (Eds). *Modern Policing*, University of Chicago Press, Chicago, IL.

Rosenbaum, D. (1988). "Community crime prevention: a review and synthesis of the literature," *Justice Quarterly*, Vol. 5 No. 3, pp. 323–95.

Siegal, L. and Senna, J. (1994). *Juvenile Delinquency, Theory, Practice and Law*, 5th ed., West Publishing Company, St Paul, MN.

Skogan, W. (1990). *Disorder and Decline: Crime and the Spiral of Decay in American Neighborhoods*, Free Press, New York, NY.

Skolnick, J. (1966). *Justice without Trial*, Wiley, New York, NY.

Smith, D. (1984). "The organizational aspects of legal control," *Criminology*, Vol. 22 No. 2, pp. 19–38.

Smith, D. and Klein, J. (1984). "Police control and interpersonal disputes," *Social Problems*, Vol. 31 No. 4, pp. 468–81.

Smith, D. and Visher, C. (1981). "Street level justice, situational determinants of police arrest decisions," *Social Problems* Vol. 29, pp. 167–78.

Sparrow, M., Moore, M. and Kennedy, D. (1990). *Beyond 911: A New Era for Policing*. Basic Books, New York, NY.

Uniform Crime Reports (1991). *Crime in the United States: Uniform Crime Reports*, Government Printing Office, Washington, DC.

Visher, C. (1983). "Arrest decisions and notions of chivalry," *Criminology*, Vol. 21, pp. 5–28.

Vollmer, A. (1936). "Police progress in the past twenty five years," *Journal of Criminal Law and Criminology*, Vol. 24 No. 2, pp. 161–75.

Walker, S. (1984). "Broken windows and fractured history: the use and misuse of history in recent police patrol analysis," *Justice Quarterly*, Vol. 1 No. 1, pp. 75–90.

Werthman, C. and Piliavin, I. (1967). "Gang members and the police," in Bordua, D. (Ed.). *The Police: Six Sociological Essays*, John Wiley & Sons, New York, NY.

Whitehead, J. and Lab, S. (1990). *Juvenile Justice: An Introduction*, Anderson Publishing Co., Cincinnati, OH.

Wilson, J. (1967). *Varieties of Police Behavior: The Management of Law and Order in Eight Communities*, Harvard University Press, Cambridge, MA.

Wilson, J. and Kelling, G. (1982). "Broken windows: the police and neighborhood safety," *The Atlantic Monthly*, March.

REVIEW QUESTIONS

1. What themes emerge from the "classic" studies of police–juvenile interactions reviewed by the authors? Which of these themes were evident in the Piliavin and Briar article at the beginning of this chapter? Which ones were *not* raised by Piliavin and Briar?

2. How do the authors say community-oriented policing (COP) is believed or expected to alter police relationships with citizens generally? With juveniles in particular? How is COP different from previous models of policing?

3. In discussing their own study of police–juvenile interactions in "Beach City," Florida,

what do the authors say they found out about police styles, attitudes, roles, and activities in neighborhoods targeted in their research? What do they conclude about the effect of COP on relations between juveniles and the police?

FURTHER READING

Becker, Harold K. (2000). New wine in old bottles: The time has come for therapeutic community policing for youth. *International Journal of Police Science and Management, 3*(2), 103–110.

Belknap, Joanne, Morash, Merry, and Trojanowicz, Robert. (1987). Implementing a community policing model for work with juveniles: An exploratory study. *Criminal Justice and Behavior, 14*(2), 211–245.

Black, Donald J., and Reiss, Albert J., Jr. (1970). Police control of juveniles. *American Sociological Review, 35*, 63–77.

Chambliss, William. (1973). The saints and the roughnecks. *Society, 11*, 24–31.

Esbensen, Finn-Aage, and Osgood, D. Wayne. (1999). Gang resistance education and training (GREAT): Results from the national evaluation. *Journal of Research in Crime and Delinquency, 36*(2), 194–225.

Grisso, Thomas. (1980). Juveniles' capacities to waive *Miranda* rights: An empirical analysis. *California Law Review, 68*, 1134–1165.

Guarino-Ghezzi, Susan. (1994). Reintegrative police surveillance of juvenile offenders: Forging an urban model. *Crime and Delinquency, 40*(2), 131–153.

Lundman, Richard J., Sykes, Richard E., and Clark, John P. (1978). Police control of juveniles: A replication. *Journal of Research in Crime and Delinquency, 15*, 74–91.

McCold, Paul, and Wachtel, Benjamin. (1998). *The Bethlehem Pennsylvania Police Family*

Group Conferencing Project. Pipersville, PA: Community Service Foundation. Available online: http://fp.enter.net/restorativepractices/BPD.pdf

Meehan, Albert J. (1993). Internal police records and the control of juveniles: Politics and policing in a suburban town. *British Journal of Criminology, 33*(4), 504–524.

Needle, Jerome A., and Stapleton, William Vaughan. (1983). *Police Handling of Youth Gangs.* Washington, DC: Office of Juvenile Justice and Delinquency Prevention.

Sampson, Robert J. (1986). Effects of socioeconomic context on official reaction to juvenile delinquency. *American Sociological Review, 51*, 876–885.

Sealock, Miriam D., and Simpson, Sally S. (1998). Unraveling bias in arrest decisions: The role of juvenile offender type-scripts. *Justice Quarterly, 15*, 427–457.

Spergel, Irving, et al. (1993). *Gang Suppression and Intervention: Problem and Response—Research Summary.* Washington, DC: Office of Juvenile Justice and Delinquency Prevention. Available online: http://www.ncjrs.org/pdffiles/gangprob.pdf

Thurman, Quint C., and Giacomazzi, Andrew. (1994). Cops and kids revisited: A second-year assessment of a community policing and delinquency prevention innovation. *Police Studies, 17*(4), 1–20.

Thurman, Quint C., Giacomazzi, Andrew, and Bogen, Phil. (1993). Research note: Cops, kids, and community policing—An assessment of a community policing demonstration project. *Crime and Delinquency, 39*(4), 554–564.

Wordes, Madeline, and Bynum, Timothy S. (1995). Policing juveniles: Is there bias against youths of color? In Kimberly Kempf Leonard, Carl E. Pope, and William H. Fey-erherm (Eds.), *Minorities in Juvenile Justice* (pp. 47–65). Thousand Oaks, CA: Sage.

Young, Michael, and Rausch, Susan. (1991). Be a winner: Arkansas' approach to involving law enforcement officers in drug education. *Journal of Drug Education, 21*, 183–189.

CHAPTER 5

The Intake Process and Diversion of Minor Offenders

Beginning in this chapter, and continuing in Chapters 6 and 7, we examine a diverse set of decisions that take place during or are related in some way to what is most commonly called the juvenile court intake process. You will recall from Chapter 1 that responsibility for making intake decisions normally falls either to an intake officer (an employee of the jurisdiction's juvenile probation department who may or may not also fulfill other duties of a probation officer) or to a prosecutor.

Barry Feld (1999) has likened this process—or, more particularly, the laws that have superceded intake officer decision making by narrowing the scope of juvenile court jurisdiction and/or transferring decision making authority to prosecutors—to the dilemma confronted during wartime by a military doctor or medic who, through a process known as "triage," must determine which wounded soldiers to care for first, directing scarce medical resources toward those whose lives can only be saved through emergency surgery while denying immediate aid both to those whose injuries are almost certainly fatal and to those whose wounds, though painful, are not life-threatening. Feld's concept of "criminological triage," though, focuses on the mechanisms and processes by which, in his view, predominantly white, middle-class, and often female status offenders and minor offenders are diverted out of the juvenile justice system altogether, serious offenders—a disproportionate number of whom are minority youth—are transferred to adult criminal court, and the remainder become the subjects of petitions for adjudication of delinquency filed in juvenile court.

This chapter focuses on the respective roles of intake officers and prosecutors in the intake process, giving special attention to the first of three conceptually distinct questions that must be resolved shortly after a juvenile is arrested or referred to juvenile court: Is the case sufficiently serious to warrant formal court intervention of any sort? We also examine in this chapter the types of diversion programs that have emerged for "nonjudicial" intervention in cases where the answer to this threshold question is "no" but outright dismissal or "adjustment" of the case with no further action of any sort is also deemed inappropriate. Chapters 6 and 7 deal, respectively, with two additional questions that arise only if the first one is answered in the affirmative: Should the child be detained (i.e., held in a secure preadjudication facility) pending the outcome of court proceedings? And does the child's age, offense, and/or prior record make transfer to adult criminal court advisable or even, depending on the jurisdiction and the facts alleged in the case, mandatory?

We begin our consideration of the threshold question—whether to file a petition seeking an adjudication of delinquency or instead to divert the child away from formal juvenile court intervention—with the IJA-ABA *Standards Relating to the Juvenile Probation Function: Intake and Predisposition Investigative Services*. The *Standards*, while not legally binding, illustrate the range of options typically available to an intake officer and outline the conditions under which the IJA-ABA Juvenile Justice Standards Project found it appropriate to file a petition, dismiss the complaint, seek a consent decree (i.e., what is more commonly known today as informal probation), or invoke a nonjudicial disposition (i.e., diversion). The *Standards* also outline recommended procedures for intake investigations, intake interviews, and dispositional conferences, and they highlight the Project's determination of the rights that should be accorded to juveniles during the intake process.

Because decision making at this stage is often either shared with or exclusively governed by a prosecutor, we will also take a brief look at standards promulgated by the National District Attorneys Association (NDAA) pertaining to the prosecutor's responsibilities with respect to determination of evidence sufficiency, filing of delinquency petitions, and diversion. (Note: Additional excerpts from NDAA's *National Prosecution Standards* appear in Chapter 8.)

The third selection reviews diversion programs implemented in the wake of the report of the President's Commission and the popularity of labeling theories in criminology during the 1970s. As students with a background in criminology and theories of crime will be aware, the labeling perspective views the process of adjudicating a child delinquent to be a highly stigmatizing experience that can lead to the youth being treated as an outcast, beginning to view himself or herself as "bad" and, consequently, falling into a life of crime simply because that is what society (and, ultimately, the child as well) expects and even demands. Just as Judge Mack saw the informal proceedings, confidentiality, and benevolent treatment of the juvenile court as a way to avoid stigmatizing the child with the "criminal" label, labeling theorists argued that even the "delinquency" label has a stigmatizing effect that can induce young people to begin trying to live up to the image others have of them and to become immersed in a delinquent role. Recall from Chapter 3 that the President's Commission—adopting the lead of Edwin Lemert (1967), a prominent early proponent of labeling theory and a consultant to the Commission who vigorously advocated "judicious nonintervention" in an appendix to the *Task Force Report*—expressed concern that official action "may produce more harm than good" and recommended both narrowing the jurisdiction of the juvenile court and using the formal juvenile justice process "only as a last resort" (see pp. 77-78). This stance, reinforced by the arguments of later labeling theorists such as Edwin Shur—who, pushing Lemert's perspective to its logical extreme, called for a policy of "radical non-intervention" centered around his injunction to "leave the kids alone whenever possible" (Shur, 1973, p. 155)—led to the proliferation of community-based and, more recently, quasi-official and even legislatively established diversion programs. The entire range of such programs is reviewed here by Mark Ezell.

Next, carrying our consideration of the intake process and diversion programs to a more specific level, excerpts from the Revised Code of Washington (RCW) addressing the decision to file a delinquency petition and the nature of diversion agreements provide a sense of the way in which both intake decision making and the diversion process operate in one state.

Finally, a diversion program very different from the one established under the Washington statute is the subject of Jeffrey A. Butts and Janeen Buck's overview of the teen court phenomenon that has taken hold in as many as 675 jurisdictions during the last decade.

REFERENCES

Feld, Barry C. (1999). *Bad Kids: Race and the Transformation of the Juvenile Court.* New York: Oxford University Press.

Lemert, Edwin. (1967). The juvenile court: Quest and realities. In *Task Force Report: Juvenile Delinquency and Youth Crime—Report on Juvenile Justice and Consultants' Papers* (pp. 91–106). Washington, DC: U.S. Government Printing Office.

Shur, Edwin. (1973). *Radical Non-Intervention: Rethinking the Delinquency Problem.* Englewood Cliffs, NJ: Prentice Hall.

Standards Relating to the Juvenile Probation Function: Intake and Predisposition Investigative Services

IJA-ABA Juvenile Justice Standards Project—Josephine Gittler, Reporter

PART II: JUVENILE COURT INTAKE

Section I: General Standards

2.1 Availability and utilization of intake services.
Intake services should be available to and utilized by all juvenile courts.

Section II: Dispositional Alternative at Intake

2.2 Judicial disposition of a complaint.
"Judicial disposition of a complaint" is the initiation of formal judicial proceedings against the juvenile who is the subject of a complaint through the filing of a petition. After intake screening, judicial disposition of a complaint may be made.

2.3 Unconditional dismissal of a complaint.
The "unconditional dismissal of a complaint" is the termination of all proceedings against a juvenile. Unconditional dismissal of a complaint is a permissible intake dispositional alternative.

2.4 Nonjudicial disposition of a complaint.
    A. "Nonjudicial disposition of a complaint" is the taking of some action on a complaint without the initiation of formal judicial proceedings through the filing of a petition or the issuance of a court order.

Source: IJA-ABA Juvenile Justice Standards Project—Josephine Gittler, Reporter. (1996). Standards relating to the juvenile probation function: Intake and predisposition investigative services. In Institute of Judicial Administration—American Bar Association. *Juvenile Justice Standards Annotated: A Balanced Approach* (pp. 155–170). Robert E. Shepherd, Jr., editor. Chicago: American Bar Association. Originally published in 1980 as a separate volume with commentary by Ballinger Publishing Company. Copyright 1996 by the Institute of Judicial Administration. Adapted by permission.

B. The existing types of nonjudicial dispositions are as follows:
    1. "Nonjudicial probation" is a nonjudicial disposition involving the supervision by juvenile intake or probation personnel of a juvenile who is the subject of a complaint, for a period of time during which the juvenile may be required to comply with certain restrictive conditions with respect to his or her conduct and activities.
    2. The "provision of intake services" is the direct provision of services by juvenile intake and probation personnel on a continuing basis to a juvenile who is the subject of a complaint.
    3. A "conditional dismissal of a complaint" is the termination of all proceedings against a juvenile subject to certain conditions not involving the acceptance of nonjudicial supervision or intake services. It includes a "community agency referral," which is the referral of a juvenile who is the subject of a complaint to a community agency or agencies for services.
C. A "community agency referral" is the only permissible nonjudicial disposition, subject to the conditions set forth in Standard 2.4 E. Intake personnel should refer juveniles in need of services whenever possible to youth service bureaus and other public and private community agencies. Juvenile probation agencies and other agencies responsible for the administration and provision of intake services and intake personnel should actively promote and encourage the establishment and the development of a wide range of community-based services and programs for delinquent and nondelinquent juveniles.
D. Nonjudicial probation, provision of intake services, and conditional dismissal other than community agency referral are not permissible intake dispositions.
E. A nonjudicial disposition should be utilized only under the following conditions:
    1. A nonjudicial disposition should take the form of an agreement of a contractual nature under which the intake officer promises not to file a petition in exchange for certain commitments by the juvenile and his or her parents or legal guardian or both with respect to their future conduct and activities.
    2. The juvenile and his or her parents or legal guardian should voluntarily and intelligently enter into the agreement.
    3. The intake officer should advise the juvenile and his or her parents or legal guardian that they have the right to refuse to enter into an agreement for a nonjudicial disposition and to request a formal adjudication.
    4. A nonjudicial disposition agreement should be limited in duration.
    5. The juvenile and his or her parents or legal guardian should be able to terminate the agreement at any time and to request formal adjudication.
    6. The terms of the nonjudicial agreement should be clearly stated in writing. This written agreement should contain a statement of the requirements set forth in subsections 2–5. It should be signed by all the parties to the agree-

ment, and a copy should be given to the juvenile and his or her parents or legal guardian.

7. Once a nonjudicial disposition of a complaint has been made, the subsequent filing of a petition based upon the events out of which the original complaint arose should be permitted for a period of [three (3)] months from the date the nonjudicial disposition agreement was entered into. If no petition is filed within that period, its subsequent filing should be prohibited. The juvenile's compliance with all proper and reasonable terms of the agreement should be an affirmative defense to a petition filed within the [three-month] period.

2.5 Consent decree.

A. A consent decree is a court order authorizing supervision of a juvenile for a specified period of time during which the juvenile may be required to fulfill certain conditions or some other disposition of the complaint without the filing of a petition and a formal adjudicatory proceeding.

A consent decree should be permissible under the following conditions:

1. The juvenile and his or her parents or legal guardian should voluntarily and intelligently consent to the decree.

2. The intake officer and the judge should advise the juvenile and his or her parents or legal guardian that they have the right to refuse to consent to the decree and to request a formal adjudication.

3. The juvenile should have an unwaivable right to the assistance of counsel in connection with an application for a consent decree. The intake officer should advise the juvenile of this right.

4. The terms of the decree should be clearly stated in the decree, and a copy should be given to all the parties to the decree.

5. The decree should not remain in force for a period in excess of six (6) months. Upon application of any of the parties to the decree, made before expiration of the decree, the decree, after notice and hearing, may be extended for not more than an additional three (3) months by the court.

6. The juvenile and his or her parents or legal guardian should be able to terminate the agreement at any time and to request the filing of a petition and formal adjudication.

7. Once a consent decree has been entered, the subsequent filing of a petition based upon the events out of which the original complaint arose should be permitted for a period of [three (3)] months from the date the decree was entered. If no petition is filed within that period, its subsequent filing should be prohibited. The juvenile's compliance with all proper and reasonable terms of the decree should be an affirmative defense to a petition filed within the [three-month] period.

Section III: Criteria for Intake Dispositional Decisions

2.6 Necessity for and desirability of written guidelines and rules.

A. Juvenile probation agencies and other agencies responsible for intake services should issue written guidelines and rules with respect to criteria for intake dispositional decisions. The objective of such administrative guidelines and rules is to confine and control the exercise of discretion by intake officers in the making of intake dispositional decisions so as to promote fairness, consistency, and effective dispositional decisions.

B. These guidelines and rules should be reviewed and evaluated by interested juvenile justice system officials and community-based delinquency control and prevention agencies.

C. Legislatures and courts should encourage or require rule making by these agencies with respect to criteria for intake dispositional decisions.

2.7 Legal sufficiency of complaint.

A. Upon receipt of a complaint, the intake officer should make an initial determination of whether the complaint is legally sufficient for the filing of a petition on the basis of the contents of the complaint and an intake investigation. In this regard the officer should determine:

    1. whether the facts as alleged are sufficient to establish the court's jurisdiction over the juvenile; and

    2. whether the competent and credible evidence available is sufficient to support the charges against the juvenile.

B. If the officer determines that the facts as alleged are not sufficient to establish the court's jurisdiction, the officer should dismiss the complaint. If the officer finds that the court has jurisdiction but determines that the competent and credible evidence available is not sufficient to support the charges against the juvenile, the officer should dismiss the complaint.

C. If the legal sufficiency of the complaint is unclear, the officer should ask the appropriate prosecuting official for a determination of its legal sufficiency.

2.8 Disposition in best interests of juvenile and community.

A. If the intake officer determines that the complaint is legally sufficient, the officer should determine what disposition of the complaint is most appropriate and desirable from the standpoint of the best interests of the juvenile and the community. This involves a determination as to whether a judicial disposition of the complaint would cause undue harm to the juvenile or exacerbate the problems that led to his or her delinquent acts, whether the juvenile presents a substantial danger to others, and whether the referral of the juvenile to the court has already served as a desired deterrent.

B. The officer should determine what disposition is in the best interests of the juvenile and the community in light of the following:

1. The seriousness of the offense that the alleged delinquent conduct constitutes should be considered in making an intake dispositional decision. A petition should ordinarily be filed against a juvenile who has allegedly engaged in delinquent conduct constituting a serious offense, which should be determined on the basis of the nature and extent of harm to others produced by the conduct.

2. The nature and number of the juvenile's prior contacts with the juvenile court should be considered in making an intake dispositional decision.

3. The circumstances surrounding the alleged delinquent conduct, including whether the juvenile was alone or in the company of other juveniles who also participated in the alleged delinquent conduct, should be considered in making an intake dispositional decision. If a petition is filed against one of the juveniles, a petition should ordinarily be filed against the other juveniles for substantially similar conduct.

4. The age and maturity of the juvenile may be relevant to an intake dispositional decision.

5. The juvenile's school attendance and behavior, the juvenile's family situation and relationships, and the juvenile's home environment may be relevant to an intake dispositional decision.

6. The attitude of the juvenile to the alleged delinquent conduct and to law enforcement and juvenile court authorities may be relevant to an intake dispositional decision, but a nonjudicial disposition of the complaint or the unconditional dismissal of the complaint should not be precluded for the sole reason that the juvenile denies the allegations of the complaint.

7. A nonjudicial disposition of the complaint or the unconditional dismissal of the complaint should not be precluded for the sole reason that the complainant opposes dismissal.

8. The availability of services to meet the juvenile's needs both within and outside the juvenile justice system should be considered in making an intake dispositional decision.

9. The factors that are not relevant to an intake dispositional decision include but are not necessarily limited to the juvenile's race, ethnic background, religion, sex, and economic status. . . .

Section IV: Intake Procedures

2.9 Necessity for and desirability of written guidelines and rules.
Juvenile probation agencies and other agencies responsible for intake services should develop and publish written guidelines and rules with respect to intake procedures.

2.10 Initiation of intake proceedings and receipt of complaint by intake officer.

A. An intake officer should initiate proceedings upon receipt of a complaint.

B. Any complaint that serves as the basis for the filing of a petition should be sworn to and signed by a person who has personal knowledge of the facts or is informed of them and believes that they are true.

2.11 Intake investigation.

A. Prior to making a dispositional decision, the intake officer should be authorized to conduct a preliminary investigation in order to obtain information essential to the making of the decision.

B. In the course of the investigation the intake officer may:

1. interview or otherwise seek information from the complainant, a victim of, witness to, or coparticipant in the delinquent conduct allegedly engaged in by the juvenile;

2. check existing court records, the records of law enforcement agencies, and other public records of a nonprivate nature;

3. conduct interviews with the juvenile and his or her parents or legal guardian in accordance with the requirements set forth in Standard 2.14.

C. If the officer wishes to make any additional inquiries, he or she should do so only with the consent of the juvenile and his or her parents or legal guardian.

D. It is the responsibility of the complainant to furnish the intake officer with information sufficient to establish the jurisdiction of the court over the juvenile and to support the charges against the juvenile. If the officer believes the information to be deficient in this respect, he or she may notify the complainant of the need for additional information.

2.12 Juvenile's privilege against self-incrimination at intake.

A. A juvenile should have a privilege against self-incrimination in connection with questioning by intake personnel during the intake process.

B. Any statement made by a juvenile to an intake officer or other information derived directly or indirectly from such a statement is inadmissible in evidence in any judicial proceeding prior to a formal finding of delinquency unless the statement was made after consultation with and in the presence of counsel.

2.13 Juvenile's right to assistance of counsel at intake.

A juvenile should have an unwaivable right to the assistance of counsel at intake:

A. in connection with any questioning by intake personnel at an intake interview involving questioning in accordance with Standard 2.14 or other questioning by intake personnel; and

B. in connection with any discussions or negotiations regarding a nonjudicial disposition, including discussions and negotiations in the course of a dispositional conference in accordance with Standard 2.14.

2.14 Intake interviews and dispositional conferences.

A. If the intake officer deems it advisable, the officer may request and arrange an interview with the juvenile and his or her parents or legal guardian.

B. Participation in an intake interview by the juvenile and his or her parents or legal guardian should be voluntary. They should have the right to refuse to participate in an interview, and the officer should have no authority to compel their attendance.

C. At the time the request to attend the interview is made, the intake officer should inform the juvenile and his or her parents or legal guardian either in writing or orally that attendance is voluntary and that the juvenile has the right to be represented by counsel.

D. At the commencement of the interview, the intake officer should:
   1. explain to the juvenile and his or her parents or legal guardian that a complaint has been made and explain the allegations of the complaint;
   2. explain the function of the intake process, the dispositional powers of the intake officer, and intake procedures;
   3. explain that participation in the intake interview is voluntary and that they may refuse to participate; and
   4. notify them of the right of the juvenile to remain silent and the right to counsel as heretofore defined in Standard 2.13.

E. Subsequent to the intake interview, the intake officer may schedule one or more dispositional conferences with the juvenile and his or her parents or legal guardian in order to effect a nonjudicial disposition.

F. Participation in a dispositional conference by a juvenile and his or her parents or legal guardian should be voluntary. They should have the right to refuse to participate, and the intake officer should have no authority to compel their attendance.

G. The intake officer may conduct dispositional conferences in accordance with the procedures for intake interviews set forth in subsections D and E.

2.15 Length of intake process.

A decision at the intake level as to the disposition of a complaint should be made as expeditiously as possible. The period within which the decision is made should not exceed thirty (30) days from the date the complaint is filed in cases in which the juvenile who is the subject of a complaint has not been placed in detention or shelter care facilities.

Section V: Scope of Intake Officer's Dispositional Powers

2.16 Role of intake officer and prosecutor in filing of petition: right of complainant to file a petition.

    A. If the intake officer determines that a petition should be filed, the officer should submit a written report to the appropriate prosecuting official requesting that a petition should be filed. The officer should also submit a written statement of his or her decision and of the reasons for the decision to the juvenile and his or her parents or legal guardian. All petitions should be countersigned and filed by the appropriate prosecuting official. The prosecutor may refuse the request of the intake officer to file a petition. Any determination by the prosecutor that a petition should not be filed should be final.

    B. If the intake officer determines that a petition should not be filed, the officer should notify the complainant of his or her decision and of the reasons for the decision and should advise the complainant that he or she may submit the complaint to the appropriate prosecuting official for review. Upon receiving a request for review, the prosecutor should consider the facts presented by the complainant, consult with the intake officer who made the initial decision, and then make the final determination as to whether a petition should be filed.

    C. In the absence of a complainant's request for a review of the intake officer's determination that a petition should not be filed, the intake officer should notify the appropriate prosecuting official of the officer's decision not to request the filing of a petition in those cases in which the conduct charged would constitute a crime if committed by an adult. The prosecutor should have the right in all such cases, after consultation with the intake officer, to file a petition.

REVIEW QUESTIONS

1. What are the basic alternatives available to an intake officer in determining the disposition of a complaint?

2. Which alternatives are considered appropriate under the IJA-ABA standards? Which ones are considered inappropriate? Why do you think the standards disallow "nonjudicial dispositions" other than community agency referrals? Is this position consistent with that taken in the report of the President's Commission that we encountered in Chapter 3?

3. In what kinds of situations do you think "unconditional dismissal of a complaint" would be considered appropriate by the people involved in preparing these standards? Under what circumstances would *you* consider it appropriate?

4. What is a "consent decree"? How does it differ from judicial disposition of a complaint? From nonjudicial disposition? What restrictions do the IJA-ABA standards place on consent decrees (i.e., what conditions must be satisfied)? In what kinds of situations would you consider this disposition appropriate?

5. Can you summarize the main criteria specified in the standards for determining the appropriate disposition in a particular case? Which criteria do *you* consider most

important? Least important? Do any of the criteria strike you as unnecessary or inappropriate? Are there other considerations (i.e., ones not specified in the standards) that you believe *should* be taken into account?

6. What are the basic intake procedures outlined in the standards? What rights do the standards specify should be granted to ju-

veniles during the intake process? Are there any aspects of the procedures that you disagree with or that you think should be modified? Explain.

7. What role in the intake process do the IJA-ABA standards accord to *prosecutors*? Do you think prosecutors should have a larger role in the process? A smaller role? Explain your response.

National Prosecution Standards: Juvenile Justice—Responsibilities of the Prosecutor for Charging Function and Diversion of Legally Sufficient Cases

National District Attorneys Association

92.2 RESPONSIBILITIES OF THE PROSECUTOR FOR CHARGING FUNCTION

a. Right to Screen Cases and File Petitions

The prosecutor should have the exclusive right to screen facts obtained from the police and other sources to determine whether those facts are legally sufficient for prosecution. If it is determined that the facts are legally sufficient, the prosecutor should determine whether a juvenile is to be transferred to adult court, charged in juvenile court, or diverted from formal adjudication.

b. Definition of Legal Sufficiency

Legally sufficient cases are those cases in which the prosecutor believes that he can reasonably substantiate delinquency charges against the juvenile by admissible evidence at trial. The charging process requires early determination as to whether the facts constitute prima facie evidence that a delinquent act was committed and that the juvenile accused committed it. If the facts are not legally sufficient, the matter should be terminated or returned to the referral source pending further investigation or receipt of additional reports.

c. Prosecutorial Disposition of Legally Sufficient Cases

The prosecutor or a designee should further review cases determined to be legally sufficient to decide whether the case will be transferred to adult court, filed as a formal petition with the juvenile court, or diverted.

d. Juveniles Held in Custody

If the juvenile is being held in custody after arrest or detention, the prosecutor should screen the facts for legal sufficiency within 24 hours (excluding Sundays and legal holidays) after receipt from the police or other referral sources, unless state law or practice provides for a shorter period. If the allegations do not substantiate a legally sufficient basis for proceeding, the matter should be terminated and the juvenile released. If the juvenile continues to be held in custody based upon legally sufficient facts, the prosecutor should determine within 72 hours (excluding Sundays and legal holidays) after receiving the facts from police and other referral sources whether the case should be transferred to the adult court, filed as a formal petition with the juvenile court, or diverted. State law or practice may provide, however, for a shorter period.

e. Juveniles Not Held in Custody.

If the juvenile is not held in custody, the facts should be screened for legal sufficiency within seven calendar days from receipt from police or other referral source, unless state law or practice provides for a shorter period. If the allegations do not substantiate a legally sufficient basis for proceeding, the matter should promptly be terminated. If the allegations do substantiate a legally sufficient basis for proceeding, the prosecutor should transfer the case to an adult court, file it as a formal petition with the juvenile court, or divert it within ten calendar days after receipt of the report, unless state law or practice provides for a shorter period.

f. Transfer or Certification to Adult Court

To the extent that the prosecutor is permitted by law to use discretion to decide whether a juvenile delinquency case should be transferred to the adult court, prosecutors should seek transfer only if the gravity of the current alleged offense or the record of previous delinquent behavior reasonably indicates that the treatment services and dispositional alternatives available in the juvenile court are:

1. Inadequate for dealing with the youth's delinquent behavior; or
2. Inadequate to protect the safety and welfare of the community.

g. Criteria for Deciding Formal Adjudication Versus Diversion

The prosecutor or a designee must further review legally sufficient cases not appropriate for transfer to adult court to determine whether they should be filed formally with the juvenile court or diverted for treatment, services, or probation. In determining whether to file formally or divert, the prosecutor or designated case reviewer should investigate to decide what disposition best serves the interests of the community and the juvenile, considering the following factors:

1. The seriousness of the alleged offense;

2. The role of the juvenile in that offense;

3. The nature and number of previous cases presented by the police or others against the juvenile, and the disposition of those cases;

4. The juvenile's age and maturity;

5. The availability of appropriate treatment or services potentially available through the juvenile court or through diversion;

6. Whether the juvenile admits guilt or involvement in the offense charged;

7. The dangerousness or threat posed by a juvenile to the person or property of others;

8. The provision of financial restitution to victims; and

9. Recommendations of the referring agency, victim, and advocates for the juvenile.

h. Qualifications of Case Screeners

Case screening may be accomplished by the prosecutor or by screeners employed directly by the prosecutor. If case screeners outside the prosecutor's office are employed, the prosecutor should have the right to review charging decisions and to file, modify, or dismiss any petition.

Screening for the legal sufficiency of facts related to a criminal incident should be conducted only by a prosecutor. Further screening of legally sufficient cases for prosecutorial disposition (transfer, filing with juvenile court, or diversion) should be conducted by or with advice of screeners knowledgeable about treatment and services for children and youth.

i. Role of the Prosecutor in Formal Filing

Formal charging documents for all cases referred to juvenile court should be prepared or reviewed by a prosecutor.

92.3 DIVERSION OF LEGALLY SUFFICIENT CASES

a. The Role of the Prosecutor in Diversion

The prosecutor is responsible for deciding which legally sufficient cases should be diverted from formal adjudication. Treatment, restitution, or public service programs developed in his office may be utilized or the case can be referred to existing probation or community service agencies. If the probation or service agency decides the case is not appropriate for their services, they must return it immediately to the prosecutor's office. The prosecutor will then make a further determination about an appropriate disposition.

b. Diversion Requires Admission of Involvement

A case should be diverted only if the juvenile admits guilt for the offense(s) charged in the written diversion contract. If the juvenile does not admit guilt, the case should be filed with the juvenile court or terminated. Admissions by the juvenile to the prosecutor or case screener in the course of investigating an appropriate prosecutorial disposition should not be used for any purpose by the prosecutor. Admissions in the juvenile's written diversion contract, however, may be used by the prosecutor in any subsequent adjudication.

c. Diversion Contract

All cases diverted require a written diversion contract between the juvenile and the supervising authority. The diversion contract should set forth the conditions of the informal disposition or diversion, together with an admission of guilt and waiver of a speedy trial and should be executed by both the juvenile and his parent or legal guardian. Diversion contracts should, in general, specify duties of the juvenile and the supervising authority that can reasonably be accomplished in three to six months. If the supervising authority determines that a juvenile has substantially breached his diversion contract, the case should be returned to the prosecutor for formal filing of a petition with the juvenile court. If the juvenile successfully complies with the contract duties, the case should be terminated with a favorable report.

d. Records of Diversion Contracts and Compliance

Records of diversion contracts and compliance or non-compliance should be maintained in the prosecutor's office. If screening is conducted outside that office, records should also be maintained in the screener's office. These records should be used exclusively by the prosecutor or designated case screeners to screen any subsequent case reports with respect to the juvenile. They should be destroyed when the juvenile reaches the age of majority.

e. Prosecutorial Review of Diversion Programs

The prosecutor should periodically review diversion programs, both within and outside the district attorney's office, to ensure that they provide appropriate supervision, treatment, restitution requirements, or services for the juvenile. The prosecutor should maintain a working relationship with all outside agencies providing diversion services to ensure that the prosecutor's diversion decisions are consistent and appropriate. . . .

COMMENTARY

. . . Standard 92.2 describes a large role for prosecutors in the charging function. This function has often been delegated by law or by practice to other agencies. While this may be a workable procedure, it is paramount that the prosecutor maintain ultimate responsibility for charging for many reasons. A major function of screening is to determine whether there is sufficient evidence to believe that a crime was committed and that the juvenile committed it. A case should only be further processed if it is legally sufficient. "Legally sufficient" means a case in which the prosecutor believes that he can reasonably substantiate the charges against the juvenile by admissible evidence at trial. These determinations should be made by a prosecuting attorney. If these determinations are, by law or practice, made initially by an outside agency, it is imperative that the prosecutor have the authority to review and revise them. The standards recommend that these decisions are best made through an intake process within the prosecutor's office.

After a determination of legal sufficiency, the next decision to be made is whether the case should be transferred to the adult court, diverted informally, or referred to the juvenile court. This decision has both legal and social implications. It should be made either by an experienced prosecutor who has an interest in juveniles or by other case screeners under the guidance of a prosecutor. The prosecutor, in exercising this function, should try to accommodate the needs of the juvenile while upholding the safety and welfare of the community.

Additionally at this stage, the prosecutor may elect to exercise his discretion to dismiss a case that may be technically sufficient but from a policy or economic point of view lacks prosecutorial merit. Continuation of the case may not serve the best interests of justice.

The large role of the prosecutor in screening is intended to eliminate at least two major abuses of the intake process. Juveniles are disserved when they are charged by non-lawyers in cases where there is insufficient evidence that they committed a crime. A lawyer, the prosecutor, should make this determination. On the other hand, the community is disserved if intake screeners continuously divert a juvenile from the court system despite an extensive background of lawbreaking. This standard seeks to halt these abuses by emphasizing the discretionary role of the prosecutor who has the primary authority to uphold the law and to evaluate what course will best achieve justice for the accused and the community.

Standard 92.2 also exhorts the prosecutor to make a prompt determination of legal sufficiency and prosecutorial disposition. The time limits suggested are ideal ones. It is recognized that some jurisdictions by law or practice make even more prompt determinations and that other jurisdictions, due to limitations in resources or the environment, have been unable to make such timely decisions. The point is that prompt determinations generally promote confidence in the system and fairness to both the victim, the community, and the juvenile. Further, prompt decisions are more likely to result in rehabilitation of the juvenile by providing more immediate attention.

The standard also recognizes that it is sometimes necessary to go beyond these time limits. Complicated cases may need additional investigation. A particularly sensitive case may require additional time so that the prosecutor can review a social history or psychological report before making a decision to, for instance, transfer a case to adult court. These exceptions should not dictate the rule. Many high volume jurisdictions have successfully instituted speedy case reviews.

It is important to note that the period described for the review of legal sufficiency encompasses only the initial review. The decision whether to transfer, charge, or divert comes later. This prompt determination is meant to uncover deficiencies in a case, so that they can be remedied, if possible, through additional investigation. If there is insufficient evidence and the deficiencies cannot be remedied, the matter should be terminated promptly and the juvenile, if in detention, should be released.

It is also important to note that the time periods begin to run after law enforcement reports the facts to the prosecutor. Delays in law enforcement reporting do not directly affect these time periods unless the prosecutor becomes aware of the facts through an alternate source, for instance at a detention hearing. Facts presented at a detention hearing commence the time limits. Prosecutors should encourage police to present facts promptly. At the same time, they should discourage law enforcement reporting that is incomplete or dependent upon extensive additional investigation unless absolutely necessary. Prosecutors must inform law enforcement that the practice of providing skeletal reports that barely describe probable cause without substantive information necessary for charging decisions is unacceptable.

In many jurisdictions, transfer of juveniles to adult court is controlled by statute or practice. In most states, the juvenile court determines whether a juvenile is to be transferred. This standard simply provides guidance for prosecutors in using discretion to the extent that they participate in this process. The provision reflects the view that the juvenile justice system should be utilized to the greatest extent possible given the level of resources available to address the juvenile's behavior. The provision further suggests that juveniles should not be transferred to the adult system unless and until a determination is made that the juvenile cannot be rehabilitated within the juvenile system or alternatives would be contrary to the safety and welfare of society or the nature of the crime dictates a transfer.

Prosecutors differ in their views about whether they should be involved in diverting less serious cases from formal adjudication. The consensus seems to be, however, that because most juveniles are in the process of developing their behavior and values, there is a unique opportunity presented at the juvenile court level to dissuade them from criminal activity. The prosecutor should seriously consider involvement in this process. For all the pessimism that abounds in the system, it is nevertheless undoubtedly true that many first-time or minor offenders will never enter the justice system again if their cases are handled properly. Treatment, restitution, or service programs often are viable alternatives to court processing. Standard 92.3 describes the opportunity for prosecutors to be involved either in diversion programs based in their offices or through referral to existing probation or community service agencies.

Diversion pursuant to this standard requires an admission of involvement in the offense. While many are critical of this requirement, the standard takes the position that it is necessary for three reasons. First, juveniles should not be sanctioned unless there is legally sufficient evidence that they committed what would otherwise be a crime or offense if they were an adult. Denial of involvement by the juvenile should weigh heavily in favor of a formal determination of guilt or innocence. Second, many juvenile justice practitioners believe that effective treatment or rehabilitation begins with an acknowledgment of wrong-doing.

Third, cases that are diverted with no admission of guilt often cannot be restored if the juvenile fails to meet the conditions agreed upon for diversion. Revival of the case is often not possible because too much time has passed and witnesses are unavailable or evidence is lost. A written admission of involvement provides evidence that the prosecutor may need if the case has to be referred to court upon failure of the diversion process.

Given this requirement for an admission of involvement, the standard delineates a careful process that should be undertaken when a juvenile case is diverted. It is critical that the juvenile and his parents understand the nature of diversion, the effect of an admission of guilt, the waiver of his rights, and his responsibilities under the diversion contract. In order to ensure that the juvenile and his parents understand this process, diversion is preceded by execution of a written contract.

REVIEW QUESTIONS

1. What role in the charging function is accorded to prosecutors in the standards for juvenile justice promulgated by the National District Attorneys Association? Are there any ways in which the role of the prosecutor outlined in these standards conflicts with the role of intake officers as outlined in the IJA-ABA standards we encountered in the previous selection?

2. What criteria are established in these standards for deciding whether to file a delinquency petition, seek transfer to adult criminal court, or divert a case away from formal court intervention? In what ways, if any, do these criteria differ from those the IJA-ABA standards set for intake officers to follow in making dispositional decisions?

3. What reasons are given in the commentary accompanying these standards for giving prosecutors a large role in the intake process and in charging decisions? Do you agree that prosecutors should play a major role, or do you think intake decisions should be made by probation officers (or other officials) as long as a prosecutor decides whether the evidence is legally sufficient before a petition is filed?

4. In what ways, if any, do these standards differ from the IJA-ABA standards with respect to diversion of legally sufficient cases (i.e., "nonjudicial disposition of a complaint," as it is called in the IJA-ABA standards)? For any differences you see, which approach do you consider preferable? Why?

5. Do the provisions for diversion outlined in the *National Prosecution Standards* seem, in your view, to represent an appropriate response to the concerns about juvenile court intervention raised in the report of the President's Commission on Law Enforcement and the Administration of Justice (see Chapter 1)? If not, what kinds of provisions would you consider more directly responsive? What provisions for diversion would *you* recommend?

Juvenile Diversion: The Ongoing Search for Alternatives

Mark Ezell

A central theme in the history of the juvenile court is the endless search for effective alternatives. The juvenile court itself was established as an alternative to handling juvenile cases in adult criminal court; houses of refuge were built to remove young offenders from jails; and probation was introduced as an alternative to reform schools. Diversion is one of the more recent chapters in this search for alternatives in that juvenile diversion programs are intended to operate as alternatives to the traditional processing of youth through the juvenile court. Diversion necessarily involves a decision by a court official to turn the youth away from usual juvenile justice system handling, and usually includes the provision of such services to the youth as individual, group, or family counseling, remedial education, job training and placement, drug and/or alcohol treatment, and recreation. Most diversion programs are funded from public resources, staffed by both professionals and volunteers, and include numerous rules and regulations with which the youth and sometimes the family must comply.

As we move into the 1990s, with a rise in juvenile arrests expected, the need for diversion remains and even increases. We will be faced with large numbers of minors for whom formal court action is ill-advised largely because alternative approaches can be more effective and efficient in reducing delinquent behavior. The purpose of this chapter is to describe and analyze the diversion process and diversion programs. The analysis is organized into the following series of questions: (1) What is diversion and why is it practiced? (2) What is the history of diversion? (3) What are the various types of diversion programs? (4) How well does diversion work? and (5) What are the critical research and practice issues?

WHAT IS DIVERSION AND WHY IS IT PRACTICED?

Although there is little agreement on a specific definition of diversion, the concept generally involves a decision to turn youth away from the official system and handle them via alternative procedures and programs. The expectation is that diverted youth will be more

Source: Mark Ezell. (1992). Juvenile diversion: The ongoing search for alternatives. In Ira Schwartz (Ed.). *Juvenile Justice and Public Policy* (pp. 45–58). New York: Lexington Books. Copyright 1992 by Lexington Books. Reprinted by permission.

successful (i.e., recidivate less) than similar youth processed in a traditional manner. Alternative definitions of diversion revolve around several questions. First, does diversion necessarily include the referral of the youth to an agency for services or does it simply mean screening the youth from formal processing? Cressey and McDermott (1973) define "true diversion" as the complete separation of the juvenile from the system with no strings attached. However, they found that instances of true diversion are rare. In most cases, the process of diversion is complemented by one or more diversion programs. Rutherford and McDermott (1976) make a useful distinction between diversion as a process and diversion as a program. Diversion as a process refers to the use of discretion by an agent of the juvenile court to remove certain cases from court jurisdiction. A diversion program receives the diverted youth for some type of intervention. The diversion process can operate without a program, but not vice versa.

Another question relates to the auspices of the diversion program. Is diversion really diversion if the agency hosting the diversion program is part of the justice system? One's answer to this question depends on one's position on labeling theory. Labeling theory would predict the following scenario:

> Official reaction to deviance invokes stigma that sets an individual apart from others as a "deviant person." Furthermore, formal dispositions are likely to entail both coercion, by threatening sanctions in response to any lack of cooperation with officials, and social control, through placing the individual under strict rules of behavior. Such coercion and social control reinforce the message that the individual is not a normal person. They also make the individual subject to further official reactions for behavior that is acceptable from others (such as violating rules of probation). These processes can lead the individual to consider him- or herself a delinquent, which will lead to increased delinquency. Official reactions thereby become the cause of further delinquency. (Osgood & Weichselbaum, 1984, p. 35)

Generally, proponents of labeling theory insist that the service agency to which the child is diverted be independent of the juvenile justice system so that stigmatization is less likely; Empey (1982) believes that allowing justice agencies to operate diversion programs subverts the goals of diversion. Others, however, are unconcerned about program sponsorship and feel that diversion's real value comes from minimizing a youth's penetration into the system. Research findings by Elliott, Dunford, and Knowles (1978) make this a meaningless debate. They found that diverted youth perceived high levels of labeling regardless of whether services are delivered through a traditional justice setting or through a separate diversion agency.

More important than the auspices of the diversion agency, however, is the question of whether the court has closed a divertee's case or retained jurisdiction. Does the youth voluntarily receive services from the diversion program? If a youth's case is still considered open by the court, then the agency, notwithstanding its official auspices, can be considered an agent of the court. Agency personnel will be expected to report the youth's attendance and/or performance to the court and the court will take whatever actions it deems necessary in that case. If the youth is cooperative and successfully completes the requirements of the particular diversion program, the case will usually be closed, but if the youth fails to attend, to cooperate, or unsuccessfully terminates with the program, the court has the option to schedule an adjudicatory hearing and prosecute the original charges. In order for this scenario to occur, the youth and his or her parents probably would have agreed to waive their rights to a speedy trial. If diversion is voluntary, as many insist it should be, the youth's decision about whether to cooperate with the diversion program should have no legal ramifications.

Another common definition of diversion is any action, decision, or program that minimizes a youth's penetration into the juvenile justice system. In this view, probation is considered diversion if the youth might otherwise have been committed to a residential program. Similarly, placement in a group home diverts youth from institutions.

This chapter specifically focuses on pretrial diversion, that is, on those practices and programs that divert alleged delinquents from juvenile court prior to an adjudicatory hearing. The concept of diversion used here specifies that a youth not headed toward the court cannot be turned away: "diversion programs must handle only youngsters who otherwise would enter . . . the justice system" (Klein, 1979, p. 153). In practice, many diversion programs operate as alternatives to station adjustments with no referrals as opposed to alternatives to traditional court processing. This practice is discussed more fully in the subsection on net-widening.

WHAT IS THE HISTORY OF DIVERSION?

Since the beginning of the juvenile court, thousands and thousands of juvenile delinquency cases have been handled informally, "adjusted" in some fashion such that the youth's case was either closed or referred to a noncourt agency. These diversions of cases away from the formal juvenile justice system were permissible because of the broad discretionary powers inherent in the jobs of law enforcement officers, court intake workers, prosecutors, and judges. Prior to the 1960s, therefore, diversion was an informal disposition used by juvenile justice officials and specific programs were rarely labeled or funded as diversionary alternatives.

As juvenile crime increased in the 1960s, the juvenile court encountered strong criticism both for its failure to reduce delinquency and for making it worse by negatively labeling youth and by mixing serious juvenile offenders with first-time, minor offenders. Most juvenile justice professionals felt that the court would do a better job by focusing on the smaller number of serious juvenile offenders and by developing alternative approaches for youth charged with less serious offenses. As a result of recommendations made by the President's Commission on Law Enforcement and Administration of Justice (1967), and because of the subsequent availability of federal grant funds, there was a rapid proliferation of diversion programs throughout the country. Sometimes formal diversion programs were implemented in addition to the existing informal diversionary practices in a community, but many times the new programs supplanted the discretionary case adjustments that had effectively functioned for decades. I will return to this issue when I discuss net-widening.

WHAT ARE THE VARIOUS TYPES OF DIVERSION PROGRAMS?

As a result of significant levels of federal funding in the late 1960s and early 1970s, a panoply of diversion programs were created, such as youth service bureaus, job training and placement programs, alternative schools, and family counseling (Roberts, 1989). Youth are either referred directly to these programs by law enforcement officers, court intake workers, prosecutors, or judges, or they are first referred to caseworkers at a youth service bureau who subsequently refer the case to one or more diversion programs.

Gensheimer and associates' (Gensheimer, Mayer, Gottschalk & Davidson, 1986) study of diversion found that all but 11 percent of the diversion interventions took place in nonresidential programs; that the median length of intervention was approximately fifteen weeks; and that the median number of contact hours was fifteen hours of service. They also found that service brokerage was the most common intervention and that group therapy was very frequently utilized.

Since the 1980s, when the juvenile justice paradigm began to shift from rehabilitation to accountability and sanctioning, there has been an increase in the use of restitution and work programs for diverted youth. Diversion program staff locate and supervise community work sites such as public parks, nursing homes, and childcare centers at which diverted youth work for a specific number of hours. Diversion staff also monitor diverted youths' progress toward making restitution to the victim(s) of the crime.

Another increasingly popular diversion program is juvenile arbitration (Ezell, 1989). Mediation and reconciliation programs are somewhat similar depending on how they are implemented. There is great variation in the implementation of arbitration, but generally the youth is referred for an arbitration hearing at which a single arbitrator or a panel decide on the appropriate sanctions. Depending on how a particular community implements this program, the crime victim may be present and participate in the hearing. The resulting arbitration agreement is flexible in-that the youth can be required to do one or more of the following: pay restitution, perform community service work, write or make a personal apology, attend a class on the consequences of crime, or participate in a counseling or drug/alcohol treatment program. If the youth complies with the arbitration contract, his or her case is closed; if not, the prosecutor has the option of taking the case to court.

There is nothing unique about a diversion intervention that differentiates it from interventions used for adjudicated delinquents. For example, a "Scared Straight" type of program can be used for either diverted or adjudicated youth or both. The key criterion for identifying a true diversion program is to determine the stage of juvenile court processing reached by the youth who is participating in the program.

HOW WELL DOES DIVERSION WORK?

The diversion research literature is quite extensive and has been reviewed numerous times. Comprehensive reviews of the diversion literature have been prepared by Klein (1979), Blomberg (1983), and Polk (1984). In addition, Gensheimer and associates (1986) conducted a meta-analysis of 103 published and unpublished outcome studies between 1967 and 1983. The purpose of this section is to summarize the current state of knowledge, add some of the more recent research findings, and highlight the issues in the recent debate over diversion. In general, "conclusions drawn by reviewers of the literature have generally painted a pessimistic view for the promise of diversionary efforts" (Gensheimer et al., 1986, p. 42).

The impact of diversion (either as a process or as a program) is expected to occur at both the individual and the system level. Theoretically, diverted youth will avoid both the stigmatization of official court handling and the criminogenic effects of associations with other delinquents, and, as a result, will not commit subsequent delinquent acts. These behavioral effects are expected to occur not only because of avoidances but also because the youth may be receiving some ameliorative service from a diversion program. At the system level, pretrial diversion is expected to reduce the number of juvenile arrests and the number of cases that go to court. In other words, if the diversion process operates as intended, the entire flow of cases into and through the juvenile justice system should be altered. When diversion is successful, and all other factors that influence juvenile arrests remain constant, arrests should decrease due to a reduction of secondary deviance as well as a less-burdened, more-efficient, and more-effective juvenile court. Notwithstanding diversion's impact on arrests, the flow of cases to juvenile court should decline.

Numerous studies have been conducted on diversion and its effect on individual youth, their families, and the court. Blomberg (1983) critically assesses both the state of knowledge about diversion and the adequacy of the research techniques employed. He concludes that "the reported findings from various evaluations of diversion programs have been mixed and fragmented" (p. 24). There have been contradictory reports of lowered rearrest rates for diverted youth versus increased misconduct and accelerated penetration into the formal system. Blomberg suggests that knowledge is incomplete regarding which diversion services are most effective for various kinds of youth, and argues that this issue should be at the top of the research agenda.

Binder and Geis (1984) recently took a strident position in defense of diversion. They argued that a cult of sociologists have "substituted rhetoric for logic in their argumentation . . . in opposition to diversion programs" (p. 624). Their prodiversion stance is not, however, bolstered by strong empirical findings. Their arguments rely solely on strong language.

The only real contribution Binder and Geis have made to the state of knowledge about diversion and related issues is the response they provoked from Polk (1984). After a careful review of diversion's record, Polk concludes that "the data on impact do not permit us at this time to reject the hypothesis that the services may be either of no benefit or even harmful to the clients experiencing the diversion program" (p. 658).

The results of the metaanalysis conducted by Gensheimer and associates (1986) are noteworthy. They conclude, "Overall, findings from this analysis do not provide substantial evidence for the efficacy of diversion programs. . . . diversion interventions produce no strong positive or strong negative effects with youth diverted from the juvenile justice system" (p. 52). The authors argue that their findings should not be the basis for the abandonment of diversion. The typical diversion client in their sample of studies was an adjudicated delinquent; they admit that this client population compromised their ability to generalize their findings to traditional diversion clients (i.e., those diverted from court prior to any adjudication).

In addition to their finding that diversion has no effect, either positive or negative, Gensheimer and associates identified two important correlations: first, the younger the diversion client, the more likely that intervention will have a positive effect; and second, "the greater number of contact hours between the youth and the service deliverer, the greater the positive effect on outcome measures" (p. 52).

Empirical studies of many community corrections reforms in general and diversion programs in particular have documented these programs' propensity to widen the net of the justice system, an unintended increase rather than an alteration of the court's reach. Explanations for the sidetracking of diversion differ somewhat, but all are in agreement that most, if not all, diversion programs have "widened the net" of the juvenile justice system. Rather than providing a true alternative to court, diversion programs have merely supplemented the court function and increased both the number of youth brought to the attention of the juvenile justice system and the number under court jurisdiction. A substantial proportion of youth served by diversion programs would not have received services and/or been supervised by the court had these programs not existed.

Saul and Davidson (1983) describe net-widening as the major unintended consequence of juvenile diversion. Instead of reducing the number of youth under court supervision, as intended, diversion has increased it. Blomberg (1983) agrees, pointing out that net-widening extends the reach of the juvenile justice system by increasing the overall proportion of the population subject to court services or control.

Esbensen (1984) indicates that no clear definition of net-widening has been agreed upon, but the following question raised by Polk (1984) accurately articulates the issues: "Is diversion serving as a process for moving young persons who have 'penetrated' the justice network outward and away from that system, or has it become a device for incorporating a whole new class of clients inside an expanding justice system?" (p. 654).

While numerous studies have documented that net-widening is one of the outcomes of diversion programs, few studies have been able to adequately identify and follow those youth who would not have been processed by the court to determine whether participation in the diversion program was harmful or beneficial. The few that have examined this question, or made conjectures about the issue, conclude that the effects of net-widening are detrimental both to individual youth and society at large (Blomberg, 1977; Fishman, 1977; Klein, 1975). Blomberg (1984) believes that net-widening reduces individual freedom, increases the number of rearrests, contributes to behavioral difficulties, and facilitates unnecessary intrusions into families. For example, Blomberg (1977) documents a case in which a youth and his family were required to attend family counseling. As a result of the father's failure to fully cooperate, and presumably other considerations, not only the boy who was originally in trouble but also his two brothers were removed from the home.

Others are equally concerned about the coercive nature of diversion programs and the complete disregard for a youth's democratic rights that diversion programs entail (Nejelski, 1976). According to Austin and Krisberg (1981), "instead of justice, there is diversion" (p. 171). In addition, Scull (1984) comments that the distinction between guilt and innocence is increasingly blurred as a result of the extension of social control.

Others see different consequences and attach different meanings and importance to net-widening. Binder and Geis (1984), for example, question the implicit assumption that no intervention is better than diversion intervention. They argue that because of net-widening, services such as counseling are provided to youth and their families where none was provided before. They add that it is doubtful that youth will outgrow their misbehavior without some societal response. Further, they are unconcerned about potential infringements of individual freedom. Youth have chosen to engage in behavior that merited intervention, and if they wish their lives to remain unconstrained by rules and regulations, they should behave accordingly, or not get caught.

Using multiple research methodologies, including a time-series design with a comparison group, Ezell (1989) documents net-widening and other unintended effects of a diversion program. Based on his research, it appeared that the operation of the diversion program caused prosecutors to reduce the probability of an alleged delinquent being sent to court but did not alter the probability of an arrested youth being placed under court supervision. The operation of the arbitration program succeeded in keeping many youth out of court but not out of the system. In addition, Ezell documented other changes in the processing of youth through juvenile court: the probabilities of youth who went to court being placed on probation or committed to a residential program both increased.

Even though it has enjoyed mixed results, diversion continues to be a popular policy. Blomberg (1983), Klein (1979), Austin and Krisberg (1981), and Lemert (1981) conclude that the promise of diversion has not been fulfilled. Lemert suggests that diversion programs have been coopted by law enforcement agencies and transformed to be more consistent with their primary goal of social control. Klein reviews a "litany of impediments" to diversion and indicates that poorly developed program rationales, the failure to target appropriate youth, and professional resistance, among other things, are largely to blame for inappropriate implementation. Both Austin and Krisberg and Blomberg argue that diversion's less-than-satisfactory results are a result of a variety of organizational dynamics.

WHAT ARE THE CRITICAL PRACTICE AND RESEARCH ISSUES?

In this section, I will identify and discuss several important issues relating to the development and operation of diversion programs as well as crucial research issues.

Practice Issues

First, better prospective targeting of the youth who should be diverted would prevent (or at least reduce) net-widening. Many juvenile diversion programs focus on youth who would not have gone to court and those who would have received little or no official response. The political and organizational forces that cause diversion programs to accept the "wrong" youth are extremely powerful and are very difficult to alter once a program is operating. Profiles of targeted youth can be developed by examining data on cases handled informally, put on probation, and committed to residential programs. Agreements on targeted youth should be achieved between law enforcement agencies, prosecutors, judges, and program staff before the program opens its doors. Better client targeting can also clarify whether the community diversion program is intended to deal with youth who were definitely headed to court or to serve as a community alternative to doing nothing. While it is true that many youth who commit minor offenses, as well as their families, are in need of social services, juvenile courts and diversion programs are not adequately designed, funded, or administered for the delivery of a wide range of human services. Court officials and diversion program staff should make referrals to appropriate community agencies; if needed services are not currently available, officials and staff should work to secure their funding. In short, diversion programs should avoid trying to be all things to all people and should focus on a limited set of service objectives.

Second, diversion programs and court officials should pay greater attention to the due process rights of juveniles accused of delinquent acts who are being considered for diversion. Currently, little attention is paid to whether the youth actually committed the alleged offense that originally brought him or her to the attention of authorities. In fact, many prosecutors divert youth on whose cases they had inadequate evidence. Therefore, the difference between guilt and innocence is left unaddressed, much less resolved. In some jurisdictions youth must admit guilt before being diverted. In others, they are not asked about their guilt but are asked to "accept responsibility" for the event. If they assert their innocence, they will not be diverted and their case will proceed to court if the prosecutor so chooses.

All too often, the youth and his or her family are asked to make their decisions without the advice of an attorney and/or in what might be considered coercive circumstances. At times, it is questionable whether the parents have the youth's best interests in mind when they agree to diversion or whether they are trying to avoid the social embarrassment of having their son or daughter go to court.

Third, juvenile justice officials should improve their ability to match diverted youth to appropriate diversion interventions and needed services, while, at the same time, communities should develop a broad variety of diversion interventions. Research as well as common sense tells us that no single intervention will work for all youth, but most communities have only one type of juvenile diversion program. This is the strength of the original conceptualization of the youth service bureau as a broker of services for diverted youth. More systematic attention should be given to matching youth to services with successful track records for youth from similar circumstances.

Fourth, in addition to developing a broad array of interventions for diverted youth, much greater care should be taken to operate programs in a way that avoids stigmatizing the participants. If labeling theory is one of the rationales for diversion, then it should be reflected in program operations. This mandate requires creativity on the part of program administrators and court officials, but by recruiting nondelinquent participants and carefully marketing the program to the community as well as other professionals who work with these youth (e.g., teachers, social workers, etc.) the self-fulfilling prophecy predicted by labeling theory can be avoided.

Research Issues

While many researchers' attempts to answer the question Does diversion reduce recidivism? have led to inconclusive answers and great debates, some are realizing that they have been asking the wrong question. A more appropriate question is What alternative works best for which types of youth? (Blomberg, 1983). Research needs to be designed so that we know which types of youth are most positively affected by an intervention. Maybe restitution programs "work best" for males and community service work is better for older youth. This type of research has to be done in order for court officials to match diverted youth to the best program as discussed above.

Researchers also need to improve the descriptions and measurements of the diversion interventions so the programs can be replicated when they are found to be effective with certain youth. Questions such as the following need to be addressed: who works with the diverted youth, what are their credentials (e.g., MSW, Ph.D., etc.) and training; what is the nature, intensity, and duration of the intervention and what theory or rationale guides it; and what are the short- and long-range goals of the intervention?

Finally, researchers should pay greater attention to the agency context of the diversion intervention and the organizational requisites for administering the program. For example, is the agency public, private for-profit, or nonprofit; what are the caseloads of the diversion staff and how are they supervised and supported; is there an automated client information system; is the agency large or small, hierarchical or flat, centralized, formalized or participatory, for example. Characteristics of the agency and its work culture have a major impact on the delivery of services but are rarely described or assessed by researchers. For example, Ezell (1989) suggested that the fact that the arbitration program he studied was organizationally located in the prosecutors office, as opposed to an external nonprofit organization, might have influenced the high level of net-widening that occurred. Not only will this information aid in the replication of successful diversion programs, but it will provide information to diversion program managers so that they can more effectively set priorities, supervise staff, and acquire and allocate resources.

CONCLUSION

There is a repetitive quality to the history of juvenile justice reform (Rothman, 1984). An examination of this series of reforms, from houses of refuge to reformatories, from probation and the juvenile court to diversion, reveals what may be viewed as well-intentioned changes that produced either dissatisfying or unknown outcomes. It also reveals a pattern of enthusiastic ideological support for innovations combined with an unwillingness or inability to critically scrutinize both the implementation and the performance of the innovation. The history of juvenile justice is an evolution of an ever-enlarging and ever-changing social control apparatus.

At the time when each reform was enacted, it appeared so sound and humane to its supporters that critical scrutiny seemed unnecessary. When viewed over a longer history, however, the policies and innovations of one generation are rejected as mistaken by the following generation, which in turn implemented new reforms that in their turn were eventually rejected, and so on.

In the 1960s, with rapidly increasing juvenile arrests and the growing belief that the juvenile court was failing, diversion became popular. While the community corrections movement created optional placements within the juvenile justice system, diversion was envisioned as an alternative to the system altogether. It was only in the late seventies that diversion began to be empirically scrutinized. Diversion's ability to reduce recidivism has received mixed reviews by researchers. However, it has consistently produced a panoply of unintended consequences, positive and negative, at both the individual and the system levels. Most diversion programs are capable of widening the net of the justice system, extending instead of altering the overall proportion of youth subject to some form of state control or supervision.

In summary, an examination of the history of juvenile justice reform reveals the following pattern. First, program and policy innovations are introduced with great enthusiasm. Accompanying the excitement is an "illusion of knowledge" (Blomberg, 1984), that is, a widely held belief that technological advances will effectively eradicate crime and delinquency. Subsequently, dissatisfaction with the outcomes grow and numerous unintended consequences are recognized. The disparity between rhetoric and reality, between intentions and outcomes, is slowly but surely documented. There is little understanding, however, of why or how this disparity arose, or from where the unanticipated outcomes came. This position is largely a result of narrowly conducted, post implementation research. A new reform is introduced and the cycle repeats itself.

With the growing fiscal crisis in America, the use of community-based alternatives to institutionalization will continue, as will efforts to divert youth from the court. In order for diversion to be effective, however, researchers and diversion staff need to cooperate to a greater extent when programs are planned, implemented, and studied. This partnership is crucial to avoid the frustrating cycle of juvenile justice reform.

REFERENCES

Austin, J., & Krisberg, B. (1981). Wider, stronger, and different nets: The dialectics of criminal justice reform. *Journal of Research in Crime and Delinquency, 18*, 165–196.

Binder, A., & Geis, G. (1984). *Ad populum* argumentation in criminology: Juvenile diversion as rhetoric. *Crime and Delinquency, 30*, 624–647.

Blomberg, T. G. (1977). Diversion and accelerated social control. *Journal of Criminal Law and Criminology, 68*, 274–282.

Blomberg, T. G. (1983). Diversion's disparate results and unresolved questions: An integrative evaluation perspective. *Journal of Research in Crime and Delinquency, 20*, 24–38.

Blomberg, T. G. (1984, April). *Criminal justice reform and social control: Are we becoming a minimum security society?* Paper presented at the Symposium on the Decentralization of Social Control, Burnaby, British Columbia.

Cressey, D. R., & McDermott, R. A. (1973). *Diversion from the juvenile justice system* (National Assessment of Juvenile Corrections). Ann Arbor: University of Michigan Press.

Elliott, D. S., Dunford, F. W., & Knowles, B. (1978). *Diversion: A study of alternative processing.* Boulder, CO: Behavioral Research Institute.

Empey, L. T. (1982). *American delinquency: Its meaning and construction.* Homewood, IL: Dorsey.

Esbensen, F. (1984). Net widening? Yes and no: Diversion impact assessed through a systems processing rates analysis. In S. H. Decker (Ed.), *Juvenile justice policy analysis trends and outcomes* (pp. 115–128). Beverly Hills, CA: Sage.

Ezell, M. (1989). Juvenile arbitration: Net-widening and other unintended consequences. *Journal of Research in Crime and Delinquency, 26*, 358–377.

Fishman, R. (1977). *Criminal recidivism in New York City: An evaluation of the impact of rehabilitation and diversion services.* New York: Praeger.

Gensheimer, L. K., Mayer, J. P., Gottschalk, R., & Davidson, W. S. (1986). Diverting youth from the juvenile justice system: A meta-analysis of intervention efficacy. In S. J. Apter & A. P. Goldstein (Eds.), *Youth violence: Programs and prospects* (pp. 39–57). New York: Pergamon Press.

Klein, M. W. (1976). Issues and realities in police diversion programs. *Crime and Delinquency, 22*, 421–427.

Klein, M. W. (1979). Deinstitutionalization and diversion of juvenile offenders: A litany of impediments. In N. Morris & M. Toney

(Eds.), *Crime and justice: An annual review of research* (pp. 145–201). Chicago: University of Chicago Press.

Lemert, E. M. (1981). Diversion in juvenile justice: What hath been wrought. *Journal of Research in Crime and Delinquency, 18*, 34–46.

Nejelski, P. (1976). Diversion: Unleashing the hound of heaven? In M. K. Rosenheim (Ed.), *Pursuing justice for the child* (pp. 94–118). Chicago: University of Chicago Press.

Osgood, D. W., & Weichselbaum, H. F. (1984). Juvenile diversion: When practice matches theory. *Journal of Research in Crime and Delinquency, 21*, 33–56.

Polk, K. (1984). Juvenile diversion: A look at the record. *Crime and Delinquency, 30*, 648–659.

President's Commission on Law Enforcement and Administration of Justice. (1967). *Task force report: Juvenile delinquency and youth crime.* Washington, DC: U. S. Government Printing Office.

Roberts, A. R. (1989). The emergence and proliferation of juvenile diversion programs. In A. R. Roberts (Ed.), *Juvenile justice policies, programs, and services* (pp. 77–90). Chicago: Dorsey.

Rothman, D. J. (1984). *Conscience and convenience: The asylum and its alternatives in progressive America.* Boston: Little, Brown.

Rutherford, A., & McDermott, R. (1976). *National Evaluation Program Phase 1 Summary Report* (U.S. Department of Justice, Law Enforcement Assistance Administration, National Institute of Law Enforcement and Criminal Justice). Washington, DC: U.S. Government Printing Office.

Saul, J. A., & Davidson, W. S. (1983). Implementation of juvenile diversion programs: Cast your net on the other side of the boat. In J. R. Kluegel (Ed.), *Evaluating juvenile justice* (pp. 31–45). Beverly Hills, CA: Sage.

Scull, A. T. (1984). *Decarceration: Community treatment and the deviant—A radical view* (2nd ed.). New Brunswick, NJ: Rutgers University Press.

REVIEW QUESTIONS

1. What is diversion, according to Ezell? What questions or considerations does the author raise in trying to explain the meaning of diversion?
2. What types of diversion programs does Ezell identify? Which ones seem most consistent with the considerations raised in your answer to the previous question?
3. How effective do diversion programs seem to be? What evidence does Ezell cite in discussing the effectiveness of diversion?
4. What is net-widening? Why does Ezell think it is a problem?
5. Ezell argues that "[r]ather than providing a true alternative to court, diversion programs have merely supplemented the court function and increased both the number of youth brought to the attention of the juve-nile justice system and the number under court jurisdiction" (p. 211). Do you agree with him? Why or why not?
6. What are the most significant concerns raised by Ezell in his discussion of practice and research issues?
7. Is there a diversion program in your community? If so, what are the criteria for acceptance into the program? What services are provided? In your view, does the program effectively divert minor offenders away from juvenile court, or does it just "widen the net" of the juvenile justice system by intervening in the lives of children whose cases should be "adjusted" without any action beyond a warning and parental notification?

Complaints, Case Screening and Diversion Agreements

Revised Code of Washington, Juvenile Justice Act of 1977 RCW 13.40.070 and RCW 13.40.080

RCW 13.40.070

Complaints—Screening—Filing information—Diversion—Modification of community supervision—Notice to parent or guardian—Probation counselor acting for prosecutor—Referral to mediation or reconciliation programs.

(1) Complaints referred to the juvenile court alleging the commission of an offense shall be referred directly to the prosecutor. The prosecutor, upon receipt of a complaint, shall screen the complaint to determine whether:

    (a) The alleged facts bring the case within the jurisdiction of the court; and

    (b) On a basis of available evidence there is probable cause to believe that the juvenile did commit the offense.

(2) If the identical alleged acts constitute an offense under both the law of this state and an ordinance of any city or county of this state, state law shall govern the prosecutor's screening and charging decision for both filed and diverted cases.

(3) If the requirements of subsections (1)(a) and (b) of this section are met, the prosecutor shall either file an information in juvenile court or divert the case, as set forth in subsections (5), (6), and (7) of this section. If the prosecutor finds that the requirements of subsection (1)(a) and (b) of this section are not met, the prosecutor shall maintain a record, for one year, of such decision and the reasons therefor. In lieu of filing an information or diverting an offense a prosecutor may file a motion to modify community supervision where such offense constitutes a violation of community supervision.

(4) An information shall be a plain, concise, and definite written statement of the essential facts constituting the offense charged. It shall be signed by the prosecuting attorney and conform to chapter 10.37 RCW.

(5) Where a case is legally sufficient, the prosecutor shall file an information with the juvenile court if:

    (a) An alleged offender is accused of a class A felony, a class B felony, an attempt to commit a class B felony, a class C felony listed in RCW 9.94A.411(2) as a crime against persons or listed in RCW 9A.46.060 as a crime of harassment, or a class C felony that is a violation of RCW 9.41.080 or 9.41.040(1)(b)(iii); or

    (b) An alleged offender is accused of a felony and has a criminal history of any felony, or at least two gross misdemeanors, or at least two misdemeanors; or

    (c) An alleged offender has previously been committed to the department; or

    (d) An alleged offender has been referred by a diversion unit for prosecution or desires prosecution instead of diversion; or

    (e) An alleged offender has two or more diversion agreements on the alleged offender's criminal history; or

    (f) A special allegation has been filed that the offender or an accomplice was armed with a firearm when the offense was committed.

(6) Where a case is legally sufficient the prosecutor shall divert the case if the alleged offense is a misdemeanor or gross misdemeanor or violation and the alleged offense is the offender's first offense or violation. If the alleged offender is charged with a related offense that must or may be filed under subsections (5) and (7) of this section, a case under this subsection may also be filed.

(7) Where a case is legally sufficient and falls into neither subsection (5) nor (6) of this section, it may be filed or diverted. In deciding whether to file or divert an offense under this section the prosecutor shall be guided only by the length, seriousness, and recency of the alleged offender's criminal history and the circumstances surrounding the commission of the alleged offense.

(8) Whenever a juvenile is placed in custody or, where not placed in custody, referred to a diversion interview, the parent or legal guardian of the juvenile shall be notified as soon as possible concerning the allegation made against the juvenile and the current status of the juvenile. Where a case involves victims of crimes against persons or victims whose property has not been recovered at the time a juvenile is referred to a diversion unit, the victim shall be notified of the referral and informed how to contact the unit.

(9) The responsibilities of the prosecutor under subsections (1) through (8) of this section may be performed by a juvenile court probation counselor for any complaint referred to the court alleging the commission of an offense which would not be a felony if committed by an adult, if the prosecutor has given sufficient written notice to the juvenile court that the prosecutor will not review such complaints.

(10) The prosecutor, juvenile court probation counselor, or diversion unit may, in exercising their authority under this section or RCW 13.40.080, refer juveniles to mediation or victim offender reconciliation programs. Such mediation or victim offender reconciliation programs shall be voluntary for victims.

RCW 13.40.080

Diversion agreement—Scope—Limitations—Restitution orders—Divertee's rights—Diversionary unit's powers and duties—Interpreters—Modification—Fines.

(1) A diversion agreement shall be a contract between a juvenile accused of an offense and a diversionary unit whereby the juvenile agrees to fulfill certain conditions in lieu of prosecution. Such agreements may be entered into only after the prosecutor, or probation counselor pursuant to this chapter, has determined that probable cause exists to believe that a crime has been committed and that the juvenile committed it. Such agreements shall be entered into as expeditiously as possible.

(2) A diversion agreement shall be limited to one or more of the following:

   (a) Community service not to exceed one hundred fifty hours, not to be performed during school hours if the juvenile is attending school;

   (b) Restitution limited to the amount of actual loss incurred by the victim;

   (c) Attendance at up to ten hours of counseling and/or up to twenty hours of educational or informational sessions at a community agency. The educational or informational sessions may include sessions relating to respect for self, others, and authority; victim awareness; accountability; self-worth; responsibility; work ethics; good citizenship; literacy; and life skills. For purposes of this section, "community agency" may also mean a community-based nonprofit organization, if approved by the diversion unit. The state shall not be liable for costs resulting from the diversionary unit exercising the option to permit diversion agreements to mandate attendance at up to ten hours of counseling and/or up to twenty hours of educational or informational sessions;

(d) A fine, not to exceed one hundred dollars. In determining the amount of the fine, the diversion unit shall consider only the juvenile's financial resources and whether the juvenile has the means to pay the fine. The diversion unit shall not consider the financial resources of the juvenile's parents, guardian, or custodian in determining the fine to be imposed;

(e) Requirements to remain during specified hours at home, school, or work, and restrictions on leaving or entering specified geographical areas; and

(f) Upon request of the victim or witness, requirements to refrain from any contact with victims or witnesses of offenses committed by the juvenile.

(3) In assessing periods of community service to be performed and restitution to be paid by a juvenile who has entered into a diversion agreement, the court officer to whom this task is assigned shall consult with the juvenile's custodial parent or parents or guardian and victims who have contacted the diversionary unit and, to the extent possible, involve members of the community. Such members of the community shall meet with the juvenile and advise the court officer as to the terms of the diversion agreement and shall supervise the juvenile in carrying out its terms.

(4) (a) A diversion agreement may not exceed a period of six months and may include a period extending beyond the eighteenth birthday of the divertee.

(b) If additional time is necessary for the juvenile to complete restitution to the victim, the time period limitations of this subsection may be extended by an additional six months.

(c) If the juvenile has not paid the full amount of restitution by the end of the additional six-month period, then the juvenile shall be referred to the juvenile court for entry of an order establishing the amount of restitution still owed to the victim. In this order, the court shall also determine the terms and conditions of the restitution, including a payment plan extending up to ten years if the court determines that the juvenile does not have the means to make full restitution over a shorter period. For the purposes of this subsection (4)(c), the juvenile shall remain under the court's jurisdiction for a maximum term of ten years after the juvenile's eighteenth birthday. Prior to the expiration of the initial ten-year period, the juvenile court may extend the judgment for restitution an additional ten years. The court may not require the juvenile to pay full or partial restitution if the juvenile reasonably satisfies the court that he or she does not have the means to make full or partial restitution and could not reasonably acquire the means to pay the restitution over a ten-year period. The county clerk shall make disbursements to victims named in the order. The restitution to victims named in the order shall be paid prior to any payment for other penalties or monetary assessments. A juvenile under obligation to pay restitution may petition the court for modification of the restitution order.

(5) The juvenile shall retain the right to be referred to the court at any time prior to the signing of the diversion agreement.

(6) Divertees and potential divertees shall be afforded due process in all contacts with a diversionary unit regardless of whether the juveniles are accepted for diversion or whether the diversion program is successfully completed. Such due process shall include, but not be limited to, the following:

(a) A written diversion agreement shall be executed stating all conditions in clearly understandable language;

(b) Violation of the terms of the agreement shall be the only grounds for termination;

(c) No divertee may be terminated from a diversion program without being given a court hearing, which hearing shall be preceded by:
   i. Written notice of alleged violations of the conditions of the diversion program; and
   ii. Disclosure of all evidence to be offered against the divertee;

(d) The hearing shall be conducted by the juvenile court and shall include:
   i. Opportunity to be heard in person and to present evidence;
   ii. The right to confront and cross-examine all adverse witnesses;
   iii. A written statement by the court as to the evidence relied on and the reasons for termination, should that be the decision; and
   iv. Demonstration by evidence that the divertee has substantially violated the terms of his or her diversion agreement.

(e) The prosecutor may file an information on the offense for which the divertee was diverted:
   i. In juvenile court if the divertee is under eighteen years of age; or
   ii. In superior court or the appropriate court of limited jurisdiction if the divertee is eighteen years of age or older.

(7) The diversion unit shall, subject to available funds, be responsible for providing interpreters when juveniles need interpreters to effectively communicate during diversion unit hearings or negotiations.

(8) The diversion unit shall be responsible for advising a divertee of his or her rights as provided in this chapter.

(9) The diversion unit may refer a juvenile to community-based counseling or treatment programs.

(10) The right to counsel shall inure prior to the initial interview for purposes of advising the juvenile as to whether he or she desires to participate in the diversion process or to appear in the juvenile court. The juvenile may be represented by counsel at any critical stage of the diversion process, including intake interviews and termination hearings. The juvenile shall be fully advised at the intake of his or her right to an attorney and of the relevant services an attorney can provide. For the purpose of this section, intake interviews mean all interviews regarding the diversion agreement process.

The juvenile shall be advised that a diversion agreement shall constitute a part of the juvenile's criminal history as defined by RCW 13.40.020(7). A signed acknowledgment of such advisement shall be obtained from the juvenile, and the document shall be maintained by the diversionary unit together with the diversion agreement, and a copy of both documents shall be delivered to the prosecutor if requested by the prosecutor. The supreme court shall promulgate rules setting forth the content of such advisement in simple language.

(11) When a juvenile enters into a diversion agreement, the juvenile court may receive only the following information for dispositional purposes:
   a. The fact that a charge or charges were made;
   b. The fact that a diversion agreement was entered into;
   c. The juvenile's obligations under such agreement;
   d. Whether the alleged offender performed his or her obligations under such agreement; and
   e. The facts of the alleged offense.

(12) A diversionary unit may refuse to enter into a diversion agreement with a juvenile. When a diversionary unit refuses to enter a diversion agreement with a juvenile, it shall immediately refer such juvenile to the court for action and shall forward to the court the criminal complaint and a detailed statement of its reasons for refusing to enter into a diversion agreement. The diversionary unit shall also immediately refer the case to the prosecuting attorney for action if such juvenile violates the terms of the diversion agreement.

(13) A diversionary unit may, in instances where it determines that the act or omission of an act for which a juvenile has been referred to it involved no victim, or where it determines that the juvenile referred to it has no prior criminal history and is alleged to have committed an illegal act involving no threat of or instance of actual physical harm and involving not more than fifty dollars in property loss or damage and that there is no loss outstanding

to the person or firm suffering such damage or loss, counsel and release or release such a juvenile without entering into a diversion agreement. A diversion unit's authority to counsel and release a juvenile under this subsection shall include the authority to refer the juvenile to community-based counseling or treatment programs. Any juvenile released under this subsection shall be advised that the act or omission of any act for which he or she had been referred shall constitute a part of the juvenile's criminal history as defined by RCW 13.40.020(7). A signed acknowledgment of such advisement shall be obtained from the juvenile, and the document shall be maintained by the unit, and a copy of the document shall be delivered to the prosecutor if requested by the prosecutor. The supreme court shall promulgate rules setting forth the content of such advisement in simple language. A juvenile determined to be eligible by a diversionary unit for release as provided in this subsection shall retain the same right to counsel and right to have his or her case referred to the court for formal action as any other juvenile referred to the unit.

(14) A diversion unit may supervise the fulfillment of a diversion agreement entered into before the juvenile's eighteenth birthday and which includes a period extending beyond the divertee's eighteenth birthday.

(15) If a fine required by a diversion agreement cannot reasonably be paid due to a change of circumstance, the diversion agreement may be modified at the request of the divertee and with the concurrence of the diversion unit to convert an unpaid fine into community service. The modification of the diversion agreement shall be in writing and signed by the divertee and the diversion unit. The number of hours of community service in lieu of a monetary penalty shall be converted at the rate of the prevailing state minimum wage per hour.

(16) Fines imposed under this section shall be collected and paid into the county general fund in accordance with procedures established by the juvenile court administrator under RCW 13.04.040 and may be used only for juvenile services. In the expenditure of funds for juvenile services, there shall be a maintenance of effort whereby counties exhaust existing resources before using amounts collected under this section.

REVIEW QUESTIONS

1. How do the statutory provisions for screening complaints and making charging decisions in the State of Washington compare with those advocated in the IJA-ABA and National District Attorneys Association standards we encountered earlier in

this chapter? Would the authors of either or both of those sets of standards be pleased with the Washington provisions? Why or why not?

2. To what extent do the diversion provisions in the Washington statute fit the various ways of defining diversion discussed by Mark Ezell in the previous selection? In answering, be sure to consider how each of the questions Ezell raises about the mean-

ing of diversion would be answered in the context of this statute.

3. Do the provisions for diversion outlined in the Washington statute seem reasonable in light of Ezell's concerns about net-widening, due process rights, availability of a range of appropriate programs, and avoidance of stigmatizing interventions? Explain your response.

Teen Courts: A Focus on Research

Jeffrey A. Butts and Janeen Buck

BACKGROUND

Teen courts are spreading rapidly across the United States. Many people view them as a cost-effective alternative to traditional juvenile court for some young offenders. Until recently, relatively little information has been available about how teen courts operate or how they affect youthful offenders. This Bulletin presents the results of a national survey of teen courts. The findings suggest that most teen courts are relatively small and were established very recently. The findings also suggest that the most established teen court programs (i.e., programs reporting longevity in operations and/or little financial uncertainty) may be those that are housed within or closely affiliated with the traditional juvenile justice system.

The survey indicates that teen courts enjoy broad community support. Their popularity appears to stem from favorable media coverage and the high levels of satisfaction reported by parents, teachers, and youth involved in teen court programs, rather than from evaluation research showing that teen courts have beneficial effects on offenders. Little research has been conducted on outcomes for teen court defendants, although some studies offer encouraging results. Recent studies have found that teen court participation may be associated with low recidivism rates, improved youth attitudes toward authority, and increased knowledge of the justice system among youth. More research is required before claims about teen court effectiveness can be substantiated.

Source: Jeffrey A. Butts and Janeen Buck. (2000). *Teen Courts: A Focus on Research.* Washington, DC: Office of Juvenile Justice and Delinquency Prevention. Adapted courtesy of the United States Department of Justice, Office of Juvenile Justice and Delinquency Prevention.

THE TEEN COURT CONCEPT

Teen courts are generally used for younger juveniles (ages 10 to 15), those with no prior arrest records, and those charged with less serious law violations (e.g., shoplifting, vandalism, and disorderly conduct). Typically, young offenders are offered teen court as a voluntary alternative in lieu of more formal handling by the traditional juvenile justice system. Teen courts differ from other juvenile justice programs because young people rather than adults determine the disposition, given a broad array of sentencing options made available by adults overseeing the program. Teen court defendants may go through an intake process, a preliminary review of charges, a court hearing, and sentencing, as in a regular juvenile court. In a teen court, however, other young people are responsible for much of the process.

Charges may be presented to the court by a 15-year-old "prosecutor." Defendants may be represented by a 16-year-old "defense attorney." Other youth may serve as jurors, court clerks, and bailiffs. In some teen courts, a youth "judge" (or panel of youth judges) may choose the best disposition or sanction for each case. In a few teen courts, youth even determine whether the facts in a case have been proven by the prosecutor (similar to a finding of guilt).

Adults are also involved in teen courts. They often administer the programs, and they are usually responsible for essential functions such as budgeting, planning, and personnel. In many programs, adults supervise the courtroom activities, and they often coordinate the community service placements where youth work to fulfill the terms of their dispositions. In some programs, adults act as the judges while teens serve as attorneys and jurors. The key to all teen court programs, however, is the significant role youth play in the deliberation of charges and the imposition of sanctions on young offenders.

Proponents of teen court argue that the process takes advantage of one of the most powerful forces in the life of an adolescent—the desire for peer approval and the reaction to peer pressure. According to this argument, youth respond better to prosocial peers than to adult authority figures. Thus, teen courts are seen as a potentially effective alternative to traditional juvenile courts staffed with paid professionals such as lawyers, judges, and probation officers. Teen court advocates also point out that the benefits extend beyond defendants. Teen courts may benefit the volunteer youth attorneys and judges, who probably learn more about the legal system than they ever could in a classroom. The presence of a teen court may also encourage the entire community to take a more active role in responding to juvenile crime. Teen courts offer at least four potential benefits:

- **Accountability.** Teen courts may help to ensure that young offenders are held accountable for their illegal behavior, even when their offenses are relatively minor and would not likely result in sanctions from the traditional juvenile justice system.

- **Timeliness.** An effective teen court can move young offenders from arrest to sanctions within a matter of days rather than the months that may pass with traditional juvenile courts. This rapid response may increase the positive impact of court sanctions, regardless of their severity.

- **Cost savings.** Teen courts usually depend heavily on youth and adult volunteers. If managed properly, they may handle a substantial number of offenders at relatively little cost to the community. The average annual cost for operating a teen court is $32,822 (National Youth Court Center, unpublished data).

- **Community cohesion.** A well-structured and expansive teen court program may affect the entire community by increasing public appreciation of the legal system, enhancing community–court relationships, encouraging greater respect for the law among youth, and promoting volunteerism among both adults and youth.

Researchers are beginning to report instances in which these potential benefits have been realized in some communities, but evaluation research on teen courts is still in the early stages. It is too soon to tell whether the positive results reported by some communities can be replicated reliably in other communities. Regardless of the limited evidence, however, teen courts are increasingly in use across the United States. . . .

NATIONAL SURVEY

As part of the Office of Juvenile Justice and Delinquency Prevention's (OJJDP's) Evaluation of Teen Courts Project, The Urban Institute recently conducted a national survey of teen courts and youth courts. With assistance from the National Youth Court Center (NYCC), which is housed at the American Probation and Parole Association and supported by funds from OJJDP, project researchers obtained addresses, telephone numbers, and personal contacts for all U.S. teen courts believed to exist as of the end of 1998, and they mailed questionnaires to nearly 500 programs. A handful of these programs had gone out of business by the time researchers tried to contact them.

Of the remaining programs, 335 (more than 70 percent) completed and returned the survey. The responses documented the range of teen court programs used by jurisdictions across the country, the characteristics of their clients, the sanctions they imposed, the courtroom models they used, the extent of community support they received, and the challenges they faced.

Program Characteristics

Recent growth in the number of teen court programs nationwide was reflected in the brief tenure of the programs responding to the national survey. Of all the programs that responded, 13 percent had been in operation less than 1 year and 42 percent had been in operation for only 1 to 3 years. More than two-thirds (67 percent) of all teen courts had been in existence for less than 5 years.

Many teen courts that responded to the survey were closely affiliated with the traditional justice system. Courts, law enforcement agencies, juvenile probation offices, or prosecutors' offices operated slightly more than half (52 percent) of the programs responding to the survey. More than one-third (37 percent) of the programs were affiliated with the courts and 12 percent with law enforcement. Private agencies operated one-quarter (25 percent) of the teen court programs.

Most teen court and youth court programs were relatively small. More than half (59 percent) of the programs responding to the survey handled 100 or fewer cases annually. Just 13 percent of the programs handled more than 300 cases per year.

Very few programs relied on private funding to meet their operational costs. More than half (59 percent) of the teen courts received no private funding; 16 percent of the programs received up to one-fifth of their funding from private sources, and 11 percent received between one-fifth and one-half from private sources.

Client Characteristics

Teen courts usually handle relatively young offenders with no prior arrests. Survey respondents reported that, on average, 24 percent of their cases involved youth under age 14 and 66 percent involved youth under age 16. More than one-third (39 percent) of the teen courts accepted only first-time offenders and another 48 percent reported that they "rarely" accepted youth with prior arrest records. Nearly all programs (98 percent) reported that they "never" or "rarely" accepted youth with prior felony arrests. Most programs (91 percent) also indicated that they "never" or "rarely" accepted youth who previously had been referred to a juvenile court.

To assess the nature of those cases typically handled in teen court, the survey asked each program to review a list of offenses and to indicate whether the program received such cases "very often," "often," "rarely," or "never." The offenses most likely to be received "often" or "very often" were theft (93 percent), minor assault (66 percent), disorderly conduct (62 percent), possession or use of alcohol (60 percent), and vandalism (59 percent).

Sanctions

The principal goal of teen court is to hold young offenders accountable for their behavior. In a system of graduated sanctions, there is a consequence for every offense. Every youth who has admitted guilt or who is found guilty in teen court receives some form of sanction. In many communities, teen court sanctions do more than punish the offender. Sanctions encourage young offenders to repair at least part of the damage they have caused to the community or to specific victims. Offenders are often ordered to pay restitution or perform community service. Some teen courts require offenders to write formal apologies to their victims; others require offenders to serve on a subsequent teen court jury. Many courts use other innovative dispositions, such as requiring offenders to attend classes designed to improve their decisionmaking skills, enhance their awareness of victims, and deter them from future theft.

Survey respondents were asked to assess a list of typical sanctions and indicate how frequently the program used each one (i.e., "very often," "often," "rarely," or "never"). Community service was the most commonly used sanction. Nearly all (99 percent) of responding teen courts reported using community service "often" or "very often." Other frequently used sanctions included victim apology letters (86 percent), written essays (79 percent), teen court jury duty (74 percent), drug/alcohol classes (60 percent), and restitution (34 percent).

Courtroom Models

NYCC divides the courtroom approaches used by teen courts into four types: adult judge, youth judge, peer jury, and youth tribunal (National Youth Court Center, 2000). Findings from the national survey suggested that the adult judge model was the most popular. Nearly half (47 percent) of the responding courts used only the adult judge model. When the number of cases handled by adult judges in programs using a mix of courtroom models was added, the adult judge model accounted for more than half (60 percent) of all teen court cases.

The next most prevalent courtroom model was the peer jury, which accounted for 22 percent of all teen court cases. More than one in four (26 percent) teen court programs used this model for at least part of their caseloads. The youth judge and tribunal models were the least used, with each accounting for just 7 percent of all cases.

The use of courtroom models varied somewhat according to the agency sponsoring the program. The adult judge model was the most popular among teen courts operated by local courts and probation agencies (58 percent) and those hosted by schools, private agencies, and other not-for-profit organizations (48 percent). There was no dominant model, however, among programs operated by law enforcement agencies or prosecutors. In fact, more than one-third (34 percent) of those programs used mixed models (i.e., a combination of two or more courtroom models). . . .

Community Support

The success of an individual teen court may depend on how well it is supported by various segments of the community. Teen court advocates have observed that it is essential for teen courts to be accepted by the larger justice system in their local area (National Youth Court Center, 2000). To examine teen court program directors' perceptions of community support for their programs, the survey asked each program to consider several prominent community groups and indicate whether each was "very supportive," "moderately supportive," "mildly supportive," or "not at all supportive."

Judges were seen as the greatest supporters of teen court programs. More than 9 in 10 teen courts rated their local judges as "very supportive" (71 percent) or "moderately supportive" (21 percent). Other groups considered "very supportive" or "moderately supportive" of teen courts included law enforcement (87 percent), court intake and probation workers (86 percent), teachers and other school officials (86 percent), and prosecutors (84 percent). In general, teen courts perceived all of the named groups to be supportive. Even the groups ranking lowest on the list (elected officials and the business community) were considered by a majority of teen courts as either very or moderately supportive (78 and 67 percent, respectively).

Problems

As small, community-based programs, teen courts face a range of challenges and obstacles. To identify the type of problems facing teen courts, the survey asked each program to review a list of typical operational problems that might cause difficulties for teen courts. Each court was asked to indicate whether it had experienced the issue as a "serious" problem, a "minor" problem, something in between, or not a problem at all.

Not surprisingly, the operational problem reported most often by teen courts was funding. Forty percent of the programs reported "some problems" (25 percent) or "serious problems" (15 percent) with funding uncertainties. Only 38 percent of the programs reported that funding uncertainties caused no problems.

Other problems that presented significant challenges for teen courts included retaining youth volunteers (i.e., attorneys, judges, and jurors) and maintaining an adequate flow of referrals. More than one-fifth (21 percent) of the programs reported having "some" problems or "serious" problems keeping teen volunteers. Nearly one-third (29 percent) reported having "some" or "serious" problems with maintaining sufficient case referrals.

Several other issues were described as presenting "some" or "serious" problems for teen courts. These issues included cases in which too much time elapsed between a youth's arrest and his or her referral to teen court (19 percent), difficulties in coordinating the efforts of teen courts with other agencies in the community (16 percent), and problems recruiting youth volunteers (19 percent) and adult volunteers (20 percent). . . .

REFERENCES

National Youth Court Center. How teen/youth courts operate. National Youth Court Center Web Site. Lexington, KY: American Probation and Parole Association. . . .

REVIEW QUESTIONS

1. What are teen courts? How do they differ from regular juvenile courts? From other juvenile justice programs?
2. What do the authors of this selection consider to be the potential benefits of teen courts? What problems did they find to be most common among the teen courts included in their survey?
3. What characteristics do teen courts tend to share and in what ways do they differ? What are the general characteristics of their clients? What sanctions are available to them? What are the most common courtroom models?
4. What is your overall assessment of the teen court concept? Do teen courts offer a viable alternative to formal juvenile court intervention for offenders who do not require severe sanctions, probation supervision, or residential placement? What, if any, are the advantages/disadvantages of teen courts as compared with other types of diversion programs?

FURTHER READING

Leiber, Michael J., and Stairs, Jayne M. (1999). Race, contexts, and the use of intake diversion. *Journal of Research in Crime and Delinquency, 36*(1), 56–86.

Lemert, Edwin. (1967). The juvenile court: Quest and realities. In *Task Force Report: Juvenile Delinquency and Youth Crime—Report on Juvenile Justice and Consultants' Papers* (pp. 91–106). The President's Commission on Law Enforcement and Administration of Justice. Washington, DC: U.S. Government Printing Office.

Mears, Daniel P., and Kelly, William R. (1999). Assessments and intake processes in juvenile justice processing: Emerging policy consid-erations. *Crime and Delinquency, 45*(4), 508–529.

Panzer, Cheri. (1997). Reducing juvenile recidivism through pre-trial diversion programs: A community's involvement. *Journal of Juvenile Law, 18*, 186–207.

Potter, Roberto Hugh, and Kakar, Suman. (2002). The diversion decision-making process from the juvenile court practitioners' perspective. *Journal of Contemporary Criminal Justice, 18*(1), 20–36.

Shur, Edwin. (1973). *Radical Non-Intervention: Rethinking the Delinquency Problem*. Englewood Cliffs, NJ: Prentice Hall.

CHAPTER

6

Detention

If diversion is not an option, or if the intake officer or prosecutor decides against it, the next decision that most likely arises is whether secure detention or, if available and appropriate under the circumstances, a nonsecure out-of-home placement, would be preferable to releasing the child to his or her parents pending the outcome of court action pursuant to a delinquency petition. In many delinquency cases the police make an initial determination to detain the child. In this situation, an intake officer or prosecutor may be asked to ratify this decision pending a court hearing. In any event, if the child is not released within a short time following arrest (usually 24 or 48 hours, as specified by statute), a detention hearing will be held before a juvenile court judge. At this hearing, which in the most typical scenario is combined with an arraignment on the delinquency petition or, if the child is already on probation, on the petition for revocation or modification of probation, the judge will seek evidence that the child, if returned to the home of his or her parents, presents a risk of (1) danger to others, (2) danger to himself or herself, or (3) failure to appear at future court hearings.

In the criminal justice system the issue of pretrial detention is handled very differently: Bail is set and the defendant either posts the specified amount (often through a bail bondsman or other intermediary), requests release on his or her own recognizance or through some other mechanism for release without bail, or awaits trial in a local jail. Only rarely, in extremely serious cases, may a court refuse to release a defendant who could afford to make bail (see *U.S. v. Salerno*, 481 U.S. 739 [1987]).

In the juvenile systems of most states, though, bail release is uncommon—if it is permitted at all. Indeed, the IJA-ABA standards explicitly forbid the use of monetary bail in any form (IJA-ABA, 1996, p. 126). Instead, release pending adjudication normally hinges on whether the child is viewed as a flight risk or as a danger to self or others. This approach, especially as regards detention decisions based on the perceived need to prevent crimes a youth might commit while awaiting adjudication, was challenged before the U.S. Supreme

Court in *Schall v. Martin*, the first selection in this chapter. The Court's response—authorizing preventive detention entirely at the discretion of the juvenile court judge so long as the purpose is not overtly punitive and the procedures followed provide a mechanism for reviewing individual cases for potentially erroneous decisions—leaves unanswered a number of troubling questions about who should be detained and what guidelines should be followed in making detention decisions.

The IJA-ABA and National Advisory Committee standards each went much further than did the Supreme Court in setting limits on the use of secure detention for youth awaiting adjudication of their cases in juvenile court. Both sets of standards established far more explicit, albeit nonbonding, guidelines for detention determinations than did the *Schall* decision. The National Advisory Committee's criteria for secure detention in delinquency cases—far more concise than those promulgated by the IJA-ABA—are included here as a counterpoint to the very flexible guidelines established by the New York statute at issue in *Schall*.

Restrictions on what are widely viewed as inappropriate uses of detention also figure prominently in the Juvenile Justice and Delinquency Prevention Act—as core requirements that states must satisfy in order to receive the full allocation of federal funding available to them through the formula grant program administered by OJJDP. Responding to persistent concerns about the harmful effects of such once-common practices as jailing juvenile detainees side-by-side with adult inmates charged with or convicted of criminal acts, and confining status offenders or even nonoffenders (i.e., dependent, neglected, or abused youth) in secure facilities alongside accused or adjudicated juvenile delinquents, the JJDP Act has long mandated that participating states must take steps to curb these abuses. From its inception in 1974, the Act mandated complete separation (often referred to as "sight-and-sound" separation) of juveniles and adults held in local jails and police lockups, and, subject only to narrowly delineated exceptions, "deinstitutionalization" (i.e., removal from secure confinement) of status offenders and nonoffenders. Beginning in 1980, the Act also mandated that participating states must avoid placing even accused or adjudicated delinquents in adult jails or lockups except in specified emergency situations. Finally, as we already learned in Chapter 1, a fourth mandate—that states take steps to reduce the extent of disproportionate minority confinement—was introduced in the 1988 amendments to the JJDP Act and made a core requirement in 1992.

In its present form (i.e., as amended most recently in the 2002 legislation reauthorizing the JJDP Act) the "separation" requirement remains absolute. The "deinstitutionalization" and "jail removal" requirements, on the other hand, are subject to elaborately structured exceptions, while the disproportionate minority confinement mandate has been reconfigured to target disproportionate minority contact with all components of the juvenile justice system. The current requirements and the statutory mechanisms for their enforcement, as they appear in the JJDP Act itself, are presented in our next selection.

Finally, shifting our attention to one of the thorniest dilemmas confronting juvenile detention center administrators today, Madeline Wordes and Sharon M. Jones tackle the problem of overcrowding, exploring the factors contributing to bulging detention facility populations, summarizing some of the consequences of crowding, and reviewing several methods that have been successfully employed to control populations by more effectively regulating admissions and length of stay. They also address issues related to the growing populations of females and racial minorities in juvenile detention centers.

REFERENCE

Institute of Judicial Administration—American Bar Association. (1996). *Juvenile Justice Standards Annotated: A Balanced Approach.* Robert

E. Shepherd, Jr., editor. Chicago: American Bar Association.

Schall v. Martin

The Supreme Court of the United States
467 U.S. 253 (1984)

JUSTICE REHNQUIST delivered the opinion of the Court.

Section 320.5(3)(b) of the New York Family Court Act authorizes pretrial detention of an accused juvenile delinquent based on a finding that there is a "serious risk" that the child "may before the return date commit an act which if committed by an adult would constitute a crime."[1] Appellees brought suit on behalf of a class of all juveniles detained pursuant to that provision. The District Court struck down § 320.5(3)(b) as permitting detention without due process of law and ordered the immediate release of all class members. The Court of Appeals for the Second Circuit affirmed, holding the provision

[1]New York Jud. Law § 320.5 provides, in relevant part:

"1. At the initial appearance, the court in its discretion may release the respondent or direct his detention.

.   .   .   .   .

"3. The court shall not direct detention unless it finds and states the facts and reasons for so finding that unless the respondent is detained;

"(a.) there is a substantial probability that he will not appear in court on the return date; or

"(b.) there is a serious risk that he may before the return date commit an act which if committed by an adult would constitute a crime."

Appellees have only challenged pretrial detention under § 320.5(3)(b). Thus, the propriety of detention to ensure that a juvenile appears in court on the return date, pursuant to § 320.5(3)(a), is not before the Court.

"unconstitutional as to all juveniles" because the statute is administered in such a way that "the detention period serves as punishment imposed without proof of guilt established according to the requisite constitutional standard." We noted probable jurisdiction, and now reverse. We conclude that preventive detention under the FCA [Family Court Act—*Ed.*] serves a legitimate state objective, and that the procedural protections afforded pretrial detainees by the New York statute satisfy the requirements of the Due Process Clause of the Fourteenth Amendment to the United States Constitution. . . .

II

. . . The statutory provision at issue in these cases, § 320.5(3)(b), permits a brief pretrial detention based on a finding of a "serious risk" that an arrested juvenile may commit a crime before his return date. The question before us is whether preventive detention of juveniles pursuant to § 320.5(3)(b) is compatible with the "fundamental fairness" required by due process. Two separate inquiries are necessary to answer this question. First, does preventive detention under the New York statute serve a legitimate state objective? And, second, are the procedural safeguards contained in the FCA adequate to authorize the pretrial detention of at least some juveniles charged with crimes?

A

Preventive detention under the FCA is purportedly designed to protect the child and society from the potential consequences of his criminal acts. When making any detention decision, the Family Court judge is specifically directed to consider the needs and best interests of the juvenile as well as the need for the protection of the community. In *Bell v. Wolfish* we left open the question whether any governmental objective other than ensuring a detainee's presence at trial may constitutionally justify pretrial detention. As an initial matter, therefore, we must decide whether, in the context of the juvenile system, the combined interest in protecting both the community and the juvenile himself from the consequences of future criminal conduct is sufficient to justify such detention.

The "legitimate and compelling state interest" in protecting the community from crime cannot be doubted. . . .

The juvenile's countervailing interest in freedom from institutional restraints, even for the brief time involved here, is undoubtedly substantial as well. But that interest must be qualified by the recognition that juveniles, unlike adults, are always in some form of custody. Children, by definition, are not assumed to have the capacity to take care of themselves. They are assumed to be subject to the control of their parents, and if parental control falters, the State must play its part as parens patriae. In this respect, the juvenile's liberty interest may, in appropriate circumstances, be subordinated to the State's "parens patriae interest in preserving and promoting the welfare of the child."

The New York Court of Appeals, in upholding the statute at issue here, stressed at some length "the desirability of protecting the juvenile from his own folly." Society has a legitimate interest in protecting a juvenile from the consequences of his criminal activity—both from potential physical injury which may be suffered when a victim fights back or a policeman attempts to make an arrest and from the downward spiral of criminal activity into which peer pressure may lead the child.

The substantiality and legitimacy of the state interests underlying this statute are confirmed by the widespread use and judicial acceptance of preventive detention for juveniles. Every State, as well as the United States in the District of Columbia, permits preventive detention of juveniles accused of crime. A number of model juvenile justice Acts also contain provisions permitting preventive detention. And the courts of eight States, including the New York Court of Appeals, have upheld their statutes with specific reference to protecting the juvenile and the community from harmful pretrial conduct, including pretrial crime.

. . . In light of the uniform legislative judgment that pretrial detention of juveniles properly promotes the interests both of society and the juvenile, we conclude that the practice serves a legitimate regulatory purpose compatible with the "fundamental fairness" demanded by the Due Process Clause in juvenile proceedings.

Of course, the mere invocation of a legitimate purpose will not justify particular restrictions and conditions of confinement amounting to punishment. It is axiomatic that "[d]ue process requires that a pretrial detainee not be punished." Even given, therefore, that pretrial detention may serve legitimate regulatory purposes, it is still necessary to determine whether the terms and conditions of confinement under § 320.5(3)(b) are in fact compatible with those purposes. . . . Absent a showing of an express intent to punish on the part of the State, that determination generally will turn on "whether an alternative purpose to which [the restriction] may rationally be connected is assignable for it, and whether it appears excessive in relation to the alternative purpose assigned [to it]."

There is no indication in the statute itself that preventive detention is used or intended as a punishment. First of all, the detention is strictly limited in time. If a juvenile is detained at his initial appearance and has denied the charges against him, he is entitled to a probable-cause hearing to be held not more than three days after the conclusion of the initial appearance or four days after the filing of the petition, whichever is sooner. If the Family Court judge finds probable cause, he must also determine whether continued detention is necessary pursuant to § 320.5(3)(b).

Detained juveniles are also entitled to an expedited factfinding hearing. If the juvenile is charged with one of a limited number of designated felonies, the factfinding hearing must be scheduled to commence not more than 14 days after the conclusion of the initial appearance. If the juvenile is charged with a lesser offense, then the factfinding hearing must be held not more than three days after the initial appearance. In the latter case, since the times for the probable-cause hearing and the factfinding hearing coincide, the two hearings are merged.

Thus, the maximum possible detention under § 320.5(3)(b) of a youth accused of a serious crime, assuming a 3-day extension of the factfinding hearing for good cause shown, is 17 days. The maximum detention for less serious crimes, again assuming a 3-day extension for good cause shown, is six days. These time frames seem suited to the limited purpose of providing the youth with a controlled environment and separating him from improper influences pending the speedy disposition of his case.

The conditions of confinement also appear to reflect the regulatory purposes relied upon by the State. When a juvenile is remanded after his initial appearance, he cannot, absent exceptional circumstances, be sent to a prison or lockup where he would be exposed to adult criminals. Instead, the child is screened by an "assessment unit" of the Department of Juvenile Justice. The assessment unit places the child in either nonsecure or secure detention. Nonsecure detention involves an open facility in the community, a sort of "halfway house," without locks, bars, or security officers where the child receives schooling and counseling and has access to recreational facilities.

Secure detention is more restrictive, but it is still consistent with the regulatory and parens patriae objectives relied upon by the State. Children are assigned to separate dorms based on age, size, and behavior. They wear street clothes provided by the institution and partake in educational and recreational programs and counseling sessions run by trained social workers. Misbehavior is punished by confinement to one's room. We cannot conclude from this record that the controlled environment briefly imposed by the State on juveniles in secure pretrial detention "is imposed for the purpose of punishment" rather than as "an incident of some other legitimate governmental purpose." . . .

. . . We are unpersuaded by the Court of Appeals' rather cavalier equation of detentions that do not lead to continued confinement after an adjudication of guilt and "wrongful" or "punitive" pretrial detentions.

Pretrial detention need not be considered punitive merely because a juvenile is subsequently discharged subject to conditions or put on probation. In fact, such actions reinforce the original finding that close supervision of the juvenile is required. Lenient but supervised disposition is in keeping with the Act's purpose to promote the welfare and development of the child. . . .

Even when a case is terminated prior to factfinding, it does not follow that the decision to detain the juvenile pursuant to § 320.5(3)(b) amounted to a due process violation. A delinquency petition may be dismissed for any number of reasons collateral to its merits, such as the failure of a witness to testify. The Family Court judge cannot be expected to anticipate such developments at the initial hearing. He makes his decision based on the information available to him at that time, and the propriety of the decision must be judged in that light. Consequently, the final disposition of a case is "largely irrelevant" to the legality of a pretrial detention.

It may be, of course, that in some circumstances detention of a juvenile would not pass constitutional muster. But the validity of those detentions must be determined on a case-by-case basis. Section 320.5(3)(b) is not invalid "on its face" by reason of the ambiguous statistics and case histories relied upon by the court below. We find no justification for the conclusion that, contrary to the express language of the statute and the judgment of the highest state court, § 320.5(3)(b) is a punitive rather than a regulatory measure. Preventive detention under the FCA serves the legitimate state objective, held in common with every State in the country, of protecting both the juvenile and society from the hazards of pretrial crime.

B

Given the legitimacy of the State's interest in preventive detention, and the nonpunitive nature of that detention, the remaining question is whether the procedures afforded juveniles detained prior to factfinding provide sufficient protection against erroneous and unnecessary deprivations of liberty. In *Gerstein v. Pugh* we held that a judicial determination of probable cause is a prerequisite to any extended restraint on the liberty of an adult accused of crime. We did not, however, mandate a specific timetable. Nor did we require the "full panoply of adversary safeguards—counsel, confrontation, cross-examination, and compulsory process for witnesses." Instead, we recognized "the desirability of flexibility and experimentation by the States." *Gerstein* arose under the Fourth Amendment, but the same concern with "flexibility" and "informality," while yet ensuring adequate predetention procedures, is present in this context.

In many respects, the FCA provides far more predetention protection for juveniles than we found to be constitutionally required for a probable-cause determination for adults in *Gerstein*. . . .

. . . [N]otice, a hearing, and a statement of facts and reasons are given prior to any detention under § 320.5(3)(b). A formal probable-cause hearing is then held within a short while thereafter, if the factfinding hearing is not itself scheduled within three days. These flexible procedures have been found constitutionally adequate under the Fourth Amendment and under the Due Process Clause. Appellees have failed to note any additional procedures that would significantly improve the accuracy of the determination without unduly impinging on the achievement of legitimate state purposes.

Appellees argue, however, that the risk of erroneous and unnecessary detentions is too high despite these procedures because the standard for detention is fatally vague. Detention under § 320.5(3)(b) is based on a finding that there is a "serious risk" that the juvenile, if released, would commit a crime prior to his next court appearance. We have already seen that detention of juveniles on that ground serves legitimate regulatory purposes. But appellees claim, and the District Court agreed, that it is virtually impossible to predict future criminal conduct with any degree of accuracy. Moreover, they say, the statutory standard fails to channel the discretion of the Family Court judge by specifying the factors on which he should rely in making that prediction. The procedural protections noted above are thus, in their view, unavailing because the ultimate decision is intrinsically arbitrary and uncontrolled.

Our cases indicate, however, that from a legal point of view there is nothing inherently unattainable about a prediction of future criminal conduct. Such a judgment forms an important element in many decisions, and we have specifically rejected the contention, based on the same sort of sociological data relied upon by appellees and the District Court, "that it is impossible to predict future behavior and that the question is so vague as to be meaningless."

We have also recognized that a prediction of future criminal conduct is "an experienced prediction based on a host of variables" which cannot be readily codified. Judge Quinones of the Family Court testified at trial that he and his colleagues make a determination under § 320.5(3)(b) based on numerous factors including the nature and seriousness of the charges; whether the charges are likely to be proved at trial; the juvenile's prior record; the adequacy and effectiveness of his home supervision; his school situation, if known; the time of day of the alleged crime as evidence of its seriousness and a possible lack of parental control; and any special circumstances that might be brought to his attention by the probation officer, the child's attorney, or any parents, relatives, or other responsible persons accompanying the child. The decision is based on as much information as can reasonably be obtained at the initial appearance.

Given the right to a hearing, to counsel, and to a statement of reasons, there is no reason that the specific factors upon which the Family Court judge might rely must be specified in the statute. . . .

The required statement of facts and reasons justifying the detention and the stenographic record of the initial appearance will provide a basis for the review of individual cases. Pretrial detention orders in New York may be reviewed by writ of habeas corpus brought in State Supreme Court. And the judgment of that court is appealable as of right and may be taken directly to the Court of Appeals if a constitutional question is presented. Permissive appeal from a Family Court order may also be had to the Appellate Division. Or a motion for reconsideration may be directed to the Family Court judge. These post-detention procedures provide a sufficient mechanism for correcting on a case-by-case basis any erroneous detentions ordered under § 320.5(3). Such procedures may well flesh out the standards specified in the statute.

III

. . . The question before us today is solely whether the preventive detention system chosen by the State of New York and applied by the New York Family Court comports with constitutional standards. Given the regulatory purpose for the detention and the procedural protections that precede its imposition, we conclude that § 320.5(3)(b) of the New York FCA is not invalid under the Due Process Clause of the Fourteenth Amendment.

The judgment of the Court of Appeals is

Reversed.

JUSTICE MARSHALL, with whom JUSTICE BRENNAN and JUSTICE STEVENS join, dissenting. . . .

The Court today holds that preventive detention of a juvenile pursuant to § 320.5(3)(b) does not violate the Due Process Clause. Two rulings are essential to the Court's decision: that the provision promotes legitimate government objectives important enough to justify the abridgment of the detained juveniles' liberty interests; and that the provision incorporates procedural safeguards sufficient to prevent unnecessary or arbitrary impairment of constitutionally protected rights. Because I disagree with both of those rulings, I dissent. . . .

. . . [F]airly viewed, pretrial detention of a juvenile pursuant to § 320.5(3)(b) gives rise to injuries comparable to those associated with imprisonment of an adult. In both situations, the detainee suffers stigmatization and severe limitation of his freedom of movement. Indeed, the impressionability of juveniles may make the experience of incarceration more injurious to them than to adults; all too quickly juveniles subjected to preventive detention come to see society at large as hostile and oppressive and to regard themselves as irremediably "delinquent." Such serious injuries to presumptively innocent persons—encompassing the curtailment of their constitutional rights to liberty—can be justified only by a weighty public interest that is substantially advanced by the statute. . . .

Appellants and the majority contend that § 320.5(3)(b) advances a pair of intertwined government objectives: "protecting the community from crime" and "protecting a juvenile from the consequences of his criminal activity." More specifically, the majority argues that detaining a juvenile for a period of up to 17 days prior to his trial has two desirable effects: it protects society at large from the crimes he might have committed during that period if released; and it protects the juvenile himself "both from potential physical injury which may be suffered when a victim fights back or a policeman attempts to make an arrest and from the downward spiral of criminal activity into which peer pressure may lead the child." . . .

Both of the courts below concluded that only occasionally and accidentally does pretrial detention of a juvenile under § 320.5(3)(b) prevent the commission of a crime. Three subsidiary findings undergird that conclusion. First, Family Court judges are incapable of determining which of the juveniles who appear before them would commit offenses before their trials if left at large and which would not. . . .

Second, § 320.5(3)(b) is not limited to classes of juveniles whose past conduct suggests that they are substantially more likely than average juveniles to misbehave in the immediate future. . . .

Third, the courts below concluded that circumstances surrounding most of the cases in which § 320.5(3)(b) has been invoked strongly suggest that the detainee would not have committed a crime during the period before his trial if he had been released. . . .

The rarity with which invocation of § 320.5(3)(b) results in detention of a juvenile who otherwise would have committed a crime fatally undercuts the two public purposes assigned to the statute by the State and the majority. . . .

If the record did not establish the impossibility, on the basis of the evidence available to a Family Court judge at a § 320.5(3)(b) hearing, of reliably predicting whether a given juvenile would commit a crime before his trial, and if the purposes relied upon by the State were promoted sufficiently to justify the deprivations of liberty effected by the provision, I would nevertheless still strike down § 320.5(3)(b) because of the absence of procedural safeguards in the provision. . . .

Appellees point out that § 320.5(3)(b) lacks two crucial procedural constraints. First, a New York Family Court judge is given no guidance regarding what kinds of evidence he should consider or what weight he should accord different sorts of material in deciding whether to detain a juvenile. For example, there is no requirement in the statute that the judge take into account the juvenile's background or current living situation. Nor is a judge obliged to attach significance to the nature of a juvenile's criminal record or the severity of the crime for which he was arrested. Second, § 320.5(3)(b) does not specify how likely it must be that a juvenile will commit a crime before his trial to warrant his detention. The provision indicates only that there must be a "serious risk" that he will commit an offense and does not prescribe the standard of proof that should govern the judge's determination of that issue.

Not surprisingly, in view of the lack of directions provided by the statute, different judges have adopted different ways of estimating the chances whether a juvenile will misbehave in the near future. . . . This discretion exercised by Family Court judges in making detention decisions gives rise to two related constitutional problems. First, it creates an excessive risk that juveniles will be detained "erroneously"—i.e., under circumstances in which no public interest would be served by their incarceration. Second, it fosters arbitrariness and inequality in a decisionmaking process that impinges upon fundamental rights. . . .

The majority acknowledges—indeed, founds much of its argument upon—the principle that a State has both the power and the responsibility to protect the interests of the children within its jurisdiction. Yet the majority today upholds a statute whose net impact on the juveniles who come within its purview is overwhelmingly detrimental. Most persons detained under the provision reap no benefit and suffer serious injuries thereby. The welfare of only a minority of the detainees is even arguably enhanced. The inequity of this regime, combined with the arbitrariness with which it is administered, is bound to disillusion its victims regarding the virtues of our system of criminal justice. I can see—and the majority has pointed to—no public purpose advanced by the statute sufficient to justify the harm it works.

I respectfully dissent.

REVIEW QUESTIONS

1. What was the issue in *Schall v. Martin*?
2. What is preventive detention? Why does Justice Rehnquist (who was later elevated to Chief Justice) believe that the New York statute authorizing preventive detention is acceptable under the due process clause of the Fourteenth Amendment to the United States Constitution? What are the "two separate inquiries" he considers necessary to examine the Constitutionality of the statute? What is his argument with respect to each one?
3. What is the basis of Justice Marshall's dissent? On what grounds does he disagree with Justice Rehnquist's reasoning as to the legitimacy of the government objectives underlying the statute *and* the adequacy of procedural safeguards for affected juveniles?
4. Do *you* think the government objectives outlined in this case are sufficiently important to justify a preventive detention statute like the one at issue here? Do you think the procedural safeguards are adequate? Why or why not?

Criteria for Detention in Secure Facilities—Delinquency

National Advisory Committee for Juvenile Justice and Delinquency Prevention

Juveniles subject to the jurisdiction of the family court over delinquency should not be detained in a secure facility unless:

   a. They are fugitives from another jurisdiction;

   b. They request protection in writing in circumstances that present an immediate threat of serious physical injury;

   c. They are charged with murder in the first or second degree;

   d. They are charged with a serious property crime or a crime of violence other than first or second degree murder which if committed by an adult would be a felony, and

     i) They are already detained or on conditional release in connection with another delinquency proceeding;

     ii) They have a demonstrable recent record of willful failures to appear at family court proceedings;

     iii) They have a demonstrable recent record of violent conduct resulting in physical injury to others; or

     iv) They have demonstrable [sic] recent record of adjudications for serious property offenses; and

   e. There is no less restrictive alternative that will reduce the risk of flight, or of serious harm to property or to the physical safety of the juvenile or others.

REVIEW QUESTIONS

1. In what ways do the criteria for detention in secure facilities outlined in this standard differ from those in the New York statute at issue in *Schall v. Martin*? Do they place significantly greater restrictions on the discretion of a juvenile court judge to order

Source: National Advisory Committee for Juvenile Justice and Delinquency Prevention. (1980). *Standards for the Administration of Juvenile Justice.* Washington, DC: U.S. Government Printing Office. Adapted courtesy of the United States Department of Justice, Office of Juvenile Justice and Delinquency Prevention.

detention? In what kinds of situations would adherence to these criteria prevent detention of juveniles who would be eligible for detention under the New York statute? Would the National Advisory Committee criteria *permit* detention in some situations where it would be prohibited under the New York statute?

2. Recall Justice Marshall's dissent in *Schall*. Do you think Justice Marshall would find the

National Advisory Committee criteria Constitutionally acceptable? Why or why not?

3. All things considered, do you think the National Advisory Committee criteria provide better guidance for detention decisions than the statute upheld by the Supreme Court in *Schall*? Justify your position.

The Juvenile Justice and Delinquency Prevention Act of 1974, as Amended Through November 2, 2002: Formula Grant Program— Core Requirements

Pub. L. No. 93-415, 42 U.S.C. § 5601 et seq. (Supp. 2003)

SEC. 5633. STATE PLANS

(a) Requirements

In order to receive formula grants under this part, a State shall submit a plan for carrying out its purposes applicable to a 3-year period. Such plan shall be amended annually to include new programs, projects and activities. The State shall submit annual performance reports to the Administrator which shall describe progress in implementing programs contained in the original plan, and shall describe the status of compliance with State plan requirements. In accordance with regulations which the Administrator shall prescribe, such plan shall— . . .

    (11) . . . provide that—

        (A) juveniles who are charged with or who have committed an offense that would not be criminal if committed by an adult, excluding—

            (i) juveniles who are charged with or who have committed a violation of section 922(x)(2) of title 18, United States Code [a federal law

prohibiting unauthorized possession of handguns by juveniles—
Ed.], or of a similar State law;

   (ii) juveniles who are charged with or who have committed a violation
of a valid court order; and

   (iii) juveniles who are held in accordance with the Interstate Compact on
Juveniles [an agreement among the states regarding procedures for
handling juveniles who cross state lines after running away from
home or absconding from placement, who are placed in treatment
settings outside their home states, or who move with their families
from one state to another while under court supervision—*Ed.*] as
enacted by the State;

shall not be placed in secure detention facilities or secure correctional facilities; and

(B) juveniles—

   (i) who are not charged with any offense; and

   (ii) who are—

      (I) aliens; or

      (II) alleged to be dependent, neglected, or abused;

shall not be placed in secure detention facilities or secure correctional
facilities;

(12) provide that—

(A) juveniles alleged to be or found to be delinquent or juveniles within the
purview of paragraph (11) will not be detained or confined in any institution in which they have contact with adult inmates; and

(B) there is in effect in the State a policy that requires individuals who
work with both such juveniles and such adult inmates, including in
collocated facilities, have been trained and certified to work with juveniles;

(13) provide that no juvenile will be detained or confined in any jail or lockup
for adults except—

(A) juveniles who are accused of nonstatus offenses and who are detained in
such jail or lockup for a period not to exceed 6 hours—

   (i) for processing or release;

   (ii) while awaiting transfer to a juvenile facility; or

   (iii) in which period such juveniles make a court appearance;

and only if such juveniles do not have contact with adult inmates and only
if there is in effect in the State a policy that requires individuals who work
with both such juveniles and adult inmates in collocated facilities have
been trained and certified to work with juveniles;

(B) juveniles who are accused of nonstatus offenses, who are awaiting an initial court appearance that will occur within 48 hours after being taken

into custody (excluding Saturdays, Sundays, and legal holidays), and who are detained in a jail or lockup—

  (i) in which—

      (I) such juveniles do not have contact with adult inmates; and

      (II) there is in effect in the State a policy that requires individuals who work with both such juveniles and adults inmates in collocated facilities have been trained and certified to work with juveniles; and

  (ii) that—

      (I) is located outside a metropolitan statistical area (as defined by the Office of Management and Budget) and has no existing acceptable alternative placement available;

      (II) is located where conditions of distance to be traveled or the lack of highway, road, or transportation do not allow for court appearances within 48 hours (excluding Saturdays, Sundays, and legal holidays) so that a brief (not to exceed an additional 48 hours) delay is excusable; or

      (III) is located where conditions of safety exist (such as severe adverse, life-threatening weather conditions that do not allow for reasonably safe travel), in which case the time for an appearance may be delayed until 24 hours after the time that such conditions allow for reasonable safe travel; . . .

(22) address juvenile delinquency prevention efforts and system improvement efforts designed to reduce, without establishing or requiring numerical standards or quotas, the disproportionate number of juvenile members of minority groups, who come into contact with the juvenile justice system; . . .

(c) Compliance with statutory requirements

If a State fails to comply with any of the applicable requirements of paragraphs (11), (12), (13) and (22) of subsection (a) of this section in any fiscal year beginning after September 30, 2001, then—

(1) subject to paragraph (2), the amount allocated to such State under section 222 [the section of the Act establishing the method for determining annual funding for each participating state—*Ed.*] for the subsequent fiscal year shall be reduced by not less than 20 percent for each such paragraph with respect to which the failure occurs, and

(2) the state shall be ineligible to receive any allocation under such section for such fiscal year unless—

  (A) the State agrees to expend 50 percent of the amount allocated to the State for such fiscal year to achieve compliance with any such paragraph with respect to which the State is in noncompliance; or

(B) the Administrator determines that the State—

(i) has achieved substantial compliance with such applicable requirements with respect to which the State was not in compliance; and

(ii) has made, through appropriate executive or legislative action, an unequivocal commitment to achieving full compliance with such applicable requirements within a reasonable time.

REVIEW QUESTIONS

1. This excerpt from the Juvenile Justice and Delinquency Prevention Act outlines four core requirements states must meet in order to be eligible for "formula" grants allocated by OJJDP. Try to identify which of the provisions has been dubbed the *deinstitutionalization* mandate. Can you tell from the provision what deinstitutionalization means in this context? What sorts of juveniles or, alternatively, what sorts of behavior, come within the scope of this mandate? What is required of states in order to be in compliance with the mandate? What problems do you think it was designed to remedy? What reasoning do you think underlies each of the exceptions to the deinstitutionalization requirement? Do you consider these exceptions appropriate? Would you add others? Why or why not?

2. Now try to identify the *separation* mandate. Why do you think this provision is often said to require "sight and sound separation"? Why do you think this mandate was included in the Act?

3. Which provision is the *jail removal* mandate? Why do you think Congress would consider jail removal important enough to require including this provision in the Act in addition to the separation mandate? What do you make of the exceptions to the jail removal requirement? Do they seem appropriate? Why or why not?

4. Can you identify the *disproportionate minority confinement* (DMC) mandate? We already encountered it in Chapter 1. How is the current version of this requirement (i.e., as amended in the 2002 legislation reauthorizing the JJDP Act) different from the original version as quoted by Pope, Lovell, and Hsia on p. 30? What is the purpose of the DMC requirement? Why do you think it was originally added to the Act's requirements? Why do you think Congress decided to change its focus? Do you think the new version provides a more—or less—effective means for combating racial bias in the juvenile justice system?

5. What mechanism did Congress provide to encourage compliance with the deinstitutionalization, separation, jail removal, and disproportionate minority confinement mandates? What happens if a state fails to meet any of these requirements? (*Hint:* Reread the subsection addressing compliance with statutory requirements.) Does this strike you as an effective way for the federal government to combat improper juvenile detention? Do you consider this method appropriate? Why or why not? Can you think of other approaches that might be more advisable?

Trends in Juvenile Detention and Steps Toward Reform

Madeline Wordes and Sharon M. Jones

The following article summarizes available data about juvenile detention use in the 1980s and 1990s, discusses possible areas of reform, and describes detention reform efforts that have been undertaken by various communities. When contemplating the causes of trends in detention, it is a truism that these populations are controlled by only two factors: admissions and length of stay. Quantitative data will indicate that the soaring national detention center population is due to increases in the number of offenders coming in the "front door" and in the length of stay of certain groups of offenders.

Data presented include the Census of Public and Private Juvenile Detention, Correctional and Shelter Facilities; juvenile court statistics from the National Center on Juvenile Justice; and local detention databases. Because national juvenile detention data are only available up to 1995, this article only addresses arrest rates for juveniles for the decade 1985 to 1995; it should be noted that in more recent years the juvenile arrest rate has generally fallen. Qualitative data about detention reform activities are from some of the National Council on Crime and Delinquency's (NCCD) projects in juvenile detention centers, including its evaluation of four sites participating in the Annie E. Casey Foundation's Juvenile Detention Alternatives Initiative (JDAI): Cook County, Illinois; Multnomah County, Oregon; New York City; and Sacramento County, California.

JDAI was inspired by the reform measures taken by Broward County, Florida in the late 1980s. As part of a federal consent decree, the county was forced to reduce extreme crowding and improve the conditions of confinement within detention. The county was able to decrease its average daily population from 161 youth in 1987–1988 to 88 youth in 1990–1991 through the use of alternatives to detention, intake screening, and assistance to the county's public defender services. Capital improvements also fostered better conditions of confinement. These achievements were made through the extraordinary cooperation and consensus of all key leaders in the county (Barton, Schwartz, and Orlando 1994). The detention reform efforts in Broward County and the JDAI sites show that the process is multidimensional and complicated and can produce positive results as well as unintended consequences.

Source: Madeline Wordes and Sharon M. Jones. (1998). Trends in juvenile detention and steps toward reform. *Crime and Delinquency,* 44(4), 544–560. Copyright © 1998 by Sage Publications, Inc. Reprinted by permission of Sage Publications, Inc.

This article does not address strategies to prevent delinquency among youth. Nor does it address the fact that juvenile detention is not uniform across the country—youth are handled very differently based on geography (Feld 1991; Krisberg, Litsky, and Schwartz 1984). There is great variation among jurisdictions in the locus of administration, staffing practices, authorization for admissions to detention, and other key factors. Detention decisions can be made by legislation, police department policy, detention center policy, court discretion, or by the decision of an individual. In addition, informal rules have long governed how detention centers are operated.

By the presentation of the national detention situation and some possible reform strategies, it is hoped that this article will encourage juvenile justice practitioners and researchers to pay more attention to the central role of detention in juvenile justice and to start to demand information about detention populations and accountability about how resources are allocated.

WHAT IS JUVENILE DETENTION?

Even though the centennial of the juvenile court is fast approaching, the role, purpose, and goal of juvenile detention in this institution is still a topic of discussion and dissent. At the most basic level, a youth who has been accused of an offense or who is arrested is often taken into custody. This youth may be held in a lockup, a jail, or a detention facility. In the case of a lockup, the law allows police to hold youth for only a short period of time (usually up to six hours). Jails, like police lockups, were intended for adults but are also sometimes used for juveniles. Generally, no services are offered in either of these facilities. Most youth (whether they are charged as juveniles or adults) are held in juvenile detention centers, which by definition are short-term holding facilities designed specifically for youth. Rudimentary educational and recreational services should be offered in most of these facilities, although in some detention centers more extensive services are available. Detention has only two generally accepted purposes: to ensure that a youth appears for all court hearings and to prevent a youth from reoffending prior to disposition (Lubow and Tulman 1995; Krisberg and Austin 1993, pp. 73–76).

In a survey of juvenile detention use commissioned in 1966, the NCCD declared that "confusion and misuse pervade detention. It has come to be used by police and probation officers as a disposition; judges use it for punishment, protection, [and] storage" (U.S. Department of Justice, Office of Justice Programs, Office of Juvenile Justice and Delinquency Prevention [OJJDP] 1997a, p. 12). In the 1970s, detention centers were regularly used to hold youth at every stage of the juvenile justice process (Schwartz and Willis 1994). Today, detention centers continue to be used for numerous and diverse populations, not just for the two main purposes of ensuring appearance in court and protecting the public.

Preadjudicated juveniles awaiting a preliminary hearing, trial, or disposition may be housed next to youth accused of very serious crimes who are being processed in the adult system. Those who have been placed in detention at the discretion of their probation officers for technical violations may be next to the severely mentally ill for whom no appropriate placement can be found. Juveniles serving a sentence in detention sleep next to those who continue to "fail" in placements and who have been rejected from any other possible placement facility. And despite federal law to the contrary, some jurisdictions place homeless and runaway youth in temporary holding cells with serious and violent juveniles until a shelter bed or parent can be found. Some of these youth will spend the majority of their adolescence in detention centers, even though staff are not trained to raise children to adulthood. Incarceration or incapacitation for these long periods of time have psychological effects that are not now fully understood. Detention is often used as the postmodern weigh station for the nation's problem children. Here we find our mentally ill, our oppositional, our angry, our troubled youth (Krisberg and Austin 1993, pp. 73–76; "Symposium" 1995).

In 1995, the year for which the most recent national data is available, there were 503 facilities holding these youth that qualified as juvenile detention facilities. Of these facilities, 450 were public facilities. On any given day in 1995, there were approximately 23,000 youth held in public detention centers and approximately an additional 7,900 held in jails (U.S. Bureau of the Census 1985–1995; Gilliard and Beck 1996). There has been a 68 percent increase in the one-day detention rate between 1985 and 1995, from 53 youth per 100,000 to 89 per 100,000 (U.S. Bureau of the Census 1985–1995).

CROWDING

Capacity also increased but not at such dramatic rates. . . . In 1984, detention facilities had more than 4,000 more beds available than were filled on an average daily basis. By 1994, however, the population exceeded capacity by more than 1,000 youth across the country. In other words, the capacity of detention centers increased 24 percent, whereas the average daily population increased 73 percent. . . .

In 1985, there were only 24 public detention facilities that were overcapacity; 11 years later, 178 facilities were crowded. When considered from the viewpoint of the effect on youth, the crowding situation looks all the more serious. In 1985, 2,732 youth were housed in facilities that were overcapacity, whereas in 1995, that number had increased to 14,932. By 1995, 56 percent of youth admitted to detention were admitted to crowded facilities (in 1984, only 15 percent were admitted to overcrowded facilities. . . . As these data show, the majority of youth now admitted to detention walk into crowded facilities, and crowding has become more the rule than the exception.

Reasons for Crowding

There are a number of possible reasons for the increase in crowding. First, the number of arrests has been increasing. Between 1985 and 1995, the number of arrests for juveniles grew by approximately 23 percent. The vast majority of youth were arrested for property crimes, and these numbers did not change much during this time period (an increase of 8 percent; U.S. Department of Justice, Federal Bureau of Investigation 1965–1992, 1993,

1994, 1995; U.S. Department of Justice, Office of Justice Programs, Bureau of Justice Statistics 1996). However, . . . the rate of drug arrests increased by 78 percent, and the violent crime index rate increased by 53 percent between 1985 and 1995.

On the other hand, the increase in arrests has not been matched by increases in the likelihood of detention. The percentage of all juvenile court cases that were detained has stayed relatively stable for all offense categories (averaging between 17 percent and 28 percent). For example, in 1984, 23 percent of drug cases were detained; in 1994, 28 percent of the drug cases were detained. Since 1987, detention was more likely in drug cases than any other category of offenses (U.S. Department of Justice, Office of Justice Programs, Bureau of Justice Statistics 1994). These data indicate that crowding is probably due in part to the gross numbers of youth brought to the front door. Additionally, they show that the causes and solutions to detention crowding should be found at the front door to detention and in state statutes regarding arrests, not necessarily in juvenile court practice.

In fact, legislation and policy around juvenile crime play a large part in the rise in detention populations. During this 11-year period, the great fluctuations in drug arrests are most likely due to varying policies and practices as part of the "war on drugs." Within this short time period, many approaches to the control of illegal drugs have been taken by police and other justice agencies, resulting either in greater or smaller arrest rates. State legislatures moved to stiffen penalties for juvenile offenders and transfer a greater number of them to adult court (Podkopacz and Feld 1995; U.S. Department of Justice, Office of Justice Programs, OJJDP 1997b).

Consequences of Crowding

There are consequences for youth, staff, and budgets in the current crisis of detention. Research has shown that youth in detention receive more punitive dispositions, even after controlling for legal and other factors (Frazier and Cochran 1986; McCarthy and Smith 1986). Growth in detained populations and more severe penalties indicate a greater pressure on probation, other supervision, and placement services.

If facilities become crowded, conditions can become untenable for staff, programs suffer, and costs skyrocket (U.S. Department of Justice, Office of Justice Programs, OJJDP 1997a). One jurisdiction faced a sudden crowding problem—350 youth over facility capacity. Youth were forced to sleep on mattresses pulled out on the floor in dayrooms, and education services were severely curtailed. In two other sites, crowding was linked to documented increases in staff/youth altercations, injuries to youth, and limitations on education. Fortunately, detention reform activities have eased crowding, and these sites implemented emergency measures to manage these populations.

The burgeoning detention population also has financial consequences. Nationally, total operating expenditures more than doubled between 1984 and 1994. Per-resident operating costs have also increased, rising from $27,745 to $36,487 in that time period (U.S. Bureau of the Census 1985–1995). These rising costs may be due to many factors, including increasing health care or staff costs or the added expenses of maintaining populations in facilities overcapacity. At this continued rate of growth, the financial burden of detaining youth will become increasingly evident.

FACTORS AFFECTING DETENTION POPULATION

The national trends in juvenile detention map a dreary picture for youth in detention. The following sections address the two possible areas of attack to manage detention populations—admissions and length of stay. Despite the "get tough" public and political environment, some jurisdictions around the country are bravely trying to accomplish innovation and reform of detention practice. As mentioned above, this section will draw on the experience of Broward County and the Casey Foundation's JDAI sites. These communities have demonstrated that there are strategies that can be effective in accomplishing detention reform. As detention rates have skyrocketed nationally, JDAI detention reform activities have helped the sites resist the national trends. It is important to note that the situation in each locale is different, and the techniques for reform are going to be dependent on the presenting detention problem. It is also necessary to recognize that measures taken to address portions of the detention population may be effective on that population but may not have an overall impact on average daily population. The lessons of these sites show us that detention reform is a complicated and multidimensional process—a series of small tugs at a massive and intractable system.

Admissions

. . . [T]he national rate of admissions has grown 40 percent between 1985 and 1995. While this rate grew for all offense types, some offense types are represented in the detention population more than others. The most striking is the population of drug offenders, which increased 200 percent between 1985 and 1989 (again, this increase is probably due to criminal justice policies in the war on drugs, as drug use was falling during that period for the detainable population) (Johnston, O'Malley, and Bachman 1994, pp. 81–86). Although fewer youth were detained on drug charges than on other types of charges, and detentions leveled off in the early 1990s, the impact of these offenders on detention is still cause for concern (U.S. Bureau of the Census 1985–1995).

Up until 1991, the rate of admission to detention for property offenders was greater than that for person offenders. However, . . . the rise in the detention rate for offenses against persons increased from 10 per 100,000 to 26 per 100,000, a 160 percent increase between 1985 and 1995. By 1995, the detention rate for person offenders was greater than that of property offenders.

Most jurisdictions looking to control the front door to detention turn first to implementing objective admissions criteria and risk assessment that identify youth who are appropriate for detention. Several jurisdictions have implemented well-planned assessment instruments, which were later validated with success (U.S. Department of Justice, Office of Justice Programs, OJJDP 1995; Steinhart 1994). Broward County and the JDAI sites implemented risk assessments and/or admissions criteria using available data, consensus about risk and seriousness of offenders, and other jurisdictions' risk assessments as models. Ideally, risk assessments would be developed empirically based on valid and reliable data. Three of the JDAI sites showed declines in admissions of between 12 percent and 14 percent between 1994 and 1996. In the other site, admissions increased, and the detention population grew to more than 70 percent over capacity after implementation of the risk assessment. As there were not adequate data at the time of development, decision makers could not have imagined this result. The instrument was greatly revised, admissions fell back to their pre-risk assessment levels, and are now controlled through the assessment instrument.

There were other obstacles to implementing risk assessment instruments as well. Once implemented, line and judicial staff may resent the perceived infringement on their judgment. One jurisdiction faced an override rate of more than 50 percent in the first year of implementation, before leaders consulted judicial staff and made changes in the instrument. This county's override rate is now between 10 percent and 12 percent.

Once having identified youth who were appropriate for detention, Broward County and the JDAI sites developed alternative programs that would provide the necessary supervision to ensure a youth would return to court for all hearings and would not reoffend while awaiting case disposition. These programs have included day reporting, shelter care, home supervision, electronic monitoring, and work projects. The JDAI sites alone have created almost 700 new program slots to date.

Ideally, these alternatives to detention programs should only supervise youth who would be detained if not for the program. However, net widening can occur when programs are implemented quickly without relevant data or without clear target populations. One county developed a total of six alternative programs, three of which began receiving youth within little more than a year. Over time, staff found that these programs had not reduced the detention population as greatly as they had anticipated. A probation unit was then established to monitor utilization of the programs, review and revise target populations, and conduct outreach to judicial and line staff. Although some net widening is still suspected, the county is now able to track how and why youth are referred to the programs.

Race and Gender Issues

Of particular note in developing risk assessments and alternatives to detention is the need to address significantly growing populations—young women and racial/ethnic minorities. National arrest rates for girls increased 41 percent between 1985 and 1995, compared to a smaller increase of 18 percent for boys. In fact, there was a dramatic 111 percent increase in the violent offense arrest rate for girls.

The national detention rate increases do not parallel the arrest rates, probably due to more serious offenses being committed by males. . . . [T]he increase in the detention rate was considerably higher for males than females. For example, in 1985, males were detained at a rate 4.3 times higher than females. Eleven years later, the rate differential increased, and males were detained at a rate six times higher than females. Across years, there was a 75 percent increase in the rate of detention for males and a smaller, yet substantial, 25 percent increase in the rate of detention for females.

There were large differences between African American and White youth in national arrest rates for violent and drug offenses. The growth rate in violent crimes was greater for White youth (69 percent) than African American youth (39 percent). However, the ratio of African American to White juvenile arrests for violence was 5 to 1 in 1995. For drug and weapons arrests, the pattern was similar but not as disproportionate; African American youth were arrested at almost three times the rate of White youth for these offenses. There was a 166 percent increase in drug arrests for African American youth compared to a 54 percent increase for Whites. In fact, in 1985 the ratio of African American to White juvenile arrest rates for drugs was 1.6 to 1, but in 1995 the ratio increased to 2.8 to 1.

. . . [E]xcept for Whites, the detention rate for all racial and ethnic groups showed very large increases from 1985 to 1995 (an increase of 180 percent for African Americans and 145 percent for Hispanics but a decrease of 13 percent for Whites). African American youth were housed in detention facilities at 2.5 times the rate of White youth in 1985. By 1995, this disproportionality had increased such that African American youth were detained at eight times the rate of Whites.

As there is some evidence that detention decisions may be racially biased, these numbers are particularly alarming (Wordes, Bynum, and Corley 1994; Pope and Feyerherm 1990a, 1990b). Risk assessments should be designed to eliminate any racial or gender bias in detention decisions. One JDAI site developed a risk assessment that seems to have reduced the disproportionate detention of minority youth (Feyerherm 1998). Alternative programs should be culturally specific to offer proper supervision for youth. One county has successfully worked with a long-standing community group to operate an evening reporting center for youth in that area of the city. The county is also in the process of developing a set of gender-specific probation programming for girls. Unfortunately, there are few examples of these types of well-balanced planning and programming for youth to reduce disproportionate minority confinement or to increase programs designed for girls.

Length of Stay

Another means to affect detention population size is to control the length of stay. The national average number of days youth were held in detention centers increased from 12 days to 15 days between 1984 and 1994 (U.S. Bureau of the Census 1985–1995). Some of this increase may be due to a growing population of youth waiting for trial as adults in the criminal justice system. Although a small number of admissions every year, these cases can be complicated and a low priority in adult judicial caseloads so they can stay in detention for long periods of time. In one of the JDAI sites, youth whose cases were being tried in adult court represented 4 percent of admissions but 20 percent of the average daily population. In another site, more than 50 percent of the beds were occupied by youth with cases in adult court.

Longer lengths of stay are probably also due to the rising population of youth who are committed to detention or who have been adjudicated but remain in detention for a number of possible reasons. Even though the national population of youth committed or adjudicated has not risen as quickly as the preadjudicated population . . ., these youth can make a large impact with a few admissions because of their long length of stay. Many of these youth remain in detention for long periods of time because no placement or proper home can be found for them; many placement facilities will not accept youth who have serious mental health problems or who have previously "failed" out of placement.

One avenue to shorten length of stay is through the use of a staff person as a detention "expediter." Although the duties of this staff person vary among jurisdictions, the expediter usually reviews all or a portion of the detention population for possible release to home or to an alternative to detention. This person is also responsible for completing any necessary paperwork associated with the release and transfer of the youth. This strategy has been successful in Broward County and several of the JDAI sites in helping to reduce length of stay for some preadjudicatory populations.

Another way these sites have attempted to reduce length of stay is through implementing case-processing reforms. For example, one county found that long case-processing times were having a significant impact on their detention center population. The county established a case-expediting system that involves the identification of certain youth at a preliminary hearing for a plea proceeding within five days. The district attorney, the public defender, and probation services were all involved in developing the program and worked to negotiate the new roles the processing system required of them. The program reduced case-processing time for selected groups of offenders. There has been a lesser impact on length of stay either because youth remain in detention facilities awaiting placement or because the change in case-processing time for the targeted offenders is not significant enough to affect the average length of stay.

One JDAI site examined data about their detention population and found that youth who have been removed from placement were occupying the largest number of beds. These youth and other "back door" offenders occupied more than half of the detention beds. Immediate measures were taken by the county to reduce the number of these youth coming back to detention: Probation administrators met with all placement providers, asked them to provide reasons why youth were terminated from their programs, and requested that the programs put into place extra provisions to prevent terminations. The county also established a committee to evaluate all placements and make recommendations for contract changes. Without this analysis of their data, the county would not have known that failures from placements and probation were such a large part of their crowding problem.

CONCLUSIONS

Unfortunately, success of these reform strategies has often been elusive. Generally, declines in average daily population as seen in the first years of the Broward County project have either not been as dramatic in JDAI sites or have not been sustained to date. In some communities, net widening did not allow detention alternatives to be used as true alternatives to detention or populations shifted from preadjudicated categories to postadjudicated or committed categories.

On the other hand, these projects do show that it is possible to reform what appears to be an intractable system. While national statistics show large increases in detention across the country, the JDAI sites were not part of this trend. The sites have been successful in targeting certain groups of youth for special case processing or alternative to detention programming. Detention reform strategies have also focused attention on this neglected segment of the juvenile justice system and have led to a general improvement in services to court-involved youth. Of note here are the communities that have been able to improve conditions of confinement in detention without the redirection of additional funds. In some communities, detention reform has led to a complete redirection in how staff interact with youth.

The United States is at a crossroads in determining what to do about juvenile crime. Although juvenile detention is almost always neglected in these discussions, this article shows how these facilities are at the nexus of how juveniles are treated in our justice systems. The National Juvenile Detention Association has recently promulgated a new definition of detention that is neither limited by place nor process: "Juvenile detention is the temporary and safe custody of juveniles who are accused of conduct subject to the jurisdiction of the court who require a restricted environment for their own or the community's protection while pending legal action" (U.S. Department of Justice, Office of Justice Programs, OJJDP 1997a, p. 33).

This definition allows for varying types of facilities and programs in which juveniles could be detained pending placement that would address public safety needs, use least restrictive environments, and not increase failure to appear rates. It also directs a wholesale change in how systems envision detention. Local, state, and national authorities will soon need to address the increasing detention population and corresponding crowding by making the difficult decisions to reduce the number of youth coming in the front doors of detention, to reduce the length of stay, or through the expensive quick fix of building more facilities to incarcerate our troubled youth.

REFERENCES

Barton, William H., Ira M. Schwarz, and Frank A. Orlando. 1994. "Reducing the Use of Secure Detention in Broward County, Florida." Pp. 1–11 in *Reforming Juvenile Detention: No More Hidden Closets*, edited by I. M. Schwartz and W. H. Barton. Columbus: Ohio State University Press.

Feld, Barry C. 1991. "Justice by Geography: Urban, Suburban, and Rural Variations in Juvenile Justice Administration." *Journal of Criminal Law and Criminology* 82(1):156–210.

Feyerherm, William C. 1998. Unpublished Report.

Frazier, Charles E. and John K. Cochran. 1986. "Official Intervention, Diversion From the Juvenile Justice System, and Dynamics of Human Service Work: Effects of a Reform Goal Based on Labeling Theory." *Crime & Delinquency* 32(2):157–76.

Gilliard, Darrell K. and Alien J. Beck. 1996. "Prison and Jail Inmates, 1995." *Bureau of Justice Statistics Bulletin*. Washington, DC: U.S. Government Printing Office.

Johnston, Lloyd D., Patrick M. O'Malley, and Jerald G. Bachman. 1994. *National Survey Results on Drug Use From the Monitoring the Future Study, 1975–1993, Volume 1, Secondary School Students*. Rockville, MD: National Institute on Drug Abuse.

Krisberg, Barry and James F. Austin. 1993. *Reinventing Juvenile Justice*. Newbury Park, CA: Sage.

Krisberg, Barry, Paul Litsky, and Ira Schwartz. 1984. "Youth in Confinement: Justice by Geography." *Journal of Research in Crime and Delinquency* 21 (2):153–81.

Lubow, Bart. 1997. *The Juvenile Detention Alternatives Initiative: A Progress Report*. Baltimore, MD: The Annie E. Casey Foundation.

Lubow, Bart and Joseph B. Tulman. 1995. The Unnecessary Detention of Children in the District of Columbia. *District of Columbia Law Review* 3(2):ix.

McCarthy, Belinda R. and Brent L. Smith. 1986. "The Conceptualization of Discrimination in the Juvenile Justice Process: The Impact of Administrative Factors and Screening Decisions on Juvenile Court Dispositions." *Criminology* 24(1):41–64.

National Center on Juvenile Justice. N.d. *National Estimates of Juvenile Court Delinquency Cases, 1986–1993* [MRDF]. Washington, DC: National Center for Juvenile Justice [producer].

Podkopacz, Marcy R. and Barry C. Feld. 1995. "Judicial Waiver Policy and Practice: Persistence, Seriousness, and Race." *Law and Inequality: A Journal of Theory and Practice* 14(1):73–178.

Pope, Carl E. and William H. Feyerherm. 1990a. "Minority Status and Juvenile Justice Processing: An Assessment of the Research Literature." *Criminal Justice Abstracts* 22(2):327–35.

_____. 1990b. "Minority Status and Juvenile Justice Processing: An Assessment of the Research Literature, Part II." *Criminal Justice Abstracts* 22(3):527–35.

Schwartz, Ira M. and Deborah A. Willis. 1994. *National Trends in Juvenile Detention*. Pp. 13–29 in *Reforming Juvenile Detention: No More Hidden Closets*, edited by I. M. Schwartz

and W. H. Barton. Columbus: Ohio State University Press.

Steinhart, David. 1994. "Objective Juvenile Detention Criteria: The California Experience." Pp. 47–68 in *Reforming Juvenile Detention: No More Hidden Closets*, edited by I. M. Schwartz and W. H. Barton. Columbus: Ohio State University Press.

"Symposium: The Unnecessary Use of Detention in the District of Columbia." 1995. *District of Columbia Law Review* 3(2).

U.S. Bureau of the Census. 1980–1991. *Population Estimates by Age, Sex, Race, and Hispanic Origin* [MRDF]. Washington, DC: U.S. Bureau of the Census [producer].

_____. 1985–1995. *Census of Public and Private Juvenile Detention, Correctional and Shelter Facilities* [MRDF]. Washington, DC: U.S. Bureau of the Census [producer].

_____. 1992–2050. *Population Projections of the U.S. by Age, Sex, Race, and Hispanic Origin* [MRDF]. Washington, DC: U.S. Bureau of the Census [producer].

_____. 1993–2050. *Population Projections of the U.S. by Age, Sex, Race, and Hispanic Origin* [MRDF]. Washington, DC: U.S. Bureau of the Census [producer].

U.S. Department of Justice, Federal Bureau of Investigation. 1965–1992, 1993, 1994, 1995. *Uniform Crime Reports, Age-Specific Arrest Rates and Race-Specific Arrest Rates for Selected Offenses*. Washington, DC: U.S. Government Printing Office.

U.S. Department of Justice, Office of Justice Programs, Bureau of Justice Statistics. 1994. *Sourcebook of Criminal Justice Statistics*. Washington, DC: U.S. Government Printing Office.

_____. 1996. *Sourcebook of Criminal Justice Statistics*. Washington, DC: U.S. Government Printing Office.

U.S. Department of Justice, Office of Justice Programs, Office of Juvenile Justice and Delinquency Prevention (OJJDP). 1995. *Guide for Implementing the Comprehensive Strategy for Serious, Violent, and Chronic Juvenile Offenders*. Washington, DC: U.S. Government Printing Office.

_____. 1997a. *OJJDP Guide to Good Juvenile Detention Practice*. Washington, DC: U.S. Government Printing Office.

_____. 1997b. Juvenile *Justice Reform Initiatives in the States: 1994–1996*. Washington, DC: U.S. Government Printing Office.

U.S. Department of Justice, Office of Juvenile Justice and Delinquency Prevention, National Institute for Juvenile Justice and Delinquency Prevention. 1984, 1985, 1986. *Juvenile Court Statistics*. Washington, DC: U.S. Government Printing Office.

Wordes, Madeline, Timothy S. Bynum, and Charles J. Corley. 1994. "Locking Up Youth: The Impact of Race on Detention Decisions." *Journal of Research on Crime and Delinquency* 31(1):149–65.

REVIEW QUESTIONS

1. What kinds of facilities are examined in this article? How do these facilities differ from jails and police lockups? From other kinds of facilities for juvenile offenders?

2. How many such facilities were in use when this study was conducted? About how many youths did they hold? Had this number increased or decreased in the previous decade? By how much?

3. What did the authors find out about the extent of crowding in juvenile detention facilities? What reasons do they suggest for crowding in these facilities? What are the consequences of crowding?

4. How do admissions and length of stay affect juvenile detention center populations? With respect to each of these factors, what policies do the authors suggest would help reduce detention populations?

5. What race and gender issues do the authors raise? What solutions do they suggest for problems related to race? In what ways, if at all, do these solutions seem responsive to the JJDP Act's disproportionate minority confinement mandate? How do the statistics the authors present on detention of girls affect your reaction to Chesney-Lind's discussion of delinquency programming for girls in Chapter 1?

FURTHER READING

Devine, Patricia, Coolbaugh, Kathleen, and Jenkins, Susan. (1998). *Disproportionate Minority Confinement: Lessons Learned from Five States*. Washington, DC: Office of Juvenile Justice and Delinquency Prevention. Available online: http://www.ncjrs.org/94612.pdf

Hsia, Heidi M., and Hamparian, Donna. (1998). *Disproportionate Minority Confinement: 1997 Update*. Washington, DC: Office of Juvenile Justice and Delinquency Prevention. Available online: http://www.ncjrs.org/pdffiles/170606.pdf

Roush, David W. (1996). *Desktop Guide to Good Juvenile Detention Practice: Research Report*. Washington, DC: Office of Juvenile Justice and Delinquency Prevention. Available online: http://www.ncjrs.org/pdffiles/desktop.pdf

Schwartz, Ira M., and Barton, William H. (Eds.). (1994). *Reforming Juvenile Detention: No More Hidden Closets*. Columbus: Ohio State University Press.

Shelden, Randall G. (1999). *Detention Diversion Advocacy: An Evaluation*. Washington, DC: Office of Juvenile Justice and Delinquency Prevention. Available online: http://www.ncjrs.org/pdffiles1/ojjdp/171155.pdf

Stanfield, Rochelle. (1999). *The JDAI Story: Building a Better Juvenile Detention System*. Part of the Pathways to Juvenile Detention Reform series. Baltimore: The Annie E. Casey Foundation. Available online: http://www.aecf.org/initiatives/jdai/pdf/overview.pdf

CHAPTER

7

Transfer to Adult Criminal Court

The final decision during the so-called middle stages of the juvenile justice process concerns whether to transfer the case to criminal court for prosecution of the juvenile as an adult. Traditionally, this decision fell to the juvenile court judge who, following a petition requesting waiver of juvenile court jurisdiction, would make a determination as to whether the youth was *amenable to treatment* within the juvenile justice system. If a youth's age, offense, and/or prior record suggested nonamenability, the case would be transferred to criminal court and the youth would be prosecuted as an adult. (Recall from Chapter 1 that the Supreme Court's decisions in *Kent v. U.S.* and *Breed v. Jones* were directed toward the procedures judges must follow in *waiving* juvenile court jurisdiction.) More recently, however, state legislatures have moved to restrict the discretion of juvenile court judges either by transferring authority for determining whether the youth should be tried as a juvenile or an adult to the prosecutor, or by legislatively excluding certain types of cases from juvenile court jurisdiction based on some combination of age, offense, and prior record.

The first selection in this chapter outlines the basic mechanisms for transfer and the variations on each basic form that are currently employed. In addition to discussing the various state legislative provisions for judicial waiver, prosecutorial direct file, and statutory exclusion, the selection addresses such supplementary provisions as reverse waiver and "once an adult/always an adult" restrictions, plus baseline standards for making transfer decisions and limiting official discretion.

Largely as a result of the growing complexity of transfer mechanisms, reliable data on the number of juveniles transferred to adult court, and on criminal court handling of young offenders following transfer, have proven remarkably elusive. One report, based on data for 1990–1994 in the nation's 75 largest counties, determined that roughly 1% of all cases handled in state criminal courts during that period involved transferred youth (Strom, Smith, & Snyder, 1998). The same study concluded that approximately 59% of transferred youth are convicted of felonies and that about 52% of those convicted ultimately serve time in prison. A more recent study, based on a national sample of criminal sentences handed down in 1996, found a somewhat higher proportion of convicted transferees going to prison—60%—with another 19% serving time in local jails (Levin, Langan, & Brown, 2000). Because of the limited and highly speculative nature of the data contained in these and a handful of other reports, however, and also because recent changes in transfer patterns have undoubtedly altered the representation of transferred youth among criminal cases, none of the available statistical examinations of criminal court processing of transferred youth appears in this chapter.

Reliable information about the influence of transfer on recidivism (i.e., commission of a new offense following release from prison or completion of probation) is, perhaps surprisingly, much more readily available. In our next selection, Donna Bishop and Charles Frazier review research on recidivism rates among transferees and the deterrent effect of transfer. Concluding that transfer is in general an ineffective deterrent, the authors go on to consider why treatment in the juvenile justice system appears more effective in reducing recidivism than the harsher punishments meted out in the adult system.

We conclude our discussion of transfer to adult court with consideration of an issue that has become increasingly controversial in the last few years: the death penalty for juveniles. We begin with a very brief statistical overview of the history and current status of the juvenile death penalty in the United States prepared by Victor L. Streib, a law professor who maintains a website documenting all death sentences and executions for juvenile offenses since January 1, 1973. In addition to detailing the historical background and legal context of the juvenile death penalty, and summarizing available information about juvenile death sentences imposed since 1973, Professor Streib's website lists the name, age, race, state, and current status of every juvenile sentenced to death in the current era as well as case summaries for all juvenile offenders currently under sentences of death. The selection included here is from the executive summary of the information available on the website.

The last two selections address the Constitutionality of the death penalty for persons convicted of offenses committed while they were juveniles. In the first of these, the U.S. Supreme Court's 1988 decision in *Thompson v. Oklahoma*, Justice Stevens outlines the Court's reasons for finding the death penalty to be unconstitutional when applied to someone under the age of 16 at the time of the offense. A very different rationale is then advanced by Justice Scalia—speaking for a deeply divided court in *Stanford v. Kentucky* the following year—for upholding the Constitutionality of executing 16- and 17-year-old murderers.

REFERENCES

Levin, David J., Langan, Patrick A., and Brown, Jodi M. (2000). *State Court Sentencing of Convicted Felons, 1966.* Washington, DC: Bureau of Justice Statistics.

Strom, Kevin J., Smith, Steven K., and Snyder, Howard N. (1998). *Juvenile Felony Defendants in Criminal Courts: State Court Processing Statistics, 1990–1994.* Washington, DC: Bureau of Justice Statistics.

Trying Juveniles as Adults in Criminal Court: An Analysis of State Transfer Provisions

Patrick Griffin, Patricia Torbet, and Linda Szymanski

INTRODUCTION

All States and the District of Columbia (hereafter included with States in this Report) allow adult criminal prosecution of juveniles under some circumstances. The following discussion of State law in this area—which is based on State statutes as amended through the 1997 legislative sessions—gives an account of the principal transfer mechanisms by which juveniles are placed in the criminal justice system at the State level for serious and violent crimes.

State transfer mechanisms differ from one another primarily in where they locate the responsibility for deciding whether or not a given juvenile should be prosecuted in a court exercising civil (delinquency) or criminal jurisdiction.

- *Waiver* provisions leave transfer decisionmaking to the State's juvenile courts: juveniles may not be prosecuted as if they were adult criminals pursuant to a waiver provision until a juvenile court judge has ordered it. Waiver provisions differ from one another in the degree of decisionmaking flexibility they allow the courts. Some make the waiver decision entirely discretionary. Others set up a presumption in favor of waiver. And still others specify circumstances under which waiver is mandatory. But under all waiver provisions, a case against a juvenile must at least originate in juvenile court and cannot be channeled elsewhere without a juvenile court judge's formal approval.

- *Direct File* provisions leave it up to the prosecutor to determine whether to initiate a case against a minor in juvenile court or in criminal (adult) court.

- *Statutory Exclusion* provisions grant criminal courts original jurisdiction over a whole class of cases involving juveniles. Under statutory exclusion, a State

Source: Patrick Griffin, Patricia Torbet, and Linda Szymanski. (1998). *Trying Juveniles as Adults in Criminal Court: An Analysis of State Transfer Provisions.* Washington, DC: Office of Juvenile Justice and Delinquency Prevention. Copyright 1998 by the National Center for Juvenile Justice. Adapted by permission.

legislature is essentially predetermining the question of criminal prosecution for itself and taking the decision out of both the prosecutor's and the court's hands.

This Report also describes statutory mechanisms by which individual cases may be moved from criminal to juvenile court (see Reverse Waiver); provisions that permanently terminate juvenile court jurisdiction over individual juveniles who have been tried or convicted as adults (see Once an Adult/Always an Adult); standards applied to waiver decisions (see Transfer Criteria); and a number of related subsidiary issues, including the extent to which transfers are allowed or required for offenses that are not violent, probable cause requirements, extraordinary evidentiary burdens, the effect of prior delinquency records in transfer proceedings, limits on prosecutorial discretion, and minimum age provisions.

TRANSFER PROVISIONS

Waiver

Discretionary Waiver

A total of 46 States give juvenile court judges discretion to waive jurisdiction in individual cases involving minors, so as to allow prosecution in adult criminal courts. Terminology varies from State to State—some call the process a "certification," "bind-over," or "remand" for criminal prosecution, for example, or a "transfer" or "decline" rather than a waiver proceeding—but all transfer mechanisms in this category have the effect of authorizing but not requiring juvenile courts to designate appropriate cases for adult prosecution.

Most discretionary waiver statutes specify threshold criteria similar to those outlined in *Kent v. United States* (383 U.S. 541, 566-67 (1966)) that must be met before the court may consider waiver in a given case: generally a minimum age, a specified type or level of offense, a sufficiently serious record of previous delinquency, or some combination of the three. [An appendix to the majority opinion in *Kent* reproduced a juvenile court policy memorandum—in force when Morris Kent was transferred—that specified criteria for waiver of juvenile court jurisdiction; this material does not appear in the excerpts from *Kent* in Chapter 3—Ed.] However, 17 States authorize discretionary waiver, at least for certain age groups, for any offense. (This is not to say that offense seriousness is not taken into account in waiver determinations in those States, only that their statutes specify no particular kind or quality of offense as a threshold for waiver consideration.)

Some States specify that the prosecutor must initiate the discretionary waiver process by filing a motion; others allow any party or the court to initiate the process.

In all States where discretionary waiver is authorized, the juvenile court must conduct a hearing at which the parties are entitled to present evidence bearing on the waiver issue. In addition, laws in seven States require a prehearing investigative report on the accused juvenile's past record and current circumstances, prepared by a juvenile probation office or some other local agency, to be submitted to the juvenile court for its consideration.

Figure 7–1

Summary of Transfer Provisions, 1997

State	Judicial Waiver			Direct File	Statutory Exclusion	Reverse Waiver	Once an Adult/ Always an Adult
	Discretionary	Mandatory	Presumptive				
Total States:	46	14	15	15	28	23	31
Alabama	■				■		■
Alaska	■				■		
Arizona	■		■*	■	■	■	■
Arkansas	■			■		■	
California	■		■				■
Colorado	■		■	■		■	
Connecticut		■				■	
Delaware	■	■			■	■	■
Dist. of Columbia	■		■	■			■
Florida	■			■	■		■
Georgia	■	■		■		■	■
Hawaii	■				(r-97)		■
Idaho	■						■
Illinois	■	■	■		■		■
Indiana	■	■			■		■
Iowa	■				■	■	■
Kansas	■		■		(r-96)		■
Kentucky	■	■				■	
Louisiana	■	■		■	■		
Maine	■						■
Maryland	■				■	■	
Massachusetts	(r-96)			■	■		
Michigan	■			■			■
Minnesota	■		■		■		■
Mississippi	■				■	■	■
Missouri	■				■		■
Montana	■			■	■		
Nebraska				■			
Nevada	■		■		■		■
New Hampshire	■		■			■	
New Jersey	■		■				
New Mexico					■	■	
New York					■	■	
North Carolina	■	■					
North Dakota	■	■	■				■
Ohio	■	■					■
Oklahoma	■			■	■	■	■
Oregon	■				■	■	■
Pennsylvania	■		■		■	■	■
Rhode Island	■	■	■				■
South Carolina	■	■			■	■	■
South Dakota	■				■	■	■
Tennessee	■					■	■
Texas	■						■
Utah	■		■		■		■
Vermont	■			■	■	■	
Virginia	■	■		■	■		■
Washington	■				■		
West Virginia	■	■					■
Wisconsin	■				■		■
Wyoming	■			■		■	

Legend: ■ indicates the provision(s) allowed by each State as of the end of the 1997 legislative session; "r" indicates repealed; * indicates by court rule.

The prosecution bears the burden of proof in a discretionary waiver hearing; however, some States designate special circumstances under which this burden may be shifted to the child (see Presumptive Waiver). Generally, the case for a waiver must be made by "a preponderance of the evidence," although a few States require a higher showing (see Clear and Convincing Evidence Standard in next chapter [i.e., in the "Additional Analyses" part of this selection—*Ed.*]). In most discretionary waiver jurisdictions, the law specifies factors a court must weigh, findings it must make, and an overall standard it must apply in making its waiver decision (see Transfer Criteria below).

Once a case has been waived to criminal court, statutes in seven States expressly provide that the criminal court may exercise jurisdiction not only over the offense that triggered the waiver, but also over any lesser included offenses.

Transfer Criteria

Nearly all of the States that authorize juvenile courts to make discretionary waivers (44 out of 46) specify broad standards to be applied and/or factors to be considered in deciding whether to waive jurisdiction. Overall, standards tend to be in the form of extremely general formulas—"the best interests of the child and the public," for instance. Lists of factors to be weighed by the courts are always considerably more specific and are usually at least loosely based on the eight factors enumerated in Kent.

The most common waiver standards call for courts to exercise their discretion to waive jurisdiction when the interests of the juvenile or the public (six States) or the interests of both (four States) would be served thereby; when the public safety (six States) or the public interest (four States) requires it; or when the juvenile does not appear to be amenable to treatment or rehabilitation within the juvenile system (four States). Most of the remaining standards combine these concepts in some way (the District of Columbia, for example, authorizes waiver if it is "in the interest of the public welfare and protection of the public security and there are no reasonable prospects for rehabilitation") or simply allow waiver whenever the court finds "good cause" (Kansas) or whenever the accused is not a "proper subject" for juvenile treatment (Missouri and Virginia). Besides requiring the court to consider "the best interests of the youth and of society" as a number of other States do, Oregon departs from the usual practice by focusing on whether the juvenile has the capacity "to appreciate the nature and quality of [his or her] conduct."

Most States that specify particular factors to be considered in waiver hearings either simply paraphrase the list from the U.S. Supreme Court's Kent opinion or list some of the Kent factors that are considered more important while omitting others. But a few States add factors of their own to the Kent list. In the District of Columbia, for example, judges considering waiver are called upon to bear in mind, besides the Kent factors, the "potential rehabilitative effect . . . of parenting classes or family counseling" on the juvenile. Arizona adds consideration of the views of the victim and any gang involvement on the juvenile's part to the usual list of factors. Maine requires the court to ask whether retaining jurisdiction would "diminish the gravity of the offense" in public opinion. In Missouri, courts must take into account any "racial disparity in certification" of juveniles for adult prosecution.

Most State statutes simply recite the factors and leave them to the consideration of juvenile court judges, without attempting to dictate precisely how they should fit into the waiver decision. In Michigan and Minnesota, however, courts are required to give the most weight to two specified factors (offense seriousness and prior record), whereas in Kentucky the law specifies that, of the seven factors the court must consider, at least two must support any decision in favor of waiver.

Mandatory Waiver

The statutes of 14 States provide for mandatory waiver in cases that meet certain age, offense, or other criteria. In these States, proceedings against the juvenile are initiated in juvenile court. However, the juvenile court has no role other than to confirm that the statutory requirements for mandatory waiver are met. Once it has done so, the juvenile court must send the case to a court of criminal jurisdiction.

Mandatory waiver must be distinguished from statutory exclusion. When an offense has been excluded by law from juvenile court jurisdiction, the case against a minor accused of that offense originates in criminal court. Under ordinary circumstances, the juvenile court has no involvement and is entirely bypassed. By contrast, although the juvenile court's involvement in a mandatory waiver case may be minimal, it receives the case initially, conducts some sort of preliminary hearing to ensure that the case is one to which the mandatory waiver statute applies, and issues a transfer order and any other necessary orders, relating to appointment of counsel, interim detention, and so on.

The mandatory waiver classification applies to statutory mechanisms that actually tie the juvenile court's hands—not those that merely seem to. So, for example, the many State laws that recite that the juvenile court "shall" or "must" transfer certain juveniles—if the public interest requires it or unless there are good reasons not to—are classified as discretionary waiver provisions. Generally, in a true mandatory waiver jurisdiction, the juvenile court is called upon only to determine that there is probable cause to believe a juvenile of the requisite age committed an offense falling within the mandatory waiver law. However, even this is not always necessary: in Indiana and South Carolina, which require mandatory waiver in cases involving juveniles with certain prior records, the juvenile court, once it has confirmed the juvenile's record, may leave the probable cause determination to the criminal court. In Connecticut, the law stipulates that, where the mandatory waiver provision applies, the juvenile's counsel is not permitted to make any argument or file any motion to oppose transfer; in fact, in those mandatory waiver situations in which a probable cause finding is necessary, the court makes it without notice, a hearing, or any participation on the part of the juvenile or his or her attorney.

Laws in a few States specify types of cases in which courts must at least consider waiver. For instance, Delaware, besides requiring waiver in certain cases, also requires that the courts give consideration to waiver in some others—as when a juvenile of at least 14 is charged with violating a restitution order or when one who is at least 16 is charged with having committed any of various listed crimes. Likewise, a Missouri law mandates that the court at least hold a waiver hearing when a juvenile is charged with any of a number of serious crimes or has already committed two or more previous felonies. However, since these laws do not affirmatively mandate waiver—only that the courts consider waiver—they have been classified as discretionary waiver provisions.

Presumptive Waiver

In 15 States, statutes (court rule in Arizona) designate a category of cases in which waiver to criminal court is rebuttably presumed to be appropriate. In such cases, the juvenile rather than the State bears the burden of proof in the waiver hearing; if a juvenile meeting age, offense, or other statutory criteria triggering the presumption fails to make an adequate argument against transfer, the juvenile court must send the case to criminal court.

It should be noted that the rebuttable presumption in these cases applies if the juvenile meets statutory critera qualifying the case for presumptive waiver treatment. It would not ordinarily apply to the question of whether the juvenile meets these criteria. For instance, in Alaska—which like many States generally requires that the prosecutor in a waiver hearing demonstrate probable cause to believe that the juvenile actually committed the crime alleged (see Additional Pretransfer Findings Required)—the prosecutor must show probable cause even when the alleged crime is one that triggers a presumptive waiver. Only when the prosecutor has met this initial burden must the juvenile come forward with evidence of "amenability to treatment" as a juvenile.

In four States, a child subject to a presumption in favor of waiver not only has the burden of proof at the waiver hearing, but must present "clear and convincing evidence" that a waiver is not justified (see Clear and Convincing Evidence Standard).

Statutory criteria triggering presumptive waiver fall into three broad categories. In some States, it is primarily the current offense that matters; in Alaska, for example, children of any age charged with certain violent felonies are rebuttably presumed to be "unamenable to treatment." (Alaska, however, is the only State that has set up a presumption against children younger than 14.) In others, older juveniles are singled out, even if the offenses of which they are accused would not otherwise trigger a presumption; in New Hampshire, the same crimes that would merely authorize consideration of a waiver in the case of a 13-year-old would presumptively require one if the juvenile involved was 15 at the time of commission. Still other States emphasize the child's prior offense history over other factors; in Colorado, if the juvenile otherwise qualifies for discretionary waiver treatment, a sufficiently serious prior delinquency record triggers the presumption all by itself.

Direct File

Statutes in 15 States define a category of cases in which the prosecutor may determine whether to proceed initially in juvenile or criminal court. Typically, these direct file provisions give both juvenile and adult criminal courts the power to hear cases involving certain offenses or age/offense categories, leaving it up to the prosecutor to make discretionary decisions about where to file them.

Of course, prosecutors often have considerable discretionary powers in this area even in the absence of formal statutory authority. In their charging decisions, for instance, they may sometimes, in effect, choose the forum in which the case will be heard. What distinguishes direct file authority is that it rests on the juvenile and criminal courts' concurrent jurisdiction over a given type of case.

Again, as is the case with other transfer mechanisms, there is wide variation among the States regarding criteria for direct file treatment, with some emphasizing offense categories, others the age of the juvenile involved, and still others the extent and seriousness of the juvenile's offending history. Generally, the minimum level of offense seriousness necessary to trigger direct file appears to be lower than that required for statutory exclusion or mandatory or presumptive waiver. Arkansas authorizes direct file treatment of a large range of offenses (including soliciting a minor to join a street gang), evidently trusting its prosecutors to make appropriate filing and resource allocation decisions. Florida allows even misdemeanors to be prosecuted in criminal court if the child involved is at least 16 and has a sufficiently serious record.

Statutory Exclusion

Twenty-eight States have statutes that remove certain offenses or age/offense/prior record categories from the juvenile court's jurisdiction. Generally, the laws of such States simply exclude anyone fitting into one of these categories from being defined as a "child" for juvenile court jurisdictional purposes. A juvenile accused of an excluded offense is treated as an adult from the beginning—that is, proceeded against (by information, indictment, or otherwise) in the criminal court that would have had jurisdiction over the same offense if it had been committed by an adult. This way of proceeding is not merely an option available to the prosecutor, as in those States that leave the determination of how to process certain offenses or age/offense categories to the prosecutor's discretion (see Direct File). Once the prosecutor has made the decision to charge a juvenile with an excluded offense, the case must be filed in criminal court—although many States provide a mechanism under which criminal courts may order excluded cases transferred to juvenile courts (see Reverse Waiver).

Some States exclude only the most serious offenses; in New Mexico, for example, only first-degree murder committed by a child of at least 15 is excluded. Others single out cases involving older juveniles. Mississippi excludes all felonies committed by 17-year-olds. It should be noted that one blanket application of this method—simply lowering the upper age limit of original juvenile court jurisdiction—excludes the largest number of juveniles for adult prosecution. Finally, as is the case with the presumptive and mandatory waiver provisions previously discussed, some States focus not so much on offense or age as on the individual juvenile's offense history. Arizona excludes any felony committed by a juvenile as young as 15, provided the juvenile has two or more previous delinquency adjudications for offenses that would have been felonies if committed by an adult.

Reverse Waiver

The laws of 23 States provide some mechanism whereby a juvenile who is being prosecuted as an adult in criminal court may petition to have the case transferred to juvenile court for adjudication or disposition. By enacting a reverse waiver provision, a State may simultaneously define a broad category of cases that it considers merit criminal court handling and ensure that its courts have an opportunity to consider whether such handling is actually appropriate in individual cases.

A statutory provision is placed in the reverse waiver category if it authorizes the State's adult criminal courts to transfer a juvenile's case from criminal to juvenile court, however it arrived in the criminal court in the first place—via direct file, exclusion, or in some instances, waiver. The reverse waiver designation applies to provisions that authorize the criminal court to transfer a case for disposition to the juvenile court, but does not apply to "blended sentencing" provisions under which the criminal court retains the case while imposing a combination of dispositions, some of which are ordinarily available only to juvenile courts. Likewise, although many States allow a juvenile who has been waived by a juvenile court to appeal the decision immediately, provisions authorizing an appeals court (as opposed to a trial-level criminal court) to order a case returned to juvenile court are not counted as reverse waiver provisions. Conversely, provisions that authorize a trial-level criminal court to make the decision either to accept jurisdiction over a case for trial, or to send it to juvenile court for adjudication, are considered reverse waiver provisions, even where (as in Virginia) they are designated "appeal" provisions.

Generally, when the reverse waiver proceeding represents the first time a court has had an opportunity to consider the appropriateness of adult prosecution in a given case—when the alleged offense is one that is excluded from juvenile jurisdiction by statute, for example, or when the prosecutor has exercised "direct file" discretion to proceed initially in criminal court—the court's decision is governed by the same kinds of broad "best interests" standards and considerations as those taken into account by a juvenile court in deciding whether to waive jurisdiction (see Transfer Criteria). In Nebraska, for example, which gives county attorneys considerable direct file discretion but requires them to consider a number of factors (including "the best interests of the juvenile and the security of the public"), the district or county court must consider the very same factors in deciding whether to retain jurisdiction over such a case in the face of the juvenile's objections.

However, six States (Connecticut, Kentucky, Mississippi, Nevada, Tennessee, and Virginia) authorize reverse waiver in some cases even when a juvenile court judge has already looked into the issues and determined that waiver to criminal court is appropriate. Under these circumstances, a reverse waiver is usually available only if the juvenile court's decision was substantially groundless (Mississippi), or if other "exceptional circumstances" can be shown (Nevada). Tennessee and Virginia have particularly anomalous reverse waiver provisions. In Virginia, as noted above, the procedure is cast in terms of an "appeal" to the adult trial court from the juvenile court's transfer decision, with the issue being whether the juvenile court's decision was in substantial compliance with the law; however, in substance the decision is the same as in other reverse waiver situations—whether or not to accept jurisdiction and retain the case for an adult criminal trial. In Tennessee, a juvenile who has been waived to criminal court is entitled to an immediate de novo rehearing on the issue at the adult criminal court level—but only if the waiver decision was made by a nonlawyer; otherwise, the juvenile must appeal the juvenile court's waiver decision following a final conviction.

Twenty of the 35 States with direct file or statutory exclusion also have reverse waiver provisions.

- **States with reverse waivers:** Arizona, Arkansas, Colorado, Delaware, Georgia, Iowa, Maryland, Mississippi, Nebraska, Nevada, New York, Oklahoma, Oregon, Pennsylvania, South Carolina, South Dakota, Vermont, Virginia, Wisconsin, and Wyoming.

- **States without reverse waivers:** Alabama, Alaska, District of Columbia, Florida, Idaho, Illinois, Indiana, Louisiana, Massachusetts, Michigan, Minnesota, Montana, New Mexico, Utah, and Washington.

Once an Adult/Always an Adult

A special transfer category has been created in 31 States for juveniles who, having once been prosecuted as adults, are subsequently accused of new offenses. Most States with "once an adult/always an adult" provisions simply require criminal prosecution of all such subsequent offenses—by means of either a blanket exclusion or an automatic waiver mechanism. Others exclude or require waiver of only a broadly defined subset of these cases—those involving juveniles of a certain age, for instance, or those in which the subsequent offense is sufficiently serious.

Nearly all once an adult/always an adult provisions stipulate that the juvenile involved must have been convicted of the offense that triggered the adult prosecution. In California, however, this is not always necessary; a subsequent charge that would ordinarily require a fitness hearing in juvenile court may be filed directly in criminal court if the juvenile involved was previously declared unfit for juvenile handling and transferred to criminal court—even if no conviction followed the original transfer—provided the original unfitness determination was based on criteria (the juvenile's delinquency history, failure of rehabilitation attempts, or both) unrelated to the juvenile's guilt or innocence of the previous charge. Likewise, in Delaware, the law does not require a conviction in the original case, provided a court (either the juvenile court in a discretionary waiver hearing or the criminal court following a reverse waiver request) had the opportunity to make a determination regarding the juvenile's amenability to the rehabilitative processes of the juvenile court. Idaho requires adult prosecution of a juvenile who has already been convicted as an adult, even if the original conviction was for a lesser offense that would not have been excluded from juvenile court jurisdiction. Mississippi requires no conviction on the first adult-prosecuted offense if the juvenile is subsequently accused of a felony.

Although most States require that, following a juvenile's conviction as an adult, all subsequent offenses be prosecuted in criminal court, three—Michigan, Minnesota, and Texas—restrict the coverage of their once an adult/always an adult provisions to cases in which juveniles are subsequently accused of felonies, and California specifies that the subsequent offense must be one for which waiver to criminal court would otherwise be allowed. Likewise, whereas most States make no distinction based on the ages of juveniles previously convicted as adults, California and Iowa limit the application of their once an adult/always an adult provisions to 16-year-olds. Oregon is the only State that leaves the once an adult/ always an adult decision to its juvenile courts, authorizing them, in connection with the waiver of jurisdiction over a juvenile of at least 16, to enter an order making waiver automatic in any subsequent case involving the same juvenile; however, if the juvenile is not convicted following the entry of such an order, the law requires that the order be vacated.

Many states require criminal prosecution of all subsequent offenses.

- **States with once an adult/always an adult provisions:** Alabama, Arizona, California, Delaware, District of Columbia, Florida, Hawaii, Idaho, Indiana, Iowa, Kansas, Maine, Michigan, Minnesota, Mississippi, Missouri, Nevada, New Hampshire, North Dakota, Ohio, Oklahoma, Oregon, Pennsylvania, Rhode Island, South Dakota, Tennessee, Texas, Utah, Virginia, Washington, and Wisconsin.

- **States without once an adult/always an adult provisions:** Alaska, Arkansas, Colorado, Connecticut, Georgia, Illinois, Kentucky, Louisiana, Maryland, Massachusetts, Montana, Nebraska, New Jersey, New Mexico, New York, North Carolina, South Carolina, Vermont, West Virginia, and Wyoming.

ADDITIONAL ANALYSES

Transfer for Nonviolent Offenses

Although State laws requiring or allowing the prosecution of juveniles as adults are commonly thought to be legislative responses to increases in juvenile violence, a surprising number of such laws authorize criminal prosecution for nonviolent offenses. Twenty-one States require or allow adult prosecution of juveniles accused of certain property offenses— most often arson or burglary. Statutes in 19 States authorize or mandate prosecution of juveniles accused of drug offenses in criminal court. Forty-six States allow waiver to criminal court for a range of offenses—personal and property, violent and nonviolent. If the accused juvenile is of sufficient age, 16 States (Alabama, Alaska, Delaware, Florida, Georgia, Idaho, Illinois, Iowa, Kansas, Maryland, Mississippi, North Dakota, Tennessee, Washington, Wisconsin, and Wyoming) permit waivers for any criminal offense; 17 (Arizona, Colorado, District of Columbia, Hawaii, Minnesota, Missouri, Nebraska, Nevada, New Hampshire, North Carolina, Ohio, Oklahoma, Pennsylvania, Rhode Island, South Dakota, Utah, and Virginia) allow or require adult prosecution for any felony; 6 (Connecticut, Kentucky, Maine, Michigan, South Carolina, and Texas) allow or require adult prosecution for any felony of a particular grade; and 9 authorize or mandate adult handling of specified offenses that do not necessarily involve violence, such as escape (Arkansas, Illinois, Michigan, and Oregon), soliciting a minor to join a street gang (Arkansas), "aggravated driving under the influence" (Arizona), auto theft (New Jersey), perjury (Texas) and treason (West Virginia). In addition, many States require or allow prosecution of juveniles as adults for misdemeanors, ordinance violations, and summary statute violations (e.g., fish and game violations).

Additional Pretransfer Findings Required

Statutes in 30 States expressly require that, before a case may be waived to criminal court, the juvenile court must find probable cause to believe that the juvenile actually committed the alleged offense. In three States, although a probable cause finding is not mandated, the list of factors for the court to consider in making its waiver determination includes the "prosecutive merit" of the case against the juvenile (see Transfer Criteria). In Maryland and the District of Columbia, on the other hand, the laws specify that, for purposes of the waiver determination, the juvenile's guilt is to be assumed.

In seven States, in addition to other findings to support a waiver order, the court must determine that the accused juvenile is not a fit subject for treatment in an institution for the mentally ill or the mentally retarded.

Clear and Convincing Evidence Standard

Generally, a prosecutor seeking a waiver to criminal court must make the case for waiver by "a preponderance of the evidence." In six States, however, a higher burden is specified: proof by "clear and convincing evidence" that waiver is justified. Under certain circumstances, the laws of four States impose the "clear and convincing evidence" burden on the juvenile who opposes waiver or seeks a transfer from criminal to juvenile court.

Special Transfer Treatment Based on Prior Record

Transfer statutes in 25 States single out juveniles with specified prior offense histories for adverse treatment. Of course, a sufficiently serious record of past involvement with the law would often be relevant to a waiver determination, and in fact this is one factor for consideration suggested in the U.S. Supreme Court's Kent decision (see Transfer Criteria). However, 25 States go further than this, either by defining a direct file or statutory exclusion category to include juveniles with previous delinquency adjudications or by requiring less of a showing for the waiver of juveniles with specified delinquency histories.

Devices to Limit Prosecutorial Discretion

Six States grant prosecutors discretion to decide when to try juveniles as adults in court proceedings but attempt to limit that discretion in some way. In Florida, for example, in cases involving specified age/offense categories, a State's Attorney must either attempt an adult prosecution or provide the juvenile court with written reasons for failing to do so. Before exercising direct file authority to prosecute juveniles as adults in Nebraska and Wyoming, prosecutors are required to give consideration to the same kinds of enumerated "factors" that are ordinarily weighed by courts making waiver determinations.

Minimum Age Provisions

Twenty-three States have at least one provision for transferring juveniles to criminal court for which no minimum age is specified. Other sections of the State statute may specify the lowest age for juvenile court delinquency jurisdiction, below which juveniles cannot be processed as delinquents in juvenile court (16 States), and/or the lowest age for criminal responsibility, below which children cannot be tried in criminal court (14 States).

As States lower the age at which youth can be transferred to criminal court, minimum age of criminal responsibility becomes important in deciding when and if a criminal court can accept jurisdiction of such youth. In two States, the juvenile code does not stipulate a minimum transfer age but the criminal code does specify a minimum age of criminal responsibility (Georgia for capital crimes; Nevada for murder).

REVIEW QUESTIONS

1. Griffin et al. outline three distinct mechanisms for transferring serious juvenile offenders to adult criminal court. They also discuss numerous variations and related provisions that have been developed by different states. How does each of these transfer methods work? What are the key differences among them? Within each approach, who has discretion to determine which juveniles are to be transferred?

2. In your view, what are the advantages and disadvantages of each transfer provision discussed in the article?

3. Recall Scott and Grisso's discussion in Chapter 1 of the influence of developmental factors in adolescents' decisions about offending and in their understanding of the criminal process. Which transfer mechanisms seem most consistent with points raised in their discussion (i.e., which ones permit the most appropriate degree of consideration for developmental factors)? Which seem least consistent?

4. What method or combination of methods for transferring juveniles into the adult criminal justice system do you think should be employed and which methods should be avoided? What is your reasoning?

Consequences of Transfer

Donna Bishop and Charles Frazier

Transfer has traditionally been justified on the grounds that the juvenile court is ill equipped to handle two classes of offenders. In the case of seriously violent offenders, the public demands heavy penalties that have been well beyond the capacity of the juvenile justice system to provide. Whether these offenders might respond to juvenile justice intervention is irrelevant: the community simply will not tolerate mild responses to heinous crimes. The other class historically targeted for removal consists of chronic offenders who have been afforded all appropriate interventions at the juvenile court's disposal and who have not responded to those efforts. In such cases, the court reasonably concludes that they are not amenable to treatment. As a last resort, they are transferred to the criminal courts, which are better equipped to incapacitate those who present a continuing threat to the public welfare.

Historically, transfer was used sparingly precisely because it was assumed that exposing juveniles to processing and punishment in the criminal courts might do them serious harm. Resort to the criminal court was appropriate only in instances where offenders were irredeemable, either on moral grounds or in point of fact. More recently, and for a variety of reasons that are beyond the scope of this chapter, legislators and justice officials have become more sanguine about criminal punishment for young offenders. They demand more in the name of desert than the juvenile court can provide and increasingly subscribe to the idea that criminal punishment has utility as a general and specific deterrent. Consequently, transfer criteria have become inclusive of a broad range of offenders who are neither particularly serious nor particularly chronic. Legislative exclusion and prosecutorial waiver statutes frequently target a broad range of offenses and offenders. In Florida, for example, the law sanctions transfer of sixteen- and seventeen-year-old first-time offenders charged with *any* felony as well as fourteen- and fifteen-year-old first-time offenders accused of any of several felonies, some of which are property crimes. Such policies are consistent with either of two conclusions. In their zeal for retribution, policy makers are willing to ignore the jeopardy into which large numbers of adolescents are placed, or they trust that

Source: Donna Bishop and Charles Frazier. (2000). Consequences of transfer. In Jeffrey Fagan and Franklin E. Zimring (Eds.). *The Changing Borders of Juvenile Justice: Transfer of Adolescents to the Criminal Court* (pp. 207–276). Chicago: The University of Chicago Press. © 2000 by The University of Chicago. Adapted by permission.

criminal punishment will ultimately prove beneficial to juvenile offenders and to society. In either event, we must be concerned about consequences. . . .

3. CONSEQUENCES FOR SOCIETY: IMPLICATIONS OF TRANSFER FOR CRIME CONTROL

Implicit in the strong rhetoric surrounding the criminalization of juvenile offending is a general deterrent purpose to dissuade juveniles from committing crimes through the threat of severe consequences, including lengthy terms of incarceration (Fagan 1995; Singer and McDowall 1988). The threat of transfer is the quintessence of the "scared straight" approach to crime control. In addition, as was discussed at the outset of this chapter, the expanded application of transfer to include offenders who are neither particularly serious nor particularly chronic suggests a specific deterrent purpose as well. There seems to be a general expectation that criminal punishments will motivate young offenders to reform. Unfortunately, assessments of the extent to which transfer achieves these dual aims are few and recent. Like so many other reforms, this one did not flow from or build on careful research.

General Deterrence

Only two studies to date have evaluated the general deterrent effects of transfer on juvenile crime. Singer and McDowall (1988; see also Singer 1996) conducted a very careful study of the effects of New York's Juvenile Offender Law, which lowered the age of criminal court jurisdiction to thirteen for murder and four other violent offenses. Using a time series design, they examined arrest rates for affected juveniles over a four-year period prior to enactment of the law and for six years following its implementation. Arrest rates for juveniles affected by the law were also compared with those of two control groups, including older juveniles in the same jurisdiction and juveniles of the same age in a nearby jurisdiction. Singer and McDowall report that the law had little if any measurable impact. It is important to note that the law received significant advance publicity and was well implemented. Consequently, the most plausible explanation is that the threat of criminal punishment had no general deterrent effect.

Jensen and Metsger (1994) evaluated the general deterrent effect of an Idaho mandatory transfer statute introduced in 1981. The law required transfer of juveniles as young as fourteen who were charged with murder, attempted murder, robbery, forcible rape, or mayhem. The researchers examined arrest rates for the five-year period prior to the new law and for five years following its implementation. They also examined rates of arrest in two neighboring states that were demographically and economically similar to Idaho. Both comparison states used discretionary waiver, as had Idaho prior to the change in the law. Jensen and Metsger found no evidence of general deterrent effects. Instead, arrests for the target offenses increased in Idaho following the introduction of mandatory transfer, while they decreased in the two comparison states.

Specific Deterrence

In order to assess the impact of transfer on offenders' subsequent behavior, researchers have compared rates of recidivism of transferred youths and those retained in the juvenile system. It is not enough simply to compare youths referenced for waiver with those waived to criminal court. As Podkopacz and Feld (1995, 1996) have shown, waiver decisions are frequently influenced by considerations regarding seriousness of the offense and prior record, which introduce selection bias. Consequently, it is essential that researchers take steps to ensure the equivalence of the groups under comparison. In this regard, two different methodologies have been employed in studies that have produced very similar results.

The first study was carried out by Fagan (1991, 1995, 1996), who conducted a natural experiment to evaluate the effects of juvenile versus criminal justice processing. He identified two counties in New York and two in neighboring New Jersey that were very similar on important socioeconomic, demographic, and crime indicators. New York and New Jersey also had very similar statutes for robbery and burglary. The key difference was that in New York fifteen- and sixteen-year-old robbers and burglars were automatically prosecuted in the criminal courts under that state's legislative exclusion statute while, in New Jersey, the juvenile courts retained jurisdiction over them. Fagan's samples consisted of four hundred robbery offenders and four hundred burglary offenders charged in 1981–82, who were randomly selected and evenly divided across the two states and four counties.

Postrelease recidivism was examined after a significant portion of the cohorts had completed their sentences and accumulated at least four years of time at risk. Several measures of recidivism were employed, including time to rearrest, prevalence of rearrest, prevalence of reincarceration, and frequency of rearrest adjusted for time at risk. While there were no significant differences in the effects of criminal versus juvenile court processing for burglary offenders, the findings for robbery offenders showed strong differences.

Transfer was associated with higher prevalence of rearrest: 76 percent of those processed in criminal court were rearrested, compared to 67 percent of those processed in juvenile court. An even greater effect was observed for the likelihood of reincarceration: 56 percent of the criminal court group were subsequently incarcerated, compared to 41 percent of the juvenile court group. Offenders prosecuted in criminal court also had higher rates of rearrest adjusted for time at risk (2.85 offenses) than those prosecuted in juvenile court (1.67 offenses), and they were rearrested more quickly (457 days compared to 553 days for those processed in juvenile court) (Fagan 1995, 249).

Differences across groups held up for the most part irrespective of the type of sanction imposed by the court. Those who were incarcerated were more likely to reoffend than those who were sentenced to probation, but those sentenced in criminal court to either incarceration or probation fared worse than their counterparts in juvenile court. Among those who had been incarcerated, those sentenced in criminal court were more likely to be rearrested and to be rearrested more quickly than those sentenced in the juvenile court. Those placed on probation by the criminal court were more likely to be rearrested and to be arrested more often than those processed in the juvenile court. In each comparison, the robbery offenders handled in the criminal court fared less well. In addition, it was determined that the effects of court type were independent of sentence length. That is, youths processed in the juvenile court had a lower probability of rearrest even after controlling for sentence length. These findings provide strong support for the utility of retaining offenders in the juvenile system.

Subsequent studies conducted by us and our colleagues (Bishop et al. 1996; Winner et al. 1997) reinforce Fagan's findings and conclusions. Our research was conducted in Florida, a state that uses prosecutorial waiver almost exclusively. In the course of other studies of prosecutorial waiver practice in the state, we had learned that, although thousands of juveniles are transferred each year, thousands of equally serious or even more serious offenders are not transferred (see, e.g., Frazier 1991). This finding provided the opportunity for a significant policy study similar to the one conducted by Fagan. Unlike Fagan's research, ours was carried out in a single state. To overcome the problem of selection bias, we used a matching procedure to pair each case transferred to criminal court with an equivalent case retained in the juvenile system. Each pair was matched on seven factors: the most serious offense charged, the number of counts charged, the number of prior delinquency referrals, the most serious prior offense, age, gender, and race. Using cases processed in 1987, we were able to generate 2,738 transfers who matched with 2,738 juveniles whose cases were retained in the juvenile system.

We assessed recidivism over the short and long terms. The short-term analysis followed cases for a maximum of twenty-four months, while the long-term follow-up tracked offenders for up to seven years. Both studies indicated that juveniles transferred to criminal court fared worse than those retained in the juvenile justice system. This was true over every comparison in the short term and over most comparisons in the long-term study.

Several measures of recidivism were employed: rearrest prevalence, incidence of rearrest, severity of the first rearrest offense, and time to failure. Over the short term, 30 percent of the transfers were rearrested, compared to 19 percent of those processed in juvenile court. Transfers were also more likely than those processed in the juvenile system to be arrested for more serious (felony) offenses. The incidence of offending was also higher in the transfer group: transfers had a rearrest rate of 0.54 offenses per person year of exposure, compared to 0.32 for those retained in the juvenile system. The transfers also reoffended more quickly (135 days) than those processed in juvenile court (227 days) (Bishop et al. 1996, 44).

Over the long term, overall differences in rearrest prevalence were no longer significant across the two groups. However, analysis by offense type indicated that transfers were more likely to reoffend in five of seven comparisons. Moreover, significant differences in rates of reoffending remained. When we calculated rearrest rates overall and for each of seven classes of offense, rates of rearrest were higher for those who had been transferred across all comparisons. Significant differences in time to failure also remained.

The Florida studies add substantively and substantially to Fagan's research. Not only do they provide a confirmation of the findings in a different jurisdiction, time frame and sociolegal context using a different transfer method, they also add new offenses to the mix. Taken together, and keeping in mind that there is no evidence of any general deterrent effect of the transfer reforms, they provide a compelling case for more limited use of transfer and more openness to the potential benefits of handling offenders within the juvenile justice system. . . .

5. DISCUSSION

From the studies that compared rates of recidivism among youths transferred to criminal court and youth retained in the juvenile system, there emerge three major findings. First, transfer appears to be counterproductive: transferred youths are more likely to reoffend, and to reoffend more quickly and more often, than those retained in the juvenile justice system. In addition, Fagan's (1991, 1995, 1996) research suggests that the differential effects of criminal and juvenile justice processing are not dependent on sentence type or sentence length. That is, the mere fact that juveniles have been convicted in criminal rather than juvenile court increases the likelihood that they will reoffend. Finally, the risk of reoffending is aggravated when a sentence of incarceration is imposed.

These findings lend themselves to several alternative explanations. It may be that processing in the criminal justice system actually promotes further offending. Alternatively, and contrary to the sentiment underlying the transfer reforms, processing in the juvenile justice system may promote law-abiding behavior. Or both of these explanations may be correct. Based on what we have learned from our interviews with young offenders and from related research, we suggest an interpretation that is consistent with both of these explanations.

We have earlier drawn upon Braithwaite's (1989) theory of shaming as a promising general theoretical perspective (Bishop et al. 1996; Winner et al. 1997). Building on social control theory, this perspective recognizes that it is through bonding or attachment to others that children learn prosocial attitudes, values, and behaviors. Children who as teens engage in serious and chronic delinquency have most often failed to develop close attachments to others. For a variety of reasons—some related to their parents, some to the children themselves—they are weakly bonded to their parents, who frequently do a poor job of monitoring and teaching appropriate behaviors (Moffitt 1999). Often the result is that these children are undersocialized, and possess traits (e.g., impulsivity, selfishness, aggressiveness) that make it more difficult for them to form positive relationships with others.

We have seen that processing in juvenile court is associated with a lower probability of reoffending. We suggest that one reason this may be so is that the juvenile system communicates messages of caring—i.e., offers of attachment—to young people whose backgrounds are often replete with alienation from and rejection by conventional adults. Time and again in our interviews with young offenders we were made aware of their sensitivity to signs of interest and concern from judges, detention workers, and juvenile program staff. Where they formed significant attachments, they appeared to be positively affected by them. Although they had behaved unlawfully, and sometimes dangerously and violently, the message they heard from the juvenile courts was most often one that encouraged their sense of individual worth and potential. For many of these youths, such messages had rarely been communicated in the primary spheres of home and school. Braithwaite suggests that these messages are reintegrative. When responses to offenders are disapproving of their law-breaking behavior but open to forgiveness and restoration, they promote the development of social bonds. Our interviews with juvenile offenders suggest that even brief positive contacts with conventional adults—say to judges or detention workers—generally have a beneficial effect, at least in the short term. For some youths, these contacts open up the possibility of trusting enough to develop other, more enduring relationships with conventional adults—e.g., with a counselor in a long-term commitment program—that may have more long-term influences on attitudes, values, and behaviors. We think it is very significant that young offenders reported to us that most "front end" and even some of the "deep end" juvenile programs they had been in were not long enough or sufficiently intense to produce real or lasting change. These observations showed insight into the complexity of their behavior as well as into the mechanics and dynamics of behavioral change.

We suggest a second reason that processing in the juvenile system was linked to lower rates of reoffending. There is now a fairly large body of empirical research demonstrating that some programs are quite effective in reducing recidivism even among serious and violent offenders. (For a recent and comprehensive review, see Lipsey and Wilson 1998.) In our own research (Bishop et al. 1998) we learned that many of these approaches were being utilized in the juvenile programs we visited. Moreover, these were the approaches that the youths themselves identified as most beneficial to them. What is most significant to us about these approaches is that they target the deficits in socialization that inhibit the formation of social bonds. For example, many serious and violent offenders have not learned how to handle impulse in productive or at least nondestructive ways. Their inability to manage anger is a source of many of the difficulties they have experienced in past relationships and, left unaddressed, will continue to interfere with the development of future attachments. These young offenders have social deficits in many other areas as well. Many have never been taught how to make polite requests, to respond to inappropriate demands or requests without losing "face," to deal with other people's anger, to work on cooperative tasks, etc. Many have not acquired the cognitive skills to anticipate the consequences of their behavior or to take the perspective of others. Programs that enhance youths' skills in these areas facilitate conventional bonding experiences. In the juvenile programs observed in our research and that of Forst, Fagan, and Vivona (1989), young offenders had more opportunities to form attachments to conventional others (especially staff), to be reinforced in conventional beliefs (by both staff and other inmates in programs), and to make commitments to conventional lines of action (e.g., in educational and vocational programs). While not without criminal learning opportunities, these juvenile programs provided opportunities for frequent, positive staff–resident interaction and program participation that emphasized conventional values and behavior.

Regardless of whether treatment in the juvenile justice system is beneficial, the criminal justice system may actually contribute to criminal behavior. Among our interviewees, we found very negative reactions to criminal court processing. Many experienced the court process not so much as a condemnation of their behavior as a condemnation of them.

Unlike the juvenile court, the criminal court failed to communicate that young offenders retain some fundamental worth. What the youths generally heard was that they were being punished not only because their behavior was bad but also because they were personifications of their behavior. If some other message was intended by the court, it failed to impress the juvenile offenders we interviewed.

It is not so much that condemnation and punishment are without value. Rather, it is more that they have value primarily when the person punished grants them legitimacy—i.e., accepts the punishment and the agents and agencies administering it as properly motivated (Matza 1964). Far from viewing the criminal court and its officers as legitimate, the juvenile offenders we interviewed saw them more often as duplicitous and manipulative, malevolent in intent, and indifferent to their needs. It was common for them to experience a sense of injustice, and then to condemn the condemners (Sykes and Matza 1957; Matza 1964; Lemert 1951, 1974), reactions that are inconsistent with compliance to legal norms (Lanza-Kaduce and Radosevich 1987; Tyler 1990).

In the institutional world of the adult prison, youths were more likely to learn social rules and norms that legitimated domination, exploitation, and retaliation. They routinely observed both staff and inmate models who exhibited these behaviors, and they observed these illegitimate norms being reinforced. In addition, youths in prison were exposed to an inmate subculture that taught criminal motivations as well as techniques of committing crime and avoiding detection. Even if the pains of punishment and confinement caused most juveniles to wish to avoid returning to prison, what they learned in prison provided a destructive counterbalance to their positive intentions.

Perhaps the most harmful effects of transfer to criminal court come in the form of informal sanctions applied in the community. While most youths who engage in delinquency will desist by early adulthood as they move into jobs and marriages that give them a sense of place and purpose, many of those who enter the criminal justice system will carry the stigma of a criminal conviction. The normal transition from risk-taking adolescence to conventional adulthood will be relatively closed to them. Stigmatization and obstruction of conventional opportunities certainly make reoffending more likely.

6. CONCLUSION

Our analysis and discussion in this chapter began by showing that a period of extensive and rapid reform has produced large increases in the number of juvenile offenders prosecuted and convicted in criminal courts and exposed to adult sanctions. Public perceptions to the contrary notwithstanding, many of these offenders are not "extreme cases," i.e., youths accused of heinous acts or chronic, hardened criminals who have repeatedly demonstrated their resistance to intervention.

We have also seen that entry of large numbers of young offenders into the criminal justice system has important systemic consequences. It places additional burdens on already overtaxed courts and corrections systems. For corrections officials, an influx of young offenders presents significant new issues related to institutional security and programming. Whether they will respond by developing age-segregated facilities and programs designed to meet the special needs of a youth population remains to be seen. Further, we have suggested that the expansion of transfer through legislative exclusion and prosecutorial waiver has created new problems of interagency articulation and may precipitate repercussive effects in the juvenile justice system which have not been heretofore addressed.

Finally, we have argued that, as a crime control policy, transfer tends to be counterproductive. Although the empirical studies on this issue are too few in number to be definitive, they strongly suggest that transfer is more likely to aggravate recidivism than to stem it. We suggest that this effect is a product of several factors, including the sense of injustice young offenders associate with criminal court processing, the multiple criminogenic effects of incarceration in the adult system (e.g., exposure to negative shaming, opportunities for criminal socialization, modeling of violence) and the stigmatization and opportunity blockage that flow from a record of criminal conviction. Compared to the criminal justice system, the juvenile system seems to be more reintegrative in practice and effect.

In short, we conclude that current transfer policies are misguided. Transfer appears to have little deterrent value. Moreover, when applied broadly to offenders who are neither particularly serious nor particularly chronic, any incapacitative gains achieved in the short run appear to be quickly nullified. While broad transfer policies may and likely do serve retributive ends, they do so at a considerable price. The same ends might be better served through modest extensions to the upper boundary of juvenile court jurisdiction. Such a course might avoid the negative effects of criminal processing, conviction, and exposure to adult correctional environments, while possibly even enhancing the prospects of rehabilitation in intensive, long-term juvenile programs. Unless and until future research negates these conclusions, the clear implication is that transfer should be reserved for those "extreme cases" to which it has traditionally been applied, where significant retributive and incapacitative benefits can be realized.

REFERENCES

Bishop, Donna M., Charles E. Frazier, Lonn Lanza-Kaduce, and Henry George White. 1998. *Juvenile Transfers to Criminal Court Study: Phase I Final Report*. Washington: Office of Juvenile Justice and Delinquency Prevention.

Bishop, Donna M., Charles E. Frazier, Lonn Lanza-Kaduce, and Lawrence Winner. 1996. "The Transfer of Juveniles to Criminal Court: Does It Make a Difference?" *Crime and Delinquency* 42:171.

Braithwaite, John. 1989. *Crime, Shame, and Reintegration*. New York: Cambridge University Press.

Fagan, Jeffrey A. 1991. *The Comparative Impacts of Juvenile and Criminal Court Sanctions on Adolescent Felony Offenders*. Final Report, Grant 87-IJ CX 4044, to the National Institute of Justice. Washington: U.S. Department of Justice.

_____. 1995. "Separating the Men from the Boys: The Comparative Advantage of

Juvenile versus Criminal Court Sanctions on Recidivism among Adolescent Felony Offenders." In *Serious, Violent, and Chronic Juvenile offenders: A Sourcebook.* Edited by James C. Howell, Barry Krisberg, J. David Hawkins, and John J. Wilson. Thousand Oaks, Calif.: Sage.

_____. 1996. "The Comparative Advantage of Juvenile versus Criminal Court Sanctions on Recidivism among Adolescent Felony Offenders." *Law and Policy* 18:77.

Forst, Martin, Jeffrey Fagan, and T. Scott Vivona. 1989. "Youth in Prisons and Training Schools: Perceptions and Consequences of the Treatment Custody Dichotomy." *Juvenile and Family Court Journal* 39:1.

Frazier, Charles E. 1991. "Deep End Juvenile Placement or Transfer to Adult Court by Direct File?" Unpublished report prepared for the Florida Commission on Juvenile Justice.

Jensen, Eric L., and Linda K. Metsger. 1994. "A Test of the Deterrent Effect of Legislative Waiver on Violent Juvenile Crime." *Crime and Delinquency* 40:96.

Lanza-Kaduce, Lonn, and Marcia J. Radosevich. 1987. "Negative Reactions to Processing and Substance Abuse among Young Incarcerated Males." *Deviant Behavior* 8:137.

Lemert, Edwin. 1951. *Social Pathology.* New York: McGraw-Hill.

_____. 1974. "Beyond Mead: The Societal Reaction to Deviance." *Social Problems* 21:457.

Lipsey, Mark W., and David B. Wilson. 1998. "Effective Intervention for Serious Juvenile Offenders: A Synthesis of Research." In *Serious and Violent Juvenile Offenders. Risk Factors and Successful Interventions.* Edited by Rolf Loeber and David P. Farrington. Thousand Oaks, Calif.: Sage.

Matza, David. 1964. *Delinquency and Drift.* New York: Wiley

Moffitt, Terrie E. 1999. "Pathways in the Life Course to Crime." In *Criminological Theory: Past to Present.* Edited by Francis T. Cullen and Robert Agnew. Los Angeles: Roxbury.

Podkopacz, Marcy R., and Barry C. Feld. 1995. "Judicial Waiver Policy and Practice: Persistence, Seriousness, and Race." *Law and Inequality Journal* 14:73.

_____. 1996. "The End of the Line: An Empirical Study of Judicial Waiver." *Journal of Criminal Law and Criminology* 86:449.

Singer, Simon I. 1996. *Recriminalizing Delinquency: Violent Juvenile Crime and Juvenile Justice Reform.* New York: Cambridge University Press.

Singer, Simon I., and David McDowall. 1988. "Criminalizing Delinquency: The Deterrent Effects of the New York Juvenile Offender Law." *Law and Society Review* 22:521.

Sykes, Gresham, and David Matza. 1957. "Techniques of Neutralization: A Theory of Delinquency." *American Journal of Sociology* 22:664.

Tyler, Tom R. 1990. *Why People Obey the Law.* New Haven: Yale University Press.

Winner, Lawrence, Lonn Lanza-Kaduce, Donna M. Bishop, and Charles E. Frazier. 1997. "The Transfer of Juveniles to Criminal Court: Reexamining Recidivism over the Long Term." *Crime and Delinquency* 43:548.

REVIEW QUESTIONS

1. Does transferring serious juvenile offenders to adult court deter other juveniles from committing delinquent acts? What evidence supports your answer?

2. Do the authors find that transfer makes it more or less likely that a juvenile will commit a new offense following release? What evidence do they offer in support of their conclusion?

3. Why do the authors of this article believe transfer is not a more effective deterrent to juvenile crime?

4. Based on your reading of this article, which of the transfer mechanisms discussed earlier in this chapter seem(s) most advisable? Which, if any, seem(s) inadvisable? What is your reasoning?

The Juvenile Death Penalty Today: Death Sentences and Executions for Juvenile Crimes, January 1, 1973–November 15, 2003

Victor L. Streib

EXECUTIVE SUMMARY

- Beginning with the first in 1642, at least 366 juvenile offenders have been executed. Twenty-two of these have occurred during the current era (1973–2003), constituting 2.5% of the total of the 881 executions during this period.

- Almost two-thirds of the recent executions of juvenile offenders have occurred in Texas, with no other country in the world actively involved in this practice.

- The most recent execution of a juvenile offender was in Oklahoma on April 3, 2003, but Oklahoma has no more juvenile offenders on death row and has not even sentenced a juvenile offender to the death sentence for 8 years.

- A total of 224 juvenile death sentences have been imposed since 1973. Of these, only 73 remain currently in force and are still being litigated. Of the other 151 sentences finally resolved, 22 (15%) have resulted in execution and 129 (85%) have been reversed or commuted.

- The U.S. Supreme Court has held that the U.S. Constitution prohibits execution for crimes committed at age 15 and younger but permits execution for crimes at age 16 or older.

- However, the Court recently has come within one vote of declaring unconstitutional all executions for crimes committed at age 17 or younger.

- The annual death sentencing rate for juvenile offenses has been declining rapidly and now is at the lowest point in 15 years.

- Of the 40 death penalty jurisdictions in the United States, 19 jurisdictions have expressly chosen a minimum age of 18, 5 jurisdictions have chosen an age 17 minimum, and the other 16 death penalty jurisdictions use age 16 as the minimum age.

- Every other nation in the world has joined international agreements prohibiting the execution of juvenile offenders, with only the United States refusing to abandon its laws permitting the juvenile death penalty.

REVIEW QUESTIONS

1. Were you surprised to discover that juvenile offenders who are transferred to adult criminal court may in some instances be subject to the death penalty? Do you consider this an appropriate response to serious juvenile crime?

2. Based on your reading of Scott and Grisso's discussion of adolescent development in Chapter 1, do you think the death penalty should be prohibited for *all* persons who commit an extremely serious offense before reaching a specific age? If so, what should be the minimum age? If not, what developmental considerations should determine the eligibility of a juvenile offender for the death penalty if the offense is one for which an adult could be executed?

3. Do the statistics compiled by Professor Streib demonstrate the presence of a general consensus among Americans either supporting or opposing the death penalty for offenders who commit extremely serious offenses before reaching the age of 18?

4. Has Professor Streib convinced you that "these may be the last days of the juvenile death penalty in America?" Why or why not?

Thompson v. Oklahoma

The Supreme Court of the United States
487 U.S. 815 (1988)

JUSTICE STEVENS announced the judgment of the Court and delivered an opinion in which JUSTICE BRENNAN, JUSTICE MARSHALL, and JUSTICE BLACKMUN join.

Petitioner was convicted of first-degree murder and sentenced to death. The principal question presented is whether the execution of that sentence would violate the constitutional prohibition against the infliction of "cruel and unusual punishments" because petitioner was only 15 years old at the time of his offense. . . .

The authors of the Eighth Amendment drafted a categorical prohibition against the infliction of cruel and unusual punishments, but they made no attempt to define the contours of that category. They delegated that task to future generations of judges who have been guided by the "evolving standards of decency that mark the progress of a maturing society." In performing that task the Court has reviewed the work product of state legislatures and sentencing juries, and has carefully considered the reasons why a civilized society may accept or reject the death penalty in certain types of cases. Thus, in confronting the question whether the youth of the defendant—more specifically, the fact that he was less than 16 years old at the time of his offense—is a sufficient reason for denying the State the power to sentence him to death, we first review relevant legislative enactments, then refer to jury determinations, and finally explain why these indicators of contemporary standards of decency confirm our judgment that such a young person is not capable of acting with the degree of culpability that can justify the ultimate penalty. . . .

The line between childhood and adulthood is drawn in different ways by various States. There is, however, complete or near unanimity among all 50 States and the District of Columbia in treating a person under 16 as a minor for several important purposes. In no State may a 15-year-old vote or serve on a jury. Further, in all but one State a 15-year-old may not drive without parental consent, and in all but four States a 15-year-old may not marry without parental consent. Additionally, in those States that have legislated on the subject, no one under age 16 may purchase pornographic materials (50 States), and in most States that have some form of legalized gambling, minors are not permitted to participate without parental consent (42 States). Most relevant, however, is the fact that all States have enacted legislation designating the maximum age for juvenile court jurisdiction at no less than 16. All of this legislation is consistent with the experience of mankind, as well as the long history of our law, that the normal 15-year-old is not prepared to assume the full responsibilities of an adult.

Most state legislatures have not expressly confronted the question of establishing a minimum age for imposition of the death penalty. In 14 States, capital punishment is not authorized at all, and in 19 others capital punishment is authorized but no minimum age is expressly stated in the death penalty statute. One might argue on the basis of this body of legislation that there is no chronological age at which the imposition of the death penalty is unconstitutional and that our current standards of decency would still tolerate the execution of 10-year-old children. We think it self-evident that such an argument is unacceptable; indeed, no such argument has been advanced in this case. If, therefore, we accept the premise that some offenders are simply too young to be put to death, it is reasonable to put this group of statutes to one side because they do not focus on the question of where the chronological age line should be drawn. When we confine our attention to the 18 States that have expressly established a minimum age in their death penalty statutes, we find that all of them require that the defendant have attained at least the age of 16 at the time of the capital offense.

The conclusion that it would offend civilized standards of decency to execute a person who was less than 16 years old at the time of his or her offense is consistent with the views that have been expressed by respected professional organizations, by other nations that share our Anglo-American heritage, and by the leading members of the Western European community. Thus, the American Bar Association and the American Law Institute have formally expressed their opposition to the death penalty for juveniles. Although the death penalty has not been entirely abolished in the United Kingdom or New Zealand (it has been abolished in Australia, except in the State of New South Wales, where it is available for treason and piracy), in neither of those countries may a juvenile be executed. The death penalty has been abolished in West Germany, France, Portugal, The Netherlands, and all of the Scandinavian countries, and is available only for exceptional crimes such as treason in Canada, Italy, Spain, and Switzerland. Juvenile executions are also prohibited in the Soviet Union.

The second societal factor the Court has examined in determining the acceptability of capital punishment to the American sensibility is the behavior of juries. . . .

While it is not known precisely how many persons have been executed during the 20th century for crimes committed under the age of 16, a scholar has recently compiled a table revealing this number to be between 18 and 20. All of these occurred during the first half of the century, with the last such execution taking place apparently in 1948. In the following year this Court observed that this "whole country has traveled far from the period in which the death sentence was an automatic and commonplace result of convictions. . . ." The road we have traveled during the past four decades—in which thousands of juries have tried murder cases—leads to the unambiguous conclusion that the imposition of the death penalty on a 15-year-old offender is now generally abhorrent to the conscience of the community.

Department of Justice statistics indicate that during the years 1982 through 1986 an average of over 16,000 persons were arrested for willful criminal homicide (murder and nonnegligent manslaughter) each year. Of that group of 82,094 persons, 1,393 were sentenced to death. Only 5 of them, including the petitioner in this case, were less than 16 years old at the time of the offense. Statistics of this kind can, of course, be interpreted in different ways, but they do suggest that these five young offenders have received sentences that are "cruel and unusual in the same way that being struck by lightning is cruel and unusual."

"Although the judgments of legislatures, juries, and prosecutors weigh heavily in the balance, it is for us ultimately to judge whether the Eighth Amendment permits imposition of the death penalty" on one such as petitioner who committed a heinous murder when he was only 15 years old. In making that judgment, we first ask whether the juvenile's culpability should be measured by the same standard as that of an adult, and then consider whether the application of the death penalty to this class of offenders "measurably contributes" to the social purposes that are served by the death penalty. It is generally agreed "that punishment should be directly related to the personal culpability of the criminal defendant." There is also broad agreement on the proposition that adolescents as a class are less mature and responsible than adults. . . .

. . .[T]he Court has already endorsed the proposition that less culpability should attach to a crime committed by a juvenile than to a comparable crime committed by an adult. The basis for this conclusion is too obvious to require extended explanation. Inexperience, less education, and less intelligence make the teenager less able to evaluate the consequences of his or her conduct while at the same time he or she is much more apt to be motivated by mere emotion or peer pressure than is an adult. The reasons why juveniles are not trusted with the privileges and responsibilities of an adult also explain why their irresponsible conduct is not as morally reprehensible as that of an adult.

"The death penalty is said to serve two principal social purposes: retribution and deterrence of capital crimes by prospective offenders." In *Gregg* [*v. Georgia*—*Ed.*] we concluded that as "an expression of society's moral outrage at particularly offensive conduct," retribution was not "inconsistent with our respect for the dignity of men." Given the lesser culpability of the juvenile offender, the teenager's capacity for growth, and society's fiduciary obligations to its children, this conclusion is simply inapplicable to the execution of a 15-year-old offender.

For such a young offender, the deterrence rationale is equally unacceptable. The Department of Justice statistics indicate that about 98% of the arrests for willful homicide involved persons who were over 16 at the time of the offense. Thus, excluding younger persons from the class that is eligible for the death penalty will not diminish the deterrent value of capital punishment for the vast majority of potential offenders. And even with respect to those under 16 years of age, it is obvious that the potential deterrent value of the death sentence is insignificant for two reasons. The likelihood that the teenage offender has made the kind of cost–benefit analysis that attaches any weight to the possibility of execution is so remote as to be virtually nonexistent. And, even if one posits such a cold-blooded calculation by a 15-year-old, it is fanciful to believe that he would be deterred by the knowledge that a small number of persons his age have been executed during the 20th century. In short, we are not persuaded that the imposition of the death penalty for offenses committed by persons under 16 years of age has made, or can be expected to make, any measurable contribution to the goals that capital punishment is intended to achieve. It is, therefore, "nothing more than the purposeless and needless imposition of pain and suffering," and thus an unconstitutional punishment.

Petitioner's counsel and various amici curiae have asked us to "draw a line" that would prohibit the execution of any person who was under the age of 18 at the time of the offense. Our task today, however, is to decide the case before us; we do so by concluding that the Eighth and Fourteenth Amendments prohibit the execution of a person who was under 16 years of age at the time of his or her offense.

The judgment of the Court of Criminal Appeals is vacated, and the case is remanded with instructions to enter an appropriate order vacating petitioner's death sentence.

It is so ordered.

APPENDICES TO JUSTICE STEVENS' OPINION [omitted—*Ed.*]

JUSTICE KENNEDY took no part in the consideration or decision of this case.

JUSTICE O'CONNOR, concurring in the judgment.

The plurality and dissent agree on two fundamental propositions: that there is some age below which a juvenile's crimes can never be constitutionally punished by death, and that our precedents require us to locate this age in light of the "'evolving standards of decency that mark the progress of a maturing society.'" I accept both principles. The disagreements between the plurality and the dissent rest on their different evaluations of the evidence available to us about the relevant social consensus. Although I believe that a national consensus forbidding the execution of any person for a crime committed before the age of 16 very likely does exist, I am reluctant to adopt this conclusion as a matter of constitutional law without better evidence than we now possess. Because I conclude that the sentence in this case can and should be set aside on narrower grounds than those adopted by the plurality, and because the grounds on which I rest should allow us to face the more general question when better evidence is available, I concur only in the judgment of the Court. . . .

The case before us today raises some of the same concerns that have led us to erect barriers to the imposition of capital punishment in other contexts. Oklahoma has enacted a statute that authorizes capital punishment for murder, without setting any minimum age at which the commission of murder may lead to the imposition of that penalty. The State has also, but quite separately, provided that 15-year-old murder defendants may be treated as adults in some circumstances. Because it proceeded in this manner, there is a considerable risk that the Oklahoma Legislature either did not realize that its actions would have the effect of rendering 15-year-old defendants death eligible or did not give the question the serious consideration that would have been reflected in the explicit choice of some minimum age for death eligibility. Were it clear that no national consensus forbids the imposition of capital punishment for crimes committed before the age of 16, the implicit nature of the Oklahoma Legislature's decision would not be constitutionally problematic. In the peculiar circumstances we face today, however, the Oklahoma statutes have presented this Court with a result that is of very dubious constitutionality, and they have done so without the earmarks of careful consideration that we have required for other kinds of decisions leading to the death penalty. In this unique situation, I am prepared to conclude that petitioner and others who were below the age of 16 at the time of their offense may not be executed under the authority of a capital punishment statute that specifies no minimum age at which the commission of a capital crime can lead to the offender's execution. . . .

For the reasons stated in this opinion, I agree that petitioner's death sentence should be vacated, and I therefore concur in the judgment of the Court.

JUSTICE SCALIA, with whom THE CHIEF JUSTICE and JUSTICE WHITE join, dissenting.

If the issue before us today were whether an automatic death penalty for conviction of certain crimes could be extended to individuals younger than 16 when they commit the crimes, thereby preventing individualized consideration of their maturity and moral responsibility, I would accept the plurality's conclusion that such a practice is opposed by a national consensus, sufficiently uniform and of sufficiently long standing, to render it cruel and unusual punishment within the meaning of the Eighth Amendment. We have already decided as much, and more, in *Lockett v. Ohio*. I might even agree with the plurality's conclusion if the question were whether a person under 16 when he commits a crime can be deprived of the benefit of a rebuttable presumption that he is not mature and responsible enough to be punished as an adult. The question posed here, however, is radically different from both of these. It is whether there is a national consensus that no criminal so much as one day under 16, after individuated consideration of his circumstances, including the overcoming of a presumption that he should not be tried as an adult, can possibly be deemed mature and responsible enough to be punished with death for any crime. Because there seems to me no plausible basis for answering this last question in the affirmative, I respectfully dissent.

REVIEW QUESTIONS

1. What reasons does Justice Stevens give to support the Court's decision to bar the death penalty for all crimes committed by persons under 16 years old? Has he convinced you that no person should *ever* be executed for an offense committed before reaching 16 years of age?

2. Justice O'Connor "concurred in the judgment" but not with Justice Stevens' reasoning. What is the basis for her position?

3. What is the basis for Justice Scalia's dissent? Is his argument consistent with the statistics presented by Professor Streib in the previous selection?

4. Is the decision in this case—and the rationale underlying it—consistent with Scott and Grisso's discussion of adolescent development in Chapter 1? Justify your response.

Stanford v. Kentucky

The Supreme Court of the United States
492 U.S. 361 (1989)

JUSTICE SCALIA announced the judgment of the Court and delivered the opinion of the Court with respect to [most aspects of the decision] and an opinion with respect to [the remaining portions], in which THE CHIEF JUSTICE, JUSTICE WHITE, and JUSTICE KENNEDY join.

These two consolidated cases [*Stanford v. Kentucky* and *Wilkins v. Missouri*—Ed.] require us to decide whether the imposition of capital punishment on an individual for a crime committed at 16 or 17 years of age constitutes cruel and unusual punishment under the Eighth Amendment. . . .

"[F]irst" among the "'objective indicia that reflect the public attitude toward a given sanction'" are statutes passed by society's elected representatives. Of the 37 States whose laws permit capital punishment, 15 decline to impose it upon 16-year-old offenders and 12 decline to impose it on 17-year-old offenders. This does not establish the degree of national consensus this Court has previously thought sufficient to label a particular punishment cruel and unusual. . . .

. . . Moreover, even if it were true that no federal statute permitted the execution of persons under 18, that would not remotely establish—in the face of a substantial number of state statutes to the contrary—a national consensus that such punishment is inhumane, any more than the absence of a federal lottery establishes a national consensus that lotteries are socially harmful. To be sure, the absence of a federal death penalty for 16- or 17-year-olds (if it existed) might be evidence that there is no national consensus in favor of such punishment. It is not the burden of Kentucky and Missouri, however, to establish a national consensus approving what their citizens have voted to do; rather, it is the "heavy burden" of petitioners to establish a national consensus against it. As far as the primary and most reliable indication of consensus is concerned—the pattern of enacted laws—petitioners have failed to carry that burden.

Wilkins and Stanford argue, however, that even if the laws themselves do not establish a settled consensus, the application of the laws does. That contemporary society views capital punishment of 16- and 17-year-old offenders as inappropriate is demonstrated, they say, by the reluctance of juries to impose, and prosecutors to seek, such sentences. Petitioners are quite correct that a far smaller number of offenders under 18 than over 18 have been sentenced to death in this country. . . . Granted, however, that a substantial discrepancy exists, that does not establish the requisite proposition that the death sentence for offenders under 18 is categorically unacceptable to prosecutors and juries. To the contrary, it is not only possible, but overwhelmingly probable, that the very considerations which induce petitioners and their supporters to believe that death should *never* be imposed on offenders under 18 cause prosecutors and juries to believe that it should *rarely* be imposed. . . .

Having failed to establish a consensus against capital punishment for 16- and 17-year-old offenders through state and federal statutes and the behavior of prosecutors and juries, petitioners seek to demonstrate it through other indicia, including public opinion polls, the views of interest groups, and the positions adopted by various professional associations. We decline the invitation to rest constitutional law upon such uncertain foundations. A revised national consensus so broad, so clear, and so enduring as to justify a permanent prohibition upon all units of democratic government must appear in the operative acts (laws and the application of laws) that the people have approved.

We also reject petitioners' argument that we should invalidate capital punishment of 16- and 17-year-old offenders on the ground that it fails to serve the legitimate goals of penology. According to petitioners, it fails to deter because juveniles, possessing less developed cognitive skills than adults, are less likely to fear death; and it fails to exact just retribution because juveniles, being less mature and responsible, are also less morally blameworthy. In support of these claims, petitioners and their supporting amici marshal an array of socioscientific evidence concerning the psychological and emotional development of 16- and 17-year-olds.

If such evidence could conclusively establish the entire lack of deterrent effect and moral responsibility, resort to the Cruel and Unusual Punishments Clause would be unnecessary; the Equal Protection Clause of the Fourteenth Amendment would invalidate these laws for lack of rational basis. But as the adjective "socioscientific" suggests (and insofar as evaluation of moral responsibility is concerned perhaps the adjective "ethicoscientific" would be more apt), it is not demonstrable that no 16-year-old is "adequately responsible" or significantly deterred. It is rational, even if mistaken, to think the contrary. The battle must be fought, then, on the field of the Eighth Amendment; and in that struggle socioscientific, ethicoscientific, or even purely scientific evidence is not an available weapon. The punishment is either "cruel *and* unusual" (*i.e.*, society has set its face against it) or it is not. The audience for these arguments, in other words, is not this Court but the citizenry of the United States. It is they, not we, who must be persuaded. For as we stated earlier, our job is to *identify* the "evolving standards of decency"; to determine, not what they *should* be, but what they *are*. We have no power under the Eighth Amendment to substitute our belief in the scientific evidence for the society's apparent skepticism. In short, we emphatically reject petitioner's suggestion that the issues in this case permit us to apply our "own informed judgment.". . .

We discern neither a historical nor a modern societal consensus forbidding the imposition of capital punishment on any person who murders at 16 or 17 years of age. Accordingly, we conclude that such punishment does not offend the Eighth Amendment's prohibition against cruel and unusual punishment.

The judgments of the Supreme Court of Kentucky and the Supreme Court of Missouri are therefore

Affirmed.

JUSTICE O'CONNOR, concurring in part and concurring in the judgment.

Last Term, in *Thompson v. Oklahoma*, I expressed the view that a criminal defendant who would have been tried as a juvenile under state law, but for the granting of a petition waiving juvenile court jurisdiction, may only be executed for a capital offense if the State's capital punishment statute specifies a minimum age at which the commission of a capital crime can lead to an offender's execution and the defendant had reached that minimum age at the time the crime was committed. As a threshold matter, I indicated that such specificity is not necessary to avoid constitutional problems if it is clear that no national consensus forbids the imposition of capital punishment for crimes committed at such an age. Applying this two-part standard in *Thompson*, I concluded that Oklahoma's imposition of a death sentence on an individual who was 15 years old at the time he committed a capital offense should be set aside. Applying the same standard today, I conclude that the death sentences for capital murder imposed by Missouri and Kentucky on petitioners Wilkins and Stanford respectively should not be set aside because it is sufficiently clear that no national consensus forbids the imposition of capital punishment on 16- or 17-year-old capital murderers.

. . . The day may come when there is such general legislative rejection of the execution of 16- or 17-year-old capital murderers that a clear national consensus can be said to have developed. Because I do not believe that day has yet arrived, I concur in [much] of the Court's opinion, and I concur in its judgment.

I am unable, however, to join the remainder of the plurality's opinion. . . . [A]lthough I do not believe that these particular cases can be resolved through proportionality analysis, I reject the suggestion that the use of such analysis is improper as a matter of Eighth Amendment jurisprudence. . . .

JUSTICE BRENNAN, with whom JUSTICE MARSHALL, JUSTICE BLACKMUN, and JUSTICE STEVENS join, dissenting. . . .

There are strong indications that the execution of juvenile offenders violates contemporary standards of decency: a majority of States decline to permit juveniles to be sentenced to death; imposition of the sentence upon minors is very unusual even in those States that permit it; and respected organizations with expertise in relevant areas regard the execution of juveniles as unacceptable, as does international opinion. These indicators serve to confirm in my view my conclusion that the Eighth Amendment prohibits the execution of persons for offenses they committed while below the age of 18, because the death penalty is disproportionate when applied to such young offenders and fails measurably to serve the goals of capital punishment. I dissent.

REVIEW QUESTIONS

1. What reasons does Justice Scalia give for upholding the Constitutionality of the death penalty for offenses committed at age 16 or 17?

2. Based on your reading of Scott and Grisso's discussion of adolescent development in Chapter 1, do you agree with Justice Scalia's conclusion that at least some 16-year-olds are sufficiently responsible for their criminal behavior to justify imposition of the death penalty? If so, would you also agree with his dissent in *Thompson*, in which he argued that some 15-year-olds are also "mature and responsible enough to be punished with death. . ."(see p. 286)? Or do you see enough of a difference between 15- and 16-year-olds to justify allowing the death penalty only for the latter? Justify your response.

3. As in *Thompson v. Oklahoma*, Justice O'Connor provided the crucial fifth vote to affirm the judgments of the Kentucky and Missouri Supreme Courts in the two cases consolidated in *Stanford*. But she only concurred in *part* of Justice Scalia's opinion. Can you tell from the excerpt with which aspect(s) of his opinion she agreed and with which parts she disagreed?

4. In October 2002 the Supreme Court declined to reconsider Kevin Stanford's death sentence (*In re Stanford*, 537 U.S. 968 [2002]). Four justices dissented from the Court's summary denial of his petition for a writ of *habeas corpus*. Writing for the dissenters, Justice Stevens argued that nearly all of the reasons given by the court just four months earlier in its decision to bar execution of mentally retarded persons (*Atkins v. Virginia*, 536 U.S. 304 [2002]) "apply with equal or greater force to the execution of juvenile offenders." After quoting extensively from Justice Brennan's dissent in the original *Stanford* case, Justice Stevens recited some of the statistics compiled on Professor Streib's website to support his argument that "a national consensus has developed that juvenile offenders should not be executed." "All of this," he argued in closing, "leads me to conclude that offenses committed by juveniles under the age of 18 do not merit the death penalty. The practice of executing such offenders is a relic of the past and is inconsistent with evolving standards of decency in a civilized society. We should put an end to this shameful practice." Do you agree with him? Why or why not? (Note: As this book goes to press, the Supreme Court has just agreed to hear a case in which it will once again be asked to rule on the Constitutionality of the death penalty for 16- and 17-year-olds. Look for the decision in *Roper v. Simmons*, No. 03-633, on the Supreme Court's website: http://www.supremecourtus.gov/index.html.)

FURTHER READING

Austin, James, Johnson, Kelly Dedel, and Gregoriou, Maria. (2000). *Juveniles in Adult Prisons and Jails: A National Assessment*. Washington, DC: Bureau of Justice Assistance. Available online: http://www.ncjrs.org/pdffiles1/bja/182503.pdf

Bishop, Donna M., Frazier, Charles E., and Henretta, John C. (1989). Prosecutorial waiver: Case study of a questionable reform. *Crime and Delinquency, 35*, 179–198.

Bishop, Donna M., Frazier, Charles E., Lanza-Kaduce, Lonn, and Winner, Lawrence. (1996). The transfer of juveniles to criminal court: Does it make a difference? *Crime and Delinquency, 42*, 171–191.

Cothern, Lynn. (2000). *Juveniles and the Death Penalty*. Washington, DC: Office of Juvenile Justice and Delinquency Prevention. Available online: http://www.ncjrs.org/pdffiles1/ojjdp/184748.pdf

Fagan, Jeffrey. (1996). The comparative advantage of juvenile versus criminal court sanctions on recidivism among adolescent felony offenders. *Law and Policy, 18*, 77–113.

Fagan, Jeffrey, and Zimring, Franklin E. (Eds.). (2000). *The Changing Borders of Juvenile Justice: Transfer of Adolescents to the Criminal Court*. Chicago: University of Chicago Press.

Levin, David J., Langan, Patrick A., and Brown, Jodi M. (2000). *State Court Sentencing of Convicted Felons, 1996*. Washington, DC: Bureau of Justice Statistics. Available online: http://www.ojp.usdoj.gov/bjs/pub/pdf/scsc9 605.pdf

Merlo, Alida V., Benekos, Peter J., and Cook, William J. (1997). Waiver and juvenile justice reform: Widening the punitive net. *Criminal Justice Policy Review,* 8(2–3), 145–168.

Podkopacz, Marcy Rasmussen, and Feld, Barry C. (1996). The end of the line: An empirical study of judicial waiver. *Journal of Criminal Law and Criminology,* 86(2), 449–492.

Singer, Simon I. (1993). The automatic waiver of juveniles and substantive justice. *Crime and Delinquency,* 39, 253–261.

———. (1996). *Recriminalizing Delinquency: Violent Juvenile Crime and Juvenile Justice Reform*. Cambridge, UK: Cambridge University Press.

Strom, Kevin J. (2000). *Profile of State Prisoners under Age 18, 1985–97*. Washington, DC: Bureau of Justice Statistics. Available online: http://www.ojp.usdoj.gov/bjs/pub/pdf/pspa 1897.pdf

Strom, Kevin J., Smith, Steven K., and Snyder, Howard N. (1998). *Juvenile Felony Defendants in Criminal Courts: State Court Processing Statistics, 1990–1994*. Washington, DC: Bureau of Justice Statistics. Available online: http://www.ojp.usdoj.gov/bjs/pub/pdf/jfdcc .pdf

Torbet, Patricia, Griffin, Patrick, Hurst, Hunter Jr., and MacKenzie, Lynn Ryan. (2000). *Juveniles Facing Criminal Sanctions: Three States That Changed the Rules*. Washington, DC: Office of Juvenile Justice and Delinquency Prevention. Available online: http://www.ncjrs.org/pdffiles1/ojjdp/18120 3.pdf

Winner, Lawrence, Lanza-Kaduce, Lonn, Bishop, Donna M., and Frazier, Charles E. (1997). Transfer of juveniles to criminal court: Reexamining recidivism over the long term. *Crime and Delinquency,* 42, 171–191.

CHAPTER 8

The Juvenile in Court: Adjudication and Disposition of Juvenile Delinquency Cases

In re Gault unquestionably sparked a revolution in juvenile court proceedings. Under *Gault,* juveniles were guaranteed the rights to notice, counsel, freedom from compelled self-incrimination, and confrontation and cross-examination of adverse witnesses. Although still not guaranteed the right to a jury trial (*McKiever v. Pennsylvania*), they now also enjoy the right to proof beyond a reasonable doubt, just like adults charged with crimes (*In re Winship*). Dispositions in juvenile courts, too, have begun to look more like sentences for adult offenders: Determinate sentencing structures designed to ensure uniform punishment by legislatively specifying the amount of time to be served in a juvenile correctional facility for a given offense have in a number of jurisdictions replaced traditional indeterminate sentencing arrangements designed both to allow the judge to tailor the sentence to the needs of the particular offender and to encourage rehabilitation efforts by making early release contingent upon evidence of significant behavioral change.

But the changes rendered by *Gault* and *Winship* did not completely transform juvenile courts into miniature criminal courts. Instead, they left in their wake a hodgepodge of procedures uneasily blending some elements of the legacy of the child savers—the informality, benevolence, and treatment orientation of traditional juvenile courts—with a new emphasis on due process and, increasingly, on punishment proportionate to the seriousness of the offense and the child's prior record. Of equal importance, the changes mandated in *Gault* and *Winship* were not implemented in equal measure throughout the country. Even today, judges in many juvenile courts are reminiscent of Judge Mack's fatherly figure wrapping an arm around a youth's shoulder, and the hearings over which they preside are marked by pronounced informality and even friendly banter between judge, juvenile, parents, and even the prosecutors and defense attorneys. In others, much to the contrary, the atmosphere is formal and highly adversarial, and proceedings follow almost exactly those in adult criminal courts except that the defendants are younger.

In this chapter we will try to decipher what really goes on in America's juvenile courts—not the idealized visions conjured up by the child savers, Judge Mack, or the justices of the United States Supreme Court. We begin with the observations of an investigative reporter who spent a full year sitting in a handful of Los Angeles County juvenile courtrooms, observing the judges, prosecutors, defense attorneys, and probation officers, not to mention the children and their parents, and gaining a front-row perspective on the operation of one juvenile court.

But knowing how one court operates does not tell us about all of them. In the second selection Barry C. Feld explores what he calls "the geography of justice"—the variations he found in levels of formality and adversariness in the juvenile courts he studied in rural, urban, and suburban communities in Minnesota.

Following this we explore the role of the prosecutor in contemporary juvenile court hearings, using the National District Attorneys Association standards for juvenile justice as our guide—just as we did in Chapter 5 with respect to prosecutor participation in the intake process. A figure rarely if ever seen in juvenile court prior to the *Gault* case, the prosecutor now appears regularly to represent the interests of "the state" or "the people." Think how different this is from the days of Frank Fisher or Mary Ann Crouse, when petitions were brought "on behalf of" the child, not "against" him or her as implied by such adversarial terminology, and juvenile court hearings were regarded as having nothing in common with criminal trials to warrant the presence of a prosecutor. The NDAA standards afford a window for us to view the dilemmas faced by prosecutors as they try to balance the adversarial role to which they are accustomed in criminal court with the still rather unique demands of today's juvenile court setting.

We then turn to the functioning of counsel for the juvenile defendant—a role theoretically ensured by *Gault* to be present in all delinquency cases but which is even now unevenly available. In the mid-1990s researchers associated with the American Bar Association's Juvenile Justice Center, in collaboration with representatives of Washington D.C.'s Youth Law Center and the Philadelphia-based Juvenile Law Center, conducted a national assessment of access to counsel and the quality of representation in juvenile delinquency proceedings. Their results are reported in the next selection. The findings confirm on a national scale what Feld had earlier discovered about legal representation in Minnesota, that many youth continue in spite of *Gault* to appear in juvenile court without counsel. They further demonstrate that high caseloads for public defenders and other attorneys representing juveniles severely jeopardize the quality of representation, that counsel is often appointed too late to be maximally effective, and that pretrial preparation and trial performance are often woefully inadequate.

A final, exceedingly important, aspect of the juvenile court adjudication process warranting our attention here—the process by which guilty pleas are accepted in juvenile court—is addressed in a selection by Joseph B. Sanborn, Jr. Based on a multi-pronged study of statutes, court rules, and appellate case decisions in the 50 states and the District of Columbia, plus extensive observations and interviews in three juvenile courts in one state, Sanborn examines the thoroughness of the pre-plea "colloquies" in juvenile court—in which judges, at least theoretically, query young defendants seeking to plead guilty in order to ascertain that the pleas are "intelligent," "voluntary," and "accurate" before accepting them.

The balance of the chapter concentrates on juvenile court disposition, or what is increasingly given the same label as its criminal court counterpart—*sentencing*. In a second selection by Barry C. Feld we are introduced to the variety of juvenile court sentencing arrangements, from the traditional indeterminate approach allowing the judge to tailor the disposition to suit the treatment needs of the individual offender, to determinate sentencing structures, mandatory minimum terms of confinement, and other statutory schemes that limit the judge's discretion by specifying fixed or presumptive sentences based on the seriousness of the offense and the child's prior record. Feld also reviews the research on juvenile court sentencing, noting in particular the influence of offense-based factors (i.e., current offense and prior record) and the race of the child on dispositions.

Finally, one of the newest and most controversial twists on juvenile dispositions—blended sentencing—is introduced in the classic discussion, by Patricia Torbet and several of her colleagues at the National Center for Juvenile Justice, of five distinctive "blends" of juvenile and adult sanctions. Similar in some respects to the transfer provisions discussed in Chapter 7, the blended sentencing structures variously authorize a juvenile court judge *or* a criminal court judge (in cases involving juveniles who have already been transferred to adult criminal court) to impose a sanction involving the juvenile correctional system, the adult correctional system, or both.

No Matter How Loud I Shout

Edward Humes

JANUARY 1994

"The first thing you learn about this place," Deputy District Attorney Peggy Beckstrand says as she conducts a brief tour of the battered juvenile courthouse she helps run, "is that nothing works."

It is 8:25 in the morning, a cold winter day, the sky as gray as an old skillet, an intermittent, muffled roar occasionally filtering into the building from somewhere outside—the steady stream of fat, full jetliners on the final approach to LAX one freeway exit to the south. Inside, the locks on the courtroom doors are snicking back, fresh piles of manila-covered court files are being placed on the judge's benches, lawyers are wading through the hundreds of kids and parents and witnesses gathered in the courthouse today, looking for a client they've never met, a witness they've never spoken to, a parent who can't believe his or her child is a criminal, evidence be damned. Dirty mint-green buses with metal cages inside them are lumbering toward court from LA's three enormous juvenile halls, carrying boys and girls wearing color-coded county-issue shirts and jeans, the color indicating their proclivity for violence or escape. The baddest kids sport coveralls in neon orange; their parents—those lucky enough to have a mom or dad interested enough to attend their court appearances—grip crumpled brown paper sacks with street clothes inside, hoping for an early release. In five minutes, court will be called into session, and the atmosphere is charged with a sweaty, anxious expectation, as if the entire building were a crowded elevator stuck between floors.

"We're drowning," Beckstrand flatly announces. She looks taller than her five feet six inches, due in part to her textbook posture. Exceedingly pale, with very long, very straight brown-blond hair, Beckstrand, a former Montessori teacher with a ribald sense of humor, enjoys a reputation for toughness that has left her decidedly unloved—and once sued—by her counterpart in the Public Defender's Office. "Look around," she says of the chaos swirling in the hallways. "It just isn't working."

She is not talking about the physical state of the place—the cracked and broken fixtures or the dysfunctional water coolers that dispense brackish water at body temperature—but of the juvenile system's broader failings, the constant aura of futility that leaves this career prosecutor regularly muttering about walking away from it all. She is not the only one. Many who work these halls have heard about the new study circulating through the system that shows, among other things, that the Juvenile Court squanders most of its time and energy, focusing on the kids who are beyond redemption while ignoring the children who could best be helped. "As if we needed a study to tell us the obvious," she says. Throughout the bureaucracy, everyone is buzzing about this study, expecting—or fearing— that it will bring massive and fundamental reform to a place that has not changed in many positive ways since the 1960s, and shows it.

Beckstrand, for one, says she would welcome a shake-up, but she openly doubts the system's ability to break its tired patterns. Her voice sounds just as tired. "We're not rehabilitating these kids, and we're sure as hell not punishing them. They can get away with murder here, and they know it. The law-breakers are winning, and we—society, those of us who obey the rules—are losing."

A young prosecutor she supervises grabs Beckstrand then, asking her to resolve one of the crises that erupt here hourly, and they disappear into a courtroom together. They pass without a glance a deputy public defender huddled on a bench with the mother of a mentally ill girl who has been charged with attempted murder after voices in her head instructed her to attack her sister with a machete. The mother is crying and shaking her head as the young lawyer explains why it will be difficult to keep the girl from being transferred to the harsh confines of adult court, due to the severity of the accusations against her and the fact that she is past sixteen years of age. "She really needs help and belongs here in Juvenile, and

I'll do everything I can to make that happen," the lawyer says. "But the problem is, the law is very tough on cases like this. The best I can do today is try for a continuance. The district attorney holds all the cards."

It is a peculiarity of Juvenile Court that two such contradictory conversations can occur here simultaneously and with total sincerity. This is because each side in the process—the prosecutors, the defenders, the judges, cops and probation officers, the crime victims, the kids on trial here and their families—sees itself as being on the one and only losing side. When a case ends in Juvenile Court, it is often hard to tell just who has won.

The setting fuels this sense of futility: This courthouse is a grim place. The gray concrete box that is the Thurgood Marshall Branch of Los Angeles's massive Juvenile Court squats next to a once graceful garden district in the city of Inglewood, a community now so profoundly distressed that parents, policemen, and civic leaders meet monthly to plot safe routes through gang turf for their schoolchildren. The courthouse occupies the sort of neighborhood where members of warring black and Hispanic gangs summon one another by beeper and cellular phone to drive-by shootings and schoolyard race riots. Three blocks from Marshall Branch, an eleven-year-old schoolgirl sporting eleven prominent gang tattoos was caught distributing flyers advertising a gang-sponsored drug, sex, and beer party. The computer-generated flyers promised "Hoochies that ram free" can enter for free—meaning young girls who provide sex on demand need not worry about the five-dollar cover charge, a deal the eleven-year-old happily promoted to her sixth-grade schoolmates. When a counselor who seized the flyers asked the girl if she was worried about AIDS, she said no, it didn't matter. She'll be dead before she's twenty, anyway.

Yet, this is also the kind of neighborhood where wealthy Angelenos regularly park their BMWs and Mercedeses, because the Thurgood Marshall Branch, one of ten juvenile courthouses spanning the huge bowl of the Los Angeles Basin, serves more than just its own troubled surroundings. Juvenile offenders from LA's most upscale communities are hauled into the same courtrooms as well, from Beverly Hills to Hollywood to Malibu to Rancho Palos Verdes—the gangbangers' parents sitting next to the bankers and moguls with their designer briefcases and tasseled loafers, all equally dazed by the odd mixture of chaos, informality, and impenetrable ritual so unique to Juvenile Court. Through a fluke of geography and bureaucracy, in one of the most racially and economically segregated regions of America, the three grimy courtrooms of Marshall Branch Juvenile Court have become the last great melting pot. Here, everyone finds a new common ground: fear. Fear of our own children.

It is a fear well grounded in fact, as juvenile crime, particularly violent crimes by kids, has ripped through the cities and suburbs of America like a new and deadly strain of virus for which no one possesses immunity. The figures are staggering: a 175 percent increase in juvenile murder rates since the 1970s, with similar boosts in juvenile crime of all kinds. Just in the last five years, violent offenses by children—murder, rape, assault, robbery—have risen 68 percent. Los Angeles, with an estimated street gang force of 200,000, a majority of them under eighteen, has been especially hard hit by this epidemic. Given such figures, it should surprise no one that the Juvenile Court each year focuses less on children in danger, and more on dangerous children, locking more away, sending more to be tried as adults, imposing stiffer sentences. And still, the fear grows. You can see it in the courthouse hallway, in the furtive glances exchanged in the never-ending line at the two dented and sticky courthouse pay phones, in the way people rush through the gauntlet of silent, staring youth who sit on the steps and railings at the courthouse entry each day. One glimpse says it all: This is not a place to come for healing. It is a place to flee, as fast as you can.

Confusion is the other principal state of mind here—and in the nine other juvenile courthouses serving Los Angeles County, with their forty-nine courtrooms and eighty thousand active cases, a system that dwarfs adult courts in most jurisdictions, the largest juvenile justice system in the world. Sweaty hands wave crumpled subpoenas and court orders like pennants, dangled anxiously in front of anyone who remotely appears to be in authority, followed by this question: Where do I go? Because most of the people asked this question are not actually in authority, but merely happen to be walking the hallway in a business suit or policeman's uniform, the most common reply is a shrug, and so dozens of people roam about aimlessly, unsure where to go.

This is what they find as they wander the Los Angeles Juvenile Court, Thurgood Marshall Branch: a waiting room, a clerk's office, and one courtroom downstairs, with one wide stairway leading to the second floor, scarred by graffiti, as are the other gray walls of this place. There is an arthritic elevator at the other end of the building, but it stinks of old urine and seems to take several minutes to pass between the two floors of this disheveled courthouse. The bathrooms are graffiti museums, the mirrors so thoroughly etched with gang insignias that the lawyers brave enough to enter cannot see enough of their own reflections to straighten their ties. The layout of the place mystifies all but the initiates: Superior Court Department 241 is on the first floor, and Departments 240 and 242 are on the second floor. There is no logic to this numbering scheme (other than judicial jockeying for the least shabby quarters), and there are no other room numbers for the courts—you have to figure out their locations on your own. There is no information counter, no posted court calendars, no map of the building, no guidance of any kind. Cryptic, hand-lettered signs, faded and yellowed with age, hang haphazardly from the walls, suspended by ancient, brittle pieces of Scotch tape, defaced by vandals and communicating nothing relevant to the day's proceedings.

The aged building, once a small municipal courthouse for adult offenders, outgrown, disused, and, finally, thrown like a gnawed bone to the space-hungry Juvenile Court, is brimming with children and their families today, their combined voices a riotous roar. The modest, casual clothes worn by most of the parents, and the bagged-out, gangster-chic clothes worn by many of the kids, make it easy to spot the lawyers in their suits and power ties, clustered together, cutting deals or interviewing witnesses three minutes before trial. These hurried mutterings in the hallway are what passes for trial preparation in this haphazard court of law, except for a rare, few, high-profile cases, "specials" in DA jargon. Snatches of conversations become intelligible as you push through the first-floor hallway, packed tight as a rush hour subway car, hot and claustrophobic: A father says, *You listen to the judge, boy,* followed by a shrill, *Fuck the judge. . . . * A woman's voice pleads, *Can my* *daughter come home today?* while someone's brother complains, *Why are they charging him with murder? He was just drivin' the car.* Next to him, a public defender wheedles with a DA, a salesman at the bazaar, pressing to close the deal: *Come on, you don't need a felony on this one, we'll cop to the misdemeanor, save some court time. . . .* The DA has her eyes closed, files tucked under each arm, trying to remember the facts of the case they're talking about, one of forty-seven she is supposed to handle that morning.

As each of the three courtrooms begin their morning calendar call, the blur of intertwining hallway conversations fades as lawyers and litigants hustle into court. There are enough stragglers, witnesses, and families waiting for their children's cases to be called to keep the hallways crowded and loud, and any respite in the noise quickly evaporates as the public address system kicks into gear. Throughout the rest of the day, conversations will be drowned out by an intermittent electronic bong, followed by the voice of one of the court bailiffs speaking over the PA summoning some child or his family or a witness or an attorney to court. During morning calendar call, the busiest time in the courthouse, the harsh screech of the loudspeakers reverberates constantly, so loud that not even the thick, heavily worn double wooden doors barring entry to each courtroom can stop the sound. These announcements frequently drown out the words of judges and lawyers in the midst of hearings, destroying any semblance of courtroom decorum, and proceedings constantly are delayed as attorneys leap up to telephone some other courtroom competing for their services via loudspeaker. The crush of cases is so great, and the public defender and the district attorney here are so understaffed, that it is not uncommon for them to have two, three, sometimes five or more cases scheduled simultaneously in different courtrooms, causing impatient judges to electronically bellow for them to come on down every few minutes. . . .

JUDGE DORN

"Call the calendar," Judge Roosevelt Dorn intones at exactly 8:30, the first words he utters each morning after climbing the bench and settling into his huge leather chair, the day's files spread out before him like the tarot. Few Juvenile Court judges (or adult court judges, for that matter) in Los Angeles start so punctually, and Dorn's recent arrival in Inglewood has shaken the courthouse crowd from its previously torpid pace. The murmur of a dozen separate conversations in the courtroom gallery evaporates. The bailiff begins reading the names of the cases to be heard that day, one by one, checking off a box on his list every time a boy or girl answers Present.

The courtroom is jammed, as it is every morning, standing room only, a constant rustling of coats, of settling into lumpy chairs, of heads poking in the door wondering if this is where they should be. Every tenth name or so, no one responds, and Dorn immediately orders an arrest warrant issued. Dorn's predecessor was not so harsh, the defense attorneys grumble to themselves. But Dorn is a stickler for punctuality, and for many of the kids, this will be the first time anyone has expected them to be on time for anything. If the child shows up later in the day (as opposed to blowing off the hearing entirely, which happens in about one in ten Juvenile Court cases), he or she will be taken into custody and locked up for a few hours, until the judge feels his message has been conveyed. "You'll not come late to Judge Dorn's courtroom again," he says to one of these latecomers, accused of emblazoning his spray-painted "tag" on several freeway overpasses.

"Yes," one attorney in the audience whispers to a colleague. "Next time he'll know not to show up at all." The lawyer starts to snicker, then falls silent and shifts uncomfortably when Dorn, who could not possibly have heard the remark, flicks a cold, prescient glance in the lawyer's direction, the teacher who can always detect the spitball's origin, even with back turned.

When the calendar call is through, the procession of cases begins in earnest. Lawyers line up in what once was a jury box (juveniles do not get trials before their peers, for obvious reasons), and compete with one another to have their cases called first, waiting to leap up and announce "Ready!" before anyone else, a kind of verbal elbowing to the head of the line. It is childish and raucous and the lawyers who get shoved aside pout and complain. Hearings for the kids in custody are supposed to have priority, but because the Probation Department is frequently tardy with both its buses and its intake reports—a child's entry into the system, the crucial passport to delinquency—this rule is often broken. Newly charged children are arraigned, their trial dates set. Older cases go to trial or, more often, get delayed, dismissed, or resolved through a plea bargain negotiated in the hallway, in which case the witnesses who wait through the morning are sent on their way, their days wasted for nothing. Perhaps they'll return for the next court date. Perhaps not.

"Call the first case," Dorn says, then closes his eyes for a moment. A very thin boy with thick spectacles is escorted from the lockup in back of the courtroom to the defense table. He sits with legs dangling from his chair, tapping the toes of his black, laceless Juvenile Hall–issue sneakers together in a slow fidget, gazing mournfully at the various players—the public defender shuffling papers for the forty-two cases she has to handle that morning, the assistant district attorney whispering to a witness in another case, the judge with his glasses now perched up on his forehead so he can scrub at his face with the palms of his hands. Dorn seems to be trying to massage away the weariness he feels from an early-morning start on the telephone, wrangling with county bureaucrats for a fresh paint job and an asbestos check for his ancient courthouse. The dingy courtroom with its cracked linoleum and sighing water cooler is still filled with parents, children, babies scrabbling and being shushed, surly teenagers with enormously baggy pants and tattoos snaking across their knuckles or up their arms, police officers sitting with arms crossed, knowing they will wait all day to testify in cases that will almost certainly be continued to another day, crime victims warily eyeing the juveniles accused of victimizing them. During a lull in the everyday din, when the cacophony of voices in the hallway and the courthouse's booming public address system briefly fall silent, you can hear the faint sandpaper sound of the dry skin of the judge's hands against his face. The boy begins to tap his sneakers together in syncopation with the rubbing. No one looks at him, speaks to him, or even seems to recognize that he is present, except for the khaki-uniformed bailiff hovering nearby, guarding against escape, or worse.

The boy is before Dorn for arraignment, his first appearance in court, a formulaic and purposely uneventful ritual. The hearing consists of a brief reading of the charges and an even briefer discussion of the contents of the court's juvenile intake form, a notoriously superficial, sometimes inaccurate two-page sheet that represents the system's sum total of knowledge about a child as he enters the court process for the first time. This is what the intake officers on duty at Juvenile Hall and in some police stations produce after each delinquency case is opened. With this, the judge must decide what to do with the child while the case slowly runs its course.

"It's a 245, Your Honor," the probation officer assigned to Dorn's courtroom informs the judge, referring to California Penal Code Section 245, assault with a deadly weapon or instrument. Tired of a bully at school, this skinny boy smashed a pipe over his tormentor's head. Then, still raging, he allegedly turned on a teacher before he was restrained. It is the boy's fourth such violent outburst in recent months, though the only one that caused major injury. The court and its investigative arm, the Probation Department, declined to act in the three previous incidents. Money and manpower is too scant to give much attention to "minor" offenses, so the system waits for someone to be seriously hurt before heaving into motion like an aged zoo lion. The boy is a twelve-year-old-bundle of anger.

Judge Dorn reads the brief summary available to him. It seems the boy once was an enthusiastic student, but a troubled home, the departure of his father, a mother who is more interested in dating than in raising an adolescent, have all taken their toll. Judge Dorn can see the boy needs help, stability, a caring guardian. He knows the biggest predictors of juvenile delinquency are a one-parent home and a failed educational experience. Studies of juvenile delinquents have confirmed this for years, as if he needed researchers and academics to tell him what he observes every day sitting on the bench: Virtually every delinquent he sees falls into one or both of these categories. But while the case is pending, the law—the boy's rights of due process—bar Dorn from doing much of anything, unless the public defender pleads him guilty on the spot. But the public defenders have a policy against doing this—first they must try to disprove or at least delay the charges. They say they are lawyers, not social workers, and their first duty is to attempt to win an acquittal—even when, strictly speaking, getting their clients off may not be in the kids' best interest. Their hard line in attempting to disprove every allegation and to exploit every legal technicality is what provokes the prosecution's lock-the-monsters-away hard line, and vice versa. And so, Dorn is left with but two options: He can release the "Pipe Kid," as a prosecutor referred to the boy in the hallway, and let him go home with his parents, or he can send him back to Juvenile Hall during the months it will take to resolve his case, on the theory that the boy is too dangerous to be free. The hall is just a temporary holding facility (though the new era of serious violent juvenile crime, combined with court backlogs, have made it far less temporary than originally intended, with stays now lasting months and even years instead of days or weeks). Services for the emotionally disturbed kids housed in the hall are minimal at best, consisting mainly of prescription drugs dispensed every night before bed, which have the additional benefit, to the staff, of making troublesome kids more manageable. The Pipe Kid cuts such a pathetic figure that Dorn is leaning toward sending him home instead, but then the mother brings him up short.

"I can't have him at home anymore," she informs the court, the large gold earring in her nose quivering as she speaks, her voice high and petulant. Her boyfriend sits next to her in his gray Budweiser T-shirt, staring at his hands folded across an ample fold of belly. Mother looks barely older than her son. "He won't listen," she fumes. "I just can't have him now."

The boy's head seems to turtle into his shoulders as she speaks, so eager is he to disappear. Someone in the audience clucks her tongue, and the mother glares in the direction it came from, though she can't quite locate the source of the disapproval. The judge nods without looking at her or the boy. "For the protection and rehabilitation of the minor, and for the protection of society, the minor is ordered detained," he announces, using that singsong voice people involuntarily adopt when they repeat the same phrase over and over, long past hearing the words. Then he returns to studying files at his bench and ribbing his face. The mother nods in satisfaction.

"We call kids like this NFC," a ponytailed narcotics investigator whispers to another onlooker in the courtroom gallery. "I see 'em all the time. You take a look at what they're doin', who their parents are, and you know: This poor kid's NFC. No fuckin' chance."

Three minutes after entering the courtroom, without ever uttering a word, without interrupting the DA's conversation with his witness or the defense attorney's shuffling of files, the boy leaves, escorted back to the holding tank. No one spoke with him or acknowledged his presence. There is a deliberately fostered anonymity to this, furthered by the practice of never calling the child by name, even as he or she sits mutely in court, life laid open for legal dissection. In Juvenile Court, a child is referred to simply as "the minor."

Small, slumped, confused, the minor avoids the eyes of the mother who doesn't want him as he rises to leave. Before he can exit with the bailiff, Judge Dorn has called the name of the next case on the docket. A fifteen-year-old girl, visibly pregnant, rises in the audience and takes the chair at the defense table, the seat still warm. Dorn sighs and studies the file.

This is what most Juvenile Court hearings look like: Little substance, much legal ritual, all flow control—the judge sits at his bench like an air-traffic controller, keeping things moving. It was not always this way, but the Supreme Court's landmark Gault decision has transformed Juvenile Court from an informal forum on children into a formal court of law where the focus is more on procedures and legal technicalities than on the welfare of children and the protection of society.

A peek into the future: Six months will pass before the Pipe Kid will see his case resolved, an eternity for a twelve-year-old. He will celebrate his thirteenth birthday in lockup, his trial postponed and rescheduled three times. The public defender representing him will play Juvenile Court's delaying game, hoping one of the People's main witnesses—the victim or the investigating officer—will fail to show up one morning, in which case the charges must be dismissed, a common occurrence here. The tactic will fail this time, though, the witnesses will show up for the third time, only to be told they can go home for good: The boy will finally plead guilty. Then he will be shuffled off to the foster home Dorn would have sent him to right away had the law permitted it. But by now, Pipe Kid is so angry at the system that he runs away after a few weeks and commits another assault and a robbery, and the process must start over again. This is the futile pattern that absorbs so much energy and time in Juvenile Court.

Perhaps more than anything else, time is the enemy here. Every day, Dorn's docket, like most juvenile judges', is swollen by a workload many times greater than judges in adult court deign to tolerate—fifty or sixty cases a day is not unusual. No one judge can deal meaningfully with such a tidal flow of human tragedy—on a busy day, and given the ninety-minute lunches and frequent breaks most judges take, the average time left per kid falls between four and five minutes.

On this day, Judge Dorn will see a total of thirty-two kids—four of them charged with armed robbery, one with attempted murder, two assaults with a deadly weapon, seven children charged with graffiti vandalism, four auto thefts, four petty thefts, three probation revocations, one case of witness intimidation, one case of resisting arrest, one disorderly conduct, three batteries, one concealed weapon charge, and one girl fighting transfer to adult court for her crimes. The kids facing these charges range in age from twelve to seventeen. By the end of the day, Dorn will have dismissed three cases because the People were unable to proceed when witnesses failed to show up (one of the missing was a police officer), sent three kids home on probation, sent another to a foster home, placed four more in the county-run detention camps, refused two recommendations to send kids to the California Youth Authority prison system, accepted four plea bargains, held one full-blown trial, continued ten other cases to various dates the following month, and arraigned three girls and two boys on newly filed charges. In one morning—a rather light one by Juvenile Court standards—Dorn has resolved more cases than most adult courts in Los Angeles do in a week.

And he is just one judge in a vast system. Taken as a whole, the ten branches of Los Angeles Juvenile Court, in twenty-eight courtrooms, each a separate fiefdom with different standards, different philosophies, and wildly different outcomes for similar cases, will handle nearly eleven hundred delinquency hearings of one kind or another this day. The most common order issued in Juvenile Court during this tidal flow of hearings is a postponement, putting off action until another day, creating months of delays in a system that is supposed to arrest the downward spiral of young people with the speed and efficiency of a hospital emergency room.

REVIEW QUESTIONS

1. In what ways do events and practices depicted by Humes support his argument that "the Supreme Court's landmark Gault decision has transformed Juvenile Court from an informal forum on children into a formal court of law where the focus is more on procedures and legal technicalities than on the welfare of children and the protection of society" (p. 301)? In what ways do they *fail* to support his argument?

2. In what other ways do the contemporary juvenile court practices described by Humes deviate from the original intent of the reformers who "invented" the juvenile court? In what ways do they remain consistent with traditional juvenile court philosophy? Can you find examples from the selection that illustrate ways in which procedural changes mandated by *Gault* and/or other Supreme Court decisions we

encountered in Chapter 3 have con-
tributed (or failed to contribute) to the
"transformation" Humes believes has occurred?

3. To what extent do you think the problems
   Humes describes are attributable to the
   original philosophy of the juvenile court as
   described by Judge Mack? To the way in

which the juvenile court was implemented
in practice (i.e., deviations from the original
intent)? To the procedural changes mandated by *In re Gault* and other Supreme
Court decisions? To pressures associated
with large caseloads? To changes in peo-
ples' attitudes concerning juvenile delinquency and juvenile justice?

Justice by Geography: Urban, Suburban, and Rural Variations in Juvenile Justice Administration

Barry C. Feld

I. INTRODUCTION

Although the same statutes and juvenile court rules of procedure apply, juvenile justice administration varies substantially in Minnesota. Juvenile courts' procedural characteristics
and sentencing practices relate consistently to urban, suburban, and rural differences in social structure. Urban courts operate in milieu that provide fewer mechanisms for informal
social control than do rural ones; consequently, they place greater emphasis on formal, bureaucratized social control. For example, the presence of counsel provides an indicator of a
court's legal formality. Attorneys appear in urban courts more than twice as often as they do
in rural courts. Structural influences on formal versus informal social control also affect the
selection of delinquents and the administration of justice. Urban courts sweep a broader,
more inclusive net and encompass proportionally more and younger youths than do suburban or rural courts. Social structure and procedural formality are also associated with
more severe sanctions. The more formal, urban courts place over twice as many youths in

Source: Barry C. Feld, (1991). Justice by geography: Urban, suburban, and rural variations in juvenile justice
administration. *Journal of Criminal Law and Criminology,* 82(1), 156–210. Copyright 1991 by Northwestern University School of Law. Reprinted by special permission of Northwestern University School of Law, *Journal of
Criminal Law and Criminology.*

pre-trial detention and sentence similarly-charged offenders more severely than do suburban or rural courts. As a result, where youths live affects how their cases are processed and the severity of the sentences they receive.

This Article examines the relationships between social structure, procedural formality, and juvenile justice administration and considers the implications of "justice by geography" for juvenile court reform.

A. Social Structure, Crime, and Justice Administration

Crime and delinquency are disproportionately urban phenomena. Criminology uses social structural features to explain variations in the distribution of crime. Classical sociological theory, for example, attributes the greater prevalence of crime in cities to urban anomie. In traditional rural communities, homogeneity and uniformity of beliefs foster informal social control, whereas in urban settings, population density, anonymity, and heterogeneity weaken social cohesion and increase reliance on formal social control. Social ecology, associated with the Chicago School, relates urban structural features such as income inequality, family structure, or racial composition to variations in crime rates.

Urbanization is associated with greater bureaucratization and formal social control as well as with higher rates of crime. Weber associated the formal rationalization of social life with urbanization and bureaucratization and argued that abstract rules would supplant more traditional methods of dispute resolution as law became increasingly rational and functionally specialized. Presumably, urban courts would be more formal and bureaucratized, emphasize rationality and efficiency, and punish on the basis of legally relevant factors such as present offense and prior record. By contrast, rural courts would be less bureaucratized and sentence on the basis of non-legal considerations.

Surprisingly, very little research has been done on the relationships between urbanization, bureaucratization, and justice administration. The few studies available document significant urban–rural differences in sentencing. Hagan found that differential treatment of racial minorities was more pronounced in rural courts than in bureaucratized urban ones. Tepperman reported that rural juvenile courts treated female offenders more leniently than males, but that gender differences declined with urbanization. Austin found that rural criminal courts considered social background factors while urban courts adhered to a more legalistic model of sentencing. Paternoster found that social context influenced charging decisions; rural prosecutors were more likely to seek the death penalty than urban ones. Myers and Talarico reported that urbanization and social context affect criminal court sentencing decisions. In short, these studies support Weberian expectations that similarly-situated offenders may be treated differently based upon their locale and that differential processing is more prevalent in rural settings and declines with urbanization and bureaucratization.

Criminology also attempts to explain variations in the administration of justice. Organizations interact with and are influenced by their external environments; for example, the expectations of police, politicians, appellate courts, news media, and the public all affect how courts perform. Criminal justice agencies operate within differing socio-political environments and depend upon their environment for legitimation, resources, and clients. As a result, external social, economic, and political variables constrain even ostensibly similar organizations. Wilson's analyses of urban police practices attributed differences in police behavior to variations in community social structure. Levin compared criminal sentencing in two metropolitan areas and attributed differences in sentencing practices to differences in the cities' political cultures. Eisenstein and Jacob identified the pivotal roles of courtroom work groups on judicial sentencing decisions in different jurisdictions.

B. Social Structural Variations in Juvenile Justice Administration—Formal Versus Informal Social Control

The traditional juvenile court's emphasis on rehabilitating offenders fostered judicial discretion, procedural informality, and organizational diversity. The broad legal framework associated with individualized justice allows judges to apply the same law very differently; descriptions of contemporary juvenile courts continue to emphasize judicial diversity.

With the imposition of formal procedures in In re Gault and the emergence of punitive sentencing goals, juvenile courts no longer can be assumed either to conform to the traditional therapeutic model or to be similar to one another. Ethnographic studies of a single juvenile court cannot be generalized to other courts in other settings. Indeed, most juvenile court ethnographies do not provide enough information about a court's social or political context to help explain its behavior.

The few studies that compare juvenile courts in different locales indicate that they are variable organizations that differ on several structural and procedural dimensions. Contrasting traditional therapeutic courts with those holding a more legalistic, due process orientation captures many of the variables in juvenile justice administration. The former intervene in a child's "best interests" on an informal, discretionary basis, while the latter emphasize more formal, rule-oriented decision-making. "Traditional" and "due process" courts may be arrayed across a continuum from informal to formal with corresponding procedural and substantive differences.

Recognizing that juvenile justice is not a uniform system vastly complicates analyses of courts' behavior. Even research that recognizes courts' diversity does not explore either the structural sources or administrative consequences of formal–informal or due process–traditional organizational variation. One recent study examined the impact of counsel on juvenile justice administration. Variations in rates of representation provided an indicator of a formal, due process orientation and were associated with differences in pretrial detention, sentencing, and case processing practices. While the presence of defense attorneys was associated with differences in juvenile justice administration, that study could not account for variations in rates of representation. Although those juvenile courts operated under statutes and rules of statewide applicability, external political, social structural, or legal variables and individual judge's policies apparently influenced courts' procedural and substantive orientations.

The present study provides compelling evidence of "justice by geography." A court's social context strongly influences the ways in which cases are selected, heard, and disposed.

Social structure is associated consistently with differences in rates of juvenile criminality, the degree of procedural formality, and juvenile justice administration. These differences are reflected in pre-petition screening of cases, the presence of counsel, pretrial detention, and sentencing practices. In urban counties, which are more heterogeneous, diverse, and less stable than rural counties, juvenile court intervention is more formal and due process–oriented. Urban formality, in turn, is associated with greater severity in pre-trial detention and sentencing practices. By contrast, in the more homogeneous and stable rural counties, juvenile justice administration is procedurally less formal and sentences more lenient. However, rural judges' exercises of discretion also result in gender differences in the processing of female offenders. What are the costs and benefits of formal versus informal dispute resolution? How do these differences in juvenile justice administration affect the lives of young people? Formulating juvenile justice policy requires an appreciation of the structural sources of local variation.

II. THE PRESENT STUDY—DATA AND METHODOLOGY

This study uses data from two sources. Minnesota county census data from 1980 provide indicators of social structure. Data collected in each county by the Minnesota Supreme Court's Judicial Information System (SJIS) for delinquency and status offense cases processed in 1986 provide information on juvenile justice administration. To facilitate analyses between the census and SJIS data sets, the county is the unit of analysis, and counties are then aggregated as urban, suburban, or rural.

The SJIS sample consists of individual juveniles against whom delinquency or status offense petitions were filed in 1986. It excludes juvenile court referrals for abuse, dependency or neglect, and routine traffic violations. Only formally petitioned delinquency and status cases are analyzed; the SJIS does not include cases referred to juvenile courts which were subsequently disposed of informally without the filing of a petition.

This study uses a youth-based data file that analyzes all 17,195 individual juveniles whose cases were formally petitioned in Minnesota's juvenile courts in 1986. Unfortunately, the Minnesota SJIS does not include data on a juvenile's family, school, socioeconomic status, or prior record of offenses or dispositions. However, each youth processed in a county's juvenile court receives a unique identifying number which is used for all subsequent purposes. By merging 1984, 1985, and 1986 annual data tapes and matching the county/youth identification numbers across years, a youth's prior record of petitions, adjudications, and dispositions was reconstructed. The data reported here reflect a youth's most current juvenile court referral as well as all petitions, adjudications, and dispositions for at least the preceding two years or more.

In this study, the offenses reported by the SJIS were re-grouped into six analytical categories. The "felony/minor" offense distinction provides an indicator of offense seriousness. Offenses are also classified as being against person or property, other delinquency, and status. Combining person and property with the felony/misdemeanor distinction produces a six-item offense severity scale. When a petition alleges more than one offense, the youth is classified on the basis of the most serious charge. The study uses two indicators of severity of dispositions: out-of-home placement and secure confinement. Out-of-home placement includes any disposition in which the child is taken from his or her home and placed in a group home, foster care, in-patient psychiatric or chemical dependency treatment facility, or correctional institution. Secure confinement is a substantial subset of all out-of-home placements but includes only commitments to county institutions or state training schools.

The classification of counties as urban, suburban and small urban, and rural uses the census concept of Standardized Metropolitan Statistical Area (SMSA) and youth-population density. In this study, counties were classified as urban if they were located within an SMSA, had one or more cities of 100,000 inhabitants, and had a juvenile population aged ten to seventeen of at least 50,000 youths. Counties were classified as either suburban or small urban if they were located within a metropolitan SMSA (suburban) or, if within their own SMSA (small urban), they had one or more cities of 25,000 to 100,000, and had a juvenile population aged ten to seventeen of more than 7,500 but less than 50,000 youths. Counties were classified as rural if they were located outside of an SMSA, had no principal city of 25,000 or greater, and had less than 7,500 juveniles aged ten to seventeen. . . .

IV. DISCUSSION AND CONCLUSIONS—VARIETIES OF JUVENILE JUSTICE

Although the same statutes and court rules of procedure apply, urban, suburban, and rural social structural features relate consistently to substantive and procedural differences in juvenile justice administration. Urban courts operate in communities with more disrupted families, more racially heterogeneous populations and less residential stability, all of which provide fewer mechanisms for informal social control. The urban counties represent less well-integrated, cohesive communities with less "mechanical solidarity" than do the suburban or rural counties. Accordingly, urban counties place greater emphasis on formal, rather than informal, mechanisms of social control. This is reflected in the deployment of police, as well as in juvenile justice administration.

The structural–geographic variation influences juvenile justice administration. In relation to their youth population, the urban courts receive a larger proportion of juveniles in all offense categories. Compared with suburban or rural courts, urban courts received a larger proportion of referrals from non-police sources, particularly probation officers and schools. The diversity of urban referral sources reflects a greater reliance on a more inclusive network of formal social control, which encompasses more troublesome youths in the community. By contrast, the suburban courts, with the lowest overall rate of juvenile court referrals, screened cases more selectively and focussed more on serious offenders and less on status offenders. Perhaps parental affluence and stability, relative to the urban or rural counties, enabled parents and court intake personnel to develop informal, alternative dispositions in lieu of formal court intervention for less serious suburban offenders. Finally, the rural courts dealt with the smallest proportions of juveniles charged with serious crimes and the largest proportion charged with status offenses.

As a result of geographic differences in delinquency, referral sources, and pre-petition screening, the juveniles appearing in the respective courts differ. Urban courts intervened more extensively in the lives of younger juveniles, especially status offenders (43.0%), as contrasted with the suburban (19.9%) or rural (15.7%) courts. Conversely, suburban and rural courts processed more serious young offenders and more older status offenders. The differences in age and offenses suggest that serious crime by younger juveniles in non-urban settings requires an immediate response, whereas for less serious offenses, rural juveniles exhaust informal community alternatives before courts invoke formal processes.

Representation by counsel provides an indicator of a court's formality or due process orientation. While the majority of youths in Minnesota appeared in juvenile courts without counsel (45.3%), geographic diversity in representation existed. The highest rates of representation occurred in the urban courts (62.6%), followed closely by the suburban courts (55.2%), while the rural courts provided only about one-quarter (25.1%) of delinquents with lawyers. The differential presence of counsel suggests basic differences in court orientation—an urban, due process or "formal rationality" model of justice versus a rural, traditional "substantively rational" juvenile court.

Earlier research reported a relationship between procedural formality and sentencing severity. This study provides even stronger support for the formality–severity relationship. The urban courts sentenced youths charged with similar offenses more severely than did the suburban or rural courts. The pattern of urban severity remained even after controlling for the present offense and prior record. Urban courts' greater use of pretrial detention reflects their reliance on formal controls and more severe intervention. Finally, the regression equations indicate that urban, suburban, and rural courts used similar "frames of relevance." Despite the substantive focus on similar legal variables, however, urban courts sentenced similarly situated offenders more severely. Other research also reports that urbanization exerts a contextual influence on sentences.

Finding "justice by geography" vastly complicates the tasks of criminologists. As this research demonstrates, there is both a theoretical and empirical relationship between variations in social structure and in juvenile justice administration. Studies which analyze and interpret aggregated data without accounting for contextual and structural characteristics may systematically mislead and obscure, rather than clarify. Both theoretically and operationally, it is necessary to refine the relationships between social structure and justice administration. What structural features influence a juvenile court's procedural and substantive orientation? How does the local culture foster a traditional or due process orientation? How do the roles of counsel operating in these diverse socio-legal settings differ?

Finding "varieties of juvenile courts" has important implications for juvenile justice policy. Recent trends in juvenile justice emphasize punishment over rehabilitation with a corresponding increase in procedural formality. What is the relationship between procedural formality and sentencing severity? Does greater urban crime engender more punitive responses, which then require more formal procedural safeguards as a prerequisite? Or, does urban bureaucratization lead to more formal procedural safeguards, which then enable judges to exact a greater toll than they otherwise might? Increases in urban crime may foster a "war-on-crime" mentality that places immense pressures on the justice system to "get tough." Urban racial diversity may foster a more repressive response to crimes by "those people" than in more homogeneous rural settings. While Minnesota traditionally favored a progressive, rehabilitative approach to many social ills, urban formality and punitiveness may reflect a more recent trend in which the ethic of care and treatment is subordinated to restoring social order.

What are the comparative costs and benefits of formal versus informal dispute resolution in juvenile courts? While the formal urban courts imposed the most severe sentences, the suburban courts were nearly as formal and yet sentenced about as leniently as the rural courts did. While the relationship between formality and severity is troubling, an uncritical embrace of the traditional, informal juvenile court does not necessarily follow. In the rural juvenile courts, female juveniles are processed differently and more severely than are either rural males or female offenders in other settings. Does rural "substantive justice" necessarily connote gender-bias and the application of a paternalistic double-standard for which informal juvenile courts are justly criticized?

The policy choices between more or less formal juvenile justice are neither simple nor straightforward. Moreover, if a court's practices are rooted in its social structure, then simply amending laws may not produce the desired change. While diversity rather than uniformity historically characterized juvenile courts, whether such extensive local variation should continue or be encouraged is questionable. Should a system of laws and court rules of procedure be applied generally and uniformly throughout the state? Should local norms and values influence the imposition of sanctions such that youths convicted of similar offenses receive widely disparate consequences? If formal legal guidelines are adopted to structure discretionary detention and sentencing decisions, will they reduce the severity of urban courts' intervention or increase the severity of rural courts? If juvenile sentencing guidelines actually limit judicial discretion, would they produce the worst of both worlds—restricting the efforts of individual judges or communities to rehabilitate their children, while perpetuating more rigid and severe sentences?

REVIEW QUESTIONS

1. What is "justice by geography"?
2. What are the basic differences between "formal" and "informal" juvenile courts as described by Feld? Which of these approaches do you consider preferable, or do you think juvenile courts should mix elements of each? What is your reasoning?
3. What were the main differences Feld found among urban, suburban, and rural juvenile courts in Minnesota? Which ones were more formal? Which were more informal? What other similarities/differences did he find among them?

4. What are the policy implications of the differences Feld found among urban, suburban, and rural juvenile courts? Does it strike you as unfair that juvenile courts operate so differently from each other? Would it be desirable to try to make them more alike? Why or why not?
5. In what ways does the juvenile court described by Humes earlier in this chapter seem to fit Feld's characterization of urban juvenile courts? In what ways (if any) does it seem more like suburban or rural juvenile courts?

National Prosecution Standards: Juvenile Justice

National District Attorneys Association

INTRODUCTION

Excellence in criminal prosecution demands excellence in all areas—including both adult and juvenile justice. Whether in response to formalization of juvenile court procedures or increased interest in juveniles and the crimes they commit, America's prosecutors are playing a larger role in the juvenile justice system. The important substantive changes in prosecutorial involvement in juvenile delinquency cases prompted NDAA's Juvenile Justice Committee to revise National Prosecution Standard 19.2, Juvenile Delinquency, originally adopted in 1977. The revised standard is designed to guide prosecutors in redefining their role. Many years have passed since the Supreme Court rendered its landmark decision, *In Re Gault,* 387 U.S. 1 (1967). The revised standard incorporates many of the lessons learned since then.

The standard is aimed at promoting justice in juvenile delinquency cases. It emphasizes the prosecutor's duty to provide for the safety and welfare of the community and victims and, at the same time, consider the special interests and needs of juveniles to the extent possible without compromising that primary duty. The standard accepts the premise that a separate court for most juvenile delinquency cases continues to be an indispensable alternative to the adult court. . . .

92.1 GENERAL RESPONSIBILITIES OF A PROSECUTOR

a. Appearance of Prosecutor

The prosecutor should appear as an attorney for the state in all hearings concerning a juvenile accused of an act that would constitute a crime if he were an adult ("a delinquent act"). This includes but is not limited to hearings for: detention, speedy trial, dismissal, entry of pleas, trial, waiver, disposition, revocation of probation or parole status, and any appeal from or collateral attacks upon the decisions in each of these proceedings.

b. Primary Duty

The primary duty of the prosecutor is to seek justice while fully and faithfully representing the interests of the state. While the safety and welfare of the community, including the victim, is their primary concern, prosecutors should consider the special interests and needs of the juvenile to the extent they can do so without compromising that concern.

c. Personnel and Resources

Chief prosecutors should devote specific personnel and resources to fulfill their responsibilities with respect to juvenile delinquency proceedings, and all prosecutors' offices should have an identified juvenile unit or attorney responsible for representing the state in juvenile matters. Additionally, the prosecutor for juvenile cases should have adequate staff support to the extent possible, given office resources including: clerical and paralegal personnel, interns, investigators, and victim/witness coordinators.

d. Qualifications of Prosecutor

Training and experience should be required for juvenile delinquency cases. Chief prosecutors should select prosecutors for juvenile court on the basis of their skill and competence, including knowledge of juvenile law, interest in children and youth, education, and experience. While the unit chief, if any, must have criminal trial experience, assistant prosecutors assigned to the unit should also have prior criminal trial experience, if possible. Entry-level attorneys in the juvenile unit should be as qualified as any entry-level attorney and receive special training regarding juvenile matters.

e. Cooperation

To the extent possible, prosecutors should cooperate with others in the juvenile justice system to promote speedy trials and efficient case processing. . . .

92.4 UNCONTESTED ADJUDICATION PROCEEDINGS

a. Propriety of Plea Agreements

The prosecutor can properly enter into a plea agreement with a defense attorney concerning a filed petition against a juvenile. The decision to enter into a plea agreement should be governed by both the interests of the state and those of the juvenile, although the primary concern of the prosecutor should be protection of the public interest as determined in the exercise of traditional prosecutorial discretion. Plea agreements, if appropriate, should be entered into expeditiously without delaying speedy adjudication and disposition, in order to protect the juvenile, the victim, and the state.

92.5 THE ADJUDICATORY PHASE

a. Speedy Adjudication

When the prosecutor decides to seek a formal adjudication of a complaint against a juvenile, he should proceed to an adjudicatory hearing as quickly as possible. Detention cases should receive priority treatment. An adjudicatory hearing should be held within 30 days if the juvenile is held in detention pending trial or within 60 days if the juvenile is arrested and released. A dispositional hearing should be held within 30 days after the adjudicatory hearing.

b. Assumption of Traditional Adversarial Role

At the adjudicatory hearing the prosecutor should assume the traditional adversarial position of a prosecutor. The prosecutor should recognize, however, that vulnerable child witnesses should be treated fairly and with sensitivity.

c. Standard of Proof; Rules of Evidence

The juvenile prosecutor has the burden of proving the allegations in the petition beyond a reasonable doubt. The same rules of evidence used in trying criminal cases in the jurisdiction should apply to juvenile court cases involving delinquency petitions. The prosecutor is under the same duty to disclose exculpatory evidence in juvenile proceedings as he would be in adult criminal proceedings.

d. Notice to Prosecutor Before Dismissal

Once a petition has been filed with the juvenile court, it should not be dismissed without providing the prosecutor with notice and an opportunity to be heard.

92.6 DISPOSITIONAL PHASE

a. Prosecutor Should Take an Active Role

The prosecutor should take an active role in the dispositional hearing and make a recommendation to the court after reviewing reports prepared by prosecutorial staff, probation department, and others.

b. Victim Impact

At the dispositional hearing the prosecutor should ensure that the court is aware of the impact of the juvenile's conduct on the victim and should further report to the court any matter concerning restitution and community service.

c. Prosecutor's Recommendation

In recommending a disposition, the prosecutor should consider those dispositions that most closely meet the interests and needs of the juvenile offender, bearing in mind that community safety and welfare is his primary concern.

d. Effectiveness of Dispositional Programs

The chief prosecutor along with the prosecutor in juvenile court should evaluate the effectiveness of dispositional programs used in the jurisdiction, from the standpoint of both the state's and the youth's interests. If the prosecutor discovers that a youth or class of young people are not receiving the care and treatment envisioned in disposition decisions, he should inform the court of this fact.

92.7 POST-DISPOSITION PROCEEDINGS

    a. Appeals and Hearings Subsequent to Disposition

       The prosecutor should represent the state's interest in all appeals from decisions rendered by the appropriate court, all hearings concerning revocation of probation, all petitions for modification of disposition, all hearings related to the classification and placement of a juvenile, and all collateral proceedings attacking the orders of that court.

    b. Duty to Report

       If the prosecutor becomes aware that the sanctions imposed by the court are not being administered by an agency to which the court assigned the juvenile or that the manner in which the sanctions are being carried out is inappropriate, the prosecutor should take all reasonable steps to ensure agency supervisors are informed and appropriate measures are taken. If the situation is not remedied, it is the duty of the prosecutor to report this concern to the agency and, if necessary, to the dispositional court.

COMMENTARY

Standard 92.1 emphasizes three aspects of the role of the prosecutor. First, the prosecutor is charged to seek justice just as he does in adult prosecutions. The prosecutor in the juvenile system, however, is further charged to give special attention to the interest and needs of the accused juvenile to the extent that it does not conflict with the duty to fully and faithfully represent the interests of the state. This call for special attention reflects the philosophy that the safety and welfare of the community is enhanced when juveniles, through counseling, restitution, or more extensive rehabilitative efforts and sanctions, are dissuaded from further criminal activity.

    Second, Standard 92.1 emphasizes the desirability of having the prosecutor appear at all stages of the proceedings. In so doing, the prosecutor maintains a focus on the safety and well-being of the community at each decision-making level. Further, because the juvenile system is increasingly adversarially based, the prosecutor fulfills an important role in addressing the arguments of other juvenile and social service advocates. The prosecutor's presence guarantees the opportunity to exercise continuous monitoring at each stage and broad discretion to ensure fair and just results.

    The standard recognizes that in some jurisdictions prosecutors are barred by statute from participating at all in juvenile proceedings. In others, prosecutors are by law or practice not involved in hearings or discussions at certain stages. For instance, in many jurisdictions the state attorney general handles all appeals. The standard suggests that prosecutors examine their systems to see whether representation of the community's interests would be better served through the presence and involvement of someone from their office at each stage of the adjudicatory process. If so, prosecutors may choose to use these standards in advocating change in existing law or practice.

Finally, the standard emphasizes professionalism in juvenile court work. It provides that attorneys in juvenile court should be experienced, competent, and interested. It suggests that the practice of using the juvenile court as a mere training forum for new prosecuting attorneys should be abandoned, because continuity of involvement in the system creates professionalism. . . .

. . .Standard 92.4 reflects the consensus that plea agreements are appropriate in a juvenile court to the extent that they are appropriate in the adult court. The appropriateness and extent to which plea agreements are used are matters of office policy to be determined by the chief prosecutor. The prosecutor should always take steps to ensure that the resulting record is sufficient to reflect the actual nature of the offense.

In juvenile courts where a plea to any offense vests full dispositional jurisdiction in the court, there is sometimes a practice to reduce the charge through a plea agreement. For instance, a provable burglary charge is reduced to theft or a sex offense to an assault. For at least these serious offenses, NDAA urges prosecutors to only enter into pleas that reflect that seriousness, unless there is a problem with proof. A provable burglary case should result in a court record that reflects commission of a burglary, not just theft. The court record can then be used as an accurate gauge of prior delinquent behavior if the juvenile is later accused of additional offenses.

A plea agreement with a juvenile should be conducted through defense counsel. Juveniles, and even juveniles and their parents, should not be involved in plea agreements when they are unrepresented by an attorney, because the danger of misunderstanding the nature of the agreement and the potential consequences are so great.

NDAA recognizes that in some jurisdictions this general rule could result in the availability of "reduced charge" pleas to represented juveniles and not to unrepresented juveniles. The rule is not meant to discriminate against unrepresented juveniles and the prosecutor is charged to exercise his discretion wisely to avoid this result.

A plea agreement should be accompanied by a recitation on the court record of sufficient facts to demonstrate a prima facie case that the juvenile has committed the acts alleged in the petition to which he is pleading guilty. When a confession by the juvenile is introduced, the prosecutor must assure [sic] that the record recites corroborative evidence establishing the crime itself. The prosecutor's recitation should be limited to the act(s) to which the juvenile is pleading guilty, except when the juvenile accepts responsibility for financial restitution with respect to dismissed charges. Where restitution is involved for dismissed charges, the court may nevertheless require a recitation to establish the basis for financial liability.

The time limits in Standard 92.5, like those in Standard 92.2, are intended to expedite juvenile cases in order to promote fair treatment to both victim and juvenile and to make the experience more meaningful for the juvenile. Many juvenile justice professionals believe that a court appearance or a disposition several months after the delinquent act is much less useful than a prompt response. Like the time limits on screening in Standard 92.2, these are suggested limits. Some jurisdictions may process cases more quickly than this while others may find it impossible, given local law and practice. NDAA recognizes, for instance, that the defense discovery process in some jurisdictions may require a longer time period. It also recognizes that good cause may exist in specific cases to extend the time period. Prosecutors may find that they can utilize these standards to convince lawmakers or other juvenile justice professionals that changes should be made to ensure prompt case processing and disposition.

Section 92.5 envisions a formal, adversarial process with respect to determination of guilt or innocence. This standard, therefore, suggests that the same rules of evidence employed in adult criminal cases in the jurisdiction should be applied to juvenile court cases. Prosecutors should strive in the juvenile court setting to maintain a distinction between a factual determination of innocence or guilt and a determination of disposition. This approach promotes fairness to both the victim and the community and enhances the integrity of juvenile court findings.

Standard 92.6 encourages prosecutors to participate in the dispositional phase because the community should be represented in this phase just as it is or should be in earlier phases. Prosecutors should also offer appropriate alternatives to the court because they have been involved with the particular juvenile's case. They are familiar with dispositional alternatives that are most appropriate. When a juvenile presents a danger to the safety and welfare of the community, the prosecutor should voice this concern. On the other hand, when appropriate, the prosecutor may offer a dispositional recommendation that is less restrictive than what the juvenile court judge may contemplate imposing. The standard recognizes that, given the scarce resources in many prosecutors' offices, it may not be practical to assign attorneys to attend disposition hearings for minor offenses. One possibility in these cases is that the prosecutor submit to the court a written recommendation on disposition.

This standard also suggests that the prosecutor should take a leadership role in the community in assuring [sic] that a wide range of appropriate dispositional alternatives are available for youth who are adjudicated delinquents. The prosecutor is challenged to assume this leadership role because he is in the unique position to help organize the community and because successful programs should serve to actually reduce crime.

Standard 92.7 suggests that the work of the prosecutor is not finished at disposition of the case. Instead, the prosecutor is encouraged to follow up on cases to ensure that dispositions are upheld, court ordered sanctions are administered, and treatment is provided. At the same time, NDAA recognizes that in some states legal restrictions do not allow such follow-up, and scarce resources prevent follow-up in other offices.

REVIEW QUESTIONS

1. What are the main responsibilities of the prosecutor in juvenile court? In what ways do you think these responsibilities are different from those of a prosecutor in criminal court? In what ways do you think the

responsibilities of a prosecutor in juvenile court *should* be different from those of a prosecutor in criminal court?

2. Were you surprised to find that the standards permit prosecutors in juvenile court

to enter into plea agreements with defense attorneys? Does it bother you to know that plea bargaining occurs in juvenile court?

3. The standards indicate that prosecutors in juvenile court should assume the "traditional adversarial role." What does this mean? Do you think prosecutors in juvenile court should be as adversarial as they are in criminal court? Why or why not?

4. Does the statement that "vulnerable child witnesses should be treated fairly and with sensitivity" suggest a different approach with child witnesses than in criminal court, or do you think this is an ethical standard that should apply equally in criminal court?

A Call for Justice: An Assessment of Access to Counsel and Quality of Representation in Delinquency Proceedings

Patricia Puritz, Sue Burrell, Robert Schwartz, Mark Soler, and Loren Warboys

In the fall of 1993, the American Bar Association Juvenile Justice Center, in conjunction with the Youth Law Center and Juvenile Law Center, received funding from the federal Office of Juvenile Justice and Delinquency Prevention to initiate the Due Process Advocacy Project. The intent of the project is to build the capacity and effectiveness of juvenile defenders through increasing access to lawyers for young people in delinquency proceedings and enhancing the quality of representation those lawyers provide. This report does not address the significant number of young people now being handled by adult criminal courts.

  This project, called for by Congress in 1992 in its reauthorization of the Juvenile Justice and Delinquency Prevention Act, has even greater importance today. The juvenile justice system in our country is at the center of public debate. The public is concerned about juvenile crime, particularly violent crime. Congress, state legislatures, and executive agencies have insisted that the juvenile courts respond with more punitive sanctions, longer periods of confinement for many youthful offenders, and increased handling of juveniles in adult criminal courts.

Source: Patricia Puritz, Sue Burrell, Robert Schwartz, Mark Soler and Loren Warboys. (1995). *A Call for Justice: An Assessment of Access to Counsel and Quality of Representation in Delinquency Proceedings.* Washington, DC: American Bar Association Juvenile Justice Center. © December, 1995 by the American Bar Association. Reprinted by Permission.

These measures have important consequences for youth in juvenile court who need effective representation to ensure that they are not held unnecessarily in secure detention, improperly transferred to adult criminal court, or inappropriately committed to institutional confinement. Society at large also has important interests as stake, including the desire for appropriate and effective sanctions for juvenile offenders and the enormous costs of increased incarceration and building new juvenile facilities at a time when state and local budgets are already severely stretched.

This report is a national assessment of the current state of representation of youth in juvenile court and an evaluation of training, support, and other needs of practitioners. The assessment sought information about excellent work being done in the field as well as problems in representation of youth. It examines all stages of representation, from the time of arrest to the time of discharge from the juvenile justice system, and covers all regions of the country, including urban, suburban, and rural areas.

THE ASSESSMENT

The assessment consisted of a national survey of hundreds of juvenile defenders, site visits to a variety of jurisdictions, interviews with people working in the field, client interviews, an extensive literature search, and meetings and consultation with the project's national Advisory Board. The assessment focused on public defenders and court-appointed counsel. We also examined the small but important role played by law school clinical programs and nonprofit children's law centers. We compared our observations with the Juvenile Justice Standards developed by the Institute for Judicial Administration and the American Bar Association.

ACCESS TO COUNSEL AND QUALITY OF REPRESENTATION

In 1967, in *In re Gault,* the United States Supreme Court established a constitutional right for children to receive counsel in juvenile delinquency proceedings. Congress expressed similar concern over the need to safeguard children's rights when it enacted the Juvenile Justice and Delinquency Prevention Act in 1974. When it reauthorized the Juvenile Justice Act in 1992, Congress re-emphasized the importance of lawyers in juvenile delinquency proceedings, specifically noting the inadequacies of prosecutorial and public defender offices to provide individualized justice. In a 1993 report, *America's Children at Risk: A National Agenda for Legal Action* the ABA's Presidential Working Group on the Unmet Legal Needs of Children and their Families also called for the juvenile justice system to fulfill children's right to competent counsel.

During the past fifteen years, a number of researchers have described and analyzed the difficulties of children in many jurisdictions in obtaining access to counsel. Others have raised serious concerns about the quality of representation when children are represented by attorneys. Some studies have taken in-depth looks at particular states, such as Minnesota and New York, while others have examined systemic problems. Commentators have noted a variety of barriers to appropriate access to counsel (including parental reluctance to retain attorneys, judicial hostility to appointment of counsel, and improper "waivers" of counsel by juveniles) and to effective representation by attorneys (such as inadequate training, high turnover, low status of juvenile court work, and insufficient support services). Overwhelming caseloads for many juvenile defenders impede both access to counsel and quality of representation.

THE ROLE OF DEFENSE COUNSEL IN DELINQUENCY PROCEEDINGS

The job of the juvenile defense attorney is enormous. In addition to all of the responsibilities involved in presenting the criminal case, juvenile defenders must also gather information regarding clients' individual histories, families, schooling, and community ties, in order to assist courts in diverting appropriate cases, preventing unnecessary pre-trial detention, avoiding unnecessary transfers to adult court, and ordering individualized dispositions. Juvenile defenders have an important role in protecting their clients' interests at every stage of the proceedings, from arrest and detention to pretrial proceedings, from adjudication to disposition to post-dispositional matters.

The assessment sought to evaluate how effectively attorneys in juvenile court are fulfilling their obligations to their clients.

ASSESSMENT RESULTS

We observed many attorneys who vigorously and enthusiastically represented their young clients. Those lawyers challenged the prosecution to prove its case through pertinent evidentiary objections, motions, arguments, and contested hearings. In court, they were articulate and prepared. Their arguments were supported with relevant facts and law. When their clients were faced with lengthy incarceration, they often provided the court with compelling alternatives. The children they represented appeared to understand the proceedings. There was ongoing communication between children and their attorneys, both in and out of court. The attorneys made good use of family members, other significant adults, experts, and potential service providers to demonstrate to the court the appropriateness of non-institutional placements.

But this type of vigorous representation was not widespread, or even very common. Often what we were told in interviews and what was reported in mail survey responses did not square with what we personally observed in courtrooms and detention centers. The assessment raised serious concerns that the interests of many young people in juvenile court are significantly compromised, and that many children are literally left defenseless.

Our intent is not to blame the many dedicated attorneys who are handling extremely difficult cases and laboring under tremendous systemic burdens. Rather, we want to highlight their problems and needs in order to build their capacity and support their ability to provide improved legal services to children and youth.

General Characteristics of Offices and Programs Surveyed

More than half of the public defender offices surveyed have at least some attorneys working exclusively on juvenile cases. In most of the offices, public defenders rotate from other courts to juvenile court, with the option of continuing to work there. In other offices, attorneys must rotate to adult criminal court in order to be promoted. Many public defenders do not stay in juvenile court very long. Among survey respondents, 55% stay less than 24 months.

Public defenders carry enormous caseloads. While caseloads varied, the average caseload carried by a public defender often exceeds 500 cases per year, and of that number, greater than 300 are juvenile cases.

Most appointed counsel who represent children in juvenile court are solo practitioners or in small firms. Their experience in law practice ranged from two years to twenty, and in juvenile court from less than one year to more than five. Their caseloads are much less than public defenders: a significant number carry under 50 cases, though approximately one-fifth carry more than 200 cases. Only about one-third handled more than 75 juvenile delinquency cases during the year preceding the survey.

Attorneys in law school clinical programs and children's law centers, whom we also surveyed, typically carry very small caseloads.

Waiver of Counsel

One of the most disturbing findings of the assessment is that large numbers of youth across the country appear in juvenile court without lawyers: for example, 34% of the public defender offices surveyed reported that some percentage of youth in the juvenile courts in which they work "waive" their right to counsel at the detention hearing. Reports by appointed counsel are very similar.

These waivers occur after an advisory colloquy in the presence of the judge slightly more than half the time (54%), but 46% of the public defenders say there is a colloquy only "sometimes" or "rarely." In addition, 45% of public defenders say the colloquy is only "sometimes" or "rarely" as thorough as that given to adult defendants and is often a meaningless technicality.

Waivers of counsel by young people are sometimes induced by suggestions that lawyers are not needed because no serious dispositional consequences are anticipated—or by parental concerns that they will have to pay for any counsel that is appointed. These circumstances raise the possibility—perhaps the likelihood—that a substantial number of juvenile waivers are not "knowing and intelligent."

Impact of High Caseloads

The assessment found high caseloads to be the single most important barrier to effective representation. High caseloads have an impact on many aspects of representation. Attorneys with heavy caseload burdens find it difficult to meet with young clients to explain the proceedings before they appear at their detention hearings, conduct thorough investigations of the circumstances of the alleged offenses, learn about youths' ties to their families and to their communities, research and write individualized pretrial motions, keep informed on community-based alternatives to secure detention, develop dispositional plans that may be preferable to institutional confinement, follow up with clients during dispositional reviews, or monitor placement problems that may arise regarding needed services or conditions of confinement.

High caseloads plagued public defenders everywhere. Almost none of the public defender offices surveyed have a cap on the number of juvenile cases they may handle. More than two-thirds of public defenders feel that caseload pressures limit their ability to represent juvenile clients effectively. More than a third of those responding said that the time available to meet with and prepare clients before their cases are called is inadequate. In addition, almost half say that the time they have to confer with clients after their case is called is inadequate.

Appointed counsel reported fewer such problems. However, for appointed counsel carrying 200 or more cases, the impact on representation was similar to that experienced by public defenders with similarly high caseloads.

Site visits revealed the problem in more detail. At several sites, children literally met their lawyers as they sat down at counsel table in the detention hearings. There was no time to investigate the charges or to obtain information from families, schools, or social service agencies. At several sites, probation officers reported that juveniles do not know who their lawyers are or what the charges are.

The impact of all this on youth in juvenile court is devastating. Children represented by overworked attorneys receive the clear impression that their attorneys do not care about them and are not going to make any effort on their behalf. One youngster said that his hearing "went like a conveyor belt."

High caseloads have a debilitating impact on attorneys as well. Burnout, job dissatisfaction, and anxiety over never having enough time to do a complete job are serious problems for many caring juvenile defense attorneys. Ultimately, the results are likely to be secure detention of youth who pose no significant danger to themselves or others, reduction in the accuracy of judicial decision-making, unnecessary transfers of juveniles to the adult system, dispositions that have little connection to public safety or children's needs, and a denial of fundamental fairness.

Appointment of Counsel

It is critical that counsel appear early in the life of the case. At first appearances in court, if judges ask about the events surrounding alleged offenses, the circumstances of arrests, the roles of other youth involved, or clients' prior contacts with the juvenile justice system, and attorneys do not have answers, they lose the initial opportunity to present clients' cases in a favorable light. Judges are left to review the uncontradicted allegations in the charging petitions. Based on incomplete reviews, judges make early determinations regarding detention that may influence cases all the way until their dispositions.

Despite the importance of early and aggressive lawyering, many public defenders and court-appointed counsel do not even meet with their clients until the proceedings have begun. Indeed, many public defenders and private counsel are not appointed until the detention hearing, and in many locations, a single attorney handles most detention hearings and accepts the appointment of counsel for a panel of attorneys, then cases are sent "downtown" for proper assignment of counsel later on, delaying the beginning of actual representation for many days.

Pretrial Preparation and Trial Performance

Inquiries into pretrial motions practice and trial performance yielded important information about a number of barriers to effective representation. High caseloads again create problems. Attorneys who barely have time to cover all of their cases on a particular day do not have the time or energy to research and write effective pretrial motions. The inadequacy (or absence) of training is another serious problem, as is lack of professional supports such as specialized texts, computerized legal research, access to paralegals, availability of bilingual staff or translators, and adequate space for interviewing and meeting with clients.

In addition, courthouse culture deters many attorneys from filing motions or aggressively pursuing sound defenses at trial. In many juvenile courts there is a high premium placed on "going along" and "getting along." Many judges frown on defense attorneys who take on adversarial roles.

Disposition

Most attorneys responding to the survey reported that they can adequately prepare for disposition. At the site visits, however, a very different picture emerged: many attorneys openly acknowledged that their representation is deficient at the dispositional phase. The main reasons cited were the lack of time to keep up with placement options and other dispositional alternatives for the client, lack of time to prepare adequate dispositional plans, and an overall lack of alternatives in the system itself.

As at the other stages of representation, high caseloads make it difficult, if not impossible, for public defenders to provide effective representation at dispositions. The problem is compounded by the lack of resources and support services.

These findings are of serious concern, particularly because dispositional hearings are often the last and most important opportunity for counsel to protect their clients' interests. Although some attorneys provide excellent representation—with social workers available to conduct client evaluations and prepare individualized dispositional plans—many are unable to provide judges with any alternatives to the recommendations of probation officers.

Post-Dispositional Representation

An alarming aspect of juvenile defense is the infrequency with which appeals are taken. Public defenders rarely take appeals in juvenile cases. Among public defender offices responding to the survey, 32% are not even authorized to handle appeals. Of the offices that do handle appeals, 46% took no appeals in juvenile cases during the year prior to the survey. Appointed lawyers also take appeals rarely. Among the appointed lawyers surveyed, three-quarters were authorized to handle appeals but four out of five took none during the prior year.

Among the public defenders surveyed, almost one-third usually end their representation at the dispositional hearing. Post-dispositional review hearings can result in release or relocation of juveniles, and afford opportunities for the court to learn what is really taking place inside juvenile justice programs. Nevertheless, many defense attorneys do not view their role at such hearings as particularly "useful."

Of those public defender offices that do represent youth at post-dispositional reviews, three-fourths usually interview the youth before the hearing, but only a little over half usually review the treatment plans and interview probation or parole officers before the review hearing. Fewer than one-third of the attorney respondents usually interview treatment staff, investigate alternative placements, or monitor implementation of treatment plans for juveniles in placement.

About forty percent of the appointed lawyers surveyed end their representation after the dispositional hearing. Those who continue to provide representation at post-dispositional review hearings generally do more than public defenders—high percentages usually interview the child before the review hearing; interview probation or parole officers before the hearing; review the treatment plan; interview the child's family; and investigate alternative placements before the hearing. However, fewer than a quarter often monitor the implementation of their clients' treatment plans.

Training and Support Services

There are serious gaps in the training available to juvenile defenders: seventy-eight percent of public defender offices do not have a budget for lawyers to attend training programs; about half do not have a training program for all new attorneys, do not have an ongoing training program, and do not have a section in the office training manual devoted to juvenile delinquency practice. About forty percent do not have a specialized manual for juvenile court lawyers, and about a third do not include juvenile delinquency work in the general training program, do not have any training manual, and do not have a training unit.

Moreover, there are significant gaps in the topics covered in public defender trainings: three-quarters of the offices do not cover pretrial motions practice; two-thirds do not cover transfer of juveniles to adult court; three out of five do not cover client-specific dispositions or detention alternatives; over half do not cover child development and issues of capacity, and half do not cover how to show amenability to treatment. Juvenile defenders repeatedly told us that they need additional training on dispositional alternatives, funding mechanisms, and working with related systems such as special education.

Similarly, only 38% of the appointed lawyers reported the availability of a criminal law training program for representing indigent juvenile defendants.

Attorneys at a number of sites voiced a need for staff social workers to assist in client needs assessment and alternative disposition plans. Others spoke of the need for basic secretarial support, investigators, paralegals, and computers. Amazingly, at one site the lawyers did not even have the very basics of law practice—desks, telephones, files, or offices. They just used the bare counsel table in the courtroom, with the judge and court clerk present, to conduct their business.

More than half of the public defender offices do not have bilingual attorneys available to communicate directly with clients who speak the first most commonly spoken language other than English, and a quarter of the offices do not have any translators available for clients who speak the first most commonly spoken language other than English.

Despite conspicuous omissions, there were some sites that had very positive training programs, many of which could be emulated elsewhere. Some offices provided extensive training prior to assigning cases to lawyers; others had creative training mechanisms such as mentoring by experienced attorneys, brown bag lunches on current juvenile justice issues, or the provision of a yearly training "allowance" per attorney.

Promising Approaches to Effective Representation

While the assessment revealed substantial deficiencies in access to counsel and the quality of representation in juvenile court, it would be incorrect to conclude that effective representation of young people cannot and does not exist. Project staff observed many individual defenders around the country who were delivering first-rate legal services to their young clients. Defender programs that appear to be of high quality have a number of characteristics in common:

- Supportive structural features of the program that make effective representation possible, including limitations on caseloads, the ability to enter the case early on, and the flexibility to represent the client in related collateral matters (such as special education);

- Comprehensive initial and ongoing training, and available resource materials;

- Adequate non-lawyer support and resources;

- Hands-on supervision of attorneys;

- A work environment that values and nurtures juvenile court practice.

The negative impact of caseload pressures at every stage of the delinquency process cannot be overstated. Some defender offices have attempted to address this problem internally, by allowing attorneys to ask for temporary relief from new case assignments if their caseload is too burdensome. Other offices provide juvenile representation through a team approach, involving social workers and investigators, as well as lawyers.

REVIEW QUESTIONS

1. What was this study designed to discover and how was it conducted?
2. What were the major findings of the study?
3. In what ways do high caseloads among public defenders and other attorneys who handle juvenile delinquency cases affect the availability and quality of legal representation for accused juvenile offenders?
4. What other factors limit the availability and quality of representation?
5. What suggestions do the authors offer for improving legal representation for juveniles in court?
6. Based on your reading of this report, has the right to counsel mandated in *In re Gault* been effectively implemented in practice? Do the findings indicate that access to counsel and the quality of representation in juvenile court are generally consistent with *Gault's* mandate? If not, what improvements would be necessary to alleviate the problem?

Pleading Guilty in Juvenile Court: Minimal Ado About Something Very Important to Young Defendants

Joseph B. Sanborn Jr.

Pleading guilty is the most critical decision facing any defendant. A plea of guilty is more significant than a mere confession of guilt; it is equivalent to a conviction, where nothing remains but to proceed to sentencing (*Kercheval v. U.S.* 1927: 223).

    Whenever a defendant pleads guilty, several concerns arise as to the legitimacy of the transaction. The criminal court has resolved this issue by requiring constitutionally that the guilty plea be entered by defendants who know what they are doing (the intelligence requirement) and are doing so freely (the voluntariness requirement; see *Boykin v. Alabama* 1969: 242–43). Many states inquire on their own whether there is a reason for believing that the defendant is the person who actually committed the crime (the accuracy requirement). The judge is charged to determine that these requirements are satisfied (see ABA 1980: ch. 14); usually a colloquy is conducted, by which a defendant is examined and convinces the judge that he or she is pleading guilty intelligently and voluntarily (McDonald 1986).

Source: Joseph B. Sanborn, Jr. (1992). Pleading guilty in juvenile court: Minimal ado about something very important to young defendants. *Justice Quarterly* 9(1):127–150. Copyright 1992 by the Academy of Criminal Justice Sciences. Reprinted with Permission of the Academy of Criminal Justice Sciences.

Intelligence ordinarily is measured by the defendant's competency to plead guilty. That is, he or she must be aware of the surroundings and the purpose of the court proceedings. The defendant also should know the nature of the charges, the consequences of pleading guilty (i.e., the rights surrendered by a plea of guilty and the effects of this surrender), and the potential sentence awaiting as a result of the guilty plea (*Boykin v. Alabama* 1969; *Henderson v. Morgan* 1976; *U.S. v. Timmreck* 1979). The honoring of any plea bargains that have been made is also essential to the intelligence issue (*Santobello v. New York* 1971). If these elements have been ascertained, consensus probably would hold that the guilty plea was offered intelligently (ABA 1980: ch. 14; Barkai 1977: 90; Decker and Kennedy 1988; McDonald 1986; Newman 1966: 32–38).

Voluntariness requires that defendants know what they are doing, and are doing so free from impermissible inducements. In other words, the judge is responsible for discovering the existence of plea agreements or other pressures on the defendant to plead guilty. Then the judge must analyze whether these agreements or pressures have overwhelmed the defendant's free choice in pleading guilty, insofar as the latter is not acting voluntarily (ABA 1980: ch. 4: 29; Arenella 1980: 512; *Boykin v. Alabama* 1969; Newman 1966: 22-31).

Accuracy is the final concern. Here, the judge's duty is to guarantee that innocent persons do not plead guilty. To ensure this, the judge usually requires the prosecution to establish a factual basis for the plea of guilty from one or more sources (the defendant's statements, a police report, witnesses' accounts) (ABA 1980: ch. 14: 32; Arenella 1980: 513-16; Barkai 1977: 91; McMunigal 1989; Newman 1966: 10–21). This task, however, is not required constitutionally (*North Carolina v. Alford* 1970).

The United States Supreme Court has addressed and answered the issues of intelligence and voluntariness when adults plead guilty in criminal court. *Boykin v. Alabama* (1969) definitively states the judge's obligations when the criminal defendant pleads guilty. The requirements attending the acceptance of a guilty plea offered by a defendant in juvenile court remain unclear, however. The United States Supreme Court has not yet determined that *Boykin* applies to juvenile court. In addition, unless a particular state has made that determination, the juvenile court judge is under no obligation to follow the *Boykin* prescriptions.

There is no published research examining the guilty plea process in juvenile court; all previous research has been dedicated to the criminal court. Most of the research prior to *Boykin* found that criminal courts should conduct colloquies so as to ensure intelligent and voluntary guilty pleas (Newman 1956, 1966). Research since *Boykin* has demonstrated that in general, criminal courts have complied with *Boykin* and that guilty pleas are tendered there intelligently and voluntarily (Arenella 1980; Barkai 1977; Decker and Kennedy 1988; McDonald 1986; McMunigal 1989). Yet we are still ignorant of the status of pleading guilty in juvenile court.

THE DIMENSIONS OF THE STUDY

Research Objective, Focus, and Design

This research sought to fill the gap in knowledge regarding the practice of pleading guilty in juvenile court. I studied both national trends and local tendencies so as to discover how, if at all, juvenile court has responded to the concerns of intelligence, voluntariness, and accuracy that accompany a juvenile defendant's guilty plea.

The research focused primarily upon what the 50 states and the District of Columbia have demanded of their juvenile court judges when youths plead guilty. Accordingly, I analyzed juvenile court statutes, court rules, and appellate court decisions from all 51 jurisdictions to see what the country has decided legislatively and judicially about pleading guilty in juvenile court.

In addition, during the summer of 1988, I spent three months observing each judge in three juvenile courts. I observed each of these judges accepting at least five guilty pleas in order to discover the nature of any colloquies given to defendants who pled guilty. Finally, I interviewed 100 workers from the three courts to ascertain how these persons perceive what should happen and what is happening when a defendant pleads guilty in juvenile court (Babbie 1989; Fitzgerald and Cox 1987). Each currently sitting judge, prosecutor, and public defender, as well as a random sample of private counsel and probation officers from all three courts, participated in the study. The interviews lasted an average of 25 minutes and were conducted during the summer of 1988. . . .

DISCUSSION OF THE FINDINGS

The statutory, court rule, and case decision research reveals that much of the country either has not addressed at all or has not fully developed standards regarding the guilty plea process in juvenile court. Even among those jurisdictions which have attempted to regulate the acceptance of guilty pleas, we find considerable diversity as to what is required in the colloquy. Only nine jurisdictions demand that youths be informed of the four constitutional rights they have before pleading guilty. Although 34 jurisdictions advise defendants of possible sentences, it is unclear whether youths are required to be warned about future sentencing implications as an adult offender. Thirty-three jurisdictions require notice of charges, but it is uncertain whether offenses must be explained in language meaningful to children. Only 19 jurisdictions appear to require an explanation to the defendant that a guilty plea means that no adjudicatory hearing will be held and that trial-related rights are thereby surrendered. Finally, only 31 and 20 jurisdictions respectively call for an investigation into the voluntariness and the accuracy of the guilty plea. Only 18 jurisdictions seem to insist that the youth personally plead guilty. Obviously, then, the nation as a whole has not devoted much effort to developing standards for the juvenile court's acceptance of guilty pleas. Nevertheless, at least 17 jurisdictions appear to have required as much of guilty pleas in juvenile court as are required in criminal court.

The observation research reveals that the guilty plea processes in the urban court differ somewhat from those in the suburban and rural courts in an "unregulated" state. Whereas the urban court conducts a comprehensive colloquy at least for those age 14 and older who plead guilty to felonies and misdemeanor weapon offenses, the suburban and rural courts simply ask the youth whether the facts as related to the court are true. More important, perhaps, colloquies would not be held in the urban court if the prosecutor's office had not been so strongly determined to preserve these guilty pleas from subsequent legal attack, so as to be able to use the adjudications in future adult court sentencing.

According to the interview data, most of the sample believed both that *Boykin* should apply to juvenile court guilty pleas and that a factual basis for the guilty pleas should be established, although the suburban and rural courts were less committed to the factual basis item than was the urban court. This finding is ironic when we consider that the factual basis is the only area of inquiry in the suburban and rural courts. Also interesting is the fact that the suburban and rural courts wanted to conduct a relatively narrow inquiry (voluntary and intelligent only) but were inclined to think that all offenders should be given this abbreviated colloquy. Not surprisingly, workers in the suburban and rural courts were more likely than their urban counterparts to comment that colloquies in their courts were deficient. Respondents expressed no particular preference as to how the inquiry was to be conducted; only the suburban and rural courts seemed to prefer that the judge ask the defendant the pertinent questions. The urban court was more likely than the others to identify a problem of comprehension among guilty plea defendants. This finding probably was attributable in part to the detail and the length of the colloquy employed there. Nevertheless, the suburban and rural courts also acknowledged that juveniles often do not seem to understand what would happen when they pled guilty in juvenile court.

THE FUTURE OF PLEADING GUILTY IN JUVENILE COURT

The legal research and the research based on observation and interviews provide some reason to believe that concerns about intelligence, voluntariness, and accuracy are not always addressed or resolved when defendants plead guilty in juvenile courts. Of course it is possible that some states have fully regulated the guilty plea process, and that research in these states would not disclose problems in this area. Then again, research in "regulated" states might unveil unintelligent and not completely voluntary guilty pleas in juvenile court. At the very least, the data in this study suggest a number of conclusions.

First, more research is needed to document what occurs when youths tender guilty pleas in juvenile court. This research examined the guilty plea practices of only three juvenile courts; thus, generalizability may well be limited. Nevertheless, this study verifies that at least some juvenile courts are not observing *Boykin*. It raises a reasonable concern that other juvenile courts (particularly, perhaps, those in other "unregulated" states) are not conducting adequate colloquies when juvenile defendants plead guilty. Only further research in both "regulated" and "unregulated" states will answer this question.

Second, various states appear to be at various stages of development with respect to regulating the guilty plea process in juvenile court. Seventeen jurisdictions currently demand in juvenile court all of what Boykin requires constitutionally in criminal court. . . ; eight states require most of what *Boykin* mandates . . . ; four states provide for relatively thorough colloquies in juvenile court. Nevertheless, nearly one-half of the states have not accomplished much in regulating the guilty plea process in juvenile court. Twelve states have developed only part of the intelligence and/or voluntariness inquiries; another 10 have ignored the issue completely.

Ideally, the 17 jurisdictions that have adopted the measures called for in *Boykin* are accepting only voluntary and intelligent guilty pleas from their juvenile defendants. It is incumbent upon the remaining 34 states to legislate or establish court rules that provide for juvenile court defendants the same constitutional protections accorded adults who plead guilty in criminal court.

There appears to be no justification for denying juvenile court defendants information about the charge(s) to which they plead guilty, the constitutional rights they have and how these rights are forfeited through a guilty plea, and the short-term and long-term sentencing consequences resulting from a delinquent adjudication. Moreover, the juvenile court judge also should find that the guilty plea is voluntarily [*sic*]—free from threats, force, or impermissible inducements. Obviously, disclosure of the existence and nature of plea bargains is critical to the judge's decision as to whether the inducement to plead guilty is impermissible or overbearing. The entire inquiry should be conducted in language that the youth understands, so as to prevent the comprehension problems that were encountered in the urban court in this study.

Finally, a factual basis, although not strictly mandated by the Constitution, should be required in juvenile court guilty pleas. Juveniles may not be able to fully comprehend the charges leveled against them or to appreciate a defense they might have, which has not been apparent to others. Requiring a factual basis would give juvenile court judges much more confidence that the correct person is pleading guilty to a bona fide crime.

The juvenile court of recent years has become increasingly punitive (Krisberg et al. 1986; Regnery 1986). The atmosphere and the sentences in juvenile court are becoming more serious. This development suggests at least two reasons why *Boykin v. Alabama* should be constitutionally applied to juvenile court. First, prosecutors will need complete and constitutionally based colloquies; without such colloquies, they risk losing the use of these adjudications in subsequent adult sentencing. Second and more important, fairness dictates that youths should understand precisely what they are doing and should know the implications of pleading guilty for both current and future considerations.

REFERENCES

American Bar Association (ABA) (1980) *Standards for Criminal Justice*. Boston: Little, Brown.

Arenella, Peter (1980) "Reforming the Federal Grand Jury and the State Preliminary Hearing to Prevent Conviction Without Adjudication." *Michigan Law Review* 78: 463–585.

Babbie, Earl (1989) *The Practice of Social Research*. 5th ed. Belmont, CA: Wadsworth.

Barkai, John L. (1977) "Accuracy Inquiries for All Felony and Misdemeanor Pleas: Voluntary Pleas but Innocent Defendants." *University of Pennsylvania Law Review* 126: 88–146.

Decker, John F. and John F. Kennedy (1988) "Judicial Admonishments in Illinois Guilty Plea Proceedings." *Loyola University of Chicago Law Journal* 19: 855–931.

Fitzgerald, Jack D. and Steven M. Cox (1987) *Research Methods in Criminal Justice: An Introduction*. Chicago: Nelson-Hall.

Krisberg, Barry, Ira M. Schwartz, Paul Litsky, and James Austin (1986) "The Watershed of Juvenile Justice Reform." *Crime and Delinquency* 32: 5–38.

McDonald, William F. (1986) "Judicial Supervision of the Guilty Plea Process: A study of Six Jurisdictions." *Judicature* 70: 202–215.

McMunigal, Kevin C. (1989) "Disclosure and Accuracy in the Guilty Plea Process." *Hastings Law Journal* 40: 957–1029.

Newman, Donald J. (1956) "Pleading Guilty for Consideration: A Study of Bargain Justice." *Journal of Criminal Law, Criminology and Police Science* 46: 780–790.

_____ (1966) *Conviction: The Determination of Guilt or Innocence Without Trial.* Boston: Little, Brown.

Regnery, Alfred S. (1986) "A Federal Perspective on Juvenile Justice Reform." *Crime and Delinquency* 32: 39–51.

CASES CITED

Boykin v. Alabama, 395 U.S. 238 (1969)
Henderson v. Morgan, 426 U.S. 637 (1976)
In re Gault, 387 U.S. 1 (1967)
In re Winship, 397 U.S. 358 (1970)

Kercheval v. U.S., 274 U.S. 220 (1927)
North Carolina v. Alford, 400 U.S. 25 (1970)
Santobello v. N.Y., 404 U.S. 257 (1971)
U.S. v. Timmreck, 441 U.S. 780 (1979)

REVIEW QUESTIONS

1. Why does the author of this study think we should be concerned about the process juvenile courts follow in accepting guilty pleas?

2. What kinds of questions must a judge ask an adult defendant before accepting a guilty plea? Why are these questions important?

3. Does the Constitution require that judges ask juveniles the same kinds of questions before accepting guilty pleas from them?

4. What did the author discover about the questions judges ask juveniles (i.e., their "colloquies") about the intelligence, voluntariness, and accuracy of guilty pleas? How do the colloquies in the juvenile courts he studied compare to those in adult criminal courts? What differences did he find among urban, suburban, and rural juvenile courts?

5. Recall Scott and Grisso's discussion in Chapter 1 of the impact of developmental factors on adolescents' understanding of court proceedings and their ability to make intelligent decisions about their cases. Based on your knowledge of adolescent development and its impact on decision making, what do you think a juvenile court judge should do, and what kinds of questions should he or she ask, to make sure that juvenile defendants fully understand the implications of a guilty plea and make sound decisions about whether to plead guilty?

Sentencing in the Juvenile Justice System: Punishment and Treatment

Barry C. Feld

Most states' juvenile court statutes contain a purposes clause or preamble that articulates the underlying rationale of the legislation to aid courts in interpreting the statutes (Walkover 1984; Feld 1988*b*). The traditional purpose of juvenile courts was benevolent: "to secure for each minor . . . such care and guidance, preferably in his own home, as will serve the moral, emotional, mental, and physical welfare of the minor and the best interests of the community" (Ill. Ann. Stat. chap. 37, paras. 701–2 [Smith-Hurd 1972]) and to remove "the taint of criminality and the penal consequences of criminal behavior, by substituting therefore an individual program of counseling, supervision, treatment, and rehabilitation" (N.H. Rev. Stat. Ann. § 169-B:1 II [1979]). In the decades since *Gault* and *McKeiver,* however, more than one-quarter of the states have revised their juvenile codes' statement of legislative purpose, deemphasized rehabilitation and the child's best interest, and asserted the importance of public safety, punishment, and accountability in the juvenile justice system (Feld 1988*b*). Some courts recognize that these changes signal basic changes in philosophical direction and acknowledge that "punishment" constitutes an acceptable purpose of juvenile courts' dispositions. In *State v. Lawley,* the Washington Supreme Court reasoned in Orwellian fashion that "sometimes punishment is treatment" and upheld the legislature's conclusion that "accountability for criminal behavior, the prior criminal activity and punishment commensurate with age, crime, and criminal history does as much to rehabilitate, correct, and direct an errant youth as does the prior philosophy of focusing upon the particular characteristics of the individual juvenile" (91 Wash. 2d at 656-57, 591 P.2d at 773 [1979]). In a similar manner, the Nevada Supreme Court endorsed punishment as an appropriate function of juvenile courts. "By formally recognizing the legitimacy of punitive and deterrent sanctions for criminal offenses juvenile courts will be properly and somewhat belatedly expressing society's firm disapproval of juvenile crime and will be clearly issuing a threat of punishment for criminal acts to the juvenile population" (*In re Seven Minors,* 99 Nev. at 432, 664 P.2d at 950 [1983]).

 1. *Juvenile Court Sentencing Statutes and Dispositional Practices.* Originally, juvenile courts fashioned indeterminate and nonproportional sentences to meet the child's real

Source: Barry C. Feld. (1998). Juvenile and criminal justice systems' responses to youth violence. In Michael Tonry and Mark H. Moore (Eds.). *Youth Violence* (pp. 189–261). Chicago: The University of Chicago Press. © 1998 by The University of Chicago. Adapted by permission.

needs (Mack 1909; Rothman 1980). In principle, a youth's offense constituted only a diagnostic symptom, and treatment personnel released the offender once they determined that rehabilitation had occurred. By contrast, when courts punish offenders, they typically impose determinate or mandatory sentences based on the gravity of the past offense. Contrasting indeterminate, nonproportional, and offender-oriented dispositions with determinate, proportional, and offense-based sentences provides another indicator of juvenile courts' increasing reliance on punishment as a response to delinquency.

 a. Indeterminate and Determinate Sentences. Most states' juvenile codes authorized courts to impose indeterminate sentences because penal therapists cannot predict in advance the course or duration of treatment necessary to attain success (Mack 1909; Ryerson 1978; Rothman 1980). While some statutes instruct judges to consider the "least restrictive alternative," most allow the court to confine a delinquent within a range for a period of years or until the offender reaches the age of majority or some other statutory limit (Feld 1988b). Traditionally, juvenile court judges exercised virtually unrestricted discretion to dismiss, place on probation, remove from home, or institutionalize a youth.

 In many states, once a judge sentences a youth to the state's juvenile correctional agency, the judge loses authority over the youth, and the correctional authority or parole board determines when to release the juvenile (Krisberg and Austin 1993). Indeterminate sentencing statutes typically provide for an unspecified period of confinement and a wide range between the minimum and maximum terms available. Corrections officials base their release decisions, in part, on youths' behavior during confinement and progress toward rehabilitative goals rather than on formal standards or the committing offense (Coates, Forst, and Fisher 1985).

 By contrast, when judges sentence juveniles under a determinate or presumptive sentencing framework, they typically impose proportional sanctions within a relatively narrow dispositional range based on the seriousness of the offense, offense history, and age. In several states, courts impose mandatory minimum sentences based on the offense for which they convicted the youth. In other states, correctional administrators determine youths' presumptive length of institutional stay or eligibility for parole shortly after their commitment based on formal standards that prescribe terms proportional to the seriousness of the offense or prior record (Coates, Forst, and Fisher 1985).

 Currently, nearly half of the states use some type of determinate or mandatory minimum offense-based sentencing provisions to regulate aspects of juvenile dispositions, institutional commitment, or release (Sheffer 1995; Torbet et al. 1996). As with legislative changes in waiver statutes, amendments to juvenile court sentencing statutes allocate to the judicial, legislative, and executive branches the power to make institutional commitment and release decisions (Guarino-Ghezzi and Loughran 1996). Determinate sentencing provisions restrict judicial sentencing discretion, mandatory minimum statutes reflect legislative sentencing decisions, and correctional or parole release guidelines enable the executive branch to determine lengths of confinement. And, as with waiver, these provisions use offense criteria to rationalize sentencing decisions, to increase the penal bite of juvenile court sanctions, and to enable legislators symbolically to demonstrate their "toughness" regardless of the effect on juvenile crime rates (Altschuler 1994). It is difficult to attribute the various statutory responses exclusively to youth violence, but rather to the political "felt need" to punish serious and persistent offenders.

   b. *Determinate Sentences in Juvenile Courts.* In 1977, the state of Washington departed dramatically from traditional rehabilitative dispositions, revised its juvenile code to emphasize "just deserts," and became the first state to enact a determinate sentencing statute for delinquents (Schneider and Schram 1983; Castellano 1986). The Washington law used presumptive sentencing guidelines to achieve offender and system accountability and based youths' sentences on the seriousness and persistence of their offending rather than their real needs. The Washington guidelines created three categories of offenders—serious, middle, and minor—and imposed presumptive, determinate, and proportional sentences based on a juvenile's age, present offense, and prior record (Fisher, Fraser, and Forst 1985). The statute provided standard dispositional ranges that include both upper and lower limits, specified aggravating and mitigating factors for sentencing within the range, and allowed a judge to depart from the standard range only when imposing the presumptive sentence would result in a manifest injustice. The guidelines prohibited confinement of a first or minor offender and provided that serious offenders serve sentences ranging from 125 weeks to three years. The Washington code revisions significantly increased the proportionality of sentences and produced a stronger relationship between the seriousness of youths' offenses and their lengths of institutional stay than prevailed under the previous, indeterminate regime (Schneider and Schram 1983; Fisher, Fraser, and Forst 1985). Despite greater equality and uniformity in sentencing, social structural and geographic variations continued to produce higher rates of referral and confinement for minority youths than for white delinquents (Bridges et al. 1995).

   Other jurisdictions also employ offense-based sentencing principles in juvenile courts. In New Jersey, Juvenile court judges consider offense, criminal history, and statutory aggravating and mitigating factors to sentence juveniles (New Jersey Juvenile Delinquency Disposition Commission 1986; N.J. Stat. Ann. §§ 2A:4A-43[a], 4A-44[a], 4A-44[d] [West 1993]). Recently, Oklahoma adopted a serious and habitual juvenile offender law that targets violent youths and those persistent offenders with three separate felony adjudications and creates a mechanism to develop determinate sentencing guidelines (Okla. Stat. Ann. tit. 10 § 7303.5.3 [West 1995]). In 1994, the Arizona legislature mandated the Arizona Supreme Court to promulgate dispositional guidelines that focused on the seriousness of a youth's present offense and prior record in order to regularize judges' institutional commitment decisions (McNulty and Russell 1995). In 1996, Texas adopted "progressive sanctions guidelines" to "ensure . . . uniform and consistent consequences and punishments that correspond to the seriousness of each offender's current offense, prior delinquent history . . . [and] balance public protection and rehabilitation while holding juvenile offenders accountable" (Tex. Fam. Code Ann. § 59.001 [Vernon Supp. 1996]). The Texas guidelines assign a youth to one of seven sanction levels based on the seriousness of the offense and attach dispositional consequences to each severity level. For some proponents of a more traditional rehabilitative juvenile court, concepts like "progressive sanctions" or "graduated sanctions" represent an effort to enlist punitive principles like determinacy and proportionality in the service of treatment goals (Wilson and Howell 1995). Combining "risk assessment" with "needs assessment" permits immediate, intermediate, and increasing intervention based on seriousness and persistence (Krisberg et al. 1995).

　　c. *Legislative Sentencing Decisions—Mandatory Minimum Terms of Confinement.* Nearly half (twenty-two) of the states use some type of offense-based guidelines to regulate judicial sentencing discretion. These statutes typically include age and offense criteria to define serious or persistent offenders and prescribe their sentences (Sheffer 1995). Juvenile codes in a number of states allow or require judges to impose mandatory minimum sentences for certain serious crimes or designated felonies (Feld 1988*b*, Sheffer 1995). Under some laws, judges retain discretion whether or not to impose the mandated sanctions, whereas others require a judge to commit a youth convicted of a defined offense for the mandatory minimum period (Feld 1988*b*; Torbet et al. 1996). In Delaware, for example, judges "shall" sentence any youth convicted of any second felony within one year to a minimum term of six months confinement (Del. Code. tit. 10 § 1009).

　　While states' nomenclatures differ, these mandatory minimum sentencing laws typically apply to "violent and repeat offenders," "mandatory sentence offenders," "aggravated juvenile offenders," "habitual offenders," "serious juvenile offenders," or "designated felons" (e.g., Ala. Code § 12-15-71.1 [1990]; Colo. Rev. Stat. § 19-1-103 [1993]; Feld 1988*b*). The statutory criteria target those violent and persistent juvenile offenders over whom juvenile courts do not waive jurisdiction either because of their youthfulness or lesser culpability. Youths charged with violent crimes like murder, rape, robbery, aggravated assault or those who have prior felony convictions constitute the primary legislative concerns. Recent amendments add to these lists of serious offenders youths charged with crimes involving firearms or who commit violent or drug crimes on school grounds (e.g., Ark. Stat. § 9-27-330[c] [1989]). And, as with changes in waiver laws, the rate of legislative change accelerates. "Since 1992, fifteen states and the District of Columbia have added or modified statutes that provide for a mandatory minimum period of incarceration of juveniles committing certain violent or other serious crimes" (Torbet et al. 1996, p. 14).

　　Most of these mandatory minimum sentencing statutes target youths similar to or only somewhat less serious or younger than those considered eligible for waiver or exclusion to criminal court. In the event that juvenile courts retain jurisdiction over serious young offenders, legislators use mandatory minimum sentences to assure that judges and corrections officials confine these youths for significant terms. For youths convicted of these serious offenses, the statutes prescribe mandatory minimum terms of confinement that range from twelve to eighteen months, to age twenty-one, or to the adult limit for the same offense (Feld 1988*b*). For example, in Georgia, juvenile court judges may sentence a youth convicted of a designated felony to the Department of Youth Services for a term of five years with a minimum period of confinement of twelve months or eighteen months, depending on the offense, in a "youth development center" (Ga. Code § 15-11-37[2] [1994]). In 1990, Alabama enacted a serious juvenile offender law that provided mandatory minimum sentences—"shall be committed"—for youths convicted of a Class A felony or felonies involving physical injury or the use of a firearm (Ala. Code § 12-15-71.1[a] and [b] [1990]). In 1993, Louisiana enacted a mandatory sentencing statute that targeted youths convicted of violent felonies, for example, rape, kidnapping, and armed robbery, and provided that the juvenile "court *shall commit* the child . . . [to] *a secure detention facility* until the child attains the age of twenty-one years *without benefit* of parole, probation, suspension of imposition or execution of sentence" (emphasis added; La. Children's Code art. 897.1 [1993]). Regardless of the statutory details, mandatory minimum sentences based on youths' serious or persistent offending preclude individualized consideration of their real needs. Moreover, mandating extended minimum terms of confinement for serious offenders increases the average length of stay, increases institutional populations, and exacerbates overcrowding (Krisberg and Austin 1993).

    d. Executive Sentencing Decisions—Correctional or Parole Release Guidelines. A number of states' departments of corrections have adopted administrative security classification and release guidelines that use offense criteria to specify proportional or mandatory minimum terms of institutional confinement (Forst, Friedman, and Coates 1985; Feld 1988*b*). These guidelines constitute still another form of offense-based sentencing. Unlike presumptive or mandatory sentencing statutes that attempt to regulate judicial sentencing discretion, administrative or parole guidelines affect only those youths whom judges commit to state correctional agencies. Except when constrained by presumptive or mandatory minimum sentencing statutes, judges in most states retain discretion over the "in-out" decision whether to commit a youth.

    The Arizona legislature required its department of corrections to adopt length of confinement guidelines; the agency created five categories based on the seriousness of the commitment offense and specified mandatory minimum terms that range in length from three to eighteen months to govern juvenile release decisions (Arizona Department of Corrections 1986; Ariz. Rev. Stat. Ann. § 8-241 [1987]). Minnesota's department of corrections adopted determinate length of stay guidelines based on the present offense and other risk factors, such as the prior record and probation or parole status (Minnesota Department of Corrections 1980; Feld 1995). Georgia's Division of Youth Services employs a "uniform juvenile classification system" that classifies committed delinquents into one of five categories of "public risk" with corresponding correctional consequences primarily based on the seriousness of the present offense (Forst, Friedman, and Coates 1985). The California Youthful Offender Parole Board decides the release eligibility of juveniles committed to the Youth Authority on the basis of a seven category scale of offense seriousness (Forst and Blomquist 1991). Other states use similar offense-based classification systems to determine institutional lengths of stay and security levels of committed youths (Guarino-Ghezzi and Loughran 1996). All of these de jure sentencing provisions—determinate as well as mandatory minimum laws and correctional as well as parole release guidelines—share the common feature of offense-based dispositions. They represent different strategies to relate the duration and intensity of a youth's sentence to the seriousness of the offense and prior record.

    2. Empirical Evaluations of Juvenile Court Sentencing. Principle of Offense and Racial Disparities. Several actors in the juvenile justice process—police, intake social workers, detention personnel, prosecutors, and judges—make dispositional decisions; their decisions cumulate and affect the judgments that others make subsequently (McCarthy and Smith 1986; Bishop and Frazier 1988). Juveniles' prior records reflect the discretionary decisions that people in the justice process make over time, and previous dispositions affect later sentences (Henretta, Frazier, and Bishop 1986). Despite recent changes in sentencing laws, juvenile court judges exercise greater sentencing discretion than do criminal court judges because juvenile courts' *parens patriae* ideology still presumes a need to look beyond the offense to the child's best interests.

Within this flexible dispositional process, minority youths are disproportionately overrepresented at every stage of the juvenile justice process (Krisberg et al. 1987; Pope and Feyerherm 1990*a*, 1990*b*). An analytic review of the juvenile court sentencing research literature concluded that "there are race effects in operation within the juvenile justice system, both direct and indirect in nature" (Pope and Feyerherm 1992, p. 41). Studies consistently report racial disparities in case processing after controls for offense variables, that inequalities occur at various stages of the process in different jurisdictions, and that discriminatory decisions amplify minority overrepresentation as youths proceed through the system (e.g., Bishop and Frazier 1996).

The discretion inherent in a *parens patriae* system raises concerns that the cumulative effect of individualized decisions contributes to the substantial overrepresentation of minority youths (McCarthy and Smith 1986; Fagan, Slaughter, and Hartstone 1987; Krisberg et al. 1987; Kempf-Leonard, Pope, and Feyerherm 1995). What methodologists call sample selection bias others might view as racial discrimination. Quite apart from overt discrimination, juvenile justice personnel may view black youths as more threatening or more likely to recidivate than white youths and process them differently (Sampson and Laub 1993; Singer 1996). More benignly, if juvenile courts sentence youths on the basis of social circumstances that indirectly mirror socioeconomic status or race, then minority youths may receive more severe dispositions than white youths because of their personal characteristics or real needs.

Minority overrepresentation may also reflect racial group differences in involvement in criminal activity. If court personnel and judges base their screening decisions and youths' sentences on the seriousness of juveniles' offenses and criminal history, then minority overrepresentation may result from real differences in the incidence and prevalence of offending by race (Wolfgang, Figlio, and Sellin 1972; Hindelang 1978). Or, the structural context of juvenile justice decision making may redound to the detriment of minority juveniles. For example, urban courts tend to be more formal and to sentence all juveniles more severely (Kempf, Decker, and Bin 1990; Feld 1991, 1993*b*). Urban courts also have greater access to detention facilities, and youths held in pretrial detention typically receive more severe sentences than do those who remain at liberty (Feld 1993*b*; Bishop and Frazier 1996). A larger proportion of minority youths reside in urban settings, and police disproportionately arrest and detain them for violent and drug crimes (Snyder and Sickmund 1995). Thus crime patterns, urbanism, "underclass threat," and race may interact to produce minority overrepresentation in detention and institutions (Sampson and Laub 1993).

a. The Principle of the Offense. Despite sometimes discrepant findings, two general conclusions emerge clearly from the research evaluating juvenile court sentencing practices. First, the "principle of offense"—present offense and prior record—accounts for virtually all of the variance in juvenile court sentences that can be explained. Every methodologically rigorous study of juvenile court sentencing practices reports that judges focus primarily on the seriousness of the present offense and prior record when they impose sentences; these legal and offense variables typically explain about 25–30 percent of the variance in sentencing (Clarke and Koch 1980; McCarthy and Smith 1986; Fagan, Slaughter, and Hartstone 1987; Bishop and Frazier 1996). In short, juvenile court judges attend to the same primary sentencing factors as do criminal court judges. Second, after controlling for legal and offense variables, the individualized justice of juvenile courts produces racial disparities in the sentencing of minority offenders (McCarthy and Smith 1986; Krisberg et al. 1987; Bishop and Frazier 1996). Other than the principle of offense—present offense, prior record, previous disposition—and age, gender, and detention status, youths' race appears as a significant factor in most multivariate sentencing studies (Pope and Feyerherm 1992; Bishop and Frazier 1996).

While youths' chronic or serious offending may indicate greater treatment needs, courts necessarily respond to their criminal behavior regardless of their ability to change it. Practical administrative and bureaucratic considerations induce juvenile court judges to give primacy to offense factors when they sentence juveniles. Organizational desire to avoid public exposure, unfavorable political and media attention, and "fear of scandal" constrain judges to impose more restrictive sentences on more serious offenders (Matza 1964; Cicourel 1968; Emerson 1969). Moreover, present offense and prior record provide efficient organizational tools with which to classify youths on the basis of the risk they pose to the public and of the scandal to the court and provide a court with a means to rationalize, defend, and legitimate its decisions.

b. Racial Disparities. The second consistent finding from juvenile court sentencing research is that, after controlling for the present offense and prior record, individualized sentencing discretion is often synonymous with racial discrimination (McCarthy and Smith 1986; Fagan, Slaughter, and Hartstone 1987; Krisberg et al. 1987; Pope and Feyerherm 1990*a*, 1990*b*, 1992). In 1988, Congress amended the juvenile justice and Delinquency Prevention Act to require states receiving federal funds to assure equitable treatment on the basis, inter alia, of race and to assess the sources of minority overrepresentation in juvenile detention facilities and institutions (42 U.S.C. § 5633[a][16] [1993 Supp.]). In response to this mandate, a number of states examined and found racial disparities in their juvenile justice systems (e.g., Bishop and Frazier 1988, 1996; Pope and Feyerherm 1992; Krisberg and Austin 1993; Bridges et al. 1995; Kempf-Leonard, Pope, and Feyerherm 1995). A summary of these evaluation studies reported that, after controlling for legal variables, forty-one of forty-two states found minority youths overrepresented in secure detention facilities, and all thirteen of thirteen states that analyzed other phases of juvenile justice decision making found evidence of minority overrepresentation (Pope 1994).

Discretionary decisions at various stages of the justice process amplify racial disparities as minority youths proceed through the system and result in more severe dispositions than for comparable white youths. The research emphasizes the importance of analyzing juvenile justice decision making as a multistage process rather than focusing solely on the final dispositional decision. For example, dramatic increases in referral rates of minority youths to juvenile courts in seventeen states result in corresponding increases in detention and institutional placement (McGarrell 1993). Juvenile courts detain black youths at higher rates than they do white youths charged with similar offenses, and detained youths typically receive more severe sentences (Bortner and Reed 1985; Frazier and Cochran 1986; Feld 1989, 1993b; Krisberg and Austin 1993). A national study of incarceration trends reported confinement rates for minority youths three to four times greater than those of similarly situated white juveniles and that judges sentenced proportionally more minority youths to public secure facilities and committed more white youths to private facilities (Krisberg et al. 1987). By 1991, juvenile courts confined less than one-third (31 percent) of non-Hispanic white juveniles in public long-term facilities; minority youths made up more than two-thirds (69 percent) of confined youths (Snyder and Siclunund 1995). Juvenile courts committed black juveniles at a rate nearly five times higher than that for white youths, and blacks made up half (49 percent) of all youths in institutions (Snyder and Sickmund 1995).

Juvenile courts, as extensions of criminal courts, give primacy to offense factors when they sentence youths. To the extent that *parens patriae* ideology legitimates individualization and differential processing, it also exposes "disadvantaged" youths to the prospects of more extensive state intervention. Of course, if states provided exclusively benign and effective treatment services to youths, then this might mute some of the concerns about racial disparities. . . .

REFERENCES

Altschuler, David M. 1994. "Tough and Smart Juvenile Incarceration: Reintegrating Punishment, Deterrence, and Rehabilitation." *St. Louis University Public Law Review* 14:217–44.

Bishop, Donna M., and Charles S. Frazier. 1988. "The Influence of Race in Juvenile Justice Processing." *Journal of Research in Crime and Delinquency* 25:242–63.

_____. 1996. "Race Effects in Juvenile Justice Decision-Making: Findings of a Statewide Analysis." *Journal of Criminal Law and Criminology* 86:392–413.

Bortner, M. A., and W. L. Reed. 1985. "The Preeminence of Process: An Example of Refocused Justice Research." *Social Science Quarterly* 66:413–25.

Bridges, George S., Darlene J. Conley, Rodney L. Engen, and Townsand Price-Spratlen. 1995. "Racial Disparities in the Confinement of Juveniles: Effects of Crime and Community Social Structure on Punishment." In *Minorities in Juvenile Justice,* edited by K.

Kempf-Leonard, C. Pope, and W. Feyerherm. Thousand Oaks, Calif.: Sage.

Castellano, Thomas C. 1986. "The Justice Model in the Juvenile Justice System: Washington State's Experience." *Law and Policy* 8:397–418.

Cicourel, Aaron V. 1968. *The Social Organization of Juvenile Justice.* New York: Wiley.

Clarke, Stevens H., and Gary G. Koch. 1980. "Juvenile Court: Therapy or Crime Control, and Do Lawyers Make a Difference?" *Law and Society Review* 14:263–308.

Coates, Robert, Martin Forst, and Bruce Fisher. 1985. *Institutional Commitment and Release Decision-Making for Juvenile Delinquents. An Assessment of Determinate and Indeterminate Approaches—a Cross-State Analysis.* San Francisco: URSA Institute.

Emerson, Robert M. 1969. *Judging Delinquents: Context and Process in Juvenile Court.* Chicago: Aldine.

Fagan, Jeffrey, Ellen Slaughter, and Eliot Hartstone. 1987. "Blind Justice? The Impact of

Race on the Juvenile Justice Process." *Crime and Delinquency* 33:224–58.

Feld, Barry C. 1988a. "*In re Gault* Revisited: A Cross-State Comparison of the Right to Counsel in Juvenile Court." *Crime and Delinquency* 34:393–424.

_____. 1988b. "Juvenile Court Meets the Principle of Offense: Punishment, Treatment, and the Difference It Makes." *Boston University Law Review* 68:821–915.

_____. 1989. "The Right to Counsel in Juvenile Court: An Empirical Study of When Lawyers Appear and the Difference They Make." *Journal of Criminal Law and Criminology* 79:1185–1346.

_____. 1991. "Justice by Geography. Urban, Suburban, and Rural Variations in Juvenile Justice Administration." *Journal of Criminal Law and Criminology* 82:156–210

_____. 1993a. "Criminalizing the American Juvenile Court." In *Crime and Justice: A Review of Research,* vol. 17, edited by Michael Tonry. Chicago: University of Chicago Press.

_____. 1993b. *Justice for Children: The Right to Counsel and the Juvenile Court.* Boston: Northeastern University Press.

_____. 1995. "Violent Youth and Public Policy: A Case Study of Juvenile Justice Law Reform." *Minnesota Law Review* 79:965–1128.

Fisher, Bruce, Mark Fraser, and Martin Forst. 1985. *Institutional Commitment and Release Decision-Making for Juvenile Delinquents. An Assessment of Determinate and Indeterminate Approaches, Washington State—A Case Study.* San Francisco: URSA Institute.

Forst, Martin, and Martha-Elin Blomquist. 1991. "Cracking Down on Juveniles: The Changing Ideology of Youth Corrections." *Notre Dame Journal of Law, Ethics and Public Policy* 5:323–75.

Forst, Martin, Elizabeth Friedman, and Robert Coates. 1985. *Institutional Commitment and Release Decision-Making for Juvenile Delinquents. An Assessment of Determinate and Indeterminate Approaches, Georgia—A Case Study.* San Francisco: URSA Institute.

Frazier, C. E., and J. K. Cochran. 1986. "Detention of Juveniles: Its Effects on Subsequent Juvenile Court Processing Decisions." *Youth and Society* 17:286–305.

Guarino-Ghezzi, Susan, and Edward J. Loughran. 1996. *Balancing Juvenile Justice.* New Brunswick, NJ.: Transaction.

Henretta, John, Charles Frazier, and Donna Bishop. 1986. "The Effects of Prior Case Outcomes on Juvenile Justice Decision-Making." *Social Forces* 65:554–62.

Hindelang, Michael. 1978. "Race and Involvement in Common Law Personal Crimes." *American Sociological Review* 43:93–109.

Kempf, Kimberly L., Scott H. Decker, and Robert L. Bin. 1990. *An Analysis of Apparent Disparities in the Handling of Black Youth within Missouri's Juvenile Justice Systems.* St. Louis: University of Missouri, Department of Administration of Justice.

Kempf-Leonard, Kimberly, Carl Pope, and William Feyerherm. 1995. *Minorities in Juvenile Justice.* Thousand Oaks, Calif.: Sage.

Krisberg, Barry, and James Austin. 1993. *Reinventing Juvenile Justice.* Thousand Oaks, Calif: Sage.

Krisberg, Barry, Elliot Currie, David Onek, and Richard G. Wiebush. 1995. "Graduation Sanctions for Serious, Violent, and Chronic Juvenile Offenders." In *A Sourcebook: Serious, Violent, and Chronic, Juvenile Offenders,* edited by James C. Howell, Barry Krisberg, J. David Hawkins, and John J. Wilson. Thousand Oaks, Calif: Sage.

Krisberg, Barry, Ira Schwartz, Gideon Fishman, Zvi Eisikovits, Edna Guttman, and Karen Joe. 1987. "The Incarceration of Minority Youth." *Crime and Delinquency* 33:173–205.

Mack, Julian W. 1909. "The Juvenile Court." *Harvard Law Review* 23:104–22.

Matza, David. 1964. *Delinquency and Drift.* New York: Wiley.

McCarthy, Belinda, and Brent L. Smith. 1986. "The Conceptualization of Discrimination in the Juvenile Justice Process: The Impact of Administrative Factors and Screening Decisions on Juvenile Court Dispositions." *Criminology* 24:41–64.

McGarrell, Edmund F. 1993. "Trends in Racial Disproportionality in Juvenile Court Processing: 1985–1989." *Crime and Delinquency* 39:29–48.

McNulty, Elizabeth W., and J. Neil Russell. 1995. *Juvenile Commitment Guidelines Departure Research Project.* Phoenix: Arizona Supreme Court.

Minnesota Department of Corrections. 1980. *Juvenile Release Guidelines.* St. Paul: Minnesota Department of Corrections.

Pope, Carl E. 1994. "Racial Disparities in Juvenile Justice System." *Overcrowded Times* 5(6):1, 5–7.

Pope, Carl E., and William H. Feyerherm. 1990a. "Minority Status and Juvenile Justice Processing: An Assessment of the Research Literature (Part I)."*Criminal Justice Abstracts* 22:327–35.

_____. 1990b. "Minority Status and Juvenile Justice Processing: An Assessment of the Research Literature (Part II)."*Criminal Justice Abstracts* 22:527–42.

_____. 1992. *Minorities and the Juvenile Justice System.* Washington, D.C.: Office of Juvenile Justice and Delinquency Prevention.

Rothman, David J. 1980. *Conscience and Convenience: The Asylum and Its Alternative in Progressive America.* Boston: Little, Brown.

Ryerson, Ellen. 1978. *The Best-Laid Plans. America's Juvenile Court Experiment.* New York: Hill & Wang.

Sampson, Robert J., and John H. Laub. 1993. "Structural Variations in Juvenile Court Processing: Inequality, the Underclass, and Social Control." *Law and Society Review* 27: 285–311.

Schneider, Anne L., and Donna Schram. 1983. *A Justice Philosophy for the Juvenile Court.* Seattle: Urban Policy Research.

Sheffer, Julianne P. 1995. "Serious and Habitual Juvenile Offender Statutes: Reconciling Punishment and Rehabilitation within the Juvenile Justice System." *Vanderbilt Law Review* 48:479–512.

Singer, Simon I. 1996. *Recriminalizing Delinquency: Violent Juvenile Crime and Juvenile Justice Reform.* New York: Cambridge University Press.

Snyder, Howard N., and Melissa Sickmund. 1995. *Juvenile Offenders and Victims: A National Report.* Washington, D.C.: Office of Juvenile Justice and Delinquency Prevention.

Torbet, Patricia, Richard Gable, Hunter Hurst IV, Imogene Montgomery, Linda Szymanski, and Douglas Thomas. 1996. *State Responses to Serious and Violent Juvenile Crime. Research Report.* Washington, D.C.: Office of Juvenile Justice and Delinquency Prevention, National Center for Juvenile Justice.

Walkover, Andrew. 1984. "The Infancy Defense in the New Juvenile Court." *University of California Los Angeles Law Review* 31:503–62.

Wilson, John J., and James C. Howell. 1995. "Comprehensive Strategy for Serious, Violent, and Chronic Juvenile Offenders." In *A Sourcebook: Serious, Violent, and Chronic Juvenile Offenders,* edited by James C. Howell, Barry Krisberg, J. David Hawkins, and John J. Wilson. Thousand Oaks, Calif.: Sage.

Wolfgang, Marvin, Robert Figlio, and Thorsten Sellin. 1972. *Delinquency in a Birth Cohort.* Chicago: University of Chicago Press.

REVIEW QUESTIONS

1. What kinds of dispositions ("sentences") did early juvenile courts impose? In what way were they "indeterminate" and why were such dispositions considered appropriate?

2. What are offense-based (i.e., determinate, presumptive, and mandatory) sentences? How are they different from the sanctions in traditional juvenile courts?

3. About how many states have begun using offense-based sentencing provisions in juvenile court? What are some examples of offense-based sentencing schemes?

4. Why do you think states have begun turning to offense-based sentencing in juvenile court? In what ways does it seem preferable to indeterminate sentences? In what ways does it seem undesirable?

5. How do correctional administrators determine length of confinement in some states?

6. What is the "principle of the offense"? How does it influence sentencing in juvenile court?

7. According to Feld, what is the primary source of racial disparities in juvenile court dispositions? Why does he think that basing sanctions on the principle of offense reduces racial disparities? What evidence does he present to support his argument?

8. All things considered, do you think it is preferable for juvenile courts to impose indeterminate dispositions oriented primarily toward treatment and rehabilitation, or should more explicitly punitive offense-based dispositions be employed? What is your reasoning?

Judicial Disposition/Sentencing Authority: Blended Sentencing

Patricia Torbet, Richard Gable, Hunter Hurst IV, Imogene Montgomery, Linda Szymanski, and Douglas Thomas

Blended sentencing statutes represent a dramatic change in dispositional/sentencing options available to judges. Blended sentencing refers to the imposition of juvenile and/or adult correctional sanctions to cases involving serious and violent juvenile offenders who have been adjudicated in juvenile court or convicted in criminal court. Blended sentencing options are usually based on age or on a combination of age and offense. For the purpose of this report, blended sentencing sanctions dispensed by either juvenile or criminal court judges are distinguished from the programming changes that have occurred within State adult and juvenile correctional systems. . . .

Five basic models of blended sentencing have emerged in recent legislation. . . . Each of the models applies to a subset of alleged juvenile offenders specified by State statute, usually defined by age and offense. In three of the models, the juvenile court retains responsi-

Source: Patricia Torbet, Richard Gable, Hunter Hurst IV, Imogene Montgomery, Linda Szymanski, and Douglas Thomas. (1996). *State Responses to Serious and Violent Juvenile Crime.* Washington, DC: Office of Juvenile Justice and Delinquency Prevention. Copyright 1996 by the National Center for Juvenile Justice. Adapted by permission.

bility for adjudicating the case. In the remaining models, the criminal court has jurisdiction for trying the case.

Moreover, the models represent "exclusive" sanctioning (either juvenile or adult sanctions), "inclusive" sanctioning (both juvenile and adult sanctions), or "contiguous" sanctioning (first juvenile, then adult sanctions). The five models "blend" sentencing options in the following ways:

- Juvenile—Exclusive Blend: The juvenile court imposes a sanction involving either the juvenile correctional system or the adult correctional system.

- Juvenile—Inclusive Blend: The juvenile court simultaneously imposes both a juvenile correctional sanction and an adult correctional sanction, which is suspended pending a violation and revocation.

- Juvenile—Contiguous: The juvenile court imposes a juvenile correctional sanction that may remain in force beyond the age of its extended jurisdiction, at which point various procedures are invoked to transfer the case to the adult correctional system.

- Criminal—Exclusive Blend: The criminal court imposes either a juvenile or adult correctional sanction.

- Criminal—Inclusive Blend: The criminal court imposes both a juvenile and an adult correctional sanction and suspends the adult sentence pending a violation or re-offense. . . .

JUVENILE—EXCLUSIVE BLEND

The New Mexico statute is the singular example of a sentencing option in which the juvenile court can impose a sanction involving either the juvenile or the adult correctional system. The legislature created a "youthful offender" category, including juveniles age 15 charged with first-degree murder; 15- to 17-year-olds charged with a felony in addition to having three prior separate felony adjudications in a 2-year period; and 15- to 17-year-olds charged with a variety of serious offenses. (These offenses are not subject to judicial waiver, and only juveniles ages 16 or 17 and charged with first-degree murder are excluded from juvenile jurisdiction.)

The juvenile court has original jurisdiction over youthful offenders, and the juvenile has the right to jury trials, counsel, open hearings, and bail. If adjudicated, the juvenile judge has discretion to impose either an adult or a juvenile sanction. For an adult sentence, the judge can impose up to the adult mandatory term. The prosecutor must file a motion within 10 days of filing a petition asking the judge to apply adult sanctions. In imposing a juvenile sanction, the judge may sentence the juvenile either to 2 years or until he reaches the age of 18, whichever is longer (unless he is discharged sooner). The Juvenile Parole Board participates in the determination of a juvenile's release date.

JUVENILE—INCLUSIVE BLEND

Minnesota, Connecticut, and Montana statutes are examples of the sentencing option that allows the juvenile court to impose a sanction involving both juvenile and adult correctional systems. The Minnesota legislature applied that option to a new legal category of juvenile referred to as extended jurisdiction juvenile prosecution (EJJP). A Supreme Court task force recommended the new category be created to provide a viable dispositional option for juvenile court judges facing juveniles who have committed serious or repeat offenses and to give juveniles one last chance at success in the juvenile system, with the threat of adult sanctions as a disincentive (Minnesota Supreme Court, 1994). The criteria for determining whether the proceeding is an EJJP include:

- A juvenile 14 to 17 years old, where a certification hearing was held and the court designated the proceeding an EJJP.

- A juvenile 16 or 17 years old who committed an offense that carries a presumptive prison commitment or who committed any felony involving a firearm, and the prosecutor designated in the petition that the proceeding is an EJJP.

- A juvenile 14 to 17 years old, and the prosecutor requested the proceeding be designated an EJJP, a hearing was held on the issue of designation, and the court designated the proceeding an EJJP.

If an EJJP results in a guilty plea or a finding of guilt, the juvenile court shall impose one or more juvenile dispositions and impose a criminal sentence, the execution of which is stayed on the condition that the offender not violate the provisions of the disposition order and not commit a new offense. The juvenile court retains jurisdiction over extended jurisdiction juveniles to age 21. Juveniles have the right to a jury trial and effective assistance of counsel.

JUVENILE—CONTIGUOUS

Four States (Colorado, for "aggravated juvenile offenders"; Massachusetts; Rhode Island; and Texas) have recently enacted a sentencing option that allows the juvenile court to impose a sanction that may remain in force beyond the age of its extended jurisdiction, at which point various procedures are invoked to transfer the case to the adult correctional system. (South Carolina's statute is longstanding; however, it is not used.) Texas has a determinate sentencing act that, by virtue of the length of the sentence imposed, is an example of a contiguous blended sentencing statute. Since 1987, a juvenile court judge or jury could impose a sentence of any length from 1 to 30 years. From the beginning, the law protected the rights of juveniles in jeopardy of such sentences by requiring (1) a grand jury to consider and approve the petition charging 1 or more of the eligible offenses and (2) a 12-person jury at adjudication and disposition phases of juvenile court proceedings.

Upon sentencing, the juvenile is incarcerated in Texas Youth Commission (TYC) facilities. The original legislation stipulated that the juvenile could be released only after a hearing before the committing juvenile court. If the juvenile is not released by age 17 1/2, the juvenile court must hold a transfer hearing to decide whether to release the juvenile from the TYC on parole or to order him transferred to the Texas Department of Corrections (DOC) to serve the balance of the sentence.

In 1995 the legislature enhanced the law to provide for determinate sentences of up to 40 years, mandatory minimum sentences for certain offenses, and 15 additional offenses for which a determinate sentence could be delivered. They also eliminated the requirement for the transfer hearing and prohibited the court or the TYC from discharging a juvenile before the completion of his sentence. The law is considered by many an effective tool for punishing violent and chronic offenders while giving them a final chance with incentive to access the rehabilitative programs of the juvenile system (Dawson, 1995).

CRIMINAL—EXCLUSIVE BLEND

The Florida statute is an example of an "exclusive blended sentence" option wherein the criminal court can impose either a juvenile or an adult correctional sanction. California, Colorado (for "youthful offenders"), Idaho, Michigan, and Virginia also enacted such provisions. The Florida legislature expanded their direct-file and exclusion provisions in 1994, thereby providing the mechanism for a wide range of juveniles to be tried in criminal court. As a balance to those measures, the legislature gave the criminal court the latitude to apply either juvenile or adult sanctions to these juveniles. Both the DOC and the Department of Juvenile Justice jointly prepare a report for the sentencing hearing regarding the suitability of the offender for disposition in their respective systems. After consideration of the report and comment by parties to the case, the criminal court judge considers a set of statutorily defined criteria to determine whether to impose youthful offender or juvenile offender sanctions instead of adult sanctions. However, a decision by the court to impose adult sanctions is presumed appropriate, and the court is not required to set forth specific findings or enumerate the statutory criteria as a basis for its decision to impose adult sanctions. If the criminal court decides to impose juvenile sanctions, the juvenile is adjudicated delinquent and committed to the Department of Juvenile Justice. If the criminal court imposes a youthful offender sanction, the juvenile is convicted as an adult and is committed to the youthful offender program within the DOC.

CRIMINAL—INCLUSIVE BLEND

Only two States, Arkansas and Missouri, have a sentencing provision that allows the criminal court to impose a sanction involving both the juvenile and adult correctional systems. In 1995 Missouri passed legislation that allows the criminal court to invoke the dual jurisdiction of both the juvenile and criminal codes when a juvenile offender has been transferred to criminal court. Juveniles ages 12 to 17 charged with any felony, or any juvenile charged with one of seven violent offenses or who committed two or more prior unrelated felonies, may be waived to criminal court. If the juvenile is found guilty, the criminal court is authorized to impose a juvenile disposition and a criminal disposition simultaneously. Execution of the criminal sentence is suspended during imposition of the juvenile disposition. The statute contains provisions for revoking the juvenile disposition and invoking the criminal sentence for violations of conditions of the imposed disposition. The Arkansas statute is rarely used. . . .

REFERENCES

Dawson, R. O. (ed.). *State Bar Section Report on Juvenile Law: Special Legislative Issue,* 9(3), August 1995.

Feld, B. C. "Violent Youth and Public Policy: A Case Study of Juvenile Justice Law Reform." *Minnesota Law Review,* 79(5), May 1995.

Minnesota Supreme Court. *Advisory Task Force on the Juvenile Justice System: Final Report.* St. Paul, Minnesota: Supreme Court, 1994.

REVIEW QUESTIONS

1. What are the five basic models of blended sentencing? What are the principal similarities and differences among them?
2. How do blended sentencing structures differ from the mechanisms for transfer to adult criminal court discussed in Chapter 7? In what ways are they similar?
3. Which (if any) of the mechanisms for blended sentencing discussed in this selection seem(s) most appropriate in response to serious juvenile delinquency? Which seem(s) least appropriate? Do any seem preferable to the basic transfer mechanisms discussed in Chapter 7? What is your reasoning?

FURTHER READING

Bazemore, Gordon, and Feder, Lynette. (1997). Judges in the punitive juvenile court: Organizational, career and ideological influences on sanctioning orientation. *Justice Quarterly,* 14(1), 87–114.

Burruss, Jr., George W., and Kempf-Leonard, Kimberly. (2002). The questionable advantage of defense counsel in juvenile court. *Justice Quarterly,* 19(1), 37–67.

Feld, Barry C. (1988). *In re Gault* revisited: A cross-state comparison of the right to counsel in juvenile court. *Crime and Delinquency,* 34(4), 393–424.

———. (1988). Juvenile court meets the principle of offense: Punishment, treatment, and the difference it makes. *Boston University Law Review,* 68(5), 821–915.

———. (1989). The right to counsel in juvenile court: An empirical study of when lawyers appear and the difference they make. *Journal of Criminal Law and Criminology,* 79(4), 1185–1346.

_____. (1993). *Justice for Children: The Right to Counsel and the Juvenile Courts.* Boston: Northeastern University Press.

Mears, Daniel P. (2002). Sentencing guidelines and the transformation of juvenile justice in the 21st Century. *Journal of Contemporary Criminal Justice, 18*(1), 6–19.

Mears, Daniel P., and Field, Samuel H. (2000). Theorizing sanctioning in a criminalized juvenile court. *Criminology, 38*(4), 983–1019.

Sanborn, Joseph B. Jr. (1993). Philosophical, legal and systemic aspects of juvenile court plea bargaining. *Crime and Delinquency, 39*(4), 509–527.

_____. (2001). A *parens patriae* figure or impartial fact finder: Policy questions and conflicts for the juvenile court judge. *Criminal Justice Policy Review, 12*(4), 311–332.

Tittle, Charles R. and Curran, Debra A. (1988). Contingencies for dispositional disparities in juvenile justice. *Social Forces, 67*(1), 23–58.

Tufts, Jennifer, and Roberts, Julian V. (2002). Sentencing juvenile offenders: Comparing public preferences and judicial practice. *Criminal Justice Policy Review, 13*(1), 46–64.

CHAPTER

9

Juvenile Corrections

Despite the ascendancy of punitive statutory schemes and "get-tough" policies in juvenile court, the treatment orientation continues to dominate the philosophy—if not always the practice—of juvenile corrections. Recall from Chapter 2 that the *parens patriae* rhetoric used by the Pennsylvania Supreme Court to legitimate involuntary commitment of Mary Ann Crouse to the Philadelphia House of Refuge in the 1830s was grounded in the reformist practices alleged to characterize what the court quaintly dubbed "the charity." Some 70 years later, Judge Mack drew upon the same rehabilitative philosophy to justify the informal character of the Chicago juvenile court, emphasizing the importance of placement in "a real school, not a prison in disguise" (see p. 63). Even during the due process revolution of the 1960s and 1970s, appellate courts continued to assert a "right to treatment" as the *quid pro quo* for the juvenile court's continued use of informal procedures that did not ensure all of the procedural safeguards (e.g., jury trials) guaranteed by the Constitution for adults facing conviction in criminal court.

Dating also from the early days of the Houses of Refuge, however, reality has often diverged radically from the rehabilitative rhetoric of juvenile corrections. Early descriptions of harsh daily regimes in Houses of Refuge (as quoted in the introduction to Chapter 2) suggest that even in the 1800s there was substantial empirical support for the decision of the Supreme Court of Illinois—bucking the otherwise nearly unbroken line of cases supporting the *parens patriae* authority to institutionalize a child without a formal trial—that, despite the rhetoric, a reformatory was indeed a prison and that placement in such an environment was indeed punishment, which could not be inflicted in the absence of conviction for a crime (*People v. Turner,* 55 Illinois 280 [1870]). And evidence is mounting that the correctional abuses to which the U.S. Supreme Court pointed in *Gault* did not emerge gradually, but were present in juvenile training schools even in the earliest days of the juvenile courts founded by Judge Mack and his Progressive contemporaries. As historian

David Rothman (1980) noted in *Conscience and Convenience,* his seminal history of Progressive Era approaches to crime, delinquency, and mental illness:

> The descent from the rhetoric to the reality of juvenile institutions is precipitous. The ideals that justified incarceration had little relevance to actual circumstances. No matter how frequently juvenile court judges insisted that their sentences of confinement were for treatment and not punishment, no matter how vehemently superintendents declared that their institutions were rehabilitative and not correctional, conditions at training schools belied these claims. . . . The closer the scrutiny of juvenile confinement, the more inadequate and, indeed, punitive, the programs turned out to be.
>
> "When is a school not a school?" asked one reformatory superintendent. "When it is a school for delinquents." (pp. 268–269 [endnotes omitted])

Today, extraordinary variation can be found in styles of juvenile correctional intervention—in both the nonresidential programs youth on probation may be required to attend and in secure and nonsecure residential facilities for adjudicated delinquents who are placed in such facilities pursuant to court order. The selections in this chapter provide an overview of some of the most intractable problems as well as some of the most promising trends in contemporary juvenile corrections. We begin with a survey of conditions of confinement in secure facilities. Conducted in 1991–1992, the study by Dale Parent and his colleagues at Abt Associates of Cambridge, Massachusetts focused on both public facilities (i.e., training schools) and facilities operated by private organizations but available for secure placement of adjudicated delinquents. (Not included in the survey were the many group homes, emergency shelters, hospitals, and other nonsecure facilities in which juveniles are also often housed. Nor did the study address conditions for those juveniles who continue to experience temporary detention in adult jails and lockups despite the JJDP Act's mandates.) Although the researchers found little evidence of the horrors earlier investigations had logged, they also discovered that few institutions were problem-free, and they catalogued an array of problems related to such diverse aspects of juvenile confinement as living space, security, controlling suicidal behavior, and health care.

Next, Paul Holland and Wallace J. Mlyniec rhetorically ask, "Whatever happened to the right to treatment?" They seek—in legislative purpose clauses and other state statutory provisions relating to juvenile corrections—an alternative legal foundation for guaranteeing rehabilitative correctional programming to replace the now largely attenuated notion of a Constitutional right to treatment grounded in the due process clause of the Fourteenth Amendment.

The final selection in this chapter turns our attention away from the shortcomings of contemporary juvenile correctional facilities and takes a long look at programs that have proven to be remarkably successful. Included in OJJDP's *Guide for Implementing the Comprehensive Strategy for Serious, Violent, and Chronic Juvenile Offenders* (we will encounter Wilson and Howell's original statement of the forward-looking and highly influential *Comprehensive Strategy* in Chapter 10), the selection begins with an effort to identify characteristics of effective juvenile correctional programs. Then, based on an extensive review of intervention programs, the authors describe a total of 14 exemplary ones—spanning all three levels of sanction identified in the *Comprehensive Strategy's* proposal for a system of "graduated" sanctions implementing progressively restrictive modes of intervention. Although discussion of published evaluations of these programs has been omitted from the selection due to space limitations, the program descriptions are included in their entirety as a means of introducing readers to the variety of intervention paradigms currently employed in the field of juvenile corrections.

REFERENCE

Rothman, David J. (1980). *Conscience and Convenience: The Asylum and its Alternatives in Progressive America.* Boston: Little, Brown.

Conditions of Juvenile Confinement

Dale G. Parent

In 1988, Congress required the Office of Juvenile Justice and Delinquency Prevention (OJJDP) to study conditions of juvenile confinement, to assess the extent to which conditions conformed to requirements of nationally recognized standards, and to make recommendations for improvement. OJJDP selected Abt Associates to conduct the study.

The study covered all 984 public and private detention centers, reception centers, training schools and ranches, camps, and farms in the United States. In 1991, these facilities held around 65,000 juveniles each day, about 69% of the confined juveniles in the United States. About 30,000 juveniles were held each day in shelters, halfway houses, and group homes, facilities that were excluded from this study. This study also excluded adult facilities that hold juveniles who were sentenced as adults and secure hospital-based treatment programs for juveniles.

To judge conditions in facilities, 46 assessment criteria were defined based on the most important needs of confined juveniles, as determined by a board of expert advisors. The criteria were arrayed into 12 topic areas, which in turn, were grouped into four categories (see Table 9.1).

To develop operational measures for the assessment criteria, we consulted requirements of nationally recognized standards, particularly those promulgated by the American Correctional Association, the American Bar Association, and the National Commission on

Table 9.1

Category	Topic Area	Number of Assessment Criteria
Basic needs	1. living space	3
	2. health care	6
	3. food, clothing, and hygiene	4
	4. accommodations	4
Order and safety	5. security	3
	6. controlling suicidal behavior	4
	7. inspections and emergency preparedness	4
Programming	8. education	4
	9. recreation	1
	10. treatment	2
Rights	11. access to community	5
	12. limits on staff discretion	6
Total		46

Correctional Health Care. For each assessment criterion, we determined conformance rates, expressed as the percentage of juveniles confined in facilities that conformed to each specific criterion. We also examined other data on conditions related to each topic area. For example, with respect to the assessment criterion on provision of volunteer programming, we collected and analyzed additional data on the number of hours of volunteer programming provided each week. For a number of particularly important topic areas, we also collected and analyzed data on pertinent outcome measures. For example, under security we computed juvenile and staff injury rates as well as escape and attempted escape rates. Under controlling suicidal behavior we computed rates of suicidal behavior in facilities.

We decided that if serious problems existed based on consideration of conformance to assessment criteria, other data on conditions, and, where applicable, outcome measures would be examined. We also conducted regression analysis to identify juvenile and facility characteristics that were related to conformity, conditions, or outcomes.

Data for the study came from the 1991 Children in Custody (CIC) Census, a special mail survey sent to all 984 facilities in August 1991, and from 2-day site visits to 95 facilities conducted between September 1991 and January 1992.

RECENT TRENDS IN JUVENILE CONFINEMENT

Before describing our findings, it is important to describe juvenile confinement trends. Admissions to juvenile facilities have risen since 1984 and reached an all-time high of nearly 690,000 in 1990. The largest increase was in detention, where admissions rose from just over 400,000 in 1984 to about 570,000 in 1990. The population of confined juveniles (based on CIC 1-day counts) has risen from about 50,800 in 1979 to about 65,000 in 1991.

The populations of all types of facilities except ranches have increased. Likewise, the number of confinement facilities has increased from 930 in 1979 to 984 in 1991; all facility types increased in numbers, except ranches.

There also have been recent shifts in characteristics of confined juveniles. The percentage who are minority rose from 53% to 63% with the biggest increases among Blacks (37% to 44%) and Hispanics (13% to 17%). The percentage confined for crimes against persons rose from 21% to 28%, drug-related offenses rose from 6% to 10% and property offenses declined from 40% to 34%. Between 1987 and 1991 the percentage of males among confined juveniles rose from 85% to 88%.

FINDINGS

Few facilities are without any deficiencies on our assessment criteria. But few facilities fail a large number of assessment criteria. This means that conditions of juvenile confinement will not be changed materially by reforms aimed only at eliminating or upgrading a small number of bad facilities. Rather, to make substantial improvements broad-scale reforms affecting routine practices in many facilities will be needed.

In three topic areas, conditions of confinement appear to be adequate: food, clothing, and hygiene; recreation; and living accommodations. We have no recommendations for improvements in these areas.

With respect to inspections and emergency preparedness, most juveniles are confined in facilities that have passed recent state or local fire, life safety, and sanitation inspections. Despite that, during site visits we observed a large number of facilities in which fire exits were not marked, fire escape routes were not posted in living units, and a few in which fire exits were blocked with furniture or other objects. *We recommend that state and local fire codes for juvenile facilities should be toughened and enforced more vigorously.*

Access to the community appears adequate for most confined juveniles. However, although almost all juveniles can place a limited number of telephone calls per week, 45% are in facilities that do not permit them to receive telephone calls. Just 71% of all confined juveniles, and 63% of those in training schools, have access to legal services while confined. Although policies generally do not discourage visitation by parents, immediate family members, or attorneys, training schools and ranches frequently are located far from juveniles' home communities (an average of more than 58 miles); therefore, distance frequently diminishes visitation.

There is high conformity to most criteria that limit staff discretion. However, search authorization is an exception: Most confined juveniles are in facilities where line staff can authorize room searches and frisks. A substantial minority are in facilities where line staff can authorize strip searches. Few facilities permit body cavity searches and rates of body cavity searching are low. However, in the few facilities that conduct body cavity searches, line staff typically are permitted to authorize them.

In three topic areas—education, health care, and treatment services—conformity to assessment criteria is generally high, but we have no data on confined youths' educational, health, or treatment needs and problems. Hence we cannot determine whether facilities provide appropriate programs or whether juveniles make progress during confinement. Three major new initiatives are needed to periodically collect such data.

We recommend that existing public health surveillance systems be expanded to include and separately track confined juveniles. We also recommend a general review of the health needs of and services received by confined juveniles based on a review of medical records of a national sample of confined juveniles.

We recommend that federal agencies support funding of a study to document educational needs and problems of confined juveniles and to evaluate the capacity of educational programs in confinement facilities to serve those needs and to address those problems.

We recommend that federal agencies support funding of a study to document treatment needs of and services received by confined juveniles, based on a study of a national sample of confined juveniles.

In four topic areas—living space, security, prevention of suicidal behavior, and health care—facilities display substantial and widespread deficiencies.

Living Space

Crowding is a pervasive problem in juvenile facilities. It is evident facilitywide, in living units, and in sleeping rooms.

In 1987, 36% of confined juveniles were in facilities whose populations exceeded their reported design capacity. By 1991, that increased to 47%. In 1991, one third of confined juveniles were in living units with 26 or more juveniles, and one third slept in rooms that were smaller than required by nationally recognized standards. To eliminate crowded sleeping rooms, slightly over 11,000 juveniles would have to be removed from the average daily population of confinement facilities, or an equal number of new beds provided in adequately sized sleeping rooms.

Facilities have responded to crowding by restricting intake (particularly in detention), by granting early releases (particularly in training schools), and by refusing to take new admissions when populations reach capacity (particularly in ranches). As a result, although crowding has become more widespread since 1987, population levels in crowded facilities have remained at about 120% of reported design capacity.

We found that rates of juvenile-on-staff injuries were higher in crowded facilities. Search rates were also higher in crowded facilities. In addition, as the percentage of juveniles housed in dormitories with 11 or more residents increased, rates of juvenile-on-juvenile injuries increased. Crowded facilities are more dangerous places for both staff and juveniles.

We recommend that large dormitories should be eliminated from juvenile facilities. No new facilities should be built that contain large dormitories. Large dormitories in existing facilities should be replaced as soon as possible.

Facilities can cushion the effects of crowding, but they cannot alter decisions by police, prosecutors, juvenile judges, and probation and parole officers that cause crowding. *We recommend that jurisdictions develop policies that regulate the use and duration of juvenile confinement and that guide future development of confinement and nonconfinement placement options.*

To do this, states need to implement a planning process that identifies decisions that affect use of confinement, identifies characteristics of juveniles processed through the system, and that documents capacities of confinement and nonconfinement placement options.

Security

Security practices are intended to prevent escapes and to provide a safe environment for both juveniles and staff. There are high levels of nonconformity with our security assessment criteria and substantial problems with escapes and injuries in juvenile facilities.

Of confined juveniles, 62% are in facilities that classify those admitted on the basis of risk and use results to make housing assignments. Just 36% are in facilities whose supervision staffing ratios conform to the assessment criterion.

In the 30 days before the mail survey nearly 2,000 juveniles (slightly over 3% of the juvenile population) and 651 staff (slightly over 1.7% of all staff) were injured in juvenile facilities. Rates of injury were highly variable. About 10% of confined juveniles were in facilities where 8% or more of the juveniles were injured in the 30 days before the mail survey, and 1% were in facilities where one fourth or more of the juveniles were injured during that time. A small number of facilities were similarly dangerous for staff. About 10% of juveniles were in facilities where 5% or more of staff were injured in the 30 days before the mail survey, and 1% were in facilities where 17 or more of staff were injured during that time.

As mentioned earlier, we found that juvenile-on-staff injury rates were higher in crowded facilities. We also found that juvenile-on-juvenile injury rates increased as the percentage of juveniles housed in large dormitories increased. Injury rates for both staff and juveniles were higher in facilities where living units were locked 24 hours a day. Interestingly, the percentage of juveniles convicted of violent crimes was not related to injury rates.

Classification is supposed to protect juveniles by assessing their propensity to violence and by separating potential predators and victims. However, we found no relationship between conformity to the classification assessment criterion and rates of injury. The reasons are not clear. It is possible that existing juvenile classification procedures do not reliably distinguish violence-prone youth or that crowding either diminishes facilities' ability to adequately separate predators and victims or increases the probability that confined youth will encounter violence-prone peers. More study of classification is needed to determine how to improve it.

During site visits, facility administrators and staff frequently said that facilities would be safer if staffing ratios improved. Our study did not support that position: We found no relationship between supervision staffing ratios and rates of injury. However, we found that higher supervision staff turnover rates were associated with increased staff-on-juvenile and juvenile-on-staff injury rates. Thus less experienced staff are more likely to be injured by juveniles and are more likely to injure juveniles.

In the 30 days before the mail survey, over 1,600 juveniles (about 2.5% of the confined population) attempted to escape from confinement facilities, and just over 800 of them (about 1.2% of the confined population) succeeded.

We found no relationship between conformity to the classification criteria and escape rates. A growing number of facilities rely on perimeter fences as an obstacle to escape. Since

1987, the percentage of facilities with perimeter fences increased from 38% to 47%. However, we found no conclusive relationship between perimeter fences and escape rates.

We recommend that juvenile justice agencies conduct detailed comparative studies of facilities with low and high escape and injury rates to identify policies and practices that can materially improve safety and security. These studies should pay special attention to procedures used to classify juveniles and the ways in which classification is used. *We also recommend extensive comparative studies of conditions in facilities with high and low rates of use of search, isolation, and restraints, to identify and test rationales for these variations in practice.*

Controlling Suicidal Behavior

Suicidal behavior is a serious problem in juvenile confinement facilities. Ten confined juveniles killed themselves in 1990. In the 30 days before the mail survey 970 juveniles committed 1,487 acts of suicidal behavior (that is, attempted suicides, made suicide gestures, or engaged in self-mutilation). Thus about 1.6% of confined juveniles engaged in suicidal behavior during this time. There were 2.4 suicidal behavior incidents for every 100 confined juveniles in the 30 days before the mail survey. If that period was typical, more than 11,600 confined juveniles engaged in over 17,800 acts of suicidal behavior in 1991.

About half the confined juveniles are in facilities that monitor suicide risks at least every 4 minutes. Most are in facilities that have written suicide prevention plans. About three fourths are in facilities that screen juveniles for indicators of suicide risk at time of admission and train staff in suicide prevention.

Our analysis showed that facilities that conduct suicide screening at admission have lower rates of suicidal behavior. We also found that as supervision staff turnover rates increased, suicidal behavior rates increased.

We found that suicidal behavior rates increased as the percentage of juveniles in single rooms increased and as the rate of short-term (1 to 24 hours) isolation increased. We found, however, that facilities frequently fail to cover housing for suicidal juveniles in their written suicide prevention plans.

Other suicide prevention measures—training staff, frequent monitoring, and written suicide prevention plans—were not associated with suicidal behavior rates. Such measures may, however, be important in preventing completed suicides.

We recommend that suicidal juveniles not be assigned to single rooms or be isolated without continuous direct supervision. We also recommend that agencies study supervision staff turnover rates and develop strategies to reduce turnover rates and to soften their impact by increased training.

Health Care

The major problems with health care are that health screenings (done at admission to identify youth who require immediate medical services) and health appraisals (complete physical examinations within 7 days of admission) often are not completed in a timely fashion. Over 90% of confined juveniles get health screenings at some point, but only 43% get them within 1 hour of admission, as required by nationally recognized standards. Similarly, 95%

get health appraisals at some point, but only 80% get them within a week. Improved timing for completion of screenings and appraisals would greatly increase conformity rates.

One third of the juveniles in detention centers have health screenings done by staff who have not been trained by medical personnel to perform health screening. Because the purpose of health screening is to identify acute injuries or health problems that require immediate attention, using untrained staff to perform the screening is cause for concern. *We recommend that juvenile justice agencies act to ensure that initial health screenings are carried out promptly at admission and to ensure that health appraisals are completed or received within a week after admission. We also recommend that juvenile justice agencies take steps to develop and ensure the use of an adequate training program for nonmedical staff who conduct health screenings.*

PERFORMANCE-BASED STANDARDS

A substantial proportion of existing nationally recognized standards focus on developing written policies and procedures, or attaining specified staffing ratios, rather than defining outcomes that facilities should achieve. Performance-based standards are more difficult to formulate because they require those who draft standards to agree on the outcomes that should be achieved. In many instances, we found that conformity to procedural standards had no discernible effect on conditions within facilities. *We recommend that organizations that develop nationally recognized standards for juvenile facilities promulgate measurable performance standards that can serve both as goals for facilities to attain and as benchmarks against which their progress can be measured.* Such standards are particularly important in areas of security, health care, education, and treatment programming.

FURTHER RESEARCH

There is substantial variation among facilities on three outcome measures—rates of escape (and attempted escape), injury, and suicidal behavior—and extreme variation among facilities on two control mechanisms—searches and isolation. Only a small amount of that variation can be explained by juvenile or facility characteristics in our analytical models. *We recommend further study of why facilities vary so dramatically in the ways they exercise control and the extent to which they provide a safe and secure environment.*

Although we discovered some important differences between crowded and noncrowded facilities, the nature of our study (that is, a national mail survey of all facilities) limited the analytic and control variables on which we could collect data. *We recommend that OJJDP support controlled research to study the effects of crowding on juvenile and staff behavior and on outcomes in detention and corrections facilities.*

On several important outcome measures our study provides data at one point in time. It is important to collect such data on a regular basis to identify trends. *We recommend that the biennial Children in Custody Census be modified to routinely collect data on staff turnover rates, use of isolation and searching, and the incidence of injuries, escapes, and suicidal behavior.*

About 30,000 juveniles are confined in halfway houses, group homes, and shelters. Another 10,000 juveniles are believed to be serving sentences in adult prisons. The number of juveniles confined in secure hospital-based treatment programs is unknown. No data exists on the conditions of confinement experienced by juveniles in these categories of facilities that were excluded from this study. *We recommend that OJJDP support additional studies of conditions of confinement for three groups of juveniles not covered in this study: (a) those placed in halfway houses, group homes, and shelters; (b) those sentenced as adults and confined in adult prisons; and (c) those confined in secure hospital-based treatment programs.*

REVIEW QUESTIONS

1. How was the study described in this report conducted? How many facilities were involved? What aspects of juvenile confinement were assessed? Can you tell what sorts of criteria were used for assessment? How was the information collected?
2. What aspects of juvenile confinement did the researchers find to be generally adequate?
3. For which aspects were the researchers unable to find sufficient information for assessment? What are their recommendations for improving collection of information relating to these topic areas?

4. What topic areas investigated in this study require the most improvement? Are the problems identified in the report generally confined to a small number of facilities or do most facilities need improvement in these areas?
5. What were the major problems with respect to living space? Security? Controlling suicidal behavior? Health care? Do the recommended reforms in each of these topic areas seem sufficient to address the problems described? Are they feasible?

Whatever Happened to the Right to Treatment?: The Modern Quest for a Historical Promise

Paul Holland and Wallace J. Mlyniec

Since the creation of the first juvenile court in 1899, state training schools have been the primary place of confinement for children removed from their homes. Although the rhetoric of the Progressive Reformers created an impression that children placed out of their homes by juvenile court judges would reside in pleasant cottages staffed with benevolent substitute parents, most children lived in large impersonal institutions. The cause of their

Source: Paul Holland and Wallace J. Mlyniec. (1995). Whatever happened to the right to treatment?: The modern quest for a historical promise. *Temple Law Review, 68,* 1791–1835. Copyright 1995 by Temple Law Review. Adapted by permission.

removal from their homes was irrelevant. Delinquent children, status offenders, and neglected children were placed together with a promise of care and rehabilitation. Notwithstanding their idyllic-sounding names and their laudatory purposes, the institutions have historically been understaffed, unhealthy, and devoid of rehabilitative programming. Many were, and some continue to be, extremely dangerous places for children. By the time the "children's rights revolution" began in the 1960s, it was clear to any observer that the promise of the juvenile court had never been fulfilled. Indeed, the United States Supreme Court stated in 1966 that "[t]here is evidence . . . that the child receives the worst of both worlds: that he gets neither the protection accorded to adults nor the solicitous care and regenerative treatment postulated for children."

Between 1972 and 1982, in an effort to ameliorate wretched institutional conditions, advocates for children filed suits in state and federal courts arguing that children confined in state training schools had both a statutory and constitutional "right to treatment." Although the cases produced few court opinions, the litigation induced many state and county governments to improve the conditions in state training schools.

The proponents of a right to treatment asserted that if a state takes custody of a child for a rehabilitative purpose, it must provide treatment to effectuate that rehabilitation. This assertion had historical validity. The rehabilitation of wayward children was the goal of the Progressive Reformers who led the juvenile court movement. The Progressives sought the creation of a juvenile court which would act as *parens patriae,* that is, "parent of the country." In the Progressives' view, the juvenile court judge was not to adjudicate and sentence the youth, but was to identify the conditions which had led him astray and to "treat" him for those conditions. The treatment provided would be guidance and care to steer the youth away from a life of crime and immorality. Thus, the original and subsequent juvenile court statutes promised that children who were removed from their families by a judge would receive the care, custody, and discipline that their parents should have provided.

Relying on the historical promise of the juvenile court and on contemporary cases concerning mental health facilities, judges began to rule that children sent to a state training school had a right to treatment.[1] The rulings were based on the purpose clauses of state juvenile codes, the substantive and procedural prongs of the Due Process Clause of the Fourteenth Amendment to the United States Constitution, and the Cruel and Unusual Pun-

---

[1]The first case to suggest a right to treatment was Inmates of Boys' Training Sch. v. Affleck, 346 F. Supp. 1354, 1367 (D.R.I. 1972) (enjoining defendants from practices which were anti-rehabilitative because they violated juveniles' equal protection and due process rights). In Martarella v. Kelley, 349 F. Supp. 575, 600 (S.D.N.Y. 1972), the court more explicitly upheld the right to treatment by stating that "[a] new concept of substantive due process is evolving in the therapeutic realm. . . . Its implication is that effective treatment must be the *quid pro quo* for society's right to exercise its *parens patriae* controls." *Id.* at 600 (quoting Nicholas N. Kittrie, *Can the Right to Treatment Remedy the Ills of the Juvenile Process?,* 57 Geo. L.J. 848, 851–52 (1969)).

ishment Clause of the Eighth Amendment.[2] Although some courts began to question the existence of the right as early as 1973,[3] the doctrine sustained litigation against state institutions for juveniles throughout the 1970s.[4]

In 1983, the United States Supreme Court wrote its only opinion about the right to treatment in the case of *Youngberg v. Romeo*.[5] Although this case involved a challenge to the training program in a mental retardation facility, it has affected litigation in the juvenile justice context as well. Similarly, cases beginning with *Rhodes v. Chapman*[6] and continuing through *Farmer v. Brennan*,[7] which curtailed the scope of the Eighth Amendment in prison conditions cases,[8] have also had an effect. These opinions have drastically limited the prospects for constitutional relief for children residing in institutions.

While some of the most egregious abuses described in the pleadings and opinions of the 1970s have abated, many training schools remain ill-equipped to provide children living in them with the education, behavior modification, counseling, substance abuse treatment, and the mental and physical health care they need. The laws of most states still promise such care. In recent years, however, a wave of legislation increasing the severity with which children who break the law are treated has compromised that promise. Legislatures have introduced punishment into juvenile codes, authorized mandatory minimum commitments in the juvenile justice system, and expanded the possibilities for prosecuting children in criminal courts. Some juvenile courts now have the power to impose a criminal sentence as part of a juvenile disposition, with the criminal sentence stayed—either temporarily or permanently—depending upon the youth's performance during the course of the juvenile disposition.

---

[2]*See, e.g.,* Nelson v. Heyne, 355 F. Supp. 451, 459 (N.D. Ind. 1973) (holding that right to treatment is guaranteed by Indiana law and United States Constitution), *aff'd*, 491 F.2d 352 (7th Cir.), *cert. denied*, 417 U.S. 976 (1974).

[3]*See* New York State Ass'n for Retarded Children, Inc. v. Rockefeller, 357 F. Supp. 752, 762 (E.D.N.Y. 1973) (holding that due process does not guarantee right to treatment).

[4]Cases continue to be filed even today but far less often than in the earlier period.

[5]457 U.S. 307 (1982). The Court held that the respondent, who was profoundly retarded and confined to a state mental facility, had a constitutionally protected interest in "minimally adequate or reasonable training to ensure safety and freedom from undue restraint." *Id.* at 319, 324. Previously, in 1975, Justice Burger had referred to the legal weakness of the arguments supporting the right in his concurring opinion in O'Connor v. Donaldson, 422 U.S. 563, 587–89 (1975) (Burger, J., concurring).

[6]452 U.S. 337 (1981). The Court held that "double celling," which is putting two prisoners in the same cell, did not violate the constitutional protection against cruel and unusual punishment. *Id.* at 349.

[7]114 S. Ct. 1970 (1994).

[8]*Id.* at 1984. In *Farmer,* a transsexual was housed with the general prison population. The Court held that "a prison official may be held liable under the Eighth Amendment for denying humane conditions of confinement only if he knows that inmates face a substantial risk of serious harm and disregards that risk by failing to take reasonable measures to abate it."

In the face of this ferment, we write this article with several purposes. We seek to re-assess the constitutional right to treatment doctrine, test its continued validity in light of recent judicial opinions and legislative changes, and suggest a different formulation of a state's obligation toward delinquent children in its care. In so doing, we show that although changes in statutes and judicial opinions will affect the lives of institutionalized children, the far greater cause for concern is the repeated failure of governments to allocate resources to effective rehabilitative programs. We will also demonstrate that even in the harsher juvenile justice system wrought by modern legislatures, states remain obligated to provide institutionalized children with a program of care and services that will assist their development. Despite the current trend, state laws preserve their original rehabilitative goals and form the heart of delinquent children's right to receive such care and services. Simply put, states are obligated to serve as the substitute parents they promise to be. They are responsible, along with parents, for ensuring that the children in their care master the identifiable skills needed to develop into responsible and productive adult citizens. This understanding of the state's role accommodates appropriate punishment and accountability alongside care and rehabilitation. Although courts can play a role in overseeing the provision of these services and in enforcing children's rights to receive them, decisions made by communities serving as parents will ultimately determine the life chances of delinquent children. . . .

IV. EFFECTIVE REHABILITATIVE CARE AND APPROPRIATE PUNISHMENT (IN THEORY AND IN STATE LAW)

As the constitutional right to treatment withered, rehabilitation lost its place as the sole purpose of juvenile justice systems in several states. Legislatures have explicitly endorsed punishment, accountability, and other principles besides rehabilitation within the juvenile justice system. Some disposition statutes, which formerly focused almost exclusively on the needs of the offender, now include mandatory minimum terms of commitment based solely on the instant offense or the child's record of offenses.

Although these developments represent a dramatic change in the design of the juvenile justice systems of some states, they do not warrant the conclusion that the provision of rehabilitative care is no longer an essential aspect of modern juvenile justice. Most state juvenile codes contain express promises of rehabilitative care. Several state courts have recently reaffirmed the rehabilitative approach to juvenile justice. Additionally, every juvenile court in the country exercises jurisdiction as *parens patriae*. For a century, this doctrine has committed the state to providing delinquent children with substituted parental care. As it has from the beginning, this means care that will enable children to develop into adults who are capable of meeting their own needs, providing for their families, and contributing positively to their communities.

Indeed, even states endorsing punishment remain committed to rehabilitation. California, for example, has authorized only "punishment that is consistent with the rehabilitative objectives" of its code and has expressly excluded retribution from the definition of "punishment" within the juvenile code. Washington's Supreme Court has stated that under the Juvenile Justice Act "the purposes of rendering a child accountable for his acts, punishing him and exacting retribution from him are tempered by, and in some cases must give way to, purposes of responding to the needs of the child." By making rehabilitation the measure of appropriate punishment, these states have manifestly reaffirmed a commitment to providing rehabilitative care to delinquent children even while they seek to achieve other goals as well.

In the District of Columbia, where the juvenile justice code does not mention punishment, the highest court, in *In re L.J.*, recognized its proper place, even in a jurisdiction "firmly committed to a rehabilitative approach." Describing the role of a modern juvenile court confronting a frightening level of violence, the court explained that "rehabilitation is not necessarily synonymous with leniency."

> [A] disposition judge may reasonably conclude that the judicial system can significantly contribute to the rehabilitation of a delinquent by teaching him that conduct does have consequences and that, so far as the judge can make them so, the results of antisocial behavior are predictable. Many, perhaps most, youngsters can respond to a rational message. If you do well, good things happen to you. If you commit a little crime, you pay a little price. If you commit a greater crime, the pain is a little greater. A first offense can be treated leniently, but if you do it again, you are subject to an escalating series of winces— and you had better believe it because the judge does not promise severe consequences and then just slap your wrist. That is an approach that a youngster can at least potentially understand.

Relying on settled notions of *parens patriae* authority rather than a recent legislative endorsement of punishment, this opinion demonstrates that appropriate punishment, like appropriate care, is inherent in the traditional conception of the juvenile court. The United States Supreme Court had long since acknowledged this. In *McKeiver v. Pennsylvania*, the Court referred repeatedly to a task force report which stated in part, "[w]hat should distinguish the juvenile from the criminal courts is greater emphasis on rehabilitation, not exclusive preoccupation with it."

The infliction of punishment has coexisted with the promise of rehabilitation for as long as delinquent children have been securely confined. The belief that confinement ever could be wholly rehabilitative and not at all punitive ignores the experience of the confined children. To them, confinement is punishment, no matter what a judge, counselor, or correctional officer calls it, and no matter how helpful or rehabilitative it actually is. Acknowledging the existence and even inevitability of punishment in juvenile justice does not render rehabilitation unattainable or dispensable. The challenge today, as ever, is to insure that meaningful rehabilitation accompanies the inevitable punishment. The problem is a practical one, not a doctrinal one. States need only take advantage of existing knowledge about what programs are effective and provide sufficient funds and facilities for their operation.

Even staunch supporters of rehabilitative programs recognize the usefulness of appropriate sanctions in assisting a delinquent child's development. Barry Krisberg has written and spoken often of the potential benefits from programs based on the principle of "graduated sanctions," which he describes as follows:

> A model system of graduated sanctions should combine reasonable, fair, humane and appropriate penalties with rehabilitative services. There must be a continuum of care consisting of a variety of diverse programs. Youths should move between different levels on the continuum based on their behavior. Offenders must understand that they will be subject to more severe sanctions should they continue to reoffend.

There is an unmistakable similarity between this description and the earlier statement quoted from *In re L.J.* This balance between discipline and support, and the limited place of punishment in the California and Florida codes are consistent with accepted notions of child-rearing. As parents may lawfully impose discipline, so may the state as it seeks to guide delinquent children in their development into responsible adults. The higher profile given to punishment and accountability in recent legislation should not divert attention away from the still-present promise to provide rehabilitative care. All children must learn discipline and responsibility.

Krisberg demonstrates the necessary interplay between sanctions and services. The Office of Juvenile Justice and Delinquency Prevention reached this same conclusion with respect to the most serious juvenile offenders and the most extreme sanction: confinement. A 1994 report concluded that "secure sanctions are most effective in changing future conduct when they are coupled with comprehensive treatment and rehabilitation services." Our own observations representing delinquent children for a combined total of thirty years add further support for these conclusions.

Because children pass beyond the jurisdiction of the juvenile justice system at a certain age, a state's failure to care properly for the children in its custody not only harms the children themselves, it undermines the community's interest in safety and order. If children leave the state's care without having learned how to behave lawfully, deal with conflict, control emotions, or relate to others, and without the ability to earn a living or to further their education, they are at grave risk of committing additional offenses, thereby causing injury to some other person and further reducing their own prospects for development. The potential harm increases if children leave the state's care with an oppositional attitude toward authority due to the juvenile justice system's lack of concern for their well-being.

Statutes and cases from several states recognize this vital interrelationship between the provision of effective rehabilitative services, the imposition of sanctions, and the protection of the public interest. Maryland offers a striking example of the way in which legislators struggle to find language to synthesize these goals. The statute governing dispositions in delinquency cases states that "[t]he priorities in making a disposition are the public safety and a program of treatment, training, and rehabilitation best suited to the physical, mental and moral welfare of the child consistent with the public interest." The clause begins with "public safety," moves to a comprehensive look at the child's needs, and then turns back to "the public interest." The importance of meaningful rehabilitative care is not lost amid the legislature's obvious and twice-stated concern for public safety. The Court of Appeals of

Maryland has "repeatedly said that the foremost consideration in a juvenile proceeding after a determination of delinquency is to provide children with a program of treatment and rehabilitation." Just as care can co-exist with punishment in a properly functioning juvenile justice system, so must a concern for public safety be tied to a responsibility to rehabilitate delinquent children. In fact, public safety cannot likely be maintained unless children receive the care which they need and which the law promises them.

V. THE RIGHT TO REHABILITATIVE CARE AND SERVICES UNDER STATE LAW

The codes of several states contain specific provisions requiring that delinquent children receive the care and services they need. Illinois, for example, guarantees to every child subject to the jurisdiction of the juvenile court the "right to services necessary to his or her proper development, including health, education, and social services." Similarly, New Hampshire's purpose clause describes the court's mission of providing "the protection, care, treatment, counseling, supervision, and rehabilitative resources which [a child within the court's jurisdiction] needs and has a right to receive," while Kentucky's juvenile code states that "any child brought before the court under [the juvenile code] shall have a right to treatment reasonably calculated to bring about an improvement in his condition." West Virginia law spells out the rights of confined juveniles in detail, including the rights to education, exercise, medical care, nutritious meals, and freedom from physical force and solitary confinement. Florida's delinquency system is charged with providing substance abuse treatment to children and families "as resources permit." A command such as this means that the agency must exhaust all resources in providing such services. The codes of Arizona and California provide that delinquent children "shall receive" "rehabilitation services" and "care, treatment, and guidance" respectively. The use of the term "right" and the command "shall receive" indicates that these statutes create rights which may be enforceable in both individual cases and class-action litigation whenever the states fail to provide appropriate services. Iowa and Texas both require that before a court can issue certain orders removing a delinquent child from his home, the court must certify that reasonable efforts have been made to prevent the need for removal. One Iowa court has recognized that "[t]he reasonable efforts requirement provides a child's attorney a strong tool for enforcing client's [sic] rights to services and family integrity." These examples demonstrate that state legislatures have not forsaken rehabilitation as a goal of the juvenile justice system even as some have introduced notions of punishment and accountability.

Several state courts have ruled that delinquent children committed to the custody of the state have rights under state law to rehabilitative treatment which will advance their development. Significantly, one of the most recent of these opinions was issued in Washington, the first state to list punishment as a goal of the juvenile justice system. In *State v. S.H.*, the Washington Court of Appeals concluded that the purpose clause of the statute imposed a duty upon the state to provide treatment to every child whose custody was based on a need for treatment. The court noted that the state did not even contest the existence of this duty. Finally, the court described the right, stating that where the length of the disposition imposed was based on the child's need for treatment, the child "must receive adequate, individualized treatment provided by qualified persons, and the treatment must continue and be beneficial to the juvenile for the length of the disposition."

The Supreme Court of West Virginia has referred to the existence of a statutory right to individualized treatment on several occasions. This right extends beyond the entitlements to services specifically listed in the code and is based instead on the "rehabilitative goal" announced in the state's purpose clause. Officials are "required to act in the best interest of the child and the public in establishing an individualized program of treatment which is directed toward the needs of the child and likely to result in the development of the child into a productive member of society." For as long as a child is subject to juvenile court jurisdiction, the court must act "to secure immediately the petitioner's placement in an appropriate juvenile rehabilitation and treatment facility whose program is designed to meet the petitioner's individual needs."

Without expressly articulating a right to rehabilitative care, the Montana Supreme Court has ruled that under that state's Youth Court Act, a trial court may not order that a delinquent child be placed at a facility which is incapable of meeting the child's recognized needs. In addition, a judge on the District of Columbia Court of Appeals has written in a concurring opinion that the District has an obligation to "adhere to applicable rehabilitative standards" in caring for the delinquent children in its custody. The fact that the author of this opinion was also the author of the opinion in *In re L.J.* provides another example of the inescapable connection between the imposition of sanctions and the provision of rehabilitative services in an effective juvenile justice system.

Courts regularly invoke the "rehabilitative" nature of the juvenile justice system as a justification for differential treatment which children (or their attorneys) perceive as detrimental to their interests, such as the denial of the right to a jury trial, or the possibility of longer confinement than would be visited upon an adult convicted of the same offense. The Washington Supreme Court rejected a jury demand, notwithstanding the statutory recognition of punishment, based on the court's conclusion that the juvenile justice system remained rehabilitative. Although both the right to a jury trial and the right to equal protection are guaranteed by the Federal Constitution, such rulings reinforce a claim for rehabilitative care under state law. It cannot be, or at least should not be, significant that the system is rehabilitative when this undermines children's claims, yet insignificant when it bolsters them. However, judicial reluctance to look behind the legislative declaration of a rehabilitative purpose and see the reality of children's experiences in inadequate facilities often thwarts efforts to make the promise a reality.

Although there is no consensus concerning the programs a state should or must operate to fulfill its obligation of adequate rehabilitative care, it is universally acknowledged that states must offer education services, both general and vocational. The importance of education to children's development and their life chances is obvious. All states require children to attend school up to a certain age. Parents who fail to ensure that their children attend school may be subject to criminal prosecutions, neglect proceedings, or the reduction of welfare benefits. States exercising *parens patriae* authority over delinquent children have the same responsibility for ensuring that the children in their care receive educational services.

The general duty to provide rehabilitative services to children in state custody necessarily includes the obligation to provide education. Specific statutory provisions granting general rights to services would necessarily include a right to receive education. Consent decrees governing juvenile justice systems contain specific provisions concerning the education of detained youth. State regulations often also contain standards for the education which delinquent children in state care are to receive. While education is not a fundamental right under the Federal Constitution, children in detention may have claims under the Due Process or Equal Protection Clauses of the Fourteenth Amendment if they are denied the education which state law promises. Many state constitutions require the legislature to provide a system of free schools wherein all the children of the state may be educated. Some variation from the program provided in the public schools would be acceptable if necessary to accommodate the state's security or disciplinary concerns. Deficiencies which cannot be justified by such concerns are illegitimate and should not be tolerated. There are few reported opinions on this subject, due in part, no doubt, to the fact that few people would claim with a straight face that children in state custody should not be educated.

Delinquent children in state care are also entitled to receive special education and related services pursuant to the Individuals with Disabilities Education Act (IDEA). Under IDEA, all states receiving federal assistance under the statute are obligated to identify all disabled children (as defined by the statute) and provide them with a free appropriate public education, including special education and related services. Special education means specially designed instruction to meet the unique needs of the disabled child. Related services means "such developmental, corrective, and other supportive services as are required to assist a child with a disability to benefit from special education." Congress has expressly listed state agencies such as departments of mental health and welfare and correctional facilities as within the statute's scope. Juvenile justice systems in any state receiving federal funds under IDEA must identify disabled children in their care, promptly devise an appropriate plan for them, and provide the necessary services. Studies and litigation from across the country have revealed grave deficiencies in all of these areas.

The cases and statutes discussed in this section demonstrate that delinquent children have rights to rehabilitative care based on state law. These rights are distinct from any constitutional claim and retain their force even within a system which avowedly punishes youths. This right includes the right to receive adequate education services, but goes much further, reaching all types of care necessary to fulfill the states' promise of rehabilitation, training, and substituted parental care. . . .

IX. CONCLUSION

In the first century of the juvenile court's existence, providing effective rehabilitative care to delinquent children has proven to be as difficult as it is important. Even in good juvenile justice systems, courts struggle with the limits of their authority and expertise, and agencies struggle to help each child amid the competing claims of other children for the same resources and the clamor of the community for protection from these very same children.

In the many dysfunctional juvenile justice systems across this country, these inherent tensions spill over into chaos that deprives children of opportunities and keeps communities fearful. There are no magic words to make these problems go away. Lawyers cannot assert a "right to treatment" and expect judges to nod, administrators to cower, nightmarish conditions to vanish, and effective programs to appear. At most, this once-prominent doctrine forbids only the most horrible abuse or neglect. Other legal arguments discussed in this article may be more robust in theory, but they cannot result in real change unless wedded to the power to appropriate funds or redesign systems. On the other hand, politicians cannot simply call for "punishment" and thereby make delinquent children, their many and various needs, and the problems in their communities disappear. Communities can turn their backs and order more fences, walls, locks, and bars, but the children will still come home someday. If they come home having been uncared for and feeling unwanted, neither they nor the community will ever benefit from their abilities. As the centennial of the juvenile court approaches, we can waste our time looking for answers in constitutions, codes, and courtrooms; or we can instead look closely at our children and ourselves, demand responsibility from both, apply the lessons of successful and failed programs, and have some reason to hope that tomorrow and the next century will be better.

REVIEW QUESTIONS

1. What is meant by the "right" to treatment? What were the arguments of early proponents of such a right? What federal court decisions upheld the existence of a right to treatment for juvenile offenders? On what statutory and/or Constitutional grounds were they based?

2. What cases do the authors of this selection point to as limiting application of a Constitutional right to treatment for juveniles in training schools?

3. Authors Holland and Mlyniec argue that the contemporary ascendance of punitiveness in juvenile justice statutes does not mean that legislatures no longer consider rehabilitation important. What evidence do they point to in support of their argument?

4. What bases do the authors find in state and federal statutes—and in court decisions interpreting potentially applicable statutes—for ensuring a right to rehabilitative care for institutionalized juvenile offenders? How does the approach taken in these statutes and cases differ from that of the early right to treatment cases?

5. In your view, how should punishment and rehabilitation be integrated in juvenile correctional facilities? Should rehabilitation programs be present in *all* such facilities? For *all* residents? Justify your position.

Graduated Sanctions for Serious, Violent, and Chronic Juvenile Offenders

Barry Krisberg, Elliott Currie, and David Onek

GUIDELINES FOR EFFECTIVE PROGRAMS

Through an extensive program search discussed below, NCCD [the National Council on Crime and Delinquency—*Ed.*] studied the characteristics of hundreds of juvenile programs. Information gained from the program search complements the findings of the research literature in identifying the crucial components of successful graduated sanctions programs. [For the seminal discussion of the graduated sanctions concept, see Wilson and Howell's *Comprehensive Strategy for Serious, Violent, and Chronic Juvenile Offenders* in Chapter 10— *Ed.*]

NCCD found that the most effective programs are those that address key areas of risk in the youth's life, those that seek to strengthen the personal and institutional factors that contribute to healthy adolescent development, those that provide adequate support and supervision, and those that offer youth a long-term stake in the community. These principles apply to youth at all stages of the continuum of care. What makes for effectiveness in aftercare or in residential treatment also works in diversion programs. What is most important, the research suggests, is not the particular stage of intervention, but the quality, intensity, direction, and appropriateness (see Andrews et al., 1990) of the intervention itself.

Although this might seem obvious, emphasis on the quality and nature of the intervention has not usually driven the development of graduated sanctions programs, particularly immediate intervention programs. Most of the discussion about how to respond to youth (including serious, violent, and chronic offenders) who have come into contact with the justice system has a laundry-list character. It lumps together everything that is not either primary prevention or "tertiary" involvement with the system—a variety of unrelated

Source: Barry Krisberg, Elliott Currie, and David Onek. (1995). Graduated sanctions for serious, violent, and chronic juvenile offenders. In James C. Howell (Ed.), *Guide for Implementing the Comprehensive Strategy for Serious, Violent, and Chronic Juvenile Offenders* (pp. 141–159). Washington, DC: Office of Juvenile Justice and Delinquency Prevention. Adapted courtesy of the United States Department of Justice, Office of Juvenile Justice and Delinquency Prevention.

and often inadequately evaluated strategies ranging from peer juries to school counseling to informal probation to intensive outreach and tracking programs.

The laundry-list approach fails to differentiate between substantive interventions (e.g., counseling, remedial education) and procedural or administrative categories (e.g., diversion). A greater problem is that there is no coherent concept of youth development—even a broad, eclectic one—underlying the numerous programs that are lumped together. Therefore, it is often difficult to determine why the programs were expected to be effective. It is therefore essential to examine the emerging literature to gain a more coherent sense of which strategies appear to be effective, which appear ineffective, and which appear promising but require more research.

The strategies that appear not to work include conventional individual psychological counseling in or out of the juvenile justice system; deterrence approaches such as Scared Straight; and most peergroup counseling strategies in which offenders talk together without substantial interventions to address their underlying issues (Dryfoos, 1990, pp. 145–147).

Slightly more effective strategies are short-term community service, restitution, and mediation programs, among others. However, the effectiveness of such programs in reducing recidivism or deflecting delinquent careers is slight at best. There is only limited evidence, for example, that restitution programs have reduced offending (Schneider, 1986). On the other hand, some evaluations suggest that they increase both the offenders' and the victims' satisfaction with the justice process, deliver significant restitution in the form of financial repayments and/or community service, and make victims less fearful of being victimized again (Umbreit and Coates, 1992).

There are common threads among programs that produce negative or inconclusive findings. Such programs often provide only one-time or short-term contact with offenders. Programs of shorter duration fail to address the key social or personal problems that contribute to the youth's delinquent behavior, and if they do address key issues, they often treat them as isolated problems separate from the rest of the young person's life. Ineffective programs rarely have a clear underlying developmental rationale. They seldom attempt to alter the youth's "ecological" or institutional situation by improving family functioning, for example, or improving work opportunities, or matching youth with appropriate schools. Programs that appear to make a difference in youth behavior are those that engage individual problems and deficits, have an underlying developmental rationale, and attempt to alter the youth's ecological and institutional conditions. Earlier reviews of the evidence (e.g., Wright and Dixon, 1977; Sechrest, White, and Brown, 1979) have repeatedly found that overall implementation factors such as the consistency and integrity of the intervention are more important than the specific intervention model or its specific theoretical underpinning. Within that general framework, however, some crucial themes are common to the most successful and carefully evaluated programs:

- They are holistic (comprehensive or multisystemic), dealing simultaneously with many aspects of youth's lives.

- They are intensive, often involving multiple contacts weekly, or even daily, with at-risk youth.

- They operate mostly, though not exclusively, outside the formal juvenile justice system, under a variety of auspices: public, nonprofit, or university.

- They build on youth's strengths rather than focusing on their deficiencies.

- They adopt a socially grounded approach to understanding a youth's situation and treating it rather than an individual or medical-therapeutic approach.

These themes apply at the substantive level. On the process or implementation level, the programs that work are usually those that, as with other successful interventions into problematic behavior, are relatively long-term and intensive, are delivered by energetic and committed though not necessarily highly trained staff, and are consistent in achieving what they set out to do.

Successful programs also have a case management component that begins at intake and follows youth through various program phases until discharge. Case management also involves the development of individual treatment plans to address the needs of each youth. These treatment plans are updated on a regular basis. Successful programs provide frequent feedback, both positive and negative, to youth on their progress. Positive behavior is acknowledged and rewarded, while negative behavior results in clear and consistent sanctions.

Other essential program components include effective education, vocational training, and counseling strategies tailored to the individual needs of juveniles. The most effective type of counseling seems to be a cognitive-behavioral approach. In addition to individual and group counseling, the counseling component must include family counseling because many problems of youth are caused or exacerbated by family dysfunction.

In addition to family issues, successful programs also typically address youth's community, peers, school, and work. Research findings suggest that youth should be treated in the least restrictive environment possible, preferably while living with their families or remaining within their communities. However, for public safety reasons, community-based treatment is not always appropriate, nor is family-based treatment when the family is dysfunctional or nonexistent.

Other key components of successful programs concern the intensity of services for youth who remain in the community. Successful community programs have low caseloads to ensure that youth receive constant and individualized attention. Frequent face-to-face contacts, telephone contacts, and contacts with parents, teachers, and employers are essential to provide close monitoring and consistent support for youth. This support is most successful if its intensity is diminished gradually over a long period.

Finally, successful programs reintegrate youth into their homes and communities gradually. Intensive aftercare services are crucial to program success, particularly for residential programs.

EFFECTIVE PROGRAMS

The principles enunciated thus far can be illustrated by examining specific intervention programs that are based on these principles. The illustrations that follow are examples of successful programs and approaches that have been carefully conceived, adequately implemented, and rigorously evaluated. Although the evidence of success is not absolutely conclusive, research on the programs has been careful and well designed, and the findings match the evidence accumulating from broader meta-analyses of delinquency intervention programs. The findings have added strength because programs found to be successful have many crucial elements in common. Evidence that one program works, therefore, is buttressed by similar evidence from the others.

Program Search Methodology

In December 1993, NCCD initiated an exhaustive search of prevention and intervention programs for serious, violent, and chronic juvenile offenders. . . .

The program search yielded information from 209 programs, including 122 intervention programs, 38 prevention programs, and 49 programs that had both prevention and intervention components. The most promising programs—based on both descriptive information and evaluation data—are discussed below. These programs, though imperfect, embody the core principles set forth in this document.

Immediate Sanctions Programs

The lack of consistent intervention with juvenile offenders soon after their initial contact with the police or other authority has long been recognized as perhaps the largest single gap in services for troubled youth. Without mechanisms to intervene predictably and early, the juvenile justice system is unable to impose swift and clear consequences for delinquent behavior and provide supports and services to address the individual, family, and community issues that typically underlie such behavior.

Too often, the juvenile justice system's response to young offenders is either too much or too little. The system may resort too quickly to secure confinement or to out-of-home placement; or it may let offenders off without significant consequences, often because facilities are overcrowded or needed services are not available; or it may shunt youth into ordinary probation in overburdened agencies that are unable to provide supervision or support.

This is not to say that every young offender needs intensive, protracted intervention. Some clearly do not, and attempting to extend such a response to the more than 1 million juveniles arrested each year would strain resources to the breaking point.

But for some youth, the failure to intervene—strategically and appropriately—means that they fall through the cracks of the juvenile justice system and of social agencies that might act on their behalf. For youth on a trajectory toward serious or repeated offending, lack of intervention can be disastrous, resulting in an all-too-common pattern: several encounters with authorities; short-term detentions with no coherent, intensive interventions; repeated offenses; and eventual incarceration in juvenile or adult corrections facilities. Another ineffective but common pattern is placement of youth in secure confinement not because community safety requires it but because it is the only way to ensure that they receive even minimal services. This practice is harmful to youth, detrimental to community safety, and enormously costly—in missed prevention opportunities and in confinement costs.

Immediate sanctions programs provide the crucial first rung on the ladder of graduated sanctions. Here are examples of four promising immediate sanctions programs.

Bethesda Day Treatment Center

The Bethesda Day Treatment Center, a private, nonprofit corporation established in West Milton, Pennsylvania, in 1983, provides intensive day treatment for preadjudicated and adjudicated youth who have committed delinquent or status offenses. Youth are referred to Bethesda from nine Pennsylvania counties.

Bethesda provides up to 55 hours of services per week to youth who reside at home. It administers both school and afterschool programs. The school program operates from 8:30 a.m. to 2:30 p.m. each day; the afterschool program operates from 3 p.m. to 7:45 p.m. Some youth attend both programs; others attend regular school during the day and come to Bethesda for the afterschool program.

The school program provides individualized education; the afterschool program focuses on a variety of treatment services. Clients' families are integrally involved in the treatment process. Treatment services include individual, group, and family counseling; drug and alcohol counseling; life skills development; and opportunities for employment. Work experiences are provided for all clients of working age; clients are required to contribute the majority of their paychecks to pay restitution, court costs, and fines.

Bethesda serves as an alternative to residential placement for some youth. For other youth returning to the community from residential placements, the program serves as part of an aftercare plan. The average length of participation at Bethesda is approximately 6 months, although some youth continue with the program for up to 12 months. The staff-to-client ratio is 1 to 3. . . .

Choice Program

The Choice program is an intensive monitoring and multiple-service program for high-risk youth at five sites in and around Baltimore, Maryland. It is similar to the Key Tracking Program that originated in Massachusetts in the 1970's in response to the State's deinstitutionalization of most young offenders. The Key program in Massachusetts has not been carefully evaluated, despite considerable statewide support and anecdotal evidence of success. Baltimore's Choice program, however, has recently undergone an encouraging, if preliminary, evaluation.

Choice is an intensive, home-based, family-oriented program operating under the auspices of the Shriver Center of the University of Maryland at Baltimore County (UMBC). The program addresses the problem of youth in the context of their families and wider communities and develops highly individualized treatment plans for each participant. Youth are referred to Choice from Maryland's Department of Juvenile Services and other public agencies. Program participants include numerous status offenders and youth arrested for minor delinquent activities. More serious, violent offenders are excluded from the program, as are youth requiring residential substance abuse treatment.

Choice is distinctive in the intensity of contact between caseworkers and clients—three to five contacts per day during the initial stages—and in the limits placed on length of service for caseworkers who usually are recent college graduates. To avoid the burnout that often accompanies long service in a program working with difficult clients, caseworkers remain with the program for approximately 1 year.

An intensive, month-long assessment period enables caseworkers to sort out the range of problems the referred youth is facing—at home, at school, or with physical health—and to identify and coordinate the resources needed to deal with them. The caseworker meets regularly with family members and school personnel and may call on outside experts including psychologists and substance abuse counselors when needed. The close and intensive daily contact allows caseworkers to closely track the client's progress and the obstacles that arise and also enables caseworkers to function as role models-offering consistent guidance and support. The typical length of participation is 4 to 6 months. . . .

Michigan State Diversion Project

Like Choice, the Michigan State Diversion Project for arrested juveniles uses college students as the principal caseworkers. The program was based on three recurring themes in research and program experience with juvenile offenders: they respond better if treated outside the juvenile justice system; the youth's community and family are the natural context for intervention; and service delivery by nonprofessionals may be both more effective and less costly than relying on credentialed professionals (see similar early findings in Wright and Dixon, 1977). . . .

The North Carolina Intensive Protection Supervision Project

The North Carolina Court Counselors Intensive Protective Supervision Project (IPS), another well-evaluated program, shares several key features with the programs already mentioned, but with some interesting differences. Unlike the other programs, IPS intervened within the juvenile justice system. Caseworkers worked intensively (initially up to several contacts a day) with offenders and arranged for additional professional services when needed. The program was designed for status offenders deemed at high risk of becoming serious, violent, and chronic offenders.

The project operated at four sites in North Carolina during the late 1980's and included an independent, randomized experimental evaluation by a team of researchers from Duke University. Each site employed a counselor who received training in the goals of the project but little special training in counseling, supervision, or therapeutic techniques. This was a deliberate choice based on the premise that if the program succeeded, it would be replicable elsewhere without the need to hire highly trained, expensive professionals. Instead, counselors would arrange for specialized services.

Youth referred to the program were deemed undisciplined by the North Carolina Juvenile Services Division and were randomly assigned to either intensive protective supervision or ordinary probation services. In the IPS project, caseloads were small—no more than 10 youth per counselor compared with 35 to 50 per counselor in regular probation. Among other advantages, this allowed IPS counselors to spend more time working with families and maintaining intensive contact with clients. During the formal assessment period, counselors met regularly with youth and their families and arranged for an external evaluation by a mental health professional. This professional identified appropriate service providers, who were then brought together in a meeting to define an individualized service plan. For up to a year, the counselor, along with contracted service providers, made regular home visits. . . .

Intermediate Sanctions Programs

Intermediate sanction programs are designed for youth whose offenses are too serious for placement in immediate sanction programs but not serious enough for placement in secure corrections. Such youth are usually repeat property offenders or first-time serious offenders. Intermediate sanctions encompass a diverse range of programs, both nonresidential and residential. Types of intermediate sanctions include intensive supervision programs, boot camps, wilderness programs, and community-based residential programs.

Family and Neighborhood Services Project

The Family and Neighborhood Services (FANS) project is a public program in South Carolina that employs the principles of "multisystemic" therapy—a "highly individualized family- and home-based treatment" designed to deal with offenders in the context of their family and community problems (Henggeler et al., 1992). Based in a community mental health center, the program represents a cooperative effort between the State's Department of Youth Services and Department of Mental Health. FANS attempts to avoid the institutionalization of seriously troubled youth. The program is rooted in a developmental model derived partly from Urie Bronfenbrenner's "ecological" approach—the idea that the adolescent is "nested" in a series of institutions (family, school, peers, and community) and that work with the youth must involve several or all of those institutions, hence multisystemic.

Youth referred to FANS from the Department of Youth Services were at imminent risk of out-of-home placement because of the seriousness of their offense histories. They averaged 3.5 previous arrests and 9.5 weeks of previous incarceration. Over half had at least one arrest for a violent crime, including manslaughter, assault with intent to kill, and aggravated assault. Seventy-seven percent of the sample were male, and 56 percent were African American. More than one-quarter lived with neither biological parent.

The program employed therapists with master's degrees who were assigned small caseloads of four families each. The therapists worked with the families on average for just over 4 months. Treatment integrity was maintained through a brief training program in the principles of multisystemic therapy and regular supervision and feedback from the program's directors. The caseworkers were available on a 24-hour basis and saw the juvenile and the family as often as once daily, most often in the juvenile's home. . . .

Lucas County Intensive Supervision Unit

The Lucas County, Ohio, Intensive Supervision Unit (ISU), begun in 1987, is operated by the juvenile court as part of the court probation department. Nonviolent felony offenders committed to the Ohio Department of Youth Services for the first time are the target population. The program does not accept youth convicted of drug trafficking or weapons offenses.

The theoretical basis for the program is the belief that delinquency is related to a breakdown of family functioning and other environmental factors. Thus, it is crucial that youth remain in their own homes and communities while they address these issues.

ISU uses case management and surveillance services and includes four phases. Youth begin the program in Phase I under house arrest. As they exhibit increased responsibility and socially appropriate behavior—measured by number of credit days earned—they move to successive phases. With each new phase, youth gain more freedom and privileges. At the start of each phase, a juvenile must pass a test on the rules and expectations of that phase.

The ISU is designed to provide control and treatment for youthful offenders. While the level of control diminishes as the youth progresses through the four phases, the treatment components remain high throughout the program. A comprehensive treatment plan is developed for each youth. The plan may include individual, family, and group counseling; psychological assessment for the youth and family; assessment for chemical dependency of the youth and family members; school evaluations and testing; random urinalysis; and restitution and community service.

ISU has a maximum enrollment of 60 youth. ISU probation officers have average caseloads of 15 youth. Initially, probation officers monitor their clients closely. The level of surveillance decreases as the juvenile moves to successive phases. In Phase I, there are two random surveillance contacts per day, two counselor contacts per week, and one meeting with the family per week. In Phase IV, there are 20 surveillance contacts, 2 counselor contacts, and 1 family meeting per month. . . .

Wayne County Intensive Probation Program

The Wayne County Intensive Probation Program (IPP) in Detroit, Michigan, is administered by the juvenile court and operated by the court probation department and two private, nonprofit agencies under contract with the court. The IPP target population is adjudicated delinquents between ages 12 and 17 who have been committed to the State Department of Social Services (DSS). The State funded program was begun in 1983 to reduce the level of delinquency commitments.

Youth referred to IPP are placed in one of three programs for casework services and supervision: the Probation Department's Intensive Probation Unit (IPU); the In-Home Care Program, operated by Spectrum Human Services, Inc.; or the State Ward Diversion Program, operated by the Comprehensive Youth Training and Community Involvement Program, Inc. (CYTCIP). The last two programs are operated by private agencies. Maximum enrollment for all three programs is 220 (170 for IPU, 100 for Spectrum, and 50 for CYTCIP).

The IPU program has the most traditional intensive supervision model of the three programs. It is characterized by low caseloads (a maximum of 10 youth per probation officer) and frequent probation officer contacts and surveillance activities. IPU operates through a system of four steps, with diminishing levels of supervision as the juvenile demonstrates more responsibility and lawful behavior. Probation officers must have two to three weekly face-to-face contacts with youth during the first phase, and at least one face-to-face contact per week during the subsequent phases. In addition, telephone contacts to check school attendance, curfew adherence, and home behavior are made on a regular basis. Youth remain in the program from 7 to 11 months.

The two private programs have different approaches. The In-Home Care Program employs a family-focused services and treatment approach based on the philosophy that comprehensive family treatment using community resources is needed to alleviate the causes of delinquent behavior. In-Home Care provides comprehensive services including supervision; individual, family, and group counseling; educational planning; recreational activities; and comprehensive employment training and placement activities. Maximum caseload ratios are one family worker for every eight juveniles. Family counselors meet with the juvenile and their families 3 to 5 times per week during the early stages of the program, and a minimum of once per week as youth demonstrate progress in the program. The length of the program is from 9 to 12 months.

The State Ward Diversion Program is a day treatment program actively involved in several key areas of youth's lives—home, family, school, employment, and community. An onsite alternative education program offers classes every weekday for 5 hours, 12 months per year. In addition to the education component, the program provides the following services: ongoing individual and group counseling; youth information groups; group parenting sessions; psychological evaluations; preemployment preparation for older youth; family outings; and structured group activities. In addition to seeing the youth onsite every weekday, the probation counselor meets with youth and parents at least once per week. Program enrollment is for a minimum of 11 months and generally does not exceed 15 months. . . .

About Face

About Face is a boot camp for nonviolent males ages 14 to 17 who were adjudicated of cocaine trafficking. Participants are sentenced to the program by the Memphis juvenile court. About Face participants spend 3 months in a nonsecure residential facility (the Memphis Naval Air Station, an active military base) followed by 6 months of aftercare. During 2 years, a total of 344 youths participated in the program.

About Face's residential program has four main components.

- Military training conducted by current and former Navy and Marine personnel. The training includes discipline, drill, physical conditioning, and leadership; however, it intentionally avoids the abusive, punitive aspects usually associated with military boot camps.

- Counseling based on a cognitive-behavioral model. Youth participate in 2 hours of group counseling each day and a minimum of 1 hour of individual counseling per week.

- Education using Navy-designed reading and math immersion techniques, computer-assisted learning, and individualized instruction. Youth receive 6 hours of education services per day, not including study time.

- Spiritual support that includes voluntary attendance at religious services conducted twice a week by members of local African-American churches.

During the About Face aftercare component, youth attend weekly 2-hour group counseling sessions and receive continued educational assistance. . . .

Similar to About Face is the Boot Camps for Juvenile Offenders program, launched by OJJDP in 1992 to create alternative intermediate sanctions for nonviolent juvenile offenders. This program emphasizes discipline, treatment, and work. The program has four phases: a screening phase to determine program eligibility; a 90-day residential phase that includes military-style drills and discipline, educational and vocational services, and drug counseling; an aftercare phase in which youth return to the community under close supervision; and a final phase with decreased emphasis on supervision and increased emphasis on education and job training. The program was launched at three sites: Mobile, Alabama; Denver, Colorado; and Cleveland, Ohio. . . .

Spectrum Wilderness Program

The Spectrum Wilderness Program is a 30-day therapeutic outdoor program for delinquent and otherwise troubled youth operated by the Touch of Nature Environmental Center at Southern Illinois University.

Each Spectrum course includes an Immersion Phase, a Training Expedition, a Major Expedition, and a Solo Experience. The specific outdoor activities vary from course to course but include backpacking, canoeing, spelunking, taking initiative, team courses, rope courses, rock climbing, and community service projects. Students also participate in daily chores including making camp, cooking, and cleaning.

In addition to outdoor skills, the program emphasizes academic skills such as reading, writing, and problem solving. Youth must write daily in both personal and group journals. They also select passages from books and read them aloud to the group.

The Spectrum program has a strong counseling component based on the group "circle" method. Circle groups meet daily to address youth's behavior problems and to recognize their successes. Conflicts that arise during the program are viewed as group problems and are worked out in the Circle. Counselors use reality therapy techniques for solving interpersonal problems through the Circle.

Spectrum groups vary in size from 7 to 11 participants. A staff team includes from three to five full-time staff with occasional support staff. The instructor-to-student ratio is normally 1 to 3. Staff provide 24-hour supervision. They lead the Circle group, provide individual counseling, give frequent feedback, teach outdoor skills, and serve as role models for the youth.

All participants have an individualized performance contract that is drawn up before the program begins. Spectrum staff, participating youth, the youth's families, and representatives from the agency that referred the youth all provide input into the individual behavior goals that make up the contract. Within 2 weeks after the course ends, Spectrum staff hold a followup meeting with these same parties to assess the juvenile's performance. . . .

VisionQuest

VisionQuest, founded in 1973, is a national program that provides an alternative to incarceration for serious juvenile offenders. VisionQuest youth spend 12 to 15 months in various challenging outdoor impact programs. Typically, the program sequence involves 3 months in an orientation wilderness camp, 5 months in an adventure program, and 5 months in a community residential program.

Most VisionQuest youth are committed to the program by the juvenile court. VisionQuest staff interview youth prior to placement to ensure that they are appropriate candidates. Youth must make four commitments before entering the program:

- To complete three high impact programs.

- To abstain from drugs, sex, alcohol, and tobacco.

- To participate for a minimum of 1 year.

- To face their problems.

The first phase of the VisionQuest program is a wilderness camp. Youth live outdoors in tepees, with a tepee family of 6 to 10 youths and 1 counselor. Here, juveniles receive an orientation to the program and undergo educational, psychological, and behavioral evaluations. They also undergo an intensive physical conditioning program in addition to their regular school work.

Next, youth may participate in an adventure program, such as a wagon train. On a wagon train, youth travel across the western States on mule-drawn wagons and assume responsibility for everything from feeding the animals to setting up nightly camps. Each wagon train consists of approximately 50 youth and 50 staff. The wagon train experience teaches juveniles the value of cooperation, self-discipline, and the work ethic.

In addition to the wagon train, youth may engage in various quests that differ in theme, scope, and duration. Examples of quests include ocean voyages, cross-country bike trips, hikes through wilderness, and breaking mustangs or camels.

After completing two wagon train or quest experiences, VisionQuest youth enter the residential program. Living in group homes prepares youth to return to their own homes by focusing on educational goals, family relationships, and plans for the future. HomeQuest offers support to youth when they return to their families and neighborhoods. This intensive program monitors school progress and home curfew, provides family counseling, and offers alternative recreational activities.

VisionQuest youth have a consistent educational plan that extends through each stage of the program. They also have individual treatment plans that are constantly reevaluated and updated. . . .

Thomas O'Farrell Youth Center

The Thomas O'Farrell Youth Center (TOYC) is located in rural Maryland, 45 minutes from Baltimore. It is a 38-bed, unlocked, staff-secure residential program for male youth committed to the Maryland Department of Juvenile Services (DJS). TOYC is operated by the North American Family Institute (NAFI), a nonprofit multiservice human service agency with headquarters in Danvers, Massachusetts. The typical TOYC youth has many prior court referrals, generally for property crimes and drug offenses. On average, youth stay at the center for 9 months, followed by 6 months of community aftercare.

The TOYC philosophy is to create a community of dignity and respect for all of its members. This positive social environment is at the core of all TOYC activities. Residents are asked to take responsibility for their behavior and to provide encouragement to fellow residents.

TOYC employs the Normative Model, a treatment theory that recognizes the importance of norms (social rules and expectations) in creating bonds among individuals. TOYC norms focus on creating and fostering expectations that respect the individual, the community, and the program. In the early stages of the Normative Model, the staff play a central role in teaching, modeling, and encouraging community values. Over time, TOYC residents assume responsibility for teaching community norms to new members and for dealing with violations of them.

The group process is at the heart of the TOYC community. Several times each day the community engages in small group discussions and problem solving. TOYC is divided into four groups of up to 10 youth each. Each group lives in separate dormitory areas, eats meals together, engages in work details as a unit, and participates in group therapy.

TOYC has a strong education program because many of its youth have special education needs. Class sizes are small, and instruction is highly individualized. Educational staff are closely involved with the other aspects of the program.

Individual and group successes, both large and small, are openly recognized at TOYC. The program uses a point system that rewards youth for excellent behavior.

The TOYC program begins with an orientation phase of at least 28 days. Orientation youth live together and participate in group sessions led by staff members who were former residents and can serve as role models. The juveniles' major task during orientation is to learn the dynamics of the group process. During phase 1, which lasts for approximately 60 days, youth acquire more knowledge about TOYC and its normative system. To move from phase 1 to phase 2, residents must demonstrate consistent and positive behavior in all aspects of TOYC life, including school attendance, work details, group meetings, and meal times. In phase 2, the resident is expected to demonstrate even higher levels of expertise in group process and community activities, including teaching the program to others. Phase 2 youth must demonstrate high levels of success in on-campus jobs and are encouraged to find part-time employment in the community. They also meet with aftercare workers to develop a community treatment aftercare plan.

TOYC operates an intensive aftercare program for participants. Each youth who completes the TOYC residential program has a specialized aftercare plan and receives postrelease services from two aftercare workers—including assistance in reentering school, vocational counseling, crisis intervention, family counseling, transportation, and mentoring. Aftercare lasts for 6 months, during which time aftercare workers contact the youth at least 12 days per month. . . .

Secure Corrections

Some offenders pose such a threat to society that they must be placed in locked, secure facilities. Such secure corrections programs should be reserved for only the most serious and violent offenders. Youth in secure programs should be provided with a wide range of rehabilitation services. Research has shown that the most effective secure corrections programs allow only a small number of participants and provide them with individualized services; large training schools have not proven to be effective in rehabilitating juvenile offenders. Examples of secure corrections programs follow.

The Violent Juvenile Offender Program
The Violent Juvenile Offender (VJO) program provided a continuum of care for violent male juvenile offenders at four urban sites: Boston, Detroit, Memphis, and Newark. VJO youth were initially placed in small, secure facilities and were gradually reintegrated into the community through community-based residential programs followed by intensive neighborhood supervision. Case management was continuous, beginning in secure care and extending through the reintegration phases.

The VJO model sought to strengthen youth's bonds to prosocial people and institutions, provide realistic opportunities for achievement, employ a system of rewards for appropriate behavior and sanctions for inappropriate behavior, and provide individualized treatment. Youth who had been adjudicated for a Part 1 index felony and who had a prior adjudication for a major felony were eligible for the program. . . .

Florida Environmental Institute
The Florida Environmental Institute (FEI), also known as "The Last Chance Ranch," targets Florida's most serious juvenile offenders. It is operated by Associated Marine Institutes (AMI), a network of affiliated residential and nonresidential programs that operates in seven States. FEI is located in a remote area of the Florida Everglades. It has a capacity of 40 youth—20 in the residential portion of the program and 20 in the nonresidential aftercare component.

FEI receives two-thirds of its referrals from the adult justice system. Under Florida law, a juvenile who has been found guilty as an adult may be returned to the juvenile justice system for treatment. FEI-referred youth average 18 prior offenses and 11.5 prior felonies. Almost two-thirds (63 percent) are committed for crimes against persons, the rest for chronic property or drug offenses.

Although FEI handles serious offenders, it is not a locked facility. Nevertheless, it is considered a secure facility because it is in an extremely remote location completely surrounded by forests and swamp. This physical isolation, in addition to a low staff-to-student ratio, protects the public's safety.

The average length of participation in FEI is 18 months, with a residential stay of at least 9 months. All but a handful of participants return to their communities after they have met strict educational, social, and behavioral objectives.

The FEI philosophy reflects the following imperatives:

- Treat youth in the least restrictive setting that is appropriate.

- Focus on education as a means of reducing recidivism.

- View hard work as therapeutic and a way to increase vocational skills.

- Employ a system of rewards for positive behavior and sanctions for inappropriate behavior.

- Promote bonding with staff role models.

- Provide a strong aftercare component.

The FEI program begins with a 3-day orientation program, during which case treatment plans are established, work projects are assigned, and the bonding process between staff and students begins. Phase 1, which emphasizes work and education, has a low staff-to-student ratio of 3 or 4 to 1. Students must earn points to move on to the second phase, where they can participate in paid work projects to help with restitution payments. Near the end of the second phase, the program's community coordinator takes the students back to their communities to assist aftercare job placements and to work on rebuilding family relationships.

In the third phase, students live in the community but maintain constant contact with the institute. Aftercare staff, with small caseloads of six, contact the students at least four times per week. They assist with job searches, family problems, and other issues. The youth must adhere to a strict curfew. If they break curfew or engage in criminal activity, they are returned to the residential part of the program. . . .

Capital Offender Program

The Capital Offender Program (COP) at Giddings State Home and School in Texas, begun in 1988, is an innovative group treatment program for juveniles committed for homicide. It is an intensive, 16-week program involving a group of eight juveniles and two or three staff members. The group meets twice a week for approximately 3 hours each session. Recently, a residential treatment component has been added to COP: the eight students live together in the same cottage until their release. Most program participants are incarcerated at Giddings for an average of 2 1/2 to 3 years.

Youth must meet four criteria to be eligible for the COP program:

- They must be committed for homicide (capital murder, murder, or voluntary manslaughter).

- They must have been at Giddings for at least 12 months and have at least 6 months remaining on their sentences.

- They must be at either a senior or prerelease level at Giddings.

- They cannot be diagnosed as psychotic or mentally retarded, or have a pervasive developmental disorder.

The primary goals of the COP program are to promote verbal expression of feelings, to foster empathy for victims, to create a sense of personal responsibility, and to decrease feelings of hostility and aggression.

The COP treatment approach focuses on group psychotherapy with an emphasis on role-playing. In addition to role-playing their life stories, participants role-play their homicidal offense, reenacting the crime first from the perpetrator's perspective and then from the victim's.

Two COP groups run concurrently, each led by a Ph.D.-level psychologist and a master's-level cotherapist. Psychologists are also available for individual counseling should a student have emotional reactions requiring more intensive support. COP psychologists receive extra training before participating in the program. . . .

CONCLUSION

The results of NCCD's intensive review of programs, along with the findings of 15 years of careful research, point the way toward an understanding of the crucial elements of success in graduated sanctions programs for young offenders. A number of past and current programs across the country have achieved credible results using some combination of these crucial elements. It can be said with confidence that some programs do work when they are carefully conceived, properly implemented, and provided with enough resources to do the job they set out to do.

Nevertheless, the evidence suggests that a new generation of programs is needed to build on these successes and move beyond them to address aspects of youth's lives that even the more effective graduated sanctions efforts typically neglect. While the successful outcomes described earlier are encouraging, they are only partial: Positive results too often deteriorate after clients leave the programs. This does not mean that the programs do not work or that their replication should become a lower priority. Rather, it means that programs for serious offenders must be enhanced and extended, especially in ways that improve offenders' chances of succeeding in the long term and becoming full, participating members of their communities.

Put simply, the effects of even good intervention programs are bound to be weakened or nullified if youth are simply returned to communities with shrinking opportunities for work, self-sufficiency, and social contribution. One of the most effective ways to address this all-too-common problem is to build a more substantial employment component into intervention programs for young offenders. The importance of employment, to be sure, varies with age (Huizinga et al., 1994): The value of a job to a 14-year-old first-time offender is likely to be less important than to a 17-year-old. By late adolescence, employment is a crucial factor in development and one of the most important predictors of later adjustment

(Sampson and Laub, 1993). Yet employment is arguably the least consistently addressed component in conventional interventions with delinquent youth. However, less conventional programs suggest the positive potential of including a systematic employment component in strategies aimed at high-risk youth.

The most interesting effort, and one with a fairly convincing evaluation, is the vocationally oriented psychotherapy program for low-income high school dropouts in Massachusetts, initiated by Milton Shore and Joseph Massimo (1963, 1973) in the early 1960's. The program strategy was simple and inexpensive. Troubled youth with a history of failure in other service programs were contacted by a trained therapist within 24 hours of dropping out of school. The core of the therapy was to place them in a steady job and to use the job placement as an entree for other services, including psychotherapy and remedial education. The services, as in the successful programs described above, were individualized, intensive, and flexible. Followup comparisons with a comparable untreated group at 5 and 10 years revealed striking differences. For example, at 10 years after the intervention, only 2 of 10 participants were deemed to have made an inadequate adjustment, with one incarcerated and one in a mental institution. The rest had experienced relatively stable employment, most had no arrests, and most were married with families. The fate of the 10 control youth, on the other hand, was bleak and virtually the opposite of the treated group: only two were judged as having made an adequate adjustment; only two were arrest-free; and five had spent time in prison, jail, or a drug rehabilitation center (Shore and Massimo, 1973, pp. 129–131).

This program never received the attention it deserved, although it is one of several employment-oriented efforts with positive results included in Wright and Dixon's review of prevention programs in the late 1970's. The small size of the samples means that the results, though striking, must be treated cautiously. The findings are supported, however, by evaluations of other work programs for disadvantaged youth. Especially relevant is the experience of the Job Corps, which has been shown to prevent a substantial amount of serious, violent crime. Though not specifically aimed at youthful offenders, the Job Corps serves a population of high-risk youth, many with a substantial history of delinquency. Another related example is the Associated Marine Institutes (AMI) program in Florida and several other States. In addition to providing support services and remedial education, AMI uses a vocationally oriented approach to teach marine-related skills.

What all these programs have in common—and what seems to account for their effectiveness—is the combination of a solid focus on a real job or serious skills training with intensive support services. The importance of real work as a strategy for preventing serious and violent juvenile offenses and deeper penetration into the justice system fits with everything known about adolescent development and the factors that protect against a variety of problematic behavior.

Yet a work component has had only a sporadic place in program development until now. That must change. Preparation for stable employment and placement in real jobs should have a prominent place in programming for older adolescents.

In designing appropriate training and placement strategies, it is important to note another frequent finding: programs tend to work better if they combine offenders with nondelinquent peers rather than isolating delinquents in one group (see Feldman, Caplinger, and Wodarski, 1983).

Linking young offenders to a broader community-oriented youth work program—perhaps modeled on existing Conservation Corps programs—could be a critical part of a comprehensive or multisystemic approach.

REFERENCES

Andrews, D.A., I. Zinger, R. Hoge, J. Bonta, P. Gendrew, and F. Cullen. 1990. "Does Correctional Treatment Work? A Clinically Relevant and Psychologically Informed Meta-Analysis." *Criminology* 28:369–404.

Dryfoos, J.G. 1990. *Adolescents at Risk: Prevalence and Prevention*. New York, NY: Oxford University Press.

Feldman, R.A., T.E. Caplinger, and J.S. Wodarski. 1983. *The St. Louis Conundrum: The Effective Treatment of Antisocial Youths*. Englewood Cliffs, NJ: Prentice-Hall.

Henggeler, S., et al. 1992. "Family Preservation Using Multisystemic Therapy: An Effective Alternative to Incarcerating Serious Juvenile Offenders." *Journal of Consulting and Clinical Psychology* 60(6).

Huizinga, D., R. Loeber, and T.P. Thornberry. 1994. *Urban Delinquency and Substance Abuse: Initial Findings*. Washington, DC: U.S. Department of Justice, Office of Juvenile Justice and Delinquency Prevention.

Sampson, R.J., and J. Laub. 1993. *Crime in the Making: Pathways and Turning Points Through Life*. Cambridge, MA: Harvard University Press.

Schneider, A. 1986. "Restitution and Recidivism Rates of Juvenile Offenders: Results from Four Experimental Studies." *Criminology* 24(3).

Sechrest, L., S.O. White, and E.D. Brown. 1979. *The Rehabilitation of Criminal Offenders: Problem and Prospects*. Washington, DC: National Academy Press.

Shore, M., and J. Massimo. 1963. "The Effectiveness of a Comprehensive, Vocationally-Oriented Psychotherapeutic Program for Adolescent Delinquent Boys." *American Journal of Orthopsychiatry* 33(4):634–642.

Shore, M., and J. Massimo. 1973. "After Ten Years: A Followup Study of Comprehensive Vocationally Oriented Psychotherapy." *American Journal of Orthopsychiatry* 43(1).

Umbreit, M.S., and R.B. Coates. 1992. "The Impact of Mediating Victim-Offender Conflict: An Analysis of Programs in Three States." *Juvenile and Family Court Journal* 43(1).

Wright, W.E., and M.C. Dixon. 1977. "Community Prevention and Treatment of Juvenile Delinquency: A Review of Evaluation Studies." *Journal of Research in Crime and Delinquency* 14:35–67.

REVIEW QUESTIONS

1. What kinds of intervention strategies, program components, and processes did the National Council on Crime and Delinquency (NCCD) find to be characteristic of the most effective juvenile treatment programs? What kinds were determined to be ineffective? What kinds were only somewhat effective?

2. The authors describe several specific programs found to be especially effective at each of three levels of a continuum of "graduated sanctions." (We will find out

more about graduated sanctions in the next chapter.) What types of juveniles are targeted by the programs highlighted at each level? What do the "effective" programs at each level have in common? What are the main differences among them?

3. Based on the program descriptions and on the authors' discussion of the characteristics of effective programs in the first part of this selection, what program or programs highlighted at each level seem(s) likely to be *most* effective in reducing future delinquency? Which seem(s) likely to be *least* effective? Why?

4. Recall Chesney-Lind's discussion in Chapter 1 of the characteristics of girls at risk for juvenile justice system involvement and the special problems associated with delinquency programming for girls. Based on what you learned about the special needs of female juvenile offenders, which of the programs highlighted at each level in this selection appear to be most appropriate for girls? Are any specifically designed for girls? Which ones are specifically indicated to accept girls? Which ones are for boys only? Which ones don't specify? If you were trying to design a program for girls at any of the three levels of sanction discussed in this selection, what aspects of the highlighted programs at that level would you consider incorporating into your program? What aspects would you avoid? Why?

FURTHER READING

Altschuler, David M., Armstrong, Troy L., and MacKenzie, Doris Layton. (1999). *Reintegration, Supervised Release, and Intensive Aftercare.* Washington, DC: Office of Juvenile Justice and Delinquency Prevention. Available online: http://www.ncjrs.org/pdffiles1/175715.pdf

Griffin, Patrick, and Torbet, Patricia. (2002). *Desktop Guide to Good Juvenile Probation Practice,* Revised Edition. Pittsburgh, PA: National Center for Juvenile Justice. Available online: http://mcjj.servehttp.com/NCJJWebsite/publications/azlist/d.htm

Howell, James C. (1998). NCCD's survey of juvenile detention and correctional facilities. *Crime and Delinquency, 44*(1), 102–109.

Howell, James C., and Krisberg, Barry. (Eds.). (1998). Juveniles in Custody. A Special Issue of *Crime and Delinquency, 44*(4).

Howell, James C., Krisberg, Barry, Hawkins, J. David, and Wilson, John J. (Eds.). (1995). *A Sourcebook: Serious, Violent, and Chronic Juvenile Offenders.* Thousand Oaks, CA: Sage.

Krisberg, Barry, Austin, James, and Steele, P.A. (1989). *Unlocking Juvenile Corrections.* San Francisco: National Council on Crime and Delinquency.

Lipsey, Mark W. (1999). Can intervention rehabilitate serious delinquents? *The Annals of the American Academy of Political and Social Sciences, 564,* 142–166.

Miller, Jerome. (1991). *Last One over the Wall: The Massachusetts Experiment in Closing Reform Schools.* Columbus: Ohio State University Press.

Moody, Edward E. Jr., and Lupton-Smith, Helen S. (1999). Interventions with juvenile offenders: Strategies to prevent acting out behavior. *Journal of Addictions and Offender Counseling, 20*(1), 2–14.

Puritz, Patricia, and Scali, Mary Ann. (1998). *Beyond the Walls: Improving Conditions of Confinement for Youth in Custody.* Washington, DC: Office of Juvenile Justice and Delinquency Prevention. Available online: http://www.ncjrs.org/pdffiles/164727.pdf

Whitehead, John T., and Lab, Steven P. (1989). A meta-analysis of juvenile correctional treatment. *Journal of Research in Crime and Delinquency, 26,* 276–295.

CHAPTER

10

The Future of Juvenile Justice

Having only recently celebrated its 100th birthday, the juvenile court is, in the words of former Academy of Criminal Justice Sciences (ACJS) President Alida Merlo, "at a crossroads." Highlighting the evident contradiction between recent reductions in juvenile crime and the get-tough correctional reforms of the current era (and in the process expressing an ideological viewpoint shared by an increasing number of juvenile justice scholars) in her Presidential Address to the members of ACJS at their 2000 Annual Meeting in New Orleans, Louisiana, she rhetorically asked her audience: "Does the system persist in this hardening of attitudes toward youths and in its disregard for the realities of adolescence, or does it adopt a softening approach? How can we modify society's tough, punitive stance toward youths and enlist public support for prevention, early intervention, and rehabilitation?" (Merlo, 2000, p. 641). Later in her address, she offered the germ of a reply:

> [W]e are at a crossroads. We can either continue to move toward more punitive juvenile justice policies, greater intolerance for adolescents, growing racism, more costly and more inhumane policies, and an ever-widening gulf between poor children and the rest of us, or we can blaze a new path. As teachers, scholars, researchers, students, and practitioners, we have the opportunity to infuse the system with a new kind of thinking—thinking that is informed by research, by the evaluation of programs, and by an understanding of the complex societal conditions that cannot be eliminated without substantial long-term investments. (Merlo, 2000, p. 657)

"Blaz[ing] a new path" can, of course, mean different things to different people. In this chapter we conclude our exploration of the juvenile justice system with three markedly differing visions for its future. In the first, portions of which were broached in the previous chapter, OJJDP stalwarts John J. Wilson and James C. Howell offer a *Comprehensive Strategy for Serious, Violent, and Chronic Juvenile Offenders*. Originally published in 1993 by OJJDP, this document provided a quasi-official blueprint for juvenile justice reform applying new policy initiatives to the traditional areas of delinquency prevention and correctional intervention. The system of "graduated sanctions" that served as the centerpiece of the *Comprehensive Strategy's* plan for the juvenile justice system has already gained considerable attention—both within OJJDP and elsewhere—as a viable alternative to the "get tough" movement, focusing instead on devising a continuum of progressively restrictive treatment alternatives through which a juvenile will progress only to the extent that interventions at lower rungs of the ladder are ineffective.

A more radical vision is offered by Barry C. Feld, who has long advocated outright abolition of the juvenile court's delinquency jurisdiction with the expectation that criminal court prosecution would ultimately be fairer for even the youngest offenders. In "Juvenile (In)Justice and the Criminal Court Alternative," Feld introduces three alternative scenarios for the future of the juvenile court: return to the informal and rehabilitative approach that served as the original cornerstone of juvenile courts; continue the movement toward a punitive juvenile court, but guarantee *all* of the procedural safeguards applicable in criminal court; or abolish the juvenile court and try young offenders in criminal court, providing for an age-graded "youth discount" at sentencing. Feld's preference among the alternatives is clear, and he effectively makes his case as he details the pitfalls of alternative juvenile court scenarios and recites the benefits of criminal court processing.

The final selection offers a middle ground between modification and reorientation of familiar approaches, as advocated by Wilson and Howell, and abandoning the juvenile court experiment altogether, as Feld would have us do. Gordon Bazemore has for the past decade been recognized as one of the chief architects of a new direction in juvenile justice most commonly known as Balanced and Restorative Justice (BRJ or BARJ). In "Restoring the Balance: Community and Juvenile Justice," Bazemore and co-author Susan E. Day outline the distinctive features of BRJ, an approach that brings together offenders, victims, and the community in a cooperative effort to repair the harm that has been done—as opposed to the exclusively offender-focused rehabilitative and punitive approaches that have until now dominated correctional philosophy and practice in both juvenile and adult justice systems. Lauded in the *Comprehensive Strategy* and elsewhere as a highly promising alternative to traditional approaches, BRJ has already gained legislative recognition in at least a dozen states that have formally adopted it as a central mission of their juvenile justice systems.

REFERENCE

Merlo, Alida V. (2000). Juvenile justice at the crossroads: Presidential address to the academy of criminal justice sciences. *Justice Quarterly, 17*(4), 639–661.

Comprehensive Strategy for Serious, Violent, and Chronic Juvenile Offenders

John J. Wilson and James C. Howell

GENERAL PRINCIPLES

The following general principles provide a framework to guide our efforts in the battle to prevent delinquent conduct and reduce juvenile involvement in serious, violent, and chronic delinquency:

- **Strengthen the family** in its primary responsibility to instill moral values and provide guidance and support to children. Where there is no functional family unit, a family surrogate should be established and assisted to guide and nurture the child.

- **Support core social institutions**—schools, religious institutions, and community organizations—in their roles of developing capable, mature, and responsible youth. A goal of each of these societal institutions should be to ensure that children have the opportunity and support to mature into productive law-abiding citizens. A nurturing community environment requires that core social institutions be actively involved in the lives of youth. Community organizations include public and private youth-serving agencies; neighborhood groups; and business and commercial organizations providing employment, training, and other meaningful economic opportunities for youth.

- **Promote delinquency prevention** as the most cost-effective approach to dealing with juvenile delinquency. Families, schools, religious institutions, and community organizations, including citizen volunteers and the private sector, must be enlisted in the Nation's delinquency prevention efforts. These core socializing institutions must be strengthened and assisted in their efforts to ensure that children have the opportunity to become capable and responsible citizens. When children engage in "acting out" behavior, such as status offenses, the family and community, in concert

Source: John J. Wilson and James C. Howell. (1993). *Comprehensive Strategy for Serious, Violent, and Chronic Juvenile Offenders.* Washington, DC: Office of Juvenile Justice and Delinquency Prevention. Adapted courtesy of the United States Department of Justice, Office of Juvenile Justice and Delinquency Prevention.

with child welfare agencies, must take primary responsibility for responding with appropriate treatment and support services. Communities must take the lead in designing and building comprehensive prevention approaches that address known risk factors and target other youth at risk of delinquency.

- **Intervene immediately and effectively when delinquent behavior occurs** to successfully prevent delinquent offenders from becoming chronic offenders or progressively committing more serious and violent crimes. Initial intervention efforts, under an umbrella of system authorities (police, intake, and probation), should be centered in the family and other core societal institutions. Juvenile justice system authorities should ensure that an appropriate response occurs and act quickly and finely if the need for formal system adjudication and sanctions has been demonstrated.

- **Identify and control the small group of serious, violent, and chronic juvenile offenders** who have committed felony offenses or have failed to respond to intervention and nonsecure community-based treatment and rehabilitation services offered by the juvenile justice system. Measures to address delinquent offenders who are a threat to community safety may include placements in secure community-based facilities or, when necessary, training schools and other secure juvenile facilities.

Under OJJDP's comprehensive strategy, it is the family and community, supported by our core social institutions, that have primary responsibility for meeting the basic socializing needs of our Nation's children. Socially harmful conduct, acting-out behavior, and delinquency may be signs of the family being unable to meet its responsibility. It is at these times that the community must support and assist the family in the socialization process, particularly for youth at the greatest risk of delinquency.

The proposed strategy incorporates two principal components: (1) preventing youth from becoming delinquent by focusing prevention programs on at-risk youth; and (2) improving the juvenile justice system response to delinquent offenders through a system of graduated sanctions and a continuum of treatment alternatives that include immediate intervention, intermediate sanctions, and community-based corrections sanctions, incorporating restitution and community service when appropriate.

TARGET POPULATIONS

The *initial target population* for prevention programs is juveniles at risk of involvement in delinquent activity. While primary delinquency prevention programs provide services to all youth wishing to participate, maximum impact on future delinquent conduct can be achieved by seeking to identify and involve in prevention programs youth at greatest risk of involvement in delinquent activity. This includes youth who exhibit known risk factors for future delinquency; drug and alcohol abuse; and youth who have had contact with the juvenile justice system as nonoffenders (neglected, abused, and dependent), status offenders (runaways, truants, alcohol offenders, and incorrigibles), or minor delinquent offenders.

The *next target population* is youth, both male and female, who have committed delinquent (criminal) acts, including juvenile offenders who evidence a high likelihood of becoming, or who already are, serious, violent, or chronic offenders.

PROGRAM RATIONALE

What can communities and the juvenile justice system do to prevent the development of and interrupt the progression of delinquent and criminal careers? Juvenile justice agencies and programs are one part of a larger picture that involves many other local agencies and programs that are responsible for working with at-risk youth and their families. It is important that juvenile delinquency prevention and intervention programs are integrated with local police, social service, child welfare, school, and family preservation programs and that these programs reflect local community determinations of the most pressing problems and program priorities. Establishing *community planning teams* that include a broad base of participants drawn from local government and the community (e.g., community-based youth development organizations, schools, law enforcement, social service agencies, civic organizations, religious groups, parents, and teens) will help create consensus on priorities and services to be provided as well as build support for a comprehensive program approach that draws on all sectors of the community for participation. Comprehensive approaches to delinquency prevention and intervention will require collaborative efforts between the juvenile justice system and other service provision systems, including mental health, health, child welfare, and education. Developing mechanisms that effectively link these different service providers at the program level will need to be an important component of every community's comprehensive plan.

Evidence suggests that a risk reduction and protective factor enhancement approach to prevention is effective. Risk factors include the family, the school, the peer group, the community, and characteristics of juveniles themselves. The more risk factors present in a community, the greater the likelihood of youth problems in that community as children are exposed to those risk factors. Prevention strategies will need to be comprehensive, addressing each of the risk factors as they relate to the *chronological development* of children being served.

Research and experience in intervention and treatment programming suggest that a highly structured system of graduated sanctions holds significant promise. The goal of graduated sanctions is to increase the effectiveness of the juvenile justice system in responding to juveniles who have committed criminal acts. The system's limited resources have diminished its ability to respond effectively to serious, violent, and chronic juvenile crime. This trend must be reversed by empowering the juvenile justice system to provide accountability and treatment resources to juveniles. This includes gender-specific programs for female offenders, whose rates of delinquency have generally been increasing faster than males in recent years, and who now account for 23 percent of juvenile arrests. It will also require programs for special needs populations such as sex offenders, mentally retarded, emotionally disturbed, and learning disabled delinquents.

The graduated sanctions approach is designed to provide immediate intervention at the first offense to ensure that the juvenile's misbehavior is addressed by the family and community or through formal adjudication and sanctions by the juvenile justice system, as appropriate. Graduated sanctions include a range of intermediate sanctions and secure corrections options to provide intensive treatment that serves the juvenile's needs, provides accountability, and protects the public. They offer an array of referral and dispositional resources for law enforcement, juvenile courts, and juvenile corrections officials. The graduated sanctions component requires that the juvenile justice system's capacity to identify, process, evaluate, refer, and track delinquent offenders be enhanced.

The Juvenile Justice System

The juvenile justice system plays a key role in protecting and guiding juveniles, including responding to juvenile delinquency. Law enforcement plays a key role by conducting investigations, making custody and arrest determinations, or exercising discretionary release authority. Police should be trained in community-based policing techniques and provided with program resources that focus on community youth, such as Police Athletic Leagues and the Drug Abuse Resistance Education (DARE) Program.

The traditional role of the juvenile and family court is to treat and rehabilitate the dependent or wayward minor, using an individualized approach and tailoring its response to the particular needs of the child and family, with goals of: (1) responding to the needs of troubled youth and their families; (2) providing due process while recognizing the rights of the victim; (3) rehabilitating the juvenile offender; and (4) protecting both the juvenile and the public. While juvenile and family courts have been successful in responding to the bulk of youth problems to meet these goals, new ways of organizing and focusing the resources of the juvenile justice system are required to effectively address serious, violent, and chronic juvenile crime. These methods might include the establishment of unified family courts with jurisdiction over all civil and criminal matters affecting the family.

A recent statement by the National Council of Juvenile and Family Court Judges (NCJFCJ) succinctly describes the critical role of the court:

> The Courts must protect children and families when private and other public institutions are unable or fail to meet their obligations. The protection of society by correcting children who break the law, the preservation and reformation of families, and the protection of children from abuse and neglect are missions of the Court. When the family falters, when the basic needs of children go unmet, when the behavior of children is destructive and goes unchecked, juvenile and family courts must respond. The Court is society's official means of holding itself accountable for the well-being of its children and family unit. (NCJFCJ, "Children and Families First, A Mandate for Change," 1993)

Earlier, NCJFCJ developed 38 recommendations regarding serious juvenile offenders and related issues facing the juvenile court system. These issues included confidentiality of the juvenile offender and his or her family, transfer of a juvenile offender to adult court, and effective treatment of the serious juvenile offender (NCJFCJ, 1984).

Finally, juvenile corrections has the responsibility to provide treatment services that will rehabilitate the juvenile and minimize his or her chances of reoffending. Juvenile courts and corrections will benefit from a system that makes a continuum of services available that respond to each juvenile's needs.

The juvenile justice system, armed with resources and knowledge that permit matching juveniles with appropriate treatment programs while holding them accountable, can have a positive and lasting impact on the reduction of delinquency. Developing effective case management and management information systems (MIS) will be integral to this effort. OJJDP will provide leadership in building system capacity at the State and local levels to take maximum advantage of available knowledge and resources.

DELINQUENCY PREVENTION

Most juvenile delinquency efforts have been unsuccessful because of their negative approach—attempting to keep juveniles from misbehaving. Positive approaches that emphasize opportunities for healthy social, physical, and mental development have a much greater likelihood of success. Another weakness of past delinquency prevention efforts is their narrow scope, focusing on only one or two of society's institutions that have responsibility for the social development of children. Most programs have targeted either the school arena or the family. Communities are an often neglected area. Successful delinquency prevention strategies must be positive in their orientation and comprehensive in their scope.

The prevention component of OJJDP's comprehensive strategy is based on a risk-focused delinquency prevention approach (Hawkins and Catalano, 1992). This approach states that to prevent a problem from occurring, the factors contributing to the development of that problem must be identified and then ways must be found (protective factors) to address and ameliorate those factors.

Research conducted over the past half century has clearly documented five categories of causes and correlates of juvenile delinquency: (1) individual characteristics such as alienation, rebelliousness, and lack of bonding to society; (2) family influences such as parental conflict, child abuse, and family history of problem behavior (substance abuse, criminality, teen pregnancy, and school dropouts); (3) school-experiences such as early academic failure and lack of commitment to school; (4) peer group influences such as friends who engage in problem behavior (minor criminality, gangs, and violence); and (5) neighborhood and community factors such as economic deprivation, high rates of substance abuse and crime, and low neighborhood attachment. These categories can also be thought of as risk factors.

To counter these causes and risk factors, protective factors must be introduced. Protective factors are qualities or conditions that moderate a juvenile's exposure to risk. Research indicates that protective factors fall into three basic categories: (1) individual characteristics such as a resilient temperament and a positive social orientation; (2) bonding with prosocial family members, teachers, and friends; and (3) healthy beliefs and clear standards for behavior. While individual characteristics are inherent and difficult to change, bonding and clear standards for behavior work together and can be changed. To increase bonding, children must be provided with opportunities to contribute to their families, schools, peer groups, and communities; skills to take advantage of opportunities; and recognition for their efforts to contribute. Simultaneously, parents, teachers, and communities need to set clear standards that endorse prosocial behavior.

The risk-focused delinquency prevention approach calls on communities to identify and understand what risk factors their children are exposed to and to implement programs that counter these risk factors. Communities must enhance protective factors that promote positive behavior, health, well-being, and personal success. Effective delinquency prevention efforts must be comprehensive, covering the five causes or risk factors [identified] below, and correspond to the social development process. . . .

Figure 10–1

Risk factors
- Individual characteristics.
- Family influences.
- School experiences.
- Peer group influences.
- Neighborhood and community.

GRADUATED SANCTIONS

An effective juvenile justice system program model for the treatment and rehabilitation of delinquent offenders is one that combines accountability and sanctions with increasingly intensive treatment and rehabilitation services. These graduated sanctions must be wide-ranging to fit the offense and include both intervention and secure corrections components. The intervention component includes the use of immediate intervention and intermediate sanctions, and the secure corrections component includes the use of community confinement and incarceration in training schools, camps, and ranches.

Each of these graduated sanctions components should consist of sublevels, or gradations, that together with appropriate services constitute an integrated approach. The purpose of this approach is to stop the juvenile's further penetration into the system by inducing law-abiding behavior as early as possible through the combination of appropriate intervention and treatment sanctions. The juvenile justice system must work with law enforcement, courts, and corrections to develop reasonable, fair, and humane sanctions.

At each level in the continuum, the family must continue to be integrally involved in treatment and rehabilitation efforts. Aftercare must be a formal component of all residential placements, actively involving the family and the community in supporting and reintegrating the juvenile into the community.

Programs will need to use Risk and Needs Assessments to determine the appropriate placement for the offender. Risk assessments should be based on clearly defined objective criteria that focus on (1) the seriousness of the delinquent act; (2) the potential risk for re-offending, based on the presence of risk factors; and (3) the risk to the public safety. Effective risk assessment at intake, for example, can be used to identify those juveniles who require the use of detention as well as those who can be released to parental custody or diverted to nonsecure community-based programs. Needs assessments will help ensure that (1) different types of problems are taken into account when formulating a case plan; (2) a baseline for monitoring a juvenile's progress is established; (3) periodic reassessments of treatment effectiveness are conducted; and (4) a systemwide data base of treatment needs can be used for the planning and evaluation of programs, policies, and procedures. Together, risk and needs assessments will help to allocate scarce resources more efficiently and effectively. A system of graduated sanctions requires a broad continuum of options.

Intervention

For intervention efforts to be most effective, they must be swift, certain, consistent, and incorporate increasing sanctions, including the possible loss of freedom. As the severity of sanctions increases, so must the intensity of treatment. At each level, offenders must be aware that, should they continue to violate the law, they will be subject to more severe sanctions and could ultimately be confined in a secure setting, ranging from a secure community-based juvenile facility to a training school, camp, or ranch.

The juvenile court plays an important role in the provision of treatment and sanctions. Probation has traditionally been viewed as the court's main vehicle for delivery of treatment services and community supervision. However, traditional probation services and sanctions have not had the resources to effectively target delinquent offenders, particularly serious, violent, and chronic offenders.

The Balanced Approach to juvenile probation is a promising approach that specifies a clear and coherent framework. The Balanced Approach consists of three practical objectives: (1) Accountability; (2) Competency Development; and (3) Community Protection. Accountability refers to the requirement that offenders make amends to the victims and the community for harm caused. Competency Development requires that youth who enter the juvenile justice system should exit the system more capable of being productive and responsible citizens. Community Protection requires that the juvenile justice system ensure public safety.

The following graduated sanctions are proposed within the Intervention component:

Immediate intervention. First-time delinquent offenders (misdemeanors and nonviolent felonies) and nonserious repeat offenders (generally misdemeanor repeat offenses) must be targeted for system intervention based on their probability of becoming more serious or chronic in their delinquent activities. Nonresidential community-based programs, including prevention programs for at-risk youth, may be appropriate for many of these offenders. Such programs are small and open, located in or near the juvenile's home, and maintain community participation in program planning, operation, and evaluation. Community police officers, working as part of Neighborhood Resource Teams, can help monitor the juvenile's progress. Other offenders may require sanctions tailored to their offense(s) and their needs to deter them from committing additional crimes. The following programs apply to these offenders:

- Neighborhood Resource Teams

- Diversion

- Informal Probation

- School Counselors Serving as Probation Officers

- Home on Probation

- Mediation (Victims)

- Community Service

- Restitution

- Day-Treatment Programs

- Alcohol and Drug Abuse Treatment (Outpatient)

- Peer Juries

Intermediate sanctions. Offenders who are inappropriate for immediate intervention (first-time serious or violent offenders) or who fail to respond successfully to immediate intervention as evidenced by reoffending (such as repeat property offenders or drug-involved juveniles) would begin with or be subject to intermediate sanctions. These sanctions may be nonresidential or residential.

Many of the serious and violent offenders at this stage may be appropriate for placement in an Intensive Supervision Program as an alternative to secure incarceration. OJJDP's Intensive Supervision of Probationers Program Model is a highly structured, continuously monitored individualized plan that consists of five phases with decreasing levels of restrictiveness: (1) Short-Term Placement in Community Confinement; (2) Day Treatment; (3) Outreach and Tracking; (4) Routine Supervision; and (5) Discharge and Followup. Other appropriate programs include:

- Drug Testing

- Weekend Detention

- Alcohol and Drug Abuse Treatment (Inpatient)

- Challenge Outdoor Programs

- Community-Based Residential Programs

- Electronic Monitoring

- Boot Camp Facilities and Programs

Secure Corrections

The criminal behavior of many serious, violent, and chronic juvenile offenders requires the application of secure sanctions to hold these offenders accountable for their delinquent acts and to provide a structured treatment environment. Large congregate-care juvenile facilities (training schools, camps, and ranches) have not proven to be particularly effective in rehabilitating juvenile offenders. Although some continued use of these types of facilities will remain a necessary alternative for those juveniles who require enhanced security to protect the public, the establishment of small community-based facilities to provide intensive services in a secure environment offers the best hope for successful treatment of those juveniles who require a structured setting. Secure sanctions are most effective in changing future conduct when they are coupled with comprehensive treatment and rehabilitation services.

Standard parole practices, particularly those that have a primary focus on social control, have not been effective in normalizing the behavior of high-risk juvenile parolees over the long term, and consequently, growing interest has developed in intensive aftercare programs that provide high levels of social control and treatment services. OJJDP's Intensive Community-Based Aftercare for High-Risk Juvenile Parolees Program provides an effective aftercare model:

> The Intensive Aftercare Program incorporates five programmatic principles: (1) preparing youth for progressive responsibility and freedom in the community; (2) facilitating youth–community interaction and involvement; (3) working with both the offender and targeted community support systems (e.g., families, peers, schools, and employers) to facilitate constructive interaction and gradual community adjustment; (4) developing needed resources and community support; and (5) monitoring and ensuring the youth's successful reintegration into the community.

The following graduated sanctions strategies are proposed within the Secure Corrections component:

Community confinement. Offenders whose presenting offense is sufficiently serious (such as a violent felony) or who fail to respond to intermediate sanctions as evidenced by continued reoffending may be appropriate for community confinement. Offenders at this level represent the more serious (such as repeat felony drug trafficking or property offenders) and violent offenders among the juvenile justice system correctional population.

The concept of community confinement provides secure confinement in small community-based facilities that offer intensive treatment and rehabilitation services. These services include individual and group counseling, educational programs, medical services, and intensive staff supervision. Proximity to the community enables direct and regular family involvement with the treatment process as well as a phased reentry into the community that draws upon community resources and services.

Incarceration in training schools, camps, and ranches. Juveniles whose confinement in the community would constitute an ongoing threat to community safety or who have failed to respond to community-based corrections may require an extended correctional placement in training schools, camps, ranches, or other secure options that are not community-based. These facilities should offer comprehensive treatment programs for these youth with a focus on education, skills development, and vocational or employment training and experience. These juveniles may include those convicted in the criminal justice system prior to their reaching the age at which they are no longer subject to the original or extended jurisdiction of the juvenile justice system.

EXPECTED BENEFITS

The proposed strategy provides for a comprehensive approach in responding to delinquent conduct and serious, violent, and chronic criminal behavior, consisting of (1) community protection and public safety, (2) accountability, (3) competency development, (4) individualization, and (5) balanced representation of the interests of the community, victim, and juvenile. By taking these factors into account in each program component, a new direction in the administration of juvenile justice is fostered.

Delinquency Prevention

This major component of the comprehensive strategy involves implementation of delinquency prevention technology that has been demonstrated to be effective. Prevention strategies within the major areas that influence the behavior of youth (individual development, family, school, peer group, and community) parallel the chronological development of children. Because addressing these five areas has been found to be effective in reducing future delinquency among high-risk youth, it should result in fewer children entering the juvenile justice system in demonstration sites. This would, in turn, permit concentration of system resources on fewer delinquents, thereby increasing the effectiveness of the graduated sanctions component and improving the operation of the juvenile justice system.

Graduated Sanctions

This major component of the comprehensive strategy is premised on a firm belief that the juvenile justice system can effectively handle delinquent juvenile behavior through the judicious application of a range of graduated sanctions and a full continuum of treatment and rehabilitation services. Expected benefits of this approach include:

- **Increased juvenile justice system responsiveness.** This program will provide additional referral and dispositional resources for law enforcement, juvenile courts, and juvenile corrections. It will also require these system components to increase their ability to identify, process, evaluate, refer, and track juvenile offenders.

- **Increased juvenile accountability.** Juvenile offenders will be held accountable for their behavior, decreasing the likelihood of their development into serious, violent, or chronic offenders and tomorrow's adult criminals. The juvenile justice system will be held accountable for controlling chronic and serious delinquency while also protecting society. Communities will be held accountable for providing community-based prevention and treatment resources for juveniles.

- **Decreased costs of juvenile corrections.** Applying the appropriate graduated sanctions and developing the required community-based resources should reduce significantly the need for high-cost beds in training schools. Savings from the high costs of operating these facilities could be used to provide treatment in community-based programs and facilities.

- **Increased responsibility of the juvenile justice system.** Many juvenile offenders currently waived or transferred to the criminal justice system could be provided opportunities for intensive services in secure community-based settings or in long-term treatment in juvenile training schools, camps, and ranches.

- **Increased program effectiveness.** As the statistical information presented herein indicates, credible knowledge exists about who the chronic, serious, and violent offenders are, that is, their characteristics. Some knowledge also exists about what can effectively be done regarding their treatment and rehabilitation. However, more must be learned about what works best for whom under what circumstances to intervene successfully in the potential criminal careers of serious, violent, and chronic juvenile offenders. Followup research and rigorous evaluation of programs implemented as part of this strategy should produce valuable information.

Crime Reduction

The combined effects of delinquency prevention and increased juvenile justice system effectiveness in intervening immediately and effectively in the lives of delinquent offenders should result in measurable decreases in delinquency in sites where the above concepts are demonstrated. In addition, long-term reduction in crime should result from fewer serious, violent, and chronic delinquents becoming adult criminal offenders. . . .

REFERENCES

Hawkins, David, and Catalano, Jr., Richard. *Communities That Care*. San Francisco: Jossey-Bass Inc. 1992.

National Council of Juvenile and Family Court Judges. "Children and Families First, A Mandate for Change." Reno: NCJFCJ, 1993.

National Council of Juvenile and Family Court
Judges. "The Juvenile Court and Serious Of-

fenders: 38 Recommendations." *Juvenile and
Family Court Journal.* Summer 1984.

REVIEW QUESTIONS

1. What is the basic rationale underlying the *Comprehensive Strategy for Serious, Violent, and Chronic Juvenile Offenders* and what are its key principles?
2. What is the "risk-focused delinquency prevention approach"? What risk factors does it address and what sorts of techniques are advocated for addressing them?
3. What is meant by the term "graduated sanctions"? What are the three levels in the

continuum of graduated sanctions outlined in the *Comprehensive Strategy* and what intervention techniques are highlighted at each level?
4. What are "Risk and Needs Assessments"? How are they used in the system of graduated sanctions outlined in the *Comprehensive Strategy*?

Juvenile (In)Justice and the Criminal Court Alternative

Barry C. Feld

THE FUTURE OF THE JUVENILE COURT: THREE SCENARIOS

For several decades, juvenile courts have deflected, co-opted, ignored, or accommodated constitutional and legislative reforms with minimal institutional change. The juvenile court remains essentially unreformed despite its transformation from a welfare agency into a scaled-down, second-class criminal court. Public and political concerns about

Source: Barry C. Feld. (1993). Juvenile (in)justice and the criminal court alternative. *Crime and Delinquency,* 39(4), 403–424. Copyright © 1993 by Sage Publications, Inc. Reprinted by permission of Sage Publications, Inc.

drugs and youth crime encourage repressing rather than rehabilitating young offenders. Fiscal constraints, budget deficits, and competition from other interest groups reduce the likelihood that treatment services for delinquents will expand. Coupling these punitive policies with societal unwillingness to provide for the welfare of children in general, much less those who commit crimes, is there any reason to believe the juvenile court can be rehabilitated?

What is the justification for maintaining a separate court system whose only distinction is that it uses procedures under which no adult would consent to be tried (Feld 1988b; Ainsworth 1991)? Whereas most commentators acknowledge the emergence of a punitive juvenile court, they recoil at the prospect of its outright abolition, emphasize that children are different, and strive to maintain separation between delinquents and criminals (Melton 1989; Rosenberg 1993). Most conclude, however, that juvenile courts need a new rationale that melds punishment with reduced culpability and procedural justice.

There are three plausible responses to a juvenile court that punishes in the name of treatment and simultaneously denies young offenders elementary procedural justice: (a) juvenile courts could be "restructured to fit their original [therapeutic] purpose" (McKeiver 1970, p. 557); (b) punishment could be accepted as appropriate in delinquency proceedings but coupled with all criminal procedural safeguards (Melton 1989; ABA 1980c); or (c) juvenile courts could be abolished and young offenders tried in criminal courts with certain substantive and procedural modifications (Feld 1984, 1988b; Ainsworth 1991).

RETURN TO INFORMAL, REHABILITATIVE JUVENILE JUSTICE

Proponents of informal, therapeutic juvenile courts contend that the experiment should not be declared a failure because it has never been implemented effectively (Ferdinand 1989, 1991). From its inception, juvenile courts and correctional facilities have had more in common with penal facilities than welfare agencies (Rothman 1980). Despite its long-standing and readily apparent failures of implementation, proposals persist to reinvigorate the juvenile court as an informal, welfare agency (Edwards 1992).

Even if a flood of resources and a coterie of clinicians suddenly inundated a juvenile court, it would be a dubious policy to recreate it as originally conceived. Despite formal statutes and procedural rules, the "individualized justice" of juvenile courts is substantively and procedurally lawless. To the extent that judges individualize decisions in offenders' best interests, judicial discretion is formally unrestricted. But without practical scientific or clinical bases by which to classify or treat, the exercise of sound discretion is simply a euphemism for judicial subjectivity. Individualization treats similarly situated offenders differently on the basis of personal characteristics and imposes unequal sanctions on invidious bases.

Procedural informality is the concomitant of substantive discretion. If clinical decision making is unconstrained substantively, then it cannot be limited procedurally either, because every case is unique. Although lawyers manipulate legal rules for their clients' advantage, a court without objective laws or formal procedures is unfavorable terrain. But without lawyers to invoke laws, no mechanisms exist to make juvenile courts conform to legal mandates. Closed, informal, confidential proceedings reduce visibility and account-ability and preclude external checks on coercive intervention.

Subordinating social welfare to social control. Focusing simply on failures of implemen-tation, inadequate social services or welfare resources, abuses of discretion, and persisting procedural deficiencies, however, systematically misleads both proponents and critics of the juvenile court and prevents either from envisioning alternatives. The fundamental shortcoming of the juvenile court is not just its failures of implementation, but a deeper flaw in its basic concept. The original juvenile court was conceived of as a social service agency operating in a judicial setting, a fusion of welfare and coercion. But providing for the social welfare of young people is ultimately a societal responsibility rather than a judi-cial one. It is simply unrealistic to expect juvenile courts, or any other legal institution, ei-ther to alleviate the social ills afflicting young people or to have a significant impact on youth crime.

Despite claims of being a child-centered nation, we care less about other people's chil-dren than we do our own, especially when they are children of other colors or cultures (Na-tional Commission on Children 1991). Without a societal commitment to adequately meet the minimum family, medical, housing, nutritional, and educational needs of all young peo-ple on a voluntary basis, the juvenile court provides a mechanism for imposing involuntary controls on some youths, regardless of how ineffective it may be in delivering services or rehabilitating offenders.

Juvenile courts' penal emphasis. When social services and social control are combined in one setting, as in juvenile court, custodial considerations quickly subordinate social wel-fare concerns. Historically, juvenile courts purported to resolve the tension between social welfare and social control by asserting that dispositions in a child's best interests achieved individual and public welfare simultaneously. In reality, some youths who commit crimes do not need social services, whereas others cannot be meaningfully rehabilitated. And, many more children with social service needs do not commit crimes.

Juvenile courts' subordination of individual welfare to custody and control stems from its fundamentally penal focus. Delinquency jurisdiction is not based on characteris-tics of children for which they are not responsible and for whom intervention could mean an improvement in their lives—their lack of decent education, their lack of adequate hous-ing, their unmet medical needs, or their family or social circumstances (National Commis-sion on Children 1991). Rather, delinquency jurisdiction is based on criminal law violations that are the youths' fault and for which the youths are responsible (Fox 1970b). As long as juvenile courts emphasize criminal characteristics of children least likely to elicit sympathy and ignore social conditions most likely to engender a desire to nurture and help, they reinforce punitive rather than rehabilitative impulses. Operating in a societal context that does not provide adequately for children in general, intervention in the lives of those who commit crimes inevitably serves purposes of penal social control, regardless of the court's ability to deliver social welfare.

Due process and punishment in juvenile court. Acknowledging that juvenile courts pun-ish imposes an obligation to provide all criminal procedural safeguards because "the condition of being a boy does not justify a kangaroo court" (*Gault* 1967, p. 28). Although procedural parity with adults may end the juvenile court experiment, to fail to do so perpetuates injustice. Punishing juveniles in the name of treatment and denying them basic safeguards fosters injustice that thwarts any reform efforts.

Developing rationales to respond to young offenders requires reconciling contradictory impulses engendered when the child is a criminal and the criminal is a child. If juvenile courts provide neither therapy nor justice, then the alternatives are either (a) to make juvenile courts more like criminal courts, or (b) to make criminal courts more like juvenile courts. Whether young offenders ultimately are tried in a separate juvenile court or in a criminal court raises basic issues of substance and procedure. Issues of substantive justice include developing and implementing a doctrinal rationale to sentence young offenders differently, and more leniently, than older defendants (Feld 1988b). Issues of procedural justice include providing youths with *all* of the procedural safeguards adults receive *and* additional protections that recognize their immaturity (Rosenberg 1980; Feld 1984).

Most commentators who recoil from abolishing juvenile court instead propose to transform it into an explicitly penal one, albeit one that limits punishment based on reduced culpability and provides enhanced procedural justice (Melton 1989; ABA 1980a). The paradigm of the "new juvenile court" is the American Bar Association's Juvenile Justice Standards. The Juvenile Justice Standards recommend repeal of jurisdiction over status offenders, use of proportional and determinate sentences to sanction delinquent offenders, use of offense criteria to regularize pretrial detention and judicial transfer decisions, and provision of all criminal procedural safeguards, including nonwaivable counsel and jury trials (Flicker 1983; Wizner and Keller 1977). Although the ABA's "criminal juvenile court" combines reduced culpability sentencing and greater procedural justice, it fails to explain why these principles should be implemented in a separate juvenile court rather than in a criminal court (Melton 1989; Gardner 1989). The ABA's Juvenile Justice Standards assert that "removal of the treatment rationale does not destroy the rationale for a separate system or for utilization of an ameliorative approach; it does, however, require a different rationale" (ABA 1980b, p. 19, note 5). Unfortunately, although the ABA standards virtually replicate the adult criminal process, they provide no rationale for a separate juvenile system.

Some commentators contend that maintaining a separate punishment system for juveniles may avoid some stigmatic effects of a "criminal" label (Gardner 1989). Others speculate that because some specialized juvenile procedures and dispositional facilities will remain, it is more practical and less risky to retain than to abolish juvenile courts (Rubin 1979). Some emphasize criminal courts' deficiencies—overcrowding, ineffective counsel, insufficient sentencing alternatives—as a justification for retaining juvenile courts, even while acknowledging that these are characteristics of juvenile courts as well (Dawson 1990). Given institutional and bureaucratic inertia, however, it might be that only a clean break with the personnel and practices of the past would permit the implementation of procedural justice and sentencing reforms.

The only real difference between the ABA's criminal juvenile court and adult criminal courts is that the former would impose shorter sentences (ABA 1980c; Wizner and Keller

1977). Particularly for serious young offenders, the sanctions imposed in juvenile court are less than those of criminal courts, and a separate court might be the only way to achieve those shorter sentences and insulate youths from criminal courts.

But, recent research suggests that there might be a relationship between increased procedural formality and sentencing severity in juvenile courts. Despite statutes and rules of statewide applicability, juvenile courts are highly variable. Urban courts, which typically are the most formal, also detain and sentence more severely than do their more traditional, rural counterparts (Feld 1991a). If procedural formality increases substantive severity, could a separate criminal juvenile court continue to afford leniency? Will juvenile courts' procedural convergence with criminal courts increase repressiveness and erode present sentencing differences? Can juvenile courts only be lenient because discretion is hidden behind closed doors? Would imposing the rule of law prevent them from affording leniency to most youths? The ABA Standards do not even recognize, much less answer, these questions.

Young offenders in criminal court. If the primary reason a child is in court is because he or she committed a crime, then the child could be tried in criminal courts alongside adult counterparts. Before returning young offenders to criminal courts, however, a legislature must address issues of substance and procedure in order to create a juvenile criminal court. Substantively, a legislature must develop a rationale to sentence young offenders differently and more leniently than older defendants. Procedurally, it must afford youths full parity with adults and additional safeguards.

Substantive justice—juveniles' criminal responsibility. The primary virtue of the contemporary juvenile court is that young serious offenders typically receive shorter sentences than do adults convicted of comparable crimes. One premise of juvenile justice is that youths should survive the mistakes of adolescence with their life chances intact, and this goal would be threatened by the draconian sentences frequently inflicted on 18-year-old "adults." However, even juvenile courts' seeming virtue of shorter sentences for serious offenders is offset by the far more numerous minor offenders who receive longer sentences as juveniles than they would as adults.

Shorter sentences for young people do not require that they be tried in separate juvenile courts. Criminal law doctrines and policies provide rationales to sentence youths less severely than adults in criminal courts (Feld 1988b; Melton 1989). Juvenile courts simply extended upward by a few years the common law's infancy presumptions that immature young people lack criminal capacity (Fox 1970b). "Diminished responsibility" doctrines provide additional rationale for shorter sentences for youths, because within a framework of "deserved" punishments, it would be unjust to sentence youths and adults alike (ABA 1980c). Although an offender's age is of little relevance when assessing harm, youthfulness is highly pertinent when assessing culpability.

Developmental psychological research confirms that young people move through developmental stages with respect to legal reasoning and ethical decision making akin to the common law's infancy defense. Even youths 14 years of age or older, who abstractly may know "right from wrong," might still not be as blameworthy and deserving of comparable punishment as adult offenders. Families, schools, and communities socialize young people and share some responsibility for their offenses (Twentieth Century Fund 1978). To the extent that the ability to make responsible choices is learned behavior, the dependent status of youths systematically deprives them of opportunities to learn to be responsible (Zimring 1982).

The Supreme Court in *Thompson v. Oklahoma* (1988) provided additional support for lesser sentences for reduced culpability even for youths above the common-law infancy threshold of 14 years of age. In vacating Thompson's capital sentence, the Court noted that even though he was criminally responsible, he should not be punished as severely. Despite a later decision upholding the death penalty for 16-year-old or 17-year-old youths (*Stanford* [*v. Kentucky*] 1989), the Court has repeatedly emphasized that youthfulness is an important mitigating factor at sentencing. The argument for shorter sentences for reduced culpability is not a constitutional claim because the Supreme Court consistently has resisted developing a criminal law mens rea jurisprudence (Rosenberg 1993). Rather, like the juvenile court itself, it is a matter of state legislative sentencing policy.

"Youth discount." Shorter sentences for reduced culpability is a more modest rationale to treat young people differently from adults than the juvenile court's rehabilitative claims. Criminal courts can provide shorter sentences for reduced culpability with fractional reductions of adult sentences in the form of an explicit "youth discount." For example, a 14-year-old might receive 33% of the adult penalty, a 16-year-old 66%, and an 18-year-old the adult penalty, as is presently the case (Feld 1988b). Of course, explicit fractional youth discount sentence reductions can only be calculated against a backdrop of realistic, humane, and determinate adult sentencing practices. For youths younger than 14 years old, the common-law mens rea infancy defense acquires a new vitality for shorter sentences or even noncriminal alternative dispositions (Fox 1970b).

A graduated age-culpability sentencing scheme avoids the inconsistency and injustice played out in binary either/or juvenile versus adult judicial waiver determinations (Feld 1987). Sentences that young people receive might differ by orders of magnitude, depending upon whether or not transfer is ordered. Because of the profound consequences, waiver hearings consume a disproportionate amount of juvenile court time and resources. Abolishing juvenile court eliminates waiver hearings, saves resources that are ultimately expended to no purpose, reduces the "punishment gap" when youths cross from one system to the other, and assures similar consequences for similar offenders.

Trying young people in criminal courts with full procedural safeguards would not appreciably diminish judges' sentencing expertise. Although Progressives envisioned a specialist juvenile court judge possessing the wisdom of a "kadi" (Matza 1964), judges increasingly handle juvenile matters as part of the general docket or rotate through juvenile court on short-term assignments without acquiring any particular dispositional expertise. In most juvenile courts, social services personnel advise judges and possess the information necessary for appropriate dispositions.

Punishing youths does not require incarcerating them with adults in jails and prisons. Departments of corrections already classify inmates, and existing juvenile detention facilities and institutions provide options for age-segregated dispositional facilities. Insisting explicitly on humane conditions of confinement could do as much to improve the lives of incarcerated youths as has the "right to treatment" or the "rehabilitative ideal" (Feld 1977, 1981). Recognizing that most young offenders return to society imposes an obligation to provide resources for self-improvement on a voluntary basis.

Procedural justice for youth. Since *Gault*, most of the procedures of criminal courts are supposed to be routine aspects of juvenile courts as well. Generally, both courts apply the same laws of arrest, search, identification, and interrogation to adults and juveniles, and increasingly subject juveniles charged with felony offenses to similar fingerprinting and booking processes as adults (Feld 1984; Dawson 1990). The more formal and adversarial nature of juvenile court procedures reflects the attenuation between the court's therapeutic mission and its social control functions. The many instances in which states treat juvenile offenders procedurally like adult criminal defendants is one aspect of this process (Feld 1984). Despite the procedural convergence, it remains nearly as true today as 2 decades ago that "the child receives the worst of both worlds" (*Kent* 1966, p. 556). Most states provide neither special safeguards to protect juveniles from the consequences of their immaturity nor the full panoply of adult procedural safeguards to protect them from punitive state intervention.

Youths' differences in age and competence require them to receive more protections than adults, rather than less. The rationales to sentence youths differently and more leniently than adults also justify providing them with *all* of the procedural safeguards adults receive *and* additional protections that recognize their immaturity. This dual-maximal strategy explicitly provides enhanced protection for children because of their vulnerability and immaturity (Feld 1984; Rosenberg 1980; Melton 1989). As contrasted with current practices, for example, a dual-maximal procedural strategy produces different results with respect to waivers of constitutional rights. Although counsel is the prerequisite to procedural justice for juveniles, many youths do not receive the assistance of counsel because courts use the adult standard and find they waived the right in a "knowing, intelligent, and voluntary" manner under the "totality of the circumstances." The Juvenile Justice Standards recognize youths' limitations in dealing with the law and provide that the right to counsel attaches when a youth is taken into custody, that it is self-invoking and does not require an affirmative request as is the case for adults, and that youths must consult with counsel prior to waiving counsel or at interrogation (ABA 1980a).

Providing youths with full procedural parity in criminal courts and additional substantive and procedural safeguards could afford more protection than does the juvenile court. A youth concerned about adverse publicity could waive the right to public trial. If a youth successfully completes a sentence without recidivating, then expunging criminal records and eliminating collateral disabilities could avoid criminal labels and afford as much relief from an isolated act of folly as does the juvenile court's confidentiality.

The conceptual problems of creating a juvenile criminal court are soluble. The difficulty is political. Even though juvenile courts currently provide uneven leniency, could legislators who want to get tough on crime vote for a youth-discount sentencing provision that explicitly recognizes youthfulness as a mitigating factor in sentencing? Even though young people presently possess some constitutional rights, would politicians be willing to provide a justice system that assures those rights would be realistically and routinely exercised? Or, would they rather maintain a juvenile system that provides neither therapy nor justice, that elevates social control over social welfare, and that abuses children while claiming to protect them?

Abolishing juvenile court forces a long overdue and critical reassessment of the meaning of "childhood" (Ainsworth 1991). A society that regards young people as fundamentally different from adults easily justifies an inferior justice system and conveniently rationalizes it on the grounds that children are entitled only to custody, not liberty (*Schall v. Martin* 1984). The ideology of therapeutic justice and its discretionary apparatus persist because the social control is directed at children. Despite humanitarian claims of being a child-centered nation, cultural and legal conceptions of children support institutional arrangements that deny the personhood of young people. Rethinking the juvenile court requires critically reassessing the meaning of childhood and creating social institutions to assure the welfare of the next generation.

REFERENCES

Ainsworth, Janet. 1991. "Re-imagining Childhood and Reconstructing the Legal Order: The Case for Abolishing the Juvenile Court." *North Carolina Law Review* 69:1083–1133.

American Bar Association—Institute of Judicial Administration. 1980a. *Juvenile Justice Standards Relating to Counsel for Private Parties.* Cambridge, MA: Ballinger.

_____. 1980b. *Juvenile Justice Standards Relating to Dispositions.* Cambridge, MA: Ballinger.

_____. 1980c. *Juvenile Justice Standards Relating to Juvenile Delinquency and Sanctions.* Cambridge, MA: Ballinger.

Dawson, Robert. 1990. "The Future of Juvenile Justice: Is It Time to Abolish the System?" *Journal of Criminal Law & Criminology* 81: 136–55.

Edwards, Leonard P. 1992. "The Juvenile Court and the Role of the Juvenile Court Judge." *Juvenile and Family Court Journal* 43:1–45.

Feld, Barry C. 1977. *Neutralizing Inmate Violence: Juvenile Offenders in Institutions.* Cambridge, MA: Ballinger.

_____. 1981. "A Comparative Analysis of Organizational Structure and Inmate Subcultures in Institutions for Juvenile Offenders." *Crime & Delinquency* 27:336–63.

_____. 1984. "Criminalizing Juvenile Justice: Rules of Procedure for Juvenile Court." *Minnesota Law Review* 69:141–276.

_____. 1987. "Juvenile Court Meets the Principle of Offense: Legislative Changes in Juvenile Waiver Statutes." *Journal of Criminal Law and Criminology* 78:471–533.

_____. 1988a. "*In re Gault* Revisited: A Cross-State Comparison of the Right to Counsel in Juvenile Court." *Crime & Delinquency* 34:393–424.

_____. 1988b. "Juvenile Court Meets the Principle of Offense: Punishment, Treatment, and the Difference it Makes." *Boston University Law Review* 68:821–915.

_____. 1991a. "Justice by Geography: Urban, Suburban, and Rural Variations in Juvenile Justice Administration." *Journal of Criminal Law and Criminology* 82:156–210.

_____. 1991b. "The Transformation of the Juvenile Court." *Minnesota Law Review* 75:691–725.

Ferdinand, Theodore N. 1989. "Juvenile Delinquency or Juvenile Justice: Which Came First?" *Criminology* 27:79–106.

_____. 1991. "History Overtakes the Juvenile Justice System." *Crime & Delinquency* 37:204–24.

Flicker, Barbara. 1983. *Standards for Juvenile Justice: A Summary and Analysis*. 2nd ed. Cambridge, MA: Ballinger.

Fox, Sanford J. 1970a. "Juvenile Justice Reform: An Historical Perspective." *Stanford Law Review* 22:1187–1239.

_____. 1970b. "Responsibility in the Juvenile Court." *William & Mary Law Review* 11:659–84.

Gardner, Martin. 1989. "The Right of Juvenile Offenders to be Punished: Some Implications of Treating Kids as Persons." *Nebraska Law Review* 68:182–215.

Matza, David. 1964. *Delinquency and Drift*. New York: Wiley.

Melton, Gary B. 1989. "Taking *Gault* Seriously: Toward a New Juvenile Court." *Nebraska Law Review* 68:146–81.

National Commission on Children. 1991. *Beyond Rhetoric: A New American Agenda for Children and Families*. Washington, DC: U.S. Government Printing Office.

Rosenberg, Irene M. 1980. "The Constitutional Rights of Children Charged with Crime: Proposal for a Return to the Not So Distant Past." *University of California Los Angeles Law Review* 27:656–721.

_____. 1993. "Leaving Bad Enough Alone: A Response to the Juvenile Court Abolitionists." *Wisconsin Law Review* 1993:163–85.

Rothman, David J. 1980. *Conscience and Convenience: The Asylum and Its Alternative in Progressive America*. Boston: Little, Brown.

Rubin, H. Ted. 1979. "Retain the Juvenile Court? Legislative Developments, Reform Directions and the Call for Abolition." *Crime & Delinquency* 25:281–98.

Twentieth Century Fund Task Force on Sentencing Policy Toward Young Offenders. 1978. *Confronting Youth Crime*. New York: Holmes & Meier.

Wizner, Steven and Mary F. Keller. 1977. "The Penal Model of Juvenile Justice: Is Juvenile Court Delinquency Jurisdiction Obsolete?" *New York University Law Review* 52:1120–35.

Zimring, Franklin. 1982. *The Changing Legal World of Adolescence*. New York: Free Press.

CASES CITED

In re Gault, 387 U.S. 1 (1967).
Kent v. United States, 383 U.S. 541 (1966).
McKeiver v. Pennyslvania, 403 U.S. 528 (1970).

Schall v. Martin, 467 U.S. 260 (1984).
Stanford v. Kentucky, 109 S.Ct. 2974 (1989).
Thompson v. Oklahoma, 487 U.S. 815 (1988).

REVIEW QUESTIONS

1. Near the beginning of this selection the author argues that "[t]he juvenile court remains essentially unreformed despite its transformation from a welfare agency into a scaled-down, second-class criminal court" (p. 396). What does he mean by this? What, in his view, are the implications for juvenile justice policy?

2. Feld introduces three scenarios for the future of the juvenile court. What are they? Which does he find most desirable? What are its benefits? What problems does he foresee with the other two scenarios?

3. What does Feld mean by a "youth discount"? Why does he think that applying such a discount in adult criminal court would be an appropriate response to concerns about the impact of developmental factors on juveniles' blameworthiness for their offenses? In what other ways does he

think adult criminal courts should alter their procedures in response to the vulnerability and immaturity of young offenders?

4. Do you agree with Feld that the delinquency jurisdiction of the juvenile court should be abolished and that all juvenile offenses should be tried in criminal court? Why or why not?

Restoring the Balance: Juvenile and Community Justice

Gordon Bazemore and Susan E. Day

In a democratic society, citizens' expectations of government agencies are critically important. Unfortunately, within our juvenile justice system, community needs have been lost in the decade-long debate over the future of the juvenile court and the relative efficacy of punishment versus treatment. A number of politicians and policymakers argue for criminalizing our juvenile justice system through "get tough," adult sentences for juvenile offenders. Some even advocate abolishing the juvenile justice system and its foundation, the independent juvenile court.

On the other hand, many proponents of the juvenile court call for reaffirming the traditional treatment mission. Increasingly, the public and even many juvenile justice professionals perceive that treatment and punishment options are, as one judge aptly put it, "bad choices between sending kids to jail or sending them to the beach."

It is doubtful that either traditional treatment or criminalized retributive models can restore public confidence in the juvenile justice system. Only through extensive, meaningful citizen participation will public expectations and community needs be met. For most juvenile justice systems, achieving this level of involvement will require substantial restructuring.

This article describes an alternative approach to addressing juvenile crime that focuses on the interests of multiple justice clients. Alternatively referred to as restorative justice, the balanced approach, and balanced and restorative justice (BRJ), this model is viewed by a growing number of juvenile justice professionals as a way to reengage the community in the juvenile justice process.

Source: Gordon Bazemore and Susan E. Day. (1996). Restoring the balance: juvenile and community justice. *Juvenile Justice,* 3(1), 3–14. Adapted courtesy of the United States Department of Justice, Office of Juvenile Justice and Delinquency Prevention.

THE LIMITS OF CURRENT PARADIGMS

. . . Advocates of reaffirming treatment argue that the system is failing because it lacks adequate resources. Critics and defenders of juvenile justice, however, argue that juvenile justice systems have failed to articulate a vision of success. If juvenile justice is underfunded, it is also underconceptualized. As closed-system paradigms, the treatment and retributive models are insular and one-dimensional. They are insular because they are offender-focused and one-dimensional because they fail to address the community's diverse interests.

Although the punitive approach may appease public demand for retribution, it does little to rehabilitate or reintegrate juvenile offenders. Punishment is often used inappropriately, resulting in amply documented negative effects. Ironically, retributive punishment may encourage offenders to focus on themselves rather than on their victims. Even increasing its severity may have little impact if we have miscalculated the extent to which sanctions such as incarceration are experienced as punishment.

In the public mind, punishment is at least somewhat related to offense. In contrast, treatment appears to address only the needs of the offender. Treatment programs often ask little of the offender beyond participating in counseling, remedial services, or recreational programs. Even when such programs "work," they make little difference in the lives of victims of juvenile crime, citizens concerned with the safety of their neighborhoods, or individuals who want young offenders held accountable for their actions.

In fact, both punitive and treatment models focus little attention on the needs of victims and victimized communities. Neither model engages them as clients or as coparticipants in the justice process. Whether treatment or punishment is emphasized, the offender is the passive and solitary recipient of intervention and service. Increasingly reliant on facilities, treatment programs, and professional experts, juvenile justice systems exclude victims and other community members from what could be meaningful roles in sanctioning, rehabilitation, and public safety.

Fortunately, treatment and retributive models are not the only options for juvenile justice. The alternative, a community-oriented system, would involve citizens in setting clear limits on antisocial behavior and determining consequences for offenders. Victims' needs for reparation, validation, and healing would be at the core of a community justice system, which would work toward building crime-resistant communities whose residents feel safe. It would emphasize the need for building relationships and involving youth in work, service, and other roles that facilitate bonding with law-abiding adults. Finally, a community justice system would articulate more meaningful roles in rehabilitating offenders and improving community safety for employers, civic groups, religious communities, families, and other citizens.

TOWARD COMMUNITY JUVENILE JUSTICE: A BALANCED AND RESTORATIVE APPROACH

- In inner-city Pittsburgh, young offenders in an intensive day treatment program solicit input from community organizations about service projects they would like to see completed in the neighborhood. They work with community residents on projects that include home repair and gardening for the elderly, voter registration drives, painting homes and public buildings, and planting and cultivating community gardens.

- In Florida, young offenders sponsored by the Florida Department of Juvenile Justice and supervised by The 100 Black Men of Palm Beach County, Inc., plan and execute projects that serve as shelters for abused, abandoned, and HIV-positive and AIDS-infected infants and children. In Palm Beach County, victim advocates train juvenile justice staff on sensitivity in their interaction with victims and help prepare victim awareness curriculums for youth in residential programs.

- In cities and towns in Pennsylvania, Montana, Minnesota, Australia, and New Zealand, family members and other citizens acquainted with a juvenile offender or victim of a juvenile crime gather to determine the best response to the offense. Held in schools, churches, or other community facilities, these family group conferences are facilitated by a community justice coordinator or police officer and ensure that offenders hear community disapproval of their behavior. Participants develop an agreement for repairing the damage to victim and community and a plan for reintegrating the offender.

- In Minnesota, Department of Corrections staff collaborate with local police and citizen groups to establish family group conferencing programs and inform the community about offender monitoring and victim support. In Dakota County, a suburb of Minneapolis, retailers and senior citizens whose businesses and homes have been damaged by burglary or vandalism call a crime repair hotline to request a work crew of probationers to repair the damage.

- In Deschutes County, Oregon, offender work crews cut and deliver firewood to senior citizens and worked with a local contractor to build a homeless shelter.

- In more than 150 cities and towns throughout North America, victims and offenders meet with volunteer mediators to develop an agreement for restitution. At these meetings, victims express their feelings about the crime and gain information about the offense.

- In several cities in Montana, college students and other young adults in the Montana Conservation Corps supervise juvenile offenders working on environmental restoration, trail building, and other community service projects. They also serve as mentors.

While many professionals have become demoralized as juvenile justice systems are threatened with extinction, others are seeking to create a new partnership between youth and victim advocates, concerned citizens, and community groups.

The balanced and restorative justice model is centered around community-oriented responses to crime.[1] Jurisdictions implementing it represent a diverse range of urban, sub-

---

[1]Balanced and Restorative Justice (BRJ) is also the title of a national action research project

urban, and rural communities. These communities share a common commitment to restructuring juvenile justice on the basis of a new mission (balanced approach) and a new value framework (restorative justice).

RESTORATIVE AND COMMUNITY JUSTICE

From the perspective of restorative justice, the most significant aspect of crime is that it victimizes citizens and communities. The justice system should focus on repairing this harm by ensuring that offenders are held accountable for making amends for the damage and suffering they have caused. The most important issue in a restorative response to crime is not deciding whether to punish or treat offenders. Rather, as Howard Zehr suggests, the three primary questions to be answered are "What is the harm?" "What needs to be done to make it right?" and "Who is responsible?"[2]

A restorative system would help to ensure that offenders make amends to their victims. Juvenile justice cannot do this alone, however. Restorative justice requires that not only government but victims, offenders, and communities be actively involved in the justice process. In fact, some have argued that the health of a community is determined by the extent to which citizens participate in community decisions. An effective justice system strengthens the capacity of communities to respond to crime and empowers them to do so. As Judge Barry Stuart notes:

> When members fail to assume responsibility for decisions affecting the community, community life will be characterized by the absence of a collective sense of caring, a lack of respect for diverse values, and ultimately a lack of any sense of belonging. . . . Conflict, if resolved through a process that constructively engages the parties involved, can be a fundamental building ingredient of any relationship. As members increase their ability to resolve disputes creatively, the ability of the community to effectively sanction crime, rehabilitate offenders, and promote public safety increases.[3]

The most unique feature of restorative justice is its elevation of the role of victims in the justice system. Victim rights has become a popular slogan, but victim needs are addressed by the system only after the needs of judges, prosecutors, probation officers, treatment providers, and even offenders are considered. Restorative justice does not define victim rights as the absence of offender rights; it focuses on the needs of victim, community, and offender. To bring balance to the present offender-driven system,

---

funded through the Technical Assistance and Training Prevention division of the Office of Juvenile Justice and Delinquency Prevention. This project provides national training and information dissemination as well as support and assistance to demonstration projects currently implementing BRJ.

[2]H. Zehr, *Changing Lenses: A New Focus for Crime and Justice* (Scottsdale, PA: Herald Press, 1990).

[3]Judge B. Stuart, notes from presentation at the annual conference of the Society for Professionals in Dispute Resolution (Toronto, Canada, 1993): 7.

however, it is necessary to give priority to victims' needs for physical, material, and emotional healing.

THE BALANCED APPROACH MISSION

The balanced approach is a back-to-basics mission for juvenile justice that supports a community's need to sanction crime, rehabilitate offenders, and ensure public safety. Toward these ends, it articulates three goals for juvenile justice: accountability, public safety, and competency development. . . . Balance is attainable when administrators ensure that equitable resources are allocated to each goal.

- **Accountability.** Crime is sanctioned most effectively when offenders take responsibility for their crimes and the harm caused to victims, when offenders make amends by restoring losses, and when communities and victims take active roles in the sanctioning process. Because the offender's obligation is defined primarily as an obligation to his victims rather than to the State, accountability cannot be equated with responsiveness to juvenile justice professionals by obeying a curfew, complying with drug screening, or writing an essay. Nor can it be equated with punishment. It is easier to make offenders take their punishment than it is to get them to take responsibility for their actions.

- **Competency.** The most successful rehabilitation ensures that young offenders make measurable gains in educational, vocational, social, civic, and other competencies that enhance their capacity to function as productive adults. When competency is defined as the capacity to do something well that others value, the standard for achieving success is measured in the community. Competency is not the mere absence of bad behavior. It should increase the capacity of adults and communities to involve young people in work, service, dispute resolution, community problem solving, and cognitive skills building.

- **Public safety.** Assuring public safety requires more than mere incapacitation. Communities cannot be kept safe simply by locking up offenders. Locked facilities must be part of any public safety strategy, but they are the least cost-effective component. A balanced strategy invests heavily in strengthening a community's capacity to prevent and control crime. A problem-oriented focus ensures that the time of offenders under supervision in the community is structured around such activities as work, education, and service. Adults, including parents, are assigned clear roles in monitoring offenders. A balanced strategy cultivates new relationships with schools, employers, and other community groups to enhance the role of juvenile justice professionals as resources in prevention and positive youth development.

The principle behind BRJ is that justice is best served when victims, offenders, and communities receive equitable attention in the justice process. The needs of one client cannot be met unless the needs of other clients are addressed. Crime severs bonds between victims, offenders, and families. Although offenders must take full responsibility for their acts, the responsibility for restoring mutual respect, understanding, and support among those involved must be shared by the community.

SMALL CHANGES YIELD LARGE RESULTS

The change at the heart of BRJ is embodied in the community-building interventions described above. BRJ collaborators, including juvenile justice and other service professionals, have discovered that even small changes in how they conduct business can have immediate and lasting effects on the dynamics of community relationships.

Communities in the United States and across the globe are making dramatic policy changes on the basis of restorative priorities. In 1989, New Zealand began requiring that all juvenile offenders over age 14 (except in the most serious cases) be referred to a family group conference in which restorative goals are addressed in meetings that include victims, offenders, support groups, families, policymakers, social workers, and others. The New Zealand law appears to have drastically reduced court workloads and the use of incarceration.[4]

Fourteen States have enacted legislation adopting the balanced approach as the mission of their juvenile justice systems. A number of States have administrative rules or statewide policies that require case managers and other decisionmakers to consider the goals of the balanced approach in dispositional recommendations. In Pennsylvania and Montana, decisionmakers are using balanced approach criteria as funding guidelines and have formed statewide groups to oversee the development of restorative justice efforts.

Balanced and restorative justice cannot be achieved by mandates or legislation alone. As the three jurisdictions that constitute the OJJDP-funded demonstration effort are learning, the new model cannot be implemented overnight. Working with different juvenile justice systems in diverse communities, administrators in Palm Beach County, Florida, Dakota County, Minnesota, and Allegheny County, Pennsylvania, are pursuing varied approaches to systemic change to build a restorative model from the ground up. These administrators have made significant progress but acknowledge that the kind of change envisioned by BRJ is quite different from past practices. This change is especially striking in the model's focus on citizen involvement, including restructuring juvenile justice agencies to more effectively engage the community.

---

[4]F.W.M. McElrae, "Restorative Justice—The New Zealand Youth Court: A Model for Development in Other Courts?" *Journal of Judicial Administration,* 4 (1994), Australian Institute of Judicial Administration, Melbourne, Australia.

BALANCED AND RESTORATIVE JUSTICE: NEW ROLES FOR CITIZENS AND PROFESSIONALS

. . . As a community justice model, balanced and restorative justice offers a new vision of how victims, offenders, and others can be involved in the juvenile justice process. . . . [T]his vision is best understood by examining how the model is viewed by its participants.

Balanced and restorative justice is a work in progress. No juvenile justice system is completely balanced or fully restorative. But if juvenile justice systems, including those most committed to the model, fail to meet the standards they have set for community and client involvement, it is not because the model is utopian. It is because administrators are constrained by management protocols designed to deliver services based on the treatment and retributive paradigms.

The innovation of balanced and restorative justice lies in its agenda for restructuring the juvenile justice system to make it community-focused rather than bureaucracy-driven. This agenda demands new values, clients, performance objectives, decisionmaking processes, program priorities, staff roles, and patterns of resource allocation. . . . [W]hile most juvenile justice agencies determine intervention priorities on the basis of current staff roles and resource allocations, juvenile justice managers who adopt the balanced approach mission are committed to making their agencies and systems value- and client-driven and outcome-oriented. Decisions are based on the premise that programs are means to accomplish restorative outcomes that address community needs. . . .

From a community justice perspective, the value of a program and the quality of its implementation is gauged in large measure by the extent to which it involves community members at all levels of implementation.

CITIZEN INVOLVEMENT AND CLIENT FOCUS

In the total quality management (TQM) movement,[5] the concept of a client involves three components: a recipient of service, a target of intervention and change, and a coparticipant who must have input into the process and be involved to the greatest extent possible in decisionmaking.

The input of each client group is needed to stimulate and maintain community involvement. Currently few citizens are involved at significant levels in juvenile justice because they are seldom asked. Although many professionals would welcome community involvement and may work hard at collaboration and service brokerage, such efforts often fail to include employers, clergy, civic leaders, and neighborhood residents. Too often, juvenile justice agencies are unable to find appropriate roles for community members who are not social service professionals or time to support their efforts. Short-term involvement

---

[5]W.E. Deming, *Out of Crisis* (Cambridge, MA: MIT Center for Advanced Engineering, 1986); L. Martin, *Total Quality Management in Organizations* (Newbury Park, CA: Sage, 1993).

is often uninteresting because it is not linked to interventions that achieve significant outcomes for offenders or victims. When citizens are asked to participate, it is often on the basis of civic duty rather than personal commitment. As Braithwaite and Mugford observe, citizens are more willing to become involved if they have a personal interest in the offender, victim, or the family.[6]

Crimes typically evoke a community of concern for the victim, the offender, families and friends, and interested citizens and community groups. As the New Zealand experiment with family group conferencing illustrates, these personal communities can be a primary resource in resolving youth crimes. It is around such microcommunities that citizen participation in justice decisionmaking is being built.

BRJ practices and programs invite a high level of citizen participation. Community involvement is never easy, but it is satisfying for citizens to help young offenders make restitution to their victims.

The more active roles for offenders, victims, and community in the juvenile justice process . . . have implications for the roles of juvenile justice professionals. The most important and difficult challenge in moving toward balanced and restorative justice will be to alter the job descriptions and professional orientations of juvenile justice staff. For those accustomed to working with offenders individually or in programs and facilities, the role change implied by the need to engage victims and communities may be dramatic. Essentially, this change may be best understood as moving from direct service provider or service broker to community justice facilitator.

. . . [T]he new roles involve juvenile justice professionals in activities with each of the three justice clients. These activities include a variety of efforts to enhance preventive capacity and to help adults provide offenders with opportunities for competency development.

GETTING THERE

. . . Robert Fulcrum tells the story of a reporter visiting the cathedral in Chartres, France, during the cathedral's construction. Hoping to get a sense of how those working on this magnificent structure understood and experienced their contribution to its completion, the reporter began asking several workmen about their jobs. The first, a stonecutter, said that his job was simply to cut the stone into square blocks for someone else to use in the foundation; the job was monotonous, and he had been doing the same thing day in and day out. Next, the reporter asked a workman who was painting stone blocks on the front of the

---

[6]J. Braithwaite and S. Mugford, "Conditions of Successful Reintegration Ceremonies: Dealing with Juvenile Offenders," *British Journal of Criminology* (1995): 34. The authors give examples of how relatives, friends, and acquaintances of young offenders, victims, and their families become vital resources in restoring and meeting the needs of crime victims while also helping offenders when asked to participate in family group conferences.

building about his job. "I just paint these blocks and nothing more," he said. "There is not much to it."

Frustrated that these workmen had little to say about the significance of working on this historical effort, the reporter moved to another part of the building and approached a man carefully cutting stained glass windows. Surely, this man felt that his work was the artistic opportunity of a lifetime. Once again the reporter was disappointed; the man said that he was very tired and somewhat bored with his task. Finally, as he walked out of the cathedral in despair, the reporter passed an elderly woman stooped and working rapidly to clean up the debris left from the stone and glass cutters, painters, and other artisans. He asked what it was that she was doing. Her answer was that she was building the most magnificent cathedral in the history of the world to the glory of God.

As this story illustrates, the key to progress toward restorative justice is viewing small steps as the building blocks of a more effective juvenile justice system.

Will balanced and restorative justice work? BRJ is not a treatment program but a model for system reform. It cannot be assessed by using traditional program evaluation technologies. The success of a restorative justice system should be measured not only by recidivism but also by victim satisfaction, offender accountability, competency development, and public safety. The success of BRJ will depend on the consistency and integrity of implementation, how well its core philosophy is understood, how effectively it is adapted to local conditions, and whether restorative justice is given a chance. Although restorative justice may not lead to immediate reductions in recidivism, the standard of comparison should be the current system. As a First Nations Community Justice Coordinator in Yukon, Canada, reminds us:

> So we make mistakes. Can you—the current system—say you don't make mistakes? . . . If you don't think you do, walk through our community. Every family will have something to teach you. . . . By getting involved, by all of us taking responsibility, it is not that we won't make mistakes, we would be doing it together, as a community instead of having it done to us. . . . We need to make real differences in the way people act and the way we treat others. . . . Only if we empower them and support them can they break out of this trap.[7]

It is the failure of current paradigms that has moved some policymakers toward radical measures to abolish the juvenile justice system. Those who wish to preserve it see balanced and restorative justice as a means to do so by crafting a new system in which juvenile justice reflects community justice.

---

[7]Rose Couch, Community Justice Coordinator, Quanlin Dun First Nations, Yukon, Canada. As quoted in B. Stuart, "Sentencing Circles: Making 'Real Differences'," monograph, Territorial Court of Yukon, Whitehorse, Yukon, Canada.

REVIEW QUESTIONS

1. What is balanced and restorative justice (BRJ)? What are its major features? How is it different from more traditional approaches?
2. Note that Wilson and Howell's *Comprehensive Strategy for Serious, Violent, and Chronic Juvenile Offenders*, which we encountered earlier in this chapter, describes the Balanced Approach as "a promising approach that specifies a clear and coherent framework" (p. 391). In what ways is the BRJ program consistent with the *Comprehensive Strategy* and in what ways is it inconsistent?
3. Do you think implementing policies consistent with BRJ should become a central objective of the juvenile justice system? Why or why not?

FURTHER READING

Ainsworth, Janet E. (1991). Re-imagining childhood and reconstructing the legal order: The case for abolishing the juvenile court. *North Carolina Law Review, 69,* 1083–1100.

Bilchik, Shay. (1998). A juvenile justice system for the 21st century. *Crime and Delinquency, 44*(1), 89–101.

Butts, Jeffrey A., and Mears, Daniel P. (2001). Reviving juvenile justice in a get-tough era. *Youth and Society, 33*(2), 169–198.

Feld, Barry C. (1997). Abolish the juvenile court: Youthfulness, criminal responsibility, and sentencing policy. *Journal of Criminal Law and Criminology, 88*(1), 68–136.

Guarino-Ghezzi, Susan, and Loughran, Edward J. (1998). *Balancing Juvenile Justice.* Somerset, NJ: Transaction.

Howell, James C. (2003). *Preventing and Reducing Delinquency: A Comprehinsive Framework.* Thousand Oaks, CA: Sage Publications.

Katzmann, Gary S. (Ed.). (2002). *Securing Our Children's Future: New Approaches to Juvenile Justice and Youth Violence.* Washington, DC: Brookings Institution Press.

Macallair, Dan, and Schiraldi, Vincent. (Eds.). (1998). *Reforming Juvenile Justice: Reasons and Strategies for the 21st Century.* Dubuque, IA: Kendall/Hunt.

Ohlin, Lloyd E. (1998). The future of juvenile justice policy and research. *Crime and Delinquency, 44*(1), 143–153.

Schwartz, Ira M. (1989). *(In)Justice for Juveniles: Rethinking the Best Interests of the Child.* Lexington, MA: Lexington Books.

Schwartz, Ira M. (Ed.). (1999). Will the Juvenile Court System Survive? A Special Issue of *The Annals of the American Academy of Political and Social Science, 564*(July).